"David Talbot's riveting account of the Kennedy Administration is heavy drama . . . brilliant journalism."

—*People Magazine* (4-starred, Critics Choice Review)

"Bracing . . . full of shocking moments and juicy tidbits."

—*Los Angeles Times*

"Those looking for new insight into John F. Kennedy's presidency will want to read this meticulously researched chronicle . . . an admirable feat of reporting, and one that will spark conversation." —*Publishers Weekly*

"Pulitzer Prize-bait . . . [a] manic and near-perfect tale of the Kennedy brothers. . . . Instead of creating yet another conspiracy theory tome, Talbot peels away the political layers of the underworld dealings, upper-crust connections, treachery, the Kennedy splendor, and rumor after rumor, and show us America's Camelot in a brand-new light." —*San Francisco Weekly*

"Although the literature about the assassination of John F. Kennedy could fill a decent-sized library, Talbot, founder of salon.com, proves there's always more to say. . . . Rather than asking us to believe a conspiracy theory, he simply ask us to understand what Bobby believed and why he believed it. . . . A persuasively written, substantive addition to the Kennedy collection."

—*Booklist*

"A hitherto hidden picture of the years 1960–1968 . . . a great work and beautifully written. . . . In a frightening point, Talbot convincingly shows how intelligence agencies have, since the death of the Kennedy brothers, insidiously fed untrue information about them to Congress and to happy conduit reporters." —*The Capital Times* (Madison, Wisconsin)

"A fascinating new look at the tumultuous Kennedy years . . . a page-turner." —*San Antonio Express-News*

"Meticulously researched and evocatively written . . . full of powerful and ironic parallels between the political issues of then and now . . . Talbot has a gift for blending the political with the personal." —*Irish Voice*

BROTHERS

THE HIDDEN HISTORY
OF THE KENNEDY YEARS

DAVID TALBOT

FREE PRESS
New York London Toronto Sydney

P

Free Press
A Division of Simon & Schuster, Inc.
1230 Avenue of the Americas
New York, NY 10020

First Free Press trade paperback edition June 2008

FREE PRESS and colophon are trademarks of Simon & Schuster, Inc.

For information about special discounts for bulk purchases,
please contact Simon & Schuster Special Sales at 1-800-456-6798
or business@simonandschuster.com

Designed by Jaime Putorti

Manufactured in the United States of America

10   9   8   7   6   5   4   3   2   1

Library of Congress Cataloging-in-Publication
Data Control No. 2007005119

ISBN-13: 978-0-7432-6918-6
ISBN-10:   0-7432-6918-7
ISBN-13: 978-0-7432-6919-3 (pbk)
ISBN-10:   0-7432-6919-5 (pbk)

*To Camille
And to our sons, Joseph and Nathaniel,
as they seek their own newer world*

ACKNOWLEDGMENTS

I must first express my gratitude to Karen Croft, who urged me to write this book and who worked with skill and dedication as my research associate. Her belief in the importance of this endeavor was a constant source of encouragement, through the dark days and the light.

I must also give special thanks to Jefferson Morley and Peter Dale Scott, two men whose research in the Kennedy assassination field long preceded my own. They generously agreed to read and comment on my manuscript and always made themselves available for enlightening discussions. Morley and Scott are owed a debt of gratitude from the nation for their long years of investigation, despite the many obstacles put in their way by government agencies and the discouraging attitudes of many of their press and academic colleagues.

I would also like to thank other experts in the Kennedy assassination field for their generous assistance, including James Lesar, Anthony Summers, Robbyn Swan, Malcolm Blunt, Ray Marcus, Vincent Salandria, Gaeton Fonzi, William Turner, Josiah Thompson, Dr. Gary Aguilar, John Simkin, Paul Hoch, Lisa Pease, Rex Bradford, Gus Russo, Eric Hamburg, and Andy Winiarczyk. They always put the higher goal of fully understanding the case above any private claims on their expertise in my dealings with them, selflessly sharing documents, sources, insights, and their time. They, too, should be heralded for their pioneering, and continuing, work in the field.

Cliff Callahan, an astute explorer of government catacombs, provided invaluable research assistance, tracking down important documents in the National Archives.

Stephen Plotkin, Allan Goodrich, Maryrose Grossman and Megan Desnoyers were helpful guides at the John F. Kennedy Presidential Library, although the continuing restrictions on Kennedy-era material remain a source of puzzlement and frustration for researchers.

Gary Mack and the staff of the Sixth Floor Museum in Dallas also provided assistance, as did the staffs of the Lyndon Baines Johnson Library, the U.S. Naval Institute, the American Heritage Center in Laramie, Wyoming, the Palm Beach Historical Society, the Museum of Television and Radio in Beverly Hills, and the State Historical Society of Wisconsin, whose archives were plumbed on my behalf by Scott Feiner.

My brother-in-law, Don Peri—whose youth was as lit up with the Kennedy flame as my own—funneled a constant stream of Kennedy artifacts from his personal archives to me.

Celia Canfield, Karla Spormann, and the staff of Tendo Communications provided shelter from the storm, and I will always be grateful.

Kelly Frankeny graciously put her bounteous design skills at the service of this project.

I was fortunate to have Martin Beiser of Free Press as my editor and sounding board. His wise judgment and instincts could always be relied upon. In an era when the art of line editing has been all but lost, Marty's deft, pen-wielding skills seem all the more miraculous.

Sloan Harris, my agent, was also a source of sharp-eyed—sometimes, *painfully* sharp—wisdom.

Few writers are as blessed with in-house editorial counsel as I am. My wife, Camille Peri, is not just a source of inspiration, but my guiding light. She tells me where I have gone wrong, and where I have gone right. And I believe her.

Finally, I am deeply grateful to the dozens of Kennedy colleagues, friends, and family members who shared with me their memories of the lives and deaths of John and Robert Kennedy. Some found it exhilarating to explore these hidden chambers from the past in a new light. Some found it excruciating. I hope this book does honor to their commitment to the truth.

CONTENTS

"I found out something I never knew. I found out that my world was not the real world."
—ROBERT F. KENNEDY, 1968

AUTHOR'S NOTE

There are many fine books about the Kennedy presidency and its violent conclusion and I have learned from all of them. But this book does not seek to retrace the familiar steps of Kennedy memoirs, histories, and biographies, or to thrash out old arguments about the JFK assassination. Instead, it looks at this brief, but operatic, swath of American history through the eyes of Robert Kennedy, and the men around the Kennedy brothers, whom they also considered brothers. Bobby Kennedy was the president's devoted partner, as well as the nation's top lawman. It has long been a mystery why he apparently did nothing to investigate his brother's shocking death on November 22, 1963. I have sought to understand this enduring mystery by not only immersing myself in the deep well of Kennedy scholarship, but by poring over newly released government documents—and most important, by re-living these years with the Kennedys' "band of brothers," as Bobby called them—the living links to the New Frontier—before this political generation disappears entirely.

What I discovered is that Robert Kennedy did not resign himself to the lone gunman theory, the official version of his brother's death. On the contrary, he immediately suspected that President Kennedy was the victim of a powerful conspiracy. And he spent the rest of his life secretly searching for the truth about his brother's murder. This book will not only shine a light on Robert Kennedy's hidden quest, it will seek to explain why he came to such a dark understanding of JFK's death.

Few men of Robert Kennedy's generation knew as much about the dark side of American power as he did. Looking at the tumultuous Kennedy presidency, and its shattering conclusion, through his eyes is an enlightening exercise. As I was completing this book, I unearthed new evidence about President Kennedy's assassination that suggested Bobby Kennedy's suspicions about Dallas were correct. These final revelations brought the book's narrative to a dramatic close.

Robert Kennedy understood that justice was an endless battle. The Kennedy brothers' murders never received the full investigative scrutiny they deserved. But following RFK's own trail is a useful place to begin.

I was a sixteen-year-old campaign volunteer for Robert Kennedy the night he was shot down in Los Angeles. It struck me then that his murder, following those of his brother and Martin Luther King Jr., had irreparably wounded America. And this feeling has never left me in all the years that have followed. For me, aggressively pursuing the hidden history of the Kennedy years was an attempt to find out where my country had lost its way, and perhaps to restore the hope and faith that I myself had lost as a young American growing up in the 1960s.

BROTHERS

1

NOVEMBER 22, 1963

Like all Americans who lived through that day, Robert F. Kennedy never forgot how he heard his brother had been shot. The attorney general, who had just turned thirty-eight, was eating lunch—clam chowder and tuna sandwiches—with United States Attorney Robert Morgenthau and his assistant by the pool at Hickory Hill, his Civil War–era mansion in McLean, Virginia, outside the capital. It was a perfect fall day—the kind of bright, crisp Friday afternoon that makes a weekend seem full of promise—and the grounds of the rolling green estate were aflame with gold and red leaves from the shedding hickories, maples, and oaks that stood sentry over the property. Kennedy had just emerged from a mid-day swim, and as he talked and ate with the visiting lawmen, his trunks were still dripping.

Around 1:45 p.m., the phone extension at the other end of the pool rang. Kennedy's wife, Ethel, picked it up—she held the receiver out to him. J. Edgar Hoover was calling. Bobby knew immediately something unusual had happened. The FBI director never phoned him at home. The two men regarded each other with a taut wariness that they both knew would only be broken when one of them left office. Each represented to the other what was wrong about America. "I have news for you," Hoover said. "The president's been shot." Hoover's voice was blunt and matter of fact. Kennedy would always remember not just the FBI chief's words, but his chilling tone.

"History cracked open" for America on November 22, 1963, as playwright Tony Kushner observed years later. But the abyss that opened for Bobby

Kennedy at that moment was the deepest of all. And it was Hoover, of all people, who brought him news of the apocalypse. "I think he told me with pleasure," Kennedy would recall.

Twenty minutes later, Hoover phoned again to deliver the final blow: "The president's dead," he said and promptly hung up. Again, Kennedy would remember, his voice was oddly flat—"not quite as excited as if he were reporting the fact that he had found a Communist on the faculty of Howard University."

Hoover's curt phone calls confirmed that the "perfect communion" between the two brothers, as the *New York Times'* Anthony Lewis described the bond between President John Kennedy and Robert Kennedy—a fraternal relationship unprecedented in presidential history—was over. But they also clearly conveyed that Bobby had suffered a death of a different kind. His own power as attorney general instantly started to fade, already to a point where the director of the FBI no longer felt compelled to show deference, or even common human grace, to his superior in the Justice Department.

For the rest of the day and night, Bobby Kennedy would wrestle with his howling grief—crying, or fighting against crying since that was the Kennedy way—while using whatever power was still left him, before the new administration settled firmly into place, to figure out what had really happened in Dallas. He worked the phones at Hickory Hill; he met with a succession of people while waiting for Air Force One to return with the body of his brother, his brother's widow, and the new president; he accompanied his brother's remains to the autopsy at Bethesda Naval Hospital; and he stayed coiled and awake in the White House until early the next morning. Lit up with the clarity of shock, the electricity of adrenaline, he constructed the outlines of the crime.

From his phone calls and conversations that day—and into the following week—it's possible to trace the paths that Robert Kennedy pursued as he tried to unveil the mystery. "With that amazing computer brain of his, he put it all together on the afternoon of November 22," his friend, journalist Jack Newfield, remarked.

RFK's search for the truth about the crime of the century has long been an untold story. But it is deeply loaded with historic significance. Kennedy's investigative odyssey—which began with a frantic zeal immediately after his brother's assassination, and then secretly continued in fitful bursts until his own murder less than five years later—did not succeed in bringing the case to court. But Robert Kennedy was a central figure in the drama—not only as his brother's attorney general and the second most powerful official in the

Kennedy administration, but as JFK's principal emissary to the dark side of American power. And his hunt for the truth sheds a cold, bright light on the forces that he suspected were behind the murder of his brother. Bobby Kennedy was America's first assassination conspiracy theorist.

Predictably, the first phone call that Bobby made on November 22 after his initial conversation with Hoover was to Kenny O'Donnell. JFK's chief of staff had accompanied the president to Dallas and was with him at Parkland Memorial Hospital when he was pronounced dead at 2:00 p.m. Tough, taciturn, Boston Irish, O'Donnell was second only to Bobby himself in his political guardianship of the president. A close friend since they roomed together at Harvard and played on the college football team, O'Donnell was the man Bobby would have wanted at the scene of a crisis if he couldn't be there himself. As a B-17 bombardier, he had flown thirty missions against Nazi Germany, was shot down and then escaped from enemy prison. In his final, legendary game as quarterback at Harvard, he ran for the winning touchdown against archrival Yale on a broken leg.

Bobby ran upstairs to phone O'Donnell from his bedroom, while Morgenthau and his assistant were led to a TV set in the drawing room at Hickory Hill. Not finding O'Donnell at the hospital, Kennedy spoke instead to Secret Service agent Clint Hill, the only officer who had performed heroically on the president's behalf that afternoon. Images of Hill rushing to leap onto the back of JFK's moving limousine would forever become part of the iconography of that eerie day.

It's not known precisely what Bobby learned that afternoon from the Secret Service man. But there was a darkness that immediately began growing in Hill and O'Donnell about what they'd seen and heard in Dallas. Neither man would ever be the same after November 22.

O'Donnell was riding immediately behind Kennedy's limousine in the Dallas motorcade, just ten feet away, along with fellow Boston Irishman Dave Powers, the White House aide and court jester. They were front row witnesses to the assassination. Powers would later say it felt as if they were "riding into an ambush." O'Donnell and more than one Secret Service man would tell Bobby the same thing that day: They were caught in a crossfire. It was a conspiracy.

Bobby Kennedy came to the same conclusion that afternoon. It was not a "he" who had killed his brother—it was a "they." This is how he put it to his friend, Justice Department press spokesman Edwin Guthman. The former Pulitzer Prize–winning *Seattle Times* reporter had become close friends with Kennedy during the 1950s when they both put themselves on the line to investigate corruption and thuggery in the Teamsters' union. Guthman was one of Bobby's "band of brothers," as the attorney general years later inscribed a picture of his young, idealistic Justice Department team. The battle cry from Shakespeare's *Henry V* appealed to Bobby's sense of heroic mission: "We few, we happy few, we band of brothers / For he to-day that sheds his blood with me / Shall be my brother . . . / And gentlemen . . . now a-bed / Shall think themselves accursed they were not here." If the perfect communion between Jack and Bobby was at the heart of the Kennedy administration, it was this wider circle of brothers—all intensely devoted to the Kennedy cause—who gave the New Frontier its blood and muscle. Bobby would quietly turn to several of these trusted aides to help him on his quest for the truth.

Guthman was having lunch with a congressman from Seattle on Capitol Hill when someone came rushing in to tell them the president had been shot. He immediately drove to Hickory Hill, where he spent the rest of the afternoon with Bobby. By now, Kennedy family members were gathering at the Virginia estate. But Bobby was also surrounding himself with "brothers" like Guthman. The two men paced endlessly together, back and forth on the backyard lawn. "There's so much bitterness I thought they would get one of us, but Jack, after all he'd been through, never worried about it," Kennedy told Guthman.

"Bob said, 'I thought they would get me, instead of the president,'" Guthman said, recalling the conversation years later. "He distinctly said 'they.'"

Guthman and others around Bobby that day thought "they" might be coming for the younger Kennedy next. So apparently did Bobby. He was normally opposed to tight security measures, which he found intrusive and perhaps even a sign of cowardice—"Kennedys don't need bodyguards," he had said, even after he began receiving death threats as the crime-busting attorney general. But that afternoon, Kennedy allowed the Fairfax County police, who rushed to Hickory Hill after the assassination without being summoned, to protect his home. Later, the police were replaced by federal marshals, who encircled Kennedy's estate after Guthman and other RFK aides spoke to Chief U.S. Marshal Jim McShane.

Bobby trusted McShane and his men. James Joseph Patrick McShane was a street-tough Irish New York cop. He had worked with Bobby as an investigator for the Senate Rackets Committee in the late 1950s and had served as bodyguard for JFK during the presidential campaign. He and his men had put their lives on the line in the civil rights battles of the South, saving Martin Luther King Jr. from a howling mob that had surrounded a church in Montgomery, Alabama, where he was preaching in May 1961. The following year, McShane and his ragtag troops had again formed a thin, bloodied line in defense of James Meredith, the black student who set off a fiery white uprising when he enrolled at the University of Mississippi. McShane was "built like a tank, had the crushed nose of the Golden Gloves boxing champ he once was, and the puffy face of a man who enjoyed booze in his off-hours," observed one chronicler of his exploits. As a New York cop, he had survived seven shoot-outs on the streets and received the NYPD's medal of honor.

It's telling that Bobby turned to McShane and his band of federal irregulars in his hour of dread, and not Hoover's more professional G-men. Even when his brother was still alive, Bobby had learned that Hoover's men could not be trusted in the administration's most dire showdowns, like those in the South. Nor did he turn to the Secret Service for protection that day. He was already trying to figure out why the agency entrusted with the president's personal safety had failed his brother.

With their youth, ambition, and deep sense of family entitlement, the Kennedys had come into office confident they could take charge of the federal government and put it at the service of their cause. But on November 22, Bobby Kennedy immediately suspected something had broken inside the government and that his brother had been cut down by one of its jagged shards. In these hours of unknown danger, Bobby followed his old tribal instincts, turning not to the appropriate government agencies, but to the tight band of brothers whom the Kennedys had always most relied upon. None of the intensely loyal men gathered around Kennedy at his home that day knew if Bobby's life too was now in danger. Nor did they know for certain in these fearful hours where the threat might come from or on whom they could depend. But they were sure that they could count on Jim McShane and his men to give their lives for the surviving Kennedy. He was one of them.

While McShane's marshals staked out the front gate at Hickory Hill and fanned out along the perimeters of the estate, Bobby worked to put faces to the conspiracy that he suspected was behind his brother's death—to find out who "they" were. No one knew more about the dark tensions within the Kennedy administration than he did. As President Kennedy struggled to command his government, clashing with hard-liners in his national security bureaucracy, he had given more and more responsibility to his brother Bobby. Among the items in the attorney general's bulging portfolio were the CIA, which the Kennedys were determined to overhaul after the agency led them into the Bay of Pigs disaster; the Mafia, which Bobby had declared war on,

telling his fellow Justice Department crusaders that either they would succeed or the mob would run the country; and Cuba, the island nation around
which raged so much Cold War sound and fury. When it came to administration policy on Cuba, Bobby was "president," General Alexander Haig, one of
the Pentagon's point men on the issue, would later say.

The CIA, Mafia, and Cuba—Bobby knew they were intertwined. The
CIA had formed a sinister alliance with underworld bosses to assassinate
Fidel Castro, working with mob-connected Cuban exile leaders. Bobby
thought he had severed the CIA-Mafia merger when the agency finally told
him about it in May 1962. But he also knew the agency often defied higher
authority. He would later describe CIA actions during the Bay of Pigs as
"virtually treason." It was this shadowy nexus—the CIA, Mafia, and Cuban
exiles—that Kennedy immediately focused on during the afternoon of November 22.

After phoning Dallas, Kennedy made a call to CIA headquarters, just
down the highway in Langley, Virginia, where he often began his day, stopping there to work on Cuba-related business and trying to establish control
over the agency's "wilderness of mirrors" for his brother. Bobby's phone call
to Langley on the afternoon of November 22 was a stunning outburst. Getting a ranking official on the phone—whose identity is still unknown—
Kennedy confronted him in a voice vibrating with fury and pain. "Did your
outfit have anything to do with this horror?" Kennedy erupted. Whatever
the anonymous CIA official told Bobby that afternoon, it did not put his
suspicions about the agency to rest.

Later that day, Kennedy would take his question to the top of the CIA.
John McCone, director of the agency, who was eating lunch in his Langley
office when his aide Walter Elder burst in to tell him the news from Dallas.
McCone immediately phoned Bobby, who told him to come right over to the
house in McLean. McCone later recalled that he was with Bobby and Ethel
in their second-floor library when Kennedy received the call telling him his
brother was dead. "There was almost nothing we could say to one another,"
recalled McCone. "We were seized with the horror of it."

After he called his mother, Rose, and brother, Teddy, to tell them Jack
was gone, a "steely" Bobby (as McCone described him) took the CIA chief
outside to the backyard and engaged him in a remarkable conversation that
would extend, off and on, for three hours that afternoon. The attorney general of the United States wanted to know whether the country's intelligence
agency had assassinated the president of the United States. Bobby would
later tell a close friend, "You know, at the time I asked McCone . . . if they

had killed my brother, and I asked him in a way that he couldn't lie to me, and they hadn't."

Bobby's remarks about his conversation with McCone have caused intense speculation. McCone, a fellow Catholic, shared a deep sense of faith with Bobby, as well as with Ethel, both of whom had consoled him after the death of his first wife. He once took a rosary ring that he carried around in his billfold for comfort to Rome, where he had a copy made and had it blessed by the pope as a gift for Bobby. Perhaps Kennedy made McCone swear to tell him the truth, as one devout Catholic to another.

In the days following the assassination, McCone would come to conclude that there had been two shooters in Dallas, in striking contrast to the official version of the crime as the work of a lone gunman, which was being ardently promoted by Hoover and the FBI. But there is no evidence that he ever came to suspect his own agency.

Bobby accepted McCone's assurance about the CIA that afternoon. But he also knew that McCone, a wealthy Republican businessman from California with no intelligence background, was not in firm control of his own agency. Kennedy himself knew more about the spy outfit's sinister exploits, including the Mafia plots, than McCone did. His brother had replaced the CIA's legendary creator, Allen Dulles, with McCone after the agency's spectacular failure at the Bay of Pigs. But McCone never worked his way into the agency's old boy network that dated back to its origins in the OSS during World War II. And there was a sense he preferred to be left in the dark on the more unpleasant stuff, that his religious principles would not countenance some of the agency's black arts. Bobby would realize that while he had taken his question to the very top of the CIA, he had asked the wrong man.

Kennedy also made inquiries about the Mafia that day. The young attorney general had built his reputation, before and after coming to the Justice Department, on a relentless crusade to crush the power of organized crime in America, which he felt was threatening to take control of the country's economy through corrupt labor unions like Jimmy Hoffa's Teamsters as well as local, state, and federal government through payoffs to politicians, judges, and elected officials. While Hoover was still focusing on the empty shell of the Communist Party USA as public enemy number one, RFK was convinced that the true "enemy within" was a corporate underworld that was gaining the power to overshadow the country's legitimate democratic institutions. "Of course it's a different era now, maybe terrorism is a greater threat these days than organized crime," said Guthman recently, sitting in his cramped office at the USC Annenberg School of Journalism, where he still lectures. "But if you look at what has happened in South and Central America, you can see Bob was right to worry about organized crime taking over our country. Where would we be if he hadn't recognized the power and importance of the Mafia and the rackets? This was a time when the chief of the FBI, Hoover, was saying there was no such thing as organized crime."

By hounding the gods of the underworld in a way no other attorney general had ever done, Bobby Kennedy knew that he had drawn their fiery wrath. He knew about the death threats made against him by Hoffa, whose control over the Teamsters' golden pension fund made him the Mafia's favorite banker. But he was undeterred. His last item of business before breaking for lunch on November 22 was the prosecution of Chicago godfather Sam Giancana on political corruption charges. Before he got the call from Hoover, he was waiting to hear from New Orleans about the verdict in Mafia lord Carlos Marcello's deportation hearing. And in Nashville, Walter Sheridan, the ace investigator who led Bobby's "Get Hoffa" squad, was monitoring the latest developments in the Justice Department's jury tampering case against the Teamster boss.

On the evening of November 22, Bobby phoned Julius Draznin in Chicago, an expert on union corruption for the National Labor Relations Board. He asked Draznin to look into whether there was any Mafia involvement in the killing of his brother. Draznin knew this meant Sam Giancana, who had been overheard on FBI wiretaps raging against a Kennedy "double-cross," after claiming to deliver the Chicago vote to JFK in 1960. "We need help on this," Bobby told Draznin that evening. "Maybe you can open some doors [with] the mob. Anything you can pick up, let me know directly."

But the man on whom Robert Kennedy relied more than any other to crawl into the country's darkest corners was Walter Sheridan. A former FBI man who had left the bureau in disgust over Hoover's methods, he had first proved himself with Bobby as an investigator for the Senate Rackets Committee where Kennedy served as chief counsel. A fellow Irish Catholic born on the exact same day as Bobby, November 20, 1925, he was as fearless as his boss in the crusade against crime and corruption. When the Kennedy Justice Department was escalating its drive against Hoffa, the death threats would not be directed solely at Bobby but at his right-hand man Sheridan as well. On these occasions, the Sheridan family home would be turned into an armed bunker.

"There would be times when the house had numerous federal marshals in it with numerous firearms stacked up behind the front door, like they were expecting a whole army to show up," recalled Sheridan's son, Walter Jr.

"Shotguns. They were expecting trouble. I was taken to school and choir practice and altar boy meetings by federal marshals—we couldn't leave home without them. This was on two occasions, when Hoffa was on trial."

Ted Kennedy later recalled, "My brother loved to tease Walter about his mild demeanor and quiet manner. But as Bobby wrote in [his book about the Mafia] *The Enemy Within*, Walter's angelic appearance hid a core of toughness. As any wrongdoer well knew, the angelic quality also represented the avenging angel."

It was Sheridan, said Ted Kennedy, to whom Bobby turned when the world was on fire. "You wanted Walter with you in any foxhole, and that is why he always seemed to get the most difficult assignments."

Sheridan was not in Washington on November 22. He was sitting in a federal court building in Nashville, where Hoffa was awaiting trial, when an associate came running in and told him, "Walt, there has just been a news flash that the president has been shot in Dallas!" Sheridan immediately phoned Bobby, but couldn't reach him. But the two brothers-in-arms would soon rejoin each other. And when Sheridan returned to the East Coast, Bobby's avenging angel would be given the most difficult assignment of his life: find out who killed the president of the United States.

Robert Kennedy had one other phone conversation on November 22 that sheds light on his thinking that afternoon. He spoke to Enrique "Harry" Ruiz-Williams, a Bay of Pigs veteran who was his closest associate in the Cuban exile community. Kennedy stunned his friend by telling him point-blank, "One of your guys did it."

The venerable Washington journalist Haynes Johnson is the source for this story. Then a young reporter for the *Washington Evening Star*, Johnson had come to know both Ruiz-Williams and Kennedy while researching a book on the Bay of Pigs. Johnson remembers almost coming to blows with Bobby, who wanted his book to focus on the Cuban heroes of the invasion like Ruiz-Williams and not the Kennedy administration's controversial actions during the ill-fated operation. "We had a very difficult conversation one afternoon at the Metropolitan Club in New York," recalled Johnson, sitting in the basement study of his Washington home. "He got very hard-eyed and didn't want to give me any information, and I said something to the effect, 'I'll be around here a lot longer than you and your brother' and he got very mad." It's a remark even more unnerving now than it must have been then. "I was young, foolish and arrogant myself at the time," shrugged the journalist. Johnson started to storm out of the club, but Bobby jumped to his feet and grabbing him by the shoulders, told him, "Don't go away, don't go away." It was the beginning of a warm relationship between the two men, the kind Bobby was in the habit of forming after first almost exchanging punches with a man.

"He was sort of a hard, passionate parish priest, the avenger type—all faith and justice," said Johnson. "I always thought of Jack, on the other hand, like an English lord."

On the afternoon of November 22, Johnson was planning to celebrate the completion of his book over lunch with Ruiz-Williams, who had been one of his principal sources. On his way to the Ebbitt Hotel, a drab establishment in downtown Washington where the CIA put up anti-Castro leaders like Ruiz-Williams, Johnson heard the news from Dallas on his car radio. As soon as Johnson reached Ruiz-Williams's cramped, sparsely furnished room, they phoned Kennedy. It was Ruiz-Williams who spoke to him. "Harry stood there with the phone in his hand and then he told me what Bobby said. . . . It was a shocking thing. I'll never forget, Harry got this look on his face. After he hung up, Harry told me what Bobby had said: 'One of your guys did it.'"

Who did Kennedy mean? When he first recounted the phone conversation, in a 1981 article in the *Washington Post*, Johnson assumed Bobby was referring to accused assassin Lee Harvey Oswald, whose name might have been known to Kennedy by then since he was arrested in Dallas at 2:50 p.m. Eastern time. Later Johnson concluded that Kennedy was probably pointing his finger in the general direction of Cuban exiles. In either case, it's important to note that Kennedy apparently never jumped to the conclusion that afternoon that Fidel Castro—the target of so much U.S. intrigue—was behind his brother's killing. It was the anti-Castro camp where Bobby's suspicions immediately flew, not pro-Castro agents. It seems that Bobby either immediately connected Oswald with anti-Castro Cuban exiles or suspected one of Ruiz-Williams's fellow exile leaders in the crime.

Bobby came to this conclusion despite the energetic efforts of the CIA and FBI, which almost immediately after the assassination began trying to pin the blame on Cuba's Communist government. Hoover himself phoned Kennedy again around four that afternoon to inform him that Oswald had shuttled in and out of Cuba, which was untrue. In reality, Oswald—or someone impersonating him—had tried only once, without success, to enter Cuba through Mexico, earlier that fall. In any case, the FBI chief failed to convince Bobby that the alleged assassin was a Castro agent.

Kennedy did not mean to implicate Harry Ruiz-Williams himself with his stunning assertion. The Cuban exile world was a "snake pit," in Johnson's words, of competing anti-Castro conspirators, some aligned with the Kennedys, some with the CIA, some with the Mafia, and some with mixed or mysterious allegiances. Bobby trusted Ruiz-Williams, more than any other anti-Castro leader, to bring order to this feverish world. "I want you to take charge of the whole thing," Bobby had told Ruiz-Williams earlier in 1963. "I'm not going to see any more Cubans unless they come through you, because they make me crazy." Throughout the year, Ruiz-Williams was in almost daily contact with Kennedy, as the two plotted ways to topple Castro, with RFK strongly backing his friend's effort to form a coalition of the more responsible exile leaders.

Ruiz-Williams had completely charmed Bobby. A U.S.-trained mining engineer, he joined the Bay of Pigs brigade though, pushing forty, he was older than most of the other volunteers. After the invasion, badly wounded, lying in a makeshift field hospital, he still tried to shoot a visiting Castro with his .45, but the gun clicked empty. Despite his ordeal, Ruiz-Williams came out of Cuban prison with a sense of proportion, unlike many of the other Bay of Pigs veterans, who were consumed with a poisonous hatred for both Castro and President Kennedy, whom they blamed for not coming to their rescue on the beaches of Cuba. He liked Bobby from the moment he met him, when he was invited to the attorney general's office after his release. "I was expecting to see a very impressive guy, very well dressed, and a big office and all that," Ruiz-Williams later told Johnson. "And when I got into his office there was this young man with no coat on, his sleeves rolled up, his collar open and his tie down. He looks at you very straight in the eyes and his office is filled with things done by little children—paintings and things like that. I liked him right away."

The feeling was mutual. Bobby invited Harry to Hickory Hill and took him on family skiing trips. "Harry was an old-fashioned buccaneer type," recalled Johnson. "He had these flashing black eyes and passion. And Bob Kennedy just liked him, he trusted him implicitly."

But the other Cuban exile leaders were a different story. Bobby, his brother's vigilant watchman, knew he had to watch them. He sent Harry to Miami to help provide security for JFK before the president traveled to Florida in November 1963, after the attorney general was informed of death threats there against his brother. Even though the city had offered the Democrats $600,000, Miami had already been ruled out by the administration as a site for the party's 1964 convention because it was feared that anti-Kennedy feeling among the Cubans there could explode.

Another Bay of Pigs veteran, Angelo Murgado, said he was so alarmed by the murderous talk about President Kennedy in Miami's Cuban exile community that he approached Bobby through anti-Castro leader Manuel Artime and offered to keep an eye on the more dangerous element and report back to the attorney general. Murgado said that he, Artime—the political leader of the Bay of Pigs brigade—and brigade veteran Manuel Reboso all met with Bobby at the Kennedy mansion in Palm Beach, Florida in 1963 to tell him of their concerns. "I was thinking we have to control and keep a sharp look on our Cubans, the ones that were hating Kennedy," recalled Murgado. "I was afraid that one of our guys would go crazy. Bobby told us to come up with a plan and do it. . . . He was fanatic about his brother, he would do anything to take care of him."

A few months after the Kennedys took office in Washington, a *New York Times Magazine* profile of Bobby described him prowling the "broader reaches of his brother's administration . . . like a Welsh collie—and with much the same quick-nipping protectiveness."

Now his brother was dead. And in the barrage of phone calls and conversations on November 22, it is clear to see where Bobby was hunting for the culprits. In those corners of the administration that had been *his* responsibility—the CIA, Mafia, Cuba.

When Bobby Kennedy told his comrade-in-arms Harry Ruiz-Williams, "One of your guys did it," he might as well have been saying, "One of *our* guys did it" or even "One of *my* guys did it." Bobby was saying that his brother had been killed by someone in his own anti-Castro operation, or by someone suspicious in the anti-Castro exile world he should have been watching. He should have been on top of this—that's the way Bobby's mind worked. Around his neck hung a St. Michael medallion, symbol of righteous power. He was supposed to know where the darkness fell, and how to keep his brother safe from it. His brother's death was his fault—this is certainly another wound that his brother's killers aimed to inflict. For they knew it would not be enough to assassinate the president—they would have to find a way to stop his avenging brother from coming after them as well, to hobble him with guilt and doubt.

But this poison dart would take a while to work its enervating effects. On November 22 and the days immediately after, Bobby Kennedy was a man on fire to find the truth.

AS DUSK FELL ON the 22nd, RFK and Guthman drove from Hickory Hill to the Pentagon, where Kennedy joined Defense Secretary Robert McNamara and General Maxwell Taylor, chairman of the Joint Chiefs of Staff. McNamara, the former Ford Motor president who had tried to tighten civilian control of the Pentagon, was the Cabinet member most admired by the

Kennedy brothers. Taylor, an intellectual military man who had fallen out of step with his colleagues for challenging the Eisenhower-era nuclear orthodoxy of massive retaliation, was also viewed as a Kennedy imposition at the Pentagon. Bobby would name a son after him. The Kennedy brothers' tensions with the military hierarchy were no less severe than those with the CIA. They were grateful to have two commanding presences like McNamara and Taylor in a military culture they otherwise thought of as a hostile camp.

While Guthman remained in the E-Ring, Kennedy, McNamara, and Taylor walked out to a Pentagon landing pad and boarded a helicopter for Andrews Air Force Base, where they waited in the gathering darkness for the arrival of Air Force One. McNamara said he could not recall if Kennedy discussed his suspicions about Dallas with him that evening: "I don't have any recollection of him saying he thought A, B or C did it."

The presidential plane heading their way in the evening gloom was a vessel of dark thoughts. In the rear compartment, Jacqueline Kennedy and Kenny O'Donnell brooded by the coffin of her dead husband, drinking from dark tumblers of Scotch that seemed to have no effect on them after the horrors of Dealey Plaza, even though the young widow had never tasted whisky before. She shrugged off Admiral George Burkley, the White House physician, when he gently tried to persuade her to change out of her gore-soaked pink Chanel suit. She was covered in rust-red stains; her husband's blood was caked even under her bracelet. But she refused to scrub herself clean. "*No,*" she hissed. "Let them see what they've done."

This would become one of the most indelible remarks from that haunted day, ever since William Manchester recorded it in his 1967 best-seller, *The Death of a President*. It's widely quoted but seldom analyzed. Like Bobby's "I thought they would get me, instead of the president," Jackie's defiant statement was filled with implications too chilling for journalists or historians to dwell upon. The feeling took hold immediately within the Kennedy inner circle that day—they were facing an organized "they," not a lone, wayward malcontent. This is not to say that they were necessarily right or that their convictions were shared by every core member of the New Frontier. But a surprising number of Kennedy loyalists did reach the same desolate conclusion as Bobby and Jackie that day, and believed it for the rest of their lives.

As Air Force One prepared to land, Jackie and O'Donnell decided that he and JFK's other close aides would carry the coffin off the plane. She pointedly told a White House military attaché, Brigadier General Godfrey McHugh, "I want his friends to carry him down." And when another general came back to the rear of the plane to tell O'Donnell, "The Army is prepared

to take the coffin off," O'Donnell shot back, "We'll take it off." But in the
end, the military would have the final word. "Clear the area," McHugh
ordered as soon as Air Force One taxied to a halt. "We'll take care of the
coffin."

This tussle over proprietorship of the presidential coffin would set the
stage for a larger drama around the JFK autopsy at Bethesda Naval Hospital,
which was ostensibly controlled by Bobby Kennedy on behalf of the family
but was actually in the hands of military officials.

Bobby hurried to Jackie on Air Force One, brushing past Lyndon Johnson
in a brusque manner the new president never forgot. "I want to see Jackie,"
LBJ's press secretary, Liz Carpenter, thought she heard him mumble. "Oh,
Bobby," Jackie exhaled as he wrapped his arms around his brother's blood-
spattered widow. It was just like Bobby, she thought; he was always there
when you needed him. Later, riding with him in the rear of an ambulance to
Bethesda, next to the coffin, Jackie reported what had happened in the hot,
bright streets of Dallas, the words rushing out of her for twenty minutes, as
she told him about the sudden explosion of violence and the chaotic aftermath at Parkland Hospital.

Bobby was also anxious to hear from the Secret Service men who had
returned from Dallas that evening. In the ambulance, Kennedy slid open the
plastic partition separating the rear from the front and spoke to Roy Kellerman, the agent who had ridden in the passenger seat of JFK's limousine in
Dallas.

"At the hospital I'll come up and talk to you," Kellerman told the president's brother.

"You do that," replied Kennedy, and shut the partition.

As Kennedy later learned when he quizzed Kellerman, a lumbering Secret Service veteran so soft-spoken his fellow agents nicknamed him "Gabby,"
the agent did not believe "it was one man." Kellerman would later tell
the Warren Commission that "there have got to be more than three shots,
gentlemen"—proof there was more than one shooter—and that a "flurry of
shells" flew into the vehicle. After her husband died, Kellerman's widow,
June, would say that he always "accepted that there was a conspiracy."

According to one account, the chief of the Secret Service himself, James
Rowley, also told Bobby that evening that his brother had been cut down in
a crossfire by three, perhaps four, gunmen. The Secret Service believed the
president was "the victim of a powerful organization," Rowley informed Kennedy. By the time he testified before the Warren Commission months later,
Rowley had changed his mind, telling the panel he believed Oswald alone

had killed the president. But the night must have grown darker for Bobby on November 22 when the head of the Secret Service told him of an organized plot more powerful than the presidency itself.

As his brother's autopsy proceeded in the morgue below, Bobby and Jackie waited in a dreary seventeenth-floor suite in the stone tower of the Bethesda Naval Hospital. They were surrounded by a retinue that now included McNamara; JFK's close friend, *Newsweek* journalist Ben Bradlee, and his wife, Tony; Bobby's sister, Jean Kennedy Smith; and Jackie's mother, Janet Auchincloss. While Bobby made a flurry of phone calls, the group consoled the young widow, still wearing her murder-scene clothes. "There was this totally doomed child, with that God-awful skirt, not saying anything, looking burned alive," Bradlee would recall.

Manchester, whose book remains the classic account of the post-assassination Kennedy drama, wrote that it was Bobby who "was really in charge in the tower suite" that evening, even making sure that his brother's personal possessions were removed from his White House bedroom to spare Jackie's feelings when she returned there. Manchester's portrait of a fully in command Bobby was later taken up by Kennedy critics such as journalists Seymour Hersh and Gus Russo, who depicted the attorney general as a feverish cover-up artist that night, working into the early hours of the morning to make sure the autopsy report would not include any evidence of his brother's Addison's disease or chronic venereal afflictions that would have damaged the JFK legend. In reality, however, RFK's dominion over the grisly proceedings in the morgue below was far from complete. The family's medical representative, JFK's personal physician Dr. Burkley, was banished from the morgue soon after the eight-hour procedure began, and he joined the Kennedy group in the tower. The autopsy itself was in the hands of three inexperienced pathologists under the constant supervision of a cadre of high-ranking military men. So crowded was the small room with uniformed officers, Secret Service men, and FBI agents that a Navy autopsy photographer would describe the scene as "a three-ring circus."

The report finally produced under this blanket of military supervision would contradict key findings of the emergency room surgeons who had first examined the mortally wounded president earlier in the day at Parkland Hospital, as well as the death certificate signed in Dallas by Dr. Burkley. For instance, where Parkland doctors saw clear evidence of an entrance wound in the throat—indicating a shot from the front—the Bethesda report was edited to conclude it was an exit wound, conforming to the theory of Oswald as lone assassin, firing from the rear.

Years later, one of the Bethesda pathologists, Dr. Pierre Finck, would testify in the case brought to court by flamboyant New Orleans prosecutor Jim Garrison—the only trial to come out of the Kennedy assassination—that it was the Kennedy family who had blocked him and his medical colleagues from properly examining JFK's throat wound by dissecting the bullet track and removing the neck organs. But the Kennedys placed no such limitations on the autopsy. The authorization form for the post-mortem examination, signed by Robert F. Kennedy on behalf of the president's widow, was left blank in the space that asked if the family preferred any restrictions on the procedure. Under persistent questioning from Garrison's assistant D.A. at the 1969 trial, Finck finally conceded that an Army general and two admirals were actually running the show in the crowded autopsy room, none of whom had medical credentials. "Oh, yes, there were admirals, and when you are a lieutenant colonel in the Army you just follow orders," Finck told the New Orleans court.

It is doubtful that Bobby—high in the seventeenth floor suite at Bethesda—was aware of how the story of his brother's assassination was being rewritten in the morgue down below. But he made one final attempt to take control after the autopsy was finally completed at well past three in the morning. Bobby took possession of his brother's brain and tissue samples, entrusting them to the care of Dr. Burkley. Over the years, this would produce waves of morbid speculation, with some suggesting it was a sign of Bobby's gloomy, unsound mind at the time and others arguing it was yet more proof of a family cover-up aimed at protecting the Camelot myth. Perhaps a more convincing explanation is that a deeply suspicious Bobby, with Burkley's assistance, was desperately holding onto any physical evidence he thought might be vital in a credible investigation in the future—that is, one under his control.

Kennedy's phone logs show that in February 1964, he also discussed taking possession of JFK's death limousine, which had been sent to a Detroit repair shop after the assassination, where—his brother's secretary, Evelyn Lincoln, informed him—it was to be "done over" for President Johnson. Perhaps the repair process—which would eliminate forensic evidence—"could be stopped," Lincoln told RFK, if Kennedy declared that he wanted the limousine to be "given to the [Kennedy] Library."

Whether or not Kennedy was intent on collecting evidence for a future investigation, it is certain that Burkley shared his dark thoughts about Dallas. Oddly, the president's physician—who should have been near the top of the Warren Commission's witness list—would never be called to testify. Nor was he questioned by the Secret Service or FBI. Nor was the death certificate he signed—which refuted the claim that JFK's throat wound was caused by a shot from behind—admitted into the official records. As far as government investigators were concerned, Burkley was a non-person.

But Dr. Burkley left his ghost world—briefly—to put on record his true opinion of what had happened to President Kennedy. JFK was the target of a conspiracy, Burkley told assassination researcher Henry Hurt on the telephone when he contacted him in 1982, refusing to elaborate. After years of public silence on the subject, this was a thunderclap.

That night at Bethesda, when Burkley was still down in the morgue, as all the beribboned men hovered over the president's cadaver, O'Donnell came down to retrieve Jackie Kennedy's wedding ring, which in a spasm of grief she had slipped onto the finger of her husband after he expired on the operating table at Parkland. O'Donnell knew she would want it. Burkley insisted on taking it upstairs himself. There she was, in the very hospital suite he had reserved for her during the final days of her last, ill-fated pregnancy. He gave it to her, while words awkwardly worked their way out of him. There was nothing to say, after the day they had been through together. She reached into her pocket and gave him one of the red roses she had been carrying in the motorcade, whose petals were slowly turning the wine-stain color of her splattered suit. He bowed his head. "This is the greatest treasure of my life," murmured the loyal doctor.

IT WAS AFTER 4:30 in the morning when Bobby and Jackie finally returned to the White House with the body of the president. Bobby walked upstairs with Jackie and her mother to make sure they could get to sleep. "A terrible sense of loss overwhelmed everybody who was present in the room," remembered family friend Charles Spalding, "and Bobby was trying to calm everybody and get them to bed." Later he asked Spalding to walk with him to the Lincoln Room, where he was going to sleep. His friend, realizing he was "terribly distraught," urged him to take a sleeping pill, which he did. Then Spalding closed the door. "All this time he had been under control. And then I just heard him sobbing. He was saying, 'Why, God? Why, God, why?' . . . He just gave way completely, and he was just racked with sobs and the only person he could address himself to was 'Why, God, why? What possible reason could there be in this?'"

After a brief, restless sleep, Bobby was up and walking the South Grounds by 8:00 a.m. that Saturday. The White House was now filled with family, close friends, and aides. Among them was actor Peter Lawford, husband of

Bobby's sister Pat, and his manager, Milt Ebbins, who had flown in from Los Angeles the night before. JFK had always enjoyed the two Hollywood men's company, pumping them for show business gossip and taking them on impromptu White House tours to show off the pomp of his new domicile. "Did you ever think you'd be in the White House with the president of the United States looking at Gilbert Stuart's painting of Washington?" a bemused Kennedy asked the Hollywood agent

Now Ebbins was back in the White House and witness to another historical tableau. The cavernous East Room had been transformed into a black-crepe-bedecked funeral hall, with the coffin of Ebbins's friend at the center, resting on a catafalque modeled on the one that had held the body of President Lincoln. A madcap mood of Irish mourning gripped the White House. "We had dinner that night, it was like an Irish wake," Ebbins recalled. "You'd never know there was a dead man upstairs in a coffin. Laughing, jokes, everything. At one point Ethel took off her wig and put it on me. That family just turns off death. They grieve alone, by themselves, I think."

Ebbins later came upon Bobby, who did not participate in the frantic dinner party, standing alone next to his brother's coffin. "I walked in and he had both hands on top of the coffin, with his head down. He was crying. I thought it was strange, because Bobby never showed his emotions." Ebbins had always thought of the younger brother as a "cold fish."

"Every time we met him, he was nice to me, but it wasn't Jack. Oh, Jack, he was something else. They were so different. Bobby had his holy grail. He was out to do something. Jack was too, but you never knew it. Eventually you did, but he would never talk about it."

But Ebbins was seeing another side of the younger Kennedy that weekend. His suffering seemed biblical.

Years later, Peter Lawford would tell a friend that during the weekend at the White House, Bobby revealed that he thought JFK had been killed by a powerful plot that grew out of one of the government's secret anti-Castro operations. Bobby reportedly told Lawford and other family members that there was nothing he could do at that point, since they were facing a formidable enemy and they no longer controlled the government.

During that gray, wet weekend, the tensions between the inner Kennedy circle and the national security team that had served the president continued to flare. Defense Secretary McNamara, who had convinced Jackie and Bobby Kennedy to lay the president to rest at Arlington National Cemetery across the Potomac from the capital, escorted groups of family and friends on four separate occasions to scout for a burial site in the cemetery. (O'Donnell and the Irish mafia, ever possessive of their fallen leader, were lobbying strenuously for Jack to be returned to the Boston soil from which he had sprung.) On his second trip, McNamara, unprotected by raincoat, hat, or umbrella, was soon soaked to the bone in a sudden downpour. None of the attending generals, safely bundled up in their own rain gear, made even a polite attempt to extend their civilian boss some cover. Artist and close family friend William Walton, who had been tapped by Jackie to help oversee the aesthetics of her husband's funeral, was flabbergasted by the military retinue's blatant show of disrespect for McNamara.

The sodden McNamara weathered the storm and oversaw the successful selection of a site, high on the slope below the white-columned antebellum mansion of General Robert E. Lee. The defense secretary was told that this was the same spot where President Kennedy had stood admiring the view, during a tour of Arlington Cemetery that he took a few weeks before his assassination. The young tour guide who escorted the president that day told McNamara that Kennedy had gazed across the Potomac at the Lincoln Memorial in the distance. "The president said that it was so beautiful, he could stay up there forever," the guide recalled.

ON SUNDAY AFTERNOON, AT 12:21 Eastern time, the second shock from Dallas struck the nation—Lee Harvey Oswald was gunned down on live television as he was being escorted through the basement of the Dallas police building. His murderer—a burly nightclub owner named Jack Ruby who shouted, "You killed the president, you rat," as he shot Oswald mortally in the stomach—professed to be distraught about the pain that the alleged assassin had caused the Kennedy family. But the killing had the feeling of a gangland hit meant to silence the accused Oswald before he could talk. In fact, Lyndon Johnson aide George Reedy thought the TV channel he was watching had cut away from coverage of the Kennedy funeral preparations to play an old Edward G. Robinson gangster movie when he first saw the shooting out of the corner of his eye.

The brazen elimination of first the president and then his accused assassin sent a deep shudder through Washington circles. On the phone with Bill Walton, Agnes Meyer, the aging, blunt-spoken mother of *Washington Post* publisher Katharine Graham, growled, "What is this—some kind of goddam banana republic?" Even former President Eisenhower was put in the same bitter frame of mind. It reminded him of a tour he had made of Haiti's national palace back in the 1930s when he was a young major. Reading the dates on the marble busts of the former heads of state that lined the wall, he was shocked to realize that two-thirds of them had been slain in office. His own country, he reassured himself, would never succumb to this type of political bloodlust. Now he wasn't so sure.

It was a worked-up Lyndon Johnson who told Bobby Kennedy about the shooting of Oswald. Entering the Blue Room of the White House, the new president greeted the surprised attorney general by urging him "to do something. . . . We've got to get involved. It's giving the United States a bad name around the world." LBJ accurately predicted the world reaction—newspapers in the free and communist camps alike howled about the "grotesque" display in Dallas, as the *Daily Herald* of London described the back-to-back murders, and openly wondered whether Oswald "was killed to keep him from talking," in the words of a Paris newspaper.

But it's uncertain how sincere Johnson was in his appeal for Bobby to join him in taking action. At this point, LBJ was still resisting calls for even a decorous investigation along the lines of the future Warren Commission. The new president seemed more concerned about the public relations aspect of the debacle in Dallas than in its actual legal resolution. In any case, Kennedy, filled with loathing for a man he immediately regarded as a usurper, never accepted the new president's challenge to work with him on the mystery of November 22. Such an alliance would have been the only way for the monumental crime to have been solved. If these dueling halves of the Kennedy legacy—antagonists out of a Shakespearean court drama—had been able to put aside their storied mutual contempt, history would have been different. But this would have been so far out of character for both men that it was never a possibility.

Later on Sunday, Milt Ebbins stood in the living room of the White House's presidential quarters with Peter Lawford, watching in grim disbelief as the TV played the shooting of Oswald over and over again. "Bobby came in, looked at the television, and then went over and turned it off. He didn't say anything. Just turned it off."

Bobby didn't want to dwell openly on the morbid spectacle in Dallas. But he wanted to quietly figure it out. It was a pattern established that first weekend, and he stuck to it for the rest of his life. He refused to cooperate with the two major public investigations of his brother's murder during his lifetime—the Warren Commission and Jim Garrison's probe—for reasons that are both understandable and perplexing. But he doggedly pursued his own secret avenues of scrutiny in a determined effort to find the truth. And Jack Ruby was one of his first investigative targets.

There was no one in America with more acute investigative instincts than Robert Kennedy when it came to organized crime. And Jack Ruby had mob written all over him. If Bobby could not have figured this out himself, anonymous tipsters quickly emerged to point him in the right direction. One week after Ruby blasted his way into the national spotlight, an unsigned communication was sent to the attorney general and former CIA director Allen Dulles, from an informer who claimed that Ruby was a mob "finger man" or hit man. "If my memory serves me right," wrote the informer, "Jack Ruby was visiting Syndicate Members in San Diego between the last months of 1961 and early months of 1962. The meeting of the Syndicate Members was at 'The Brass Rail,' a bar-restaurant. . . . It is used as a homosexual bar, much as the New York Syndicate under the former Gallo gang used some dozen homosexual bars as 'fronts.'"

Immediately after Oswald was gunned down, Bobby put his right-hand man, Walt Sheridan, on Ruby. An FBI memo dated November 24, 1963, shows that within hours of the shooting, Sheridan turned up evidence that Ruby had been paid off in Chicago by a close associate of Jimmy Hoffa. According to the memo, Sheridan reported that Ruby had "picked up a bundle of money from Allen M. Dorfman," Hoffa's chief advisor on Teamster pension funds and the stepson of Paul Dorfman, the labor boss's main link to the Chicago mob. Robert Peloquin, an attorney in the Justice Department's criminal division, was quickly dispatched to Chicago to check out the story about the Ruby payoff. Informed of this mission by the chief of the Chicago FBI office in a November 25 memo, an irritated J. Edgar Hoover scribbled on the document, "I do wish Department would mind its own business and let us mind ours."

A few days later, Julius Draznin, the federal labor lawyer whom Bobby had asked to look into a possible Chicago Mafia role in the assassination, provided further evidence about Ruby's background as a mob enforcer. Draznin submitted a report on November 27 that detailed Ruby's labor racketeering activities and his penchant for armed violence. Later, Kennedy would remark that when he saw Ruby's phone records, "The list was almost a duplicate of the people I called before the Rackets Committee."

Bobby opened up another line of investigation the weekend after the assassination. Still brooding about the collapse of security around his brother, he quietly asked family friend Daniel Patrick Moynihan, then an assistant secretary of labor, to explore whether Hoffa had been involved and whether the Secret Service had been bought off. Bobby knew that Moynihan was not an experienced investigator like Sheridan, but with a background in the longshoreman's union, the fellow Irishman was presumed to have some useful contacts and expertise about labor corruption. Moynihan would later hand Kennedy a confidential report stating there was no evidence the Secret Service had been corrupted.

Even before Dallas, Bobby Kennedy seemed to be losing confidence in the ability of the Secret Service to protect his brother against the numerous dangers that surrounded him. At the time of the assassination, Kennedy was backing a bill, H.R. 4158, which would have given the attorney general the authority to appoint the agents who protected the president, instead of the Secret Service. Rowley, the agency's chief, acknowledged in his testimony before the Warren Commission that he was adamantly opposed to the bill, asserting that the transfer of authority to RFK's office would "confuse and be a conflict in jurisdiction."

On Tuesday, four days after the assassination, Kennedy spoke again with Clint Hill, following up the phone conversation he had with him on November 22 when the Secret Service agent was still in Dallas. There is no record of this conversation, but the security lapses in Dallas were so flagrant, Kennedy would certainly have wanted to know what happened from an agent like Hill whom the family deeply trusted. ("Clint Hill, he loved us, he was the first man in the car," Jackie would later tell Theodore H. White.)

The Secret Service had selected an unsafe motorcade route through downtown Dallas, culminating in the slow, hairpin turn onto Elm Street where the president met his death. The tall buildings, grassy knoll, and overpass that turned Dealey Plaza into a perfect crossfire shooting gallery were not secured. Motorcycle patrolmen protecting the presidential limousine followed loosely behind instead of tightly surrounding the vehicle. There were no Secret Service men on the limousine's running boards, and agents were also ordered to stay off the rear of the vehicle. The Secret Service later spread the story that it was JFK himself, anxious that the crowd's view of the first couple not be obscured, who insisted on this. But this has been effectively refuted by researcher Vincent Palamara, who interviewed numerous agents, all of whom said the order came from Secret Service officials, not the president.

Clint Hill, riding in the Secret Service follow-up car, was the only agent to sprint for the limousine when the shots rang out. He did this despite being ordered to stay put by the agent in charge of his vehicle, Emory P. Roberts. Hill reached the limousine as the first lady was crawling onto the trunk, where, he realized to his horror, she was trying to retrieve a piece of her husband's skull. He clambered aboard the car and pushed Jackie safely back in.

Despite his heroism, Hill was plagued for years afterwards by the fact that he had not reached the limousine sooner. In 1975, after retiring from the Secret Service, he agreed to be interviewed by Mike Wallace of *60 Minutes*. On camera, the former agent's face was convulsed with pain. At one point, Wallace later recalled, Hill broke down in sobs, but he insisted on continuing with the interview. His eyes rimmed in red, his head jerking as he fought to choke his emotions, Hill dragged on a cigarette and forced himself back to Dealey Plaza. If he had only reacted a split second sooner, he could have taken the fatal head shot instead of Kennedy, said Hill.

"And that would have been all right with you?" Wallace asked.

"That would have been fine with me."

"You got there in less than two seconds, Clint . . . you surely don't have any sense of guilt about that?"

"Yes, I certainly do. I have a great deal of guilt about that. Had I turned in a different direction, I'd have made it. It's my fault. . . . And I'll live with that to my grave."

Remembering the interview years later, Wallace wrote, "I've never interviewed a more tormented man."

It surely is one of the more poignant ironies of November 22 that a man who performed more bravely than anyone else there that day was one of the most severely punished.

ON THE MONDAY FOLLOWING the assassination, Bobby put aside his investigative work to bury his brother. In his funeral tailcoat, he marched past the solemn crowds lining the streets, following the flag-draped gun carriage that carried his brother from the Capitol rotunda to St. Matthew's Cathedral and then his final resting place in Arlington. Walking slowly down Pennsylvania Avenue with Jackie and Teddy, he retraced the steps that Jack had taken a thousand days earlier to begin his presidency. In the old news footage, the utter bleakness of the day is all written in Bobby's eyes.

Ed Guthman and Nicholas Katzenbach, the deputy attorney general, had tried to prevail upon Bobby to ride in a closed limousine, for security reasons, instead of walking in the funeral procession. But he waved them off. It was the beginning of a recurring dispute between Guthman and Bobby over his safety that would drag on until the day he died. "He was never afraid. After his brother was killed, a bunch of us would talk to him about getting security, but he always brushed it off."

By midnight, the friends and family who had filled the White House for the funeral had deserted it, leaving only the president's brother and widow.

"Shall we go visit our friend?" Bobby suggested. The two drove past the Lincoln Memorial and over the Potomac to the sloping lawn below the Lee mansion whose panoramic vista Jack had marveled at weeks earlier. In the night gloom, brightened only by the grave's fluttering eternal flame, the two knelt and prayed.

The day after the funeral, the Kennedys began converging as usual for Thanksgiving at the family compound in Hyannis Port. Jackie arrived by plane with her children, Caroline and John Jr., after visiting her husband's grave in the morning. Teddy and his family also flew to the compound, as well as his sisters Pat, Eunice, and Jean and their families. "It was a bleak day," on the Cape that Thanksgiving, the *New York Times* reported. "The landscape, rust-colored with the dead leaves of scrub oaks, seemed more desolate than the gray, restless waters of Nantucket Sound." The *Times* reported that when Jackie arrived, she went directly to her father-in-law's house, avoiding her own, which was filled with mementos of the late president. One of the more touching, the newspaper observed, was a watercolor painting in the hall commemorating a happier family gathering, with a touch of Kennedy humor. It depicted a victorious JFK returning to his family's cheers at the prow of his racing sloop Victoria—in a pose that called to mind "Washington Crossing the Delaware"—after winning his party's presidential nomination in Los Angeles.

Bobby could not face Thanksgiving at Hyannis Port, with a clan now hollowed of the two men who had once been its center—Jack and Joe, the powerful patriarch who had been robbed of speech and confined to a wheelchair since suffering a stroke in 1961. Instead, Bobby stayed at Hickory Hill for the holiday with Ethel and their seven children. About twenty people, the usual mixture of Justice Department colleagues and press friends, were invited for brunch. Bloody Marys were served. Bobby and Ethel "were putting up their usual good fronts," recalled Sheridan, who had just returned from the Hoffa trial in Nashville. "But you could tell, looking at him, of the strain."

Bobby steered Sheridan away from the party—he wanted to know what his investigator was finding out about the assassination. Sheridan suspected that the Teamster boss was involved. "I remember telling him what Hoffa had said when John Kennedy was killed. . . . I didn't want to tell him, but he made me tell him," recalled Sheridan. "Hoffa was down in Miami in some restaurant when the word came of the assassination, and he got up on the table and cheered. At least that's what we heard."

That weekend Bobby took his family to the Kennedy mansion in Palm Beach, where he gathered around him the band of brothers who had fought alongside him, from the 1950s underworld probes to the New Frontier crusades—including Sheridan, Guthman, and White House press secretary Pierre Salinger. It was a wrenching weekend, with Bobby alternately possessed by numbing grief and savage anger. Salinger, the former San Francisco journalist whose life Bobby had forever transformed after recruiting him for his Senate rackets investigation, remembered the weekend years later with a shudder: "I mean, he was the most shattered man I had ever seen in my life. He was virtually non-functioning. He would walk for hours by himself. . . . From time to time, he'd organize a touch football game. . . . But they were really vicious games. I mean it seemed to me the way he was getting his feelings out was in, you know, knocking people down. Somebody, in fact . . . broke a leg during one of those games. I mean they were really, really tough."

Bobby also continued to be driven by investigative zeal that weekend. He conferred with Sheridan about Oswald and Ruby. Bobby asked him to fly to Dallas and make some private inquiries. "The key name was Marina Oswald [widow of the alleged assassin]—he wanted Walt to check in to see what she really knew," Richard Goodwin, the JFK speechwriter and aide, told me.

"The thing about Bob was he was going to deal with the truth, whatever it was," Guthman said. "He was going to work hard to find it out. And the people who worked for him, like Walter, that's the way it was for them too. He was someone Bob trusted totally. He was a first-class investigator. It was always hard facts with Walter, there was not going to be any bullshit."

After sending Sheridan to Dallas, Bobby dispatched another trusted Kennedy family intimate, Bill Walton, to Moscow, one week after the assassination. Walton carried with him a secret message for the Soviet government from Bobby and Jackie. It was the most astounding mission undertaken at the request of the Kennedy family in those astounding days after the death of JFK.

WILLIAM WALTON WAS THE ideal man to play the role of confidential courier. There was no one the Kennedys trusted more. If Bobby had his loyal band of brothers, JFK attracted the devotion of his own circle of male friends. And none of these men enjoyed a more easy compatibility with the president than Walton, whom JFK fondly called "Billy Boy."

"I was always surprised that he thought I was as close a friend as he did," Walton recalled years later. "He kept drawing me into things. I was even in his bedroom in the White House. I never expected to be there. Finally we were totally intimate. I think he was deeply fond of me. I was of him. I haven't had many male friends as close as he became finally.

"I was not subservient to him in the way you see so many people. My position was independent. And to tell you the truth, [when we first met], he thought I was a lot more famous than he was."

Walton met Kennedy in the late 1940s in Georgetown, where the young unwed congressman was living with his sister, Eunice, and Walton was turning the second floor of his Victorian-style home into a studio, after leaving journalism to try his hand at painting. Walton, a former *Time* magazine war correspondent who won a Bronze Star after parachuting into Normandy with General James Gavin's 82nd Airborne Division, had known JFK's late brother and sister, Joe and Kick, in London. He flew one mission with Joe's naval aviation outfit about a month before the eldest Kennedy brother died on a treacherous bombing run. Eight years older than JFK, Walton must have conjured memories of his heroic older brother in Jack.

But if Walton had the resume of a man's man, he was equally at ease in the company of women, with whom his relationships tended to be "sweet and safe and jolly," in the words of one such female companion, Martha Gellhorn, the distinguished war reporter and ex-wife of Ernest Hemingway. Walton also enjoyed a "sweet and safe" friendship with Jackie Kennedy.

He met her in Washington before she was married, when she was "just a wonderful-looking, kooky, young" inquiring photographer for the now-defunct *Times-Herald*. He immediately was drawn to her "fey, elfin quality" and her curiosity about books and art. She liked his bohemian style, with his fondness for wearing tight blue jeans and work shirts years before it became a popular look, and his love of gossip. Walton was twenty years older than the wide-eyed gamine, but he had a wonderful, boyish spirit and crooked grin that brought to Gellhorn's mind "a clever and funny Halloween pumpkin." Like other women, Jackie was also surely drawn to Walton's valiant effort at single fatherhood, raising son Matthew and daughter Frances by himself after he was divorced from his mentally unstable wife.

After the Kennedys moved into the White House, the first couple made Walton a frequent sidekick, finally giving him an official role in 1963 as the chairman of the Fine Arts Commission, where he and Jackie joined hands to save Washington's historic blocks from the wrecking balls of philistine developers. She sent him flirtatious notes on White House stationery, including a collage featuring a photo of Walton with the inevitable cigarette in hand and the inscription: "Hate cigarettes—but I simply can't resist those Marlboro men! Will you be my Valentine?"

He was in a "unique position," Walton later noted, because he was equally close to both Jack and Jackie. They each confided their secrets in him and they used him to communicate with each other. "I figured out later that I was a real link for both of them. You can well imagine how tough that period is in anybody's life . . . it is the eye of the hurricane." Walton—witty, worldly, dishy—helped ground them both. They could act around him as if they were still the young, carefree couple they had been back in Georgetown.

One summer day Walton brought an architectural model of his proposed renovations for Lafayette Square, which JFK had taken a strong interest in, to Hyannis Port, where the Kennedys were vacationing. "[Jack] got down on the floor and just loved it. And played with it. And Jackie came in and said, 'You two,'" Walton recalled with a laugh. "And later another time she caught us on his bedroom floor. He was supposed to be taking a nap, meaning he just had on his underpants, and it was like 2:30 in the afternoon. He'd had a little sleep, and then I'd been let in because I had a crisis on something that had to be decided that afternoon. We're on the floor with another [model], and she went out and got her camera and took pictures and sent me a copy of it. And it said, 'The president and the czar,' because the newspapers had started calling me 'czar of Lafayette Square.'"

"Bill thinks that Jack's flirtatiousness with men is a part of his sexual drive and vanity," Walton's friend, Gore Vidal, recorded in his journal in September 1961. Vidal, who years later called his friend "the only civilizing influence in that White House," enjoyed encouraging Jackie's own naughty side.

That summer he teamed up with Walton to escort Jackie, with whom he had a family connection, on an adventure in Provincetown, already a gay mecca. "Jackie and Bill Walton arrive at the Moors Motel at 5:30," Vidal wrote in his journal. "That morning Jackie had been pondering over the phone to me—should she wear a blond wig 'with braids' in order not to be recognized. Instead, she wears a silk bandana, a jacket, capri pants, and looks dazzling. Bill wears a dark blue sports shirt; and the usual lopsided grin. . . . They came into my room at the motel. No one about. Jackie flung herself on the bed— free!"

The first lady of the United States and her male companions then plunged into a night of frivolity that could surely never be repeated in today's dreary, political climate, with its all-seeing media eye. They attended a performance of Shaw's *Mrs. Warren's Profession* at the Provincetown Playhouse—bad enough considering the scandalous history of the play about prostitution and the hypocrisy of Victorian high society, which was banned in Britain for eight years after it was written in 1894. But after the play, the merry trio then went bar-hopping, ending up in a dimly lit watering hole whose upstairs bar was frequented by lesbians. "Jackie was fascinated but dared not look in," Vidal noted.

Bill Walton was very discreet about his sexual yearnings, which by this point in his life were decidedly homosexual. Friends like Vidal—who ran into him again that September in Provincetown "cruising the Atlantic House, very relaxed"—certainly knew, as did fellow JFK pals like Ben Bradlee, who assumed he was "gay as a goose." Did JFK and Jackie know? The ever-discreet Walton, who died in 1994, never said whether he revealed his sexuality to the first couple. Walton's son, Matthew, said he would "bet a thousand to one against it." Still, the three shared sexual confidences and Jack was comfortable enough to ask Walton to squire his mistresses to White House events. If JFK was aware of his friend's secret life, he was clearly self-assured enough about his own sexuality not to feel threatened by it. In fact, as Walton remarked to Vidal, he seemed to thrive on male, as well as female, adoration.

Bobby, on the other hand, did not share his brother's casual polymorphous perversity. Vidal, who carried on a notorious feud with the younger Kennedy through much of the 1960s, sensed homosexual panic in Bobby's taut, angry attitude toward men such as himself. "I couldn't stand Bobby," said Vidal, recalling the two men's poisoned relationship years later. "There are certain visceral dislikes that surface in people. It surfaced in me certainly—and in him." Vidal thought Bobby had the blunt personality of an Irish cop. "The two people Bobby most hated (a rare distinction, because he hated so many people) were . . . Jimmy Hoffa and me," the author remarked.

Despite the whiff of homophobia in Vidal's nostrils, Bobby never seemed discomfited by Walton. They had worked closely together in the 1960 presidential campaign. "Bill had everybody's ear—he had direct access to Jack and Bobby," said Justin Feldman, a Kennedy organizer who loaned space in his New York law office to Walton during the campaign. "They completely trusted him. Bobby talked to him several times a day during the campaign. The Kennedys trusted him with the tough assignments. At one point, Bobby didn't like the stories being written about Jack by a reporter in the *New York Post*. I was sitting with Walton in our office when he got Bobby on the speaker phone to discuss the situation. Bill told him, 'Mission accomplished.' Bobby said, 'How did you do that?' Walton said, '[The reporter] is coming to work for us. You'll be paying him $1,000 a week.'"

Bobby, the driving engine behind his brother's campaign, valued loyalty to his family's political cause above all else. And he knew Walton was deeply devoted. "My father was a believer," Matthew Walton recalled. "You might call him an idealist in the sense that there was nothing in it for him—certainly not money. He never really believed in a political movement before JFK."

"Bill was disinterested—he was not out to get glory for himself, nor was he feathering his nest in the current tradition," added Vidal. "He wanted nothing for himself other than to be amused, which he was, by court life."

When his service to Jack came to a stunning end on November 22, 1963, Walton was overcome. He was leaving the West Wing lobby with Pat Moynihan shortly before JFK's death was officially announced, when Moynihan pointed to the White House flag, which had just been lowered: "Bill, you might as well see that." Walton visibly sagged.

"Let's walk out the way he would have expected us to," said Walton, trying to hold himself together. But he couldn't. Moynihan had to help him into a cab at the Northwest Gate.

But there was still the family, Bobby and Jackie. And they needed Walton again that week, after he had helped oversee a proper ceremonial departure for his friend. They were to entrust him with a final, highly confidential task. "He was exactly the person that you would pick for a mission like this," said Vidal.

BILL WALTON HAD BEEN scheduled to fly to the Soviet Union on November 22, at the request of JFK, to help open a dialogue with Russian artists. The artistic exchange mission was part of Kennedy's peace offensive, which was gathering momentum that year, with his eloquent olive branch speech at American University in June and the nuclear test ban treaty in August. Walton was to visit Leningrad and Moscow, where he was to oversee the opening of an American graphic arts exhibit for the U.S. Information Agency. Walton canceled his flight after hearing the news from Dallas. But Bobby later urged him to go ahead with his travel plans, and to carry a secret message from him and Jackie to a trusted contact in the Soviet government. On November 29, one week after the assassination, Walton took a Pan Am flight to London, and after connecting to Helsinki, arrived in Leningrad on an Aeroflot plane the following day. After touring the Hermitage in Leningrad, Walton flew to Moscow, where he would spend the next two weeks.

Moscow was in the grip of its usual frigid winter, and Walton was fighting a bad cold, blowing his nose into a red handkerchief as he went unflaggingly about his busy schedule. He chatted with Russian artists at the USIA exhibit and visited their studios, the state-sanctioned variety as well as underground ones, to view their work. He went to a poetry reading in a crowded hall, where passionate young fans ran to the stage to scribble questions on bits of paper for the poets after they finished their recitals. "Poets in Moscow have fans as devoted as American bobbysoxers are to movie stars," a bemused Walton later observed. "They debate the relative achievements of their heroes and heroines."

Walton was also invited to take tea with Mrs. Khrushchev at the House of Friendship, a government-sponsored club where foreign dignitaries were fêted. The wife of the Soviet leader immediately turned the conversation to Jackie Kennedy, whom she had met in Vienna during the 1961 summit. "She is so strong and so brave," she said, her eyes welling up. "My heart aches for her and for the two children who probably won't even remember their father."

Everywhere Walton went in Leningrad and Moscow, people wanted to talk about his dead friend. "When I arrived, he had been dead a week," Walton later recalled. "Tough old bureaucrats would brush aside a tear as they spoke of him. In several studios the painters stood in one minute of silent tribute before we began our talk about the arts. In one house the cook, crippled by age, hobbled on crutches from the kitchen and with tears coursing down her cheeks gave me a handful of paper flowers to put on John Kennedy's grave. The emotion was so genuine, the feeling so deep, that one wondered how this young man, in such a brief presidency, could have gotten through to the people of this distant land."

The Russians Walton met credited the young president with trying to ease the doomsday terror of the Cold War. "He was a man of peace." This, observed Walton, "was the universal epitaph" for his friend as he traveled the land held in mutual nuclear bondage with the United States.

"I could see that President Kennedy's death was as disrupting to the USSR as to everyone else. With him the Russian leaders felt they had established personal contact. Over and over they emphasized how much more important personal connections are than cumbersome diplomatic contacts between great powers."

Among those Walton spoke with about the violent transformation of the U.S. government was Soviet journalist Aleksei Adzhubei, the son-in-law of Khrushchev. Over three glasses of throat-soothing hot tea and a cognac, Walton tried to reassure the well-connected *Izvestia* editor that America had not been taken over by a "reactionary clique." He asserted that President Johnson "has indicated a real desire" to continue JFK's policies. Walton must have "bit his tongue" as he passed along these assurances about LBJ, as one report of the meeting later observed, for he "detested" the new president, and the

feeling was mutual. Like Bobby, he shuddered to think of the Texan occupy-
ing JFK's office.

Despite what he told Adzhubei over tea and cognac, Bill Walton had a
much more disturbing secret message for the Soviet government, which he
delivered as soon as he arrived in Moscow. Bobby had asked Walton to meet
with Georgi Bolshakov, a Soviet agent formerly stationed in Washington,
through whom the Kennedys had communicated confidential messages to
Khrushchev at critical points in their administration, including the Cuban
Missile Crisis. The squat, pug-nosed, jovial Bolshakov was a frequent visitor
to Bobby's Virginia home and to his spacious Justice Department suite,
where he would sweep unannounced into the attorney general's office, with
Kennedy's diligent secretary Angie Novello running frantically after him. So
closely associated was he with Kennedy circles that *Newsweek* dubbed him
the "Russian New Frontiersman." Official Washington frowned on the back
channel between the Kennedys and Bolshakov. But that did not deter Bobby
from pursuing the relationship.

"One time Bob wanted to invite Georgi to a party of government officials
on board the presidential yacht, the *Sequoia*," recalled James Symington, the
attorney general's administrative assistant, in a recent interview. "But Mc-
Cone from the CIA said, 'If he gets on the boat, I get off.' McCone was appalled at the idea of swanning around with some Soviet agent. But Bob was
looser than that. Bob had no illusions about Bolshakov—he had no illusions
about anyone. He knew perfectly well what Bolshakov was. But he knew
how to read him. And he knew he could be useful. It was impossible for JFK
and Khrushchev to speak directly, so it was important for the Kennedys to
have a back channel to communicate with the Kremlin."

Now Bobby was using Bolshakov one more time to relay a top-secret
message to the Soviet leader. The attorney general instructed Walton to go
directly to Bolshakov in Moscow, without first checking in to his quarters at
the U.S. Embassy. Bobby did not want the new U.S. ambassador Foy Kohler,
whom he regarded as anti-Kennedy, to know about the Bolshakov meeting.
Kohler was a hardliner who thought Khrushchev was more dangerous than
Stalin. "He gave me the creeps," Bobby later recalled of Kohler, adding that
he didn't regard him as someone "who could really get anything done with
the Russians." Kohler was equally cool to Kennedy. During the 1961 Berlin
crisis, when Kohler was the State Department official in charge of the Soviet
Union, he remembered, "Bobby would sit there across the table with those
cold blue eyes as if to say, 'You son of a bitch, if you ever let my brother down,
I'm going to knife you.'"

Walton delivered his remarkable message to Bolshakov at Moscow's ornate Sovietskaya restaurant. What he heard must have reminded the Russian of an unsettling encounter he had had with Bobby the year before in Washington. As Bolshakov came out of an August 1962 meeting with JFK at the White House, where he was asked to relay a conciliatory message to Khrushchev, Bobby heatedly confronted his Russian friend: "Goddamn it, Georgi, doesn't Premier Khrushchev realize the president's position? Every step he takes to meet Premier Khrushchev halfway costs my brother a lot of effort. . . . In a gust of blind hate, his enemies may go to any length, including killing him."

Now, in Moscow, Bobby Kennedy's representative was reporting that the attorney general's worst fears had come true. What Walton told Bolshakov over their meal at the Sovietskaya stunned the Russian. He said that Bobby and Jackie believed that the president had been killed by a large political conspiracy. "Perhaps there was only one assassin, but he did not act alone," Walton said, continuing the message from the Kennedys. There were others behind Lee Harvey Oswald's gun. J. Edgar Hoover had told both Bobby and Jackie that Oswald was a Communist agent. But despite the alleged assassin's well-publicized defection to the Soviet Union and his attention-grabbing stunts on behalf of Fidel Castro, the Kennedys made it clear that they did not believe he was acting on foreign orders. They were convinced that JFK was the victim of U.S. opponents. And, Walton told Bolshakov, "Dallas was the ideal location for such a crime."

Despite this provocative remark, the Kennedy courier apparently did not mean to implicate President Johnson in the crime. But he shared with Bolshakov the Kennedys' true scornful feelings about JFK's successor. Johnson was "a clever timeserver" who would be "incapable of realizing Kennedy's unfinished plans." More pro-business than JFK, Johnson was certain to stock his administration with a legion of corporate representatives. The one hope for peaceful relations between the two countries was Robert McNamara. Walton described the defense secretary as "completely sharing the views of President Kennedy on matters of war and peace."

Walton then discussed Bobby's political future. He said he planned to stay on as attorney general through 1964, and then he planned to run for governor of Massachusetts, an idea Kennedy had already floated in the press. He would use this office as a political base for an eventual race for the presidency. If he succeeded in returning to the White House, he would resume his brother's quest for détente with the Soviet Union. Some Russians he spoke with, added Walton, regarded Bobby as more of a hard-liner toward

Moscow than President Kennedy. "This is untrue," Walton assured Bolshakov. The younger brother might have a tougher shell than JFK had, Walton
acknowledged. But "Robert agreed completely with his brother and, more
important, actively sought to bring John F. Kennedy's ideas to fruition."

The remarkable meeting between Walton and Bolshakov was first recounted in *One Hell of a Gamble,* a widely praised 1997 book about the
Cuban Missile Crisis by Timothy Naftali, a Yale scholar at the time and now
director of the Richard Nixon Presidential Library, and Aleksandr Fursenko,
chairman of the history department at the Russian Academy of Sciences.
Though the book itself—which was based on secret documents from a
variety of Soviet agencies and government bodies, including the KGB and
Politburo—attracted wide coverage in such publications as the *New York
Times, Washington Post, Business Week, Foreign Affairs, The Economist,* and
The Nation, none of these reviews saw fit to highlight Walton's extraordinary
mission on behalf of the Kennedys, certainly one of the book's more eye-
popping disclosures.

Newsweek's Evan Thomas, a dean of Washington journalism, did zero in
on the book's account of the Moscow mission in his 2000 biography of Robert Kennedy, wagging his finger at Kennedy for this "irresponsible and potentially mischievous act of backdoor diplomacy." But Thomas completely
ignored the most provocative part of Kennedy's communication—his views
on the assassination—and focused solely on Bobby's anti-Johnson sentiments and political ambitions. Bobby's astonishing secret message to Moscow, one of the most revealing glimpses we have from those days of his
thinking about the assassination, would disappear down the media hole as
soon as it was made public.

Bolshakov immediately delivered a report on what Walton told him to his
superiors at the GRU, the Soviet military intelligence agency. It undoubtedly
added to the gloom at the Kremlin, where the Kennedy assassination was
already viewed as a backlash by hard-line elements in the U.S. national security establishment against JFK's bid for rapprochement with the Soviets.
When Khrushchev heard about Kennedy's death, he had broken down and
wept. "He just wandered around his office for several days, like he was in a
daze," a Soviet official told Pierre Salinger.

Robert Kennedy's post-Dallas, back-channel message to Moscow is a
stunning historical footnote. The man who bared his soul to the Soviets
that week is, after all, the same man who had served as counsel for the notorious red-baiting senator from Wisconsin, Joe McCarthy. The man who led
the administration's relentless drive to overthrow Fidel Castro and stop the

spread of Communism in Latin America. The man so enthralled by the adventures of James Bond, the supremely elegant and implacable foil of Soviet skullduggery, that he wrote fan letters to Bond's creator, Ian Fleming.

Robert Kennedy's views of the Soviet threat had, like his brother's, become more complex with time and experience. But the Soviet Union was still his country's most feared enemy, with whom his brother had parried and thrusted all over the world, from Berlin to Cuba to Southeast Asia. Nonetheless, the ground beneath his feet had given way for Bobby Kennedy on November 22. The world was, in an instant, deeply different. The enemy lines no longer seemed so certain that week. Suddenly the attorney general of the United States regarded the government of our leading enemy as less alien than our own. He was eager to share his darkest suspicions with Moscow, taking pains to hide this extraordinary communication from the U.S. embassy there. What is even more remarkable than the fact that Kennedy engaged in an "irresponsible act of backdoor diplomacy" is the fact that such an intensely patriotic man, someone who was viscerally anticommunist, felt driven to do so.

There is no other conclusion to reach. In the days following his brother's bloody ouster, Robert Kennedy placed more trust in the Soviet government than the one he served.

Why did Kennedy feel so estranged from his own government that he was willing to take such an extreme step? To understand his conspiratorial frame of mind in the days after Dallas, we must understand the inner workings and tensions of the Kennedy administration in the years leading to the assassination. John F. Kennedy's body was not long in the ground when his administration began to be enshrouded in the gauzy myths of Camelot. Years later these myths would be shredded by the counterlegend of a decadent monarch, a sexually frenzied and heavily medicated leader whose reckless personal behavior put his nation at risk. Neither of these versions conveys the essential truth of the Kennedy administration. Missing from the vast body of literature on the Kennedy years—including the sentimental memoirs, revisionist exposés, and standard texts—is a sense of the deep tumult at the heart of the administration. The Kennedy government was at war with itself.

2

1961

John Kennedy was haunted by the specter of cataclysmic war. An avid reader of history from boyhood on, he was acutely aware of how the Great War had been stumbled into by the great powers, decimating the flower of Europe's youth and leaving behind scarring images of muddy, blood-soaked trenches and the dead stillness of poisoned air. "All war is stupid," he had written home from the Pacific in 1943, while fighting the next war, the one that World War I—the war to end all wars—had led to. The death of his older brother, Joe, in a fiery aerial explosion over the English Channel during a suicidal mission, brought home the raw misery of it all. "He was very close to my brother Joe, and it was a devastating loss to him personally, and he saw the enormous impact that it had on my father," Ted Kennedy told me. "He was a very different person when he came back from the war. I think this burned inside of him."

But it was the Cold War, with its constant threat of instant annihilation, that confirmed the ultimate absurdity of war. Kennedy came to recognize that war in the nuclear age was unthinkable. "I think that the principal reason Kennedy ran for the presidency was he thought the Eisenhower-Dulles policy of massive retaliation and all of that was heading the country toward nuclear war," said Theodore Sorensen, contemplating his days with JFK years later in the offices of his Manhattan law firm. "He felt the policy of massive retaliation—in which we supposedly kept the peace by saying if you step one foot over the line in West Berlin or somewhere else, we will respond by an-

nihilating you with nuclear weapons—he felt that was mad. He also felt it
was a policy that had no credibility and would *not* prevent Soviet pressures
or incursions in one place or another."

But John Kennedy did not run for the White House in 1960 against the
scowling anticommunist Richard Nixon as a peace candidate. He was too
politically shrewd for that. Kennedy had seen the owlish, high-minded Adlai
Stevenson, darling of the Democratic Party's liberal establishment, soundly
defeated twice by Republican war hero Dwight Eisenhower. From the Mc-
Carthy era on, flag-waving Republican candidates had beaten their Democratic opponents by portraying them as soft and effete defeatists, no match
for our brutal and implacable enemies. (It was a winning political formula
that Republicans would use throughout the Cold War and then successfully
retool, at least for a time, with the "war on terror.") John Kennedy, however,
was no Adlai Stevenson. The party's liberal wing—regally presided over by
the sainted widow of the Democrats' gloried past, Eleanor Roosevelt—hated
him for it, scorning Kennedy as slick and vague—"a gutless wonder," in Harry
Truman's bitter formulation. Mrs. Roosevelt wondered, with reason, how the
author of *Profiles in Courage*, a book extolling political leaders who put prin-
ciple ahead of expediency, could have avoided taking a stand against McCar-
thyism, the greatest threat to American democracy of the day. If only the
glamorous young senator "had a little less profile and a little more courage,"
she tartly remarked.

But the Kennedy family had no interest in being beautiful losers like
Stevenson, whose inevitable defeats were embraced by liberals as confirmation of their own natural superiority. Winning was always the goal with the
Kennedys, and they knew how to do it. The Kennedy brothers might have
been raised in Brahmin comfort and been educated at the most elite New
England schools, but when it came to the brawling world of politics, they
were not that far removed from the Irish saloons of their forefathers.

In his 1960 presidential race, John Kennedy faced the most cunning and
dirty politician on postwar America's national stage, Richard Nixon. JFK beat
him by playing every bit as dirty—and more important, by grabbing the war
club that Republicans like Nixon used to beat Democratic contenders, and
using it against "Tricky Dick" instead. Kennedy stunned Nixon by thumping
his chest louder than his opponent on the nuclear arms race and on Cuba,
where Fidel Castro's revolutionary government was dramatically breaking
away from U.S. dominion. Prodded by his Georgetown friend Joseph Alsop,
a syndicated newspaper columnist with close ties to the CIA, JFK sold voters
on the alarming idea that we were falling dangerously behind the Soviets in

the nuclear arms race. The "missile gap" turned out to be a myth, the creation of Air Force intelligence analysts and credulous newsmen, as Kennedy would be informed by a Pentagon arms expert soon after moving into the White House. But during the campaign, the missile gap hue and cry succeeded in putting Nixon on the defensive, as did Kennedy's clarion call to support Cuban "freedom fighters" in their crusade to take back the island from Castro.

Nixon felt especially flummoxed by Kennedy's call for liberating Cuba, since the vice president was plotting to do just that, along with the CIA and a band of Cuban émigrés. Because he was obligated not to reveal the top-secret plan, Nixon was tongue-tied during the fourth and final presidential debate when Kennedy called for Cuba's liberation. "I had no choice but to take a completely opposite stand and attack Kennedy's advocacy of open intervention in Cuba," Nixon wrote in his 1978 memoirs. "I shocked and disappointed many of my own supporters. . . . In that debate, Kennedy conveyed the image—to 60 million people—that he was tougher on Castro and communism than I was." Nixon, a master of the black arts of electoral politics, had finally met his match.

Kennedy edged out Nixon by a whisper of a margin on Election Day, but liberal JFK supporters like John Kenneth Galbraith, the economist who had been Kennedy's tutor at Harvard and esteemed advisor in the campaign, worried about the costs of victory, especially JFK's promise to help free Cuba. Journalists and historians have made much of the Kennedy family's alleged deal with Chicago mobsters to deliver votes in their key city. But no pact would prove more decisive, or more costly to Kennedy, than the one he made with Vulcan, god of fire and metal. By invoking the gods of weapons and war, Kennedy succeeded in banishing the Democrats' image of Stevensonian weakness and replacing it with a vigorous new muscularity. But the champions of aggressive foreign policy who thrilled to Kennedy's militaristic rhetoric now expected the new president to deliver. As Kennedy prepared to take office, they eagerly awaited a massive U.S. arms buildup and a bold effort to roll back communism in Cuba.

If the new president was committed to expanding America's nuclear arsenal, he was even more determined never to use it. This seemingly contradictory position was vividly displayed in Kennedy's ringing inaugural address. The speech revealed a man with "one foot in the Cold War, and one foot in a new world he saw coming," as Kennedy advisor Harris Wofford described the new president. With its double-edged message of bellicose vigilance and pacific idealism, the speech appealed to a broad political spectrum.

While Kennedy vowed the nation would "pay any price, bear any burden, meet any hardship, support any friend, oppose any foe to assure the survival and the success of liberty," he also dispensed with the usual Soviet-bashing rhetoric and invited our enemy to join us in a new "quest for peace, before the dark powers of destruction unleashed by science engulf all humanity in planned or accidental self-destruction." Likewise, he offered a post-colonial vision to the Third World, and Latin America in particular, where the United States would help "in casting off the chains of poverty" in an "alliance for progress"—but immediately followed this with a veiled warning to those revolutionary groups in the region who sought to follow Castro's path, vowing to "oppose aggression or subversion anywhere in the Americas."

The inaugural was an inspired work of oratory, whose soaring rhetoric succeeded in making its aggressive interventionism as well as its ambitious humanitarianism seem of a whole. Calling on powers both dark and light in our nature, it was cheered by everyone from Norman Thomas on the left to Barry Goldwater on the right. Only a speech this deftly written could have thrilled both the pacifist poet Robert Lowell, who had served prison time during World War II as a conscientious objector, and one of that war's most ferocious lions, Admiral Arleigh Burke. After Kennedy's speech, Lowell was moved to declare his joy "that at long last the Goths have left the White House." Old "31-Knot" Burke—President Eisenhower's crusty, saber-rattling chief of naval operations and certainly a man Lowell would have considered one of those "Goths"—was no less enthused. "I was there [at the inauguration] along with the other [Joint] Chiefs [of Staff], and I have never heard a better speech," Burke later recalled. "I thought, 'This is a magnificent speech. It's the best statement of the policies in which I believe that I have ever heard.' . . . I was extremely proud on that day."

As Kennedy neared his trumpet blast of a conclusion that inaugural day—hatless and coatless in the biting, bright winter air, warmed only by the passion of his soon to be famous words ("And so, my fellow Americans: ask not what your country can do for you . . .")—he took a sweeping part of the nation "with him through a membrane in time, entering the next decade, and a new era," in author Thurston Clarke's words. Electrified by the bold poetry of JFK's vision that day, many more Americans were willing to follow him through that membrane into the future than had voted for him in November.

Looking back, Ted Sorensen, Kennedy's essential collaborator, saw nothing contradictory about the inaugural address. It embodied, he said, Kennedy's fundamental philosophy of peace through strength. "The line in the inaugural address that is the most important is not 'Ask not what your country can do for you.' It's 'For only when our arms are sufficient beyond doubt can we be certain beyond doubt that they will never be employed.' That was the Kennedy policy in a nutshell. He wasn't for unilateral disarmament—on the contrary, he wanted to build an overwhelming nuclear advantage, so we'd never have to use them, the Soviets would never dare challenge us."

IT'S ONE THING TO write a speech that artfully weaves together opposing views and unites opposing constituencies in a burst of applause. It's another to govern consistently based on such a delicately balanced philosophy. The world of power has a way of reducing subtleties and complexities to their lowest common denominator. Ted Sorensen's experience in the first year of the Kennedy White House is revealing in this regard.

Sorensen was more than just John Kennedy's speechwriter—he was one of the better angels of his nature. He helped Kennedy stay in touch with the liberal conscience that underlay the president's carefully manufactured political enterprise. He knew how to tap into the soaring vision in JFK and how to give it wing in Kennedy's speeches. Hired at the age of twenty-five to be a writer and advisor for Kennedy as the rising politician entered the Senate in 1953, Sorensen quickly learned how to crawl inside his employer and channel his thoughts. "Ted Sorensen is getting to be a mirror image of me, reflecting even what I am thinking," Kennedy told his old Navy crony Paul "Red" Fay. During the decade they spent together, Sorensen would later say, John F. Kennedy "was the only human being who mattered to me." Sorensen's first marriage would become a victim of his devotion to Kennedy. He separated from his wife Camellia during the 1960 presidential campaign and divorced her in July 1963 after fourteen years of marriage.

Still bitter from his loss, Nixon lashed into the two men's eloquent political partnership in an interview with *Redbook* magazine in June 1962, charging Kennedy was a "puppet who echoed his speechmaker" during the 1960 campaign. "It's easier for Kennedy to get up and read Sorensen's speeches, but I don't think it's responsible unless he believes it deeply himself."

Jackie Kennedy—forced to yield much of her husband to Sorensen, especially during the 1960 race—had a better grasp of the dynamic between JFK and the man nearly a decade his junior. Far from a puppet master, the devoted Sorensen was "a little boy in so many ways" who "almost puffs himself up when he talks to Jack," Jackie told a reporter during the campaign with ill-concealed spite. Nixon himself was more generous in his appraisal of Sorensen, telling *Redbook* that Sorensen "has the rare gift of being an intellectual who can completely sublimate his style to another intellectual"—a kind of "passionate self-effacement," in the apt description of Thurston Clarke, who carefully analyzed the working relationship between the two men in his 2004 study of the JFK inaugural, *Ask Not*.

Right-wing opponents of President Kennedy, searching for vulnerabilities in his administration during its first year, sensed something weak and exposed in Kennedy's unique relationship with Sorensen. The speechwriter was not like the rough-and-tumble Irish mafia political operators surrounding Kennedy. The studious young aide, with his slicked down hair and horn-rim glasses, represented JFK's more intellectual and idealistic side. More important, while Kennedy had created a winning political persona as the World War II hero of PT-109 fame, Sorensen embodied the antiwar sentiments that JFK's enemies suspected were really in command of the new presidency despite its tough rhetoric. To these conservative critics, there was something weak and feminine about the team of boyishly handsome, tousled-haired young men who had taken over the government from the reliable old general who had commanded it before them. And in the fall of 1961, these critics zeroed in on Sorensen, the elegant voice of the administration, as the symbol of its weakness.

Unlike Kennedy and many of his other top men, Ted Sorensen had never gone to war and never even served in the military. He had registered in 1948 as a conscientious objector and later escaped service in the Korean War as a father. "I was not against service, I was against killing," Sorensen, told me years later. "I'm not sure that pure pacifists would describe me as a pacifist. I was willing to risk my life [in a noncombatant role]. I believed and still do that there is such a thing as just wars. I think ridding the world of Hitler was justified."

Born into a Unitarian household in Lincoln, Nebraska, Sorensen was raised to view war with a deeply skeptical eye. His father, a crusading attorney and progressive politician named C.A. Sorensen, had sailed on Henry Ford's Peace Ship to Stockholm in 1916, as part of the automobile pioneer's desperate attempt to head off World War I by convening a European peace conference. The attorney, who was also counsel to the women's suffrage movement, met his Russian Jewish wife, Annis Chaikin, when he represented the ardent young feminist against charges of radicalism and pacifism during World War I. Their son Ted would meet his first wife, Camellia, a Quaker who shared the Sorensen family's antiwar philosophy, when she came to attend services at their Unitarian church, since there was no Friends Meeting House in Lincoln.

Knowing Ted Sorensen's background as a Unitarian and conscientious objector, President Kennedy was careful to keep him out of high-tension meetings with the Joint Chiefs of Staff, like one that took place in the White House during the height of the Cuban Missile Crisis. "I'm sure that would have provoked them further," said Sorensen, chuckling today at the polarities JFK had to manage within his administration. "I don't think they ever regarded me as one of their strongest advocates," the former CO drily added.

But Kennedy's opponents would not allow him to keep Sorensen's beliefs discreetly concealed. In September 1961, the White House aide's pacifism exploded as a public issue when Walter Trohan, the Washington bureau chief of the anti-Kennedy *Chicago Tribune*, wrote that "the man behind President Kennedy's rocking chair in a world [filled] with war tensions, escaped military service as a conscientious objector." Republican presidential hopeful Barry Goldwater promptly turned the *Tribune* article into a political issue by inserting it into the *Congressional Record*, remarking, "I can't help but wonder at the thoughts of the fathers and mothers of American boys who are right now being called up for active military service when they learn that one of the president's closest advisors is an objector because of conscience."

Sorensen insists today that Kennedy simply brushed aside the controversy: "It didn't bother the president at all." But it was just one more unsettling fact about the new administration that gnawed at the national security chiefs, who believed that the country's defense rested first and foremost on their shoulders no matter who occupied the Oval Office. They knew, of course, about family patriarch Joe Kennedy's shameful record of appeasement toward the Nazis, which cut short his service as President Roosevelt's ambassador to England and ruined his political future. Now they saw his son surround himself in the White House with men they regarded as Cold War appeasers. From the very beginning of his administration, the young president himself was regarded with a wary suspicion by Washington's warrior culture. They feared JFK was a lightweight who might very well put the nation at risk, a physically and morally compromised man whose victory had been purchased by his cunning crook of a father.

For these men, Kennedy's inauguration was not an occasion for celebration. During the inaugural ceremony, while waiting for a luncheon in Eisenhower's honor at the exclusive F Street Club, a group of senior military officials, including Admiral Arthur Radford, former chairman of the Joint Chiefs, stood grimly watching the TV as the new president called upon the nation to follow him into the future. The military men were focused less on Kennedy's inspiring words than on his forehead, which was perspiring profusely in the frigid winter air. "He's all hopped up!" shouted out General Howard Snyder, the retiring White House physician. Snyder, who had access to FBI and Secret Service files on Kennedy, told Radford that Kennedy—who suffered from Addison's disease—was "prescribed a shot of cortisone every morning to keep him in good operating condition" and on this particularly stressful day he had obviously been administered an extra dose, resulting in his heavily beaded brow. Snyder worried aloud about the nation being placed in the hands of a man so obviously medically impaired: "I hate to think of what might happen to the country if Kennedy is required at three a.m. to make a decision affecting the national security."

It would not be long before Kennedy did face the first such crisis of his administration—and the way he handled it confirmed the warrior elite's worst fears about him.

JACK KENNEDY AND THE CIA seemed made for each other. The spy agency's cloak and dagger derring-do appealed to the James Bond–loving imagination of the young president. But the agency's main attraction was its promise of accomplishing strategic objectives on the cheap and sly, without embroiling the nation in the rampant, unpredictable violence of all-out war.

Kennedy had moved smoothly through the Georgetown social milieu of the CIA's bright, young, Ivy League–educated men. Joe Alsop (Groton '28, Harvard '32), who presided over salon gatherings frequented by the CIA elite with his unique combination of effete mannerisms and Cold War machismo, helped pave the rising young politician's entrance into this world. Among those he introduced to Kennedy was his old Groton friend Richard Bissell, who had been plucked from academia by spymaster Allen Dulles and later groomed as his successor. Some CIA hands were still wary of Kennedy from the McCarthy days, when Jack looked the other way while Bobby served as counsel for the demagogic senator, whose witch hunt grew so feverish that its flames began to lick at the CIA itself, menacing bright young idealists in its top ranks like Cord Meyer and William Bundy, until Dulles boldly told the boozy politician with the five-o'clock shadow of a movie crook to take his business elsewhere. The WASPy agency's snubbing of the crude, publicity-grubbing Irish-Catholic McCarthy echoed the Kennedys' own treatment at the hands of the Protestant establishment. But Jack was too smooth to bring up old tribal resentments like this as he deftly navigated his way through the intelligence culture during his run-up to the presidency.

Bissell was a tall, bespectacled man whose professorial bearing concealed a ruthless character. His wealthy Connecticut family had colonial roots, with one ancestor serving as a spy for General George Washington. Like Dulles, who came from a family of secretaries of state and international financiers, he had a proprietary sense about America. During the 1960 campaign, Bissell responded enthusiastically to Kennedy's aggressive international posture, seeing in him someone like himself—a bright, young leader who would not be content with the global status quo but would seek to roll back the advances of communism, not simply by waving the big nuclear stick, like Eisenhower, but by confronting the Soviets with a variety of counterinsurgency and espionage methods more suited to the world of modern conflict. Meeting privately with Kennedy during the campaign, Bissell, who still worked for a Republican administration, told him he could not flaunt his choice for president, but made no secret of his support for Kennedy.

The Republican Dulles, hedging the agency's bets, voted for Nixon. But Nixon would nurse a deep resentment against the agency for the rest of his life, believing that the CIA director secretly briefed his Democratic opponent about the Bay of Pigs plan, giving Kennedy an edge in the final debate. He also suspected the agency helped tip the election to Kennedy by delaying the Cuba invasion until after the election, depriving Nixon of an October surprise.

After Kennedy's victory, Bissell wrote a friend that he looked forward to the new administration because "I think Kennedy is surrounded by a group of men with a much livelier awareness than the Republicans of the extreme crisis that we are living in. . . . What I really mean is that the Democrats will be far less inhibited in trying to do something about it. My guess is that Washington will be a more lively and interesting place in which to live and work."

Dulles, for his part, did not expect any significant change in his role under Kennedy. The spymaster and his late brother—Eisenhower's secretary of state, John Foster Dulles—had largely run America's foreign policy between the two of them during the 1950s. And he expected to continue the family's policies undisturbed under the new, inexperienced president. Kennedy confidante Bill Walton was stunned to hear Dulles declare his sense of entitlement out loud at a dinner party at journalist Walter Lippmann's home after Kennedy took office. "After dinner," Walton recalled, "the men sat around awhile in an old-fashioned way, and he started boasting that he was still carrying out his brother Foster's foreign policy. He said, you know, that's a much better policy. I've chosen to follow that one." The loyal Walton, who detested Dulles (the feelings were mutual), rang his friend in the White House at dawn and told Kennedy everything the CIA director had said the night before. "God damn it!" a furious Kennedy responded. "Did he really say that?"

For Dulles and Bissell, the world had been their espionage playground under Eisenhower, with their agents romping freely from Iran to Guatemala to Indonesia to the Congo. Under Kennedy, their splendid "monkey business"—as agency masterminds referred to their 1954 military coup in Guatemala—promised to become even more unrestrained. Ike made an effort to tighten the reins on Dulles and his outfit in his second term, but he finally threw up his hands. "I'm not going to be able to change Allen," Eisenhower conceded to his national security advisor, Gordon Gray. He learned to live with a CIA director who firmly believed that the "gentlemen" of U.S. intelligence were not bound by the same moral code that other mortals were.

Dulles and Bissell were sublimely untroubled by any scruples when they plotted the overthrow of the duly elected government of Guatemala's president Jacobo Arbenz, who was deemed too left-wing and too hostile to the continued reign of United Fruit, the corporate colossus that was represented by the Dulles brothers' former Wall Street law firm. Indeed the top two CIA officials waved the coup's success as a gleaming trophy when, less than three months after Kennedy took office, they persuaded the new president to go ahead with the CIA operation against Castro that had been set in motion by Eisenhower the year before.

Bissell, the principal architect of the Arbenz coup, would reassemble the key members of his Guatemala team for the Bay of Pigs operation, including Tracy Barnes, David Atlee Phillips, Howard Hunt, and David Sanchez Morales. These men would soon find, however, that Cuba was no Guatemala. The doomed Bay of Pigs mission would lead to the downfall of spymaster Allen Dulles and the ambitious man in line to succeed him, Richard Bissell. And it would abruptly terminate JFK's romance with the spy agency, turning the Kennedy brothers and their national security apparatus explosively against one another.

IT WAS THE EVENING of Tuesday, April 18, 1961, the day after some 1,500 U.S.–trained Cuban exiles landed on the moonlit shores of their native land to wage war on Fidel Castro. By Tuesday, the invaders' situation was dire, with what remained of Castro's motley air force in control of the skies over the Bay of Pigs and the exile brigade pinned down by relentless enemy fire in the vast Cienaga de Zapata swamp surrounding the landing site, whose primordial muck was infested with crocodiles, mosquitoes, and huge buzzing flies. The brigadistas' supplies and ammunition were running low. It was agonizingly clear to CIA officials in Washington that their attempted liberation of Cuba was hours from a crushing, degrading defeat. The mood at Quarters Eye, the old Army barracks near the Lincoln Memorial that still served as the CIA's headquarters, was frantic.

White House advisor Walt Rostow, already established as the administration's hard-liner against Third World insurgency, drove over to the CIA quarters in his Volkswagen to check in with Bissell, his old Yale professor. He found the normally unflappable espionage wizard unshaven and haggard, surrounded by a number of his distraught men, several of whom were shouting and demanding that Bissell do more to save the brave Cubans the CIA had sent into battle. "We've got to persuade the president! The president must send the Air Force in," one of Bissell's men pleaded.

Kennedy had repeatedly made it clear to Dulles and Bissell that he would not commit the full military might of the United States to the Bay of Pigs operation. He knew that such a display of gunboat diplomacy would destroy his effort to transform the United States' image in the hemisphere from bullying Yankee imperialists to benevolent partners for reform in the new "alliance for progress" he had promised in his inaugural. And he feared that such a heavy-booted action might provoke a dangerous countermove by the Soviets against West Berlin. The president insisted that the exiles' invasion not create a lot of "noise"—a stricture he would continue to place on all anti-Castro operations during his days in office, to the immense frustration of the CIA and Pentagon. To make sure that the brigade soldiers themselves knew that they could not expect to be reinforced by the U.S. Marines, he had sent a military aide to their Central American training camps to deliver the message directly. Kennedy—who was intrigued by the legend of Fidel Castro, the only other leader in the hemisphere whose charisma could rival his own—was taken by the idea that the Bay of Pigs invaders could slip quietly into Cuba and start an insurgency in the mountains, as the bearded revolutionary had done almost five years earlier. The prospect of the Cuban people themselves taking back their country from the Communist dictator was vastly preferable in Kennedy's mind to a counterrevolution enforced by U.S. bayonets.

But that evening at Quarters Eye, Rostow realized that Bissell and the other CIA men had never truly believed that Kennedy would stick to his ban on direct U.S. intervention. "It was inconceivable to them that the president would let [the operation] openly fail when he had all this American power," Rostow later wrote. In the heat of battle, the CIA expected Kennedy to cave and send in warplanes and troops. Realizing it was the agency's last chance to convince Kennedy to do so, Rostow prevailed on Bissell to go to the White

House to make his case one final time directly to the president. Rostow phoned Kenny O'Donnell, who by now also realized the invasion "was going in the shit house," and reaching him in the Oval Office, set up a meeting for late that night.

It was minutes before midnight when the extraordinary meeting convened. Kennedy, McNamara, Vice President Johnson, and Secretary of State Dean Rusk had all just come from the annual Congressional Reception in the East Room and were still wearing their white ties and black tails. They were joined by General Lyman Lemnitzer, chairman of the Joint Chiefs, and Admiral Burke, the Navy chief, both of whom were in full dress uniform. Bissell presented his case for U.S. intervention to the assembled group in urgent tones, "acutely aware of the desperation of those whose lives were on the line," he later recalled. The invasion was "on the brink of failure," he told them, but there was "still hope." Burke was "very much on my side," recalled Bissell. The two men implored Kennedy to unleash the military.

"Let me take two jets and shoot down the enemy aircraft," pleaded Burke.

Kennedy refused. He reminded Bissell and Burke that he had warned them "over and over again" that he would not commit U.S. combat forces to save the operation.

The president was beginning to realize that his top military and intelligence chiefs did not take his instructions that seriously. Kennedy would later learn that the Bay of Pigs operation had been riddled with insubordinate behavior. Up until the moment he finally approved the invasion, Kennedy repeatedly emphasized to Bissell that he reserved the right to abort the operation. But Bissell had sent a very different message to the military leaders of the Bay of Pigs brigade in their Guatemala training camp. They were informed that "there are forces in the administration trying to block the invasion" and if these "forces" succeeded, the brigade leaders were to mutiny against their U.S. advisors and proceed with the invasion. This stunning act of CIA defiance would provoke a public furor when it was later revealed by Haynes Johnson in his 1964 book about the Bay of Pigs. Burke, it was subsequently disclosed, had also flirted with insubordination on the first day of the invasion, "leaning on his orders" in the polite description of a sympathetic chronicler and sending the U.S. aircraft carrier *Essex* and helicopter landing ship *Boxer* close to Cuban shore, in violation of Kennedy's order to keep U.S. ships fifty miles away.

The blunt-spoken admiral grew increasingly angry during the midnight White House meeting as Kennedy repeatedly brushed aside his and Bissell's pleas. Finally, Burke asked for just one destroyer, so he could "knock the hell out of Castro's tanks."

"What if Castro's forces return the fire and hit the destroyer?" Kennedy appropriately asked.

"Then we'll the knock the hell out of them!" roared the admiral. The man who had commanded a destroyer squadron in the South Pacific during World War II, winning fame as "31-Knot" Burke for his speed and daring during the battles of Empress Augusta Bay and Cape St. George, was grappling with someone who had been a junior ensign on a PT boat in the same seas—and the blustery Navy commander was appalled to find himself in such an ignominious position.

But the junior ensign was now president, and he was not easily intimidated. "Burke, I don't want the United States involved in this," Kennedy snapped, beginning to lose his own temper.

"Hell, Mr. President," the Navy chief shot back loudly, "but we *are* involved!" Burke wanted to be "as forceful as I could be in talking to the president," he later recalled. But Kennedy was unmoved.

As the meeting finally came to an end shortly before 3:00 a.m., the president stood by his decision to keep U.S. forces out of the Bay of Pigs and the mission met its doom later that day, with more than 200 brigadistas killed and nearly 1,200 captured and marched off to Castro's prisons. The country's military and intelligence chiefs had clearly believed they could sandbag the young, untested commander-in-chief into joining the battle. But he had stunned them by refusing to escalate the fighting.

"They were sure I'd give in to them and send the go-ahead order to the *Essex*," Kennedy said to Dave Powers. "They couldn't believe that a new president like me wouldn't panic and try to save his own face. Well, they had me figured all wrong."

What JFK suspected about the CIA—that the agency knew all along that its plan was doomed to fail unless Kennedy could be panicked into sending in U.S. forces at the eleventh hour—was confirmed years later. In 2005, a secret internal CIA history of the Bay of Pigs was finally released to the public. The 300-page document contained proof that Bissell concealed the operation's bleak prospects from Kennedy when he briefed him about it for the first time shortly after JFK's election. The internal history quoted a CIA memo dated November 15, 1960, that was prepared for Bissell before the Kennedy briefing. In it, the agency conceded that "our concept . . . to secure a beach with airstrip is now seen to be unachievable, except as joint Agency/ DOD [CIA/Pentagon] action." In other words, "The CIA knew that it couldn't accomplish this type of overt paramilitary mission without direct Pentagon participation—and committed that to paper and then went ahead and tried it anyway," explained Peter Kornbluh of the National Security Archive, the George Washington University–based research group that made public the CIA document. Furthermore, there is no evidence that Bissell informed Kennedy of the CIA's bleak assessment.

It is also now known that the CIA still pushed ahead with the ill-fated mission, even after it discovered that the cover for the clandestine invasion had been blown. One of the operation's key CIA planners, Jacob Esterline, later admitted to a government panel that the agency discovered in advance that the plan had been leaked to Soviet intelligence. "There was some indication that the Soviets somewhere around the 9th [of April] had gotten the date of the 17th," Esterline said, in secret testimony that was later revealed through the indefatigable National Security Archive.

Charles Bartlett, the Washington correspondent for the *Chattanooga Times* and old Kennedy friend who had introduced JFK to his future wife at a 1951 dinner party, also got advance word about the invasion—not from his friend in the White House, but from Castro's former Washington lobbyist, Ernesto Betancourt. "He came to see me after Kennedy had just been in office a few weeks," Bartlett recently recalled. "And he said, 'The CIA is about to make a huge mistake. Terrible things are about to happen and Castro knows all about it.' I was walking around the Oval Office later and it would have been easy to tell Jack. But I figured he had all these pressing appointments, let's not hit him with another one. So I took the information to Allen Dulles. It was the stupidest damn thing I've ever done. He was sitting there in his office at the CIA smoking his pipe. He said, 'Oh, I don't know anything about this. I'll look into it and give you a call.' So I get a call about five days later, but by then the boats were already going ashore. Dulles was really the wrong guy to tell."

Dulles clearly did not care whether Castro and his Soviet patrons knew the invasion was coming, because his agency regarded the band of Cuban exiles who were about to hit the beaches as mere cannon fodder, a device to trigger the real invasion by the U.S. military—one that would be so overwhelming it would quickly sweep aside any resistance. When this cynical calculation failed, short-circuited by the surprisingly resolute Kennedy, Dulles and the CIA high command were stunned. For years they had gotten their way in Washington, with the Dulles brothers running the government as a family franchise, and the secretive agency deceiving and manipulating President Eisenhower under the convenient Cold War cover that dangerous times called for drastic measures. But now a new president was signaling that those days were over.

Dulles believed that "great actions require great determination" and "at the decisive moment of the Bay of Pigs operation," Kennedy showed himself lacking in this quality of leadership. He thought that Kennedy was "surrounded by doubting Thomases and admirers of Castro." On the evening the invasion collapsed, sitting down for dinner with Richard Nixon—the man who had spearheaded the plan as vice president—a visibly distraught Dulles asked for a drink, exclaiming to Nixon, "This is the worst day of my life!" Nixon agreed that Kennedy lost his nerve when he failed to send in U.S. war planes to cover the invasion. This lament about the lack of air cover would become the central fixation of Kennedy critics for decades to come. They were convinced that air strikes could have saved the day for the would-be liberators of Cuba.

As for Bissell, the chief architect of the Bay of Pigs would remain silent about the disaster until shortly before his death in 1994. In his final interview, the former CIA golden boy whose glittering intelligence career would come to an end in the Zapata swamp, made a strange, unnerving remark about his onetime White House patron: "I was probably taken in by Kennedy's charisma. He was such a complicated mix of accomplishments and mistakes that when he died, my children didn't know whether to laugh or cry."

The Bay of Pigs catastrophe sent shock waves through the agency, particularly among the agents who had worked closely with the Cuban émigrés on the operation. CIA men muttered darkly among themselves that Kennedy was guilty of "criminal negligence" or even worse. Years later, Robert Maheu, the shadowy private intelligence operator whom the CIA had asked to serve as a go-between with the Mafia in their plots to kill Castro, would testify bitterly to the Church Committee that the bloodiest crimes in the whole Cuba saga were not those committed by mobsters or CIA agents but by President Kennedy. "I think I rattled some cages. I said something like: 'Senator, I find it difficult to understand all the time and money that is being spent to determine if our country plotted to murder a foreign leader—a murder that never took place—when there is no [effort] to turn the spotlight on the murders that in fact did take place,'" recalled Maheu in his memoir. "I tell you everybody jumped out of their seats."

"Are you saying that murders *actually* took place?" Church asked.

"I said, 'yes,' but my explanation wasn't what he was expecting. The murders I meant were the boys killed during the botched Bay of Pigs invasion."

Anti-Kennedy spleen seeped into the Cuban exiles from their CIA handlers, like Howard Hunt. The night Kennedy was elected, "the Cuban barrio in Miami went wild with joy," noted Hunt in his 1973 memoir, since JFK's campaign rhetoric had raised exuberant expectations about the overthrow of Castro. But after the Bay of Pigs, the hatred of Kennedy became just as florid in Little Havana. The United States now owed the Cuban people a blood debt "so tremendous that it can never be paid," Hunt declared. Captain Eduardo Ferrer, who led the exile air force, bluntly explained the shift in opinion about Kennedy: "The [Bay of Pigs] failure was Kennedy's fault. Kennedy was a little bit immature, a little bit chicken. Today, 90 percent of the Cubans are Republicans because of Kennedy, that motherfucker."

The Bay of Pigs disaster was also viewed with great distress in the Pentagon, where Kennedy's hesitation was seen as sending a dangerous signal of U.S. weakness to Moscow. "Pulling out the rug," said Joint Chiefs Chairman Gen. Lemnitzer, was "unbelievable . . . absolutely reprehensible, almost criminal." General Lauris Norstad, Supreme Commander of Allied Forces in Europe, told a friend that the failed invasion was the worst American defeat "since the war of 1812."

"Their big mistake was that they didn't realize the tremendous importance of the operation or the effect it would have on the world," said Admiral Burke in an oral history for the Naval Institute over a decade later, still furious at Kennedy and his civilian team. "They didn't realize the power of the United States or how to use the power of the United States. It was a game to them. . . . They were inexperienced people."

"Mr. Kennedy," Burke added, "was a very bad president. . . . He permitted himself to jeopardize the nation."

The heavens ripped open for the Kennedy administration following the Cuba crisis and they never came back together. Cuba was the Iraq of its day, no more than a swath of sugar cane afloat in the Caribbean, but to the national security elite who determine such things, it was where the forces of good and evil were arrayed against one another, the epicenter of a struggle that would come close to a literally earth-shattering climax. And in his first test in this supreme confrontation, Kennedy was judged by military and intelligence officials to be a dangerously weak link at the top of the chain of command. He would never again enjoy their complete trust or loyalty.

PRESIDENT KENNEDY, FOR HIS part, was equally estranged from his national security team after the Bay of Pigs. "I've got to do something about those CIA bastards," he raged. He also lashed out at the Joint Chiefs, with their rows of colorful ribbons that boasted of all their military experience: "Those sons-of-bitches with all the fruit salad just sat there nodding, saying it would work." While the president famously took responsibility for the debacle in public, CIA and Pentagon officials knew that he privately spread the word that they were to blame. Never again, he told liberal advisors like Arthur Schlesinger Jr., would he be "overawed by professional military advice."

Weeks after the fiasco, playing checkers at his Cape Cod family compound with his World War II pal Red Fay, whom he had installed as assistant secretary of the Navy, Kennedy was still fuming. "Nobody is going to force me to do anything I don't think is in the best interest of the country," he said, referring to the intense pressures that had been put on him to escalate the Bay of Pigs fighting. "We're not going to plunge into an irresponsible action just because a fanatical fringe in this country puts so-called national pride above national reason."

Kennedy grew more passionate, thinking about the carnage that would have resulted from an all-out U.S. assault on the island. "Do you think I'm going to carry on my conscience the responsibility for the wanton maiming and killing of children like our children we saw [playing] here this evening? Do you think I'm going to cause a nuclear exchange—for what? Because I was forced into doing something that I didn't think was proper and right? Well, if you or anybody else thinks I am, he's crazy."

In his fury, Kennedy threatened to "shatter the CIA into a thousand pieces, and scatter it to the winds." He did not follow through on this vow, but after waiting for a politically expedient interval, he did fire Dulles and Bissell. And shortly after the Cuba fiasco, when the Joint Chiefs urged him to respond to the advances of Communist insurgents in Laos by invading the remote Southeast Asian country, Kennedy did not hesitate to rebuff their advice. "After the Bay of Pigs, Kennedy had contempt for the Joint Chiefs," Schlesinger recalled before his death in early 2007, over drinks in the hushed, stately rooms of New York's Century Club. "I remember going into his office in the spring of 1961, where he waved some cables at me from General Lemnitzer, chairman of the Joint Chiefs, who was then in Laos on an inspection tour. And Kennedy said, 'If it hadn't been for the Bay of Pigs, I might have been impressed by this.' I think JFK's war hero status allowed him to defy the Joint Chiefs. He dismissed them as a bunch of old men. He thought Lemnitzer was a dope."

But Kennedy was acutely aware of how formidable the institutional powers were that he confronted. While still reeling from the Bay of Pigs, the president took his concerns to an old family friend, liberal Supreme Court

justice William O. Douglas. "The episode seared him," said Douglas, recalling their conversation. "He had experienced the extreme power that these
groups had, these various insidious influences of the CIA and the Pentagon,
on civilian policy, and I think it raised in his own mind the specter: Can Jack
Kennedy, president of the United States, ever be strong enough to really rule
these two powerful agencies? I think it had a profound effect . . . it shook
him up!"

Since he had won the White House by the slimmest of margins, Kennedy thought it politically wise to retain icons from the Eisenhower era like
Dulles in his administration, even though friends like journalist Ben Bradlee
had urged him to replace the aging "godfather of American intelligence." In
the case of Dulles, his reappointment might also have been a reward for
his discreet—and wily—political assistance to the Kennedy campaign. JFK
"came into government the successor to President Eisenhower, who was a
great general, a great military figure. . . . He retained the same people in all
these key positions whom President Eisenhower had," recalled Bobby Kennedy in a 1964 oral history. "Allen Dulles was there, Lemnitzer was there,
the same Joint Chiefs of Staff. He didn't attempt to move any of these people
out. . . . They had had the experience; they had had the background; they
evidently were trusted by his predecessor. So he thought he could trust
them."

But when he realized he could not, Kennedy moved to get rid of this old
guard or sideline them. After the cataclysm in Cuba, JFK pulled away from
these national security "wise men" and began to surround himself with his
most trusted personal advisors, men who had fought with him in the political
trenches and were known for their intense loyalty as well as liberal passion:
Sorensen, O'Donnell, Salinger, Schlesinger, Galbraith. He asked Sorensen
to start advising him on foreign affairs even though the young aide had never
traveled beyond the country's borders.

Above all, Kennedy turned to his brother. On the morning that the Cuba
mission began to fail, Kennedy tracked down Bobby at a newspaper editors'
convention in Williamsburg, Virginia, where he was speaking, urgently asking his brother to "come back here." Like Sorensen, Bobby had no foreign
policy experience, but he would move into the center of national security
decision making for the rest of his brother's presidency. Kennedy offered his
younger brother the CIA, but Bobby thought it politically ill-advised. While
he rejected the position of CIA director, however, the attorney general began
to unofficially take on the responsibility of supervising the agency for his

brother. At this juncture, it seemed JFK would have put Bobby in charge of every vital part of his government if he could have.

This is the point where the Kennedy administration began becoming "a family affair," in the words of Berkeley scholar Peter Dale Scott, with the two Kennedys at the center, encircled by the small group of men they considered their band of brothers. "Kennedy couldn't work through the CIA, the Pentagon or even the State Department. There was so little institutional support in Washington for the Kennedys' policies. The bureaucracies were very committed to the Cold War," Scott observed.

Their close relationship fortified the two brothers, gave them confidence that they could take charge of a government that was in many ways hostile to their enterprise. "They were totally loyal to each other," recalled Fred Dutton, who served as JFK's Cabinet secretary, in an interview not long before his death in 2005. "They almost didn't need to communicate with each other, they almost knew what the other person was thinking and doing. Bob's sole focus was to make sure everything was working for his brother. He gave him everything. He did all the unpleasant tasks for Jack. . . . Bob had no problem running interference for his brother, handling the messy things. He was willing to be Mr. Bad Guy."

Cabinet members felt excluded from the meshing of fraternal minds that often replaced formal discussions, Dutton said. "The two brothers often held these sessions by themselves, they'd go off in the corner of the room away from the rest of the Cabinet and staff. During a crisis like the Bay of Pigs, you'd see them talking off to the side of the room. There was a level of conversation they engaged in that not even the senior staff was privy to."

In the beginning, Bobby brought a militant energy to foreign policy councils, especially on Cuba, a reflection of his youthful anticommunism and his deep resentment over the humiliation his brother suffered at the hands of Castro. A government postmortem on the Bay of Pigs that Bobby spearheaded with General Maxwell Taylor in late spring 1961 declared there could be "no long-term living with Castro as a neighbor" and Bobby demanded in meetings about Cuba that the "terrors of the earth" be invoked against the dictator. But over time he would fall under the sway of his brother's more temperate personality and philosophy.

John Kennedy was more viscerally antiwar than has been recognized in some quarters, where he has continued to be portrayed as an aggressive Cold Warrior, even a forerunner to Ronald Reagan. "I am almost a 'peace-at-any-price' president," he once confided to Bill Walton.

"[JFK] brought into the presidency the knowledge of history that many presidents didn't have when they became president," recalled Robert McNamara during a fortieth anniversary retrospective on the administration at the Kennedy Library. "And I think his view was that . . . the primary responsibility of the president is to keep the nation out of war if at all possible."

While Kennedy's foreign policy councils included hawks like Dean Acheson and Paul Nitze, what set apart his presidency from previous Cold War administrations was the surprising presence of pacifists like Sorensen and global visionaries like Chester Bowles, who sought to align the United States with the revolutionary nationalism sweeping the developing world. And it was these voices of peace and progressivism to which JFK seemed more attuned, as Acheson discovered during the 1961 Berlin Crisis when the president rejected his bellicose counsel, prompting Truman's old, mustachioed secretary of state to harrumph about Kennedy, "Gentlemen, you might as well face it. This nation is without leadership."

After Bowles, a liberal patrician from the Stevenson wing of the party, took office as Kennedy's number two man at the State Department, he lost no time in recruiting other innovative foreign policy thinkers, including legendary CBS newsman Edward R. Murrow, George Kennan, and Roger Hilsman. The wave of progressive policymakers brought to Washington by the new Kennedy administration shook the centurions of the old order. J. Edgar Hoover tried mightily to block Murrow's appointment as head of the United States Information Agency, digging as far back as his childhood to find subversive evidence about the television journalist, who had antagonized the FBI chief with his broadsides against the anticommunist excesses of Joe McCarthy. But Murrow finally was confirmed by the Senate, and with Kennedy's backing he promptly began cleansing the agency of its hard-line Cold War propaganda and rehabilitating victims of the McCarthy-era blacklist by finding jobs for them in his agency.

As Murrow told senators during his confirmation hearing, the fundamental message that Kennedy wanted delivered to the world was "that we as a nation are not allergic to change and have no desire to sanctify the status quo." When McCarthy's old Senate ally Bourke Hickenlooper of Iowa brought up Murrow's muckraking CBS documentaries and asked why we couldn't follow the Soviet lead and keep our propaganda more upbeat, the newsman, barely restraining himself, shot back: Because we live in a free society and you couldn't convincingly "tell the American story" if you masked all its flaws.

To his deep disappointment, Murrow would never become more than a second-string advisor for Kennedy. But the president still valued his voice at National Security Council meetings, where he could be counted on to help JFK fend off the more alarming militaristic proposals. His advice on the Bay of Pigs—he was one of the few in Kennedy's circle to warn against it, calling the venture unworthy of a great power and destined to fail—went unheeded. But Kennedy made certain his voice was heard on other issues, from nuclear arms control to Vietnam. Young foreign policy maverick Roger Hilsman would consider him "a staunch ally" in the movement within the Kennedy administration to shift U.S. policy from its regimented Cold War line.

Never before in the Cold War had Washington's halls of power seen the likes of men like Sorensen, Bowles, and Murrow. These men's very presence in high-level national security meetings, along with the president's boyish-looking brother, was seen as an affront by the military and espionage chieftains, who prided themselves on having won a global war against fascist dictatorships and were now pursuing a Cold War victory over communist dictatorships. The national security elite regarded these Kennedy reformers as fuzzy-thinking intruders, out of their depth in the deadly serious arena of global hostilities.

One of the crusading liberals on the Kennedy team who attracted the most suspicion was Richard Goodwin, the thirty-one-year-old White House aide who had moved from his entry-level post as Sorensen's speechwriting assistant to the president's point man on Latin America. Goodwin had no foreign service or national security experience. He was simply a young Boston liberal who shared the president's reform instincts when it came to Latin America. In the months after the Bay of Pigs, President Kennedy would signal his disgust with the national security establishment by making the free-wheeling Goodwin his chief advisor on Cuba. Goodwin's brief stewardship of the explosive Cuba issue is a colorful and little-known chapter in the Kennedy presidency. It vividly demonstrated the Kennedys' ambivalent approach toward the Castro regime. And it soon provoked a sharp backlash.

CHE GUEVARA WAS STALKING Dick Goodwin. Cuba's economic minister, whose revolutionary charisma rivaled that of Fidel Castro himself, knew where the young Kennedy aide would be that night—at a birthday party for a diplomat that was being held in a small apartment in a quiet, dark residential neighborhood of Montevideo, Uruguay's capital city. Guevara arrived at the diplomat's party about an hour after Goodwin with two bodyguards in tow, wearing his trademark olive fatigues, black beret, and combat boots. The Cubans slowly circled the buffet table, sampling the heavy cream cakes that are a Uruguayan specialty. Women broke away from their tangos to swarm around the handsome, bearded revolutionary leader, a fate to which he was accustomed. But, as Goodwin later recalled, "I had no doubt he had come to talk with me. Had I been wiser and more experienced, I would probably have left. But what the hell, I told myself in the highest tradition of Kennedy-style machismo, an American didn't have to run away just because Che Guevara had arrived." If he got in hot water for meeting with the enemy, the White House aide rationalized, he could point out it was just a "chance encounter." But the real reason he stayed, Goodwin admitted, "was curiosity about this romantic figure of revolution. I wanted to talk with him."

Guevara had chosen his prey well. Goodwin was one of the young, progressive New Frontiersmen who seemed to be open to a dialogue with the enemy. To Washington hard-liners, he represented the worst of the administration—an intellectual, dreamy-eyed product of Harvard Law, who had rejected a sober career in corporate law to tilt at windmills on behalf of the American people. As a congressional investigator, Goodwin had helped expose fraud in popular TV game shows. He then was hired by the equally idealistic Ted Sorensen to work under him as a junior speechwriter for the White House–bound Senator John Kennedy. In the White House, Goodwin specialized in Latin American affairs, helping JFK develop the bold Alliance for Progress program that promised to shift U.S. policy away from propping up oligarchies and military dictatorships toward uplifting the poverty-plagued masses. The product of a Jewish working-class neighborhood in Boston, Goodwin, with his wild foliage of eyebrows and unruly hair, brought an ethnic brashness to Washington's traditionally WASPy foreign policy councils.

When controversy began to swirl around JFK's reform-minded Latin policy aides like Goodwin during the early months of the administration, the president came to their defense: "My experience in government," Kennedy told a news conference in June 1961, "is that when things are noncontroversial, beautifully coordinated and all the rest, it may be that there is not much going on. . . . We are attempting to do something about Latin America and there is bound to be ferment. If the ferment produces a useful result, it will be worthwhile."

There was a pungent air of ferment that night in August 1961 in Montevideo. Guevara surely knew it was his last chance to speak with Goodwin before the young Kennedy official returned home from a conference of Latin American finance ministers, where the new Alliance for Progress had been warmly endorsed by every representative except Che. The two men had been cautiously circling around each other during the twelve-day conference, which was held ninety miles away from the shabbiness of Montevideo, in a converted casino at the Uruguayan resort of Punta del Este. Guevara had noticed that Goodwin liked to relieve the tedium of the meetings by smoking cigars and he delivered a challenge to him through an Argentinian delegate: "I bet he wouldn't dare smoke Cuban cigars." When Goodwin relayed word that he certainly would if he could get his hands on some, the Cuban leader promptly sent him a polished-mahogany box, beautifully decorated with an inlaid Cuban seal amid a rainbow of national colors, filled with aromatic Havanas. With the gift was a typewritten note from Guevara: "Since I have no greeting card, I have to write. Since to write to an enemy is difficult, I limit myself to extending my hand."

Coming just four months after the U.S.-backed Bay of Pigs invasion, it was a remarkable gesture on the part of the revolutionary leader. When Guevara followed up the next day by inviting Goodwin to sit down with him for an informal talk, the Kennedy aide quickly got clearance from the chief of the U.S. delegation, Treasury Secretary Douglas Dillon. But on the final day of the conference, Guevara—who the press had already proclaimed was "stealing the show" at the conference, his impassioned oratory easily outshining the businesslike efforts of the pinstriped, former Wall Street banker Dillon—delivered a fiery denunciation of the Alliance for Progress. He pointed out, with some accuracy, that Kennedy's generous program should be credited to the Cuban revolution, since the United States had been blissfully unconcerned with Latin American poverty until Castro and Guevara's bearded guerrillas paraded victoriously into Havana. He then denounced the Alliance as a futile effort to reform Latin societies because "one cannot expect the privileged to make a revolution against their own interests." Real change in the medieval barrios and fields would come only through the armed uprising of the oppressed, as it had in Cuba. Dillon quickly responded with harsh words of his own, declaring that the United States eagerly awaited "the day when the people of Cuba once more have regained their freedom from the foreign domination and control to which they are presently subjected." The meeting with Guevara, Dillon informed Goodwin, was off.

But Guevara was not easily deterred. He now had Goodwin cornered in the narrow confines of the Montevideo apartment. After the revolutionary made it known that he wanted to speak with Goodwin, the two men were introduced. Goodwin immediately told him that he would be happy to listen to whatever he had to say, but he had no authority to negotiate anything. That was fine with Guevara, and they retreated to a small sitting room where they could hear each other over the party's samba music. At first Guevara sat

on the floor, with Goodwin quickly following suit so Che could not "outpro-
letarianize" the American. But when the Brazilian and Argentinian officials
who were acting as intermediaries for the momentous meeting insisted the
two men take the seats in the room, Guevara settled into a couch, and Goodwin sat facing him in a heavily upholstered chair. In a confidential memo on
the meeting that Goodwin later wrote, he observed that "behind the beard
Che's features are quite soft, almost feminine, and his manner is intense. He
has a good sense of humor."

The Goodwin-Guevara encounter was loaded with political meaning.
There they sat, their knees almost touching. On one side of the room was the
man whose intense visage, with the dashing beret and beard, was already
achieving iconic status—a man who had rejected the privileges of his afflu-
ent Buenos Aires upbringing to become a doctor for the destitute and
scorned, and then, after observing first-hand how the CIA destroyed a progressive, democratically elected government in Guatemala, had dedicated
himself to the armed liberation of Latin America. On the other was an idealistic young American, who believed—like the youthful president he served,
a man who had also broken from the narrow interests of his wealthy background—that the oppressive oligarchies that dominated the region could be
peacefully transformed if the forces of the democratic left in those countries
received the powerful support of the United States. One was a legendary
revolutionary. The other drew on revolutionary rhetoric to infuse the president's speeches and policies with the same sense of passion. "We are the
revolutionary generation in a revolutionary world," Goodwin would proudly
announce to a gathering of young volunteers for the Peace Corps, Kennedy's
international assistance program that would inspire imitative efforts by Fidel
Castro.

Guevara broke the ice that evening with a sharp joke, thanking Goodwin's
government for the Bay of Pigs, since the stunning Cuban victory helped
consolidate the Castro regime's control over the country. Goodwin said perhaps Guevara's government would return the favor and attack the U.S. military base at Guantánamo, a provocative act that Che knew would lead to an
invasion of his country. In fact, as Che had accurately charged in a speech at
the Punta del Este conference, some Washington officials wanted to stage
such an assault as a pretext for war. "Oh no," Guevara replied with a laugh.
"We would never be so foolish as that."

As the tensions in the small room lifted, Guevara got to the heart of the
matter. He realized that a true understanding between the two countries was
impossible, but he floated the possibility of a "modus vivendi." To achieve

this state of coexistence, Che suggested that his government would be willing to address the Kennedy administration's two major concerns about Cuba. It would agree not to make any political or military alliances with Moscow, to ensure Washington that Cuba would not become the Soviet outpost it feared. His government would also reconsider its unofficial policy of aiding insurrections in other Latin countries, a policy that the Kennedy administration denounced as "exporting revolution." In return for these agreements, Guevara said, the United States would promise not to support the overthrow of the Cuban government by force and would lift the trade embargo that had been imposed on the country.

It was nearly six in the morning when the discussion finally ended. Guevara and Goodwin rose and shook hands, promising not to reveal the meeting to anyone except their respective leaders, Castro and Kennedy. "I liked him a lot, actually," Goodwin recalled many years later, over a pasta dinner at a favorite restaurant in a mini-mall not far from his home in Concord, Massachusetts. "We got along well, talking all night long, until dawn. He was hoping to find a way for our two countries to live together, he laid the whole thing out. He was very honest." After bidding farewell to each other that dawn, the two men walked into the next room, where a few hardy couples were still dancing. The Kennedy aide then rushed back to his hotel and made notes of their remarkable conversation, before the presidential 707 carrying the American delegation flew back to Andrews Air Force Base.

When Goodwin returned to the White House and reported on his meeting with the infamous Che Guevara to JFK, the president showed no annoyance with his young aide's act of freelance diplomacy, only curiosity about the charismatic revolutionary and what he had to say. While talking with Goodwin, Kennedy spied him holding the contraband box of Cuban cigars, which were outlawed under the U.S. trade ban. "Are they good?" the president asked. "They're the best," Goodwin replied, prompting Kennedy to immediately open Che's gift and sample one of the Havanas. "You should have smoked the first one," Kennedy told Goodwin. "It's too late now, Mr. President," he responded. Kennedy gave a sheepish grin, and continued puffing on the illicit Cuban export.

Kennedy asked Goodwin to "write up a complete account and circulate it to Rusk, Bundy, and the others." The memo Goodwin produced for the foreign policy high command was properly restrained, but his enthusiasm for Guevara's peace feeler was nonetheless obvious. And Che apparently felt the same excitement about the meeting. The morning after their nightlong talk, the Argentine diplomat who had helped arrange the meeting phoned Goodwin to say that "Guevara had thought the conversation quite profitable, and had told him that it was much easier to talk to someone of the newer generation." This no doubt appealed to Goodwin's boss, whose youthful restlessness often drove him also to circumvent his government's clogged and cautious bureaucratic channels.

Goodwin sent a second memo to Kennedy on Cuba policy in the wake of the Punta del Este conference and his marathon conversation with Che. Don't make Cuba a geopolitical obsession, the aide advised Kennedy—it only inflames anti-U.S. passions in the region and strengthens Castro's hand.

The flurry of excitement in the Kennedy White House over the Cuban peace initiative was quickly doused by bitter political fallout from the meeting. Che was an electric rail in hemisphere politics, a crackling force that could not only ignite major upheavals in the anxiety-ridden ruling classes of Latin America, but also convulse the giant to the north. When word of the Che-Goodwin encounter got back to Washington, it set off a political storm. A Republican congressman denounced Goodwin's "so-called chance meeting" with Guevara and charged that the young Kennedy aide was a "kid playing with fire." Goodwin was forced to explain himself before a Senate subcommittee. Fortunately for the administration, it was chaired by a sympathetic Wayne Morse of Oregon, and Goodwin's appearance quickly turned into a "pleasant session," in the words of the New York Times. But the right would not let go of the incident, and months later attack dogs like Goldwater were still demanding Goodwin's head. The conservative senator lumped the young aide together with other notorious administration liberals like Bowles, Stevenson, and Schlesinger, calling on President Kennedy to get rid of the men who had been "wrong from start to finish in their attitudes and recommendations for American policy in the Cold War."

JFK's right-wing opponents accurately sensed something ambivalent within the administration when it came to Cuba. If someone like Dick Goodwin was the White House's point man on Cuba, what did that say about the administration's anti-Castro resolve? Hard-liners suspected that the Kennedy brothers' war of words with the Castro brothers was just that— words. Secretly the Kennedys were prepared to live with this Communist outpost, charged their conservative critics, no matter how inflamed their rhetoric grew or how loudly Bobby hectored the CIA to destabilize the Castro regime.

Chronicles of the Kennedy administration inevitably focus on the brothers' so-called "Cuba obsession." There is no denying that Cuba's revolutionary government was a major focus for the brothers. But it was not simply a morbid one. John Kennedy had an intellectual and even playful curiosity about the Cuban experiment and its leaders that would eventually lead him to explore openings in the cold wall that had been erected between the two nations. Guevara's August 1961 Montevideo peace gambit would prove premature, but it would not be the last time that President Kennedy would consider such a bold chess move with Cuba. In fact, he never shut off the option, as his right-wing critics suspected. Montevideo became a running theme of his presidency—the back-channel escapade, the valiant attempt to end-run the dead, bureaucratic forces of Cold War stasis and break through to a less dangerous world.

In the midst of the Guevara storm, JFK expressed irritation with Goodwin's Cuban flirtation. But the truth is, Kennedy was just as fascinated by Cuba's charismatic leaders. Journalist Laura Knebel, who like her husband, Fletcher, covered the Kennedy White House as well as the Cuban revolution for *Look* magazine, observed JFK's personal obsession with Guevara. Knebel, one of the few women journalists whom Kennedy respected, had a bantering relationship with him. She often challenged him on his Latin policies, a special area of interest for her. He tweaked her for what he thought was her overly sympathetic coverage of the seductive Guevara. "When I'd talk to Kennedy, he would ask me about Guevara, and when I went to Cuba, Guevara would talk about Kennedy—as an imperialist, of course," Knebel later recalled. "They were both cool, pragmatic, very smart characters. That's when he said, 'Something gives me the feeling you've got the hots for Che.' That made me sore as hell. I felt put down. I protested. Hadn't he seen the photo of me and Che arguing during the interview? 'Yeah,' said the president, 'but that kind of hostility often leads to something else.'"

New York Times reporter Tad Szulc, another Latin America correspondent who enjoyed good access to Kennedy, saw JFK's fascination with Guevara's boss, Fidel Castro, as well. The fascination was mutual, observed Szulc, who came to know the Cuban leader while writing a 1986 biography of him. Both men, wrote Szulc, "had superb minds and a vision of history. They had never met but were fascinated by each other as adversaries and as national leaders. I know it from discussing Castro with Kennedy in the short years when they were simultaneously in power . . . and discussing Kennedy with Castro over a quarter of a century later."

As president, Kennedy felt politically compelled to keep the heat on Castro, whom national security hard-liners and the media (particularly Henry Luce's hawkish *Time* and *Life* magazines) had succeeded in turning into a bearded bogeyman. But after the Bay of Pigs, JFK clearly preferred to clash with Castro ideologically rather than militarily. Kennedy was confident that he could compete with Castro's charisma for the hearts and minds of the Latin American public.

With his youth, Catholicism, movie-star looks, and progressive appeal, JFK thought he could out-market even the dashing Fidel and Che in the war of ideas, selling democratic reform as an alternative to armed revolution. Kennedy did, in fact, succeed in electrifying Latin America during his brief presidency, during which he made three trips to the region. Huge crowds inevitably greeted his appearances with a frantic adoration that threatened not just Castro, but the beribboned generals and wealthy despots who stiffly greeted the American president. On Kennedy's trip to Bogotá, Colombia in December 1961, a crowd of 500,000—nearly half the city's population—poured into the streets to greet him. While there, Kennedy attacked dictatorships of the left and the right, and declared that his Alliance for Progress program could only be accomplished within the framework of democratic societies. At a dinner hosted by Colombia's president, Kennedy insisted that democracy had an "unparalleled power" to reshape societies and that it could meet "new needs without violence, without repression."

Castro was intrigued by Kennedy's Latin America offensive, years later admitting to Szulc that JFK's Alliance for Progress was an "intelligent strategy" that sought the same goals as the early phase of the Cuban revolution, including agrarian reform, social justice, and a better distribution of wealth. But, like Guevara, he believed it was doomed to fail because the region's ruling cliques would not allow real reform. Castro's prediction seemed borne out during the Kennedy years, when reactionary forces responded to the winds of change that the Alliance for Progress had helped set loose in the continent by overthrowing democracies in Brazil, Argentina, and Peru. The Kennedy administration made known its displeasure at these antidemocratic coups, withholding recognition of the puppet government that replaced President Arturo Frondizi in Buenos Aires for nearly three weeks—longer than it took the Soviet Union—and slapping economic, diplomatic, and military sanctions on the military junta that took over following the July 1962 putsch in Peru. The *New York Times* proclaimed Kennedy's response to the Peruvian coup "the most significant turn in U.S. hemispheric foreign policy since the inception of the Alliance for Progress 16 months ago."

Kennedy's action put the administration on the side of democratic reform in a region where the U.S. historically supported repression. Eduardo Frei, one of Chile's last democratic presidents before his country's 1973 fall into military tyranny, expressed his amazement over Kennedy's progressive policies in a letter to Dick Goodwin, which the aide framed and hung in his White House office: "Latins were astonished that this young Yankee was trying to force them to agree on radical social change. It was as if the positions of decades had been reversed."

President Kennedy was serious about reforming U.S. policy in Latin America, according to Goodwin. Soon after moving into the White House, Kennedy summoned Goodwin to the Oval Office, where the aide found him poring over congratulatory telegrams from Latin leaders. "There's even one from that bastard Somoza," said Kennedy, referring to Nicaragua's gangster-like dictator, "saying that my election has given him new hope for Nicaragua's democracy. Draft an answer saying that's my hope too—democracy for Nicaragua. That ought to scare him."

Later in their conversation, Kennedy ripped into the United States' Latin policy, in impassioned language that could have come from Castro or Guevara: "We can't embrace every tinhorn dictator who tells us he's anticommunist while he's sitting on the necks of his own people. And the United States government is not the representative of private business. Do you know in Chile the American copper companies control about 80 percent of all the foreign exchange? We wouldn't stand for that here. And there's no reason they should stand for it. All those people want is a chance for a decent life, and we've let them think that we're on the side of those who are holding them down. There's a revolution going on down there, and I want to be on the right side of it. Hell, we are on the right side. But we have to let them know it, that things have changed."

But, as Goodwin discovered, Kennedy's foreign policy bureaucracy was not ready for the sweeping changes in Latin policy that he had in mind.

The former Kennedy advisor is now standing in the study of his Concord home, as an evening snow falls gently outside. His mane has grown long now, his eyebrows are more impressively lawless than ever. The room is crowded with Kennedy memorabilia. He picks up an object, a box with a polished sheen. It's empty of Che's cigars now, but he's kept it all these years as a reminder of a different time, when anything seemed possible.

Looking back, Goodwin now sees a link between Kennedy and Guevara as "children of the '60s": Despite their obvious political differences, they both believed that the world could be changed through heroic exertions. "That is why, as the times changed," he would write in *Remembering America*, his memoir of the decade, leaders like this "would have no successors. There would be no place for romantics in the triumphant ascendance of bureaucracy."

Goodwin said that as a young, progressive White House aide, he never felt any personal antagonism from hard-line opponents in the government "except when I dealt with Latin America—then I got it from these old-line CIA guys down there who would be pulling off various capers. They were totally Cold Warriors. Kennedy took a longer view of our future and the hemisphere, of how to build a solid bulwark of democracy there. But they were fighting the Cold War . . . they were just concerned with individuals and regimes, whether we liked them or didn't like them. And anybody who seemed the least like a socialist was a threat, whereas that was not Kennedy. He wanted to ally himself with the democratic left in Latin America, so he had a whole different outlook and approach."

Dick Goodwin was a benign influence in White House foreign policy councils. His advice that President Kennedy defuse the Cuba crisis by simply ignoring Castro became the prevailing sentiment in the White House in the months after Punta del Este. In a September 1, 1961, memo, he told the president that "our public posture toward Cuba should be as quiet as possible." Kennedy agreed. The Castro threat should be handled through a multilateral Latin American strategy involving economic and diplomatic measures, the president told a visiting South American leader, rather than turning it into a high-drama showdown of "Castro versus Kennedy, because a debate of this kind would only enhance Castro's prestige."

As long as the maverick Goodwin was in the West Wing, the president was assured of a partner in his ongoing battles with the hard liners on Latin policy. But, as with Chester Bowles, the young aide increasingly became a target of conservatives and JFK's own foreign policy bureaucracy, which resented Goodwin's trespassing on its turf. The Cold War regime that had taken over in Washington after World War II, dominating the presidencies of Democrat Truman as well as Republican Eisenhower, was not prepared to cede power to the new Kennedy government. This was soon made clear to the president's team by the nation's top military commanders.

"CERTAINLY WE DID NOT control the Joint Chiefs of Staff," said Arthur Schlesinger when asked near the end of his life about the extent to which President Kennedy controlled his own government. The eminent historian, who played the roles of court chronicler and roving liberal conscience in the Kennedy White House, spoke in a voice feeble with age. But his words were nonetheless chilling, considering the high nuclear stakes of the Kennedy years.

In a 1994 interview with the *Boston Globe*, Schlesinger elaborated on

Kennedy's fears about the military. "Kennedy's concern was not that Khrushchev would initiate something, but that something would go wrong in a *Dr. Strangelove* kind of way," he said, referring to Stanley Kubrick's macabre Cold War satire in which a rabidly anticommunist Air Force general loses his marbles and launches World War III. Haunted by fears of an accidental nuclear war, Kennedy strived to keep "tight controls [on the military] right down the line." But he never fully succeeded.

President Kennedy's tensions with the Joint Chiefs during his first year in office were aggravated by the strenuous efforts of his defense secretary, Robert McNamara, to gain control of the "military-industrial complex"— the increasingly powerful "conjunction of an immense military establishment and a large arms industry" that Eisenhower warned about as he bade farewell to the nation in what would become his most famous speech. The old general could have added bellicose members of Congress to this militaristic nexus—and in fact his original draft called it a "military-industrial-congressional complex"—as well as the octopus of far-right organizations, retired military officers' associations, and defense industry trade groups that had sprung up during the Cold War to lobby for higher arms spending and belligerent policies. During his eight years in office, Eisenhower battled heroically to restrain the defense budget against relentless pressure from this complex. But he did little to change the Cold War policies that fueled this militaristic fervor. Kennedy, on the other hand, came into office committed to a major defense buildup as well as a deescalation of the Cold War. By pumping more money into the military-industrial complex, he made it even more powerful, complicating his efforts to slow the momentum towards war.

While presiding over a massive arms buildup, Defense Secretary McNamara simultaneously tried to impose rational controls over the spending, bringing a cost-benefit managerial philosophy from his days as a Ford executive that was alien to the Pentagon, where the military services indulged freely in expensive cost overruns and duplicate weapons systems. The military chiefs, backed by their defense industry and congressional allies, strongly resisted as McNamara and his young, horn-rimmed "whiz kids" tried to take control of the defense spending process.

The warrior culture also raged against the efforts of McNamara—and the young defense intellectuals from the Rand Corporation he brought into the Pentagon—to transform the country's nuclear strategy. Alarmed by the massive overkill of the Joint Chiefs' SIOP (Single Integrated Operational Plan), the military blueprint that called for a planet-threatening fusillade of

nuclear fire in the event of war, Kennedy and McNamara ordered the exploration of limited nuclear war scenarios and sought to impose tighter civilian
controls over the country's vast nuclear arsenal. War in the nuclear age, Kennedy told advisors, was too important to be left in the hands of generals.

General Curtis LeMay—the cigar-chomping, notoriously gung-ho Air
Force chief upon whom actor Sterling Hayden would model the demented
General Jack D. Ripper in *Dr. Strangelove*—made no secret of his loathing
for the administration. "Everyone that came in with the Kennedy administration . . . were the most egotistical people that I ever saw in my life," snarled
LeMay. "They had no faith in the military; they had no respect for the military at all. They felt that the Harvard Business School method of solving
problems would solve any problem in the world. . . . As a matter of fact, I had
a man tell me, 'No, General, this is not the kind of weapon system that you
want to use, this is what you need.' This man was in knee pants when I was
commanding the division in combat. He had no experience in the use of
weapons at all."

Years after he left the Air Force, in an oral history for the Lyndon Johnson
Library, LeMay was still venting in remarkably savage terms, calling the
Kennedy crowd "ruthless," "vindictive," morally debased vermin whom LBJ
should have "stepped on" when he took over the White House, "like the
cockroaches they were."

Despite the Kennedy team's "ruthless" reputation, LeMay showed no
reluctance to publicly challenge the administration's defense policies during
its first year in office. The Air Force chief stunned the capital in July when
Washington Post columnist Marquis Childs reported that he casually predicted that nuclear war would break out in the final weeks of the year.
LeMay made the hair-raising announcement to a senator's wife at a Georgetown dinner party, telling the shocked woman that war was "inevitable" and
that it would likely incinerate such major U.S. cities as Washington, New
York, Philadelphia, Los Angeles, Chicago, and Detroit as well as level most
Soviet cities. Asked by the senator's wife if there was anywhere she could flee
to safety with her children and grandchildren, LeMay advised her she might
try deserted sage brush country in the far West. After the ensuing uproar in
Washington, LeMay felt compelled to deny the story. But Kennedy officials
knew it reflected the Air Force general's true beliefs.

Years later, an elderly McNamara reflected on the man who ran his Air
Force. As always, the former defense secretary was coolly rational in his assessment of LeMay. But his description of the man who presided over most
of the nation's nuclear arsenal was no less jolting for its matter-of-fact tone.

Here was a top military leader, McNamara acknowledged, who frankly and firmly advocated a preemptive nuclear war to rid the world of the Soviet threat. "LeMay clearly had a different view of the Soviet problem than most of the rest of us did," McNamara said. "LeMay's view was very simple. He thought the West, and the U.S. in particular, was going to have to fight a nuclear war with the Soviet Union, and he was absolutely certain of that. Therefore, he believed that we should fight it sooner rather than later, when we had a greater advantage in nuclear power, and it would result in fewer casualties in the United States."

McNamara took issue with his Air Force chief, telling him that even though the United States enjoyed a clear nuclear advantage over the Soviet Union, we could not be certain of destroying the enemy's ability to respond. "I believed then, and I think I was absolutely right, that we did not have a first-strike capability. We couldn't launch our 5,000 missiles and destroy so many of their 350 missiles that we could be assured that the remainder would not inflict unacceptable damage on us. Therefore LeMay and I were just totally opposed. I told him, 'Look, you're probably right that *if* we had to fight a war with the Soviet Union, we'd have fewer casualties today than if we had to do it later. But it's not clear that we have to fight them. So for God's sake, let's try to avoid it.'"

Kennedy and McNamara, despite their early explorations into how nuclear war might be "managed," would finally conclude that there was no such thing as a winnable nuclear war—considering how many people would be vaporized or poisoned in such a holocaust. But LeMay was of a different opinion. "It depends on how you define 'win,'" said McNamara. "LeMay defined it as ending up with more nuclear warheads than your opponent had. I would define 'win' as no more than acceptable casualties."

McNamara managed to stay on civil terms with LeMay, whom he had served as an analyst during World War II, when the general was first making his name as a Shiva of war, laying waste to much of Japan with his infamous firebombing campaign. "I thought he was the ablest combat commander of any senior military man I met during my three years of service in World War II," McNamara said. But other members of Kennedy's national security team had decidedly hostile encounters with LeMay and his top Air Force commanders.

Carl Kaysen, one of the Harvard scholars brought into the White House as an advisor, recalled a particularly toxic meeting with LeMay's longtime associate, General Thomas Power of the Strategic Air Command—a man even LeMay considered "not stable" and a "sadist." "I went out to SAC for a meeting with Tom Power, with [McNamara whiz kid] Adam Yarmolinsky," Kaysen recalled. "He just acted extraordinarily hostile to us. In fact, as we compared notes later, we felt that we might never get out of there. His atti- tude was, What the hell are you civilians doing here at SAC talking about our nuclear strategy and messing around—it's none of your goddam business."

Kennedy personally despised LeMay—"I don't want that man near me again," he once spat out, after walking out on one of the general's briefings. "A prick like LeMay—Kennedy didn't trust him as far as he could throw a marble pillar," Charles Daly, one of Kennedy's White House political aides, says today. But in June 1961, Kennedy felt politically compelled to promote LeMay to the Joint Chiefs as commander of the Air Force. "He wanted to be protected on his right flank," Kaysen explained. JFK knew that if he pushed LeMay into retirement, he would create an uproar in the Air Force and there would be one more retired general on the political circuit, denouncing his "no-win" policies.

General David Shoup, head of the Marine Corps, was the only member of the Joint Chiefs with whom Kennedy was able to build a decent relation- ship. A few days after promoting LeMay, Kennedy, deeply estranged from his top military men, would prevail on Maxwell Taylor, the maverick military thinker who had fallen out of step with Eisenhower, to come out of retire- ment and take a specially created position in the White House as his military advisor. The Joint Chiefs immediately recognized the move for what it was— a "screw you" attempt to keep them out of his hair.

IN SUMMER 1961, KENNEDY came under increasing pressure from mili- tary and intelligence officials to consider launching a preemptive nuclear strike against the Soviet Union. The president was informed that far from suffering a "missile gap," the United States actually enjoyed a growing lead in land-based nuclear missiles. According to a National Intelligence Esti- mate delivered that year, the Soviets had only four intercontinental ballistic missiles in place—all of them on low alert at a test site—while the U.S. had 185 ICBMs and over 3,400 deliverable nuclear bombs at the time. This clear "window" of nuclear superiority would eventually close as Soviet nuclear weapons production began to catch up. While it remained open, Washington was a hothouse of militaristic fever, which accounts for LeMay's intemperate remarks about an imminent nuclear war at the July dinner party.

On July 20, at a National Security Council meeting, Kennedy was pre- sented an official plan for a surprise nuclear attack by the Joint Chiefs chair- man, General Lemnitzer, and Allen Dulles, who would remain at the helm of the CIA until the fall. Lemnitzer, whose intellectual abilities the president found wanting, presented the doomsday plan "as though it were for a kindergarten class," according to Schlesinger, and a disgusted Kennedy got up in the middle of the meeting and walked out. "And we call ourselves the human race," he bitterly remarked to Secretary of State Dean Rusk afterwards.

The relationship between Kennedy and his Joint Chiefs "reached a new low," in the words of New York Times military correspondent Hanson Baldwin, that month, when the president ordered FBI agents to "invade" the military commanders' Pentagon offices to determine the source of a press leak about military contingency plans to deal with the developing Berlin Crisis. Kennedy's action was "degrading," the chiefs complained to Baldwin, one of their more sympathetic ears in the press, and they predicted that the leaks would not be pinned on them. Years later, in an oral history for the U.S. Naval Institute, Baldwin would charge that he too had been subjected to an FBI probe during the Kennedy presidency, when Bobby dispatched agents to investigate an article he wrote about Soviet missile defenses. "The Kennedys used intimidation and pressure to force people into line. They used it quite often," said Baldwin, reflecting a point of view widely held in the military world he covered. "From my observation of many years in Washington dealing with many presidents, back to FDR, the Kennedys were the most retributive and the most ruthless of any of them."

By the last week of July, Kennedy found himself caught up in a growing storm, buffeted by the winds of war both at home—within his military—and overseas in Berlin. "Nuclear conflict was very much in the air that week," wrote University of Texas political historian James K. Galbraith, the son of John Kenneth Galbraith, in a revealing article about the first-strike pressures on Kennedy. Khrushchev was escalating tensions over Berlin, the divided city that had long been a Cold War flashpoint, by threatening to let his East German clients close off access to West Berlin. Kennedy's generals and hardline advisors like Acheson, who were convinced that the president's failure of will at the Bay of Pigs had led directly to his humiliation at the hands of a bullying Khrushchev at the Vienna summit in June, thought he was in danger of being pushed around yet again in Berlin. They urged him to take a firm stand, and Kennedy asked his advisors for a Berlin scenario that envisioned a limited nuclear war.

But in the end, JFK threaded the needle on Berlin, as he would do repeatedly during his administration, avoiding either an explosive confrontation or embarrassing capitulation through an artful dance combining tough speech, symbolic military measures, and back-channel diplomacy. "The Berlin Wall was allowed to remain intact when constructed in August of 1961, a symbolic column of [American] soldiers was sent through to West Berlin, and a fallout shelter program was undertaken in the United States," noted Galbraith. "But [Kennedy] did not engage the Soviets." LeMay's nuclear Armageddon would be averted—at least until the next showdown.

As usual, the military found Kennedy's moderation unsatisfying. General Lucius Clay, the hero of the 1948–49 Berlin Blockade whom Kennedy had installed as his top military envoy in the divided city during the latest crisis, seemed anxious to find ways to challenge the tense but peaceful truce that prevailed in Berlin during the fall. In October, Clay precipitated a nerve-wracking confrontation with the Russians at the Berlin Wall, the first time in history that American and Soviet tanks had ever faced each other. Valentin Falin, Soviet ambassador to West Germany, said Moscow later learned that Clay had ordered his tank commanders to knock down the Berlin Wall—as he had instructed them to practice doing in a nearby forest without informing the White House. If that had happened, Falin said, the Soviet tanks would have returned fire and we would have slid "closer to the third world war than ever"—just the kind of accidental inferno sparked by trigger-happy generals that Kennedy deeply feared.

In the midst of this unnerving showdown, Kennedy felt compelled to soothe not only Soviet pride but that of his military commander. "I know you people over there haven't lost your nerve," he told Clay over the phone. The confrontational general was not mollified by this presidential pat on the back, however. "Mr. President," he shot back, "we're not worried about our nerves. We're worrying about those of you people in Washington."

In the end, Kennedy succeeded in outmaneuvering his general, secretly instructing Bobby, the "little brother" whom Clay said he could "not abide," to communicate with his back-channel Soviet friend Georgi Bolshakov and work out a mutual withdrawal of the opposing tanks "without damage to each other's prestige."

IT WAS THE CRUSTY World War II–vintage commanders like Burke and LeMay with whom Kennedy clashed most fiercely during his first year in the White House. But his supporters in Washington worried that JFK's problems with the military ran deeper than that. Arkansas Senator J. William Fulbright, one of Kennedy's closest allies on the Hill, was among those who viewed with alarm the rise of what he saw as a politicized military culture, one that was extremely right-wing and blatantly insubordinate.

The far-right indoctrination of the military had its roots in the Eisenhower era, McNamara aide Joseph Califano later noted, when a 1958 National Security Council directive encouraged the military to educate its troops and the public about the dangers of communism—"tasks many officers pursued with gusto." Ironically, Califano observed, Bobby Kennedy had played a role in kicking off this propaganda offensive when he was counsel for the McClellan Committee, which reacted to the widely publicized brainwashing of U.S. POWs in North Korea by calling for more effective anticommunist indoctrination in the ranks. By the time Kennedy entered the White House, there was widespread right-wing agitation within the military, with anticommunist seminars and conferences sponsored by the military proliferating on bases at home and overseas and far-right films and tracts by groups like the John Birch Society flooding the barracks.

The controversy over the politicization of the military exploded into public view in the spring when the *Overseas Weekly*, an independent newspaper popular with GIs stationed abroad for its racy tabloid fare, broke a story about the flamboyant indoctrination efforts of Major General Edwin A. Walker, commander of the 24th Infantry, a crack, front-line division in West Germany. Walker, a hero in World War II and Korea, had always been something of an eccentric. He volunteered to lead a paratroopers unit against the Nazis without ever having jumped from a plane—"How do you put this thing on?" a puzzled Walker asked a subordinate as his plane lifted off the ground for his first jump. But the war in Korea set him on his collision course with civilian authority, after he became convinced that America's elected officials wanted no better than a "stalemate" with international communism. A diehard segregationist, he was further disillusioned when he was ordered by President Eisenhower to lead the Army unit that enforced the integration of Little Rock schools in 1957.

The following year Walker joined the loony-right John Birch Society—whose candy-maker founder had famously denounced Eisenhower as "a dedicated, conscious agent of the Communist conspiracy"—and began lavishing Bircher propaganda on the men under his command. The general, a lifelong bachelor who grew up on a Texas ranch, found it hard to distinguish American liberalism from godless Communism. Among the targets of his wrath were Eleanor Roosevelt, Adlai Stevenson, *Mad* magazine, and Harvard University. "General Walker," reported an aide, "thought Harvard was the bad place, the factory where they made Communists. He was sure death on Harvard." This was undoubtedly one more source of his estrangement from the Kennedy White House, which was practically a hiring hall for the elite university. Walker believed the administration was stocked with "no-win" Ivy

Leaguers and "confirmed Communists" like Edward R. Murrow, whose appointment as Kennedy's USIA director caused the general to "practically have a tantrum," according to *Newsweek.*

In April, the *Overseas Weekly* reported that Walker not only communicated his low opinion of leading American liberals and Kennedy officials in speeches to his troops, but instructed them how to vote, using a political index prepared by a group so far to the right that it did not even give Barry Goldwater a perfect score. In doing so, Walker broke various Army regulations and federal laws, including the Hatch Act, which prohibits political activity by government employees. In June, Walker was relieved of his command and transferred to the Army's European headquarters in Heidelberg—a relatively mild reprimand considering his violations. But Walker's punishment immediately made him a martyr in far-right circles, both in and out of the military.

The ensuing political melee quickly demonstrated that Walker's extremist agitation had an alarmingly wide base of support in the officer corps, where Hanson Baldwin reported that he was regarded as a "soldier's soldier." An aggrieved Army captain told the *New York Times,* "I feel the general is being crucified. And I think the men feel the same way." It was revealed that Walker's indoctrination program had been endorsed by none other than General Lemnitzer, the country's top military leader, who wrote in a letter to the far-right officer that he found his efforts "most interesting and useful."

As the military establishment flexed its political muscle, two young legislative aides to Senator Fulbright looked on with growing apprehension. They saw the political effects of this right-wing agitation back in the senator's home state of Arkansas, where military officers were joining with Christian fundamentalists in an anticommunist crusade that targeted liberal politicians and legislation as subversive. They looked overseas at the restive right-wing generals in France who, angry at President De Gaulle's attempts to reach a peaceful settlement of the Algerian war, were threatening to overthrow him. (In September, De Gaulle would be the target of an unsuccessful assassination attempt by right-wing extremists.) And they wondered if there was the growing possibility of such a coup in Washington.

The two aides took their fears to Senator Fulbright, who cornered McNamara at a party and urged him to take action. Soon after receiving a memo on the dangers of rising militarism that was prepared by Fulbright's aides, the defense secretary issued a directive that limited military officers' ability to promote right-wing causes at public events. McNamara and Fulbright were immediately denounced by South Carolina Senator Strom Thurmond, a major general in the Army Reserve, and other congressional mouthpieces for the military-industrial complex. Thurmond charged that McNamara's directive was a "dastardly attempt to intimidate the commanders of the U.S. Armed Forces" and "constitutes a serious blow to the security of the United States."

Fulbright decided to stand up on the Senate floor to answer Thurmond and take his message about the menace of militarism before the American people. The man who had grown up on an Arkansas hog farm to become a Rhodes scholar, university president, and chairman of the powerful Senate Foreign Relations Committee had been considered a potential secretary of state by Kennedy. Indeed, the brilliant, independent-minded statesman— one of the few who warned the new president against the Bay of Pigs invasion—could have been featured in a sequel to Kennedy's *Profiles in Courage* if it had not been for the residue of segregationism he carried with him from his home state and which cost him the top post in the State Department. Fulbright was the only member of the Senate to vote against funds for Joe McCarthy's witch-hunt expedition during the fevered height of his inquisition.

On August 2, the tall, lanky Fulbright rose to his feet and in his soft Ozarks drawl offered the nation a civics lesson in the vital importance of keeping the military out of political affairs in a democracy. Fulbright's speech echoed the passage in Eisenhower's farewell address that warned against "the acquisition of unwarranted influence . . . by the military-industrial complex." If the country allowed such "a disastrous rise of misplaced power," Ike had counseled, it would "endanger our liberties or democratic processes." But Eisenhower himself had helped create the Frankenstein of a politicized military with his 1958 directive on the indoctrination of troops. Now Fulbright was telling his fellow citizens it was time for the military to return to its barracks and leave the political arena to elected officials.

Fulbright declared that military officers at the highest levels, including the National War College, were being steeped in propaganda produced by far-right groups, with the approval of the Joint Chiefs. They were being indoctrinated with the message that "sellouts" in Washington were undercutting the military's effort to defeat communism. They were being taught that President Kennedy's domestic legislative program—"including continuation of the graduated income tax, expansion of Social Security (particularly medical care under Social Security) and federal aid to education"—was another front in the communist assault on America.

"If the military is infected with the virus of right-wing radicalism, the danger is worthy of attention," Fulbright told his Senate colleagues and the public. "If, by the process of the military educating the public, the fevers of both groups are raised, the danger is great indeed."

As he reached his conclusion, Fulbright dramatically raised the specter of a military coup, invoking "the revolt of the French generals as an example of the ultimate danger." The Washington echo chamber quickly picked up Fulbright's dire warning, with columnist Marquis Childs writing that "in one country after another in recent years, the intervention of the military in politics has had disastrous consequences . . . [Military officers] do not have the right to impose their political opinions on the troops whom they command. Nor is theirs the right to try to share policy by public speeches that directly oppose what the Government is undertaking." Syndicated columnist Drew Pearson also rang the alarm bell, writing that "certain Pentagon brass hats were lining up with industrial right-wingers to foment a sort of neo-fascism despite the fact they were wearing Uncle Sam's uniform."

In reaction, Strom Thurmond pushed the Senate Armed Services Committee to open hearings on the "muzzling of the military." In September, McNamara was hauled before the committee, where Thurmond and his colleagues hammered him for six hours one day on his censorship of military officers. "The military establishment is an instrument—not a shaper—of national policy," the slick-haired, bespectacled defense secretary reminded his Senate interrogators in his supremely rational, Mr. Spock fashion.

McNamara was testifying in the marble-walled Caucus Room of the Old Senate Office Building—the same hearing room that was the scene of McCarthy's downfall seven years earlier during the Army-McCarthy hearings. But the extremist fervor that filled the Caucus Room that day made it clear that the spirit of McCarthy was still alive in Washington. Throughout his testimony, McNamara was loudly booed by the 250 spectators in the room while Thurmond was cheered. As a weary McNamara finished his testimony that day, he was swarmed by dozens of suburban housewives wearing "Stop Communism" tags, who had trooped to Capitol Hill to support Thurmond's crusade. Newsweek later reported that "an attractive mother of four in a blue frock, trapped McNamara as he stuffed his briefcase" and demanded whether he had read General Walker's Strangelovian "Pro-Blue" propaganda literature. When he politely murmured that he had not, the woman exploded: "You haven't! Why, it's the best statement against Communism. I believe our armed forces should get this material."

The same month, as the Armed Services Committee forced McNamara to defend his injunction against political activism in the military, the

Army brazenly signaled its defiance of the order by staging another anticommunist spectacle. In late September, the Fourth U.S. Army sponsored a two-day propaganda show that drew thousands of people to San Antonio's municipal auditorium, where reactionary speakers like General A. C. Wedemeyer denounced the Kennedy administration for "appeasing" the Soviet Union and the Episcopal Church for supporting the civil rights activism of the Freedom Riders.

The following month, in response to the San Antonio rebellion and other anti-Kennedy seminars organized by the military, McNamara felt compelled to issue another ban against political agitation in the ranks. And once again the Armed Services Committee announced it would subject the McNamara crackdown to congressional scrutiny.

The Cold War lobby was on the offensive, with retired military leaders and other far-right activists loudly calling for the impeachment of the president and other prominent liberals like Supreme Court Chief Justice Earl Warren. One retired Marine colonel went further and called for Warren's hanging, while a retired Marine general suggested a coup was in order if the "traitors" could not be voted out.

Kennedy finally grew exasperated. In October, while hosting an off-the-record luncheon with a group of Texas newspaper publishers in the White House, Kennedy was crudely confronted by the reactionary publisher of the *Dallas Morning News*, E. M. (Ted) Dealey. As the president idly chatted with the newspaper businessmen, the Texan stunned the gathering by haranguing Kennedy directly to his face, reading from a five-hundred-word statement that he suddenly whipped from his pocket in which he berated the commander-in-chief as if he were an errant copy boy. "We can annihilate Russia and should make that clear to the Soviet government," Dealey lectured Kennedy. But unfortunately, he continued, "The general opinion of the grassroots thinking in this country is that you and your administration are weak sisters. We need a man on horseback to lead this nation, and many people in Texas and the Southwest think that you are riding Caroline's tricycle."

Kennedy flushed visibly and fixed Dealey with a hard look. "The difference between you and me, Mr. Dealey," Kennedy shot back, "is that I was elected president of this country and you were not. I have the responsibility for the lives of 180 million Americans, which you have not. . . . Wars are easier to talk about than they are to fight. I'm just as tough as you are—and I didn't get elected president by arriving at soft judgments."

Kennedy had been slow to react to the threat from the extreme right. That August, when the subject of the John Birch Society had come up in conversation with Gore Vidal over canapés and vin rose at Hyannis Port, JFK seemed to airily dismiss the danger. The president took the "frenzy of the far right a lot less seriously than I," Vidal observed. But by the fall, Kennedy's attitude was no longer complacent. He dispatched Bobby to meet with the Reuther brothers—they discussed over breakfast how the liberal leaders of the United Auto Workers union could help mount an effective media campaign to counter the thunder from the right. The president also asked his staff to begin giving him monthly reports on far-right activities and ordered the director of the IRS to investigate organizations receiving tax exemptions.

But most important, Kennedy realized, it was time for the president of the United States to personally speak out. He needed to take to the road and explain to the American public why his pragmatic policies to extricate the country and the world from the Cold War's death grip made more sense than the simplistic, militaristic approach of the right. Kennedy turned once again to Sorensen, whose eloquence he always called upon when he needed a passionate rejoinder to his critics and a stirring appeal to the American people's better instincts. JFK would travel widely that fall, delivering several key speeches on how America should navigate its way through the "long twilight struggle" of the Cold War. His travels would take him from Chapel Hill, North Carolina—on the doorstep of his senatorial nemesis, South Carolina's Thurmond—to Los Angeles, then a bastion of right-wing ferment and home to a quarter of the John Birch Society's membership. In directly confronting his critics, Kennedy would be forced to clarify what he stood for and what America's role should be in a fast-changing world where "heroes are removed from their tombs, history rewritten, the names of cities changed overnight."

After being battered by Cold Warriors for nearly a year, Kennedy finally stepped into the ring that fall and began to fight for what he believed, to define his administration. The battle was, at last, joined.

IT WAS SATURDAY EVENING, November 18, 1961. On stage at the Hollywood Palladium, the cavernous dining and dancing hall where Lawrence Welk and his Champagne Music Makers normally presided on weekends, the president of the United States was giving his right-wing critics hell. To raucous applause from the 2,500 assembled Democrats, Kennedy, chopping the air for emphasis, scorched the "crusades of suspicion" and "discordant voices of extremism" that were echoing throughout the land. For months, the president had been forced to listen to their incessant din—the cries of "treason in high places" from the John Birch Society, whose paranoia had found fertile ground in regions with large fundamentalist populations like the Los Angeles Basin; the loud complaints from generals and admirals about Kennedy's "no-win" policy; the charges of weakness and cowardice from Texas blowhards like publisher Dealey; the calls from vigilante groups like the Minutemen for Americans to arm themselves in preparation for the imminent day when Washington would fall to Communist hands. Now Kennedy—standing on the gold foil-lined stage, in front of a giant reproduction of the presidential seal—was slashing back at all this madness in a speech that targeted his fanatic enemies with icy precision.

In periods of high tension like the Cold War, Kennedy told his audience, "there have always been those on the fringes of our society who have fought to escape their own responsibility by finding a simple solution, an appealing slogan, or a convenient scapegoat." In the current "period of heightened peril," with the world held hostage by the constant threat of nuclear war, this paranoid strain in American politics was flourishing, Kennedy observed. "Men who are unwilling to face up to the danger from without are convinced that the real danger is from within. They look suspiciously at their neighbors and their leaders. They call for a 'man on horseback' because they do not trust the people. They find treason in our churches, in our highest court, and even in the treatment of our water." This last twist of the presidential knife was directed at the colorful theory, popular in far-right circles at the time, that the fluoridation of water was a Communist plot.

"They equate the Democratic Party with the welfare state, the welfare state with socialism, and socialism with communism. They object, quite rightly, to politics intruding on the military, but they are very anxious for the military to engage in politics."

But, Kennedy concluded, he was confident that Americans—"whose basic good sense . . . has always prevailed"—would reject these "counsels of fear and suspicion."

Kennedy's hard-hitting speech—which the *Los Angeles Times* would the next day call "a scornful 21-gun presidential blast"—was loudly cheered by the Democratic Party faithful who filled the Palladium that night, including Hollywood celebrities like Frank Sinatra, Nat "King" Cole, and Ralph Bellamy, who helped provide the evening's entertainment. But outside the Palladium, where the paranoid legions Kennedy had lashed out at were noisily gathered, it was a different story. An estimated three thousand right-wing protesters—more than the number of Kennedy supporters gathered inside—paraded up and down on both sides of the street, spilling off the sidewalks and snarling traffic. Wearing red, white, and blue paper hats, they shouted anti-Kennedy slogans, sang "God Bless America," and waved signs reading "Unmuzzle the Military," "Disarmament Is Suicide," "Get the Reds Out of the State Department," and "Stamp Out Communism."

Kennedy, who was ushered quickly into the Palladium hours before he spoke, did not see the armies of the night who were massing against him. But the next day he would be forced to confront their passions in a surprising place. Kennedy, who loved to bask in the sun and celebrity atmosphere of Southern California, woke the next morning in his presidential suite at the Beverly Hilton, looking forward to a relaxing Sunday. In the afternoon, the president would ride leisurely down Wilshire Boulevard in an open convertible, waving at openmouthed pedestrians. His motorcade—which consisted of only two police cars (one in front of the president's convertible and one in back) and a car filled with reporters—glided through Santa Monica to its destination, the Spanish-style oceanfront home of Kennedy's sister Pat and her husband, Peter Lawford. There, the president would enjoy himself, swimming in the pool and dining with Hollywood friends Angie Dickinson and Mrs. Billy Wilder on a lunch of cold vichyssoise, stuffed brandied squab with wild rice, a vegetable dish of peas and onions, and mixed green salad with Italian dressing, all finished off by chocolate tarts and coffee.

But Kennedy's Sunday did not begin so smoothly. That morning, he and his old political crony Dave Powers were driven from the Beverly Hilton to the nearby Church of the Good Shepherd on Santa Monica Boulevard. After settling into a pew ten rows from the front, Kennedy soon found himself and the other worshippers being lectured about the necessity of vigilance in a dangerous world in a sermon delivered by Father Alfred Kilp. It was immediately clear what kind of message Father Kilp was sending the presidential captive in his audience. Catholics took pride in the first member of their faith to win the White House. But Kennedy's church, with its strong anti-communist legacy, had also become a beachhead for the John Birch Society. Robert Welch, founder of the group, claimed that 40 percent of its membership was Catholic and he proudly displayed a letter from none other than Cardinal Cushing, the Kennedy family's favorite prelate, praising Welch as a "dedicated anticommunist."

In his sermon Father Kilp invoked the terrible vision of an America under communist rule—one where Catholic schools would be closed and churches turned into "such profane uses as theaters or even garages."

"Be alert, pray and meditate," the priest counseled his flock, "because if you do not, you may wake up and find yourself a second-rate citizen of a satellite nation or a dispossessed Catholic."

The day after Kennedy was lectured in his own church about the need for anticommunist vigilance, he came under strong return fire from the John Birch Society itself, whose leaders were stung by the president's frontal assault on them as a band of paranoid fanatics. Kennedy's fiery speech at the Hollywood Palladium was "another example of talk tough and carry a big pillow," declared John Rousselot, a Bircher congressman from San Gabriel. "The only thing we can be assured of is that the organized, powder-puff left wing will herald this speech as a great blow for sound diplomacy and 'peace in our time.'"

Kennedy's anti-right campaign also drew an angry response from Senator Barry Goldwater, around whom the growing conservative movement was gathering as the standard-bearer to face Kennedy in 1964. The real "radicals" in American politics, sniped Goldwater at an Atlanta press conference, were "in the White House." The Arizonan called Kennedy a "wagon master" who is "riding on the left wheel all the time."

The explosions on the political right as Kennedy took off from Los Angeles International Airport on Sunday night to return to Washington demonstrated that he had hit his targets. Kennedy's eloquent offensive in fall 1961 was a turning point in his administration. His muscular response to the zealotry of the far right gave the American people a clear view of the path along which he wanted to lead them out of the gloomy Cold War thicket.

JFK's coast-to-coast counterattack on his right-wing opponents had begun with an October 12 speech at the University of North Carolina's Kenan Stadium, where he disparaged those thundering patriots who believed America's challenges in the world could be resolved by swaggering and sloganeering. "We shall be neither Red nor dead, but alive and free," declared Kennedy in the final line of his speech, alluding to the morbid right-wing slogan of the day, "I'd rather be dead than Red."

After Chapel Hill, Kennedy came west, launching another barrage against the right in Seattle on November 16 before heading south to John Birch country in Los Angeles for the most spectacular showdown in his anti-right speaking tour. In his speech at the University of Washington, the president reiterated his theme that there was nothing "soft" about averting nuclear war and that America showed its true strength by refraining from using its military might until all other avenues were exhausted. And he made a startling declaration that seemed to retreat from the aggressive posture struck in his inaugural speech. Despite its overwhelming power, he said, the United States could not play the role of global sentinel. "We must face the fact that the United States is neither omnipotent or omniscient, that we are only

6 percent of the world's population, that we cannot impose our will upon the other 94 percent, that we cannot fight every wrong or reverse each adversity, and that therefore there cannot be an American solution to every world problem." To those on the right who believed in America's divine and unlimited powers, this was nothing less than sacrilege.

"You must read the University of Washington speech," said its co-author Ted Sorensen years later, sitting in his law office at Paul, Weiss, a bronze bust of the man he served on his desk. "It's one of Kennedy's great speeches on foreign policy, a direct refutation of the hard-liners. Had Kennedy lived, there is no doubt in my mind, we would have laid the groundwork for détente. The Cold War would have ended much sooner than it did."

"I think my brother had a very healthy sense about the power of this country," Ted Kennedy recently remarked. "He had a sense of its military power, but also of its moral power. And how both could be used, with a sense of proportion, which is very rare for a young leader. You don't see that kind of judgment even in older people."

DURING HIS WESTERN SPEAKING tour, JFK invited his White House predecessor to ride with him in his helicopter during a swing through Texas to attend the funeral of legendary Speaker of the House Sam Rayburn. Kennedy and Eisenhower were later spotted standing next to the whirlybird on the tarmac at Perrin Air Force Base, locked in animated conversation. "Mr. Kennedy gestured repeatedly with his left hand and appeared to be explaining something to General Eisenhower," the Associated Press later reported. "General Eisenhower listened intently and shook his head affirmatively several times." The two men then shook hands and parted.

Five days later, on November 18, the old general added his influential voice to Kennedy's campaign against "the rise of extremists" in the country and the politicization of the military. Speaking out during an interview with Walter Cronkite of CBS News, the World War II hero said it was "bad practice—very bad" for an officer, even when testifying on Capitol Hill, to express opinions "that are contrary to the president's."

"I don't think the United States needs super-patriots," Eisenhower declared. "We need patriotism, honestly practiced by all of us, and we don't need these people that are more patriotic than you or anybody else."

But the superpatriots in Washington soon demonstrated their power again. One week after Kennedy returned to the capital from Los Angeles, in an administration shuffle that would become known in Beltway circles as "the Thanksgiving Day massacre," the president served the head of his most prominent liberal foreign policymaker—Chester Bowles—to his baying critics on the right. Bowles, it was announced on November 26, was being removed as under secretary of state and being given a vague Flying Dutchman role in the administration as a roving ambassador. The man who had seen himself as a counterweight to the forces of militarism within Kennedy's government would now, to his opponents' glee, be dispatched far from the center of power—winding up literally halfway around the world by summer 1963, when he was posted as ambassador to India. The self-described foreign policy "radical" who had urged the president to abolish the CIA after the Bay of Pigs would cause his enemies no more trouble for the rest of Kennedy's tenure.

In the State Department the old guard, who had recoiled from Bowles's efforts to align the United States with the revolutionary ferment sweeping through the Third World, raised glasses to toast Bowles's downfall. The trouble with Bowles, sneered one veteran diplomat, was that when he "saw a band of black baboons beating tom-toms, [he] saw George Washingtons."

During an emotional meeting in Bowles's office, Sorensen told his fellow Unitarian liberal that he was a victim of Washington's powerful Cold War lobby. But the number two man at the State Department was not helped by his sour relationship with Bobby Kennedy, who had never forgiven Bowles for refusing to campaign for his brother in the 1960 Wisconsin primary, out of allegiance to fellow liberal Hubert Humphrey, and for what Bobby believed was a cowardly attempt to run for cover after the Bay of Pigs fiasco.

The two had also clashed in early June during discussions about how to handle the rapidly deteriorating situation in the Dominican Republic, where plotters would soon assassinate the vicious dictator Rafael Trujillo, and the Kennedys were eager to see a stable, U.S.-friendly government installed. "The tone of [a June 1 State Department] meeting was deeply disturbing," Bowles would later write in a confidential memo. "Bob Kennedy was clearly looking for an excuse to move in on the island. At one point he suggested, apparently seriously, that we might have to blow up the [U.S.] consulate to provide the rationale. . . . The entire spirit of this meeting was profoundly distressing and worrisome, and I left at 8:00 p.m. with a feeling that this spirit which I had seen demonstrated on this occasion and others at the White House by those so close to the president constitutes a further danger of half-cocked action by people with almost no foreign policy experience, who are interested in action for action's sake, and the devil take the [hindmost]." When Bowles succeeded in blocking Bobby's intervention plans, the young Kennedy—still very much in his hotheaded phase, particularly when it came to Caribbean political intrigue—dismissed him as a gutless bastard.

Bowles's downfall highlighted a weak strain in the Kennedy presidency. So eager were the brothers to prove their toughness that they sometimes made examples of their liberal cohorts, rather than stand firm against their public lynching. "The McCarthy years had pounded into [the Kennedy crowd's] heads a sense of inferiority, insecurity and a sense that they weren't quite trusted by the members of the Establishment," Bowles later reflected. They needed the blood of sacrificial lambs like Bowles to prove they could be equally as merciless as Republican Cold Warriors.

It was the president's own misfortune. "Kennedy's inability to bring out the best and draw on the wisdom of Bowles was the president's loss," remarked Kennedy aide Harris Wofford. "He badly needed someone close to him who had a basic moral reference point."

The Thanksgiving massacre also claimed another liberal victim: Dick Goodwin. Kennedy bowed to the political pressure by transferring his freewheeling Cuba point man to the State Department, where the "young Jew," in Goodwin's words, would be kept under tight "WASP supervision." Goodwin's enemies crowed over his demotion, telling the *Washington Daily News* that a "major irritant" in Latin American policy had now been removed.

Kennedy would continue to phone Goodwin with questions about Latin policy, but it was not the same. Goodwin felt like "a rejected lover," banished to a hostile wing of the president's government, where he would not last long. He would later escape to Sargent Shriver's more hospitable Peace Corps. And on November 22, 1963, he was to be named a special consultant on the arts—a post far removed from the inner foreign policy councils where he could cause his enemies trouble.

ROBERT KENNEDY LATER SAID that his brother regarded 1961 as "a very mean year." His confidence in his own national security team had been shattered by the humiliation in Cuba. He had been bullied on the one side by Khrushchev and by his own military chiefs on the other. The world had slithered closer to extinction during the Berlin Crisis. "Fucked again," exhaled Kennedy, when just as the global situation seemed at its darkest, he learned that the Soviets were resuming nuclear weapons testing. "I want to get off," said JFK after a particularly gloomy White House meeting held to discuss this latest destabilizing development.

"Get off what?" Bobby asked him.

"Get off the planet."

The president was in a reflective mood on the Saturday evening after Thanksgiving. He was spending the holiday weekend with family and friends up at Hyannis Port. After working all day on his forthcoming budget, he joined the festive group at his father's house in the family compound, where everyone was gathering for cocktails and dinner. After the plates were cleared away, Kennedy suggested that his friend Red Fay—whom he had made assistant secretary of the Navy, as Admiral Burke rightly and bitterly suspected, primarily to enjoy his lively company—entertain the group with his trademark rendition of "Hooray for Hollywood." After "Grand Old Lovable," as Kennedy called his Republican friend, finished the song, Teddy—the best singer in the family—belted out "Heart of My Heart" and sister Eunice also took her turn in the spotlight. Then everyone insisted that the president himself entertain them. "Do you know 'September Song'?" Kennedy asked Teddy's wife, Joan, who was playing piano.

It was an odd selection, considering the frivolity of the evening. Written by Kurt Weill, the German Jewish composer who had fled the Nazis in 1933 after his avant-garde musicals sparked fascist riots, the song was a little masterpiece of melancholic beauty. Though Weill wrote it for *Knickerbocker Holiday*, his 1938 effort to adapt to the lighter moods of the Broadway stage, "September Song" was suffused with the wistful world-weariness of old Europe.

Joan played the song's haunting chorus and Jack began to sing:

> *"Oh, it's a long, long while from May to December*
> *But the days grow short when you reach September;*
> *When the autumn weather turns the leaves to flame,*
> *One hasn't got time for the waiting game."*

A hush fell over the room as Kennedy delivered the next lines of the song in a speaking voice:

> *"Oh, the days dwindle down to a precious few,*
> *September, November!*
> *And these few precious days I'll spend with you*
> *These precious days I'll spend with you."*

The following month, Kennedy's small group of confidants grew smaller, when, six days before Christmas, his father suffered a stroke while playing golf in Palm Beach. It was the final blow in this harshest of years. The hard-charging entrepreneur—who had been deeply wired into the highest and lowest enclaves of power, from kings to mobsters—had put all of his relentless drive and paternal devotion at the service of his sons. Joe Kennedy's emotional tides rose and fell with those of his son in the White House. When Jack was reduced to tears by the Bay of Pigs debacle, Joe had spent much of the day on the phone with him and Bobby. "At [the] end, I asked him how he was feeling," his wife Rose later recorded in her diary, "and he said 'Dying'—the result of trying to bring up Jack's morale." Now the once powerful patriarch could no longer offer his son solace or counsel, his speech reduced to one word by his calamity, the word "no," which he uttered in angry frustration over and over.

Joe Kennedy suffered his stroke just five days after J. Edgar Hoover reported to Bobby that FBI bugging devices had caught Chicago godfather Sam Giancana complaining bitterly about being betrayed by the Kennedys. The gangster made provocative references to Joe Kennedy and a deal that had been struck with the mob to deliver the Chicago vote to JFK in 1960. Giancana's fury over the alleged double-cross was volcanic.

Considering how often his sons sought his counsel, it's likely that Bobby had brought this disturbing information—which was now in the hands of the blackmailing Hoover—to his father. The old man knew what savage enemies that Mafia bosses—and the reptilian FBI chief—could be for his already beleaguered sons. The stress on the father must have been terrible. And now he was unable to help them.

"The tragedy was Joe Kennedy getting a stroke," Gore Vidal said. "He could have settled the problem with the Mafia in two minutes."

Vidal has long suspected that the Mafia played a key role in the events in Dallas. "I lived for years in a house in southern Italy. When the chief of police of all Italy arrives in Palermo, in an open car with his wife, they blow him up in public view for everyone to see, in precisely the same scene that happened in Dallas. Typical Mafia killing."

With his father incapacitated, it would fall to Bobby—the son Joe knew was as hard as he was—to try to protect the family. "Bobby's a tough one, he'll keep the Kennedys together, you can bet," the old man once said.

As the brothers' enemies proliferated in places high and low, the task seemed daunting.

3

1962

Bobby Kennedy rarely shouted or raised his voice when he got angry. But there was no mistaking his mood when he was not pleased with you. "When he lost his temper, he would fix you with an icy cold look—you knew you were wiped out," recalled Fred Dutton, who as a Kennedy insider from JFK's 1960 presidential race to RFK's 1968 run, saw him in various states of pique.

At four o'clock on the afternoon of May 14, 1962, the attorney general's glinting blue eyes were focused sharply on two men from the CIA who were sitting in his spacious, walnut-paneled office on the fifth floor of the Justice Department. CIA counsel Lawrence Houston and Colonel Sheffield Edwards, the agency's chief of security, had been summoned by Kennedy to discuss a highly delicate matter. The attorney general wanted them to explain why the agency was trying to block the prosecution of a private eye who had been caught the year before bugging the telephone in comedian Dan Rowan's Las Vegas hotel room. The case would expose national security secrets, the CIA men told Kennedy, because the private eye had been hired by the shadowy CIA intermediary Robert Maheu as a favor to Chicago godfather Sam Giancana, who suspected that Rowan was sleeping with his girlfriend, singer Phyllis McGuire. Why was Maheu so interested in keeping Giancana happy? Because, the intelligence officials informed Kennedy, the CIA had enlisted the gangster in a plot to assassinate Fidel Castro.

It was at this point during the half-hour meeting that Robert Kennedy's

eyes grew icy and his jaw tightened, giving the CIA men "a definite impression of [his] unhappiness." Kennedy had spent years as a Senate investigator
and now as attorney general trying to waken the country to the dangers of the
growing merger between legitimate authority—unions, corporations, political institutions—and criminal forces. Now the CIA, an agency that he and
his brother already found deeply suspect, was informing him that it had entered into the assassination business with the very Mafia lords he was trying
to bring to justice. Kennedy fixed the two obviously discomfited CIA couriers
with a hard look. "I trust that if you ever do business with organized crime
again—with gangsters," he said in a voice seething with sarcasm, "you will let
the attorney general know."

The CIA men assured Kennedy that the Mafia plots had been terminated. But, probably unbeknownst to the two agency messengers, the murderous intrigue was still alive. In fact, around the same time Houston and
Edwards were conveying their assurances to Kennedy, the CIA's point man
on Cuba, William Harvey, was delivering poison pills to Giancana confederate Johnny Rosselli, to eliminate the Cuban leader.

In later years, CIA officials and other political opponents of the Kennedys would insist that Bobby's outrage that day had been an act, that he was
already aware that the Mafia had been enlisted in the government's crusade
against Castro. They would say that Kennedy was simply scolding the CIA
because he wanted to be fully informed of the agency's underworld dealings
in the future, not because he wanted the sinister plots against Castro shut
down.

But Houston himself, who as the bearer of bad news that afternoon was
in the best position to read the attorney general's immediate reaction to the
Mafia scheme, later testified that he "got the impression at that time that
[Kennedy] did not know about" the CIA's underworld pact. Under questioning from the Church Committee, the Senate panel formed in 1975 to investigate CIA involvement in assassination plots and other nefarious business,
Houston observed that Kennedy "was disgusted that he had been placed in
that position" by the CIA—where he would be forced to drop an organized
crime case because of the agency's shady intrigues.

RFK's right-hand man at the Justice Department, John Seigenthaler, also
believes that Kennedy's anger that afternoon was genuine. "I remember when
Bob found out about the plots against Castro, he was absolutely furious,"
recalled Seigenthaler, a Pulitzer Prize-winning journalist for the *Nashville
Tennessean* who served as the attorney general's administrative aide until
mid-1962. "When the two fellows from the CIA came over, I took them into

Bob's office and was there for part of it. It was a very testy, cold discussion. My impression was that the silliness had stopped, and there would be nothing in the future unless the administration approved it. I could tell that Bob was genuinely furious at that meeting. He was not putting on a show for me. He didn't want the administration embarrassed. . . . I mean you're talking about something that would have driven Robert Kennedy right up the side of a wall, and it did when he found out about it. Whatever anybody might think about him, you just don't know the man if you think that's something he might go for. It violated his most basic principles. Advance knowledge of a conspiracy to assassinate Castro would have been antithetical to his most basic beliefs. I don't think there's any evidence of it and I don't believe you'd ever find it."

Robert Kennedy's meeting with the two CIA officials still looms large in historical debates about the Kennedy administration. Was he truly shocked and enraged by the agency's dark dealings? Or was the younger Kennedy actually the driving force behind the government's murderous plots against Castro? Two warring camps have angrily engaged each other over these questions in the past four decades, with Kennedy partisans on one side and CIA apologists on the other. At stake is nothing less than the Kennedy brothers' moral standing in history and the reputation of the intelligence agency.

Another crucial question hovers over this debate: Were the Kennedys in control of their own intelligence apparatus? Yes, CIA officials and their advocates in the media have long insisted—the Kennedys were not only in control, they were so zealous and single-minded in their pursuit of Castro, the man who had humiliated the highly competitive brothers in their showdown at the Bay of Pigs, that they drove intelligence officials past acceptable bounds in their pursuit of the Cuban leader. But Kennedy partisans have been equally insistent that the two brothers were simply not this kind of men, that using underworld cutthroats as agents of U.S. foreign policy would have been anathema to them.

The debate began while Robert Kennedy was still alive, and it continued long after he was dead. Years after the younger Kennedy's 1968 assassination, Seigenthaler went to a Georgetown dinner party, a soiree with the usual mix of journalists, policymakers, and spooks. Among the guests was Richard Helms, the master CIA bureaucrat who had emerged as the real power in the agency soon after the downfall of Dulles and Bissell, even after JFK appointed John McCone as CIA director. "It was clear that McCone was out of the loop—Dick Helms was running the agency," Seigenthaler had quickly concluded. "Anything McCone found out was by accident."

During the party, Helms—an urbane and calculating man who, unlike other CIA veterans, never drank more than his limit of one martini—maneuvered himself into Seigenthaler's path. "In his own super-secret, egocentric way, without saying anything directly, Helms brought up the Castro plots and began pointing fingers at the Kennedy administration," Seigenthaler recalled. "He was very careful, because he knew I was a Kennedy loyalist, but he was also being cute, saying things like, 'The Castro plots? You don't want to go there.' He was snide and sly."

In 1975, Helms—by then dispatched to Tehran as U.S. ambassador but still very much the keeper of CIA secrets—tried to point the finger even more bluntly at the late Robert Kennedy. By then, news of past CIA abuses was beginning to surface in Washington's post-Watergate climate. One morning, Helms took Secretary of State Henry Kissinger to breakfast and made it plain where he was going to pin the blame if government investigators got too close to agency secrets: "Helms said all these stories are just the tip of the iceberg," Kissinger later reported to President Ford at an urgent meeting in the Oval Office. "If they come out, blood will flow. For example, Robert Kennedy personally managed the assassination of Castro." Helms's threat, which his friend Kissinger was all too eager to relay, might have helped ensure that the CIA inquiry that was later launched by the Ford administration, under the cautious chairmanship of Vice President Nelson Rockefeller, did not delve too deeply into the agency's hidden chambers.

Kennedy loyalists like Seigenthaler have a very different view of the relationship between the brothers and their intelligence agency. It was not the Kennedys who were flogging the agency to take deadly action against foreign enemies—it was the CIA's own unchecked passions, they contend, that led it astray. "I thought and I still feel that the CIA was always a rogue agency—it did wet work on its own," Seigenthaler says today in a soft Tennessean drawl. "The concept of plausible deniability, under which the CIA took action with the so-called tacit consent of the president, gave men like Helms the excuse to do whatever they wanted. They were way too in thrall to 007. My own instinct was that the relationship between the CIA and the Kennedy White House was not a healthy one. The administration was particularly vulnerable with someone like McCone in charge over there—he was in over his head. . . . And Bob shared that feeling—he didn't have any confidence that John McCone had the slightest idea of what the CIA was doing.

"We were caught in the reality of the Cold War and the agency obviously had a role to play," Seigenthaler continued. "But I don't think the Kennedys believed you could trust much of what they said. . . . We were trying to find our way out of the Cold War, but the CIA certainly didn't want to."

Seigenthaler's Kennedy ties date back to 1957, when he tried to share the fruits of his investigative reporting on Nashville labor racketeering with Bobby, who was making a name for himself at the time as the chief counsel for the McClellan Committee, the Senate panel that was probing organized crime's corrupt inroads into America's economy and politics. Bobby's brother-in-law, Sargent Shriver, arranged a meeting between the two men in New York, where Seigenthaler was leading a seminar on investigative reporting at Columbia University. The journalist hurried downtown for the meeting, arriving ten minutes early, only to have the brash Bobby—dressed in his overcoat and ready to leave—accuse the journalist of being tardy, insulting his regional roots in the process. "Are you Southerners always late?" Kennedy snapped. He brushed past Seigenthaler, telling him to get in touch with his assistant. A few weeks later, after being summoned to Bobby's Washington office, the newspaper reporter was again snubbed by RFK, who shunted him off once more to his aide. By now, Seigenthaler knew what he thought of Kennedy: "What a rich little prick!"

Three weeks later, Seigenthaler began to change his opinion. While working in the newsroom of the *Tennessean* one afternoon, he unexpectedly got a phone call from Kennedy. For the next forty-five minutes, Bobby peppered the investigative reporter with detailed questions about Teamster corruption in Tennessee, making it plain that he had read every article that Seigenthaler had written on the subject. Then he told the reporter he was sending two investigators to Nashville the next day and asked if he could help them. Seigenthaler agreed.

"From that point on, I grew more and more impressed with Bobby Kennedy and I thought the little snot was a great guy, and our relationship warmed tremendously," remembered Seigenthaler. "Who would have guessed?"

Seigenthaler had passed the Kennedy test. He would now join the band of brothers that included fellow journalists like Ed Guthman and Pierre Salinger, investigators like Walt Sheridan, and political comrades like Kenny O'Donnell—men whose lives would be forever changed, first by Bobby's reformer zeal, and then by his brother's presidential mission. For Seigenthaler, the bond with RFK would grow deeper when he asked the journalist to help him with the memoir of his anti-crime campaign, which would become the 1960 bestseller *The Enemy Within*. Seigenthaler moved into Kennedy's

Hickory Hill mansion, editing the manuscript as Bobby turned out the pages in longhand, and taking long walks with him in the afternoon. It was during those walks that Seigenthaler "got to know Bob Kennedy better than I got to know anybody during my whole life," he later recalled. "He was completely candid with me about everything."

As he grew closer to Kennedy, Seigenthaler's early impressions of him as an arrogant, entitled prince began to evaporate. The Kennedy brothers could have chosen the idle lives of "little rich boys" sunning themselves on a "beach somewhere," the journalist concluded, but instead they had chosen lives of public service. They were willing to take risks to change America. And Seigenthaler decided he would join their cause, doing "everything in my power to make Jack Kennedy president." And, after that, putting his body on the line for Bobby Kennedy at the Justice Department.

In May 1961, during the administration's first civil rights crisis—prompted by violent attacks on a bus filled with Freedom Riders traveling through Alabama—Seigenthaler was dispatched by the attorney general to monitor the situation. Alabama Governor John Patterson had promised Seigenthaler that the civil rights activists would be protected, but as their Greyhound bus reached Montgomery, its convoy of state police cars suddenly melted away, and the bus riders were left to the mercy of an ugly crowd wielding chains and ax handles. Kennedy aide John Doar was reporting to the attorney general on the alarming events from a phone booth near the Montgomery bus terminal where the Freedom Riders were besieged. "The passengers are coming off," he alerted Bobby. Then his voice grew agitated: "Oh, there are fists, punching. A bunch of men led by a guy with a bleeding face are beating them. There are no cops. It's terrible. It's terrible. There's not a cop in sight. People are yelling, 'Get 'em, get 'em.' It's awful."

Seigenthaler could not restrain himself. Seeing a girl being smacked in the face and hit over the head as she tried to escape the mob, he went to her rescue. She warned him: "Mister, get away. . . . You're only going to get killed. This is not your fight." He tried to push her into his car, but was suddenly clubbed from behind. While FBI agents stood watching, Seigenthaler collapsed to the ground, where he was kicked as he lay unconscious. He awoke in a Montgomery hospital.

Kennedy was furious when he heard what had happened to his aide; he was also moved by his courage. "You did what was right," Kennedy told Seigenthaler when he reached him by phone in the hospital. Still woozily recuperating in his hospital bed, Seigenthaler murmured, "Let me give you some advice. Never run for governor of Alabama."

It was Bobby who took on the most explosive issues for his brother's administration, from civil rights to Cuba to organized crime. He always seemed to be in the thick of combat, and his own band of brothers at the Justice Department was right there with him. But despite his belligerent reputation, it was not the life that Robert Kennedy had imagined for himself.

When his newly elected brother asked him to become his attorney general—at the urging of their shrewd, tribalistic father, who wanted someone Jack could utterly trust in the top legal post—Bobby initially resisted. He was tired of "chasing bad men," he told his brother. He didn't want to spend the rest of his life doing that. Maybe he would go home to Massachusetts and do something there, maybe run for governor or become a college president. Bobby took Seigenthaler with him one bitter cold morning after the election to Jack's Georgetown house, to give his brother his final decision over a breakfast of bacon and eggs. But in the end, of course, he dutifully took the job. "I need you in this government," Jack told his brother. And Seigenthaler knew that was that. Bobby's fate was determined. He would, in fact, end up doing precisely what he wanted to avoid—chasing bad men for the rest of his life.

NO ONE OF HIS era came to know more than Robert Kennedy about the dark side of American power. As Arthur Schlesinger observed, Bobby knew how the country was really run—"the underground streams through which so much of the actuality of American power darkly coursed: the FBI, CIA, the racketeering unions and the mob." He had learned from his father, who attempted to steer these streams for the benefit of the Kennedy family. He had learned as a crime-busting Senate investigator. He had learned as his brother's tough, undefeated campaign manager. And he would learn, most of all, as the attorney general, when his crusades turned the full fury of these dark powers against the two brothers' administration.

The younger Kennedy threw himself into these dangerous battles with a mixture of bravery, arrogance, idealism, and Irish fatalism. "You won't have any trouble finding my enemies," he told a *Life* reporter in January 1962 with what struck the reporter as a satisfied smile. "They're all over town." Bobby's bravado recalled his childhood days when he had forced himself to do whatever he feared most. Slow to master swimming as a boy, he had thrown himself off a yawl into Nantucket Sound to either sink, or finally swim. "It showed," a bemused Jack would observe, "either a lot of guts or no sense at all."

When RFK became attorney general at age thirty-five, he was still very much a work in progress. Before the president-elect took him outside his Georgetown house to anoint him as his choice for attorney general in front of the press throng assembled on N Street, he had to tell his kid brother to go upstairs and comb his hair. Standing before the battery of news cameras next to his smoothly self-assured older brother, Bobby looked like a sheepish schoolboy getting an award he didn't deserve.

Compared to his cool-running older brother, he seemed a cauldron of youthful passions. The men who knew them both, like Charles Bartlett, did not see Jack's subtlety of mind in Bobby. Ted Sorensen's first impressions of the younger Kennedy were far from reassuring. He struck Sorensen as "militant, aggressive, intolerant, opinionated, somewhat shallow in his convictions . . . more like his father than his brother."

As a thirteen-year-old, Bobby had summed himself up this way in a school composition titled "A Portrait of Myself": "I have a pretty good character on the whole, but my temper is not too good." It remained an accurate assessment after he became the second most powerful man in Washington. Even fellow Democrats tagged Bobby "Raúl," after the younger Castro brother who was Fidel's militant enforcer. Adlai Stevenson crowned him "the black prince."

"The great difference between Bobby and John F. Kennedy in those days was that everything was black and white for Bobby," said Pierre Salinger, recalling the early years of the brothers' political saga. "But John F. Kennedy had the facility to see the fact that life was not a black and white proposition, that there were a lot of gray areas in life."

Reflecting on the two brothers years later in his office at the *Washington Post*, retired editor Ben Bradlee said, "I think there was less hidden business in Jack. There was no inner turmoil in Jack. Bobby was always a crusader, campaigning against the people who hurt the people he loved."

The attorney general brought a messianic sense of purpose to his brother's administration. Believing that men lost their juice for battle by middle age, RFK surrounded himself at the Justice Department with aides as young and dedicated as himself. Ed Guthman remembers looking around the attorney general's expansive office, during a meeting there one afternoon in late 1961. Kennedy was sitting on his desk in a typical pose—no suit jacket, shirtsleeves rolled up, legs folded under him Indian-style. The sober government office had been transformed into a colorful salon decorated with his children's wildly impressionistic crayon scrawlings on the walls, a varnished sailfish over the mantelpiece, and a stuffed tiger near the fireplace. The menagerie was completed by the attorney general's lumbering, black 125-pound Newfoundland, Brumus—a beast of "passable intelligence and overwhelming love for mankind," in the words of *Look* magazine journalist Fletcher Knebel, who "drools on everybody, including the boss, who frequently has to wipe one of his expensive New York-tailored suits after Brumus's happy salivations." Surveying Kennedy's assembled staff that day, Guthman realized that, at forty-two, he was the oldest person in the room.

Kennedy's young staff responded to his crusading spirit, warm and open management style, and transparent emotions. In the eyes of most of his staff, Bobby's passions made him temperamentally suited for the role of an avenging attorney general.

The question that still haunts the Kennedy legacy, however, is did RFK's righteous fervor push him, and his brother's administration, to extreme lengths in their campaign against the Castro regime? After the Bay of Pigs debacle, the wily, charismatic dictator undeniably became an obsession of the Kennedy brothers, particularly Bobby, who was given the mission of solving the Cuba problem. "The bearded fellow," as he contemptuously referred to him, would join his most wanted list, along with other "tyrants" like Jimmy Hoffa. The attorney general brought an intensity to the anti-Castro crusade that was not as evident in JFK, a passion that seemed born of the younger brother's more visceral anticommunism and Catholicism. According to anti-Kennedy revisionists like journalist Seymour Hersh, Bobby's mandate was clear: It was "to murder Fidel Castro and overthrow his government."

But there is no compelling evidence to support this. While Bobby did indeed browbeat CIA officials to do more to disrupt the Cuban government, assassination was not among the measures he urged upon the agency. In fact, the Kennedys' views of the Castro regime became less and less absolutist as time went on. The administration would adopt a contradictory, two-track strategy toward the Castro regime, wielding not just sticks but carrots, as the Kennedy brothers attempted to navigate their way out of the crisis atmosphere that characterized their first two years in office.

Dick Goodwin tells the story of the day in November 1961 when he led Tad Szulc, who was being considered for an administration job, into the Oval Office to meet with President Kennedy. The president stunned the *New York Times* reporter by asking him, "What would you think if I ordered Castro to be assassinated?" The journalist told him he did not think the United States should be involved in this type of thing. Kennedy said, "I agree with you completely." He then said he was under intense pressure from officials within his government to take this extreme step, but that he was "glad" that Szulc agreed with him because he felt that for "moral reasons" the United States must never resort to this sinister activity.

As with Bobby's angry response to the CIA couriers who informed him of the Mafia plots, Kennedy critics charge that JFK staged this dialogue with Szulc to give himself cover in case the murder plots were later revealed. But Goodwin finds this far-fetched. "It struck me that if Kennedy were in fact involved in a plot to kill Castro, he hardly would have told that to a reporter from the *New York Times*, who the day after Castro was killed would be sitting on the biggest story in the world! I can't go into his mind and find his motives, but I just don't think that someone as media-savvy as Kennedy would do something like this."

When Goodwin brought up the Szulc discussion with Kennedy several days later, the president reiterated his opposition: "We can't get into that kind of thing, or we would all be targets."

Years later, in 1984, Szulc talked about his remarkable Kennedy meeting with Castro himself. The Cuban leader listened with rapt interest, telling the journalist that it confirmed his belief that Kennedy had nothing to do with the CIA attempts on his life. He was convinced that if Kennedy had lived, they would have worked out their differences, he told Szulc.

More recently, Robert Kennedy's widow, Ethel, raised the subject of the assassination plots with Castro during a visit with the Cuban leader in Havana. She waited until his translator had left the room before broaching the matter. Castro pretends not to be fluent in English, but he actually speaks it very well. When they were alone, Ethel addressed Fidel directly. "I want you to know something," she said, looking up at the tall, graying figure whose story was so entwined with that of her family. "Jack and Bobby had nothing to do with the plots to kill you." Castro met her eyes. "I know," he said.

But if President Kennedy thought he had shut down the Castro assassination intrigue, he could not be certain when it came to the CIA. "You could never be sure with the CIA," Goodwin observed. "They were doing things on their own."

Goodwin recalled Kennedy's anger when he informed him that the CIA had secretly supplied rifles to assassins who were plotting to kill Dominican Republic dictator Rafael Trujillo. "Tell them no more weapons," exclaimed Kennedy. "The United States is not to get involved in any assassinations. I'd like to get rid of Trujillo, but not that way." But Trujillo was terminated that way, when his car was fired upon while driving on a deserted stretch of highway on May 30, 1961.

The CIA's defiance of Kennedy's leadership was most flagrant when it came to Cuba. The agency felt increasingly whipsawed by the Kennedy brothers—flayed, on the one hand, to produce more results in their secret sabotage campaign against the island, but scolded when their actions created too much political fallout. Hard-liners in the agency and elsewhere in the government bitterly complained about what they regarded as a two-faced Kennedy policy.

As Robert Kennedy struggled to master the Cuba problem, he was also straining to control the CIA, the agency that his brother had vowed to shatter into pieces, but which had only grown more powerful and unaccountable as it pursued its lavishly funded covert war with Castro. The intelligence organization, still bitter over the president's handling of the Bay of Pigs, deeply resented the younger Kennedy's intrusion into the Cuba arena and chafed under his management, which spy officials regarded as full of brash theatrics but largely ineffectual. At the same time the relentless RFK was badgering CIA officials to take more action against the Cuban regime, and abrasively challenging their authority, he and his cool-headed brother were imposing strict limits on what the agency could do. It was an unhealthy state of affairs. The relationship between the younger Kennedy and the intelligence czars grew increasingly poisonous. By the final days of the Kennedy reign, the brothers would find themselves more at war with their own national security regime than they were with the one in Havana.

IN THEIR ATTEMPT TO take control of their government, the Kennedys often turned to mavericks who operated outside bureaucratic channels. When Dick Goodwin was forced out of the Cuba command post in late 1961, they selected another wild card, the legendary counterinsurgency expert Edward Lansdale, to fill the vacancy. By November 1961, the Kennedys had concluded that their quiet approach toward Havana was not working. Castro seemed to be hardening into a Soviet-controlled Communist dictator with revolutionary ambitions for the rest of Latin America, and the political pressure to do something about his regime was growing. That month the president inaugurated a new covert operation, codenamed "Mongoose," that would be aimed at toppling the Castro regime from within by instigating a Cuban revolution. "My idea is to stir things up on the island with espionage, sabotage, general disorder, run & operated by Cubans themselves with every group but Batistaites and Communists," read Robert Kennedy's notes on the

November 3 White House meeting where the president authorized Operation Mongoose. "Do not know if we will be successful in overthrowing Castro but we have nothing to lose in my estimate."

The Kennedys were convinced that the gung-ho Lansdale was just the man to serve as operations chief for Mongoose, reporting directly to RFK. A dashing-looking, mustachioed Errol Flynn type, he had become a Cold War celebrity in the 1950s by almost single-handedly helping Philippines leader Ramón Magsaysay defeat a left-wing insurgency and later creating and propping up Ngo Dinh Diem's regime in South Vietnam. Lansdale's bold counterinsurgency strategy, which drew on his background as a California advertising man, was aimed at winning the hearts and minds of Third World populations. Though Graham Greene denied it, Lansdale was rumored to be the model for Alden Pyle, the fatally naïve do-gooder in *The Quiet American*, Greene's prescient 1955 novel about the doomed American enterprise in Vietnam. But Lansdale proudly embraced his fictional portrayal as Edwin Hillandale—the American military officer at the center of the 1958 best-seller, *The Ugly American*, which was written by two acquaintances of his, William Lederer and Eugene Burdick. Although the term later became an epithet for clueless, culturally insensitive Americans abroad, the protagonist of *The Ugly American* was actually a sympathetic character. Like Lansdale, who ventured into jungle villages where he entertained natives with his harmonica, Hillandale was willing to get his hands dirty in his counterinsurgency efforts—hence the "ugly American," as opposed to the aloof "beautiful Americans" stationed abroad who never left the comforts of their U.S. embassy suites and remained blissfully ignorant of local customs and conditions.

The book meshed with JFK's activist foreign policy philosophy and he incorporated its themes into his 1960 campaign. And Lansdale would later strike Kennedy as the ideal choice to take on Castro, using the revolutionary leader's own guerrilla tactics to bring him down.

There was a romantic aspect to the Lansdale legend that strongly appealed to the Kennedys. He was brave and risk-taking and uninhibited by bureaucratic protocols. Though he initially enlisted in the Army during World War II, he had later been assigned to the OSS and he spent his subsequent government career floating between intelligence and the military, where he had risen to become an Army brigadier general. This gave Lansdale an aura that was independent of both the CIA and the Pentagon, neither of which fully trusted the lone ranger. A Lansdale-run Operation

Mongoose, the Kennedys realized, had the potential to cut out the CIA hierarchy and Joint Chiefs of Staff, an obvious Kennedy aim when it came to Cuba. Lansdale played to RFK's distrust of the CIA elite in a memo he wrote the attorney general soon after Mongoose was launched, suggesting that they go around "Dick Bissell" and "the CIA palace guard" and work with a middle-management CIA official named Jim Critchfield as their agency liaison, a man Lansdale thought they could rely upon.

The freewheeling attorney general and his equally independent-minded point man on Cuba seemed intent on yanking the island away from the national security bureaucracy and creating their own special team to deal with it. In a December 7, 1961, memo, Lansdale complained that the CIA's "smash and grab" raids on Cuba—which often utilized militant exiles who would not have met Robert Kennedy's more exacting criteria, including men linked to Batista and the mobsters who helped prop him up—were out of step with the Mongoose philosophy, which held that sabotage expeditions should only be carried out when they helped build a popular movement inside Cuba against Castro.

Lansdale invoked the democratic ideals of the American Revolution to justify the U.S. operation against Castro. "Americans once ran a successful revolution," wrote Lansdale in a program review of Mongoose dated February 20, 1962. "It was run from within, and succeeded because there was timely and strong political, economic, and military help by nations outside who supported our cause. Using this same concept of revolution from within, we must now help the Cuban people to stamp out tyranny and gain their liberty."

But underneath the shiny, new democratic marketing, Lansdale's overseas missions pretty much fit the old imperialist mold. In the Philippines, he had managed Magsaysay's political career like a corrupt ward heeler, spreading around a suitcase full of CIA cash to ensure his man's 1953 presidential victory and once slugging Magsaysay so hard he knocked him out when the candidate tried to deliver a speech written by a Filipino instead of one by his American handlers. The counterinsurgency wizard delighted in telling the story of how he terrorized the rebellious Huks into fleeing a part of the Philippine jungle where they had been strong by making the superstitious rebels believe the area was infested with vampires:

"When the Huks came . . . the last man [of their patrol] was silently grabbed by the [government] patrol. When the Huks were out of the vicinity, the captured Huk was held down, two holes punched in his throat, held up by the heels, and drained of blood. The body was carefully placed back on the trail. The returning Huks found the body. The vampire evidence was compelling. The Huks deserted their strongly held jungle area before dawn."

Lansdale's grotesque vampire stunt later became notorious in the Philippines, with one journalist writing in 1986 that the tale "makes Filipinos vomit. Lansdale would never dare desecrate the body of a white American. . . . But not the Filipinos, who are dung, who are of an inferior race and whose bodies may be desecrated, drained of blood and left to rot in the jungles."

Lansdale never attempted anything so grisly in Cuba. But his grab bag of raids, propaganda tricks, and psychological war stunts—including his plan to stage a Second Coming of Christ by having a U.S. submarine off the Cuba coast fire some star shells into the sky, thereby inciting Catholics on the island to rise up and overthrow Castro—fell ludicrously short of endangering the Havana regime. It was one thing to send the primitive Huks scurrying in the Philippines jungle. It was quite another to unseat the brilliant and charismatic Fidel Castro, whose rule was growing steadily stronger through his popular social reforms and his increasingly sophisticated repressive machinery.

CIA officials loathed Lansdale, whom they derided as a "con man" and a "mystic," fearing that he would cut them out of the Cuba account, which was becoming the government's biggest, most lavishly financed battlefront in the Cold War. They connived to find ways of bringing him down, and were quick to point out Mongoose's notable lack of results.

Bobby Kennedy was forced to acknowledge Mongoose's obvious misfires, but he stuck with the program through most of 1962, until the October missile crisis highlighted its utter failure. The operation served the Kennedys' purpose that year. As the Democrats headed toward the midterm congressional elections in November, the brothers were under sharp pressure to prevent Cuba from becoming an explosive issue. The Luce press, the media's leading champion of Cold War machismo, kept up a steady drumbeat that year to get tough on Castro, starting with a January 19 *Life* magazine editorial that warned JFK he must take strong unilateral action against this "captured beachhead [of] Communist imperialism" if our Latin allies proved too timid to act. Meanwhile, Barry Goldwater was denouncing the administration's "do-nothing policy toward Cuba," and restive Cuban exiles were charging that President Kennedy was secretly settling for coexistence with Castro. As his brother's political guardian, Bobby realized that Mongoose at least provided the president some cover. It gave the appearance that the administration was not simply ignoring Castro, as Goodwin had advised, but was now taking the offensive.

The Kennedys were aware that the calls for an all-out U.S. military invasion of Cuba would grow louder as the November elections drew closer. As Admiral Burke prepared to leave the Navy in summer 1961, eased out by the administration he had come to revile, JFK had called him into the Oval Office to debrief him about Cuba. The president surely realized that Burke was soon to become a political thorn in his side and he wanted to hear what his line of attack on Cuba would be. "He asked me if I thought we would have to go into Cuba," Burke later recalled. "I said yes. He asked whether we could take Cuba easily. I said yes, but it was getting more and more difficult. He asked what did I think would happen if we attacked. I said all hell would break loose but that some day we would have to do it." By the following year, Goldwater was declaring that "something must be done about Cuba . . . if it takes our military, I wouldn't hesitate to use it."

President Kennedy had no intention of invading Cuba. But he and his brother knew that to do nothing in the fevered climate of the day would be political suicide. So they settled on the middle option, Operation Mongoose, as the safest. Picking an ad man like Lansdale to run it made perfect sense. The operation was "mostly for show," griped the CIA's point man on Cuba, Bill Harvey. As the more savvy CIA officials undoubtedly realized, that was the point. Lansdale's Cuba show, starbursts and all, was supposed to dazzle the American people. It would reassure them that something was being done. Polls showed that the public—poked and prodded by a media whose belligerence rivaled that of the Hearst press in the "Remember the *Maine!*" era—did indeed want *something* done. But, fortunately for the Kennedys, Americans stopped short of demanding war. So the Kennedys kept the Pentagon and CIA in check, while assuaging the public's vague anxieties about Cuba by fruitlessly harassing the Castro regime.

CIA and Pentagon officials were not fooled or assuaged. They knew that Operation Mongoose had no chance of succeeding and that a military invasion was the only way to remove the "humiliating" Communist outpost in the Caribbean, as Goldwater called it. For the rest of the Kennedy administration, military leaders and intelligence officials would strain and conspire to force the president to take this drastic step, as they had during the Bay of Pigs debacle. And their anger and frustration steadily grew as the Kennedys kept deflecting their bellicose pressures.

On July 18, 1962 CIA director John McCone dined with Bobby, using the occasion to urge tough action on Cuba. McCone had already advised RFK that "Cuba was our most serious problem. I also added, in my opinion, Cuba was the key to all of Latin America; if Cuba succeeds, we can expect most of Latin America to fall." Over dinner, the CIA chief drove home these points. But Kennedy was not buying McCone's argument. Bobby acknowledged that the Mongoose effort was "disappointing" so far, but he could not be persuaded that the United States should unleash its full military might against Havana. "He urged intensified effort but seemed inclined to let the situation 'worsen' before recommending drastic action," a discouraged Mc-Cone later wrote in his notes on the dinner.

In the ideological war to define the Kennedy administration, which broke out soon after the president was laid to rest in Arlington and continues to this day, national security officials insisted that the Kennedy brothers were "out of control" on Cuba, pushing them to take absurd measures against Castro like the Mongoose folly. This would become the standard version of the Kennedys' Cuba policy in countless books, TV news shows, and documentaries—it was rash, obsessive, treacherous, even murderous. But this is not an accurate picture of Kennedy policy. What in truth bothered national security hard-liners was not how "out of control" the brothers were on Cuba—it was how *in* control they were. They were enraged by the way that Bobby Kennedy, and eccentric lieutenants like Lansdale, were installed over them. And they were infuriated by the restrictions imposed on their military ambitions. Frustrated in their campaign to declare war on Cuba, intelligence officials declared war instead on the Kennedys, particularly the insufferable kid brother who was put in charge of supervising them. And without telling either the president or the attorney general, they took another ominous step. They renewed their sinister contract with the Mafia to eliminate Fidel Castro.

ON A BRIGHT SPRING afternoon, Cynthia Helms sits in the sunroom of her comfortable home in a leafy Washington neighborhood near Battery Kemble Park. She is surrounded by photos of her late husband, Richard, who died in his sleep in their upstairs bedroom in 2002 at age eighty-nine. There are framed shots of Helms with every president he served—with the notable exception of Kennedy. Late in the administration, the CIA man realized he didn't have one of the "customary" autographed pictures of JFK, and he phoned Kenny O'Donnell at the White House to get one. But three days later, Kennedy was dead.

Cynthia Helms's hair, once a striking red, is now cloud white. She wears a no-nonsense outfit this afternoon—light cotton blouse and tan slacks. She is a bright, well-read, unflappable woman. On a side table is a copy of Ian McEwan's latest novel, *Saturday*.

During World War II she served her native England as a WREN (Women's Royal Naval Service). Afterward she married a Scottish surgeon and "went directly with him to the Mayo Clinic, where I cried for months" when she realized she had made a mistake. She gave birth to four children, then divorced her husband, and moved to Washington, D.C., where she met Helms at a party at the Lebanese embassy, marrying him in 1968. She remained married to Helms the rest of his life, throughout his controversial career as CIA director and later ambassador to Iran—no easy task. "I nearly wrote a book about CIA wives," she says. "I think they had a really difficult time. You go to a foreign country and your husband's gone all night and you don't know where he is. And you can't ask. There were many divorces."

But she learned to accommodate her husband's private ways. She knew when to press him and when not to—like the days he came home from the office with what she called his "Oriental look—totally inscrutable." It was better not to ask him anything those evenings. Her husband was "terribly discreet." And drinking wouldn't loosen his tongue, as it did with many gin-swilling CIA old boys. "He just had a martini on Friday nights—one martini," she says. "Very disciplined."

But Helms did not conceal his true feelings from his wife about Robert Kennedy, even though the spymaster had long since stopped working for him when they met and Kennedy would die the year the couple was wed. "My husband was not particularly an admirer of Robert Kennedy's," says Cynthia Helms with British understatement. "He felt he was obsessed with Cuba. He was just obsessed. It was very hard for people in the government to handle." Helms also thought Kennedy was a phony, says his widow. By the end of his life, Kennedy was widely admired for being one of the few white politicians in racially polarized America who could cross lines and appeal to diverse audiences. But Helms was disdainful. "He really didn't feel that Bobby was—how can I put it? He thought his interest in civil rights was political."

So strong was the animus of top CIA officials like Helms against Robert Kennedy that it outlasted both men's lives. Revulsion for the Kennedys, and for Bobby in particular, would be channeled by aging Helms associates like CIA veteran Sam Halpern, whose disparaging remarks about the reign of Camelot were widely quoted in history books and documentaries until his own death in 2005.

Richard Helms effectively took over the CIA in February 1962 when his

bitter rival, Dick Bissell, finally walked the plank for the Bay of Pigs and
Helms replaced him as covert operations chief. It was the agency's number
two post, but Helms—who had served under Allen Dulles in the OSS—had
the same proprietary sense about the CIA that his old boss did and he quickly
overshadowed Dulles's replacement, John McCone, as the real center of
power at Langley. For the rest of the Kennedy presidency, Helms was the key
intelligence figure with whom Robert Kennedy engaged. While Helms
treated McCone as a harmless front man—a white-haired, well-groomed
CEO type who "stepped straight from central casting in Hollywood," as he
later wrote in his posthumously published 2003 memoir—he regarded Bobby
as his true rival for leadership of the spy agency.

Like most of the CIA's upper ranks, Helms was a product of WASP afflu-
ence and entitlement. The grandson of a prominent international banker and
the son of an Alcoa executive, he was raised in Europe and educated alongside the future shah of Iran at the fashionable Le Rosey School in Switzer-
land. After graduating from Williams College as "the most likely to succeed,"
he married the heiress to the Barbasol shaving fortune, but this first match
ended in divorce. He was pursuing a career in journalism, the highlight of
which was landing an interview with Hitler as a young Berlin correspondent
for the United Press, when World War II broke out and he was recruited into
the intelligence world. Tall, well-dressed, his thinning hair slicked straight
back, Helms carried himself with a supremely self-confident air. He was a
fixture of the Georgetown salons and tennis courts, where he worked the
Washington press and charmed his dinner partners. "A former foreign correspondent, he observes much and can recall precisely what few American
husbands ever note in the first place—what gown each woman wore to dinner and whose shoulder strap was out of place," noted the *New York Times*.

Helms viewed the younger Kennedy as a cunning political enemy who
had to be carefully monitored and managed. He smoldered as the attorney
general poked his nose into agency affairs and barraged him with directives.
Helms resented it when Kennedy abruptly ordered him to drive in to Washington from Virginia to attend Mongoose meetings at 9:30 every morning.
"Given the travel time involved in getting about in Washington at that hour,"
he later sniffed, "there seemed to be more than a whiff of a disciplinary flavor
in this decision."

Helms dismissed the Mongoose sabotage efforts as no "more than pinpricks" against Castro and he bridled at Kennedy's "hammering us for results." He later complained that under Bobby's "relentless" reign, he was
"getting my ass beaten. You should have enjoyed the experience of Bobby

Kennedy rampant on your back." While thrashing the spymaster's behind, Kennedy had only "a slight idea what was involved in organizing a secret intelligence operation," Helms bitterly concluded. The espionage chief grimly considered his dilemma: He was saddled with an obnoxious brat of an overseer who had a direct line to his older brother in the White House—and both of them seemed determined to "upend" the intelligence agency he was dedicated to protect, while leaving Castro safely in power.

RFK had a similar disregard for Dick Helms. "I didn't trust Helms and I don't think Bob did either," said John Seigenthaler. "Bob would make snide remarks about him. I think the Kennedys thought they could energize and breathe fresh air into damn near every agency in the government. Maybe it was idealistic. But I think Bob in particular believed it. He was shaking up everything. Still, there were a couple places where the bureaucracy was entrenched and impenetrable. Bob didn't think there was any way to break through the crust of the CIA. That only meant to him that they should not be trusted."

Dick Helms was a smooth enough bureaucrat to know how to contain his bitter resentment of the president's meddling brother. But the man he put in charge of the agency's Cuba operations lacked Helms's knack for dissembling. Bill Harvey was a hard-drinking, ill-tempered former FBI man from the Midwest known for strutting around with a revolver stuffed in his waistband. When he took over the CIA's Miami-based Cuba operation, he named it in typically cocky fashion "Task Force W" after the nineteenth century soldier of fortune William Walker who seized Nicaragua as his private empire and was later executed by a Honduran firing squad. Squat-figured and bug-eyed, due to a thyroid condition, and often drunk, Harvey had nonetheless made a name for himself as a daring spymaster in postwar Berlin by digging a tunnel underneath Soviet lines to eavesdrop on the enemy. (The fact that the Russians discovered the tunnel before they suffered a significant intelligence setback did not tarnish Harvey's reputation within a Cold War Washington hungry for espionage heroes.) When the James Bond–bedazzled JFK asked to meet the CIA agent who came closest to 007, Lansdale walked Harvey over to the White House. The bemused president asked the pear-shaped, pigeon-toed, balding agent if he had as much luck with women as Bond.

Privately, Harvey called the Kennedy brothers "fags" but he reserved a special loathing for Bobby, whom he routinely referred to as "the little fucker." Often admonished by the attorney general for making too much "noise" with his Cuba raids, he considered the Kennedys cowards who were not serious about removing Castro. "After Bill Harvey takes over in early '62, we did have a small success . . . maybe we knocked out a transformer," recalled Sam Halpern, who served as Harvey's Task Force W assistant. "It was a minor thing but it made headlines in Cuba and it made the headlines in Miami . . . and the attorney general gets on the phone to Bill Harvey . . . Bill gets chewed out by Bobby Kennedy on the phone. Harvey tells the attorney general that people are going to talk about it; it's going to be on radio, it's going to be on television. That's the facts of life. You can't hide these things."

As time passed, Harvey grew increasingly irritated by Kennedy's hands-on management and was not afraid to show it. RFK and Lansdale, whom Harvey and his aides dismissed as a "screwball," sometimes paid visits to Task Force W's headquarters, which were housed in former Navy barracks on the University of Miami's secluded south campus. Harvey made it clear that they were not welcome. During one of his visits to the JM/WAVE station, as the sprawling center of covert anti-Castro operations was code-named, Kennedy ripped a piece a paper out of an office teletype, but Harvey immediately grabbed it from his hands. "You have no right to read that," he growled at Kennedy in his gravelly voice. On another occasion, an impatient Kennedy complained that Harvey's station was not infiltrating enough opera-tives into Cuba, offering to train more men himself at his Hickory Hill estate if necessary. "What will you teach them, sir?" the CIA man shot back. "Baby-sitting?"

Nothing the Kennedys did, short of launching a massive U.S. military invasion of the island, would have pleased CIA officials like Helms and Har-vey. This was, they believed with good reason, the only certain way of ousting the Castro regime. But the Kennedys would do little more than engage in pointless "boom and bang" exercises, in Halpern's dismissive phrase, and play around with far-fetched coup schemes involving exile leaders who had no serious chance of replacing Castro. Bobby had a weakness for these brave if deluded Don Quixotes, often driving CIA officials to distraction by going around them and conferring directly with these Cuban plotters. And he was especially fond of exile leaders who rejected CIA sponsorship, vowing to take back their country by themselves.

One such man was Ernesto Betancourt, the former Washington emissary of Castro's revolutionary movement who had tried to warn JFK against the doomed Bay of Pigs mission through Kennedy press pal Charles Bartlett. In 1962 Betancourt fell in with one of many Cuban exile groups with visions of toppling Castro before Christmas, the ELC (*Ejercito Libertador de Cuba*). That September he met with Bobby Kennedy, exciting the attorney general with his talk of sparking a popular uprising in Cuba by the end of the month. And yes, this remarkable feat could be accomplished without the CIA, an agency, he bitterly told a receptive Bobby, that has typically "relegated Cubans to the status of tools, while the Americans called the signals." Betancourt painted a picture of a Cuba in full revolt: ELC slogans splashed on walls all over the island, bridges and factories blown to pieces, Castro's militia under fire throughout the countryside. It was then that Betancourt's guerrillas would land on Cuba's beaches and infiltrate the island, to begin coordinating the final assault on Havana. And this time they would be successful, unencumbered by the inept leadership of the CIA.

Kennedy immediately called Helms and told him of the Betancourt plan. One can only imagine the delight with which the consummate CIA bureaucrat greeted this latest Bobby scheme to "work outside the framework" of the agency to unseat Castro. Helms and Harvey promptly moved to squelch the plan, dispatching an agent named Charles Ford to assess the Betancourt brainstorm and to inform Kennedy of its futility. Ford told RFK that "in the frank opinion of the CIA, there is little likelihood of there being 15,000 persons ready to carry out even a partially successful revolt; that CIA does not believe such a revolt will take place, and that in the unlikely event that it does occur, it will be ruthlessly and totally suppressed." It was a harsh but accurate assessment and Kennedy was forced to accept the agency's logic. Meanwhile, Ford reported to his CIA superiors that one of the ELC men surrounding Betancourt was tied to a suspected Castro spy who had been sent to the United States to penetrate the group and kill its leaders. This undoubtedly confirmed Helms's and Harvey's view of Kennedy as an amateur spook whose antics only distracted the professionals from their real work.

Despite the enthusiasm of CIA officials for a military assault on Cuba, the agency's own analysts took a dim view of the prospects for such an invasion. In an April 10, 1962, memo to Director McCone, Sherman Kent, chairman of the CIA's Board of National Estimates, drew a sobering picture of what would likely happen if U.S. troops stormed the island. Over four decades later, the Kent memo still has a startling, revelatory power.

The good news, Kent wrote McCone, is that initial resistance from Castro's forces would melt within a few days of the U.S. invasion. Euphoria would reign as Washington promised to turn over control of the nation as soon as possible to a government that was representative of the Cuban people. Then the situation would quickly deteriorate, Kent predicted. "Substantial numbers" of Castro's forces would survive the initial U.S. assault and "would continue a guerrilla resistance" in the country's interior. Much of the Cuban population would support this resistance against what they would perceive as a U.S. attempt to "reimpose upon the Cuban people the yoke of 'Yankee imperialism.'" Establishment of a pro-U.S. government would be "greatly hindered by the persistence of terroristic underground resistance in the cities" and guerrilla resistance in the countryside. "Pacification of the country, to the extent necessary to permit the development of a credible . . . regime, might be long delayed," Kent noted. As a result, the U.S. military would be forced into a "prolonged" role as an occupation force, which would become a sitting target for terrorist violence. This would provoke American soldiers to take "arbitrary measures against the general population," deepening resentments against the U.S. occupation and adding fuel to the resistance. Meanwhile, the United States' international standing would suffer badly as a result of its unilateral military action, isolating the country from its allies in NATO and Latin America and heightening suspicions about U.S. power in the rest of the world.

It was a nightmare scenario that would be played out more than once in America's future. And it was precisely the quagmire that President Kennedy feared would suck him down if he followed his national security officials' advice, first on Cuba and later on Vietnam.

But buckets of cold water like the Kent memo did nothing to dampen the Cuba war fever in the Pentagon and CIA headquarters. The Joint Chiefs of Staff continued to have contingency plans for a Cuba invasion drawn up, none of which had the same bad ending as the Kent scenario. One of the most insidious documents ever produced by the U.S. government was delivered by General Lemnitzer, the chairman of the Joint Chiefs, to Robert McNamara on March 13, 1962. The top-secret memo, which was signed by the country's highest military commanders, urged the administration to stage a variety of shocking incidents to create a rationale for invading Cuba. Among these were faking attacks on the U.S. military base at Guantánamo and on Latin countries such as the Dominican Republic, Haiti, Guatemala, and Nicaragua and blaming the Castro government; simulating Cuban shoot-downs of U.S. civilian and military aircraft (phony "casualty lists in U.S. newspapers would cause a helpful wave of national indignation," noted the memo); and blowing up an American ship in Guantánamo Bay and pinning it on Cuba, an incident the memo compared to the mysterious explosion of the U.S. battleship *Maine* in Havana harbor in 1898, which helped spark the Spanish-American War.

But the Joint Chiefs' most cold-blooded suggestion was to mount a terror campaign in Miami and other Florida cities "and even in Washington" that would create international revulsion against the Castro regime. This violent campaign would be directed at Cuban refugees in America, the chilling memo read. "We could foster attempts on lives of Cuban refugees in the United States even to the extent of wounding in instances to be widely publicized. Exploding a few plastic bombs in carefully chosen spots, the arrest of Cuban agents and the release of prepared documents substantiating Cuban involvement also would be helpful in projecting the idea of an irresponsible government." The military leaders did not spell out how their exploding bombs would be limited to only wounding, not killing, their unsuspecting victims and how they could be assured that the only casualties would be innocent Cuban refugees, and not American bystanders. But the U.S. military has long been overly confident in its precision.

There is no record of how McNamara responded to this cynical proposal by his top military officers when Lemnitzer met with him that Tuesday afternoon. But the sinister plan, which was codenamed Operation Northwoods, did not receive higher approval. When I asked him about Northwoods, McNamara said, "I have absolutely zero recollection of it. But I sure as hell would have rejected it. . . . I really can't believe that anyone was proposing such provocative acts in Miami. How stupid!"

Like the president, McNamara regarded Lemnitzer with barely disguised contempt. "McNamara's arrogance was astonishing," said a Lemnitzer aide. "He gave General Lemnitzer very short shrift and treated him like a schoolboy. The general almost stood at attention when he came into the room. Everything was 'Yes, sir,' and 'No, sir.' "

Lemnitzer even fell afoul of fashion-conscious Jackie Kennedy. "We all thought well of him until he made the mistake of coming into the White House one Saturday morning in a sport jacket," she contemptuously remarked, underlining how class and culture, not just politics, divided the Kennedy White House from the military.

Lemnitzer, a far-right ideologue whose endorsement of General Edwin Walker's paranoid indoctrination of Army troops had raised the suspicions of Senator William Fulbright's Foreign Relations Committee, was equally dismissive of the Kennedy crowd. He thought their administration "was crippled not only by inexperience but also by arrogance arising from failure to recognize [their] own limitations. . . . The problem was simply that the civilians would not accept military judgments."

On March 16, three days after his meeting with McNamara, Lemnitzer was summoned by President Kennedy to the Oval Office for a discussion of

Cuba strategy that was also attended by McCone, Bundy, Lansdale, and Taylor. At one point the irrepressible Lansdale began holding forth, as usual, on the improving conditions for popular revolt inside Cuba, adding that once the glorious anti-Castro revolution began, "we must be ready to intervene with U.S. forces, if necessary." This brought an immediate reaction from Kennedy, ever alert after the Bay of Pigs about being sandbagged into a military response in Cuba. The group was not proposing that he authorize U.S. military intervention, was it? "No," Taylor and the others immediately rushed to assure him.

But Lemnitzer could not restrain himself. He jumped in at that moment to run Operation Northwoods up the flagpole. The general spared the president the plan's more gruesome brainstorms, such as blowing up people on the streets of Miami and the nation's capital and blaming it on Castro. But he informed Kennedy that the Joint Chiefs "had plans for creating plausible pretexts to use force [against Cuba], with the pretexts either attacks on U.S. aircraft or a Cuban action in Latin America for which we would retaliate."

Kennedy was not amused. He fixed Lemnitzer with a hard look and "said bluntly that we were not discussing the use of U.S. military force," according to Lansdale's notes on the meeting. The president icily added that Lemnitzer might find he did not have enough divisions to fight in Cuba, if the Soviets responded to his Caribbean gambit by going to war in Berlin or elsewhere.

Despite the president's cold reaction, the Joint Chiefs chairman persisted in his war campaign. About a month after the White House meeting, Lemnitzer convened his fellow service chiefs in "the tank," as the JCS conference room was called. Under his direction, they hammered out a stern memo to McNamara insisting "that the Cuban problem be solved in the near future." That would never be accomplished by waiting around for Ed Lansdale's fairy-tale popular uprising, the memo made clear. There was only one way of getting the job done: "The Joint Chiefs of Staff recommend that a national policy of early military intervention in Cuba be adopted by the United States."

Lemnitzer was wearing out Kennedy and McNamara's patience. After a National Security Council meeting in June, the president took the general aside and told him he wanted to send him to Europe to become NATO's new supreme allied commander. Kennedy would replace Lemnitzer as the nation's top military man with the more amenable Max Taylor. He would have one less warmonger to harass him about Cuba.

• • •

WHEN IT BECAME CLEAR to Richard Helms that President Kennedy was not going to take Cuba by military force, "the gentlemanly planner of assassinations," as biographer Thomas Powers anointed him, took it upon himself to rekindle the Mafia plots against Fidel Castro. Helms did not tell the Kennedy brothers, nor did he notify his nominal superior at the CIA, John McCone. He simply ordered his Cuba man, Bill Harvey, to renew the contract on Castro. Equally frustrated by the Kennedys' cautious handling of the Havana regime, Harvey lost no time in re-contacting his friend, Mafia emissary Johnny Rosselli.

Just days before the agency's Lawrence Houston and Sheffield Edwards assured Bobby Kennedy that the CIA-Mafia collaboration had been shut down, Harvey handed poison pills prepared in CIA labs to Rosselli. But the plotters apparently decided that firing at Castro with long-range rifles during one of his public appearances had more chance for success than an attempted poisoning. So soon afterwards, Harvey and Ted Shackley, head of the JM/WAVE station, rented a U-Haul truck, packed it full of rifles, handguns, and explosives, and drove it one night to a dark parking lot in Miami, where Rosselli stood waiting in the shadows. The CIA men handed the mobster the keys to the truck. He in turn passed the weapons to henchmen from the Cuban exile world, including men he had done business with ever since the lurid glory days of Batista. The assassination conspiracy against Castro—a three-headed Gorgon featuring the CIA on top, flanked by the Mafia and its Cuban accomplices—was again in motion.

This time Harvey cut out Chicago godfather Sam Giancana and Florida godfather Santo Trafficante, both of whom had been involved in the original Mafia plot. But he felt he could trust Rosselli, whose contacts with the CIA dated back to Guatemala in the 1950s, where the gangster got involved in political intrigues on behalf of gambling interests and the powerful fruit companies. Rosselli was a smooth operator, a polished link between the criminal underworld and the above-ground world of power. The two men made an odd couple—the sharply groomed and deeply tanned mobster with his alligator shoes and $2,000 watch and the rumpled, frog-faced government man in his drab brown suits. But Harvey convinced himself that Rosselli was not just a slick hoodlum from the mean streets of East Boston, but an American patriot. He gave Rosselli the false cover of an Army colonel and granted him complete access to the JM/WAVE headquarters, where the gangster met on a daily basis with CIA assassin David Morales.

Testifying before the Church Committee, Harvey got defensive when

Rosselli's name came up. "I was not dealing with the Mafia as such, pardon my saying so," the CIA man insisted. "I was dealing with, and only dealt with, an individual who allegedly has had contacts with the Mafia. He is charged, but not provably charged, with having been a part of the so-called Chicago Family." Harvey sounded more like his old friend's Mafia lawyer than a high-ranking U.S. intelligence official. He seemed all too comfortable in the criminal world. Bill Harvey was a "thug" in the blunt assessment of CIA colleague John Whitten. Former Senator Gary Hart, one of the more active members of the Church Committee, is still unnerved by the ease with which Harvey crossed into the underworld. "He became best friends with Rosselli and they vacationed together," Hart recalled. "I find this totally bizarre. . . . I don't like CIA agents who become family friends with the Mafia." While growing up, Sally Harvey, the spy's adopted daughter, learned to call her father's gangster friend "Uncle Johnny."

In his 2003 memoir, Helms seemed to hang the CIA-Mafia rap on the conveniently deceased Harvey. Helms claimed that he was as flabbergasted as anyone else when he first heard about the plot. "After checking into it, I told Bill Harvey—who agreed entirely—to close it down," wrote Helms. This assertion was false from beginning to end, and Helms provided no evidence to support it.

Blaming Harvey seemed to be Helms's fall-back position. In 1975, when Helms was brought first before the Rockefeller Commission and then the Church Committee to testify about the Castro plots, he tried to pin the blame, as he had threatened to do over breakfast with his friend Henry Kissinger, squarely on Robert Kennedy. Helms was treated gently by the Republican-run Rockefeller panel, which was stocked with members—like the resilient General Lemnitzer—who were perfectly happy to hear the Kennedys charged with Cuban treachery. But the spymaster came under tougher questioning from the Democratic-controlled Church Committee, and he was compelled to bob and weave before the senators.

Helms appeared before the panel headed by Idaho Democrat Frank Church on a sweltering July afternoon. His testimony, which was delivered in a closed session in the Russell Senate Office Building, was a masterpiece of evasion, innuendo, and deception. "I don't want anybody on this committee to think I am being slippery," Helms told the senators at one point. But this is precisely what he was, as he feigned ingratiating cooperation with the legislators while twisting them into knots with bureaucratic double-speak.

"I never liked assassination," Helms assured the senators, in a bid to claim the moral high ground. But they could not imagine how much pressure that Bobby Kennedy was bringing down on the agency to do something—anything—to get rid of Castro.

"Since he was on the phone with you repeatedly, did he ever tell you to kill Castro?" Senator Church asked him point blank. "No," Helms admitted. But he could not leave his answer as simple as that. "Not in those words, no." He never received a direct assassination order from Kennedy, that is true, Helms acknowledged. And far be it from him "to put words in a dead man's mouth"—that would not be "fair of me," he said. Nonetheless, Helms got the distinct impression in conversation with Kennedy that "we have to find a way to . . . get rid of this fellow." Helms simply got the "feeling that [Kennedy] would not be unhappy if [Castro] had disappeared off the scene by whatever means."

Helms's testimony was filled with winks and nods about Robert Kennedy, but no proof. When pushed by the committee, Helms admitted that Kennedy had been kept in the dark about Harvey's poison pills and guns and was deceived by the CIA when its emissaries told the attorney general that it was no longer working with the Mafia. (Harvey himself conceded to the Senate panel that if RFK had wanted to kill Castro, he, Harvey, would have been the last person that Kennedy would have put in charge of the operation.) The CIA death plots against Castro preceded the Kennedy administration, Senate investigators would conclude, and they continued long after the Kennedy presidency ended.

When his Bobby-made-me-do-it defense began to crumble, Helms fell back on Plan B, which was apparently throwing Harvey over the side. The truth, Helms confided to the Church Committee, was that he had "very grave doubts about the wisdom" of the whole Mafia scheme. But Harvey "tried to convince me that he had been in the FBI a long time" and this is the way G-men "handled these matters and so forth." Besides, he really didn't take the Harvey-Rosselli cloak and dagger stuff all that seriously anyway. "I thought that Harvey was sort of on a wild good chase, frankly."

As his usual mask of self-assurance began to wilt under the questioning, Helms even began to point a finger at his oblivious former boss, John McCone. Helms admitted that he and Harvey had decided to keep McCone blissfully ignorant about the Castro plots—because McCone was "taking over a new job" and the murderous intrigue was "going to look very peculiar to him." But then he contradicted himself by charging that McCone "was involved in this up to his scuppers just the way everybody else was that was in it. I have no reason to impugn his integrity. On the other hand, I don't understand how it was he didn't hear about some of these things that he claims he didn't."

McCone did not know about the CIA's dark side because he did not look hard enough. But Helms also did not want him to know. This was the secret core of the agency, the inner sanctum to which only Helms—and a few other top officials whose spy service dated back to the OSS days—had access. The intelligence world was a unique realm with its own rules and codes of behavior. Helms, in his patronizing way, tried to explain this to the senators on the Church Committee. "When you establish a clandestine service [like] the Central Intelligence Agency," he enlightened them, "you established something that was totally different from anything else in the United States government. Whether it's right that you should have it, or wrong that you should have it, it works under different rules . . . than any other part of the government."

When McCone was brought before the Church Committee, he was put in the embarrassing position of admitting that he did not control the agency that President Kennedy had entrusted to him. JFK's CIA director did not find out about the Mafia conspiracy until August 1963, he told the committee, when he read about it in a Chicago newspaper. He immediately confronted Helms with the newspaper account, but his number two man falsely assured him the plot was old news. "He was very clear that this was something that had been canceled, in 1961, before I took office," said McCone.

It was not until an investigator for the Rockefeller Commission informed McCone in 1975, a dozen years after his conversation with Helms, that he realized his second-in-command had lied to him and that the Mafia plots had continued throughout his CIA tenure. "The fact that this happened is very disturbing to me," an unnerved McCone said at the time. "Because it gives some credibility to the accusation that some things have gone on in the CIA that have been unsupervised and uncontrolled."

This is precisely the conclusion that the Church Committee came to when it released its final report in April 1976, concluding that the CIA had acted like "a rogue elephant."

A disturbing suspicion ran throughout the Church hearings, like a dark thought that can only be faced in a dream. If the CIA was capable of working hand in hand with bloody Mafia assassins against Castro, what else was the agency capable of? This is why the Castro plots and the revelations of CIA treachery against other foreign leaders exploded in the media at the time and continue to echo in the national conscience even today. When men with the dark, unlimited license that Helms argued should be accorded the CIA are set loose upon the world, they can also perform their shadowy deeds closer to home.

During his appearance before the committee, Ted Sorensen made an eloquent case for why President Kennedy would never have approved the CIA's "wet work." Assassination, Sorensen told the senators, "was totally foreign to his character and conscience, foreign to his fundamental reverence for human life and his respect for his adversaries, foreign to his insistence upon a moral dimension in U.S. foreign policy and his concern for the country's reputation abroad, and foreign to his pragmatic recognition that so horrendous but inevitably counterproductive a precedent committed by a country whose own chief of state was inevitably vulnerable, could only provoke reprisals and inflame hostility on the part of those anti-U.S. forces whose existence was never dependent upon a single leader. Particularly ludicrous is the notion that one of his background would have ever knowingly countenanced the employment for these purposes of the same organized crime elements he had fought for so many years." It was a noble statement of the administration's philosophy, which held that the U.S. government should not resort to the ways of the jungle, even if our enemies did. But, as Sorensen acknowledged, it was not shared by all of Kennedy's government.

"I don't think the president ever fully succeeded in getting a handle on what the CIA was doing," Sorensen told the committee. This statement received no headlines, but it was a frighteningly simple description of the limits of democratic power. Why couldn't Kennedy control his own intelligence agency, Sorensen was asked? "If I knew the answer to that, your committee's problem would be much easier," he replied. But he tried to unravel it for the senators. "I think it was a large organization which had been accustomed for many years to operating with a degree of independence. Its officials regarded themselves as highly sophisticated individuals who had an understanding of the realities of the world that they do not feel people in the White House and the State Department shared."

Kennedy's intelligence apparatus grumbled under his command, testified Sorensen. "While President Kennedy was alive, there were reports around town of CIA officials expressing doubt as to his toughness, courage, and ability to recognize all the hard things that had to be done."

Dissatisfied with Kennedy's leadership, agency officials like Helms simply began to ignore it. They undertook drastic actions against Cuba without informing the president, his brother, or his CIA director. Some of these actions were discovered by Kennedy, many were not. Some would escape even the curiosity of the Church Committee and other congressional panels that explored the hidden chambers of the Kennedy years. These incidents dramatically illustrate how brazen the CIA had become in the pursuit of its own unauthorized Cold War policy.

ON AUGUST 22, 1962, the S.S. *Streatham Hill,* a British freighter under Soviet lease, limped into San Juan harbor in Puerto Rico after damaging its propeller on a reef. The ship, which was bound for Russia, was carrying 80,000 bags of Cuban sugar. To facilitate repairs, over 14,000 bags were offloaded and stacked in a warehouse under U.S. customs bond because of the embargo on Cuban products. Sometime while the repairs were underway, CIA agents slipped into the warehouse and contaminated the sugar with an emetic. "It would have made whoever ate the sugar feel very lousy," Carl Kaysen, a Kennedy national security advisor, later said.

Kaysen found out about the CIA sabotage when he intercepted a cable that had not been meant for his eyes. He immediately informed President Kennedy, who flew into a rage.

"I just read a book review by Tom Powers where he wrote that CIA officials never do anything the president doesn't want done," Kaysen said. "But I simply don't have that kind of observation."

Kaysen, a Harvard political economist, was brought into the White House by his former academic colleague McGeorge Bundy. His views were not predictably dovish—during the 1961 Berlin Crisis he had helped prepare a plan for a limited nuclear war that had outraged Sorensen. Still, he recognized that poisoning a shipment of sugar meant for unsuspecting Russian consumers was a highly provocative act that crossed the administration's boundaries. The president strongly agreed.

"Kennedy got very angry and said eating the sugar could kill a sick person, an old person or a child," Kaysen recalled. The president promptly phoned McCone at his Langley office and told him to report to the White House. It is not known whether McCone authorized the act of sabotage, but in any case, he knew he was about to be tongue-lashed for his agency's reckless behavior. On his way into the Oval Office, the CIA director confronted Kaysen, lighting into him for blowing the whistle on the agency. "What the hell are you interfering in this business for?" McCone erupted.

"But after Kennedy chewed him out, [McCone] came out of the president's office and put his arm around my shoulder like he was my buddy," recalled Kaysen, now a professor at MIT.

Kennedy ordered McCone to do whatever was necessary to stop the contaminated sugar from reaching Russia. William Sturbitts, a CIA agent involved in the economic sabotage of Cuba, later told a Rockefeller Commission investigator that the United States simply arranged for a sugar firm to buy the cargo from the Russians. But according to Kaysen, the contaminated cargo was disposed of in a more dramatic way: CIA agents again stole into the warehouse and this time torched the sugar bags.

The CIA was capable of even more shocking insubordination in its secret war on Castro. The same month that the agency poisoned the S.S. *Streatham Hill's* cargo without the president's knowledge, the Kennedy brothers dispatched a New York attorney named James Donovan to Havana to negotiate the release of 1,113 Bay of Pigs prisoners still held captive by Castro. It was the beginning of a diplomatic initiative that would again raise the possibility of a peace agreement between the two countries, a discussion that had been dormant since the political firestorm in 1961 over the Goodwin-Guevara meeting.

Bobby Kennedy had selected Donovan as the brothers' emissary to Castro because of his storied success in negotiating the release of U-2 pilot Francis Gary Powers after he was shot down over the Soviet Union during a 1960 spying mission. Donovan had led a colorful life, serving as the OSS general counsel during World War II and later as OSS prosecutor at Nuremberg, where he presented shocking photographic evidence of Nazi leaders' crimes. Donovan (who was no relation to legendary OSS founder Colonel William "Wild Bill" Donovan, but liked to joke he was his illegitimate son) had the Irish gift of gab, and he loved to banter and philosophize while smoking and drinking. The lawyer hit it off with Castro, a nighthawk who loved nothing better than to swap stories and opinions until dawn. The voluble Cuban leader would summon Donovan late at night from the decaying villa outside Havana where he was staying, bringing the American lawyer to the presidential palace or a mistress's apartment, where they would talk until morning's early glow. After months of negotiations, which were severely complicated in October 1962 by the missile crisis, Donovan and Castro finally worked out an agreement under which the prisoners were freed in return for $53 million worth of U.S. food, medicine, and equipment.

As the last of the prisoners boarded a plane on a tropical December night in Havana, the ebullient Donovan turned to Castro—who stood in the airport surrounded by aides and machine gun–toting militiamen—and joked that, considering all the American consumer goods he had won for the Cuban people, he was thinking of capitalizing on his popularity on the island. "I think the next election I'm going to come back here and run against you," Donovan told the Cuban leader, loud enough for his retinue to hear, "and furthermore, I think I can take you." Castro slowly digested this, Donovan later recalled. "He is a tremendous ham actor, you see. Then he looked around, and in an equally loud voice he said, 'You know, Doctor, I think you may be right. So there will be no elections.'"

Encouraged by the successful Bay of Pigs settlement, Donovan continued making trips to Cuba to negotiate the release of others held in Castro's prisons, including twenty-two U.S. citizens, among whom were several CIA agents. The relationship between the two men grew warmer, as the energetic Castro entertained Donovan at his presidential palace in Havana and his beach resort at Varadero and took him on excursions around the island, including a trip to the Bay of Pigs, where the Cuban leader gave a detailed account of how his forces had defeated the invaders. Castro invited Donovan to three Cuban baseball championship games and to fishing expeditions on his boat. During an impromptu visit to a medical school, Castro led three hundred medical students in a round of cheers for his American friend: "Viva Donovan!"

Bobby Kennedy asked John Nolan, a young Washington lawyer who had worked on the 1960 campaign, to accompany Donovan on the Cuba trips. Kennedy, who found Donovan grating to deal with, trusted Nolan, who would later become his administrative aide, to be his eyes and ears on these high-stakes missions. "Bob wanted me to deal with Donovan because he wasn't very fond of him," Nolan told me. "They were just very different people. Bob was fast on the uptake, witty, sometimes brusque, very action-oriented. Jim was very philosophical—he liked to lean back in his chair with a Scotch and cigarette and analyze the situation. Bob was not comfortable with his style."

Nolan was relieved to find how accommodating Castro was, in striking contrast to the villainous caricature of the Cuban leader in the American media. "During the time that we were with him, Castro was never irrational, never drunk, never dirty. In his personal relationships with us and in connection with the negotiations, he was always reasonable, always easy to deal with. There were no tantrums, fits. He was a talker of very significant proportions. I mean, he would come over at midnight or one o'clock in the morning and stay all night talking. But he wasn't a conversational hog. He'd ask questions, listen for answers, give his own viewpoints. He was easy to talk to, a good conversationalist."

Donovan and Nolan soon realized that Castro was opening up a bigger diplomatic subject than simply the release of prisoners: he was interested in exploring a resolution of the U.S.–Cuba conflict. Returning from a Cuba trip in April 1963, Nolan phoned RFK from Miami to tell him about Castro's intriguing peace feelers. Bobby expressed strong curiosity about the man who loomed so large in Washington's fevered dramas. "What do you think?" he asked Nolan. "Can we do business with that fellow?" The president was also very interested in the message that Castro was communicating through Donovan and Nolan. JFK told his advisors that "we should start thinking along more flexible lines." He did not want to impose conditions on any future negotiations with Castro that might drive him away.

Jim Donovan was the kind of man who thought any problem could be worked out with enough time and talk. He grew increasingly excited by the idea that he could mediate the most bitter conflict in the hemisphere. "Before falling asleep at night, I think Jim would see himself as the man who brought peace to Cuba and the United States," said Nolan, looking back today at his colorful partner, who died in 1970 at the age of fifty-three. "He would refer to himself as a 'meta-diplomat.'"

But Donovan's old associates in the intelligence world did not share his enthusiasm about the embryonic Cuba peace venture. The CIA was well aware of Donovan's discussions with Castro. After every trip to Cuba, he and Nolan were debriefed by agents in a Miami safe house. "I couldn't tell what the CIA thought about Donovan's peace talks," said Nolan. "The agents who debriefed us were just apparatchiks—they just sat there taking notes as Jim rambled on." But years later Nolan later got a strong idea of how the agency felt about the Donovan peace initiative.

On their final trip to Cuba, in April 1963, Donovan and Nolan brought with them a gift for water-enthusiast Castro—a skin-diving suit. "We knew that Castro liked to skin dive, and I don't know whether it was Jim's idea or whether it was suggested by someone in the CIA, but a skin-diving suit was purchased at Abercrombie & Fitch in New York," recalled Nolan. "The guy who purchased it was a lawyer for the agency, and he bought and delivered it to Donovan. Then we flew to Havana and were driven to Castro's beach house at Varadero and the following day we drove with Castro to the Bay of Pigs. When we got there, we went out on Castro's boat and he put on the skin diving suit and jumped into the water, where he speared a half dozen fish. Then he climbed out of the water, took the suit off, and we had lunch. That was the last I saw of the suit or heard about it until thirteen years later. Flash forward to the Church Committee hearings. You can imagine how I felt when I heard the evening news that day."

What Nolan heard on TV that evening in 1975 stunned and infuriated him. Among the schemes devised by the CIA to kill Castro, the Senate investigation revealed, was a plan to give him a skin-diving suit dusted "with a fungus that would produce a disabling and chronic skin disease" and a scuba "breathing apparatus contaminated with tubercle bacilli." The CIA's scientific wizard of extermination, Dr. Sidney Gottlieb, told the committee that a diving suit had been purchased and contaminated, but he did not know if it was actually delivered.

It is uncertain whether the diving suit Donovan delivered to Castro was the one prepared in the CIA death labs. Perhaps it was and the toxins failed to do their job. CIA spokesman Sam Halpern claimed it was not—he said that the plan was dropped because Donovan had already given Castro a suit on his own initiative.

But Nolan was convinced that the CIA intended to use him and Donovan—two men who were pursuing peace with Castro on behalf of the Kennedy administration—to kill the Cuban leader instead. After he heard the shocking news story that evening in 1975, the former Kennedy aide picked up his phone to confront a CIA official he knew. "I said, 'Did you see that story about what was disclosed at the Church hearings today?' And he said, 'Don't worry, it never happened. That was just some crazy idea some guy at the agency had and nothing ever came of it.' And I said, 'What happened to the guy?'—thinking they should have taken him out and shot him! And he said, 'Nothing happened to him—he was just a squirrel in the basement laboratory.'

"This plot was clearly hatched without Jim Donovan's or my knowledge. Obviously he and I were not going to be part of anything that would be injurious to Castro."

But, it seems, the CIA was not above contemplating using two Kennedy peace envoys as unwitting assassins. If the diving suit that Donovan and Nolan carried to Cuba was indeed contaminated, the agency showed as much disregard for the safety of these two Kennedy envoys as it did for Castro's life.

Donovan and Nolan might have been treated with callous disregard by the CIA, but the man they reported to—Robert Kennedy—was treated as an enemy leader, a hostile strongman who had to be kept under constant surveillance. The agency felt the need to maintain this vigilant watch over the attorney general even after his brother's assassination, when his power was greatly diminished. In March 1964, JM/WAVE station chief Ted Shackley wrote a memo to his CIA boss, Desmond FitzGerald, boasting of his success at recruiting Miami journalists as CIA assets, including Al Burt, the Latin America foreign news editor for the *Miami Herald*. It was essential for the CIA to enlist journalists like Burt, Shackley wrote, to ensure that the huge

JM/WAVE station, the agency's second largest operation after its Langley headquarters, did not attract "the publicity spotlight" of the southern Florida media. Media assets like Burt also gave JM/WAVE "an outlet into the press which could be used for surfacing certain select propaganda items," as well as serving as useful informers for the agency, Shackley noted.

One of the more intriguing ways that Shackley thought Burt could be of use was by passing along inside information about Bobby Kennedy. Among Burt's contacts, Shackley reported, was a press colleague named Edmund Leahy, whom Burt "regards . . . as being particularly interesting." This was because Leahy, who was the *Miami Herald*'s Washington bureau chief, was the father of a young woman named Jane, who "is a secretary in the office of Attorney General Robert Kennedy."

There is no evidence that either Edmund Leahy or his daughter, Jane, spied on Robert Kennedy for the CIA. According to John Nolan, the senior Leahy was friendly with Bobby Kennedy, but not a confidant—"just one of the fifty or so Washington journalists whom Bob knew at the time." And Nolan, who supervised Jane Leahy when he worked as the attorney general's administrative aide, insisted she would never have betrayed Kennedy. "I can guarantee you that she was not a source for her father on anything that could be considered confidential," he told me. "She was fiercely independent, hard to get along with. I would think that if her father ever asked her for inside information, that would be unthinkable. I can just imagine her reaction if her dad asked her to find out what Bob was doing about the [CIA-supported Cuban exile group] Alpha 66. She'd bop him on the head."

Shackley could have dropped Ed Leahy's name in his memo simply to pump up his standing with his superiors at agency headquarters. But his boast about having a potential source inside the attorney general's office does reveal much about the CIA's attitude toward Robert Kennedy. RFK was the top lawman in the nation, he was the brother of the martyred president. Yet he was someone that the intelligence agency regarded as a proper target for surveillance.

THEY WATCHED HIM AS he swam in his pool and romped in his back-yard with his seven children. They watched him as he drove alone in his convertible to and from work. They were surprised to discover that he never had bodyguards with him. The CIA was not the only organization that was interested in keeping Robert Kennedy under surveillance. The attorney general was also being watched by agents of the International Brotherhood of Teamsters, the country's largest and most powerful union. Like the CIA, the

Teamsters, under the iron-fisted leadership of Jimmy Hoffa, had formed a sinister alliance with organized crime. Hoffa had been the principal target of Kennedy's anti-crime drive ever since the Senate Rackets Committee hearings in the late 1950s. Now Hoffa and his Mafia allies, enraged by the attorney general's increasingly effective crackdown on them, were targeting him.

One day in August 1962, Hoffa was talking in his office at the "Marble Palace," the Teamsters' grand Washington headquarters, with one of his lieutenants, Ed Partin, a big ex-boxer and ex-con who ran the union's Baton Rouge local. Hoffa, who kept his taut, compact body in shape by working out in the basement gym every day, was thrumming with angry energy. Suddenly he sprang from behind his immense desk and beckoned Partin to join him at his big picture window, with its panoramic view of the Capitol dome three blocks away. Hoffa asked his confidant if he knew anything about plastic explosives. "I've got to do something about that son of a bitch Bobby Kennedy. He's got to go," he growled.

Hoffa told Partin he was considering two different ways of eliminating Kennedy—by torching his Virginia house or by shooting him with a long-range rifle as he drove in his convertible. Hoffa seemed to favor the first idea, having someone toss plastic explosives into the Kennedy home after he had retired for the night. "You know, the SOB doesn't stay up too late," Hoffa observed. "I've got a rundown on him . . . his house sits here, like this, and it's not guarded." With his finger, Hoffa drew a diagram of the Kennedy estate's layout for Partin. If Kennedy somehow survived the incendiary explosion, he "and all his damn kids" would be consumed in the flames since "the place will burn after it blows up." The sniper scheme was apparently Hoffa's backup plan. The perfect time to shoot Kennedy, he said, would be while he was driving in his open car, preferably somewhere in the South, where the assassination could be blamed on white supremacists opposed to the Kennedys' civil rights policies.

In the end, Hoffa was too shrewd to carry out something as risky as this. "If Bob Kennedy's house had blown up back then, [or] if he had been shot," said Walter Sheridan, the chief of Kennedy's "Get Hoffa Squad" at the Justice Department, "there's one name we'd have put at the top of the list, in about five minutes . . . Jimmy Hoffa." But the Teamster boss was unwise in his choice of confidants. Ed Partin soon became a government informant, telling federal investigators not only about Hoffa's death threat against Kennedy but also about his jury tampering efforts in a Nashville trial.

Kennedy would use the jury tampering information to finally win a conviction of the cagey Teamster leader in 1964. But when Sheridan told the attorney general about Hoffa's death threat in September 1962, he shrugged it off and climbed into his closely watched convertible.

Sheridan took the threat more seriously. When Bobby was traveling, Ethel would sometimes ask the aide to come over to the house to make sure the family was safe. Ethel and the kids occasionally spotted big black cars packed with burly men in dark suits gliding slowly by on the road out front. The family would get terrifying letters and phone calls. "We know where your kids go to school and we know how they get there." "Do you know what hydrochloric acid can do to your eyes?" "Boom!"

Bobby despised the idea of living under a security blanket. The front door at Hickory Hill was usually left gapingly open. The only warning system was the cattle guard at the foot of the driveway, whose old iron pipes would send up a racket whenever a car rolled over them. That and the howls from shaggy Brumus and the rest of the family's bestiary whenever someone arrived. A sign on the front lawn announced: "Trespassers Will Be Eaten." But the worst damage Brumus had ever inflicted was to nip at the soft parts of unsuspecting guests as they sprinted by the lumbering Newfoundland in backyard football games. Out of concern for his family, Kennedy occasionally permitted Chief Marshal Jim McShane to set up a patrol on the road outside, Chain Bridge. But he took no precautions for himself.

Kennedy had been tangling with gangsters, labor racketeers, hit men, and extortionists for years. He and his investigators had been threatened and strong-armed by a rogue's army of dangerous characters. But Bobby had developed a reckless sense of bravado, a sense of Kennedy invincibility that his enemies found impressive even as they discussed his demise. You had to hand it to the son of a bitch, Hoffa told Partin—he had guts for strutting around unprotected. But no one was invulnerable, the Kennedy brothers' enemies realized. Not even the two most powerful men in the country.

Bobby Kennedy's anti-crime crusade drew lethal fury that September from two other ominous sources: Carlos Marcello, the powerful Mafia godfather whose dominion included New Orleans and Dallas, and his close ally Santo Trafficante, the Florida crime lord who had joined forces with the CIA in its original murder plot against Castro. Both Mafia bosses had close financial ties with Hoffa, who had turned the Teamsters' pension fund into a piggy bank for the mob. Meeting with prospective business partners at his swampland farm on the west banks of the Mississippi that month, Marcello—like Hoffa, the target of relentless Justice Department pursuit—flew into a rage at the mention of Bobby Kennedy's attempts to deport him. But it was Bobby's brother at whom the Mafia kingpin took aim: "You know what they say in Sicily: If you want to kill a dog, you don't cut off the tail, you cut off the head. The dog will keep biting you if you only cut off its tail." Marcello told his visitors that he had made up his mind that President Kennedy had to go, but his assassination had to be arranged in such a way that a "nut" would be set up to take the blame—"the way they do in Sicily."

The same month, during a meeting with a wealthy Cuban exile named Jose Aleman at Miami's Scott Bryant Hotel, Trafficante bitterly complained about the Kennedy campaign against his business associate Hoffa and assured Aleman that President Kennedy's days were numbered. "Kennedy's not going to make it to the election. He is going to be hit."

Trafficante had operated the wildly lucrative sin franchise in pre-Castro Havana on behalf of all the Mafia families until he was imprisoned by the new regime, which threatened to stand him in front of a firing squad before his crime associates bribed Cuban officials to release him. (According to some reports, Jack Ruby was one of the mob couriers who delivered the bribe money to Havana.) Trafficante's lawyer, Frank Ragano, estimated that his client lost over $20 million when the revolutionary government seized the Mafia's casinos, clubs, and hotels. Trafficante told his lawyer that the Kennedys' "soft" policies towards the Castro regime ensured that the Mafia would never reclaim its tropical assets.

Bobby's reputation as a scourge of the underworld defined his early political career. But years later, in summer 1975, Richard Helms and his former—but still steadfast—CIA lieutenant, Sam Halpern, tried to demolish this image. While testifying before the Church Committee, the two CIA veterans told an eye-popping story—one that seemed to turn the image of Bobby Kennedy as an anti-crime crusader on its head. According to Helms and Halpern, Robert Kennedy had ordered the CIA to help him establish contacts with the Mafia, to determine if the mob's old network in Cuba could be reactivated to work against, and even kill, Castro. In response to Kennedy's order, Helms and Halpern testified, they had enlisted Charles Ford, the same agent used to squelch Bobby's illusory plan to cut out the CIA on Cuba. Helms and Halpern claimed that Ford was asked to serve as Kennedy's intermediary with the underworld—under the appropriate-sounding alias "Rocky Siscalini."

Following the Senate hearings, Halpern continued to circulate this story to the media, including journalist Seymour Hersh, who featured it in his book, *The Dark Side of Camelot*. "I don't know how Bobby Kennedy squared that in his own mind," Halpern told Hersh. "On the one hand, he allegedly was going after the Mafia to destroy them; on the other, he was using them for information about Cuba. Maybe it was a deal he made with them. Who knows?"

Hersh is a Pulitzer Prize–winning journalist whose exposés of Vietnam war atrocities and U.S. military abuses at Iraq's Abu Ghraib prison, among other investigative feats, have won him wide respect. But he was led astray on *The Dark Side of Camelot* by his strong reliance on untrustworthy sources like Halpern—a man who worked so diligently during his life to undermine the Kennedys' image and shield the CIA's that it seemed this was his intelligence mission. In a frank interview with *New York* magazine in 2005, Hersh acknowledged that his journalism is deeply dependent on his sources in the national security world: "I'm not working with guys outside the system," he said. "You do understand that, don't you? I'm not outside the system in what I do. I'm really not." Never were the limitations of this journalistic practice more evident than in his book about the Kennedys. As one critic wrote in the *Los Angeles Times*, Hersh's book "turns out to be, alas, more about the deficiencies of investigative journalism than about the deficiencies of John F. Kennedy."

The explosive story about RFK and Charles Ford was difficult to check out because both men were dead. And Halpern could provide Hersh with no conclusive evidence. But it turns out that Ford left behind his own statement on the subject, a document that apparently escaped Hersh's attention because it was declassified a year after his book was published—and the document directly contradicts the Helms and Halpern story. On September 19, 1975, Ford wrote a confidential memorandum for the CIA's internal record, detailing what he had told Church Committee investigators when they came calling on him the day before. "The main, if not the only, point of concern to the [Senate] investigators is whether I was directed to sally forth and initiate contact with members of the underworld in the U.S. and who directed me to do so," wrote Ford. "Once again, I explained that my job was broader than this by a long shot, and that I was never directed to take the initiative in establishing contacts with the underworld." Ford added that the investigators were very interested in his meetings with Attorney General Kennedy, but he explained to them that these meetings focused on the efforts of a Cuban exile group to foment an anti-Castro uprising, not on Mafia assassination plots. (Ford was probably referring here to his September 1962 meetings with Kennedy to throw water on the quixotic plan to topple Castro without the CIA's involvement.)

The Ford memo strongly suggests that Helms and Halpern fabricated their story about Bobby Kennedy and the Mafia. It was not Bobby Kennedy who was crawling about in the underworld, but the Central Intelligence Agency. Officials like Helms and Halpern tried to deflect public outrage over their unseemly collusion by pinning the blame on the late attorney general. It was a particularly scurrilous smear job because Kennedy had literally risked his life to fight the Mafia. Kennedy's primary motivation in taking on organized crime was his fear that it was becoming intertwined with government and business and threatening to corrupt the social contract that held together American democracy. There was no more shocking example of this than the CIA-Mafia merger. Kennedy's anti-crime crusade threatened not just the lucrative fiefdoms of men like Hoffa, Marcello, and Trafficante, but shady power alliances like the one that targeted Castro. No federal official had ever poked so sharply at such a hornets' nest of dangerous adversaries. As Hoffa told Partin during his murderous musings that summer day, Bobby Kennedy "has so many enemies now they wouldn't know who had done it."

Even before he became attorney general, Kennedy knew how entwined American power was becoming with criminal forces. He learned, as the ruddy-cheeked, young chief counsel for the Senate Rackets Committee, when a Mafia man brought in for questioning defiantly told him, "You can't touch me. I've got immunity." When Bobby asked him, "Who gave you immunity?" the gangster replied, "The CIA. I'm working for them, but I can't talk about it. Top secret." When Kennedy checked out the gangster's story, he was sickened to find out it was true.

The CIA—and its predecessor, the OSS—had been using the Mafia to do their dirty work since World War II, when the government enlisted mob bosses Meyer Lansky and Lucky Luciano to help guard against enemy sabotage in the New York harbor and to supply intelligence from their contacts in Italy. Later, in postwar Italy, U.S. intelligence used Luciano and his notorious colleague Vito Genovese to help eliminate the growing Communist threat there.

Kennedy learned too about the merger of the underworld and overworld when distinguished senators and governors came before his committee to argue on behalf of organized crime despots, and when executives from Fortune 500 companies sheepishly testified about the deals they cut with burly gangsters to assure labor peace.

And Robert Kennedy learned as he was digging into the dirty history of racketeering in America, when he came across the name of his very own father. It was the buccaneering enterprise of Joseph P. Kennedy that had made possible his political career and that of his brother. His father's aggressive climb to wealth and power illustrated with painful clarity for the younger

Kennedy how ambitious families sprouting towards the sun often begin their journeys in the muck.

BOBBY KENNEDY CAME FACE to face with a world that few young men of his class and privilege had to confront when he became chief counsel of the Senate Select Committee on Improper Activities in the Labor or Management Field. It was fall 1956 and he was just twenty-nine years old. His work on the Senate panel, better known as the Rackets Committee or the McClellan Committee after the Arkansas Democrat who chaired it, took Bobby down a hole into an underworld of cold-blooded killers, union thugs, crooked politicians, brothel queens, and pinstriped executives with tawdry secrets. It also introduced him to brave labor reformers, incorruptible cops and judges, and heroic newspaper reporters. With his romantic and religious frame of mind, Kennedy saw this colorful tableaux of human greed and turmoil as not just a struggle over who would control the nation's economy, but a battle for the country's very soul. He had missed World War II, where his older brothers had proved their courage, but this would become Bobby's war.

Armed with a staff of thirty-five investigators, forty-five accountants, twenty stenographers, and assorted clerks—more than a hundred people in all—Kennedy ran the biggest juggernaut of federal scrutiny on Capitol Hill. It was a restless operation. The young counsel and his investigators did not remain hunkered down in their warren of offices below the street floor of the old Senate Office Building. They roamed the country in search of malefactors, as well as the honest witnesses and incriminating evidence they needed to put them away.

On a tip from a prisoner at Joliet, Bobby found himself one day digging in an Illinois farm field for the body of a newspaperwoman who the convict said had been killed by local mobsters. With Kennedy was one of his committee investigators, Jim McShane, the pug-faced former New York cop who would be called upon by Kennedy in many dire circumstances in the years to come. The two men shoveled away without finding anything, urged on by the con, who insisted he was telling the truth: "May I have syphilis of the eyes, and may my mother be a whore, if she isn't buried here," he declared. Kennedy later wryly observed that he knew little "about the man's mother or his eyes, but Jim McShane and I both knew, after hours of digging, that the woman's body was not there." When the angry farmer whose fields were being excavated by the Senate investigators suddenly appeared with his three corn-fed sons, that settled it—Kennedy and McShane beat a hasty retreat.

On other occasions, McShane and his fellow investigators had guns drawn on them. Kennedy was offered bribes. A man mistaken for a Kennedy spy by Teamster goons in Detroit was hung out a tenth floor window of the union building by his heels. But the reform machine chugged forward, unearthing hundreds of eye-opening tales of corruption, violence, and abuse of power. Stories about men who were killed or savagely beaten or driven to suicide after standing up to tyrants like Hoffa. Men who had acid thrown in their faces, or cucumbers shoved all the way into their intestines. Walter Sheridan—the quiet, friendly investigator whose appearance Bobby described as "almost angelic"—would impress his boss by solving the mystery of an Indianapolis cab company owner who had vanished. There was nothing left of him to be found. Nothing but the records of the man's final phone calls, which his wife handed over to the sweet-faced Sheridan when he knocked on her door. The calls were to Jimmy Hoffa and his henchmen.

Kennedy brought the characters at the heart of these lurid stories parading into the grand, dignified setting of the old Senate building's Caucus Room, so America could see the rot and brutality that often lay beneath the jeweled thrones of power. It was the same ornate Beaux Arts room where other historic investigations had unfolded, including the probes into the Titanic disaster and the Teapot Dome scandal. Crystal chandeliers hung from the room's high, richly detailed ceilings; carved eagles adorned its wooden benches. It was here, Kennedy noted, "where the star of Senator Joseph McCarthy rose and fell." The young Senate counsel had once been drawn to the McCarthy crusade, but now he had discovered an "enemy within" that he believed was more threatening to the American way of life and more deserving of his fury than communism.

Sitting next to committee chairman John McClellan—a balding man three decades his senior with a hardscrabble Arkansas face and the deep, austere tones of a Southern minister—Bobby Kennedy seemed an unlikely crime-buster. He had the fresh-faced good looks and high-pitched voice of a Boston schoolboy. When he began questioning the hard-looking men who sat before him, men who had torn and scratched for their illegal slice of the American Dream, they found it hard to take him seriously. Hoffa winked at him. Sam Giancana giggled. But they soon realized they were in the crosshairs of a ferociously intelligent and doggedly prepared man who was determined to prove that he was tougher than they.

Kennedy brought his confrontations with these men vividly to life in his 1960 book, *The Enemy Within*. He accused Hoffa of "personalizing" their battle in his book. But Kennedy himself brought a razor-sharp eye for detail to his descriptions of Hoffa and the other crime bosses that was nothing but personal. Hoffa and his lieutenants were "often bilious and fat, or lean and cold and hard," he wrote. "They have the smooth faces and cruel eyes of gangsters; they wear the same rich clothes, the diamond ring, the jeweled watch, the strong, sickly-sweet-smelling perfume." Kennedy returned to the subject of these men's smell. It was feminine to him. It seemed to underscore how their brutality was the work of strutting bullies, not real men. "I was riding up in the elevator on my way to the hearing room when I was almost overcome by a heavy, sickly-sweet smell," Kennedy wrote, describing a brush with a Hoffa hood named Joey Glimco. "I tried to remember what madam was testifying that day, until I got out and, walking down the hall with Glimco to the caucus room, realized that he was the source of the oppressive odor."

Kennedy seemed to get a charge from sparring with these men. One day the notorious New York labor enforcer Joey Gallo, who controlled the city's jukebox business, strolled into his office "dressed like a Hollywood Grade B gangster." His shirt, pants, and coat were all black. He had long, pomaded hair curling down the back of his neck. He leaned over and felt Kennedy's carpet: "It would be nice for a crap game."

Kennedy was not amused. His committee had heard testimony from a jukebox distributor who had dared to resist Gallo's crooked union. Gallo's thugs jumped him after a meeting, cracking his skull open with steel bars. The man had shuffled into the Senate hearing room, a "thin, wan, pathetic figure," still barely able to speak.

As Gallo reached out to shake hands with Kennedy that day, the young investigator said, "So you're Joey Gallo, the Jukebox King. You don't look so tough. I'd like to fight you myself." The gangster demurred. "I don't fight," he told Kennedy.

Bobby's older brother had sought to define himself with a lofty book about courage in politics. But *The Enemy Within* was a much grittier revelation of its author's true character than JFK's *Profiles in Courage* was of his. While John Kennedy chronicled the bravery of men he admired from a historical distance, Bobby wrote about men with whom he had personally clashed or whose life-and-death heroics he had passionately championed. He had climbed down into the underworld he was describing. He was part of the story.

The rackets investigation defined Bobby the way World War II had defined Jack. And it made the two men brothers in arms. When Bobby talked his brother into joining him on the McClellan Committee, to make sure it was politically balanced enough to prevent Republican senators from declaring open season on organized labor, it afforded JFK one of his few displays of genuine courage during his Senate career. The experience would also help shape the Kennedy presidency. The young, dedicated investigators and reporters Bobby gathered around him on the committee—O'Donnell, Salinger, Sheridan, Seigenthaler, Guthman—would become the heart of his brother's administration. It was fitting that JFK would announce his campaign for president in the Senate Caucus Room, where he and his brother had done battle with what Bobby bluntly called a "conspiracy of evil."

But Joseph Kennedy worried that his two sons had made a horrible error. In late December 1956, when Bobby went to Hyannis Port to celebrate Christmas with his family, his father confronted him about the labor rackets hearings, which had just begun. Joe Kennedy didn't think the family should get mixed up in something like this. Bobby's sister Jean later reported that the two men clashed with a kind of fury she had never seen erupt between them. Their father feared that Bobby's investigative work would hurt Jack's presidential chances by turning the labor movement against the Kennedys, Jean recalled. But there was clearly something more behind this unprecedented father-son tempest. Joe Kennedy was deeply alarmed by the path that his son was taking. What demons would Bobby stir up as he went crashing about the underworld with his avenging angels? "The old man saw this as dangerous," recalled longtime Kennedy family crony Lem Billings. "He thought Bobby was naïve."

Joe Kennedy loved his sons more than anything else in life. His dominating presence in his children's lives is part of American lore. But less appreciated is the Kennedy patriarch's ever-watchful love. This paternal attentiveness shines through in the flurry of correspondence he dashed off to his offspring, particularly his sons, as he traveled the globe in his empire-building days. He instructed them on everything from manners and grooming to global affairs; he comforted them when they were homesick and dispirited at boarding school; he inspired them with grand visions of their future if they worked hard enough. Joe Kennedy was not just a tower of protective male strength in his children's lives, he was a nagging, nurturing mother hen, who constantly instilled in them a sense of family pride and self-worth.

"After long experience in sizing up people, I definitely know you have the goods and you can go a long way," Joe pep-talked a seventeen-year-old Jack. But he needed to apply himself. Joe worried that his son was gliding a little too nonchalantly through his adolescence. Bobby, at sixteen, needed a different kind of love from his father. He lacked Jack's easy self-confidence, he brooded about things. "I wouldn't be too discouraged about the football team," his father bucked him up. "After all, the value of playing football isn't primarily playing on the first team—it's the opportunity to meet a lot of nice boys and to get the practice of playing teamwork."

As the Kennedy brothers prepared to challenge the gods of the under-world—who, unmolested by the FBI, were enjoying a golden reign in post-war America—their father feared for his sons' safety, and for good reason. Joe Kennedy knew these sorts of men, he had done business with them, they had helped him make a fortune in liquor distribution, both during and after the bootlegging days. He knew what they were capable of.

Kennedy was precisely the type of predatory capitalist whom his son would summon before the Rackets Committee, a shrewd, law-skirting entre-preneur who took his business opportunities and his partners where he found them. He was a master at exploiting the wildly profitable frontiers of Ameri-can enterprise, from his days as a Wall Street speculator to movie baron to whiskey bootlegger. Running liquor during Prohibition brought the kind of windfall profits the drug trade does today. But it also meant doing business with the Mafia if you valued your life, and Kennedy went right to the top to ensure the security of his business. He forged a partnership with Frank Costello, the dapper, politically wired "prime minister of the underworld" who began each day after leaving his fashionable Central Park West pent-house by getting groomed at the Waldorf-Astoria Hotel barbershop. By the late 1940s, as Jack began the political career his father had urged upon him, Kennedy had cashed out of the liquor business, selling his distribution com-pany, Somerset Importers, to New Jersey mobster Longy Zwillman. But the stain on the Kennedy name would remain an indelible part of the family's folklore.

"Yes, he was amoral, sure he was," observed *New York Times* columnist Arthur Krock, whom Kennedy treated as a family retainer. "I think only a Ro-man Catholic could possibly describe how you could be amoral and still be religious. That is, how you can carry an insurance policy with the deity and at the same time do all these other things. . . . I never had any idealism from the time I was a young reporter about anybody who touched the edges of politics or big business. So I was not shocked in the least. I expected, and still do, that politicians and big businessmen don't have any morals." But Bobby Kennedy held public men to different standards.

Joe Kennedy flew down to Washington some days to watch his two sons confront the country's most infamous gangsters and racketeers in the ornate Senate hearing room. One can only imagine the feelings of pride and fear that must have collided within him as he watched Jack and Bobby clash with the sort of men he knew from his secret business world. When Bobby knew his father was going to be there, committee staff members observed, he acted in a nervous sort of way that he never seemed to when facing off against the hoodlums. As his father walked into the Senate Caucus Room, in his expensive New York–tailored suits and his banker's homburg hat, "Bob was a little keyed up, a little tense," recalled Ruth Watt, the McClellan Committee's chief clerk. "There was a strong paternal influence over all the Kennedys. [Joe Kennedy] really was a strong, strong person. . . . When their father came to town, everybody hopped! I remember one time he came during the hearings and he was going back to Boston. They had Eastern Airlines, Jack Kennedy's office, the SEC, and somebody else working on one reservation for him to get back to Boston!"

Bobby had enormous respect for his powerful father. But by plunging ahead with the rackets investigation, over his father's impassioned objections, he had risked the sort of dramatic Oedipal split that both men had so far managed to avoid. Bobby was the son most like him, Joe Kennedy always liked to say—"he hates like me." But Jackie Kennedy, who would draw so close to her husband's younger brother, thought Bobby was "the least like his father." Rose Kennedy saw the devout, sensitive side to her son. Never as emotionally effusive as her husband with their children, she was still calling Bobby her "own little pet" even when he was sixteen. In his role as the scourge of organized crime, Bobby had found a way to combine his father's raging will with his mother's religious purity. But Joe Kennedy knew how dangerous an enterprise this was.

Ruth Watt was an experienced Capitol Hill aide whose level-headed administrative skills helped ensure that the rackets hearings ran smoothly. But when some of the more menacing characters came before the committee, she felt deeply unnerved. "The scariest one," she thought, was New York godfather Vito Genovese, who had murdered his way to the top of the Mafia, forcing Joe Kennedy's old bootlegging partner Frank Costello into early retirement along the way. "I would stand in back of where the senators were when he was testifying, and he had the coldest eyes. He would look right through you and just make chills. He was about the coldest individual I think I've ever seen."

With Bobby leading the witness interrogations, the hearings were fueled by a barely contained fury. He wanted America to shudder with the same outrage he felt when these men, who preferred the dark shadows of power, were summoned into the glare of the TV lights that filled the Caucus Room. The hearings, which dragged on for two and a half years and summoned more than 1,500 witnesses, provided the younger Kennedy with a national stage on which to wage his holy war for America's soul. On days when celebrated villains were scheduled to appear before the committee, Bobby made sure that his older brother was there. He was already staging JFK's presidential bid, and he knew these theatrical duels with the leading men of crime would add to his brother's national luster. Hoffa would vow that if Bobby thought he was going to use him to get his brother elected president, it would "be over my dead body." But that's precisely what the younger Kennedy had in mind. "Two tousle-haired brothers from Boston are catching attention in Washington just now as young men who may have big careers ahead," *U.S. News & World Report* informed its readers as the rackets hearings began making headlines.

On the days that handsome young Senator Kennedy strode into the Caucus Room, a bolt of media excitement crackled through the air. "I remember one day that [Jack] came into a hearing, it must have been when they knew he was going to run for the presidency because the press was flocking around him," recalled Watt. "He hadn't had any lunch and [his secretary] Evelyn Lincoln came in with a tray of lunch for him, and he took it and went into the telephone booth to try to eat it. The press was like this around him, so he never ate his lunch. I remember it very well, because he was in that little telephone booth with his lunch. No matter what he did it was news. When the Kennedys were around, you felt it in the air."

The hearings made Bobby into a media sensation too. An effusive Jack Paar introduced him to his national *Tonight Show* audience on July 23, 1959 as "the bravest, finest young man I know." Bobby, still unused to the media glare, came across as a shy, doe-eyed, slope-shouldered boy. At the end of the interview, the emotionally candid Paar blurted out that his guest was "like a baby." But Bobby turned into a hard-jawed prosecutor that night when he began cataloging the many sins of Jimmy Hoffa and his cronies. "They feel they're above the law," Kennedy told Paar's audience. "They feel they can fix judges and juries. Mr. Hoffa has said every man has his price. This country can't survive if you have somebody like him operating. He won't win in the end."

The McClellan Committee dragged a variety of notorious figures into the national spotlight. Among them were men who would loom large in the lives of the Kennedys, such as mobsters Carlos Marcello, Santo Trafficante, and Sam Giancana—each of whom would later join the secret war on Castro that would bring together the Mafia, the CIA, and Cuban exiles. (Even the name of a petty Chicago hood named Jack Ruby would surface during the long hearings, in connection with the Mafia's Cuba intrigue.) But no witness filled the Senate hearing room with as much explosive tension as Jimmy Hoffa. The confrontations between the Teamster boss and the Kennedy brothers were epic. Even his more cool-headed older brother seemed to absorb Bobby's heat when he sparred with Hoffa.

"I'd like to say something, Senator," Hoffa burst out on one occasion, his voice full of contempt and provocation. Since the Kennedys, in their hatred for him, were trying to single him out from the rest of the labor movement for special federal punishment, why not "spell it out in the law, exempting everyone but Hoffa, okay?" JFK cut him off, his normally smooth sense of Senate formality suddenly gone. "We're exempting everyone but hoodlums and racketeers and crooks," he shot back, in a rush of anger and harsh Boston vowels.

But nothing matched the hatred and fury of the matches between Hoffa and Bobby Kennedy. To Kennedy, the labor boss represented the chilling nexus between the America that most people knew, the country of laws and ideals, and the one where the codes of the jungle prevailed. By the time Hoffa appeared before the Rackets Committee, he was on his way to amassing the kind of power that would make newspaper publishers, business tycoons, senators, governors—even presidential hopefuls—pay him respect. He dreamed of the day when he would take over one of the political parties—it didn't matter to him whether it was the Republican or Democratic. As Robert Kennedy knew, this impressive national clout was built on blood and corruption.

In the Senate Caucus Room, the two men went at each other for hours, day after day. Committee member Barry Goldwater was astonished by the "animal anger" between them. "We were like flint and steel," Hoffa said. "Every time we came to grips the sparks flew."

At the witness table, Hoffa's beady eyes flashed with a sharp intelligence. Despite ceaseless battering from Bobby and the committee members, the grimly determined labor boss never gave ground, always slipping away when it seemed he was backed into a corner. Occasionally Hoffa would weary of the bobbing and weaving and simply smack Kennedy with an epithet. "You're sick. That's what's the matter with you—you are sick," he spat at Kennedy one afternoon after a testy exchange with the Senate counsel.

But the most intense confrontations between Kennedy and Hoffa were silent. Kennedy later vividly described the eerie malevolence that seeped out of Hoffa as the two men engaged in combat: "In the most remarkable of all my exchanges with Jimmy Hoffa, not a word was said. I called it the 'look.' It was to occur fairly often, but the first time I observed it was on the last day of the 1957 hearings. During the afternoon, I noticed that he was glaring at me across the counsel table with a deep, strange, penetrating expression of intense hatred. I suppose it must have dawned on him about that time that he was going to be the subject of a continuing probe—that we were not playing games. It was the look of a man obsessed by his enmity, and it came particularly from his eyes. There were times when his face seemed completely transfixed with this stare of absolute evilness. It might last for five minutes—as if he thought that by staring long enough and hard enough he could destroy me. Sometimes he seemed to be concentrating so hard that I had to smile, and occasionally I would speak of it to an assistant counsel sitting behind me. It must have been obvious to him that we were discussing it, but his expression would not change by a flicker.

"During the 1958 hearings, from time to time, he directed the same shriveling look at my brother. And now and then, after a protracted, particularly evil glower, he did a most peculiar thing: he would wink at me. I can't explain it. Maybe a psychiatrist would recognize the symptoms."

They were a study in opposites. With his sawed-off, tightly coiled body, his blunt-cut, shiny Brylcreemed hair, and his cheap gabardine suits and floodwater pants, Hoffa looked every bit the working stiff he once had been. Born in a backwater Indiana town—the son of a coal driller who died when Jimmy was seven, leaving the family penniless—Hoffa had to scrap his way to the top. He led his first strike at the age of seventeen, a successful wildcat action on the loading docks of Detroit. To match the brute power of the trucking and warehouse companies he was fighting, Hoffa had to use his fists, turning to gangsters for more muscle when the labor battles grew uglier. As he shouldered his way up the Teamster ranks, he used the same blunt force to enforce discipline in his organization. The drivers and warehousemen for whom Hoffa brought home the bacon saw him as their hero, one of their own. But Bobby Kennedy saw him as a traitor to the labor movement, a man who sold out his hardworking membership by turning over their pension funds to hoodlums, cutting shady deals with employers, and crushing union dissent with savage violence.

Hoffa, in turn, looked at the Kennedy brothers as "spoiled rich kids" who never had to work a real day in their lives. With their boyish haircuts and well-cut suits, and their chosen aura, they represented everything that Hoffa had been denied. He drew from this deep pool of class resentment when he publicly attacked the brothers, dismissing their crusade to clean up the union movement as a ploy to emasculate organized labor. "All this hocus-pocus about racketeers is a smoke screen to carry you back to the days when they could drop you in the scrap heap," he told Teamster members, adding that when big business fat cats used thugs as strikebreakers, no one raised a fuss, but "now we've got a few and everybody's screaming."

But in some ways, Hoffa and Kennedy were cut from the same cloth. Both men were tireless warriors who were less interested in lavish pleasures than they were in their higher causes—extending the power of the Teamsters in one case, and the power of his family in the other. "A Saturday night ice cream was Jimmy's puritan style for a night on the town," recalled Hoffa's lawyer Frank Ragano. "He always appeared to be out of place in swanky restaurants and supper clubs, as if he knew that his inelegant clothes, white socks, and rough, ungrammatical speech disqualified him from acceptance in such places." Bobby was equally Spartan in many ways. "He has little of the president's peripheral interest in social intercourse and intellectual fashion," a *Life* magazine cover story noted about Bobby in January 1962. "He does not enjoy nightclubs, the theater or big parties and shuns them when he can. He will occasionally sip at a drink or puff at a cigar, but for real debauchery he turns to chocolate ice cream with chocolate syrup and extra-ice-cold milk."

With the brutal clarity that only a diehard enemy can have, Hoffa saw another connection that bound him to Bobby Kennedy. He reminded Bobby of his father. "I'm no damn angel," Hoffa growled. "I don't apologize. You take any industry and look at the problems they ran into while they were building up—how they did it, who they associated with, how they cut corners. The best example is Kennedy's old man." This is how the real world worked, Hoffa knew—powerful men on their way up, whether they were self-made tycoons like Joe Kennedy or labor moguls like himself, had to "cut corners." Snot-nosed "Booby," as he liked to call him, just didn't get it.

Or maybe he did. While clawing his way through the tunnels of American corruption, Bobby Kennedy came upon proof of his father's involvement with the underworld, according to Rackets Committee member Barry Goldwater. "It just killed him," Goldwater said.

Years later, Robert Lowell asked Bobby what character in Shakespeare he would like to be, and he picked Henry the Fifth. Of course. Young Prince Hal, the monarch in waiting who rebels against the heavy family expectations hanging over him—until he finally proves his worth on the battlefield. Bobby used Henry's famous speech before the Battle of Agincourt to inspire his own troops at the Justice Department. But it was Henry's father he wanted to talk about that day. He read to Lowell the death speech of Henry the Fourth, in which the dying king ruefully considers the lot of powerful patriarchs—those "foolish over-careful fathers [who] have broke their sleeps with thoughts, their brains with care, their bones with industry." And for what? Only to bequeath their children a poisoned inheritance, "the canker'd heaps of strange-achieved gold."

"Henry the Fourth. That's my father," Bobby told Lowell.

It was a legacy that Robert Kennedy seemed determined to make pure. If his father had sold his soul in pursuit of fortune and power, he would redeem the family name through his own righteous works. Even if that meant betraying his father's partners in crime.

ON AUGUST 16, 1962, FBI director Hoover sent Attorney General Kennedy one of the disturbing memos about his family that he delighted in waving in his face from time to time. They usually had to do with Jack's reckless philandering. Like a loathsome troll tucked furtively under the castle drawbridge, Hoover had kept careful watch on the amorous comings and goings of the handsome Kennedy prince over the years. But this "personal memo" concerned the attorney general's father and his organized crime ties. Joe Kennedy had courted the top G-man over the years, telling him with buttery flattery in 1958 that the FBI was "the greatest organization in the Government and you have performed the greatest public service of any man that I know." Kennedy had prevailed upon his sons to keep the aging director in his post, figuring it was better to have Hoover and his secret files inside the administration tent than outside. This was how the FBI chief repaid the favor, now that the founding father was stricken and confined to a wheelchair.

"Before the last presidential election," the memo read, "Joseph P. Kennedy (the father of President John Kennedy) had been visited by many gangsters with gambling interests and a deal was made which resulted in Peter Lawford, Frank Sinatra, Dean Martin and others obtaining a lucrative gambling establishment, the Cal-Neva Hotel, at Lake Tahoe. These gangsters reportedly met with Joseph Kennedy at the Cal-Neva, where Kennedy was staying at the time."

Hoover could have told the attorney general more. He knew that in Joe Kennedy's drive to ensure his son's presidential victory, old Joe had conferred with some of the top Mafia leaders in the country, including some of those Bobby dragged before the Rackets Committee. One of these meetings took place at Felix Young's restaurant in New York during the heat of the 1960 campaign. "I took the reservation, and it was as though every gangster chief in the United States was there," recalled Edna Daultyon, who worked at the time as hostess at the restaurant. "I don't remember all the names now, but there was John Rosselli, Carlos Marcello from New Orleans, the two brothers from Dallas, the top men from Buffalo, California and Colorado. They were all the top people, not soldiers. I was amazed Joe Kennedy would take the risk."

Through Frank Sinatra and other intermediaries, Kennedy also arranged deals with mobsters to help deliver the vote in the crucial West Virginia primary, where "walking-around money" traditionally played a key part in the outcome, and to pull off a landslide in Chicago (where the mob wards later skewed 80–20 for Kennedy) to ensure Illinois went Democratic in November. According to one witness, Kennedy went so far as to personally meet with Chicago godfather Sam Giancana in the chambers of an accommodating Cook County judge. This was the same snickering hoodlum with whom Bobby had clashed just months earlier in a headline-making exchange at the rackets hearings when he questioned the gangster's manhood: "I thought only little girls giggled, Mr. Giancana."

Much has been written about the Kennedy effort to steal the 1960 vote. But what Joe Kennedy knew from his own hard-won experience in the trenches of politics and business is that American democracy is not the crystal vessel our textbooks hold aloft. It's a roughly contested thing. Elections are often brokered, votes bought or stolen or uncounted. And in 1960, as Kennedy knew, the outcome of the presidential race would likely depend to a significant extent on corrupt machines and underworld bosses. JFK's rivals had their own hoodlum backers—despite his father's entreaties, Marcello supported Lyndon Johnson at the Democratic convention and Nixon in the general election, contributing $500,000 to the Republican candidate. And Hoffa predictably threw the full weight of the Teamsters against Kennedy, holding union meetings across the country to mobilize the vote for Nixon, and matching Marcello's contribution with another half million dollars raised from other crime lords. In return for Hoffa's support, which was credited with delivering Ohio into the GOP column, the vice president intervened with Eisenhower Attorney General William Rogers to sit on an indictment of the Teamster leader.

And when it came to stealing votes, Kennedy was certainly not the lone culprit in the 1960 presidential race. As political reporter Theodore H. White found out when he investigated the Illinois vote outcome, there was a good reason that Nixon did not challenge that state's final count: "The Republicans stole as many votes as the Democrats." Chicago Mayor Richard Daley knew how the game was played—his Democratic machine had to steal at least as many votes in elections as the Republicans did in downstate Illinois, where the GOP prevailed. Daley quickly silenced Republican protests over the 1960 Chicago vote by challenging the GOP to back a statewide recount. "He challenged them—he said he'd pay for half the recount statewide, and they said, 'No, thank you,'" Daley's son, William, recently recalled with a wry laugh. "Once you got out of Cook County, it was all pretty much rural Republican in those days. And they used paper ballots instead of the old machines we used in the city, so there was even more opportunity for fraud."

Of course, politics were not pure in 2000 either, when Bill Daley ran Al Gore's presidential campaign. There were many Democrats that year who wished Daley and his candidate had demonstrated the brawling political instincts of his father and the Kennedy family during the sordid Florida recount spectacle, when the bare-knuckled Bush machine humiliated the Gore team, as it clung proudly to its Marquis of Queensbury rules of political pugilism.

By contrast, the Kennedy family knew how to fight to win. And they were under no illusions about the back-alley cunning of Richard Nixon. The Kennedys were prepared to do whatever it took to outmaneuver their Republican opponent.

The difference between John Kennedy and his rivals is that after winning the 1960 election, a down and dirty contest during which both campaigns resorted to unsavory measures, he refused to pay off the political debts that he had incurred.

There is no evidence that Bobby Kennedy participated with his father in the underworld wheeling and dealing that took place during the campaign. Nor did JFK take the lead on these negotiations. The family founder seemed to be operating on his own typically brash initiative when he contacted his old associates in the criminal world to help deliver the election for his son. "If Jack had known about some of the telephone calls his father made on his behalf to Tammany Hall–type bosses during the 1960 campaign, Jack's hair would have turned white," Kenny O'Donnell later said. Still, Bobby and Jack were not naïve about their father; they were both too shrewd to be completely unaware of the levers he was pulling on behalf of the campaign. When a friend warned JFK, "You know, the old man is hurting you," he replied, "My father is working for his son. Do you want me to tell my father to stop working for his son?"

What is certain is that no matter what special favors their father arranged in the underworld, once he and his brother took office, Robert Kennedy showed no reluctance in going after the Mafia bosses who had inserted themselves into American politics. On the contrary, the young attorney general unleashed a furious campaign against the crime lords, the likes of which they had never experienced. The message was brutally clear: You might give money to the Kennedys, but you can't buy the Kennedys.

Hoffa could see it coming, right after the election. He knew that he "was in the soup worse than ever. Nobody had to tell me that [Bobby] was really going to go after my scalp now. I knew that my worst days were still in front of me."

When he took over the Justice Department, Kennedy breathed new life into the organized crime unit and created a special task force under Sheridan to hunt Hoffa. He lit a fire under Hoover, who had famously denied the existence of the Mafia, prompting gangsters to laugh off the FBI as "Famous But Incompetent." When Hoover proved an obstacle to Kennedy's anti-crime drive, he simply went around the bureau, using agents from the Treasury Department, Internal Revenue Service, and Narcotics Bureau as his shock troops. He offered incentive awards to his team of young prosecutors to come up with ingenious new ways to put mobsters and crooked politicians behind bars. The number of indicted gangsters shot up from 121 in 1961 to 615 in 1963—among them were such notorious figures as Carlos Marcello, Mickey Cohen, Teamster hoods Anthony Provenzano and Joey Glimco, as well as Hoffa himself. Kennedy's crime-busters were also in relentless pursuit of Santo Trafficante and Sam Giancana. It was getting so hot for the criminal underworld that FBI wiretaps picked up mobsters' conversations in which they talked of abandoning their line of work until the Kennedys were out of office.

The hard-charging attorney general seemed to pursue gangsters who were tied to the Kennedy family name with a special wrath. He ordered FBI agents to dog Sam Giancana's every step—they trailed him into restaurants, shined their lights into his Oak Park home, and interfered with his golf game. Even when the mobster exploded at his FBI tormentors one day at O'Hare Airport, threatening that "one of these days we are going to tell all" about the Kennedys, the attorney general did not let up. Kennedy's top aides flirted with authoritarian measures to bring down the Chicago godfather.

"My boss, [criminal division chief] Jack Miller, called me in one day," recalled former Justice Department prosecutor Ronald Goldfarb. "I was the expert on the fairly refined area of law called contempt. They said to me: What do you think of this idea? The grand jury calls in Giancana and we offer him total immunity on everything he's ever done in his whole life, as long as he agrees to talk about every crime the Mafia has ever committed. Of course he can't possibly do that, so he's got to go to jail, and the federal rule is you can only throw someone in jail for contempt for the life of a grand jury, which is eighteen months. But they had a plan: The day Giancana gets out of jail, they say, we call him back to another grand jury and ask him the same question. This goes on and on. Life imprisonment for Sam Giancana! So I think, oh my God, they're really thinking of doing this—they're going to take the Mafia leaders one by one and put them in jail indefinitely. And so they ask me, Can we do this? And I remember saying to them, 'Yes, technically you could do that. But it would be outrageous, we'd be viewed as fascistic, overbearing prosecutors, it would take the law way too far. I strongly recommend against it.'

"So the notion that we were pulling our punches with people like Giancana because we knew that he had helped Kennedy's campaign, or was hooked up with Sinatra, or was helping the CIA kill Castro—that's just absurd."

Goldfarb, a young Yale Law graduate, had defied his New York liberal friends—who were leery of RFK's aggressive law and order image—to join Bobby's crusade. He quickly fell under the attorney general's spell, embracing his conviction that they were chasing not simply everyday criminals but "massively rich and powerful" corrupters of the American system—"perfect villains," in Goldfarb's description. "I felt so admiring of Kennedy. I thought, Wow, this guy is dead straight, he is totally supportive of us in every way. Every time I won a case, he would invite me to a restaurant, he was a nice guy. Incredible integrity. So nobody is going to tell me that he made us compromise or capitulate or anything like that, because I was there. It didn't happen."

But in later years, Goldfarb, author of a 1995 book that argued JFK was assassinated by the Mafia, would shake his head at Bobby Kennedy's wild courage. "He was burning the candle at both ends, pressing the mob like he did even after his family had used them for favors," the former Justice Department prosecutor told me. "How in God's name he thought he was ever going to get away with this, I don't know. But they were the Kennedys—they came from a family where the father had done all of that, and they still reached the absolute top. I couldn't have slept at night knowing what Bobby did! But these people were different."

It was not just his father's unsavory associates who complicated Bobby Kennedy's Justice Department reign, it was his brother's. On the afternoon of March 22, 1962 the ever-scheming Hoover arrived at the White House, where he was greeted by the president, who sat down with him for lunch in the Executive Mansion dining room. Hoover told Kennedy that he had evidence of the president's madly indiscreet affair with a dark and curvy young beauty named Judy Campbell, who had been introduced to JFK by Frank Sinatra. Hoover also knew that Kennedy was sharing his mistress with none other than Sam Giancana. (Recent evidence suggests that Campbell might have been steered Kennedy's way by the Mafia.) The president's ever-watchful brother also knew everything. One of his investigators had come across the affair the month before while tracking a paper trail of racketeers' phone calls and immediately told his boss, who informed his brother. Sending Hoover over to the White House might have been Bobby's way of drilling into his sexually daring brother the urgency of stopping his liaison before it became a presidency-threatening scandal.

That summer, another Justice Department investigation prompted Bobby to again warn his brother to cut off a risky relationship, this one with Sinatra. A young Florida attorney named Doug McMillan, who had recently joined the Justice Department, had compiled a dossier on the underworld ties of the singer, who had helped swing the entertainment industry behind Kennedy's candidacy and had been master of ceremonies at JFK's inaugural ball. McMillan, fully aware of the family connection, was nervous about presenting his evidence to his boss. But the attorney general listened respectfully and then asked the young lawyer to put all the details in a memo, which he did, presenting it to his boss on August 3, 1962. Shortly thereafter, JFK famously cut Sinatra out of his life, to the singer's volcanic rage. When the president had Sinatra notified that he would no longer be staying with him during his Palm Springs vacations, the singer reportedly took a sledgehammer to the helicopter landing pad that he had constructed in anticipation of the presidential visits.

Sinatra's fury was undoubtedly mixed with panic. He had helped enlist his underworld friends in the Kennedy campaign, but then the family brushed him aside. "They treat him like a whore," a contemptuous Johnny Rosselli was overhead telling Giancana on the phone. That's the way the Kennedys treated friends, he said: "You fuck them, you pay them, and then they're through." Giancana fumed in graphically violent language about Sinatra, and his failure to get the Kennedys to honor the deal that old Joe had allegedly made with the underworld during the 1960 race. The singer, who knew that Joe's stroke in December 1961 had eliminated any chance of a sit-down between the family and the Mafia, bemoaned his bad luck. "Why, oh why, did Joe get that fucking stroke?" Sinatra's valet heard him wail.

Giancana later said that the only thing that saved Sinatra's life was his sublime talent. The gangster felt a rush of mercy toward Old Blue Eyes during a moment of coital bliss with his girlfriend, singer Phyllis McGuire. One night, he told a Chicago associate, "I'm fucking Phyllis, playing Sinatra songs in the background, and the whole time I'm thinking to myself, Christ, how can I silence that voice? It's the most beautiful sound in the world. Frank's lucky he got it. It saved his life."

Rosselli was also feeling double-crossed by the government. He had put his services at the CIA's disposal for free, out of patriotic duty. But Bobby Kennedy saw no reason to honor the intelligence agency's debts. "Here I am helping the government, helping the country," Rosselli told a Las Vegas associate on a plane trip to Washington in 1962, "and that little son of a bitch is breaking my balls."

BOBBY KENNEDY WAS NOT intimidated by these dragon blasts from the underworld. The only obstacle in the way of his crime crackdown, as far as he was concerned, was J. Edgar Hoover. Frustrated by Hoover's foot dragging, Kennedy and his team resorted to building their own makeshift investigative force. "The feeling was very simple—we felt that we could not look to the FBI for any major assistance, and when we did our requests would have to be screened through Hoover," recalled John Cassidy, who was a lawyer in Kennedy's organized crime section. "You'd ask them to go interview a witness or a suspect and they'd ask you a hundred questions, most of which came down to 'why?' It took a long time to move that forward, to the point where we looked elsewhere for investigators. We found postal inspectors, we found customs people, we found the IRS. We ran around the FBI, because they weren't getting things done."

According to Ed Guthman, Kennedy took the same initiative in the civil rights arena when he realized the FBI was also useless there. The Justice Department built its own "intelligence unit" in the embattled South, said the attorney general's former press secretary and confidant. "We learned shortly after the attack on the Freedom Riders in Alabama that the FBI knew the Klan was going to attack, but they didn't do anything and they didn't warn anybody. So we knew we couldn't rely on the FBI to deal with whatever crisis came up in the South, and as a result we formed our own intelligence unit." Guthman told me that the Kennedy Justice Department sent a wave of young staff attorneys into the South to get information. "Another part of our intelligence operation was my relationship with the press," he said. "The reporters covering the civil rights battles would be all over the place and they would tell me everything they knew."

Ignoring organized crime and civil rights, RFK's two overriding issues, Hoover continued to insist that communism was the nation's primary threat. Kennedy dismissed this notion when he took office, saying "it is such non-sense to have to waste time prosecuting the Communist Party" when most of its dwindling membership consisted of undercover FBI agents.

Hoover's reluctance to pursue the Mafia has been ascribed to his zealous bureaucratic protectiveness—a fear that shifting resources from everyday crime to the more complex rackets would result in less impressive arrest numbers, as well as expose his agents to the Mafia's seductive bribery. It also has been given more tawdry explanations. The legendary lawman was reportedly not immune to the corrupting influence of the mob, consorting with Joe Kennedy's favorite gangster Frank Costello and other underworld figures, who helped make him a fortune by supplying him with gambling tips. Other reports suggest that lifelong bachelor Hoover was a victim of sexual blackmail by the Mafia.

What is certain is that Hoover snooped on the Kennedys with more relish than he did on organized crime bosses. The attorney general was locked in a malignant minuet with his FBI chief. At times Kennedy took his father's lead and tried to win him over with flattery. Other times RFK and his circle flaunted their scorn for Hoover. Bobby and wife Ethel sometimes set loose their high-spirited brood on the prim director's office, where the kids would go toppling into his giant flowerpots. "My father would send us kids into Hoover's office to raise hell, overturn stuff on his desk, to get a rise out of him," Joseph Kennedy II, RFK's oldest son, remembered with a laugh. "And having Brumus, this huge Newfoundland, come romping in and slobbering all over his office—that probably didn't go over too well either," quipped his older sister, Kathleen Kennedy Townsend.

Hoover suspected that the Kennedys were plotting to replace him in their second term, give him the "MacArthur treatment" and send him off to pasture with trumpet blasts and flying colors. But he had other plans. According to William Sullivan, the FBI's number three man, Hoover assiduously compiled all the dirt he could find on JFK, "which the president, with his active social life, seemed more than willing to provide. . . . I was sure he was saving everything he had on Kennedy, and on Martin Luther King Jr., too, until he could unload it all and destroy them both. He kept this kind of explosive material in his personal files, which filled four rooms on the fifth floor of headquarters."

Looking back on their administration after his brother's death, Bobby said that he realized the FBI director was a "dangerous" man—a "menace to democracy" and a "habitual blackmailer," whose poisonous power over presidents and other politicians came from his voluminous secret files. Hoover "acts in such a strange, peculiar way," Kennedy said in a remarkably frank 1964 interview that was intended to be read only by future historians. "He's rather a psycho." But, said Bobby, he and Jack thought "that we could control" him, "that we were on top of, that we could deal with [him] at the appropriate time. That's the way we looked at it."

The Kennedys thought they could control Hoover, suggested one family member, because Jack and Bobby and their top aides were aware of Hoover's secret life. This was confirmed by Kenny O'Donnell Jr., who said that his father and the Kennedy brothers knew Hoover "wore funny clothes. That's why they had a stalemate. They knew enough about Hoover and Hoover thought he knew something about them."

Ironically, the sexually closeted Hoover spread homosexual rumors about Robert Kennedy. Hoover ally Lyndon Johnson tried to get some mileage out of these rumors at the 1960 Democratic convention when he was vying with JFK for the presidential nomination. Several days before the convention, Theodore White received a phone call from someone who later became a high Johnson administration official. "I think you should know that John Kennedy and Bobby Kennedy are fags," the caller told the journalist. "We have pictures of John Kennedy and Bobby Kennedy in women's dresses in Las Vegas this spring at a big fag party. This should be made public." The caller promised to deliver the photographic evidence to White in twenty-four hours, but the pictures never arrived.

The Kennedy brothers' boyish good looks set off homophobic anxiety attacks among many of their enemies, including the sexually repressed Hoover. The hedonistic Jack and his cultured wife were not discomfited by having gay confidants in their circle. And those who came to know Bobby quickly recognized the empathy underneath his tough-guy exterior. Both brothers seemed soft in a way that deeply unnerved their hard-line opponents. But this particular whispering campaign about the Kennedys, who were notoriously heterosexual, never went anywhere.

ON JULY 2, 1962, producer Jerry Wald informed Bobby Kennedy that the screenplay based on *The Enemy Within* was completed. The film project, which Wald had been working on for over a year with screenwriter Budd Schulberg, was close to Kennedy's heart. The Kennedys were well aware of the silver screen's mesmerizing powers. It was *On the Waterfront*, the powerful 1954 movie about the mob's reign of terror on the New York docks, that had inspired Bobby to launch his crusade against racketeering. When Wald showed him a list of prospective screenwriters for *The Enemy Within*, Kennedy had quickly chosen Schulberg, who won an Oscar for *On the Waterfront*. Meeting with Kennedy at Hickory Hill to discuss the project, Schulberg won him over by telling him he thought *The Enemy Within* was about something bigger than bad men or corrupt unions—it was about how "something at the core of our society was beginning to rot." This is precisely what the radical reformer in Kennedy had hoped to convey with his book—that the very centers of American power were in danger of being corrupted. By harnessing Hollywood's magic, Kennedy thought his warning message would finally get the public's full attention.

The attorney general asked Sheridan and Guthman to assist Schulberg on the script. Paul Newman was approached to play Bobby in the movie. By July 1962, Schulberg believed, *The Enemy Within* was headed toward becoming "not merely a sequel to *Waterfront* but a significant extension of that film on a national scale." Then, eleven days after telling Kennedy the cameras were ready to roll, Jerry Wald dropped dead of a heart attack at the age of forty-nine in his Beverly Hills home. Schulberg feared that the project would die with him. He thought that the rotund, ebullient independent producer—maker of hits like *From Here to Eternity*, *Peyton Place*, and *Key Largo*—was the only one in Hollywood who had the courage and the clout to make the movie. Schulberg was right.

After Wald's death, a labor racketeer paid a visit to the deceased producer's studio, 20th Century Fox. Walking brazenly into the office of the studio president, he announced that if 20th Century Fox went ahead with the project, it would be plagued by labor troubles—Teamsters would refuse to deliver prints of the film to theaters, stink bombs would be thrown into cinemas where it was shown. The studio abruptly dropped the film.

Kennedy convinced Schulberg to produce *The Enemy Within* himself, and he began searching for financing. But the two men soon found out how much muscle organized crime had in Hollywood. Some studios were under the direct control of the Mafia, Schulberg later wrote, "and, of course, those studios rejected [the film] out of hand." Columbia, which had released *On the Waterfront*, showed a brief interest in *The Enemy Within*. But then the movie company got a warning from a Hoffa attorney—a letter that was "disturbingly extra-legal," Schulberg recalled—and a studio meeting to discuss the film was suddenly canceled. Schulberg's cast also became infected with fear. One star showed up at Schulberg's house drunk one night

Joseph P. Kennedy Sr. was a ferocious, but loving, force in the lives of his sons, Ted, Jack, and Bobby. His fortune—scraped together on the frontiers of American capitalism—paved his sons' way to political glory. But Bobby suspected that his father, like Shakespeare's Henry IV, had bequeathed them a poisoned inheritance, "canker'd heaps of strange-achieved gold." *Courtesy JFK Library*

The Kennedy brothers probe a witness during a session of the Senate rackets hearings in May 1957. The mammoth investigation into labor and business corruption helped usher the brothers onto the national stage. But, as their father feared, it made Jack and particularly Bobby targets of bitter enmity in the criminal underworld. *Courtesy Corbis*

Bobby and trusted aide Walter Sheridan (center) spar with their long-time nemesis, Teamster leader Jimmy Hoffa Sheridan was Kennedy's "avenging angel" in his war on organized crime. Later, he would enlist Sheridan in the most secret and urgent investigation of their lives—to find the truth about the assassination of President Kennedy. *Courtesy Nancy Sheridan*

White House press secretary Pierre Salinger (left) chats with Kenny O'Donnell, JFK's political aide. O'Donnell, whose life was entwined with that of the Kennedy brothers, never recovered from their assassinations. Without the Kennedys, said one old Boston friend, "O'Donnell was the music without the harp." *Courtesy JFK Library*

Bobby confers with family friend William Walton during a break from the 1960 presidential primary campaign on the back roads of West Virginia. After JFK's assassination, Bobby and Jackie Kennedy would entrust Walton with a stunning secret mission—to visit Moscow and assure Soviet authorities that the Kennedys did not suspect them of plotting the crime. The president, Walton confided, was the victim of a powerful domestic conspiracy.
Courtesy JFK Library, photo by Robert Lerner

Kennedy speechwriter Theodore Sorensen brought a soaring poetry to JFK's efforts to articulate a post-Cold War future, a visionary quest that culminated in the president's historic "Peace Speech" at American University in June 1963. Sorensen, who was raised in a pacifist Unitarian family, drew the ire and suspicion of Washington hawks. *Courtesy Getty*

Edwin Guthman (second from left), walking with Ethel and Bobby Kennedy, was one of RFK's "band of brothers"—a crusading newspaper reporter who put his career on hold to join the Kennedys' New Frontier. Guthman, who knew how many enemies Bobby had made during his own crusading career, pleaded in vain with his friend to surround himself with more protection during his public appearances. *Courtesy JFK Library*

Robert F. Kennedy confers with John Seigenthaler during the 1960 presidential campaign. "What a rich little prick!" Seigenthaler thought when he met Bobby. But he later put his body on the line for RFK's civil rights battles. *Courtesy John Seigenthaler, photo by Jacques Lowe*

White House aide Richard Goodwin antagonized hardliners by urging a hands-off policy on Cuba and by meeting with Che Guevara at a Uruguay dance party in August 1961. In later years, Goodwin confided his suspicions about JFK's assassination to Bobby, a plot that the Kennedy aide thought had grown out of the CIA-Mafia war on Castro. *Courtesy Getty*

The Kennedy clan and advisors gather in the family's Hyannis Port compound to nervously await the official outcome of the presidential race the morning after the election, which had still not been conceded by Richard Nixon. Waiting with JFK, from the left, are Walton, Salinger, Ethel, Bobby, RFK's secretary Angie Novello, and campaign aide William Haddad. JFK's whisper of a victory gave the young president-elect a tenuous hold on the machinery of government. *Courtesy Woodfin-Camp NYC, photo by Jacques Lowe*

Bobby warily eyes FBI chief J. Edgar Hoover during a meeting at the bureau. The attorney general came to view Hoover as a "menace to democracy," whose poisonous power over politicians came from his voluminous secret files. The Kennedys, who compiled their own compromising information on Hoover, thought they could control him. But as soon as President Kennedy was cut down in Dallas, Hoover made it clear to the attorney general that he would no longer defer to him. *Courtesy Woodfin-Camp NYC, photo by Jacques Lowe*

Soviet leader Nikita Khrushchev greets President Kennedy at the Vienna summit in June 1961. Despite their jousting over Berlin, Cuba, Vietnam, and other Cold War hot spots, the two leaders came to develop an appreciation for one another as they tried to steer their nations from the nuclear abyss. Hearing the news from Dallas, Khrushchev broke down and sobbed in the Kremlin. Khrushchev was convinced that Kennedy was killed by militaristic forces in Washington bent on sabotaging the two leaders' efforts to reach détente. Less than a year later, the Soviet leader was forced out of power by his own hardliners in a bloodless coup. *Courtesy JFK Library, photo by Look/Stanley Tretick*

Fidel Castro holds forth in a Harlem restaurant during his 1959 visit to New York. JFK was convinced that he could compete with the Cuban leader's revolutionary charisma, winning over the people of Latin America with U.S. aid and promises of democratic reform. In the final months of the Kennedy administration, JFK opened up a diplomatic back channel with Castro to explore peace with his rival, who said that Kennedy could become "the greatest president of the United States." *Courtesy Getty*

ABC news correspondent Lisa Howard rubs elbows with Che Guevara. Howard, who carried peace feelers between Havana and Washington, became one of Castro's lovers in the process. CIA officials regarded Howard's efforts with cold disdain. Her partner in the peace effort, UN diplomat William Attwood, later concluded that when word of the Kennedy-Castro back channel spread throughout the febrile world of spies, gangsters, and militant Cuban exiles, the results were explosive. *Courtesy Getty*

and told the screenwriter he was afraid he would be killed if he appeared in the movie.

The Enemy Within never made it to the screen. Schulberg had grown up a Hollywood prince, the son of movie mogul B.P. Schulberg. He had written one of Hollywood's masterpieces, winner of the 1955 Academy Award for Best Picture. Bobby Kennedy was known as the second most powerful man in the country. But they could not get a movie made over the blunt opposition of organized crime. It was a stunning lesson in the dark workings of American power.

THE CHAIRMAN OF THE Joint Chiefs of Staff marched into the president's office at 7:59 p.m. He had been summoned by his commander-in-chief, but it was the general—with his rugged jaw, gray-flecked hair, and silver stars— who seemed to radiate the most authority in the room. Even when the president told the general why he had been brought to the White House, his commanding self-confidence seemed to remain intact. The president had made a shocking discovery: his Joint Chiefs chairman was plotting to overthrow his government and replace it with a "regular damn South America junta," in the president's words. He confronted the military man with irrefutable evidence of his treason, but the general did not immediately crumble. He lashed viciously into the president. "You have lost the respect of the country," he told him. "Your policies have brought us to the edge of disaster. Military morale has sunk to the lowest point in thirty years." In his eagerness to make peace with the Soviet Union, the president had acted as recklessly as "a naïve boy."

The president was shaken by the general's defiance. The plot had been exposed, but the president was still uncertain of victory. He knew that the power of the U.S. military establishment had been growing unchallenged ever since World War II. He knew that the general enjoyed heroic stature among the American people. He knew that after living for years in the shadow of nuclear terror, the public was ripe for a military strongman who promised them security. When people "feel helpless, they start going to extremes," the president had mused aloud with his most trusted aides when he first heard about the coup plot. "Look at the history—Joe McCarthy, then the Birch society. . . . The climate for democracy in this country is the worst it's ever been. . . . People have seriously started looking for a superman."

After their taut confrontation in the Oval Office, the general finally agreed to submit his resignation. In return the president agreed not to make

public the military conspiracy and to allow its masterminds to quietly re-
tire to civilian life. It was a compromise that underlined the Democratic
president's sense of moderation and restraint, but perhaps his political weakness too.

At the White House press conference where he later announced the
general's resignation, the president denied reports of an attempted coup. The
beleaguered leader did not want to further undermine confidence in his government. The American military is deeply indoctrinated in the principles of
the Constitution, the president lectured the assembled reporters, so such
treason is foreign to our officer corps. "I am sure the American people do not
believe that any such thought ever entered the mind of any general officer in
our services since the day the country began," the president said, as he concluded the conference. "Let us pray that it never will." For those who knew
how close to the brink the country had really come, the president's reassurances must have seemed bleakly hollow.

These were not real-life scenes from the Kennedy presidency, but fictional scenes inspired by the increasingly ominous mood in the capital. They
take place at the end of *Seven Days in May*, the bestselling novel about a
military coup that comes chillingly close to success. Written by Washington
journalists Fletcher Knebel and Charles W. Bailey, the political potboiler
lacked literary flair, suffering from cardboard characters and corny dialogue.
But its spooky scenario struck a chord with the public when it was published in September 1962, after nearly two years of well-publicized tensions
between civilian and military officials in the Kennedy administration. Knebel, a White House correspondent for *Look* magazine, said he got the idea
for *Seven Days in May* after interviewing the country's always disturbing
Air Force chief, Curtis LeMay, who at one point shocked the journalist by
going off the record to fume against President Kennedy's "cowardice" at the
Bay of Pigs.

Knebel and his co-author were not just expressing their own anxieties—
and those of the public—about the stability of the Kennedy presidency. They
were channeling the fears of the Kennedy brothers themselves. Both men
were haunted by the premonition that their administration would end violently. They raised the subject of a coup or assassination with eerie frequency
during their brief hold on power. Surely no American presidency, with the
possible exception of Abraham Lincoln's, has been so filled with intimations
of its own mortality. Yet, oddly, this chronic concern of the Kennedys has
received scant attention in histories of the administration.

JFK made a habit of shocking his friends with the morbid specter of his own bloody demise. One day, JFK was sailing off Palm Beach with Grant Stockdale, an old friend and fund-raiser whom he appointed ambassador to Ireland. JFK began shooting off rounds from a .22 rifle over the empty ocean expanse and he urged his friend to join him. Stockdale said, "Not on your life, not with all the Secret Service around and me with a gun in my hands." JFK then turned thoughtful and said, "Stock, do you think I'll be assassinated?" His friend rushed to reassure him: "Chief, don't even think about such a thing. Of course you won't."

Kennedy brought up the subject on several occasions with Charlie Bartlett, even discussing at length with him what kind of president Lyndon Johnson would make after his own violent departure. One day, the two men were taking a relaxing drive on a backcountry road in Virginia. Suddenly a car shot past the Secret Service car that was trailing the president and then roared past JFK and his friend. "He was shaken a little bit by this car going by," Bartlett recalled. "And he said, 'Those fellows should have stopped them. . . . The Secret Service should have stopped that car.' And then he disliked the fact that he was showing concern, and he said, 'Charlie, that man might have shot you.' But the thing was obviously on his mind."

John Kennedy had highly sensitive political nerve endings. He was acutely attuned to the dark rumblings in Washington. And so were journalists like Knebel, who enjoyed good access at the White House. Knebel had known Kennedy since his days in Congress, when he recognized the dazzling young politician from Boston as a comer. "He was just good copy, that's all— with the money and the flashiness and the beautiful wife and the whole thing, you know?" Knebel later said. "Also, I felt strongly that he was going someplace, so I just began hanging around his office."

Like his wife, fellow *Look* staff writer Laura Fletcher Knebel, he developed a genial, sparring relationship with JFK. Once, after showing Kennedy a 15,000-word profile of him that he had written for an upcoming book about the 1960 presidential race, Knebel was sharply challenged by the candidate on one of his facts. Knebel had written about a well-documented loan that Joe Kennedy had made to the publisher of the *Boston Post* during JFK's 1952 Senate race. Soon after, the *Post*'s editorial page switched allegiance from Republican candidate Henry Cabot Lodge to JFK.

"The way you write this, about that '52 election, any reader would think that we had bought that paper for the editorial support," Kennedy objected.

"Frankly, that's the implication I want to leave because I think that's what happened," Knebel shot back.

The two men continued squabbling at some length over Knebel's characterization of the deal until Kennedy finally got him to agree to insert a strong denial from family finance man Stephen Smith. Their dispute resolved, JFK then walked Knebel to his door. Years later, the journalist laughed at the memory of what Kennedy did next. "This was a trait about Kennedy that reporters just loved, it just killed them." Opening the door for Knebel, Kennedy said, "You know, we had to buy that fucking paper or I would have lost the election."

"How shrewd that guy was, you know?" the journalist later marveled. "That strange, whimsical, almost magical quality that that guy had about him; he did have it. It wasn't something that was painted on by the press or that was manufactured. It was real."

Knebel made sure that Kennedy got an early copy of *Seven Days in May* before it was published. JFK quickly devoured the book, as did his brother and others in their circle. Then Kennedy contacted Hollywood director John Frankenheimer, maker of the soon-to-be-released film *The Manchurian Candidate*—another Cold War thriller JFK admired—and encouraged him to turn *Seven Days in May* into a movie. So began a remarkable, little-known footnote of the Kennedy years, when the president appealed to his Hollywood friends to help him awake the nation to the threat of far-right treason.

The president wanted to send his enemies in Washington a message. "Kennedy wanted *Seven Days in May* to be made as a warning to the generals," Arthur Schlesinger said years later over glasses of Perrier and lemon in the book-lined drawing room of New York's Century Club. "The president said the first thing I'm going to tell my successor is 'Don't trust the military men—even on military matters.'"

"President Kennedy wanted *Seven Days in May* made. Pierre Salinger conveyed this to us," Frankenheimer recalled. "The Pentagon didn't want it done. Kennedy said that when we wanted to shoot at the White House, he would conveniently go to Hyannis Port that weekend."

JFK had also encouraged the production of Frankenheimer's *Manchurian Candidate*, which starred the president's yet-to-be excommunicated friend Frank Sinatra. Destined to become a Cold War classic, the 1962 film was a perverse dream that tapped into the political psychosis of the era. In *The Manchurian Candidate*, brainwashing Communists and scheming right-wing extremists are amoral equivalents; they join forces to assassinate a president and dispose of American democracy. Kennedy was an avid fan of the darkly lurid 1959 Richard Condon best seller on which the film was based. When United Artists suddenly got cold feet about the movie, fearing that it might exacerbate Cold War tensions, Sinatra persuaded Kennedy to intervene with the studio. The president maintained an active interest in the movie's production. "He was really interested in the facts of the project," Sinatra recalled. On August 29, 1962, Kennedy gave *The Manchurian Candidate* a special screening at the White House.

John Kennedy clearly grasped Hollywood's dreamlike power to conjure the public's deepest fears and hopes. As with Bobby's *Enemy Within* project, JFK showed his communications savvy by turning to Hollywood on *Seven Days in May*. But there is also something poignant about his entreaty. The fact that the president of the United States was driven to enlist the support of show business friends in his struggle with the military underscores how embattled he must have felt.

Frankenheimer and an A-list of Hollywood liberals responded to the president's call. Kirk Douglas's production company acquired the rights to the novel even before it was published and he agreed to co-star in the film with Burt Lancaster as the mutinous General James Mattoon Scott and Frederic March as peace-loving President Jordan Lyman. The Defense Department "shunned" the *Seven Days in May* project, Knebel later reported, after Frankenheimer refused to submit the script (by future *Twilight Zone* creator Rod Serling) for "consideration," as military censors euphemistically called the process. But with Kennedy's support, Frankenheimer filmed scenes at the White House and staged riots outside on Pennsylvania Avenue—mock battles between opponents and supporters of "President Lyman" that echoed the real-life clashes swirling around the Kennedy administration.

Months later, *Look* magazine ran a photo essay by Knebel on the making of *Seven Days in May*, including shots of overturned government cars burning in the streets of Washington. The journalist revealed the rampant anxieties that the movie's production had set off within the government: "At the outset of filming, the moviemakers had a call from still another arm of government. The Secret Service was alarmed at a spurious report that the movie involved a President's assassination." Three days after the magazine's publication date, Kennedy was dead. A strange and melancholy air would hang over the film when it was finally released in February 1964, despite the fact that in the story, at least, the good guys won.

The day Kennedy was assassinated, Paramount Pictures, the distributor of *Seven Days in May*, planned to run an ad for the film, using a quote from one of its fictional military conspirators: "Impeach him, hell. There are better ways of getting rid of him." The studio yanked the ad at the last minute, fearing it was too provocative, "narrowly avoiding an embarrassing coincidence on the very day the president was shot," *Variety* later reported. But several media commentators found the movie itself too disturbing when it was released. An opinion writer in the *Los Angeles Herald-Examiner* questioned whether movies like *Seven Days in May* should be made. "The world is on too short a fuse," he argued, and pictures like this damaged "the American image abroad." A *Los Angeles Times* columnist felt compelled to reassure his readers that a military coup could not really happen in America, quoting none other than retired admiral Arleigh Burke to support his case. Meanwhile congressmen, including Melvin Laird, a future secretary of defense, called for the movie to be clearly labeled fiction before it was shown overseas.

Seven Days in May was one of several nerve-wracking political features to come out of the Kennedy years, including *The Manchurian Candidate, Dr. Strangelove,* and *Fail-Safe.* Together they weave a jittery picture of American democracy "as an excitingly perilous arena," in the observation of film critic J. Hoberman. "Shot in sober black and white and populated by demagogues, dupes and traitors, such movies were delirious news bulletins that set American presidents and presidential candidates in the midst of some personal or public Armageddon." Hollywood, in short, was trying to tell America something about the country's precarious political situation. With most of the Washington press corps remaining cheerfully oblivious to the ominous tensions building in the nation's capital, "the delirious news bulletins" had to come from the country's dream factory.

Critics would later call these films masterpieces of political paranoia. But Frankenheimer rejected the description in an interview near the end of his life. "Paranoia only exists if the circumstances are totally untrue," he pointed out. And America was fraught with dangerous circumstances in those years, he said. As for *The Manchurian Candidate,* he said, history has "vividly demonstrated that there are lots and lots of plots to assassinate presidents and high-ranking figures for political gain. . . . There's a certain grotesque reality about *The Manchurian Candidate.* And as far as *Seven Days in May* is concerned, we know that there was a very definite group in the military that would have, at one point, liked to have taken over the government . . . .The extreme right has been very, very effective in undermining quite a few things that could've changed the destiny of this country."

Her husband never believed the lone gunman theory of President Kennedy's demise, said Evans Frankenheimer, widow of the director, who died in 2002. She said that John Frankenheimer would discuss his ideas about the assassination with Bobby Kennedy, with whom he drew close in

1968, while filming his presidential campaign ads. Both men agreed there were other forces at work in Dallas besides Oswald.

When President Kennedy read the advance copy of *Seven Days in May* that Knebel had sent him, in late summer 1962, he was confident that he could head off any such disaster before it befell the country. The day after reading the book, JFK went sailing on the *Honey Fitz* with his old World War II pal, Red Fay. As the assistant Navy secretary, Fay served as a window for the president into the hostile military culture. Fay too had read an early copy of *Seven Days in May* and he was eager to hear JFK's opinion of the book. Could a military coup really happen here?

"It's possible," JFK told his sailing mate in a calm voice. "It could happen in this country, but the conditions would have to be just right. If, for example, the country had a young president, and he had a Bay of Pigs, there would be a certain uneasiness. Maybe the military would do a little criticizing behind his back, but this would be written off as the usual military dissatisfaction with civilian control. Then if there were another Bay of Pigs, the reaction of the country would be, 'Is he too young and inexperienced?' The military would almost feel that it was their patriotic obligation to stand ready to preserve the integrity of the nation, and only God knows just what segment of democracy they would be defending if they overthrew the elected establishment."

Finally, said the president, "if there were a third Bay of Pigs, it could happen." He paused, as Fay absorbed this chilling scenario. "But it won't happen on my watch," Kennedy added.

Just weeks later, however, the Kennedy administration would suffer two more shocks to the system, with one crisis following hard on the heels of the other. Both crises deepened the same jagged fracture lines in the government that the Bay of Pigs had first chiseled. They reinforced the conviction in some Washington quarters that this was a failing presidency. And, as Kennedy sensed would happen, there were now those who felt a patriotic obligation to do something about it.

"I HAVEN'T HAD SUCH an interesting time since the Bay of Pigs," President Kennedy dryly remarked. His brother was in an equally mordant mood. "The attorney general announced today he's joining Allen Dulles at Princeton University," he deadpanned. It was nearing midnight on September 30, 1962. The Kennedys were huddled in the Cabinet Room with a handful of their closest advisors, including O'Donnell and Sorensen. The president was nervously pacing the room, while Bobby crouched over a telephone connecting him to the University of Mississippi, where a race riot sparked by the arrival of James Meredith—who would become the first black student to enroll at Ole Miss—was rapidly blossoming into a full-blown Southern insurrection against the federal government.

As the night wore on, Bobby continued to monitor the deteriorating situation by phone, talking to his top two men at the scene, Deputy Attorney General Nicholas Katzenbach and Ed Guthman, who relayed increasingly frantic reports from a pay phone booth in the Lyceum, the old administration building where they were holed up. Outside the historic, colonnaded structure—where wounded Confederate soldiers had once been nursed—raged what some would call the last battle of the Civil War. A motley federal force—comprising a few hundred marshals and hastily deputized prison guards, border patrolmen, alcohol and tobacco agents, and the like—were desperately trying to hold off over 2,500 students, Klansmen, squirrel hunters, and even off-duty lawmen, who, armed with bricks, metal pipes, gas-filled Coke bottles, and shotguns, were trying to overrun the citadel. As they charged, they filled the warm night with blood-curdling rebel yells and cries to "lynch the nigger." A majority of the federal marshals were Southerners themselves and were no champions of school integration. But under the command of the attorney general's favorite New York Irishman, Jim McShane, they resolutely held their ground during the long, bloody siege, using only tear gas guns to repel the rioters. The marshals were under strict orders not to draw their sidearms, unless the mob came close to grabbing Meredith, who was passing the night, with odd serenity, on a dormitory cot not far from the Lyceum.

"Stay right by Meredith. Shoot anybody that puts a hand on him," Robert Kennedy told his men.

James Meredith, an eccentric and visionary twenty-eight-year-old Air Force veteran, was possessed by a religious-like belief in his mission, which he described as a "Divine Responsibility" to end "White Supremacy" in his native Mississippi. He had been inspired to undertake this dangerous endeavor after hearing President Kennedy sound freedom's trumpet in his inauguration speech. Meredith had the supreme equanimity of a man who didn't much care whether he lived or died in the process. But the federal marshals were frantic to save his skin, as well as their own. And, as their tear gas supplies ran perilously low and the attacks on their thin line of defense outside the Lyceum grew more vicious, they were not confident they would succeed.

Inside the Lyceum, the scene was bloody bedlam. A young marshal from

Memphis had been shot in the throat, severing his jugular vein, and he was dragged inside the building, jetting blood onto the walls and tile floor. (The marshal, Graham E. Same, would expire and come back to life four times that night, but would miraculously survive.) Dozens of other marshals with broken and bleeding limbs were splayed on the floor. Others were collapsed against the blood-splattered walls, crying inside their gas masks. There was no doctor at this point in the siege and few medical supplies. A persistent sniper was blasting away at the Lyceum's windows. A swirling, eye-stinging haze of tear gas came drifting into the building from the ferocious battle outside.

Kenny O'Donnell, who at one point relieved Bobby on the phone in the Cabinet Room, was shaken by what he was hearing. "Guthman's so scared he can't talk. Helpless feelings on the other end of that phone." And these were two men who had weathered the firestorm of World War II combat.

"How's it going down there?" the attorney general asked Guthman when he got back on the phone.

"Pretty rough," Guthman told him. "It's getting like the Alamo."

A pause. Then Bobby replied, "Well, you know what happened to those guys, don't you." The black Irish humor again. The exchange would be widely quoted in later reports on the battle of Ole Miss, as a way of underlining the Kennedys' grace under pressure.

There were indeed flashes of Kennedy wit throughout the long night. But what comes across most vividly in listening to the tapes from the Cabinet Room and Oval Office that later surfaced, thanks to the secret recording system installed in the White House by the president, is the Kennedy brothers' mounting rage. It started when they began puzzling over the Army's ass-dragging pace that night, its strange failure to promptly relieve the bloodied and outnumbered federal marshals. It grew when mad-eyed, beetle-browed General Edwin Walker—recently forced into retirement—suddenly appeared in the college town, dressed in a natty black suit and his trademark gray Stetson, and showed up later at a Confederate monument on campus, where he rallied the ragtag army of race-haters. And it boiled over as Army officials offered a series of excuses for why their troops were moving so slowly to prevent the lynching of James Meredith and the slaughter of his federal guard. The question that comes searingly through these presidential transcripts is: Why is the military being so unresponsive to the commander-in-chief?

"General Walker's been out downtown getting people stirred up," Bobby Kennedy told the Cabinet Room group at one point. "Well, let's see if we can arrest him," he said over the phone connecting him to Oxford, Mississippi. "Will you tell the FBI that we need an arrest warrant?"

Mention of the mutinous retired general prompted a strong reaction from the president. "General Walker," JFK said disgustedly to the room. "Imagine that son of a bitch having been commander of a division up till last year. And the army promoting him."

The president's comment raised the specter of a military coup in Sorensen's mind. "Have you read *Seven Days in May*?" he asked the president.

"Yeah," said Kennedy.

"It's pretty interesting," remarked Sorensen. "I read it straight through."

Kennedy, a voracious and sophisticated reader, then subjected the book to a sharp literary critique. The novel was marred by "awful amateurish dialogue" and the portrayal of the president was "awfully vague," but the treasonous General Scott made a strong impression on Kennedy.

His brother brought the group back to the disturbing reality of General Walker. "He's getting them all stirred up. If he has them march down there with guns, we could have a hell of a battle."

Later, gruesome reports from the blood-spattered Lyceum flowed into the Cabinet Room. Even the normally calm and collected Nick Katzenbach—who had gone down with his B-26 over the Mediterranean in 1943, spending the rest of the war in a German prison camp, from which he twice escaped—was starting to lose his cool, demanding to know when the Army was going to rescue them. Bobby Kennedy could not tell him. "Damn Army!" cursed RFK about a quarter past midnight. "They can't even tell if the MPs have left yet!"

More than ninety minutes had now passed since the attorney general had ordered troops from the 503rd Military Police Battalion—the Army's riot-control SWAT team—to move from Memphis to Oxford. But Army Secretary Cyrus Vance and Major General Creighton Abrams, who was in charge of the military operation (and would later command the war in Vietnam), seemed at a maddening loss to explain the soldiers' delay. The president barraged Vance with at least fifteen phone calls that night, trying to find out what was going on with his troops. The army secretary, suffering from a ruptured disc, lay on his office floor as the president berated him. "Where's the Army?" Kennedy shouted at Vance. "Where are they? Why aren't they moving?"

Army officials would later explain that it was simply a case of bad planning, resulting from the Kennedys' original desire to avoid a dramatic display of military force in the South and the Army's inexperience in domestic operations of this sort. The 503rd's frantic road trip that night produced the comic spectacle of Army officers in full battle gear rolling into backcountry gas stations in their jeeps and demanding Tennessee-Mississippi highway maps.

Henry Gallagher, a twenty-three-year-old second lieutenant who was leading an Army convoy to Ole Miss, was so desperate to find his way there that he ordered his jeep driver to kidnap a Navy shore patrolman with a Southern accent who seemed to know the area. "I said that we were all from up north and didn't have the foggiest idea where the town of Oxford was. I said that he had to come with us," recalled Gallagher. "He was incredulous. 'Sir, I can't do that. I'm on duty here at this gate. My captain will go crazy wondering where I am.' I said something to the effect that we were all under orders from President Kennedy and he had to go with us. I motioned to [my driver]. He came around and picked up the startled SP in a bear hug and placed him in the back of the jeep."

But in the Cabinet Room that night, which throbbed with the taut nerves of a war room, the Army's stumbling performance seemed more than a comedy of errors. It felt like insubordination. This was how far relations between the White House and Pentagon had sunk by this point in the Kennedy administration. In their high-anxiety mood, the Kennedy brothers and their advisors sensed something sinister in the military's farcical incompetence. They were outraged by how indifferent the Army seemed to presidential orders.

"I'll be a son of a bitch if the president of the United States calls up and says, 'Get your ass down there,'" said O'Donnell, his Irish rising. "Yeah, I would think they'd be on that fucking plane in about five minutes."

"I have a hunch that Khrushchev would get those troops in fast enough," he added, with bitter sarcasm.

JFK expressed his disgust at once again being jerked around by men in uniform: "They always give you their bullshit about their instant reaction and split-second timing, but it never works out. No wonder it's so hard to win a war."

Robert Kennedy had never seen his brother so angry during his presidency—not during the humiliations of the Bay of Pigs and the Vienna summit, not during the nerve-wracking showdown over Berlin or tense negotiations over Laos. "People are dying in Oxford!" JFK erupted at General Abrams. "This is the worst thing I've seen in forty-five years. I want the military police battalion to enter the action. You are to proceed to the campus forthwith." Bobby himself told a reporter the next morning that "last night was the worst night I ever spent." He was his brother's point man on civil rights, he was supposed to be in control of volatile situations like this. But the night seemed on the verge of exploding into the most spectacular nightmare of the Kennedy presidency, a racial bloodbath that would tear the country apart and savage America's image abroad as a beacon of freedom.

O'Donnell later offered a riveting, you-are-there account of the rising feelings of calamity in the Cabinet Room as the Mississippi night burned on: "Clearly, we are very panicked by all this right now, that [Meredith] might be killed, federal marshals killed and troops potentially killed, [it's] going to be a political catastrophe as well as a devastating set of events for everyone who is directly involved. . . . The implications both at home and across the globe are enormous. . . . Nick is on the phone from Oxford and Bobby is on the phone from the Cabinet Room. The president is pacing back and forth in the Cabinet Room listening to the conversation. He is as upset as I have ever seen him. The president is now seeing the full portent of this problem, all the implications if things go terribly wrong and a real fear that there will be a blood bath there. . . . The president and the attorney general were, to say the least, a little unhappy with the military. The president required a memorandum explaining to him in detail why they had failed to mention what was really critical information to us in deciding the strategy for deployment. The president was just livid, absolutely livid. . . . The tempo of violence is increasing minute by minute now in Oxford. It becomes clear that the most horrible possibility is now in existence—that the marshals will be overwhelmed and that Meredith and now really the president's own men, meaning Nick and the others, are in danger of their lives. The marshals are clearly being overwhelmed and many of them have been very seriously injured at this point.

"The president is on the phone almost every minute now. First he began with the Pentagon to get some answers. He quickly became exasperated with this conversation, so he hung up and called the base in Memphis again to find out what is going on. He gets the general [Abrams] directly and the guy finally admits that they have not loaded the helicopters, they are all there now, but there is a new problem. The president can't imagine, what is the new problem? Well the problem is, the general admits, they are not sure where they are going or how to get there. The president is stunned. You know, we are sitting staring at each other. This is supposed to be the greatest military in the world! They explain to the president that when they laid out all these plans and briefed the attorney general, it was all based on a mission during the daytime. That now it has become a nighttime mission, they are not sure they can get there in the helicopters at night and they do not know where to land. I mean, here we are sitting in the Cabinet Room of the White House and they are literally saying to the president, 'Where should we land? We do not know where to land.' He could not believe it."

During the Bay of Pigs, President Kennedy had learned that he could not safely delegate responsibility for a high-stakes operation to the CIA. On the night of Ole Miss, he and his advisors discovered that they could not rely on the military to carry out even a domestic operation against "a few hundred students and rednecks," in Sorensen's caustic words. Surveying the frantic scene in the Cabinet Room, O'Donnell was struck by the grotesque absurdity of what he was witnessing: the president of the United States forced to play the role of air traffic controller, conferring with his staff on where to land the helicopters and then dialing a lowly sergeant on the ground in Oxford to make sure there would be trucks to pick up the troops when they landed. The uniformed grunt on the other end of the president's phone proved to be the most proficient military man with whom Kennedy talked that night. "The president joked maybe we should put him in charge," O'Donnell observed.

It was not until 2:15 in the morning—when the first wave of heavily-armed MPs finally came storming through the flames toward the Lyceum— that the Kennedy war room could begin to relax. (By some calculations, the troops began arriving more than three hours after the Army promised they would. But Robert Kennedy later estimated the military's delay at more than five hours.) A deep-throated roar went up from the battered marshals. Their tear gas supplies were all but depleted, and they were just minutes away from being overrun by the mob. The soldiers were thunderstruck by the scene that greeted them, with burning cars, the crackle of gunfire, and the moans of the wounded creating a hellish battlefield tableaux. "I could not believe what I saw," recalled Lieutenant John Migliore. "I could not believe I was on the campus of a university in the United States of America." But the worst was over now. Faced with the full might of the U.S. military, the rioters soon began to disperse.

By then two men were dead—a reporter for Agence France-Presse and a local jukebox repairman—and a total of 166 federal marshals were wounded. Dozens of soldiers, students, and rioters were also injured in the Battle of Ole Miss. Some three hundred people were arrested, men and boys of all ages who had come from all over the Deep South and from as far away as California. They had flooded into the mossy, idyllic college town in response to the racist rallying cries of rebel leaders like General Walker, who urged them to "bring your flags, your tents and your skillets" and take a final stand for Southern sovereignty against the tyranny of federal race-mixing. The attorney general's office even received an FBI report about a Wisconsin segregationist who planned to fly a surplus military plane to battle in Oxford.

The Mississippi tempest left another cloud of ill will and distrust over White House–Pentagon relations. The attorney general vented his anger with the military by going after General Walker as ferociously as he pursued gangsters. The morning after the riot, Walker was arrested by federal marshals and flown to a Missouri psychiatric prison, where he was to undergo examination before standing charges on insurrection. The *New York Times* observed that committing the general to a mental hospital "was regarded as unusual." But Bobby Kennedy was in no mood for judicial restraint. He summoned Cy Vance's aide Joe Califano, who was considered the Pentagon expert on the zealous general, and made it clear that his job was to keep Walker behind bars. "There was no discussion of Walker's rights," Califano recalled in his memoir, "no echoes of the right to bail that was stressed in my criminal law course at Harvard. 'Whatever it takes to keep him locked up in that hospital, that's what we need,' was the message from the attorney general as he stared at me. I knew Kennedy had mercilessly chewed out Vance for not getting Army troops to Oxford in time to avoid the violence. His chilling glare at me said, 'Maybe you guys in the Army can at least get something right.'" But Walker's attorney appealed to his far-right sympathizers in Congress, calling his client "the United States' first political prisoner," and the insurrectionary general was released seven days later.

The Ole Miss crisis also drove a permanent wedge between the Kennedy administration and the white South, a political crack that the brothers had been desperately trying to caulk over, at least until JFK was safely reelected. But as the Kennedy brothers finally went to bed on the dawn of October 1, they knew a historic turning point had been reached. The old Democratic coalition could no longer be held together; it was a house divided and would soon fall.

"The president, angry and distraught, goes home about six o'clock that morning," remembered O'Donnell. "We all went home, I went home and Bobby did as well. We went home knowing for the moment that we had at least saved the lives of those involved—but in fact whatever cordiality that ever existed between the Southern states and the rest of us was now at an end. There was to be no more pretense and this issue [integration] would not and could not be detained any further. . . . The president, besides being just personally deeply disturbed, also realizes that this glossing over of the great national problem and the attempt to reach some sort of consensus with the

Southern states, with its congressmen and senators, is now at an end. The bitter feelings from this incident will spill over for a long time to come."

Raised in a privileged world of country clubs and prep schools, the Kennedy brothers were slow to recognize that the entrenched evils of racism had to be fully confronted by the government in order for the American journey to continue. In the beginning, they saw the exploding demands for racial equality as a political problem that had to be managed rather than as a moral imperative. "The problem with you people," a peevish and arrogant Bobby snapped at NAACP lawyer [and future Supreme Court Justice] Thurgood Marshall, "is that you want too much too fast." During JFK's first year in office, Martin Luther King Jr. famously remarked that President Kennedy seemed intellectually supportive of the civil rights movement, but emotionally disengaged. "I'm convinced that he has the understanding and the political skill, but so far I'm afraid that the moral passion is missing." But pushed and pulled by the heroism of the civil rights crusaders, and the righteous power of their cause, the Kennedy brothers—first Bobby, then the cooler Jack—began to change. By the time Ole Miss erupted, the Kennedys were viewed as hostile foreign leaders in the white South because of their growing support for civil rights. "If Khrushchev was running against Kennedy here, Khrushchev would beat him," groused a Mississippi voter. "And if Bob Kennedy was the candidate, Khrushchev would beat him worse."

In the days following the bloody insurrection, Attorney General Kennedy ordered young Justice Department aides to roam the Ole Miss campus and the town of Oxford and report back to him on the mood of the smoldering battleground. Oxford was a seat of culture and learning, home of Nobel Prize–winning novelist William Faulkner, who had died the summer before the conflagration at his stately Greek Revival house, Rowan Oak.

Faulkner had predicted something like the Ole Miss insurrection before his death, writing that white Southerners would embrace "another Civil War, knowing they're going to lose," rather than bow to desegregation of their schools. The writer's nephew, Murry, had bravely and loyally led the local National Guard unit during the battle of Ole Miss, rushing to the aid of the federal marshals despite the outrage of his fellow Southerners and at one point scurrying with a squad to the defense of a black church that was on the verge of being torched by rednecks. He suffered two broken bones during the riot when a flying brick struck his arm.

But even among the educated people of Oxford, the sentiments about the Kennedys were raw. When the attorney general phoned Captain Falkner (as his wing of the family spelled their name) after the uprising to congratulate him on a "job well done," the reaction was far from soldierly pride. "Later I told the troop of my call and conversation," Falkner remembered. "Rather than the compliment being a morale booster, it had an adverse effect, making us more disgusted than ever."

Robert Kennedy's men brought back disturbing reports and documents from the Mississippi front, primitively racist artifacts that he stored in his Justice Department files like the archeology of a lost civilization. Much of it revealed the underlying sexual panic behind the anti-Meredith furor—the fear that incoming black male students would defile the pure white magnolia of Southern womanhood. (The president was "really disgusted" by the sexual phobias on florid display at Ole Miss, O'Donnell later remarked.) Leaflets depicting fresh-scrubbed, blonde coeds in the arms of grossly caricatured black "coons" littered the campus. "How would you like it if your exquisitely formed White child was no longer White?" read one. "Pink cheeks no longer pink. Blue eyes no longer blue . . . It's [sic] sensitive mind no longer sensitive but ape like? It's beautiful body no longer beautiful but black and evil smelling?" Another leaflet urged that Meredith be socially isolated like "a piece of furniture of no value," while Klansmen meanwhile explored a more direct approach, plotting to kidnap and lynch him at the earliest opportunity. A student newsletter called Rebel Underground attacked the Kennedy brothers as "the KKK—Kennedy Koon Keepers," while the Mississippi Junior Chamber of Commerce denounced the administration's act of "tyranny," branding it "one of the most tragic events in the history of [our] beloved country—federal force against a sovereign state . . . education at bayonet." A bumper sticker read: "The Castro Brothers Have Moved into the White House."

One leaflet distributed to white soldiers stationed on campus tried to stir up mutinous passions in the ranks. "Do not be tricked into fighting your fellow Americans," read the appeal to the Army troops. "KENNEDY is out to destroy AMERICA because he is a sick, sick COMMUNIST. . . . If you will join with your fellow Americans here in Mississippi, no force on earth can conquer us. Together with all other GOOD AMERICANS, we will remove RED JACK KENNEDY and all the other communist PARTY politicians from office, and go on from there to wipe the HELL-SPAWNED FILTH of COMMUNISM from the face of the earth."

James Symington, who had replaced John Seigenthaler as RFK's administrative aide, was one of the young men Kennedy dispatched to Ole Miss. Symington, the son of Senator Stuart Symington of Missouri, arrived in Oxford the morning after the riot in a small government plane. "The marshal who picked me up at the local airport told me to cover my head with my coat as we drove into town in case a brick came through the window," Symington recalled in a recent interview. The young Kennedy aide questioned dozens of people who had been arrested during the riot, as well as preachers, newspaper publishers, judges, and other local dignitaries. The testimony he collected from the Mississippi Delta was almost uniformly distressing. Young rioters told him they didn't want to get into any trouble, but they were following orders from their daddies or preachers.

"One preacher let me into his church," said Symington, "and told me, 'You represent a tyranny.' I said, 'How do you think black people feel living in Mississippi with no rights?' He said, 'Well, it's better to have a lot of little tyrannies than one big one.'" Another minister told Symington that telephone linemen had observed "hillbillies camping in the woods, waiting for the troops to leave so they could come in for Meredith." (The military occupation of Oxford would last for nearly ten months. A small squad of federal marshals stayed on to protect Meredith through his graduation.)

Later Symington was asked to speak to a group of Ole Miss grad students. "I went to a little house in town. I brought my guitar to sing some old folk songs, which I did in those days. I was greeted at the door by a young man with a tall glass, the kind you'd fill with milk, but it was filled to the top with bourbon. I said, 'How about a little ice in that.' He said, 'We don't water our drinks in Mississippi.'

"I walked into the kitchen and I saw a whole tray of skinned squirrels. Then I went and sat in the living room and played some songs on my guitar. They brought out the squirrels and gave me one to eat. One guy told me, 'You've got to stick your fork right in there, like it's a lobster, and get that white blob. What do you think that is, Yankee?'

"And I said, 'First of all, I'm not a Yankee—I'm from Missouri, and that's a border state. And I think it's the brain.'

"And they shouted, 'That's right!' I stuck it as far down my gullet as it would go so I wouldn't gag on it and swallowed. And they whooped and hollered.

"We kept drinking the bourbon and they told me, 'You gotta understand— we *love* our niggers down here.' And I said, 'Well that's just grand—so why can't they go to school with you?' And they said, 'That's not the way we love 'em.'"

Someone brought Robert Kennedy a souvenir from the battle of Ole Miss—a white federal marshal's helmet that had been dented by a flying missile. Kennedy kept the battered helmet on display in his office for the rest of his tenure as attorney general, as a graphic reminder of what the administration was confronting.

When it came time for President Kennedy to honor the heroism that was displayed in Oxford during that long night, he did not hand out citations to anyone from the U.S. Army or the FBI. He summoned five ragged warriors from the ranks of the federal marshals. During a White House ceremony, Kennedy told the men that if they had not stood their ground and James Meredith had been lynched, "it would have been a blow from which the United States and Mississippi would not have recovered for many years."

Ole Miss drove home two unavoidable conclusions for the Kennedy administration: the U.S. Army could not be trusted to settle a domestic crisis, and the South was hostile territory. The crisis stirred new doubts within JFK's inner circle about how firmly the president was in control of his own military. And the battle of Oxford—with its jolting images of U.S. troops in action, not against Castro's Cuba, but against the American South—incited more dark muttering among Kennedy's opponents about the president's leadership.

James Meredith had forced a U.S. president to send troops into the South for the first time since the Civil War to protect the human rights of black Americans. "I wasn't there as a student—I was there as a soldier," the courageous and messianic Meredith later declared. "I was a general. I was in command of everything."

There were many defenders of the old order, not just in the South but in the military and the Washington establishment, who regarded this as a grossly improper use of the armed forces. Barry Goldwater denounced the display of military power as an unconstitutional federal attempt to seize the schools. Republican candidates in the forthcoming midterm elections made a point of standing on stage with Confederate flags fluttering behind them, a vivid symbol of the emerging GOP majority in the South. The Republican Senate contender in South Carolina compared Kennedy to Hitler, charging that his Ole Miss actions had "the earmarks of a cold-blooded, premeditated effort to crush the sovereign state of Mississippi into submission." When a high school band struck up *Dixie,* the Senate campaigner whooped, "I just hope that song could be heard all the way from Oxford, Mississippi, to Washington, D.C.!"

The explosion of violence in Mississippi would have reverberated even louder in Washington and across the country if another concussion of a still greater magnitude had not quickly blown it off the front pages. This crisis emanated, once again, from Cuba.

• • •

IT WAS 9:45 ON the morning of Friday, October 19, 1962, four days after a U-2 spy plane had spotted several medium-range ballistic missile sites under construction in a remote area in the west of Cuba. The United States and Soviet Union were locked in the first week of the Cuban Missile Crisis, a thirteen-day dance of death that Arthur Schlesinger Jr. would later declare "the most dangerous moment in human history." President Kennedy was straining to pick just the right steps in this tremulous choreography, so the world did not go stumbling over the nuclear edge. He and the two men who had emerged as his wisest advisors, his brother Bobby and Robert McNamara, were trying to steer the decision-making process toward the idea of a naval blockade of Cuba, to stop the flow of nuclear shipments to the island and to pressure the Soviets into a peaceful resolution of the crisis. But virtually his entire national security apparatus was pushing the president to take military action against Cuba. Leading the charge for an aggressive response were the members of the Joint Chiefs of Staff, who were urging the president to launch surprise air strikes on the island and then invade. On the morning of October 19, the nation's top military commanders filed into the Cabinet Room to convince Kennedy to adopt their position. No meeting between a leader and his national security advisors has ever been so laden with consequence. And no meeting during the Kennedy presidency so dramatically illustrates the divisions between the head of state and his military chiefs.

Attending the meeting with the president were Joint Chiefs Chairman Maxwell Taylor, Air Force Chief of Staff Curtis LeMay, Chief of Naval Operations George Anderson, Army Chief of Staff Earle Wheeler, and Marine Corps Commandant David Shoup, as well as McNamara. Taylor was ostensibly a Kennedy man, inserted into his position by the president to inject some intellectual sophistication into the Pentagon. Shoup lacked Taylor's intellectual gifts but also tried to position himself as a New Frontiersman, spreading the word that he had supported JFK's election and clashing with Senator Strom Thurmond over the far right's attempts to indoctrinate the Marine Corps. ("I didn't feel that we needed to have Strom Thurmond and his henchmen determine for me what I taught the Marines about communism," Shoup later remarked. "I thought it was rather ridiculous.") But Kennedy expected trouble from crusty, cigar-chomping Curtis LeMay—who had been advocating a preemptive nuclear strike on Russia since the early 1950s, after taking over the Strategic Air Command. LeMay dismissed Cuba as a "sideshow," and bluntly recommended that the United States "fry it." The president also knew he could not count on support from George Anderson, the tall, handsome, straight-arrow naval chief known for lecturing his sailors to follow a morally clean path. Anderson, whose good looks earned him the nickname "Gorgeous George," had proven to be as abrasive as his predecessor, Arleigh Burke, openly challenging the Kennedy-McNamara attempts to take control of defense spending and the weapons procurement process. And Wheeler, a by-the-numbers general, was still stinging from JFK's furious scolding following the Army's sluggish performance at Ole Miss.

LeMay was in the habit of taking bullying command of Joint Chiefs meetings. With his sagging jowls and chronic scowl, he came across as a bulldog marking his territory. He blew cigar smoke in the faces of anyone who disagreed with him and communicated his boredom and contempt by leaving ajar the door to the bathroom that was located off the Joint Chiefs conference room while he relieved himself with raucous abandon. The Air Force chief reverted to the same confrontational style with Kennedy in the Cabinet Room that morning. The loathing between the two men was mutual and complete. They had already clashed over the developing crisis, at a White House meeting held the day before. Kennedy had asked LeMay to predict how the Russians would respond if the United States bombed Cuba. "They'll do nothing," LeMay blandly replied. "Are you trying to tell me that they'll let us bomb their missiles, and kill a lot of Russians and then do nothing?" an incredulous Kennedy shot back. "If they don't do anything in Cuba, then they'll certainly do something in Berlin." JFK was always sensitive to how a move on one square of the Cold War chessboard might trigger a countermove somewhere else.

After the meeting, the president was still shaking his head over the general's blithe prediction. "Can you imagine LeMay saying a thing like that?" Kennedy wondered aloud to O'Donnell when he got back to his office. "These brass hats have one great advantage in their favor. If we listen to them, and do what they want us to do, none of us will be alive later to tell them that they were wrong."

At the Friday meeting, LeMay bluntly declared that "we don't have any choice except direct military action." And he obstinately repeated his prediction from the day before, insisting that there would be no Soviet response to an air strike on Cuba. "I don't think [the Russians] are going to make any reprisal if we tell them that the Berlin situation is just like it's always been. If they make a move, we're going to fight." LeMay made no effort to hide his disgust with Kennedy's blockade strategy. It reeked of cowardly Neville Chamberlain, he growled. The general was certainly crafty enough to know what he was doing when he raised the specter of Munich. He must have known how it would put Kennedy on the defensive, with its reminder of his father's shameful performance as ambassador to London. Kennedy's blockade scheme was "almost as bad as the appeasement at Munich," he needled the president.

Emboldened by LeMay, the other chiefs jumped into the fray, repeating the Air Force general's call for immediate military action. "I do not see that, as long as the Soviet Union is supporting Cuba, that there is any solution to the Cuban problem except a military solution," Admiral Anderson lectured Kennedy. Even Taylor and Shoup endorsed LeMay's bellicose position. But Kennedy evaded the chiefs' attempts to back him into a corner. When a rambling, inarticulate Shoup offered the passing observation that the Soviet Union already had the ability to strike the United States without the Cuba missiles, Kennedy seized on this side comment. Maybe the installation of the new missiles was not such a destabilizing development, the president suggested—perhaps it was not worth risking nuclear war over. "No matter what they put in there, we could live today under [this threat]," Kennedy mused aloud.

This conciliatory sentiment provoked another outburst from LeMay. "If we leave them there," the general fumed, the Communist bloc would wield a "blackmail threat against not only us but the other South American countries." Then the Air Force chief did something remarkable. He decided to violate traditional military-civilian boundaries and issue a barely veiled political threat. If the president responded weakly to the Soviet challenge in Cuba, he warned him, there would be political repercussions overseas, where Kennedy's government would be perceived as spineless. "And I'm sure a lot of our own citizens would feel that way too," LeMay added. With his close ties to militaristic congressional leaders and the far right, LeMay left no doubt about the political damage he could cause the administration. "In other words, you're in a pretty bad fix at the present time," LeMay told Kennedy.

It was an ugly, sneering comment—particularly in the grave atmosphere of the moment—and Kennedy did not let it pass. "What did you say?" he quickly responded.

"You're in a pretty bad fix," LeMay repeated, holding his ground.

"You're in there with me," the president tartly replied. Then Kennedy laughed, a strained and mirthless laugh. "Personally," he added, drilling home the point for LeMay.

Ted Sorensen later expressed astonishment at LeMay's provocative behavior in the Cabinet Room that morning. "In that meeting, what LeMay said is almost out of *Seven Days in May*," exclaimed Sorensen in a recent interview. "Telling Kennedy this is like Munich, this is too soft, and the American people will think so too! That's what outraged me—a general telling the president of the United States what the people think."

After an hour, Kennedy left the meeting, followed by McNamara. The confrontation with his top military men had clearly disturbed the commander-in-chief. Later he told an aide that the administration needed to make sure the Joint Chiefs did not start a war without his approval, a chronic fear of JFK's. "I don't want these nuclear weapons firing without our knowing it," he said. "I don't think we ought to accept the chiefs' word on that one."

Kennedy had reason to question the Joint Chiefs' loyalty. After he and McNamara left the Cabinet Room that morning, the president's secret taping system continued to record the military chiefs' conversation, unbeknownst to them. As soon as the president and his defense secretary were gone, the chiefs began profanely condemning Kennedy's cautious, incremental approach to the crisis. Shoup, the supposed Kennedy loyalist, took the lead in the angry attack, as if to show his fellow generals where his allegiance truly resided. JFK always took a gradual approach in "every goddamn" crisis, Shoup vented bitterly to his colleagues. You can't "go in there and frig around with the missiles," he cursed, or "you're screwed."

"That's right," LeMay seconded.

"You're screwed, screwed, screwed."

Kennedy was hung up on "the political action of a blockade," Wheeler chimed in, rather than letting his military men solve the problem.

The military chiefs' scorn and frustration with the president came pouring out in a torrent of "insubordination," as Sorensen later described it. "What they said after he left the room about their commander-in-chief was outrageous," he said.

With each passing day of the missile crisis, Kennedy knew that the pressures on him were growing to resolve it militarily. As he came out of the Cabinet Room that morning, he bumped into Sorensen, whom he had wisely kept out of the meeting to avoid provoking the Pentagon chiefs. "He burst out of the meeting, hot under the collar, and he said, 'You and Bobby have to get a consensus on this [blockade] thing.' And he pointed at the meeting and he said, 'They all want war.' He just felt that with the kind of pressure rising in that quarter, he knew time was going to run out."

As the crisis progressed, LeMay's right-hand man, Tommy Power—whose psychological temperament even LeMay acknowledged was "not stable"—

took it upon himself to raise the Strategic Air Command's alert status to DEFCON-2, one step from nuclear war. General Power clearly thought he knew better than the president of the United States how to handle the Russians. To make sure Moscow got the message, Power deliberately sent the alert in the clear, so the Soviets could immediately read it. Was the White House aware of this Strangelovian move by the head of the country's nuclear air forces? "No, we were not," Sorensen flatly says today.

It was not until years later that surviving members of the Kennedy administration learned just how dangerous the military pressure on JFK was. At a conference held in Havana in October 2002 to mark the fortieth anniversary of the Cuban Missile Crisis, former Kennedy officials were stunned to hear from their Russian counterparts how cocked and ready Soviet nuclear forces were during the showdown. "The Joint Chiefs were pushing to take out the missiles with a surprise attack," recalled Schlesinger, who attended the Havana gathering. "But as we discovered at the conference, the Soviet military had forty thousand troops in Cuba, not the ten or twelve thousand we expected. And the Soviet commanders in Cuba were equipped not only with strategic missiles but with tactical nuclear missiles, and they had the delegated authority to use them to repel an American invasion. I was sitting next to Bob McNamara in Havana when the Russian general who had been head of the Red Army contingent in Cuba in 1962 suddenly revealed this. McNamara nearly fell out of his seat. We never had any expectation of that."

The Havana conference, observed Sorensen, "brought to my mind and Arthur's and Bob McNamara's—all of us who participated—as never before, how close the world came to stumbling into a nuclear exchange that would have escalated very quickly on both sides to a nuclear holocaust that would have left both countries in ruins, and soon most of the world as well." The Joint Chiefs, Sorensen continued, "were certain that no nuclear warheads were in Cuba at the time. They were wrong." If Kennedy had bowed to their pressure, Sorensen grimly concluded, the world would have been reduced to smoking rubble.

"There isn't any learning period with nuclear weapons," McNamara remarked during the Havana conference. "You make one mistake and you destroy nations."

This is what McNamara tried to impress upon his military chiefs as the crisis was unfolding. After initiating the blockade, Kennedy ordered his defense secretary to keep close watch over the Navy to make sure U.S. vessels didn't do anything that would trigger World War III. There was to be no shooting at Soviet ships without McNamara's approval. But Admiral Anderson bridled under the defense secretary's hands-on control, clashing with McNamara in the Navy's Flag Plot room, the Pentagon command center where the blockade was being monitored. In a choleric outburst that would be dramatized in the 2000 film *Thirteen Days*, the admiral told his civilian boss that he didn't need his advice on how to manage a blockade, the Navy had been carrying out such operations since the days of the Revolution. "I don't give a damn what John Paul Jones would have done," McNamara angrily replied. "I want to know what you are going to do—now." Anderson suggested that McNamara leave the room: "Mr. Secretary, you go back to your office and I'll go to mine and we'll take care of things."

"Apparently it was the wrong thing to say to somebody of McNamara's personality," the insubordinate admiral later remarked. As McNamara left the Flag Plot, he told his aide Roswell Gilpatric, "That's the end of Anderson."

Like his fellow chiefs, Anderson was eager to use the missile crisis "to solve the Cuban problem" by invading the island. "It could have been rather bloody, but I would say with a relatively low degree of casualties on the part of the American forces," the admiral remarked in a 1981 interview for the U.S. Naval Institute. "I think the Cuban people would have immediately rallied to our support and I think we could have installed a good government in Cuba, and I think with the proper warnings to the Russians and care on our part, my belief is that there would not have been a military confrontation between the Russian troops that were there and ours, because there were relatively few Russians there. I don't believe under any circumstances they would have fired those offensive weapons against the United States or it would have been nuclear warfare."

Anderson was never given the opportunity to test his theories. Several months after the missile crisis, Kennedy and McNamara pushed the admiral out of the Navy, dispatching him as ambassador to Portugal, where he would become chummy with dictator Antonio Salazar, whom he described as "an extremely polite, decent, quiet man." Before leaving the Pentagon, Anderson dropped by McNamara's office, where the defense secretary tried to give him a parting handshake. The admiral, who regarded McNamara as a "vindictive" and "deceitful" man, refused his hand. "Shake hands with you? Hell, no." McNamara invited him to sit down for a talk. "Mr. Secretary, your idea of integrity is so far removed from anything we are brought up with in the military," the admiral brusquely told him during a lengthy conversation. "It's the difference between night and day." According to Anderson, McNamara burst into tears at this. Years later, you could still feel the admiral's contempt. The Kennedy civilians were nothing but crybabies in suits.

The Joint Chiefs were not alone in trying to maneuver the United States into war over the Cuban missile installations. The CIA also played a dangerous game during the crisis. CIA director John McCone, who was the first administration official to charge the Soviets were inserting missiles into Cuba, made no secret of his desire for a shooting war over the new threat. In the weeks before the crisis exploded, the agency began leaking information about the missiles to friendly reporters like Hal Hendrix of the *Miami News*—who later won a Pulitzer for his "scoops"—as well as to Republican Senator Kenneth Keating of New York, who used the intelligence tips to politically embarrass the Kennedy administration.

During the height of the crisis, President Kennedy instructed the CIA to immediately stop all raids against Cuba, to make sure that no flying sparks from the agency's secret operations set off a nuclear conflagration. But, once again, the agency asserted its right to determine its own Cuba policy, independent of the president's will. In defiance of Kennedy's order, Bill Harvey mobilized sixty commandos—"every single team and asset that we could scrape together"—and dropped them into Cuba, in anticipation of the U.S. invasion that the CIA hoped was soon to follow. When somebody in the JM/WAVE station tipped off Robert Kennedy to Harvey's reckless act, the attorney general hit the roof, ripping into the CIA official at a Mongoose meeting for risking World War III. An unrepentant Harvey shot back that if the Kennedys had taken care of the Cuba problem at the Bay of Pigs, the country would not be stuck in the current mess. The attorney general stormed out of the room. Years later, at his appearance before the Church Committee, the CIA man was still dismissive of Kennedy's concerns, shrugging them off as "persnickety."

But for the Kennedys, it was one more demonstration of the intelligence agency's cowboy nature. "Of course, I was furious," Bobby later said, recalling Harvey's wildly provocative act. He was astounded that a CIA official would risk nuclear doomsday "with a half-assed operation like this."

Watching the eruption between Kennedy and Harvey, McCone knew that the career of his Cuba point man had just imploded. "Harvey has destroyed himself today," the CIA director told an aide. The Kennedy "tirade" against Harvey was "so severe," according to an FBI memo, "that McCone felt it would be appropriate to move Harvey from Washington, D.C., for a few days." Later, Dick Helms came to Harvey's rescue, transferring him to the agency's Rome station, where he would be out of Kennedy's line of fire.

The legendary spy would drink his way through his brief Roman exile, until he was brought back to CIA headquarters.

Before Harvey departed for Rome, his colleagues threw him a bon voyage party, where they staged a dramatization of the life and death of Julius Caesar, with Harvey in the lead role. As the sketch concluded, someone shouted, "Who was Brutus?" In a flat voice, Harvey said, "Bobby," a man whom by then he regarded as "treasonous."

His career was essentially finished. But throughout his decline and fall at the CIA, Harvey continued to stay in touch with his old Mafia comrade-in-arms Johnny Rosselli. The two men were spotted together in Florida, Los Angeles, and Washington, D.C., conferring over their usual refreshments—martinis for the spy and Smirnoff on the rocks for the gangster. When Harvey retired from the agency and set up his own law firm in Washington, Rosselli dropped by to see his old friend and threw him some business. The retired spy refused to distance himself from the mobster, even under pressure from the agency. Bill Harvey never apologized for the odd relationship. "Regardless of how he may have made his living in the past," Harvey would later tell Senate investigators, Johnny Rosselli was a man of "integrity as far as I was concerned." The gangster was loyal and dependable "in his dealings with me," said Harvey. He had "a very high estimate" of the man.

President Kennedy's isolation within his own government was never so glaringly apparent as it was during the Cuban Missile Crisis. During the ExComm meetings (Executive Committee of the National Security Council) where Kennedy thrashed out his strategy, he could count on only his brother and McNamara for support. Bobby, who matured from a kneejerk hawk to a wise and restrained diplomat during the nerve-punishing crucible, played an especially critical role. "Thank God for Bobby," Dave Powers heard the president remark one morning as his brother strode into another tension-filled ExComm meeting. The humanity-threatening crisis forced the younger Kennedy to confront a fundamental question about the use of power in the nuclear age. "What, if any, circumstance or justification gives . . . any government the moral right to bring its people and possibly all people under the shadow of nuclear destruction?" he asked himself. As Schlesinger later observed, it was a question few statesmen ever raised and few philosophers answered.

Robert Kennedy was the key courier for his brother in the delicate back-channel negotiations that finally brought an end to the crisis, secretly meeting with Georgi Bolshakov until the Kennedys realized that their old Soviet chum had been used by Moscow to deceive them, and later Ambassador Anatoly Dobrynin. In his memoirs, Nikita Khrushchev offered a startling account of RFK's emotional conversations with Dobrynin, in which Kennedy stressed how fragile his brother's rule was becoming as the crisis dragged on. It was not the first time in the Kennedy presidency that Bobby had communicated this alarming message to the Russians. But in this high-stakes moment, Kennedy's plea struck Khrushchev as especially urgent.

After the attorney general paid an unofficial visit to the Soviet embassy one evening, Dobrynin reported to Moscow that "Robert Kennedy looked exhausted. One could see from his eyes that he had not slept for days. He himself said that he had not been home for six days and nights. 'The president is in a grave situation,' Robert Kennedy said, 'and he does not know how to get out of it. We are under very severe stress. In fact we are under pressure from our military to use force against Cuba. . . . President Kennedy implores Chairman Khrushchev to accept his offer and to take into consideration the peculiarities of the American system. Even though the president himself is very much against starting a war over Cuba, an irreversible chain of events could occur against his will. . . . If the situation continues much longer, the president is not sure that the military will not overthrow him and seize power. The American army could get out of control."

On another occasion, Khrushchev wrote, Bobby Kennedy "was almost crying" when he phoned Dobrynin. "I haven't seen my children for days now," he told the Soviet ambassador, "and the president hasn't seen his either. We're spending all day and night at the White House; I don't know how much longer we can hold out against our generals."

Kennedy loyalists like Schlesinger—who prefer to see the brothers' management of the crisis as certain and masterful, which in many respects it was—suggest that Bobby Kennedy's emotional pleas to the Soviets were a tactic to win leverage in the negotiations. President Kennedy was never afflicted by doubts when it came to standing up to the Pentagon, Schlesinger observed recently: "JFK had a great capacity to resist pressures from the military. He simply thought he was right. Lack of self-confidence was never one of Jack Kennedy's problems. We would've had nuclear war if Nixon had been president during the missile crisis. But Kennedy's war hero status allowed him to defy the Joint Chiefs. He dismissed them as a bunch of old men."

Still, as Schlesinger has acknowledged, Kennedy was not firmly in control of his own military. And the repeated references to coups and *Seven Days in May* scenarios that pop up in presidential transcripts and recollections about the administration make it plain that JFK himself, and his closest advisors, worried about the stability of the government.

So did Khrushchev. "For some time we had felt there was a danger that the president would lose control of his military," he later wrote, "and now he was admitting this to us himself." Moscow's fear that Kennedy might be toppled in a coup, Khrushchev suggested in his memoirs, led the Soviets to reach a settlement of the missile crisis with the president. "We could sense from the tone of the message that tension in the United States was indeed reaching a critical point."

Thirteen days after the crisis began, Khrushchev announced that he would withdraw the missiles from Cuba. The Soviet decision was heralded as a major U.S. victory, a dramatic demonstration of the power of American resolve. The Kennedys encouraged this media spin, though they had secretly made their own concessions to end the showdown, agreeing to quietly withdraw aging Jupiter missiles from U.S bases in Turkey and pledging not to invade Cuba. This latter concession was particularly critical from the Soviet point of view, since it was the military threat hanging over Cuba that had prompted Khrushchev to install the missiles. Washington officials would later insist this pledge was not binding because Castro refused to allow U.S. weapons inspections of Cuba to make sure the missiles were gone. But Kennedy and future presidents would nonetheless honor the no-invasion pledge. It essentially ensured the survival of the Cuban revolution, and though Castro did not see it that way at the time, Khrushchev correctly called it "a great victory" for the embattled island.

While the Kennedy media offensive successfully sold the story that "the other guy blinked," Washington hardliners saw the resolution of the crisis differently. A few days after Khrushchev's announcement, the president summoned the Joint Chiefs to the Oval Office to thank them for their role in the crisis, a particularly gracious gesture considering the friction between the commander-in-chief and his generals. But LeMay was in no mood to celebrate. "It's the greatest defeat in our history," he thundered at Kennedy. "We should invade today!" The anti-Kennedy rage was widespread among the upper ranks, where it was felt the president had flinched at the perfect opportunity to dismantle Cuba's Communist regime. "We had a chance to throw the Communists out of Cuba," a disgusted LeMay later fumed. "But the administration was scared to death [the Russians] might shoot a missile at us."

Daniel Ellsberg, the defense analyst who later became famous for leaking the Pentagon Papers, was consulting with Air Force generals and colonels on nuclear strategy when the missile crisis ended. He was struck by the "fury" within the Air Force after the Kennedy-Khrushchev settlement. "There was virtually a coup atmosphere in Pentagon circles," Ellsberg recalled. "Not that I had the fear there was about to be a coup—I just thought it was a mood of hatred and rage. The atmosphere was poisonous, poisonous."

The CIA also knew the missile crisis was a turning point on Cuba. When Kennedy gave Khrushchev "assurances against [the] invasion of Cuba," CIA official George McManus wrote in a memo on November 5, "Operation Mongoose died." Mongoose had always been more for show, McManus noted, a smoke and mirrors operation designed "to remove the political stain left on the president by the Bay of Pigs failure." But now, the CIA bleakly concluded, the Kennedy administration was dropping even the pretense of overthrowing Castro.

For those militants who were part of the massive juggernaut organized to destroy the Castro regime, the peaceful resolution of the missile crisis was a betrayal worse than the Bay of Pigs. They watched the U.S government go to the brink of launching a devastating assault on Cuba, only to see Kennedy nimbly sidestep the final reckoning at the last minute. It was the closest they would get to realizing their political dreams, and they had been crushed. "Talk about the word treason at the Bay of Pigs, this was even bigger for us, the people involved," said Rafael Quintero, who was one of the sixty commandos recruited by Harvey to parachute into Cuba during the missile crisis.

As the year 1962 came to an end, the world was in a safer orbit. Those thirteen sleepless days and nights had won John Kennedy his place of glory in history. "People no longer thought that world war between the Soviet Union and the United States was inevitable," Sorensen observed years later. The young president had navigated his way through the most dangerous shoals ever faced by an American leader, tacking just enough one way to avoid impeachment or a coup and sailing just enough the other way to avoid nuclear annihilation. Afterward, there was a shift in the world's mood, a hint of light through the iron clouds that had been darkening the planet since the start of the Cold War's long, deadly slog. Like men elated by a narrow escape from death, Kennedy and Khrushchev felt emboldened to pursue peace with a new vigor.

Kennedy and Khrushchev had drawn closer to each other during the thirteen-day ordeal, exchanging private letters and confidential messages. JFK was especially moved by one letter, a "cry from the heart," as one U.S. diplomat called it, in which Khrushchev pleaded that the Russian people were neither "barbarians" nor "lunatics" and wanted to live as much as the American people. Therefore it was up to Kennedy and him to stop tugging on the "knot of war" before it became so tight that neither man could untie it.

Khrushchev later said that he developed "a deep respect" for Kennedy during the crisis. "He didn't let himself become frightened, nor did he become reckless. . . . He showed real wisdom and statesmanship when he turned his back on right-wing forces in the United States who were trying to goad him into taking military action against Cuba."

There was more understanding than ever between the two leaders. But both men were increasingly estranged from their own governments. As Khrushchev had steered his country toward a peaceful way out of the crisis, his military advisors had "looked at me as though I was out of my mind or, what was worse, a traitor." But the Soviet leader had defiantly pursued his course. "What good would it have done me in the last hour of my life to know that though our great nation and the United States were in complete ruin, the national honor of the Soviet Union was intact?"

It was a strange and perilous turning point in the Cold War, a time when the leaders of the two nuclear powers found themselves out of step with their own national security bureaucracies. Khrushchev was acutely aware that Soviet political history was an epic of blood and treachery, of sudden, violent exits from the stage. But he was not the only superpower leader who feared for his own safety.

4

1963

A thunderous roar erupted from the stadium crowd as the glamorous president and first lady glided into the Orange Bowl in a gleaming white convertible. A sea of Cuban and American flags flapped wildly in the stands. John F. Kennedy strode briskly across the grass to the ranks of men in crisp khaki uniforms, greeting them and shaking their hands. Some of the men were on crutches, but they stood proudly erect in the dazzling Miami sunshine. It was Saturday morning, December 29, 1962. The men of Brigade 2506, survivors of the Bay of Pigs and Castro's prisons, were finally free and Kennedy was there to welcome them home. Several of his advisors had strongly warned the president against going to the Orange Bowl ceremony, including Kenny O'Donnell, who worried about the political fallout from what would certainly be an emotionally volatile event. "Don't go there," he told Kennedy, when the president phoned him from the family's Palm Beach mansion, where he was spending the Christmas holidays. "After what you've been through with Castro, you can't make an appearance in the Orange Bowl and pay a tribute to those rebels. It will look as though you're planning to back them in another invasion of Cuba." But Bobby—always more febrile on the subject of Cuba than Jack—convinced his brother to go. It turned out to be a disastrous decision.

When one of the Brigade leaders, Erneido Oliva, presented Kennedy with the rebels' flag, which they had hidden during their imprisonment, the normally reserved JFK suddenly lost his cool. "Commander, I can assure you," he declaimed in a rising voice, "that this flag will be returned to this Brigade in a free Havana."

The Brigade members, more than eleven hundred strong, instantly shot to their feet, cheering lustily. Shouts of "Guerra! Guerra!" and "Libertad! Libertad!" swept the stadium. Some rebels broke down in tears.

Kennedy's advisors were stunned. Goodwin, who had written the Orange Bowl speech, later said that JFK went "off script . . . that line about bringing back the flag to a free Cuba was not in the text. He was carried away by the moment." But a declassified CIA memo dated December 28, 1962, reveals that the dramatic flag exchange was carefully choreographed in advance by Bobby Kennedy and exile leaders. In any case, JFK's warlike cry was O'Donnell's worst fear come true. The president's eruption seemed to promise that the United States would back another invasion of the island. "Diplomatically, it was the worst possible gesture that a president of the United States could have made at that time," he later wrote.

JFK himself soon realized his mistake. A few days later, he met with reporters in his Palm Beach house to clarify his Cuba policy. His administration had no intention of supporting another rebel invasion or imposing a new regime on Cuba, Kennedy made clear, unless Castro committed his own dramatic act of aggression. Once again, the president had blown wind into the Cuban rebels' sails, only to quickly deflate their billowing hopes. It was the same ambivalent pattern that had characterized administration policy since the Bay of Pigs. The Kennedys would talk tough about the Castro regime and stoke Cuban exiles' passions, and then tug sharply backwards on the reins of war.

The Kennedy two-step on Cuba contained a certain political logic—it was intended to restrain Khrushchev and Castro's Latin American ambitions and defuse right-wing pressures at home, while stopping short of war. But it inflamed tempers in the Cuban exile community, where the Kennedy name became synonymous with betrayal. A violent rage began to fester in Miami's political tropics, a shadowy world where shifting alliances of exiles, gangsters, and spies plotted labyrinthine conspiracies and dreamed of revolutionary glory. During JFK's Orange Bowl appearance, a would-be assassin lurked in the crowd, carrying a duffel bag with a disassembled, scoped rifle. The Secret Service and Miami police were later tipped off about the suspect, who was described as a young Cuban male with a strong muscular build, but were unable to track him down.

By the summer of 1963, the whirl of intrigue in the anti-Castro underground was reaching a fever pitch. Confusion reigned as the Kennedys tried to impose control over the action-oriented Cuban exile groups like the Cuban Student Directorate (DRE) and Alpha 66, turning off and then on their raids against Cuba as it suited administration policy. The CIA claimed these anti-Castro groups were out of its control, but the rebels were heavily dependent on agency funding and it was never certain whether the groups' frequent defiance of Kennedy policy was in fact instigated by their spymasters in Langley and Miami.

The DRE was a particular favorite of the CIA. Founded in 1954 as a Catholic student group militantly opposed to the dictator Batista, it later shifted its underground operations against Castro, moving its headquarters to Miami in 1960. The group's most notorious exploit—a nighttime August 1962 raid when two of its speedboats opened fire on a beachfront Havana hotel in an assassination attempt on Castro—was explained away by the State Department as an act of freelance buccaneering that was executed without the government's knowledge or support. But, in fact, the daring raid had been carefully plotted at the CIA's JM/WAVE station in Miami.

These were strange days marked by the emergence of mysterious characters. In August 1963, the DRE became entangled with a puzzling young man named Lee Harvey Oswald. He presented himself to the group's New Orleans chapter as a sympathizer with the anti-Castro cause, but then created a spectacle by handing out pro-Castro leaflets and scuffling with DRE members in the street. Was the mysterious ex-Marine, who had defected to the Soviet Union and had then returned to the United States with surprising ease, a left-wing adventurer of some sort—or was he playing out some clandestine role with the CIA-backed DRE? Once again, the truth was murky.

The DRE was not the only Cuban exile group that crossed paths with Oswald that summer. According to Bay of Pigs veteran Angelo Murgado, he and a team of fellow Cuban exiles not only observed Oswald's suspicious activities in New Orleans in August 1963, they reported on him to Bobby Kennedy.

Murgado was aligned with the Cuban exile faction led by Manuel Artime, the Brigade's political leader. Like Murgado, Artime had fought briefly alongside Castro, but as a devout Jesuit-trained medical student, he had quickly grown alienated from Fidel's communistic initiatives, and he fled the island with the CIA's assistance. Artime was an artful operator. A conservative Catholic, he established himself as the CIA's "golden boy," building a close friendship with the reactionary agent Howard Hunt. But he uttered enough liberal pieties to also win the Kennedys' support, telling one fellow Brigade leader that "the only way we could control the Communists in Cuba was with love" and lecturing U.S. officials that the government that replaced Castro must embrace social reforms to avoid sliding backwards to the medieval cruelty of the Batista era. Artime enjoyed access to Bobby Kennedy, meeting with him in his Washington office, at Hickory Hill, and at the family's Palm Beach mansion. A secret Defense Department background sheet on the Brigade leader described him as "intelligent, aggressive, energetic, hotheaded and dogmatic"—a profile that also neatly fit the young attorney general. But RFK never fully trusted Artime, as he did Harry Ruiz Williams. He was too close to the CIA. And, in the end, Artime was all about Artime.

According to Murgado, he participated with Artime's group in CIA-backed raids on Cuba, contaminating sugar cane fields and livestock with toxins. Some Brigade veterans enlisted in the U.S. military, but Murgado chose to join the CIA's covert war on Havana. Trained in intelligence-gathering methods, he began to detect suspicious activity among some of his fellow exiles in the Miami Cuban community, a dangerous level of chatter aimed at President Kennedy. He took his concerns to Artime, who was initially reluctant to do anything about them for fear of betraying Cuban comrades. But, said Murgado, Artime finally agreed to set up a meeting with Bobby Kennedy where they could alert him to the threats against his brother.

Today, Angelo Murgado is a graying, stocky man in his mid-sixties with a voluble, colorful personality. The story he recounted was spiced with earthy vernacular and the rich tang of his Cuban accent. He spoke freely about his interactions with Bobby Kennedy, but abruptly closed the door on questions relating to fellow Cuban exiles and the assassination of JFK.

Murgado said that he and Artime first met with Bobby at the Kennedys' Mediterranean-style, red tile–roofed mansion on North Ocean Boulevard in Palm Beach. The only other person who attended this meeting was another Bay of Pigs veteran affiliated with Artime named Manuel Reboso. (Artime died of cancer in 1977 and Reboso reportedly left the United States and could not be located.) At their first meeting, Murgado said he was stunned to see the *Rex*, the flagship of the CIA's secret war on Cuba, anchored in the Atlantic waters outside the Kennedys' home. "We used to load speedboats on the *Rex*, get within three miles of Cuba and then put the speedboats with raiders in the water," Murgado told me. "I asked Manolo [Artime], 'What the hell is the *Rex* doing outside Bobby's home?'" To the exiles it was one more indication of how closely RFK was trying to hold the Cuba operation.

At the meeting, Murgado told the attorney general of his alarm about the growing anti-Kennedy passions in Cuban exile circles. "I told him that we have to keep a sharp look on these Cubans. I was afraid that one of our guys would go crazy. And he said, 'You mean to tell me that some heat could come from the [anti-Castro] Cubans? And I said, 'Yes. The same way that a lot of people are trying to hit Castro, there are a lot of people trying to hit the president of the United States. . . . We have a lot of crazy sons of bitches and they're willing to pull anything.'"

Artime tried to downplay the threat, according to Murgado, but Bobby fixed on it with a scorching intensity. "He was a fanatic kamikaze about covering his brother's ass. You could tell that was the main thing that drove him. Nothing would be able to get to the president if Bobby was standing in the middle. I wish I could have a brother who felt 20 percent of what Bobby felt about his brother. I would be the happiest cat in the world. That's why I loved him so much. Even today, even right now, talking to you about him, I get very emotional. Cubans are fucking highly emotional. We're talking about someone with a heck of a lot of conviction, and a heck of a pedigree."

Murgado said that Bobby asked him to keep an eye on alarming Cuban exile activity and report back to him. "We asked, 'Why don't you tell the president and use the CIA or FBI?' And he said, no, no, no—he didn't trust any of the agencies. And he didn't want to load his brother down with this situation. So we went outside the CIA and we did this on a personal basis with Bobby." The attorney general paid Murgado's expenses out of his own pocket, according to the Bay of Pigs veteran. "He would ask us, 'What did you guys spend?' And we'd say, '$86.05.'" Murgado could not produce any proof of these payments. But setting up private intelligence operations that he tightly controlled was a well-established practice of Bobby Kennedy's throughout his political career.

In the summer of 1963, Murgado's surveillance work led him to New Orleans, where he came across a curious gringo named Lee Harvey Oswald. Murgado and his compadres watched Oswald one day as he distributed his pro-Castro propaganda on the street. They later saw stacks of Oswald's pamphlets in the office of Carlos Bringuier, one of the local DRE delegates who had confronted Oswald in a raucous shouting match that New Orleans police would report appeared staged. (Bringuier was a vehemently anti-Kennedy exile leader who had vowed to defy the administration's crackdown on his group's Cuba raids.)

Murgado's team came to the conclusion that Oswald was an FBI informant. "He was a peon in a game run by what I call 'the invisible government.'" To shed light on Oswald's murky game, Murgado said they went so far as to contemplate eliminating him to see who would take his place in the clandestine operation. But they were warned by the FBI to leave town. "We were about to sanitize Oswald—you know, kill the motherfucker!—and the FBI stopped us."

After returning to Florida, Murgado met with Bobby again at his Palm Beach house, where he reported on his surveillance targets, including the mysterious Oswald. He showed Kennedy newspaper photos taken of Oswald handing out his pro-Castro pamphlets. He told the attorney general that as far as he could determine Oswald was tied to the FBI. Bobby had never heard of Oswald, according to Murgado, but he did not seem concerned about him because of his apparent government role and the conversation quickly moved on to other matters. Murgado would not think seriously about Oswald again until November 22.

Murgado is indisputably a colorful character. He said that he changed his name to Angelo Kennedy in the 1960s in memory of the fallen president he had served. He admitted that, after JFK's assassination, he and the rest of Manuel Artime's band became so cynical about the U.S. government that they continued to accept CIA subsidies to overthrow Castro while running contraband liquor, tobacco, and guns out of Nicaragua. (Despite reports to the contrary, he insisted they did not traffic in drugs.) After his career as a self-described "mercenary" came to an end, Murgado worked as a Miami building code inspector. In 1999 he was arrested for pocketing cash in return for zoning favors, later pleading guilty to the bribery charges. (He struck a deal with prosecutors that kept him out of jail.)

All this made Murgado a controversial figure in assassination circles when he suddenly popped into the spotlight in 2005 before just as quickly disappearing back into the shadows. But the anti-Castro underworld was never the exclusive domain of shining knights. It had more than its share of tarnished heroes and intrepid rogues, as does any exile community in the shadow of American empire that runs on broken dreams and ruthless ambitions. Despite his checkered past, Murgado's story about Oswald and RFK has not been refuted.

If Murgado's story is to be believed, it has historical significance. Assassination researchers have long speculated about whether Bobby Kennedy was already familiar with the name Oswald when it suddenly exploded on the American stage on the afternoon of November 22. Was this the man to whom Bobby was referring when he told anti-Castro leader Harry Ruiz Williams that afternoon, "One of your guys did it"? Did RFK immediately associate Oswald with the covert war against Castro because of Murgado's intelligence report? Or did he brush quickly past Oswald when Murgado brought him up because, as some researchers have suggested, he already connected the name to the administration's secret war? The Murgado story may provide an important key to Bobby's understanding of the crime. It could help explain why the president's brother cast his suspicions immediately towards the anti-Castro underworld on the afternoon of November 22.

AS THE DAYS DWINDLED down to November, the Kennedys struggled to control the sprawling operations related to Cuba. Some of these activities were sanctioned by the administration, some were not. Sometimes one arm of government subverted official government policy. Sometimes the Kennedys themselves seemed to contradict their own policy, ordering contingency plans for another Cuba invasion while opening a secret back channel to Castro to explore peace. And all the while, the CIA pursued its own agenda, with an unsavory cast of accomplices that included mobsters and the type of hot-headed exiles that gave Murgado nightmares. It was Bobby's job to stay on top of this sulfurous miasma—a task that took on a frantic urgency as the threats against his brother multiplied. Murgado shook his head in wonder at the daunting burdens that seemed piled on Bobby's shoulders. "He seemed to have twenty irons in the fire at any one time. I don't know how a human being has the capability to fight on all those fronts at the same time. It was beyond my comprehension."

In April 1963, two years after the Bay of Pigs, Cuban exiles' seething frustration with the Kennedy administration burst into public view when José Miró Cardona, a distinguished Havana law professor who had briefly served as Castro's first premier, angrily resigned as president of the Miami-based Cuban Revolutionary Council, the loose coalition that tied together anti-Castro rebel groups. Miró charged that the administration's crackdown on Cuba raiding expeditions following the missile crisis proved that JFK had cut a deal with Khrushchev to "coexist" with Castro. The Kennedys had sold out the liberation movement, he dramatically declared: "The struggle for Cuba is in the process of being liquidated by the [U.S.] government."

On April 5, days before issuing his heated denunciation of Kennedy policy, Miró had visited the attorney general in his office, where he found him surrounded by his rampant children and slobbering dog. The proud sixty-year-old jurist told RFK that his honor was at stake—he had stood with the Kennedys because the president had promised him the previous year that the United States would launch a military invasion of Cuba, but his brother had reneged on his pledge. In the history of Cuba, no man had ever been more "insulted" than he, Miró told Bobby. With his high forehead, oversized spectacles and graying mustache, Miró exuded a grave, professorial intensity. He spent four hours in the attorney general's office, sternly presenting his case. But Kennedy was unmoved. He told Miró that the exile groups could not continue launching raids on Cuba "right under our nose and without any control." To make matters worse, said the attorney general, the groups brayed loudly about their exploits at press conferences. As for a military invasion of the island, Bobby continued, Miro could forget it: "Doctor, we have told you from the very beginning that there is not going to be any invasion or military action."

Two days later, an outraged Miró reported back to his CIA contact about his meeting with Kennedy. After leaving the Justice Department, the exile leader told the CIA official, he vented so bitterly to a Kennedy aide that he doubted "the president and attorney general would ever forgive what [I] said." The administration tried to muzzle Miró before he could fire his anti-Kennedy blast in public. Before leaving Washington, the exile leader received a call from a White House aide who "threatened that [he] would be labeled a traitor," according to a report by the CIA, which closely monitored the political storm. But Miró proudly retorted that "he could never be a traitor to the United States because he was not a citizen of the United States and that his first and only loyalty was to Cuba."

Miró's public break with the administration opened the floodgates of anti-Kennedy fury in the Cuban exile world. Desmond FitzGerald, the CIA official who had replaced Bill Harvey as the agency's chief Cuba man, reported to Director McCone on April 11 that "there appears to be a movement within the Cuban Brigade to organize a formal request for the return of the Brigade flag, which was presented to President Kennedy at the Orange Bowl ceremony." This would have been a stinging political embarrassment for the administration, coming at a time when Republican critics like Richard Nixon were chiding the White House for its flip-flopping Cuba policy. Under President Kennedy, sniped Nixon that month, we had "pledged the Cuban exiles that their flag would fly in Havana, then pledged ourselves not to invade." The once and future Republican standard bearer announced that it was time "to do whatever is necessary to force the removal of the Soviet beachhead in Cuba."

Bobby Kennedy maneuvered on multiple fronts to defuse the Cuban political bombshell. He worked feverishly to make sure that Brigade veterans, whom he called the "cream of Cuba," were taken care of, pulling strings to find them jobs and legal help and even moving two exile leaders into his neighborhood, renting houses for them down the road from Hickory Hill. He smoothed the way for more than two hundred brigadistas to join the U.S. Army, where they underwent training at Fort Benning, Georgia for what they hoped would be a more successful assault on Cuba. He explored the possibility of creating a special Peace Corps unit for Cuban exiles and investigated how the government could channel others into law enforcement careers. Brigade family members thought of Bobby as their social worker. In June several exile wives wrote him to seek his help in getting their welfare payments continued.

JFK was cool and calculating in his handling of Cuba policy, greenlighting raids on the island when he wanted to send Moscow a warning signal and shutting them down when he wished to improve Soviet relations. He tended to regard Cuba as a sideshow, a pawn in the great superpower chess game. But Bobby took the Cuban exiles' passionate cause more to heart, developing particularly strong sympathies for the Brigade veterans. Always attracted to men whose courage had been tested in battle, RFK embraced Brigade heroes like Artime, Oliva, and Williams. He appalled snobbish CIA officials like FitzGerald, who viewed the Cuban exiles with contempt, by entertaining them at his home and inviting them on family skiing trips. "Yes, I do think he felt a sense of guilt or obligation to them," said John Nolan, Bobby's point man on Cuba. "It was not just for political reasons, though he was clearly not ignorant of that. I think he felt indebted to them. He made himself available to the Brigade leaders any place, any time, day or night."

While Bobby's sympathies were genuine, he was constantly on alert for how the Brigade's political disgruntlement could hurt his brother. In July, the attorney general's office was informed of a disturbing development in Brigade circles. According to a confidential State Department memo sent to Kennedy's office on July 19, 1963, two militant, far-right Bay of Pigs veterans identified only by their last names, "Llaca" and "Andreo," were plotting a bold gambit to compel the Kennedy administration to intervene in Cuba. (These were likely Enrique Orbiz Llaca and Jose Santos Andreu.) The two men were attempting to "organize an exile raid with the objective of seizing a town in Cuba, preferably one with a weak security set-up but a strong radio station, and start broadcasting appeals for U.S. Marines to come to the rescue." If the Kennedy administration did not respond by sending in military forces, the rebellion would be crushed, creating a political nightmare for the White House along the lines of Moscow's bloody repression of the 1956 Hungary uprising. This, the memo pointed out, seemed to be the real goal of the plotters. After the freedom fighters were martyred by Castro's forces, "Kennedy, having stood by doing nothing, would be open to the charge that he abandoned the rebels when he had a perfect pretext to act. Results: JFK would enter the lists in '64 a branded coward and traitor to his word."

The plot by Llaca and Andreu—who both boycotted the Orange Bowl ceremony in protest against JFK—was sinister enough on its own terms. But what made the scheme even more unsettling was the two exiles' source of support. Llaca and Andreu were "backed by the same Bircher-type Republicans who figure in the Goldwater movement," according to the State Department memo. These were the same well-heeled "movers and shakers," the memo further illuminated, who were also underwriting the Citizens Committee for a Free Cuba. This anti-Castro propaganda group was founded in 1962 by Paul Bethel, a former head of the U.S. Information Agency in Cuba who was close friends with David Atlee Phillips, the agency's disinformation chief for the Guatemala coup and the Bay of Pigs. Other prominent members of the group included the Kennedys' old bête noire, retired admiral Arleigh Burke; William Pawley, a right-wing Miami businessman deeply embedded in the intelligence world; CIA-linked Miami newspaper reporter Hal Hendrix; and the formidable Clare Boothe Luce—wife of Time-Life media baron Henry, journalist, playwright, former ambassador to Italy, and a woman who was also closely affiliated with the intelligence agency.

In other words, the Llaca-Andreu plot represented a perfect political storm for the Kennedys, a dangerous convergence of the brothers' most avid enemies—coming together from the worlds of anti-Castro extremism, right-wing wealth, and U.S. intelligence to shake the White House. There is no record of how Robert Kennedy responded to this threat. Apparently the two exiles never succeeded in taking control of a Cuban town. But this was not the only brazen enterprise that summer aimed at humiliating the Kennedys. Nor was it the only plot involving Pawley and the Luces.

ON A BRIGHT JUNE morning in 1963, the *Flying Tiger II*, a sixty-five-foot yacht owned by William Pawley, slipped away from its dock on fashionable Sunset Island in Miami's Biscayne Bay and headed for the Florida Straits. It was the beginning of a high-stakes expedition that its planners hoped would damage the Kennedy presidency so badly that voters would decide to terminate it in 1964. On board the boat was a collection of venomously anti-Kennedy characters who would later attract the attention of the Warren Commission and other assassination investigators. Among them were John Martino, a former security expert in the Havana casinos run by Santo Trafficante who later hooked up with Johnny Rosselli to assemble anti-Castro hit teams; William "Rip" Robertson, a veteran of the CIA's Guatemala and Bay of Pigs operations who had shifted his allegiance to the Somoza dictatorship in Nicaragua; and Eduardo Pérez, better known as Eddie Bayo, a heroic Castro guerrilla who had turned against the revolution, joining the violent exile band, Alpha 66, one of the more defiantly anti-Kennedy groups.

It was Bayo and Martino who had kicked off the expedition when they began circulating a letter that had supposedly been smuggled out of the anti-Castro underground in Cuba. The letter claimed that two Soviet colonels stationed in Cuba knew where Russian nuclear weapons were hidden on the island in violation of the Kennedy-Khrushchev missile crisis settlement. The two Russians wanted to defect and win asylum in America. Right-wing circles in the United States had been buzzing with rumors of Soviet treachery ever since the superpower leaders negotiated an end to the nuclear crisis. Kennedy was certain to run for reelection the next year on his act of diplomatic glory that pulled the world back from the precipice. If JFK's political enemies could produce shocking proof that he had been tricked by the Soviets, they were certain the American people would turn against his presidency.

As soon as Bayo and Martino began waving around the letter, the right-wing anti-Kennedy machinery churned into gear. After hearing the story, a conservative journalist named Nathaniel Weyl, who had testified against Alger Hiss in the early 1950s, phoned Jay Sourwine, chief counsel for the Senate Internal Security Committee. This was the notorious witch-hunting panel chaired by Senator James O. Eastland, the powerful Mississippi racist who had clashed swords with the Kennedys over Ole Miss. If the two Soviet defectors testified before Eastland's committee, the administration would be forced to defend itself in a decidedly hostile forum. But Weyl's friend, fellow conservative journalist Ralph de Toledano, had a better idea. After Toledano conferred with Barry Goldwater, it was decided that "the Russians would be immediately invited to Goldwater's ranch in Arizona," Weyl later recalled, "that [the senator] would call a press conference, enabling them to tell their story to the world, and that he would also give them enough money so they could start a new life in America."

The publicity stunt would be a stunning one-two punch against the Kennedy presidency. The media spectacle would not only humiliate Kennedy before the eyes of America and the world, it would rocket-propel the campaign of the man who was determined to replace him.

To mount the expedition, the plotters turned to a wealthy businessman with a mysterious background, Bill Pawley. The sixty-seven-year-old Pawley had led the kind of colorful life that was the stuff of "old-time dime novels," as his *New York Times* obituary later remarked, combining overseas financial exploits with cloak and dagger intrigue. After making a fortune in the Florida real-estate boom of the 1920s, Pawley developed airlines in Cuba and China and sold them to Pan American Airways. In China he helped organize the Flying Tigers, the legendary team of American pilots who fought against Japan before Pearl Harbor. After the war, he turned his attention to Latin America, buying Havana's bus system and serving as ambassador to Peru and Brazil. This was his official resume, but unofficially Pawley was part of the CIA's old boy network. A close friend of Allen Dulles, he used his diplomatic and business covers to carry out clandestine tasks on behalf of the agency, playing a key role in the Guatemala coup and talking President Eisenhower into approving the Bay of Pigs plan.

Pawley was an enthusiastic proponent of assassination as a foreign policy tool, especially when it came to Castro. He would pay any price if someone could just get close enough to eliminate the Cuban leader, Pawley mused aloud. When Eisenhower appointed him in 1954 to a CIA review panel known as the Doolittle Committee, Pawley made sure that its final report gave Dulles the full license the CIA director desired to fight the Cold War his way. In the face of "an implacable enemy," the report concluded, the United States had to learn how to fight even more viciously than its opponents. "There are no rules in such a game," the panel lectured, in language that reflected Pawley's black-and-white world view. The American people might not like it, but they would have to grow accustomed to "this fundamentally repugnant philosophy."

Vociferously anticommunist, Pawley railed against alleged Castro sympathizers in the State Department, whom he blamed for losing Cuba. He chaired the Nixon presidential campaign in Florida, after working closely with the vice president on the secret Cuba invasion plan. Following the Bay of Pigs, he blamed the disaster on President Kennedy's "betrayal."

Afterwards, Eisenhower arranged a meeting between JFK and Pawley to see if his old advisor's hawkish views might sway the young president. The encounter—which took place in the Oval Office on May 9, 1962—was a disaster. Kennedy began by asking Pawley what he should do about Cuba in the wake of the Bay of Pigs. "I think we have to drop ten thousand Marines in the environs of Havana," the brash tycoon replied. Pawley knew a sugar plantation on the outskirts of the city "that would be an excellent assembly area." Afterward, another thoughtful suggestion occurred to the old Cuba hand, which he sent off in a letter to the CIA: The president might want to consider invading the sovereign country on a day when the United Nations was conveniently not in session. Kennedy, Pawley later complained, gave him the brush-off, never again asking him for advice despite Eisenhower's repeated recommendations that he do so.

But Pawley continued to operate his own private war on the Castro regime. After the DRE's abortive attempt to blow up the Cuban leader at the seaside Hotel Icar, the millionaire soldier of fortune adopted the daring young militants. He even convinced some of his wealthy acquaintances to sponsor DRE speedboats, "much the way Catholic schoolchildren used to sponsor foreign orphans whom they called 'pagan babies,'" according to one mordant observation. One of these adoptive mothers was Clare Boothe Luce, who referred to the three-man crew she sponsored as "my young Cubans," bringing them to New York on several occasions to shower them with maternal affection. Luce later claimed that the earliest revelations about Russian missile sites in Cuba—which politically embarrassed the Kennedy administration when they were fed to Senator Kenneth Keating of New York—came from her young speedboat rebels. "The information they came out with was remarkably accurate," she later gushed proudly.

The swashbuckling Pawley brought the same entrepreneurial gusto to his covert operations that he did to his far-flung business ventures. He was willing to carry out the high-risk jobs that the CIA, with whom he maintained close ties, thought unwise to officially undertake. He was a wildcat operator with friends high up in "the Company" and he gave them a convenient cloak of deniability. At the CIA's request, he had tried to talk his old friend Fulgencio Batista into leaving his palace as Castro's guerrillas closed in on Havana, in a last-ditch effort to head off the revolution by replacing the despised despot with a military junta. He had also tried and failed to persuade the Dominican Republic's bloodthirsty Rafael Trujillo to do the same in a midnight meeting, shortly before CIA-armed assassins took the matter into their own hands. When Pawley got a phone call from Senator Eastland, asking him to organize the secret Cuban mission that JFK's enemies hoped would bring down his presidency, the millionaire told him he would have to check with the CIA, only agreeing to undertake the high-risk mission after getting agency approval and assistance.

Ever the hands-on operator, the dapper, bespectacled, gray-haired tycoon was on board the *Flying Tiger II* as it sailed into Cuban waters. He had frisked every man who boarded his yacht, to make sure there were no Castro double agents who might hijack the boat. Just to make sure, he had the three CIA men on board keep their machine guns trained on Bayo and his Cuban commandos during the trip.

Like the Llaca-Andréu affair, the Bayo-Pawley mission was a perfect convergence of Kennedy haters. In addition to the men from the anti-Kennedy trinity—the CIA, Mafia, and anti-Castro exile underworld—there were two representatives from the Luce press, a *Life* reporter named Richard Billings and a freelance photographer hired by the magazine (neither of whom were known for any anti-Kennedy fervor). Pawley was uncomfortable with the idea of having the media along for the ride, but his government superiors approved it. The expedition's sponsors thought a spread in the popular picture magazine would ensure maximum political impact. And according to Weyl, they were concerned that Kennedy might frustrate their plans by having the yacht intercepted and the Russian defectors whisked away "to an undisclosed location . . . on the grounds of national security." To make sure Kennedy did not spoil their plans, Weyl recalled, "The Russians would be photographed on board by a *Life* magazine camera man. Henry Luce would see that their revelations reached the world."

Sitting atop his Time-Life empire, Luce was one of the country's most powerful media moguls as well as one of the most influential proponents of American global power. The son of a Presbyterian missionary, Luce believed that the United States had a messianic duty to save the world through the spread of capitalism and American values. "The American mission is to make men free," he declared, a philosophy he avidly promoted in his publications during the Cold War, which he believed should be fought not just to contain communism but to eradicate it.

Despite their sharp differences over war and intervention, Luce and Joseph P. Kennedy shared a long-term friendship, "a good, tough one that both men enjoyed," in the words of Time-Life political correspondent Hugh Sidey. It was the comfortable, cigar-puffing accommodation of two powerful, self-made men and apparently it was undisturbed even when Kennedy slept with Clare during a visit the Luces made to the U.S. embassy in London before the war. Joe Kennedy went to Luce's Waldorf-Astoria apartment to watch JFK accept the Democratic nomination. "It was a memorable moment in my life," Luce later recalled. "It's quite a thing to sit with an old friend and watch his son accept the nomination for president of the United States."

Joe Kennedy failed to persuade Luce to support his son for president, but the Luces were both in attendance on the biting cold January afternoon when JFK was sworn in. The press lord was heartened to hear echoes of his own exuberant American theology in the new president's vow that we shall "oppose any foe to assure the survival and the success of liberty." His wife predicted that Kennedy would prove to be Eisenhower's equal as a leader, and, as a bonus, he was decidedly more pleasing to look at. "The Kennedy clan is fun to watch and very easy on the eyes," she noted.

But the Luces grew dismayed with Kennedy after the Bay of Pigs, using their magazine pulpit to routinely scold the administration for its perceived weaknesses. Turning her pen against the young president she had once favored, Clare lectured him that Cuba was an issue "not only of American prestige but of American survival." By spring 1963, relations between the Time-Life juggernaut and the Kennedy administration were so frayed that JFK tried to mend fences by inviting the Luces to lunch at the White House. The afternoon quickly went sour. Luce browbeat Kennedy at length about the urgency of going to war with Cuba until the president finally lost his patience. When JFK suggested that Luce was a "warmonger," the lunch came to an abrupt end. The Luces got to their feet before dessert was served and marched out of the White House.

Luce went directly back to the Time-Life headquarters in midtown Manhattan, where he convened a remarkable meeting of his top editorial command. He told his editors that if the Kennedy administration could not be counted on to confront the communist bastion in the Caribbean, Time-Life Inc. would. The corporation began channeling funds to anti-Castro raiders, paying them for exclusive stories on their escapades and even providing life insurance for the commandos and the correspondents who accompanied them. "With this directive," wryly remarked Warren Hinckle and William Turner, authors of *Deadly Secrets*, their revealing 1981 book on the secret war against Castro, "Luce, the great editorial innovator, invented a new form of journalism for which he is yet to be credited . . . paramilitary journalism." But the Bayo-Pawley raid, to which Henry Luce contributed $15,000 (with Pawley himself kicking in another $22,000), had an even more disturbing mission. It was designed not only to wound the Castro regime, but to bring down an American presidency. If his son ever "shows any signs of weakness in general toward the anti-Communist cause, or to put it more positively, any weakness in defending and advancing the cause of the free world," Luce had once warned his friend Joe Kennedy, "why then we'll certainly be against him." The press baron was now making good on his threat.

The fact that Luce, an old family friend, was willing to underwrite such an extraordinary assault on the Kennedy presidency shows how fractured the country's elite circles had become over JFK's policies. The young president's fitful attempts to break away from the country's Cold War regimen ignited a backlash from the old guard, who felt Kennedy was putting the country at risk.

Like the Llaca-Andreu enterprise, the Soviet defector caper also proved to be a bust. On the night of June 8, 1963, the *Flying Tiger II* dropped anchor ten miles off Cuba's Oriente province. The city of Baracoa was "lit up like a church" in the murky distance, Pawley later recalled. Bayo and a dozen or so commandos piled into a speedboat loaded with CIA-supplied weapons that was to zip them ashore. The raiding party was never heard from again. Pawley, who had pleaded with Bayo not to crowd the speedboat with so many men, concluded that the craft sank before it could reach land. Others thought the raiders were captured or killed by Castro's forces. In any case, no Russian defectors were ever spirited out of Cuba. Later, some researchers concluded that the defector story was a hoax created by Bayo and Martino to cover the smuggling of high-powered weapons into Cuba to assassinate Castro. But Weyl insisted to the end of his life this was not the case. When he was approached by the plotters "to find a yacht and meet the defectors at sea," the journalist noted in his 2003 memoir, they knew he did not "have any access to assault weapons." They came to Weyl for one simple reason: because he was part of the anti-Kennedy propaganda network. There was no doubt about the purpose of the failed mission, Weyl wrote: it was "to defeat Kennedy."

There is a curious end note to the William Pawley story. Years later, the elderly international adventurer came under the suspicion of Kennedy assassination investigators. Some conjectured that Pawley would have been precisely the type of independent operator to whom the CIA would have subcontracted the extremely delicate "executive action" assignment in Dallas. Gaeton Fonzi—a Florida-based investigator for the House Select Committee on Assassinations, which reopened the JFK case in the late 1970s—put Pawley high on his list of people he planned to interview for the congressional investigation. But on January 7, 1977, one week after Fonzi sent his target list to the committee, Pawley was found by police at his Sunset Island mansion, slumped in bed and dying of a bullet wound to the chest. Investigators, who said the eighty-year-old Pawley had been suffering from "nervous disorders," concluded the gunshot was self-inflicted. He left a brief handwritten note for his wife, Edna: "The pain is more than I can bear."

WHEN IT CAME TO Cuba, the Kennedys were masters of artifice. Their sleight of hand was designed to keep the Caribbean hot spot off the front pages and ensure that it would not burst into flames as an issue in the 1964 presidential race. Did they intend to invade Cuba again before the election to finally finish off Castro? The president vehemently denied it in public, but then quietly ordered the Pentagon and CIA to prepare for such an invasion. The Kennedys told one thing to certain Cuban exile leaders, and the opposite to others. Even decades later, conflicting testimony from administration insiders and a tortuous government documents trail led JFK researchers into confusing thickets and contrary conclusions.

In 2005, two independent researchers, Lamar Waldron and Thom Hartmann, published a massive, 904-page book in which they argued that President Kennedy was indeed preparing to topple Castro, even naming the date on which the plot was to take place—December 1, 1963. According to the authors, the Kennedys were scheming with a high Cuban official to stage a coup and then invade the island to guarantee the installation of a friendly Havana regime. The book, *Ultimate Sacrifice*, was based on seventeen years of exhaustive research and it contained many shiny nuggets that shed light on the administration's Cuba policy and the assassination of JFK. But its claim that Kennedy was backing a coup/invasion plan just days before his assassination was unconvincing.

The authors can be forgiven for their erroneous conclusion. Throughout 1963, Cuba policy was wrapped in fog and shadow. Confusion seemed to be the point. While Bobby Kennedy was telling José Miró Cardona that the administration had no intention of invading Cuba, he was filling Brigade leaders Manuel Artime, Erneido Oliva, and Harry Ruiz-Williams with hopes that they would soon be in Havana. He encouraged Artime to set up training camps in Nicaragua, with the support of the dictator Somoza; he let Oliva believe that he would spearhead the invasion, leading the unit of U.S.-trained Brigade veterans from Fort Benning; and he told Williams that he would head the post-Castro provisional government, arousing so much anticipation in his Cuban friend that he began naming his Cabinet ministers.

Bobby conferred frequently with exile leaders throughout 1963. They phoned the attorney general so often that in July he asked them to lay off "because of the increasing frequency of rumors linking him with certain enterprises against Cuba," according to a CIA memo. RFK met with Artime, Williams, and other rebels as late as November 17 and was scheduled to meet with them again on November 21 or 22, stated an Army memo.

In January 1963, soon after Artime and Oliva were released by Castro, Bobby invited them to Hickory Hill, where he assured the two exile leaders "that the administration was committed to the liberation of Cuba," Oliva recalled. "We felt that this time victory would be the outcome." That is why he continued to believe in the Kennedys, Oliva wrote years later in an article explaining why he had personally handed the Brigade's holy relic, its banner, to the president at the Orange Bowl. Oliva, a former Cuban army officer, was one of the heroes of the Bay of Pigs. He led the 370 men under his command with brilliance and courage, at one point grabbing a 57mm cannon and standing down a Stalin tank rumbling directly toward his company. After he was captured, Oliva was visited one night in prison by Che Guevara. Cuba's revolutionary leaders could not understand why Oliva, the Brigade's only black leader, had joined the Yankee assault on their brave new society. Why did he leave Cuba? Che asked him. Because it had been taken over by Communists. Was he afraid of being executed? "Yes," Oliva replied. He was "also afraid of the dentist when he took out four teeth."

Oliva never wavered in his belief that President Kennedy was going to invade Cuba, even after hearing about the deal JFK struck with Khrushchev after the missile crisis. "The president who failed us at the Bay of Pigs was truly and sincerely remorseful," Oliva wrote years later. Up until the day JFK died, Oliva insisted, the president was working "to rectify his historic mistake and to free Cuba."

Perhaps Bobby Kennedy believed this as well. Maybe he really imagined that glory would finally shine on these exile leaders, the ones whose courage and values he so admired. The administration was certainly preparing for such an eventuality throughout 1963. Military contingency plans on Cuba went flying back and forth between government offices, elaborate documents that war-gamed how Washington would respond in the unlikely event that this or that occurred in Cuba—or in Berlin or Laos, since JFK was always prepared to make a move on the island if the Soviets made a threatening move elsewhere on the superpower chess board.

But more likely, the deeply empathetic attorney general just could not bring himself to tell the truth to the rebel leaders: the Kennedys were simply not willing to go to war to liberate the island. Joseph Califano was in a prime position to witness Kennedy's tortured efforts to assuage Brigade veterans. As Army Secretary Cyrus Vance's young special assistant, he was put in charge of the effort to integrate the Bay of Pigs combatants into the U.S. military. Califano was disturbed by Kennedy's inability to level with the exiles. "Most troubling (and greatly complicating my job)," Califano wrote in his 2004 memoir, RFK "could not admit to them, and perhaps even to himself, that the United States was unlikely to support another invasion."

Kennedy came closest to the truth with Harry Williams when he told him there would come a time when their interests would diverge. There will be a point when "the national interests of the United States and the interests of you people of Cuba who want to go back will not be in accordance," the

exile leader later recalled Bobby cautioning him. It was Bobby's way of warning his friend, but it did nothing to dampen Williams's optimism about the
coming liberation of his homeland.

Robert McNamara confirmed to me that President Kennedy had no serious intention of invading Cuba after the missile crisis, despite the contingency plans and training operations conducted by the military. Did Kennedy
plan to invade Cuba in 1963? "No, absolutely not," McNamara replied.
"And we had given a guarantee to Cuba and the Soviets [after the missile
crisis] that we would not invade. Now that guarantee was associated with
Khrushchev's agreement to remove the missiles, which he did, but under
the supervision of the U.N., which he did not. Therefore, technically, we
maintained there was no guarantee. But as a matter of fact and practice,
there has been."

Dick Goodwin agreed that Kennedy had no desire to invade. Launching
such an operation in 1963, he insisted, would have been a reckless and
senseless act, the kind of folly Kennedy had no stomach for after weathering
two crises in two years on Cuba. "Why would he have done it? Castro was
really no threat to us anymore, once the Russians took their missiles out of
there. I think the idea of trying to overthrow Castro just before the [1964]
election is just absurd. Anything could go wrong. It would have been a
breathtaking risk and an unnecessary one."

Bobby Kennedy succeeded in keeping alive the hopes of Artime, Oliva,
and Williams, but the CIA looked suspiciously on all his conniving and
dreamweaving with the rebels. The attorney general continued to bark at
intelligence officials, demanding that they inflict more damage on the Castro
regime, but they knew the Kennedys were not serious about bringing it down.
Des FitzGerald—the handsome, tennis-playing, former Wall Street lawyer
who had taken the drunken, disheveled Bill Harvey's place—had a less poisoned relationship with RFK. But the brash attorney general still phoned
him at home, haranguing the autocratic CIA blueblood as if he were a towel
boy at the country club. FitzGerald's stepdaughter Barbara Lawrence still
vividly recalls the nerve-rattling weekend phone calls that her stepfather received from Bobby at their Virginia country home: "The phone would ring
and it would be Robert Kennedy. I have a picture in my mind of my stepfather coming out to this sort of enclosed porch area that we had down at
the farm, having just been on the phone with Bobby, and he was just pul-
sating."

FitzGerald raged against the way the president's brother was microman-
aging Cuba policy and running his own secret game with the exile leaders he

favored. And the CIA man dismissed the Kennedy brothers' actions on Cuba as showy gestures that would produce flying sparks and little else, comparing their theatrics to "tying a rock to a wire and throwing it across high-tension lines."

The Kennedys' most extravagant bit of anti-Castro showmanship in 1963 was their decision to help build Artime's private army. The brothers were prepared to generously support exile leaders like Artime as long as they agreed to set up their operations outside the United States, at a safe distance from Washington. The administration cut a deal with Nicaragua's Somoza, the tyrant whom JFK had gleefully disparaged to Dick Goodwin soon after taking office, that allowed Artime to set up his training camps there. Kennedy was undoubtedly aware of the irony—and cynicism—in doing business with one notorious dictator in order to get rid of another. But the brothers' main concern was to contain the Cuban exile problem, and offloading the militants to Central America had a certain political logic.

The CIA saw through the Kennedys' plan and grew irritated with agency golden boy Artime when he did not. The more affiliated Artime became with Bobby, the less the CIA trusted him. The overseers of the agency's Cuba operation stewed as they watched the administration funnel money and re-sources to Artime's private army, suspecting that the attorney general was once again trying to cut the agency out of the action. When Artime, a slight young man with thick, dark eyebrows and a rasping voice, visited Washing-ton, the CIA put him in a secure house in Maryland that was heavily bugged. The rebel leader's exotic girlfriend aroused agency suspicions—she was a bisexual who had shared the beds of Batista and a Venezuelan dictator and had undraped her body for pornographic display. Langley worried that Artime's colorful sex life could damage his reputation if somebody leaked the salacious details. And who did headquarters fear might do such a thing? Members of the CIA's own Cuba task force, who resented Artime's favored status with the Kennedys.

There was another sexual affair in Washington on which CIA officials were avidly eavesdropping that season. This one concerned another sexually adventurous leader whose political and personal lives were of great interest to the agency: the president of the United States.

ON FRIDAY MARCH 8, 1963, the president and first lady held what would be their last dinner dance in the White House. The guest of honor was World Bank president Eugene Black, but he was really just an excuse for the Ken-nedys to throw a big party for their friends. Not understanding his role as a convenient cover, Black invited so many people that the Kennedys had to tell their own crowd to eat somewhere else and show up for the dance at 10 p.m. This was when the fun really began. Ben Bradlee and his wife, Tony, whom Jackie once told were the first couple's best friends, came upon their hosts in the upstairs hall. "Oh, Tony, you look terrific," gushed the first lady in her breathy voice. "My bust is bigger than yours, but then so is my waist." The spirits were flowing that night—thirty-three bottles of champagne and six bottles of more bracing stuff had been consumed so far by the hundred-odd guests, JFK reported to his friends. (The president was keeping close tabs because he suspected the White House liquor stockpile was being raided.) Kennedy was in a festive mood. Looking around the candle-lit Blue Room, where the dance was being held, he surveyed the luxurious supply of glamorous female guests (who had been "imported from New York," Bradlee later observed) and sighed, "If you and I could only run wild, Benjy."

Of course, Kennedy *was* running wild, though Bradlee would later insist he never knew. And among his many secret lovers, perhaps the most intriguing was Mary Pinchot Meyer, the sister of Bradlee's wife. Meyer was a more formidable partner than any of the White House playmates JFK enjoyed and cast aside with careless, Rat Packlike ease. A free-spirited blonde in her early forties, she was the product of the eccentric, blue-blooded Pinchot family. After divorcing the brainy, intense CIA propaganda master Cord Meyer, she had refashioned herself as a Georgetown bohemian, setting herself up as a painter in a studio behind the Bradlees' N Street house.

Mary Meyer had arrived at the White House that chilly late-winter night in typically unconventional style, showing up among the sea of gowned women wearing a summer chiffon dress that had belonged to her great grandmother. At one point, Meyer disappeared long enough that people began asking, "Where's Mary?" recalled her sister, Tony Bradlee. Finally, her escort for the evening, Blair Clark, an old Harvard classmate of JFK, went searching for her. When he found his date, her face was flushed and the hem of her dress was wet. "She had been upstairs with Jack, and then she had gone walking out in the snow," remembered Clark. "So there I was, the 'beard' for Mary Meyer."

The president's mistress was upset and left early that night. Some speculated that Kennedy had tried to break off the relationship. Bobby, the constant watchman, arranged for her to get home, steering her toward a White House limousine and helping her into the back seat. Earlier that night, Adlai Stevenson, JFK's too gentle liberal adversary—a man used to receiving women's confidences, while his younger rival took other favors—was taken aback when Jackie, his dinner table partner, began sharing intimacies with him about her marriage. "I don't care how many girls" Jack has slept with, she told him, "as long as he knows it's wrong and I think he does now. Anyway that's all over, for the present."

But Kennedy's affair with Mary Meyer was not over. She continued to see the president at the White House, mostly when Jackie was absent, and at convenient events like Joe Alsop's Georgetown salons. (White House entry logs recorded thirteen visits by Meyer over a two-year period.) The relationship apparently started in late 1961 and lasted until the day Kennedy died.

They had met when they were both in prep school—the charming, scrawny Choate senior had cut in on her while she was dancing with her date, William Attwood (who would later serve Kennedy on an important diplomatic mission), at a school dance in 1935. They met again in San Francisco after the war, when she accompanied her new husband to the United Nations' founding conference, which Kennedy was covering for the Hearst papers. The two men took an instant dislike to each other, a mutual hostility that never faded away, even when the Meyers moved next door to Hickory Hill, which was first owned by Jack and his new bride before they sold it to Bobby and Ethel.

Cord and Mary Meyer were a tragic golden couple out of the pages of Fitzgerald. A tall, strikingly handsome aspiring poet at Yale, Cord's life had been shattered during World War II, when a grenade tumbled into his foxhole on Guam and exploded in his face. He survived, but his left eye was turned to "useless jelly," as he later wrote in "Waves of Darkness," a short story based on his war trauma that won the O. Henry Prize in 1946 for best first-published story. After he returned home from the war, his twin brother was killed in the savage fighting on Okinawa. Meyer vowed to honor those "who fell beside me" in the war and "to make the future for which they died an improvement upon the past."

Historical circumstances beyond his control had forced him to learn how "to destroy," the sensitive young Marine had written in a plaintive diary entry during the war. But now he threw himself into the peace movement, helping organize the American Veterans Committee, a liberal rival to the American Legion, and becoming president of the United World Federalists, which envisioned a globe under the calm and rational dominion of one government. With his curled locks and resplendent smile, a visage made only more endearing by his war-scarred face, Meyer became the heartthrob of liberal campus coeds, who stuck his picture on their dorm room walls. He was someone to watch, voted one of America's ten most outstanding young men by the

Jaycees. (A young congressman from California named Richard Nixon was another.) And then, in 1951, he suddenly disappeared from the public eye. He joined the CIA.

Meyer would always insist that he did not betray his youthful idealism by entering the Cold War's dark underworld. He simply decided that as long as the forces of Stalin and communist tyranny stood in the way, world peace was not possible. His crusade remained the same, he told friends, even if he now operated undercover. Meyer was part of a wave of idealistic, anticommunist liberals who enlisted in the CIA after the war. He would rise to become the number two man in the agency's clandestine operations—known by critics as "the department of dirty tricks." Along the way, he secretly financed labor unions, youth groups, writers' organizations, and literary journals—a mission he saw as building a bulwark against the global communist propaganda offensive. The once promising writer, who considered abandoning his intelligence career early on for a career in the book publishing industry, must have gained a private satisfaction from playing the role of secret patron. But when Meyer's covert philanthropy was exposed in the late 1960s, his detractors charged that it was an insidious corruption of the country's liberal infrastructure.

Cord Meyer never entirely let go of his youthful creative temperament. Even his close friendship with the CIA's gaunt master of black arts, the legendary James Jesus Angleton—the deeply spooky figure in charge of keeping the agency pure of communist infiltration—made sense in this context. They were the agency's bohemians. Before ascending to his exalted position within the espionage world, Angleton, like Meyer, had been a youthful Yale poet, editing a literary journal, *Furioso*, that published the work of e.e. cummings and Ezra Pound. The CIA's counterintelligence chief approached his work with artistic eccentricity, trying to divine the secret stratagems of world communism from within his sepulchral, heavily draped office at Langley. He would emerge at midday to take his customary lunch at the Rive Gauche in Georgetown, where he was often joined by Meyer, floating through the afternoon on a stream of cocktails, red wine, and cognac like a Left Bank libertine. It is not surprising that Meyer, with his visionary and artistic inclinations, would be drawn to Angleton. The half-Mexican, anglophilic spymaster was part of the WASPy CIA culture, and yet he hovered above it. With his sunken cheeks and burning eyes—a face his wife described as springing from El Greco—James Jesus Angleton seemed like the haunted prophet of American intelligence.

While Meyer insisted that he had not fundamentally changed, something hardened within him, particularly after he and other CIA liberals were targeted by a McCarthy witch hunt in 1953. Allen Dulles came to his defense, saving his job, and he was ushered through a bureaucratic cleansing process by Richard Helms. During his purgatory, Meyer found solace in reading Kafka's *The Trial*. Afterwards, observed Helms's biographer Thomas Powers, "a note of harshness and rigidity entered [Meyer's] political thinking; he became more Catholic than the Pope, and from a commitment to peace and international amity he gradually shifted toward a purely anti-communist fervor."

Meyer fell increasingly under the spell of the gloomy, Byzantine views of his CIA mentor Angleton. "Cord entered the agency as a fresh idealist and left a wizened tool of Angleton," observed Tom Braden, Meyer's boss early in his intelligence career. "Angleton was a master of the black arts. He bugged everything in town, including me. Whatever Angleton thought, Cord thought."

Mary Meyer was not happy with the way that the young world-reformer she had married was changing. At Georgetown parties Cord Meyer became a hectoring, self-righteous presence, sending other guests fleeing to far corners of the room. Even the passionately anticommunist saloniere, Joe Alsop, found him repellent, describing him as "a bright but rebarbative man with a certain genius for making enemies." The couple grew apart. Mary began startling other CIA wives with her own remarks, which were openly critical of the agency's ways. When their middle son, nine-year-old Michael, was fatally run down by a car on the curving road outside their McLean home in 1956, the marriage began to shatter. "Such a thing can either make or break a marriage," observed a friend of the couple. "In their case it broke it."

Mary divorced her husband two years later, a bitter break-up in which Cord "acted like a 17th century cuckold," according to another friend, denouncing her as "an unfit mother" and comparing her "to the whore of Babylon." She immediately took her life in the opposite direction of her ex-spouse's rigid world. Mary threw herself into the Washington art scene, starting an affair with a younger artist—the rising abstract painter Kenneth Noland—and embracing a pre-hippie lifestyle that included a wardrobe of peasant blouses and blue tights and a round of Reichian therapy, which promised enlightenment through orgasmic release.

It's easy to understand why JFK was entranced by her. The Mary Meyer who came into his life once again when he was in the White House was the same blonde beauty with sparkling green-blue eyes whom he had met when they were both teenagers. But now her mischievous and witty personality possessed something deeper, an earthy and wry wisdom that must have matched his own acute sense of life's absurd tragedy. Unlike most other women in Kennedy's circle, including the more refined Jackie, Mary could more than hold her own in a roomful of men. She got the joke. "When he was with her, the rest of the world could go to hell," observed Kennedy biographer Herbert Parmet.

While Kennedy enjoyed many erotic adventures in the White House, James Angleton observed, with Mary it was more serious. They "were in love," the espionage official stated with conviction. "They had something very important." Angleton's wife, Cicely, was a good friend of Mary. But his information did not come from her. The spook had more direct sources, he told reporters during a weirdly confessional period late in his life: he had bugged the rooms and telephones in Mary's Georgetown house. Angleton's voyeurism is disturbing on several levels. There is the alarming specter of a CIA official spying on a president's private life; there is the creepy perversity of peeping into the bedroom of a close friend's ex-wife. And there is another twist, which Ben Bradlee suggested to me: "I think [Angleton] was perhaps even in love with Mary. They were great, great friends, and he was a very odd stick, Jim."

The CIA official's snooping might have been prompted by a disturbing mix of illicit motives. But what is important here is what he found out about the relationship between Kennedy and Mary Meyer, in addition to its erotic details. Angleton would later tell reporters that the lovers experimented with drugs, smoking marijuana and dabbling with LSD. According to the spy, Meyer and Kennedy took one low dose of the hallucinogen, after which, he noted with a cringe-inducing delicacy, "they made love."

The CIA was no stranger to drug experimentation. The agency's secret funding of LSD research, on witting and unwitting subjects (including at least one person who committed suicide while on a bad trip), has been credited with spawning the 1960s counterculture, the ultimate in unintended consequences. The CIA's interest in psychedelic drugs lay in their possible military use; the agency was intrigued by LSD's potential to control enemy minds. But Mary Meyer had something very different in mind with her drug experimentation. She wanted to turn on the Washington power structure in the interests of world peace. And there was no better place to start this sweeping transformation of the capital's political consciousness than with her powerful lover.

When America's intelligence czars found out about Mary Meyer's daring acid experiment, it must have blown *their* minds. Here was one more stark piece of evidence that they were dealing with an aberrant presidency. Kennedy was not only injecting himself with bizarre drug cocktails to control his chronic back pain and to boost his energy; he had now fallen under the erotic sway of Cord Meyer's peculiar ex-wife, a woman who seemed increasingly unhinged to her old CIA friends after the death of her son and her divorce. And the president's unconventional mistress was engaged in a mind-control experiment aimed not at the Kremlin, but the White House.

To carry out her psychedelic peace mission, Meyer sought the help of Timothy Leary, the handsome Boston-Irish rogue who was becoming known as the country's leading proponent of LSD's revolutionary powers. When she showed up at his office at Harvard's Center for Personality Research in spring 1962, the forty-one-year-old psychology professor was still clinging to academic respectability. Except for his white tennis shoes, the bespectacled Leary still looked every inch the tweedy, tenure-track Ivy League scholar. But he had fallen under the watchful eye of the more conservative overseers at Harvard—an institution he respected but came to regard as a "finishing school for Fortune 500 executives"—as well as his drug research rivals at Langley. The attractive middle-aged woman who was leaning provocatively against his door that day was, like him, a renegade—in her case from the CIA world. And Leary—who collected women, celebrities, and trouble—was impressed by what he saw: "Good looking. Flamboyant eyebrows, piercing green-blue eyes, fine-boned face. Amused, arrogant, aristocratic."

As he would later write, she addressed him in a cool voice: "Dr. Leary, I've got to talk to you." She stepped presumptuously into his office and held out her hand. "I'm Mary Pinchot. I've come from Washington to discuss something very important. I want to learn how to run an LSD session."

Mary told Leary that she had a friend in Washington "who's a very important man." This man was intrigued by her LSD experiences and wanted to try the drug himself. She wanted Leary's advice about how to guide him through his psychedelic journey. Though Mary didn't name her powerful friend, she left little doubt who he was. "I've heard Allen Ginsberg on radio and TV shows saying that if Khrushchev and Kennedy would take LSD together they'd end world conflict," she told Leary. "Isn't that the idea—to get powerful men to turn on?"

Leary agreed it was worth a try. "Look at the world," he said. "Nuclear bombs proliferating. More and more countries run by military dictators. No political creativity. It's time to try something, anything new and promising."

Over the next year and a half, Mary continued to pop in and out of Leary's life, picking his brain about acid experimentation protocol and soliciting doses of the drug to take back to Washington. Ironically, Leary had known Cord, but not Mary, from their days in the American Veterans Committee, where the two young visionaries had clashed. Leary was surprised that someone as free-spirited as Mary could have been with a man whose personality he found implacable. "Mary was so much more outgoing and much more fun and much more lively [than Cord]—he was a monster machine," Leary later said.

In middle age, Mary's ex-husband was settling into a bitter acceptance of the world's grim realities. "You have to live with sorrow," Cord would tell a visitor to his Georgetown house, a domicile the visitor described as "remarkable for its museum-like neatness." Meyer was sitting on his sofa, cleaning his pipe. "What was Carlyle's remark? I think it was Carlyle," he mused aloud. "Somebody told him, 'I accept the universe,' and he answered, 'You damn well better.'"

But Mary Meyer did not accept the universe. She still burned with the utopian fever of her and Cord's visionary youth. She would use the transcendent power of sex and drugs—the magical charms that the emerging sixties generation thought could change the world—to enchant the Washington power structure.

Even the evangelistic Leary found Mary's ambition "scary." One can only imagine how alarming it was to the intelligence officials who were eavesdropping on Mary and her affair with the president.

In winter 1963, Mary asked to see Leary again, meeting him in her room at Boston's Ritz-Carlton Hotel. A visibly tense Mary told the acid guru that her Washington drug experiments were still proceeding smoothly, but that her affair had been "exposed publicly." A friend of hers, she said, "got drunk and told a room full of reporters about my boyfriend." She was apparently referring here to the notorious incident in January 1963 when Phil Graham, the increasingly erratic publisher of the *Washington Post* who would later commit suicide, grabbed the microphone at a newspaper industry conference in the Biltmore Hotel in Phoenix and delivered a disjointed harangue during which he exposed the affair between JFK and the president's "favorite" mistress, Mary Meyer. (Kennedy promptly dispatched an Air Force plane with Graham's psychiatrist on board to pick up the publisher, who was tranquilized and hospitalized for several weeks.) Graham's bombshell was covered up, Mary told Leary. "I've seen it a hundred times in media politics," she said. "The manipulation of news, cover-ups, misinformation, dirty tricks."

The last time Leary saw Mary, he recalled, she was deeply distraught. She phoned him at the Millbrook estate in upstate New York, where he had moved his research after leaving Harvard, and asked him to pick her up in the local village. As they drove through the splendor of the autumn country-side, where the trees glowed with what Leary described as a "Technicolor" intensity, Mary told him that her Washington drug experiment had come crashing down. "It was all going so well. We had eight intelligent women turning on the most powerful men in Washington. And then we got found out. I was such a fool. I made a mistake in recruitment. A wife snitched on us. I'm scared." Mary burst into tears. She told the drug researcher he must be very careful now. "I'm afraid for you. I'm afraid for all of us." Leary thought she was being paranoid. He reached over to stroke her hair. But her alarm began to seep into him. If she ever showed up at the estate, Mary asked him, could she hide out there for awhile? Leary assured her that she could. Then she bid farewell to him. Leary never heard from Mary Meyer again.

In 1965, after returning from an around-the-world trip, Leary tried to track down his old friend. Remembering that Mary was a Vassar graduate, he called the alumni office to find her whereabouts. The secretary who cheerily answered the phone grew somber when Leary gave her Mary's name. "I'm sorry to say that she is, ah, deceased," she told Leary. "Sometime last fall, I believe." Digging frantically through old *New York Times* clippings he got from a contact at the newspaper, Leary began sobbing as he found out what happened. The previous October, while taking an afternoon walk along the old Chesapeake and Ohio Canal in Georgetown, Mary had been shot twice, once in the head and once through the heart. There was no evidence that Mary, who left her purse at home, had been robbed or sexually assaulted. A suspect had been arrested—a twenty-five-year-old African-American day laborer named Ray Crump Jr. But Crump was later acquitted of the crime and it was never solved.

The murder of Mary Meyer would become one of the more baffling and bizarre subplots in the Kennedy drama. Assassination researchers have pored over accounts of the crime, seeking possible links between the murders of the two secret lovers. The spectral appearance of James Angleton in the Meyer murder story greatly contributed to the fog of suspicion floating around the case.

Following the murder, Ben and Tony Bradlee got an urgent overseas phone call from Mary's friend Anne Truitt, who told them Mary had kept a diary containing sensitive information. Mary had requested that it be destroyed if anything ever happened to her, said her friend. When the Bradlees went looking for the journal, first at Mary's house and then at her studio, they found a sheepish Angleton apparently in hot pursuit of the revealing notebook. The first time, the spy—known as "The Locksmith" in CIA circles—was already inside Mary's house, rummaging through her belongings. On the second occasion, the Bradlees found him trying to pick the lock on Mary's studio. The spook slinked off, with barely a word. The story grew even weirder the next day when Tony Bradlee, after finding the diary and reading about her sister's affair with JFK, handed it over to Angleton so he could safely dispose of it—as if the CIA was the only power on earth capable of destroying a document. But Angleton did not do away with the diary, and when he admitted this to Tony years later, she demanded that he return it. Later, she claimed, she burned it in her fireplace. "None of us has any idea what Angleton did with the diary while it was in his possession, nor why he failed to follow Mary and Tony's instructions," Bradlee wrote in his 1995 memoir, an account that left more unexplained than answered.

Bradlee was still vague about the Angleton incident in an interview for this book, ascribing the CIA official's illegal entry and attempted break-in to his eccentricity and his possible amorous obsession with Mary. "I thought Jim was just like a lot of men, who had a crush on Mary," the legendary former *Washington Post* editor said, sitting in his office at the newspaper, where he occupies emeritus status. "Although the idea of him as a lover just stretches my imagination, especially for Mary, because she was an extremely attractive woman. And he was so weird! He looked odd, he was off in the clouds somewhere. He was always mulling over some conspiracy when he wasn't working on his orchids. It was hard to have a conversation with him. I bet there are still twelve copies of Mary's diary in the CIA somewhere." Bradlee denied that the diary contained any secrets about the CIA or other revealing information, beyond the passages about her romance with JFK. "I thought about this when I wrote my book. I don't think there's anything hidden away in my psyche that I haven't come clean on."

At Mary's funeral in the National Cathedral, the solemn, gray stone fortress overlooking Georgetown, Cord Meyer wept uncontrollably. He was consoled during the ceremony by his two closest friends in the CIA, Richard Helms and James Angleton, who sat on either side of him in the pew. A memo written at the time by William Sullivan, the number three man in the FBI, revealed that Helms and Angleton "have been very much involved with matters pertaining to the death and funeral of Mrs. Mary Pinchot Meyer." In an interview years later with Mary Meyer's biographer, Nina Burleigh, Helms could not recall just what it was about Mary's passing that had required so much of his attention.

Friends of Mary told Burleigh they felt her killing was in some way connected to her relationship with Kennedy, but they had no proof. During the final months of her life, reported her biographer, Mary seemed to be the target of a disturbing surveillance, with her Georgetown house broken into on more than one occasion, including once when she and her two sons were sleeping upstairs. "What *are* they looking for in my house?" she was heard to plaintively ask.

In his 2003 book about Washington, D.C.'s intrigue-filled society world, *The Georgetown Ladies' Social Club,* author C. David Heymann told a remarkable story about visiting a fading Cord Meyer in his Washington nursing home, just six weeks before his death. Who did he think had killed his ex-wife, Heymann asked Meyer? "The same sons of bitches that killed John F. Kennedy," the mortally ill CIA man reportedly "hissed." But the credibility of some of the author's earlier work had been challenged, and his story about Meyer's final testament received scant attention. The truth about Mary Meyer's murder would remain clouded in the same mists that enveloped the demise of her lover.

What is clear is that Mary Meyer's personal life was of intense interest to the CIA, before and after her death. Angleton was fully aware of the ecstatic sway she had over the president. And he believed that she actually influenced administration policy, nudging it in a more dovish direction. In some circles, this made her a figure to watch closely. "With her combination of access and disregard for convention, Mary Meyer became a female type, the classic dangerous woman," wrote Burleigh.

Mary Meyer was John Kennedy's link to a post–Cold War future that neither of them would live to see. She connected him to the phantasmagoria of sex, drugs, and mind exploration that would light up the late sixties. The tightly controlled JFK only allowed himself to sample these pleasures, but that was certainly enough to send a shiver of fear through the national security command. CIA officials were deeply involved in drug research aimed at rendering an enemy harmless. They worried that Kennedy was being similarly disarmed.

A friend of Mary later told the story of the time she brought a half dozen marijuana joints to the White House. Kennedy smoked three of them before they finally took effect. As he closed his eyes and let the reefer carry him away, he mused dreamily, "Suppose the Russians did something now." The Cold Warriors with a window on the president's extracurricular exploits no doubt wondered the same.

• • •

AS AN ORATOR, JOHN Kennedy is known primarily for two speeches—his anthemic "ask not" inaugural address in which he challenged Americans to new heights of national purpose and his dramatic June 1963 "Ich bin ein Berliner" speech in which he confronted a communist system that was forced to wall in its own people. Video images from these two ringing addresses have become enshrined in the national memory through endless replay.

But Kennedy's greatest moment as the voice of his nation came two weeks before his tumultuous Berlin appearance, on the morning of June 10, when he delivered the commencement address at American University in Washington. The president's Peace Speech, as it became known, caused little stir at the time. But it carried one of the most radical messages ever delivered by an American president: it is possible to live peacefully in the world with even the most formidable enemies. This was a concept with profound implications during the deep freeze of the Cold War.

President Kennedy delivered his visionary remarks from a stage wrapped in red, white, and blue bunting that had been erected on the university's Reeves Athletic Field. Looking out at the crowd assembled under a bright, cloudless sky, Kennedy made history by proposing an end to the Cold War. It was time for Americans and Russians alike to break free of militarism's cold grip, he said. The public had been indoctrinated to believe that peace was impossible, he told the audience, but that was not true. "Our problems are man-made—therefore, they can be solved by man." Political speeches during the Cold War era typically vilified the Communist enemy and glorified the American way of life. But, remarkably, the American University speech challenged Americans, as well as Russians, to rethink their attitudes toward peace and each other. "Every graduate of this school, every thoughtful citizen who despairs of war and wishes to bring peace, should begin by looking inward—by examining his own attitude toward the possibilities of peace, toward the Soviet Union, toward the course of the Cold War and toward freedom and peace here at home," declared Kennedy. His call for national introspection about the defining conflict of the day marked a sharp break from the period's triumphalist rhetoric.

Kennedy then did something equally startling—he sought to humanize the Russians, our Cold War bogeyman. Americans might "find communism profoundly repugnant . . . but no government or social system is so evil that its people must be considered as lacking in virtue." With this ice-breaking statement, Kennedy launched into a passage of such sweeping eloquence and empathy for the Russian people—the enemy that a generation of Americans had been taught to fear and hate—that it still has the power to inspire. This passage ended with poetic cadence: "We all inhabit this small planet. We all breathe the same air. We all cherish our children's future. And we are all mortal."

The president concluded his speech by vowing that America would "never start a war. We do not want a war. . . . This generation of Americans has already had enough—more than enough—of war and hate and oppression." It was a stark rejoinder to the hard-liners in his administration who were pushing for a preemptive military solution to the Cold War.

The Peace Speech received a muted reaction. After one week, it elicited only 896 letters from the public. (A bill on the cost of freight brought over 28,000 into the White House during the same week.) Goldwater and other Capitol Hill Republicans paid scant attention, succinctly—and predictably—brushing aside the speech's "soft stand." Moscow signaled its pleasure with the speech by allowing the Voice of America to broadcast it into Russia and by reprinting the full text in *Izvestia*. But eleven days after the speech, Khrushchev used it to win points with his Central Committee, strangely mirroring Kennedy's domestic enemies by belittling the president's call for peace as an expression of weakness. (Privately, however, the Soviet leader called it "the best speech by any president since Roosevelt.")

The Peace Speech has grown more lustrous with time, with historian Michael Beschloss anointing "the lyrical address" as "easily the best speech of Kennedy's life." This estimation is shared by surviving dignitaries of the administration. At a "Recollecting JFK" forum at the Kennedy Library in October 2003, Robert McNamara grew euphoric when the speech was evoked. "Let me comment on this speech," he told the audience. "Most of you, probably all of you, have never read it, never heard it. Please read it. It's one of the great documents of the twentieth century."

In a recent interview, the former defense secretary elaborated on the speech's historic significance. "The American University speech laid out exactly what Kennedy's intentions were," McNamara told me in a voice gravelly with age. "If he had lived, the world would have been different, I feel quite confident of that. Whether we would have had détente sooner, I'm not sure. But it would have been a less dangerous world, I'm certain of that."

Kennedy's landmark speech was nothing less than an attempt to end the nuclear stare-down between the two superpowers that had held the world in its thrall for over a decade, ever since the Soviets had begun their own atom bomb testing in 1949. In recent years, it has become fashionable for conservatives and hawkish liberals to claim Kennedy as one of their own. But

Kennedy's impassioned American University address clearly demonstrated he was no longer a Cold War liberal. "No, Kennedy was not a hawkish Cold Warrior," Ted Sorensen remarked years later. He was a pragmatist, said Sorensen, who was deeply aware of how human folly led to tragedy. And he was determined to demilitarize relations between the nuclear powers before catastrophe could strike.

Kennedy, a realist, understood that the journey to end the Cold War would stretch "a thousand miles," but he was determined to take the first step. Though he was under no illusions about the Soviet system and its ambitions, he yearned to break free from the fevered spell of anticommunist demonology. Ever since World War II, America had been dominated by "a permanent war establishment," in the words of maverick sociologist C. Wright Mills. This war establishment—which included the country's militarized executive branch and corporate sector as well as the defense colossus headquartered in the Pentagon—justified its existence by creating a constant, free-floating state of anxiety and animosity. "For the first time in American history, men in authority are talking about an 'emergency' without a foreseeable end," Mills wrote in his durable 1956 work, *The Power Elite*. "Such men as these are crackpot realists: in the name of realism they have constructed a paranoid reality all their own." But the Kennedy presidency tried to secede from this reign of fear. The boldness of this attempt has not been fully appreciated by historians.

The Peace Speech was the masterpiece of the Kennedy-Sorensen creative partnership. Here was the heart of the administration laid bare. The speech was born of JFK's deepest aspirations as a world leader—and his sharp sense of political timing. But the soaring, utopian language was Sorensen. Presidential historian James MacGregor Burns has suggested that leaders rarely achieve greatness without taking their nations to war. But what the American University address eloquently argued was that great leadership in the nuclear age came from avoiding war—a spasmodic exchange of fire and poison that would mean "all we have built, all we have worked for, would be destroyed in the first twenty-four hours," as Kennedy told the audience that morning.

By the spring of 1963, JFK realized that the window for peaceful progress that had opened after the Cuban Missile Crisis was quickly closing, as hardliners in Washington and Moscow reasserted their control. When Pope John XXIII, who had been deeply alarmed by how close humanity had come to extinction, enlisted Norman Cousins—editor of the liberal magazine *Saturday Review* and a longtime peace activist—to serve as an informal emissary between the Vatican, Washington, and Moscow, Kennedy readily agreed to discuss strategy with the amateur diplomat. When Cousins returned from a trip to Russia—where Khrushchev had entertained the emissary at his Black Sea retreat, plying him with rounds of vodka and playing badminton with Cousins's two teenage daughters—JFK eagerly debriefed him.

The president greeted Cousins in the Oval Office, where the citizen-diplomat sat on a large sofa as Kennedy grilled him. Outside, on the White House lawn, busloads of high school musicians began noisily warming up for a musicale that had been organized by the first lady. "This is Jackie's department, but Jackie is away," the president apologetically told his visitor. True to Kennedy fashion, he first wanted to know all the personal details about Cousins's meeting with Khrushchev. How plush was his country estate? How energetically could the portly Soviet leader wield his racket during badminton? The magazine editor assured Kennedy that his Russian counterpart—despite his age, physique, and considerable intake of vodka at lunch—had acquitted himself rather well in the game, which left him "neither winded nor flushed."

Then the discussion moved on to more serious matters. Cousins told JFK that Khrushchev was eager for a new chapter in U.S.-Soviet relations. He agreed with Kennedy that the two nations could begin by signing a ban on the nuclear arms testing that was dusting the earth with radioactive poison. "You want me to accept President Kennedy's good faith?" Khrushchev exclaimed at one point, sitting in a chair facing Cousins in his dacha's glass-enclosed terrace. "All right, I accept President Kennedy's good faith. . . . You want me to set all misunderstandings aside and make a fresh start? All right, I agree to make a fresh start."

As Cousins reported on his conversation with the Soviet leader, Kennedy sat quietly in his rocking chair with his eyes fixed intently on the peace courier. While Khrushchev clearly desired diplomatic progress, Cousins continued, the Russian leader also stressed that he was under intense political pressure to maintain a militant Cold War stance. This prompted a revealing reply from Kennedy.

"One of the ironic things about this entire situation is that Mr. Khrushchev and I occupy approximately the same political positions inside our governments," the president observed. "He would like to prevent a nuclear war but is under severe pressure from his hard-line crowd, which interprets every move in that direction as appeasement. I've got similar problems. Meanwhile, the lack of progress in reaching agreements between our two countries gives strength to the hard-line boys in both, with the result that the hard-liners in the Soviet Union and the United States feed on one another, each using the actions of the other to justify its own position."

When Cousins suggested that Kennedy blast through the impasse with "a breathtaking new approach, calling for an end to the Cold War and a fresh start in American-Russian relationships," Kennedy was intrigued. He asked Cousins to confer on the speech with Ted Sorensen, a fellow Unitarian with whom he was friendly.

The idea of two anti-war Unitarians working on a presidential speech to redefine U.S.-Soviet relations would surely have been deeply disturbing to national security apparatchiks, as Kennedy knew. The president instructed Sorensen to keep his working draft under tight wraps and not circulate it as usual to the Pentagon, CIA, and State Department for comments. Like Sorensen, Cousins's pacifist inclinations were well-known. He was a co-founder of the Committee for a Sane Nuclear Policy (SANE) and had widely publicized the horrors of nuclear war by bringing twenty-four young Japanese women who had survived the bombing of Hiroshima to the U.S. for medical treatment. The final draft of the American University speech reflected both men's Unitarian philosophy.

"The language in the speech is Unitarian language—lines like man's problems are made by men and can be solved by men," said Sorensen, sitting in his New York law office. Sorensen has made a longtime practice of not claiming authorship of Kennedy's speeches, but his creative pride in the American University address is obvious. "I don't want to take anything away from JFK, but that speech represents my personal philosophy more than anything else out there in the world today. It's the one I'm proudest of."

There was a dramatic international backdrop to Kennedy's speech that morning. On that same day, a Chinese delegation was arriving in Moscow to deliver a harsh demand to the Kremlin: the wobbly Khrushchev must stop begging for peace with the untrustworthy Americans and adopt a tougher line. Faced with an increasingly bitter Sino-Soviet split, and struggling to maintain its leadership of world communism, would Moscow seek a pact with China or the United States?

When Kennedy, towards the end of his speech, announced that high-level talks would soon begin in Moscow to reach a comprehensive nuclear test-ban treaty and vowed that in the meantime the United States would not conduct nuclear tests in the atmosphere as long as other nations did not, it was "the breathtaking" bid to blow through the diplomatic bottleneck that Cousins had urged the president to make. It worked. Less than a month later, Kennedy and Khrushchev signed the Limited Test Ban Treaty, which as

Sorensen proudly observed, was the first major arms control agreement "in that terrible era known as the nuclear age"—and the first significant diplomatic thaw in the Cold War. It was the American University speech that released these doves into the air. But it took all of Kennedy's political determination and wiles to capitalize on the speech's momentum and secure the treaty.

As Kennedy emissary Averill Harriman was negotiating the treaty in Moscow that July, it became clear that the original goal of banning underground tests as well as atmospheric tests would be impossible. Administration officials knew that they could not succeed in pushing a comprehensive test ban through the Senate unless the Soviets agreed to demonstrate they were not cheating on the hard-to-detect underground tests by allowing numerous on-site inspections. But the Soviets insisted that inspections of their weapons facilities be strictly limited, out of fear that NATO spies would exploit them for their own purposes. The compromise was a Limited Test Ban Treaty that focused solely on atmospheric tests, which were much easier to monitor. Though the treaty was not as far-reaching as originally hoped, it was still a momentous occasion when it was initialed by the negotiators on the evening of July 25. The night before, Khrushchev had invited Harriman to share his box at the closing ceremony of a U.S.-U.S.S.R. track and field meet. As the crowd cheered the two men, the wealthy, immaculately groomed Harriman looked over at his squat, bald host—a man with the rustic manners and raw emotions of his peasant roots. He saw that Khrushchev's eyes were filled with tears.

Kennedy knew that even a limited test ban would face stiff political opposition at home. Treaty opponents were initially caught off guard by the speed at which the administration moved the agreement along. But as soon as it was initialed, they swung into action. The president faced his usual band of antagonists. The principal spokesman for the opposition was Dr. Edward Teller, the Hungarian-born physicist known as "the father of the hydrogen bomb" who, with his clotted Eastern European accent and Groucho Marx eyebrows, had established himself as one of the more flamboyant advocates of American militarism. Teller drew on his expertise to downplay the dangers of atmospheric testing, but as Kennedy knew from his own scientific advisors, radioactive strontium was already being detected in the bones and teeth of American children. Behind Teller was the lobbying might of the military-industrial complex, the well-financed network of weapon-makers trade groups, retired military officers associations, and brigades of flag-waving superpatriots that regularly directed fire at Kennedy policies. But what worried the president most were the secret machinations within his own government.

Carl Kaysen, a deputy national security advisor for Kennedy, recently recalled one of the Pentagon's more disturbing maneuvers during the test ban drama. It occurred while the administration was still considering a full ban, including controls on underground testing. "There was a complicated argument within the government over whether you could detect underground tests," said Kaysen. "I tended to be the Bundy staff member who interacted with the scientific crowd on nuclear matters. At one point, we needed to confer with a man named Carl Romney, who was in charge of the Air Force operation that monitored underground testing. He ran these seismic networks we had in Iran and Pakistan, which tried to tune in on underground Russian explosions. So I tried to get a hold of Romney for the White House. But the Air Force hid him! They literally hid him! This was about as near as you could come to mutiny. After a lot of back and forth, he finally got dug out of whatever hole he was hiding in."

Kennedy was further enraged when he learned that the CIA was trying to sabotage the treaty in the Senate, where the agreement faced a tough ratification process. The president discovered that McCone was dispatching nuclear experts from the agency to persuade senators that Moscow could not be trusted to abide by the treaty. JFK's relationship with the CIA director had never recovered from the missile crisis, when McCone made a point of spreading the word throughout Washington that he had seen the Russian missiles coming long before Kennedy finally acted. Despite his efforts to cultivate Bobby, McCone was wearing thin on the president's brother, too. The attorney general worried that with the 1964 election approaching, Mc-Cone—a lifelong Republican—might be a disloyal fifth column within the administration.

Dean Rusk cautioned Kennedy to put off addressing the nation about the treaty until he had consulted with key senators. But Kennedy knew that the best way to sway the Senate was by mobilizing the public. The president went before the TV cameras on the night of July 26, one day after the treaty was initialed. "I speak to you tonight in a spirit of hope," he told the nation-wide audience. The United States and Soviet Union were caught in the coils of an endless and increasingly ominous arms race, said Kennedy. But "yester-day a shaft of light cut into the darkness." He urged the Senate to ratify the test ban so America could "step back from the shadows of war and seek out the way of peace."

Kennedy realized that passage of the treaty was far from certain. He was told that congressional mail against the test ban was running at a lopsided fifteen to one. Years of Cold War indoctrination about the demonic Russians could not be dispelled by one presidential broadcast. But Kennedy was determined to put everything he had into winning the treaty. He shocked White House aides by declaring that he would "gladly" sacrifice his reelection for the sake of the arms agreement. The two-month battle that Kennedy waged on behalf of the treaty is a profile in presidential courage. The hard-fought campaign, which highlighted Kennedy's skills as a political warrior, demonstrated how much a president can win when he is willing to lose all.

Soon after his TV address, Kennedy began organizing his own grassroots network to counter the anti-treaty offensive of the military-industrial complex. Once again, he called on Norman Cousins, asking him to help activate "a whirlwind campaign for educating and mobilizing public opinion." Drawing on his contacts in the peace movement, the crusading journalist quickly assembled a citizens' coalition of business, labor, entertainment, scientific, and religious leaders to back the treaty. Meeting with Cousins and other coalition representatives in the Cabinet Room on August 7, Kennedy told them they faced formidable opposition from the military world. The generals simply did not want any limitations on the nuclear arms juggernaut, said the president. "In fact," he told the group, "some generals believed the only solution for any crisis situation was to start dropping the big bombs." When he challenged their thinking, asking "how bombing would solve the problem," said Kennedy, the military men would become "far less confident or articulate." The president's startling revelation about the Pentagon's trigger-happy instincts surely drove home the urgency of their task for the citizens' committee.

Before Cousins and his group dispersed, Kennedy assured them that they could call upon him to speak personally with any individuals or organizations they felt necessary. Cousins immediately took the president up on his offer, arranging a special meeting between JFK and editors of the major women's magazines. The peace activist shrewdly recognized the enormous potential power of women voters, who could be roused to action by concerns about the health of the planet and their children. At the meeting, the president stressed the importance of the test ban for world peace, and his remarks were duly printed in all of the women's magazines, which had a combined circulation of 70 million. "It was the first time that the influential women's magazines had come together in a joint publishing venture of this kind," Cousins later noted—a testament to his magazine industry connections and Kennedy's political charm.

Kennedy did not limit himself to public campaigning on behalf of the treaty; he also masterfully worked the levers of power behind the scenes. As the arms agreement headed for the Senate floor, the president worried that his predecessor in the White House—the old general whose opinion on matters of war and peace still carried great weight—might torpedo it. Eisenhower had signaled his opposition to the treaty, but JFK had a card up his sleeve. After Kennedy took office, new evidence against Eisenhower's chief of staff Sherman Adams, who had resigned under a cloud of corruption charges, was brought to the attorney general's office. Bobby resented the swipes taken at his brother by Ike, who had begun tossing barbs like, "I read that the word 'victory' has been expunged from certain New Frontier dictionaries." The thin-skinned attorney general was not inclined to spare Eisenhower's former aide the embarrassment of federal prosecution. But Ike asked Senate Republican leader Everett Dirksen to intervene with JFK and ask him "as a personal favor to me" to terminate the case. "He'll have a blank check in my bank if he will grant me this favor," Eisenhower reportedly said. Over Bobby's angry objection, the president agreed. Now JFK was calling in his chit.

Kennedy buttonholed Dirksen and made it clear to the influential Republican that he wanted both him and Eisenhower to reverse themselves and back the test ban. "Mr. President, you're a hell of a horse trader," Dirksen responded. "But I'll honor my commitment, and I'm sure that General Eisenhower will."

An air of expectation hung over the Senate chamber when the legislator from Illinois with the familiar gray-white poodle-fluff of hair and rumbling bass voice strode onto the floor. He began reading from a prepared text, confessing that his earlier concerns about the treaty had been misplaced. But then he abruptly put down the pages in his hand and launched into a flowery extemporaneous defense of the arms agreement that was pure Dirksen in all his bombastic splendor. "The whole bosom of God's earth was ruptured by a man-made contrivance we call a nuclear weapon . . . Oh, the tragedy. Oh, the dismay. Oh, the blood. Oh, the anguish . . . A young president calls this treaty the first step. I want to take a first step." By the time Dirksen modulated to his conclusion, Kennedy knew the treaty would pass. Victory came on September 24, 1963, when the Senate voted by a surprising margin, 80 to 19, to ratify the Limited Test Ban Treaty.

"No other accomplishment in the White House ever gave Kennedy greater satisfaction," Sorensen later said. At the signing ceremony in the Treaty Room on the third floor of the White House, the president used sixteen pens to write his name on the document, handing them as souvenirs to the dignitaries gathered around him. He then picked up a final pen, dipped it in the ink, and slashed a bold line underneath his signature. "This one is mine," said Kennedy with a satisfied smile, slipping the pen into his pocket.

ONSTAGE IN THE MAIN hall of the Kennedy Library, the ghosts of presidencies past are trying to assign historic blame for the great imperial disaster of their times, the Vietnam War. They sit stiffly side by side, these representatives of the Kennedy, Johnson, and Nixon administrations, in the I. M. Pei–designed glass-walled atrium with its sweeping backdrop of the white-capped waters of Boston Harbor. Jack Valenti—the short, chirpy, perennial Washington insider—sits in for LBJ, whom he served as a special assistant; Henry Kissinger—all glowering jowls in his sunken old age—and Alexander Haig—full of knowing winks and sly, sidewise glances—speak for Nixon, whose darkly cunning Realpolitik they helped shape; and at the end of the table primly sits the bespectacled Ted Sorensen, one of the last living links to the inner sanctum of the Kennedy White House. At age seventy-seven, the survivor of a stroke, Sorensen is still a vigilant keeper of the Camelot flame. But his eyes sometimes have a clouded, faraway look, as they do this afternoon.

The illustrious panel has convened on this bright, late-winter day in March 2006 for a forum titled "Vietnam and the Presidency." The event—which is introduced by JFK's sole surviving heir, the ever-poised Caroline Kennedy Schlossberg—is similar to many Kennedy Library functions where Sorensen has held forth. But the picture of the Kennedy administration that is emerging during the two-day conference is one that Sorensen clearly finds disturbing. The assumption that underlies the forum is that Kennedy, Johnson, and Nixon all bear equal responsibility for the war that laid waste to Indochina and a generation of Americans. There is a continuum that runs from the low-level combat of Kennedy's term to the apocalypse that loomed in the future. At least that seems to be the consensus of the ruminating scholars, journalists, and public officials who have converged on the Kennedy Library, for the benefit of an overflow crowd and C-SPAN viewers. A genial Jimmy Carter, beamed onto a vast video screen in the main hall, voices this conventional wisdom: "My understanding as a young, non-politician— I was just a peanut farmer then—was that the commitment to go to Vietnam was made basically by the Kennedy administration . . . it was initiated by President Kennedy."

Sorensen's eyes suddenly come alive. It's up to him, once again, to set the record straight on the Kennedy presidency. There were only 16,000 U.S.

military advisors in Vietnam at the time and JFK had no intention of escalating the war, he declares; it was a minor blip on the administration's screen. "Vietnam was *not* central to the foreign policy of the Kennedy presidency," he tells the library audience. "Berlin was, Cuba, the Soviet Union—but not Vietnam. Vietnam was a low-level insurrection at that point." Kennedy sent three fact-finding missions to Vietnam, Sorensen points out, and all three urged him to dispatch combat divisions and to bomb North Vietnam. "JFK listened" to his hawkish advisors, "but he never did what they wanted."

But even here, at the Kennedy Library, with the president's daughter sitting in the audience, Sorensen's points seem to get lost. The discussion quickly moves on. A moist-eyed Valenti reveals how torn up inside LBJ was by his war. "He told me that sending young men out to die is like drinking carbolic acid every morning." Kissinger irascibly swats away a question from a member of the audience who wonders whether there is anything for which the distinguished foreign policymaker would like to apologize. "There is no reason that the people who ask that sort of question have a more elevated moral standing than us," he intones in his guttural, Jabba the Hutt voice. He didn't need to come here today, he grumbles—he did it as a favor to Caroline Kennedy and her family. In place of the war crimes tribunals and congressional investigations that never followed America's disastrous Cold War ventures, we have decorous public forums like this one. And even this restrained event proves too nettlesome for Kissinger.

Is Kennedy really to be lumped in with Nixon and Johnson, with all the gore on their hands? Confusion still seems to reign in historical circles. "I think the issue of how JFK would have acted differently than LBJ [in Vietnam] is something that will never be settled, but intrigues biographers," Kennedy chronicler Robert Dallek has airily stated. But the truth is—thanks to the work of scholars like Peter Dale Scott, John Newman, David Kaiser, Howard Jones, James K. Galbraith, and Gareth Porter—a clear picture *has* emerged of Kennedy's intentions in Vietnam. A conclusive body of evidence indicates that JFK formally decided to withdraw from Vietnam, a process he planned to begin by bringing home 1,000 military personnel in December 1963 and finish in 1965, after his reelection gave him the political cover to complete what he knew would be a controversial action.

The American public actually first learned of Kennedy's Vietnam intentions years ago, from the remembrances of administration insiders like Kenny O'Donnell. In spring 1963, after Senate Democratic leader Mike Mansfield gave Kennedy his unvarnished opinion about the dismal prospects for victory in Vietnam, JFK told O'Donnell that he agreed the United States must withdraw. A U.S. pullout would prompt a "wild conservative outcry," said the president, so he would not complete the troop phase-out until after the 1964 election. But then he was willing to take the heat, Kennedy told O'Donnell: "In 1965, I'll become one of the most unpopular presidents in history. I'll be damned everywhere as a Communist appeaser. But I don't care. If I tried to pull out completely now from Vietnam, we would have another Joe McCarthy red scare on our hands, but I can do it after I'm reelected. So we had better make damned sure that I *am* reelected."

JFK kept his Vietnam plans hidden from his national security bureaucracy, which was hell-bent for war—the military confrontation with communism that Kennedy had repeatedly denied his bellicose advisors, in Cuba, Berlin, and Laos. To avoid an open showdown with the Washington war lobby and maintain his public image as a Cold War militant—which Kennedy realized was still a political necessity in early 1960s America—he avoided publicizing his Vietnam withdrawal plans. As Gareth Porter illuminated in his important 2005 book, *Perils of Dominance*, Kennedy operated on "multiple levels of deception" in his Vietnam decision making, making minor concessions to the hawks to prevent a public split within his administration, while artfully deflecting demands for escalation and engaging in quiet, back-channel diplomacy. It was a brilliant shadow dance that succeeded in keeping America out of war as long as Kennedy was alive.

The only White House document that gave some indication of Kennedy's plan for a phased withdrawal was NSAM 263, issued on October 11, 1963. It revealed the president's intention to bring home 1,000 military advisors by the end of 1963, but specifically directed that no formal announcement be made about this imminent withdrawal. Because JFK left behind an indefinite paper trail, and a blur of ambiguous public statements, it was easy for his war-minded successors to take control of his legacy and present the jungle inferno as a direct result of his policies.

"The documentary record does not prove that Kennedy was going to get out, because he did not want to even hint at this at the time," Daniel Ellsberg observed in a recent interview. "He could not have wanted the generals to know that. He said it to several people, but he never put it in writing. It was understandable, but it was a bad decision because he died and the war went on."

Kennedy kept his political enemies in the dark by never making a public speech on Vietnam during his presidency. But, as Sorensen observed, you can find JFK's true feelings about wars of national liberation by reading two surprisingly prescient speeches he gave on the Senate floor, one about Vietnam and the other on Algeria. The central theme of these two speeches, which rattled the foreign policy establishment at the time, is the same: it is folly for Western powers to resist the rising aspirations of developing nations. Kennedy, one of the most well-traveled presidents in history, had seen the bleak fate of French colonialism at close hand, during a trip to Vietnam he took with Bobby in 1951. On April 6, 1954, the young senator from Massachusetts rose to his feet and warned President Eisenhower not to get caught up in France's doomed enterprise: "I am frankly of the belief that no amount of American military assistance in Indochina can conquer an enemy which is everywhere and at the same time nowhere, an 'enemy of the people' which has the sympathy and covert support of the people." This is as succinct a warning about the perils of imperial hubris as has ever been uttered by an American leader. And unlike some of his successors in the White House, Kennedy clearly heeded his youthful insight.

Kennedy's elusiveness on Vietnam was typical of his presidential style. "He never made a decision that he didn't have to make, until time came that he had to make it," Sorensen says. This reluctance was undoubtedly reinforced by the fractious state of his administration. As the only man in the room who consistently opposed military escalation in Vietnam, the president was compelled to operate in a stealthy fashion to avoid becoming completely isolated within his own government. By the time Vietnam began to reach a crisis point late in Kennedy's term, much of his national security bureaucracy—weary with the president's sly maneuvers to keep the country out of war—was in flagrant revolt against him. The Pentagon and CIA were taking secret steps to sabotage his troop withdrawal plan. And even trusted advisors like Harriman, the Moscow-friendly globe-trotting tycoon whom Kennedy thought he could rely on to help broker a deal on Vietnam, were brazenly undercutting his peace initiatives.

As the political situation in Vietnam deteriorated in fall 1963, the limits of Kennedy's oblique management style became apparent. Frustrated by the growing instability of South Vietnam's Diem regime, U.S. officials split over whether to back a military coup to replace it, with Kennedy himself vacillating back and forth on the question. In October, the growing feud between Ambassador Henry Cabot Lodge, who supported a coup, and Saigon CIA station chief John Richardson, who backed the increasingly autocratic President Ngo Dinh Diem, erupted into public view. Richard Starnes, a Saigon correspondent for the Scripps-Howard newspapers, filed a remarkable report on the rift, quoting "a high U.S. official here" who charged the CIA with insubordination. The official called the agency a "malignancy" and said he "was not sure even the White House could control [it] any longer." He then added this eyebrow-raising observation: "If the United States ever experiences a [coup attempt] it will come from the CIA and not the Pentagon. . . . [The agency] represents a tremendous power and total unaccountability to anyone." Starnes's stunning report prompted the *New York Times'* venerable Arthur Krock to warn Kennedy to get control of his administration. "This is disorderly government," the old Kennedy press retainer sternly admonished JFK in his October 3 column. "And the longer the president tolerates it, the greater will grow . . . the impression of a very indecisive administration in Washington."

The CIA's unaccountability in Vietnam brought cries for Congress to "turn a permanent floodlight on the citadel of secrecy," the *New York Times'* Ben Bagdikian reported later that month. Intelligence executives, noted Bagdikian, were "appalled" at the idea of more congressional scrutiny of their machinations. But they had little to fear. For the rest of the Cold War, despite occasional congressional foot stomping, the CIA continued to operate largely unsupervised.

The sense of an administration in growing conflict with itself only increased on November 1 when South Vietnamese military plotters dragged Diem and his brother Nhu out of church, handcuffed the two men and threw them in the back of a truck, where they were stabbed and shot in the head. (The coup was facilitated when the CIA withdrew Richardson from Saigon, allowing the agency to cooperate with the South Vietnamese generals behind the plot.) Kennedy was not opposed to a change of government in Saigon if it brought the kind of stability that could help ease a U.S. withdrawal. But he was sickened and depressed by the bloody disposal of the Catholic leader and his brother, butchered like animals in a rolling abattoir. Robert McNamara, who was with Kennedy when he got news of the brothers' assassinations, later remarked that he had never seen the president more upset: "He literally blanched." The murders "shook him personally," Michael Forrestal, Kennedy's specialist on Southeast Asia, observed. They "bothered him as a moral and religious matter [and] shook his confidence . . . in the kind of advice he was getting about South Vietnam."

The center was not holding for John Kennedy in the final weeks of his life. The violent overthrow of Diem not only exacerbated the feeling of chaos in Vietnam, it underlined the limits on Kennedy's ability to control events, in Saigon as well as in Washington. The president who prided himself on his mastery of foreign policy—a man who had been tutored by old pro Joe Kennedy in the wily arts of power—felt the reins slipping from his hands.

After hearing about Diem, JFK called Mary Meyer—whom he turned to in moments of duress—and asked her to join him at the White House for the afternoon. It was the last time they saw each other.

Ironically, the only top national security advisor who came around to supporting Kennedy's Vietnam pullout plan was the man who would go down in history as one of the war's most reviled architects, Robert Strange McNamara. After returning from a fact-finding trip to Vietnam in October, the defense secretary met with Kennedy in the White House, telling him, "I think, Mr. President, that we must have a means of disengaging from this area, and we must show our country what that means." It was McNamara who encouraged Kennedy to withdraw 1,000 soldiers by the end of the year.

But McNamara abruptly shifted his Vietnam thinking under Kennedy's successor, dutifully realigning himself with the Johnson administration's escalating violence. The numbers cruncher with the shiny, shoe-polished hair and whiz-kid wire-rims would become an icon of failure, the reigning symbol of the tragic folly of fighting a war against impassioned peasant warriors with the cold logic of a statistician. Why did he allow himself to become the brains of the war under LBJ after plotting with JFK to disengage from it? "Oh, I don't want to talk about that," McNamara told me with the clipped, authoritative voice of a CEO shutting down a disagreeable topic at a board meeting.

The Vietnam War mastermind reemerged in 1995 as a critic of the war, publishing a remarkable mea culpa called *In Retrospect* and following up with *The Fog of War*, Errol Morris's 2004 Academy Award–winning documentary in which McNamara strove to make sense of his life and its hard-earned lessons. But despite the confessional frame of mind that he has adopted late in his life, McNamara is still selective about his revelations. Here is one of the most intriguing personalities that the world of American power has ever produced, all exposed nerves one moment and buttoned-down reserve the next. McNamara has asserted that he and Curtis LeMay, whom he served under during World War II, could have been prosecuted as war criminals if the United States had lost the war. And yet he still loyally dodges questions about Lyndon Johnson's moral responsibility for Vietnam. He can speak with clinical detachment about the mass civilian casualties for which he bears responsibility in Japan and Vietnam, and yet tears up at the memory of the death of one U.S. airman. He seems both the most human of men to occupy a top post in the American military machine and the most chilling.

As Admiral Anderson, McNamara's Pentagon adversary, caustically noted, the defense secretary cried easily—a trait that seems to have grown with age. Reliving his life in *The Fog of War*, McNamara's memories of his seven years as defense secretary inevitably choked him up. "My wife got ulcers from it, my son probably did," he told the camera. "But it was the best years of our lives." As he spoke, his watery eyes and twitching mouth betrayed a riot of suffocated emotions.

If his years with Johnson ravaged his family, his years with Kennedy were clearly Robert McNamara's brief and shining moment. He was helping the young president keep peace in the world, helping keep rational restraints on the country's military leviathan. And then came Dallas. Robert McNamara would go from glory to infamy. The man whom Kennedy wanted to make secretary of state in his second term, co-architect of his plans for world peace, would instead go down in history as a warmonger. The tears are not just for the fallen president—they're for McNamara himself, and what he lost.

Other hawks who served with Kennedy, from LBJ on down, claimed there was a seamless narrative between the two Democratic administrations on Vietnam. It would have been easy for McNamara to take the same self-serving line. But he didn't. He told the truth in his memoir—Kennedy intended to get out—even though it made his own jarring shift from dove to hawk seem all the more bizarre. Of course, McNamara is a company man— he is still loyal to Kennedy, as he is to Johnson. But there is something more at work in his need to set the record straight on JFK and Vietnam. Perhaps he is also being true to his younger self, the brilliant New Frontiersman who was going to make the world a better, safer place.

It would not have been easy for Kennedy to disengage from Vietnam, McNamara said. According to the former Pentagon chief, JFK did not completely reject the assumptions of the Cold War; he still believed in the domino theory that held if Vietnam fell to the Communists, it would lead to the collapse of other free countries throughout the region. But in the end, McNamara said, JFK would have steered the country away from the cataclysm. "My belief is that Kennedy would have had a hell of a problem deciding what to do, because he believed in the domino theory. However, he also believed, as he stated before he died, that it was South Vietnam's war and the people there had to win it—the United States could help them, but not win it for them. These might have been two contradictory positions. But in the end, I believe he would have decided that the latter position—we couldn't win the war for them—was more powerful than the domino view."

"He kept the peace." That's what Kennedy often said he wanted as his epitaph. And against all odds, he succeeded in doing just that, remarked McNamara—the man who failed to do so. In the dangerously militarized atmosphere of the Cold War—and under relentless pressure from generals, CIA officials, congressional hawks, and his own national security advisors— Kennedy again and again slipped the knots of war. "I think his view was that the primary responsibility of the president is to keep the nation out of war if at all possible," McNamara observed at the "Recollecting JFK" forum. Kennedy maintained the peace, his defense chief pointed out, when many powerful figures in Washington believed that nuclear war with the Soviet Union was inevitable. "They were certain of that." McNamara painted a sobering picture for the audience of life in Cold War Washington. There were men in power who believed that America could claim victory even if the country lost 20 or 30 million people. "That's perfectly absurd," said McNamara. "It sounds today absurd to you, I'm sure." But you weren't in power during this period of mass psychosis, he told the crowd. You don't know what it was like. "You lived the Cold War twenty-four hours a day, 365 days a year . . . those were the attitudes." But Kennedy stood firmly against these mad delusions. "And he won. We averted a nuclear war. We came that close, but we avoided it."

Then Kennedy died, and his antagonists got their war. But it was a smaller war, not the one that the generals wanted, and the planet survived. He and Lyndon Johnson made sure of that, says McNamara today. He deservedly takes a deep sense of satisfaction from that.

When *The Fog of War* was released, McNamara appeared onstage at his alma mater, the University of California at Berkeley, to talk about the film's lessons of war and peace. As the sell-out crowd filled Zellerbach Hall, there was a taut suspense in the air. Would McNamara be safe at this former center of antiwar protest, where the graying audience still had searing memories of his past role? But the old warrior did not hesitate to march onstage. He was on a mission to confront his ghosts, said his middle-aged son Craig, who drove from his organic walnut farm near Davis, California to accompany his father that night. There was a time when the war had torn them apart too.

The Berkeley audience was surprisingly respectful. They applauded McNamara's passionate jeremiads. "We human beings killed 160 million other human beings in the twentieth century," he exclaimed. "Is that what we want in this century? I don't think so!" But loud sighs greeted his refusal to publicly criticize the Bush administration's war in Iraq, even though he had earlier voiced strong criticisms of the war as "morally wrong" in the Canadian press. "I'm not going to comment on President Bush," he told the audience. Ever the loyal government man.

In the auditorium that evening was Daniel Ellsberg, the one-time defense intellectual who dared to break ranks by leaking the Pentagon Papers, the government's own damning report on the Vietnam War. It was the path not taken by McNamara, who called Ellsberg a traitor at the time. But Ellsberg himself, who once viewed McNamara with similar contempt, now has more complicated feelings about the former Pentagon chief. He talked about them at his home in the East Bay hills before the event.

"McNamara believes that he kept Curtis LeMay and the others from doing to Hanoi what they did to Tokyo and Hiroshima in World War II," said Ellsberg. "And he did do that. It's possible that no one else in his position could have held back the U.S. Air Force from firebombing or nuking Vietnam, turning it into the parking lot that LeMay wanted to. So yes, that's how McNamara lives with himself—very easily: 'I had my finger in the dyke, I am the boy who kept this disaster from happening. No one else could have prevented the Joint Chiefs from forcing Johnson to let them loose on Hanoi. I worked for months and years to prevent that holocaust, and no one else could have succeeded.' That's a pretty strong argument for his place in history."

McNamara, for his part, when later told that Ellsberg was in the Berkeley audience, seemed undisturbed. "I hadn't any idea. If I had known, it would not have bothered me."

McNamara is liver-spotted and stoop-shouldered now. He says that his computer brain has memory lapses. But he has the wisdom of an old soldier. Looking back, he can see his fatal mistakes with the same clarity he had before he made them. He likes to quote these days from T. S. Eliot's "Four Quartets":

> *What we call the beginning is often the end*
> *And to make an end is to make a beginning . . .*
> *We shall not cease from exploration*
> *And the end of all our exploring*
> *Will be to arrive where we started*
> *And know the place for the first time.*

LISA HOWARD WAS WAITING for Fidel. It was a ritual with which foreign journalists—as well as visiting dignitaries—were all too familiar. It had taken months for the ABC newswoman just to get a visa out of the Cuban government. She assiduously worked her contacts in the diplomatic corps, including Russian First Deputy Premier Anastas Mikoyan. But in the end, it was Jim Donovan, Bobby Kennedy's unofficial Havana go-between, who finally finagled permission for her. Howard arrived in Havana on April 1, 1963, taking up quarters in the Hotel Riviera, a gleaming, Miami-style high-rise overlooking the city's seafront. And then she waited some more—three weeks more—while Castro pondered her request for a TV interview.

The thirty-seven-year-old Lisa Howard was an anomaly in the broadcast news world of the Kennedy era, a sexy, stylish, high-profile woman in a business that was the almost exclusive domain of rumpled, sober-faced, middle-aged men. Howard was one of a handful of TV newswomen in the early 1960s that included Nancy Dickerson of NBC and Nancy Clark of CBS. A former actress, she made the leap from Off-Broadway theater and TV soap operas—she was regular on CBS's *The Edge of Night* in the late 1950s—to broadcast journalism through sheer determination, after deciding that her acting career was stalled. As the United Nations correspondent for Mutual Radio Network, she developed a reputation for brash enterprise, becoming the first American journalist to score an interview with Khrushchev. (She snagged the Soviet leader by using her theatrical wiles, slipping past guards at the Russian consulate in New York by dressing as a maid and then embracing Khrushchev as he walked by her.) Hired away by ABC in 1961 to cover the Kennedy-Khrushchev summit in Vienna, she continued to make a name for her splashy journalistic coups—years before the rise of Barbara Walters and a future generation of female TV icons—and was rewarded by being given her own show, *The News Hour with Lisa Howard*.

The blonde and curvy Howard, whom *Newsweek* had declared "startlingly good-looking," was willing to use what she called her "natural advantages" to finally land the interview with Castro. After midnight on April 21, the newswoman was awakened in bed at the Riviera by a diplomat friend who told her to come downstairs to meet Castro. She slipped into a low-cut brown cocktail dress and went down to the lobby, where the Cuban leader greeted her and escorted her into the hotel nightclub, where they talked until after five in the morning. Castro was charmed by Howard. He asked an aide to take photos of them, using a Polaroid camera given to him by his old friend Donovan. In the pictures, a glamorous, bare-shouldered Howard sits snugly next to the uniformed Castro at a cocktail table, regarding him with a bright-eyed intensity. Castro later agreed to be interviewed on camera by Howard, sitting for a forty-five-minute chat in the hotel's twentieth floor penthouse suite.

The interview, the first Castro had granted a U.S. network since 1959, was a major coup for Howard and ABC.

After Howard returned to the United States, she went to the White House, where a curious Kennedy debriefed her. She shared the details of her Castro encounter with the gossip-hungry Kennedy, including the revelation that she had slept with the Cuban leader. "She talked with Jack about it," Howard's friend, the equally dishy Gore Vidal, later reported, "and mentioned that Castro hadn't taken his boots off. Jack liked details like that." In her diary, Howard wrote that Castro "made love to me efficiently."

But Howard had something more weighty to convey to the president. She told Kennedy that Castro was clearly eager to open a dialogue with him. Howard, whose path to Castro had been paved by Donovan, was continuing the peace mission that the New York lawyer had begun the previous year.

The newswoman delivered the same message to the CIA when she discussed her Cuba trip with agency officials, a common Cold War practice among journalists returning from Communist outposts. But CIA officials were not as enthusiastic about Howard's news as the president. Just as they had done with Donovan's peace initiative, agency executives moved swiftly to short-circuit Howard. In a May 2, 1963, memo, McCone sternly advised that the "Lisa Howard report be handled in the most limited and sensitive manner" and "that no active steps be taken on the rapprochement matter at this time." Administration hard-liners even considered trying to block ABC from broadcasting Howard's interview. "Public airing in the United States of this interview would strengthen the arguments of 'peace' groups, 'liberal' thinkers, Commies, fellow travelers, and opportunistic political opponents of the present United States policy," as well as provide Castro with a coast-to-coast audience for his "reasonable line," cautioned an analysis sent to White House national security advisor McGeorge Bundy.

The memo's fears were well-founded. When ABC broadcast the interview on May 10, Castro did indeed come across as a sympathetic and reasonable character. He applauded the Kennedy administration for taking "some steps in the way of peace," including cracking down on the "piratical" raids on his country, and left the door open for a reconciliation with the United States. But with administration hawks blocking peace talks, Howard's peace initiative soon stalled.

Lisa Howard was not easily discouraged, however. She brought the same single-minded determination to her Cuba mission as she did to her journalistic exploits. According to Howard's daughter, Fritzi Lareau—who was a teenager at the time—her motivations were largely emotional. "She fell for Castro," Lareau told me, recalling her "wild" and "iconoclastic" mother. Lareau remembered her mother bluntly asking her stepfather, film producer Walter Lowendahl, whether she should take her diaphragm to Cuba before she left on one of her frequent trips there. (Lowendahl agreed she should. According to Lareau, her stepfather was not happy with her mother's adventures, but the German immigrant suffered his wife's exploits with European equanimity.) "She liked powerful men. And Fidel was very macho. And, of course, the peace mission appealed to her dramatic sensibility, because it was very grand, it was on a world playing field. It was secretive and exciting."

In September, seeking to revive the peace initiative, Howard enlisted her friend, UN diplomat William Attwood, a former journalist who, like the TV newswoman, had no qualms about crossing the lines into politics. Attwood, the Choate classmate of JFK who kept finding himself preempted by Kennedy when he took a young Mary Pinchot (later Meyer) to a school dance, had shifted back and forth between journalism and politics throughout his career. In 1959 he took a leave of absence from *Look* magazine, where he was the globe-trotting foreign editor, to write speeches for Adlai Stevenson, switching to Kennedy's team the following year during his presidential campaign. After his election, Kennedy named Attwood ambassador to Guinea, which was seen as an important Cold War battleground in Africa at the time, and later made him a deputy to UN ambassador Stevenson.

Bill Attwood had a solid East Coast establishment pedigree—from Choate to Princeton to Army intelligence in World War II (he later became a captain in the Thirteenth Airborne Division) to a career in international journalism and diplomacy. But his years overseas gave him a more skeptical perspective than his elite contemporaries on the Cold War hysteria back home. He looked with dismay on "the creeping police state" mentality in Washington and called the cloak and dagger activities of the CIA "often ludicrous." When Attwood interviewed the young, victorious Castro in 1959 for *Look* magazine—rambling over the Cuban countryside in a car with him, with the correspondent's wife, Simone, squeezed onto the lap of a machine-gun-cradling bodyguard—he saw a tragic hero rather than a pariah, a charismatic leader who could have chosen the West over the East if Washington had played it differently.

Attwood had a natural sympathy for Latin America's underdogs, who were finally starting to bite back after years of exploitation. He understood why men like Fidel and Che had turned against America. He later recalled a story told by Guevara. When the future revolutionary was a young man in

Buenos Aires, a U.S. navy ship steamed into port, disgorging hundreds of sailors. One "very large" American sailor grabbed Che's girlfriend in a dance hall and when he objected, the man snarled, "Sit down and shut up, you little nigger."

"Ever since," noted Attwood, "the word 'America' made Che think of a huge hand pressing down on his head and the word 'nigger.' Thus are lifelong guerrillas often created."

When Lisa Howard told Attwood that Castro would like to restore communications with Kennedy and offered to set up an informal meeting at her apartment between him and Cuba's UN representative, Carlos Lechuga, the diplomat responded enthusiastically. In a memo he wrote for Stevenson and Averill Harriman—who he was told was the best direct channel to Kennedy—Attwood suggested that "we have something to gain and nothing to lose by finding out whether in fact Castro does want to talk." If the peace bid succeeded, the diplomat observed, "it could remove the Cuban issue from the 1964 campaign." Stevenson was intrigued. But "unfortunately," he sagely cautioned, "the CIA is still in charge of Cuba." Nonetheless, Stevenson took the proposal to Kennedy, who gave him clearance to pursue the dialogue. Harriman too said he was "adventuresome enough" to like the idea, but advised Attwood to also get the approval of Bobby Kennedy, the administration's point man on Cuba. Stevenson was not keen for Attwood to meet with the attorney general, whom he still considered bullheaded on Cuba. But Attwood dutifully phoned the Justice Department, arranging to see RFK on September 24.

The night before Attwood flew to Washington, Howard arranged for him to meet Lechuga at a cocktail party in her brownstone apartment on East Seventy-fourth Street, where the newswoman loved to entertain the likes of Che and Adlai Stevenson, impressing guests with her eighteen-foot ceilings, antiques collection, and leaded-glass windows. The two diplomats repaired discreetly to a corner of her living room, where Lechuga told Attwood that Castro had read Kennedy's American University speech with avid interest. Attwood talked of spending time with Fidel in 1959, when the Cuban leader gave him a message for the American people—"Let us be friends"—before shoving some cigars into his shirt pocket and urging him to return one day. Lechuga suggested that Attwood finally take up Castro's offer and come back to Havana to renew their conversation.

The next day, Attwood reported all this to Bobby Kennedy in his office. Instead of pouring cold water on the rapprochement idea, as Stevenson feared he would, Bobby responded favorably. He thought it would be too risky for Attwood to visit Cuba, since it would probably leak out and create a political furor in Washington. But he nevertheless felt the peace dialogue was "worth pursuing" and he suggested that secret talks with Castro could be held in another country, such as Mexico, or at the United Nations.

JFK was even more enthusiastic. At a White House meeting on November 5, Bundy told Attwood that the president was "more in favor of pushing towards an opening toward Cuba than was the State Department, the idea being—well, getting them out of the Soviet fold and perhaps wiping out the Bay of Pigs and maybe getting back into normal."

Once again, Kennedy himself was the most forward-looking person on his foreign policy team. Years later, his Hollywood crony Milt Ebbins confirmed that JFK was intent on normalizing relations with Cuba. "He would have recognized Cuba," Ebbins said in an interview for this book. "He told me that if we recognize Cuba, they'll buy our refrigerators and toasters and they'll end up kicking Castro out." JFK sidekick Red Fay agreed that Kennedy was determined to make peace with Cuba. "Jack figured that once the missiles got taken out of Cuba, he didn't think there was any reason why we should have a confrontation with Cuba," the former assistant Navy secretary told me at his home in the Presidio Heights neighborhood of San Francisco, sitting in a study strewn with Kennedy memorabilia and nautical artifacts. "As a result of that, he felt we could settle the whole thing with Cuba and get it all behind us."

In the final days of his life, Kennedy sent two dovish messages to Castro. One was delivered in a November 18 speech before the Inter-American Press Association in Miami, when Kennedy declared that the only obstacle to peace between the United States and Cuba was Havana's support for revolutionary upheavals in other Latin countries. "This and this alone divides us," Kennedy emphasized. "As long as this is true, nothing is possible. Without it, everything is possible." Schlesinger, who helped write the speech, later told Attwood that it was meant to help his diplomatic effort by signaling that the president was truly interested in opening a peace channel with Castro.

But JFK always felt compelled to brandish an arrow as well as an olive branch when he spoke in public about Cuba. This was particularly true in Miami, hotbed of anti-Castro fervor. True to this double-edged strategy, Kennedy's November 18 speech carried harsh rhetoric as well, maligning the Castro government as a "small band of conspirators" which "once removed" would ensure U.S. support for a democratic, progressive Cuba. Desmond FitzGerald took credit for injecting this militant language into the speech, and the CIA spun the president's remarks to its friendly media contacts as a get-Castro tirade. "Kennedy Virtually Invites Cuban Coup," the *Dallas Times Herald* blared. And the CIA-cozy Hal Hendrix of the *Miami News* wrote that JFK's speech "may have been meant for potential dissident elements in" Castro's government. The fact that both Schlesinger and FitzGerald could claim credit for the same speech demonstrates how the administration's Cuba policy was a battleground between competing factions.

But the CIA was fully aware of which direction on Cuba Kennedy was tilting in his final days. Unknown to Lisa Howard and Bill Attwood at the time, as they worked the phones in her apartment on behalf of the JFK-Castro peace initiative, the agency was listening in. In one call to Havana, Howard was overheard excitedly describing Kennedy's enthusiasm for rapprochement. The newswoman had no sense of the shock waves she was causing within the halls of Washington power. "Mother was very naïve, she was an innocent," said Lareau. "She didn't really understand all the dynamics. She was like a bull in a china shop—she just went all out for what she wanted, and she was not that concerned about the consequences."

The agency was determined to derail the administration's secret peace bid. At a White House meeting on Cuba on November 5, Helms urged that the administration slow down the Attwood initiative, proposing that the government "war game" the peace scenario "and look at it from all possible angles before making any contacts" with Castro.

Despite the agency's resistance, the peace feelers continued. Kennedy's second cordial message was delivered to Castro personally by French journalist Jean Daniel, editor of the socialist newsweekly *L'Observateur*, on the day the president was assassinated. Before leaving for Havana, Daniel had met with Kennedy in the White House, where the president took a conciliatory line toward Cuba. Sounding like the Alliance for Progress crusader instead of the Bay of Pigs invader, Kennedy told Daniel that America's Cuba policy during the Batista era was characterized by "economic colonization, humiliation and exploitation," adding, "We'll have to pay for those sins." If Castro stopped acting as the Soviet Union's agent of subversion in Latin America, Kennedy suggested, the United States would lift its economic blockade of Cuba. Daniel later said that the president was clearly "seeking a way out" of the impasse between the two countries. When the French journalist met with Castro, the Cuban leader was riveted by his report on his White House meeting, asking him to repeat Kennedy's remarkably honest assessment of America's shameful policy during the Batista years. "He has come to understand many things over the past few months," Castro mused aloud.

But on the very day that Daniel was conveying JFK's conciliatory message to Castro (and Kennedy would ride to his doom in Dallas), CIA officials were taking covert steps to strangle the peace initiative. On November 22, in a stunningly duplicitous act of insubordination—without informing the president, attorney general, or CIA director—Richard Helms and Desmond FitzGerald arranged for a poison pen to be delivered in Paris to a disaffected Cuban military officer named Rolando Cubela for the assassination of Castro. Like the agency's plan to kill Castro with a toxic wet suit, hatched during the Donovan peace mission, the Cubela plot was clearly designed to snuff out the Attwood-Howard initiative. The CIA hoped that Castro's assassination would trigger a military coup. But even if the Cubela plot failed and was exposed, it was certain to deeply embitter relations between the two countries.

The agency's dark intrigue bore out Stevenson's warning to Attwood that "the CIA is in charge of Cuba." In any case, Attwood grimly noted years later, that's the way the spy outfit acted—"and to hell with the president it was pledged to serve."

The CIA tried to frame Robert Kennedy for the Cubela plot. When Cubela asked his agency contacts to meet personally with the president's brother, FitzGerald took the extraordinary step of flying to Paris to falsely assure the assassin of RFK's support. Meeting Cubela, who was given the code name AM/LASH, at a CIA safe house in the city, FitzGerald introduced himself as "Senator James Clark," a personal representative of Kennedy's. But the president's brother had no idea the CIA was using his name. Helms and FitzGerald agreed that it would be "totally unnecessary" to inform Kennedy of their gambit. When later confronted with evidence of his duplicity by the Church Committee, in the 1970s, Helms was forced to explain why he had kept Kennedy in the dark. "It wasn't that I was being smart or tricky or hiding anything," Helms insisted, although that's precisely what he was being. "I just thought this is exactly the kind of thing . . . he's been asking us to do, let's get on with doing it." The intelligence czar later embroidered on his lie in an interview with journalist Evan Thomas, suggesting that he concealed the Cubela meeting from Kennedy for RFK's own good, because the risk-taking attorney general might have flown to Paris to deliver the assassination tools himself. "Bobby wouldn't have backed away [from the Cubela meeting]," said Helms. "He probably would have gone himself."

The CIA continued to plot with Cubela until 1966, when he was arrested by Cuban counterintelligence and sentenced to thirty years in jail. But as it turned out, it was Kennedy's assassination, not Castro's that terminated the efforts to reconcile the two countries. After Dallas, the Attwood back-channel talks sputtered briefly along, with Castro again using a Lisa Howard interview to express his continued interest in peace. But in January the Johnson administration pulled the plug on the talks, to avoid handing the Republicans a potential campaign issue in the 1964 election. In a memo written three days after JFK's assassination, Gordon Chase, the White House point man on the secret negotiations, observed that "President Kennedy could have accommodated with Castro and gotten away with it with a minimum of domestic heat [but] I'm not sure about President Johnson. For one thing, a new president who has no background of being successfully nasty to Castro and the Communists (e.g., President Kennedy in October 1962) would probably run a greater risk of being accused by the American people of 'going soft.'" The other reason rapprochement with Cuba would now be "more difficult," Chase noted, was that Kennedy's accused assassin, Lee Harvey Oswald, "has been heralded as a pro-Castro type"—a portrayal of Oswald that was aggressively promoted by the CIA and its client groups in the Cuban exile community like the DRE, starting immediately after the shots were fired in Dealey Plaza.

Howard doggedly continued her citizen's diplomacy through early 1964, despite a growing disdain for her efforts in the Johnson White House and CIA, but her life took a tragic arc. In September, she threw herself in typically dramatic fashion into the New York Senate race that pitted Bobby Kennedy against Republican incumbent Kenneth Keating. Joining with other high-profile liberals who harbored resentments against Bobby, like Gore Vidal, Howard formed a Democrats for Keating group at a meeting in her apartment. Ironically, Keating had played a very belligerent role on Cuba, goading the Kennedy administration to take military action against the island and dismissing Castro as "just a puppet" of the Soviet Union after he appealed for peace in his first TV interview with Howard. But Howard, frustrated by the failure of her Cuba peace bid, focused blame curiously on Bobby, even though he had given the effort his approval.

"She was trying to make peace and she was convinced Jack and Bobby wanted war," recalled Vidal. "She was most resentful of it and she saw this would be a good opportunity to punish Bobby." The Kennedys not only made

enemies on the right with their two-track strategy towards Cuba—they alienated some on the left as well.

Soon after her plunge into the Senate campaign, Howard was fired by
ABC for her highly publicized partisanship. A network executive brusquely
told the *New York Times*, "She's being canned. She doesn't fit. She's a mystery
girl. We just don't want her on the staff." The once high-flying TV correspondent was outraged by her abrupt excommunication from the airwaves. She
filed suit against ABC, claiming that she had been "blacklisted" for her political activities. Deprived of her prominent TV platform, Howard seemed
lost. "Lisa Howard Pleads to Be Visible Again," read the plaintive headline of
a *New York Times* story on her lawsuit. Her lawyer told the newspaper that
monetary compensation could not offset the terrible damage done to Howard by depriving her "of daily exposure to her audience."

In April 1965, months after her dismissal, Howard crashed a New York
Radio and Television Correspondents Association meeting held in the ABC
corporate conference room where Bobby Kennedy was a featured speaker.
She confronted Kennedy at the forum, questioning his effectiveness as a
political leader. The next day, ABC public relations executive James C.
Hagerty felt compelled to apologize for Howard's behavior in a letter to Kennedy: "The report of her conduct towards you, as relayed to me, burned me
up. This is just a note to express my personal regrets even though Miss Howard is no longer working for us—and that's a story in itself. . . . I'm just sorry
it happened while you were a guest in our building." Kennedy himself took
the incident in stride—at least Howard didn't level the usual "ruthless Bobby"
charge at him, he quipped. "My slogan next time," he wrote in his reply to
Hagerty, "is going to be: 'Re-elect Robert F. Kennedy Senator—He is too
inefficient to be ruthless.' Anyway, thank you for writing. With the problems
that exist for everyone," Bobby added, his days still shrouded by Dallas, "Lisa
Howard is rather inconsequential."

"Mother was basically having a mental breakdown by that point," said
Lareau. "She had lost the most important thing in her life—her career, her
position. She was a public person, an exhibitionist—she loved being on camera, at the center of attention. So when all of this disappeared, she felt like
her whole world was falling apart."

Her mother was also afflicted by an addiction to sleeping pills that began
during her first trip to Cuba. "She used to stay up all night waiting for Fidel,
and then she couldn't sleep the next day, so she would take pills."

Howard's spiral downward continued that summer when she suffered a
miscarriage. On July 4, after being released from the hospital, she drove to a

pharmacy in East Hampton, where she and her husband were spending the summer. She altered a sleeping pill prescription to read 100 instead of 10 and promptly downed most of the barbiturates with a Coke. Police found her wandering dazed and glassy-eyed in the drugstore parking lot, mumbling about her miscarriage. They drove her to a hospital but she collapsed and died before they could get her inside. A medical examiner said she had taken enough sleeping pills to kill five people. "It wasn't a cry for help," said Lareau. "She was determined to die." Lisa Howard pursued death as aggressively as she had pursued life.

IN CONTRAST TO HIS friend Lisa Howard, Bill Attwood's career flourished in the post-Kennedy years. After serving as President Johnson's ambassador to Kenya, he returned to journalism, becoming editor-in-chief of Cowles Communications, publishers of *Look*, in 1966 and then president and publisher of *Newsday* in 1970. But as the years went by, Attwood was increasingly haunted by the assassination of JFK. He began to wonder whether there might be a link between Kennedy's secret Cuba peace efforts and his murder. In October 1975, he wrote a letter to Senator Richard Schweiker of Pennsylvania, who, along with fellow Church Committee member Gary Hart of Colorado, had persuaded Frank Church to let them form a subcommittee to investigate the Kennedy assassination. "I think the Warren Commission is like a house of cards," Schweiker announced to the press at the time. "It's going to collapse." In his letter, Attwood told Schweiker that while he found it "hard to disbelieve the Warren Report," he had some suspicions about the possible involvement of anti-Castro Cubans in the assassination. And he encouraged Schweiker to investigate the back channel that Kennedy opened with Castro as a possible motive for his killing.

As the years went by, Attwood's suspicions deepened. He communicated with conspiracy researchers. He discussed the assassination with Castro during a February 1977 trip to Havana that was intended to revive his long-dormant peace mission, this time on behalf of newly inaugurated President Carter. During a lengthy conversation one evening in the presidential palace, Castro told Attwood that Kennedy's American University speech showed that "he'd have been a great president had he lived." The Cuban leader then recalled the exploratory peace talks between Attwood and his UN representative, Lechuga. "This is why Kennedy was killed," Castro told him, pinning the blame on "a conspiracy of right-wing elements who could see U.S policy in Cuba and Vietnam about to change."

Attwood was beginning to think along similar lines. He later gave an eye-opening interview to Anthony Summers, a former BBC journalist whose 1980 book on the assassination, *Conspiracy*, was a landmark in Kennedy research, applying rigorous reporting skills for the first time to the crime. Attwood told Summers that he suspected the phone calls he and Lisa Howard made to Havana from her apartment were tapped by the CIA. When word of Kennedy's secret peace track filtered down the agency ranks, Attwood conjectured, to the level where zealous operatives worked with equally feverish exiles, the results might have been explosive. "If word of a possible normalization of relations with Cuba leaked to these people, I can understand why they would have reacted violently," Attwood said, "This was the end of their dreams of returning to Cuba, and they might have been impelled to take violent action. Such as assassinating the president."

Arthur Schlesinger concurred with Attwood's assessment, telling Summers, "Undoubtedly if word leaked of President Kennedy's efforts, that might have been exactly the kind of thing to trigger some explosion of fanatical violence. It seems to me a possibility not to be excluded."

It should have been front-page news when someone of Attwood's prominence—backed up by a former Kennedy administration insider who was one of the country's leading historians—raised such provocative questions about the assassination. But Attwood's statement quickly disappeared into the media black hole where JFK revelations are routinely consigned.

Nonetheless Attwood continued to speak to the press about his suspicions late into his life. "We thought there was more to Dallas than we'd been told," his widow, Simone, said in an interview.

In January 1986, Attwood repeated what he told Summers in a phone conversation with British TV producer Richard Tomlinson, telling him he suspected "disgruntled CIA operatives and Cuban exiles." Attwood's "theory," Tomlinson wrote in his notes of the conversation, was "that the secret negotiations with Cuba were the last straw as far as the conspirators were concerned. It was then that they took the decision to kill Kennedy." His "critical mistake," Attwood remarked, was "to use phones which were tapped by the CIA. Until that point, only six people knew about the [peace] negotiations." But "there were elements within the CIA which were violently opposed to rapprochement with Cuba."

In the United States, the only reporter who took an interest in Attwood's provocative statements about the JFK assassination was someone from the *Advocate*, his hometown paper in New Canaan, Connecticut. Attwood shared with him his dark speculations about Dallas. "I knew there were people in the agency—one of them worked with me later—who felt strongly that

Kennedy had let them down by normalizing relations with Cuba. These were fairly nutty people." Attwood concluded his interview in his local paper by urging his fellow citizens not to forget the crime of the century.

"If you don't get to the bottom of these things, if you let it lie, then we're all part of the cover-up."

But when Attwood died of heart failure in 1989, at age sixty-nine, the truth was still out of reach, fathoms below in the cold, dark unknown.

5

DALLAS

President Kennedy looked tired and somber as he stood at the lectern in the spacious State Department Auditorium on Halloween 1963. There were dark bags beneath his eyes and his shoulders stooped, as if from pain or fatigue. It was the second to last press conference of his administration, a forum in which he generally sparkled. These were occasions for the deft and charming president to show off, and he did so often, holding sixty-four news conferences in his 1,037 days in office. Though he was invariably well-prepared, he always seemed spontaneous and light on his feet. There was no sign of effort in his smooth replies and displays of mischievous wit. A reporter tried to break through his easy self-confidence at one press conference. "The Republican National Committee recently adopted a resolution saying you were pretty much of a failure," he poked Kennedy. "How do you feel about that?" With a comic's sense of timing, JFK waited for the nervous chuckling in the auditorium to fade before responding. "I assume it passed unanimously."

But Kennedy seemed downcast at his October 31 news conference. The questions he was asked that day vividly demonstrated the pressures he was under: What were his intentions in Vietnam? Should U.S. generals stationed overseas be given the authority to order nuclear strikes, as Senator Goldwater has urged? Was the president expecting a white backlash against his civil rights policies in the forthcoming Philadelphia municipal elections? Castro has captured several CIA agents and is threatening to execute them—would he care to comment?

A woman reporter sensed the president's heavy spirit. She reminded him that after the Bay of Pigs she had asked him how he liked being president. Now, prompted by his dark mood, she repeated the question. It was a choice opportunity for Kennedy to exhibit his wit, to neatly deflect the emotionally probing query with a joshing jab at his Republican opponents or a self-deprecating quip. But, instead, he grew philosophical. In a voice oddly meditative for a man soon to announce his reelection bid for the White House, he mused that he found the job "rewarding." And then he invoked the wisdom of the ancient Greeks, as his brother would often do in seeking solace after he was gone. "I have given before to this group," Kennedy told the 304 reporters assembled in the auditorium's tiered seats, "the definition of happiness of the Greeks, and I will define it again. It is the full use of your powers along the lines of excellence. I find, therefore, the presidency provides some happiness."

It was hardly a ringing endorsement of the job. Despite his solemn mood, however, Kennedy was looking forward to the 1964 election. He predicted the race would pit him against Goldwater, a man with whom he had developed a friendly relationship in the Senate but who represented the opposite pole of the political spectrum. By fall 1963, JFK had settled on a peace theme for his reelection campaign—and he sensed that the American people, tired of being held captive by nuclear terror, would reward him with victory. The 1964 campaign would offer a stark choice—the emerging détente of the Kennedy-Khrushchev era versus the Cold War militance of the far right. In the final months of his life, he felt increasingly confident that he could carry his peace message even into Republican strongholds.

He did just that on September 26 before a Mormon Tabernacle assembly in Salt Lake City, declaring that America must learn to live in "a world of diversity" where no one power dominated global affairs. "We must first of all recognize that we cannot remake the world simply by our own command," the president intoned. "When we cannot even bring all of our own people into full citizenship without acts of violence, we can understand how much harder it is to control events beyond our borders." To the astonishment of the jaded Washington press pack covering the president's speech, the conservative crowd cheered and cheered.

Nonetheless, Kennedy knew the 1964 campaign would be bitterly fought. He was aware of how polarized the country had become as a result of his efforts to end the Cold War and racial segregation. Because of his civil rights policies, the South was in hot flight from the Democratic coalition where it had resided since the New Deal.

Kennedy's June 1963 TV address announcing the introduction of civil rights legislation in Congress was a moral high point of his administration. But it was the final insult to a traditional Southern order built on white supremacy. The president asked Sorensen to write the speech on the spur of the moment, after watching TV in the Oval Office as another Southern governor—this time Alabama's George Wallace—defied federal orders to integrate a Dixie university. Swinging around in his chair from the television set, Kennedy said to Sorensen, "We better make that speech tonight." The White House speechwriter had two hours to craft the history-making address. "Scramble is putting it mildly," Sorensen said. "While I was typing away, the president came into my office—I believe it was the only time in his presidency that he came into *my* office—and said, 'How's it coming?' And I said, 'Don't worry, I'm just finishing some revisions now.' And he said, 'Whew, I thought I was going to have to go on national television ex tem.' "

JFK's TV address on civil rights, along with his Peace Speech that same month, defined where the administration was moving on the two burning issues of the day. "We are confronted primarily with a moral issue," he told the American public with a stirring simplicity. "It is as old as the scriptures and is as clear as the American Constitution. The heart of the question is whether we are going to treat our fellow Americans as we want to be treated. If an American, because his skin is dark, cannot eat lunch in a restaurant open to the public, if he cannot send his children to the best public school available, if he cannot vote for the public officials who represent him, if, in short, he cannot enjoy the full and free life which all of us want, then who among us would be content to have the color of his skin changed and stand in his place?"

The president had at last dropped his cautious, pragmatic pose on civil rights—his doomed strategy to hold together the old Democratic Party coalition—and addressed America's original sin with the passion it demanded. And once again, he turned to Ted Sorensen—the Nebraska progressive who in his youth had formed the Lincoln Social Action Council to fight racism in his hometown—to help him find the right words to inspire the better angels of our nature.

"One hundred years of delay have passed since President Lincoln freed the slaves, yet their heirs, their grandsons, are not fully free. They are not yet freed from the bonds of injustice. They are not yet freed from social and economic oppression. And this nation, for all its hopes and boasts, will not be fully free until all its citizens are free."

JFK told his brother, who had become the administration's battering ram on civil rights, he feared the speech would be his "political swan song." Because he had finally put his full eloquence behind the cause of equal rights, the president knew he was facing the mass defection of white voters not only in the South but in ethnic neighborhoods that were resisting integration in the North. A Gallup Poll in early November found that the president's popularity had sunk to 59 percent, after hitting 77 percent following the Cuban Missile Crisis. Republican leaders gathering in Charleston, South Carolina, on November 9 confidently predicted that Goldwater would sweep the South in 1964, even taking Texas out of the Democratic column. George Wallace, who had theatrically faced off against the Kennedy administration on the steps of the University of Alabama, told a cheering Dallas audience on November 18 that "the American people are going to save this country next year" by removing Kennedy from the White House. The press began wondering whether Kennedy's reelection was becoming less of a sure bet, with *Look* magazine declaring "JFK Could Lose" and *Time* speculating that "Barry Goldwater could give Kennedy a breathlessly close race."

Kennedy could lose most of the old Confederacy and still win reelection in 1964, but he could not afford to lose Texas, which he had narrowly taken in 1960 with the help of his wily Lone Star running mate, Lyndon Johnson. He needed the state's twenty-four electoral votes and he needed to tap its riches for his campaign war chest and this is why he planned a two-day trip there in late November. The trip was a political necessity, but Kennedy and his staff dreaded it. "It's a real mess," Kenny O'Donnell told White House advance man Jerry Bruno in October. Texas's increasingly conservative white voters had turned sharply against Kennedy's liberal policies and open war had erupted in the state's Democratic Party between conservative Governor John Connally and liberal maverick Senator Ralph Yarborough. Connally, Kennedy's former Navy secretary, was well along the path that would eventually take him into the Republican Party. Fearing that the president could poison his own reelection chances in 1964, Connally made no secret of his opposition to the trip.

If Connally could not stop JFK from coming to his state, he was determined to control his itinerary, shuttling the president to exclusive fundraisers and limiting his public exposure so Texas Democrats would not suffer from an anti-Kennedy backlash. Tall, well-groomed, and blessed with the jutting-jawed good looks of a cowboy matinee hero, Connally seemed cut from the same cloth as the wealthy ranchers and oil men whom he politically served. He tried to intimidate the fireplug-shaped Bruno, when Kennedy's emissary met with him in the governor's mansion to plan the presidential visit. Towering over Bruno in his cowboy boots and surrounded by his aides, Connally began dictating the schedule for Kennedy's trip. If the president didn't like it, he informed Bruno, he could stay at home. "At one point," recalled JFK's advance man, "they brought in lunch: a juicy steak for Connally, a sandwich for me. And I'll tell you, if you've spent most of your life working with your hands, you know what they're trying to tell you with a move like that."

Connally was dead set against a presidential motorcade in Dallas, but the populist Yarborough lobbied aggressively for it. "Yarborough, the 'People's Senator,' felt the trip was too heavy on visits with fat cats and didn't provide enough of a chance for ordinary Texans to see the president," recalled Texas politician Ben Barnes, a Connally protégé who helped him organize the trip. The White House sided with Yarborough on the motorcade and let Connally know where he stood in the chain of command. "The president is not coming down to be hidden under a bushel basket," O'Donnell told Johnson aide Bill Moyers.

Privately, however, Yarborough and Kennedy's aides had deep misgivings about Dallas. The frontier boom city was a vortex of all the whirling passions that had bedeviled the Kennedy presidency. When *Dallas Morning News* publisher Ted Dealey insulted the president to his face in the White House, telling him he was not "the man on horseback" the nation needed but a pantywaist "on Caroline's tricycle," he knew he was speaking for most of his hometown, which voted for Nixon in 1960 by the widest margin of any major city. In the final days of the campaign, even native son LBJ had come under assault, when he and wife, Lady Bird, were spat upon and roughly jostled by a "mink coat mob" of right-wing women in the lobby of the city's plush Adolphus Hotel. A month before Kennedy was scheduled to visit Dallas, Adlai Stevenson—whose liberalism and UN ambassadorship made him a favorite target of the far right—was heckled off a stage in Dallas and then set upon by a mob outside the auditorium, who gobbed him, struck him over the head with a picket sign (which read "IF YOU SEEK PEACE, ASK JESUS"), and rocked his car as he tried to escape. "For a minute or two I thought we were going to be turned over," recalled Dallas department store mogul Stanley Marcus, who was accompanying Stevenson that day. "I told the driver step on it . . . [blast] your horn and get out of here in a hurry, which he did, and fortunately we didn't hit anybody [because] we were surrounded and I think we were in imminent danger of being manhandled."

Dallas was the city of retired General Edwin Walker, the apocalyptic "Christian Soldier" who electrified his fellow citizens with his attacks on

Kennedy's "defeatist" foreign policy and "socialistic" domestic agenda. JFK, he declared, was rapidly turning the American eagle into a "dead duck." It was a seething mecca for John Birchers, Minutemen, and Christian Crusaders.

Various people tried to warn JFK against going to Dallas, including Billy Graham, David Brinkley's wife, Ann, and Stanley Marcus. On a flight to Little Rock, William Fulbright—the man who had spearheaded the administration's Senate attack on the alarming politicization of the military—begged the president to cancel his trip, calling Dallas "a very dangerous place. I wouldn't go there. Don't *you* go." But Kennedy was determined to go. When Bobby and O'Donnell read a letter from a Democratic Party official in Texas imploring the president to stay away from Dallas because of the city's extreme animosity toward him, they didn't even pass it on to JFK. "If I had suggested cutting such a large and important city as Dallas from the itinerary because of [the] letter, the president would have thought that I had gone out of my mind," O'Donnell later noted.

Riding through the streets of Dallas in an open car would later come to exemplify the legendary Kennedy recklessness. It was pointed to as a prime example of the family's arrogant defiance of the fates. Joe Kennedy had brought up his children to be blithe daredevils, it was said, indoctrinating them with the powerful myth of Kennedy invincibility. But JFK would have strenuously rejected this interpretation of his decision to go to Dallas. Kennedy had long since stopped believing in the sublime exceptionality of his family. It was World War II that had destroyed this family myth, a young JFK wrote in a remarkably revealing 1947 letter to Claiborne Pell. The war had "savaged" his family, he confided to Pell, taking the lives of his older brother, sister, and brother-in-law. "It turned my father and brothers and sisters and I upside down and sucked all the oxygen out of our smug and comfortable assumptions. We still, with the old battles long over, have great confidence: great Kennedy confidence, which is the main strength of our tribe. But we sons and daughters no longer have that easy, witless, untested and meaningless confidence on which we'd been weaned before the war. Our father had us pretty well trained to appear to ourselves and others as unbeatable and immortal—a little bit like Gods. Now that's over with. Now, after all that we experienced and lost in the war, we finally understand that there is nothing inevitable about us. And that's a healthy thing to know."

It was Kennedy's sense of political duty that compelled him to Dallas, not recklessness. He knew there was nothing inevitable about his reelection. Lyndon Johnson would bury Goldwater in 1964, but his landslide was triggered by the seismic post-Dallas grief that shook the nation. Kennedy knew the election would be close. If he hoped to be reelected president, he could not let himself be run out of major cities in the country, no matter how hostile they seemed. He refused to cede any part of the nation to his enemies on the far right. In fact, he planned to use his trip to Dallas to denounce the threat of extremism in American life.

Here is what Kennedy planned to tell his audience at the Dallas Trade Mart on November 22, 1963, when he arrived there: Americans must stop listening to the voices of "nonsense" that blared "peace is a sign of weakness." The most effective way to demonstrate America's strength was not to brandish its awesome weapons and threaten its enemies. It was to live up to the country's democratic ideals, "practic[ing] what it preaches about equal rights and social justice," and pursuing peace instead of "aggressive ambitions." Kennedy had been warned not to inflame the city's right-wing passions, but he was undeterred. If the speech lit up Ted Dealey, so be it. Reading an advance copy of the Trade Mart address, Robert MacNeil—who was covering the Dallas visit for NBC News—was filled with a kind of pride, even though he had long maintained a journalistic skepticism toward Kennedy's seductive charms. "On reading this speech, I felt a surge of the intellectual power and rational force that he represented. I felt warmed by it and was looking forward to the moment when he would loose his barrage on the citizenry of Dallas."

Going to Dallas was a risky but essential mission, and the president fully embraced it. It was not LBJ who had strong-armed Kennedy into going, as some Johnson haters in the Kennedy camp later bitterly charged. In fact, Johnson was just as fearful of the political backlash against the administration in his home state as Connally was. Taking his New Frontier themes—peace and racial equality—into an Old Frontier state, Kennedy would directly engage with the rugged electorate of Texas and try to persuade them that his policies were in their best interest. Riding through the streets of Dallas in an open car filled with the radiance of the young first couple, the politically astute president knew, was a dramatic way of connecting directly with the people he hoped to win over with his vibrant message. The heroism of Kennedy's mission was underscored by his realization that it carried not just political risk but physical danger.

Kennedy took the threatening atmosphere in Dallas in fatalistic stride. When Dealey's newspaper ran a caustic, anti-Kennedy ad on the morning of November 22, he shrugged it off, but he knew that it would disturb Jackie. Framed in a funereal black border, the ad—which was paid for by right-wing oil baron H. L. Hunt's son, Nelson, and future Dallas Cowboys owner Bum

Bright—accused JFK of selling out the country to the Communists. "We're heading into nut country today," he told his wife that morning before their short plane ride from Fort Worth to Dallas. "But, Jackie, if somebody wants to shoot me from a window with a rifle, nobody can stop it, so why worry about it?"

JFK, who often broached the subject of assassination during his contentious years in office, seemed particularly preoccupied with the specter during his Texas trip. There was good reason for this. In the weeks preceding Dallas, he was informed of two serious assassination plots against him—one in Chicago and the other in Tampa. We can now conclude that Kennedy was, in fact, being methodically stalked in the final weeks of his life.

On Saturday, November 2, a motorcade that was to take the president from Chicago's O'Hare Airport to Soldier Field, where he would watch the Army-Air Force football game with Mayor Richard Daley, was abruptly canceled after the FBI informed the Secret Service of a plot to shoot the president before he reached his destination. The conspiracy, which was detailed in the 2005 book *Ultimate Sacrifice* by assassination researchers Lamar Waldron and Thom Hartmann, involved a four-man sniper team (at least two of whom were Cuban exiles) and a fall guy named Thomas Arthur Vallee with an Oswald-like profile (a troubled ex-Marine with an apparent affinity for guns and extremist politics). Kennedy was to be ambushed as his limousine made a slow, hairpin exit from the expressway onto Jackson Street—similar to the 90-degree turn his car would take onto Elm Street in Dallas shortly before the shots rang out there—passing a tall warehouse building where Vallee worked, not unlike the Texas School Book Depository. Vallee, who was arrested by Chicago police two hours before Kennedy's plane landed at O'Hare, later claimed that he was framed by someone with special knowledge of his background, namely his "CIA assignment to train exiles to kill Castro."

Later that month, another plot to kill Kennedy was exposed by law enforcement officials in Tampa, where the president was scheduled to ride in a lengthy motorcade on November 18 from MacDill Air Force Base to a speech at the National Guard Armory and then a second speech at the International Inn. "The Tampa attempt," noted Waldron and Hartmann, who interviewed former Tampa Police Chief J. P. Mullins and other officials about the plot, "had even more parallels to Dallas than Chicago." A key suspect in the Tampa plot, a Cuban exile named Gilberto Lopez, seemed stamped from the same strange mold as Oswald. Like the accused Dallas assassin, Lopez had earlier defected to Russia and masqueraded as a pro-Castro member of the Fair Play for Cuba Committee. Despite the plot—

which Waldron and Hartmann assert was aborted when one of its architects, Florida Mafia boss Santo Trafficante, was tipped off that it had been exposed—Kennedy went ahead with the motorcade. He even stood up in the moving limousine and waved to the crowds, to the distress of Secret Service agents and Tampa police officials assigned to protect him. Kennedy did not take the risk lightly—one Florida official later observed that he was under obvious strain that day—but he refused to let the growing threats against him preempt another motorcade so soon after Chicago and curtail his contact with the American people. JFK was also well aware of the electoral importance of Florida, the only other southern state besides Texas that he planned to aggressively contend in 1964.

By the final month of his life, John Kennedy seemed a marked man, encircled by a tightening knot of treachery. On the weekend of November 16, as the president took up residence in the family's Palm Beach mansion to work on his important olive branch/war arrow speech about Cuba that he planned to deliver in Miami, a suspicious group of Cuban exiles moved into the house next door. The group was led by a wealthy Bay of Pigs veteran named Alberto Fowler, who bitterly blamed the president for the brigade's defeat. Fowler later told the *New Orleans Times-Picayune* that he was simply trying to annoy Kennedy by blasting loud Cuban music all weekend. But his apparent role as an intelligence operative—after Dallas he tried to spread the false story that Oswald was a Castro agent and he later infiltrated Jim Garrison's New Orleans investigation of JFK's murder—point to a more disturbing explanation for his sudden appearance as Kennedy's neighbor.

Robert Kennedy was fully aware of the Chicago and Tampa plots, and while there is no evidence he knew about Fowler's odd stalking of the president, he was keenly conscious of the growing intrigue against his brother in the Cuban exile world. Bobby was Jack's protector, but he was also his political point man. The two roles must have clashed in a particularly disturbing way for Bobby in November 1963. Like his brother, he fully grasped how important the Texas trip was for their political ambitions. But he was growing increasingly apprehensive about Jack's safety, to the point where he was maneuvering to take away presidential protection duties from the Secret Service and bring them under his control in the attorney general's office. Like Kenny O'Donnell, the "third Kennedy brother" in the administration, Bobby could not bring himself to try to block Jack's Texas trip. The Kennedys were supposed be tough enough to ride out dark nights of foreboding. But Dallas disturbed him. Perhaps both brothers had a sense of what was coming.

On November 20, Bobby turned thirty-eight. He was in a gloomy, wry mood at the surprise party thrown for him at the Justice Department, mocking himself for being a drag on his brother's reelection chances. "Who do you think clinched the South for President Kennedy?" he exclaimed like a politician on the stump, while his staffers looked down in embarrassment. "Robert Kennedy, that's who!" No matter how maniacally he worked for his brother, it was never enough for Bobby. Later he went over to the White House for the annual reception for the judiciary. He talked to his brother about his forthcoming Texas trip. Why did Jack have to go on political missions like this, Bobby asked? "You are president and those duties are enough," he told his brother. There was a sad, wistful quality to his complaint, and of course, he knew exactly why Jack had to go.

JFK tried to jostle his younger brother out of his mood. "But, Bob, '64 is coming and I can't wait." Remember what Lord Tweedsmuir said, the president reminded his brother, invoking the Scottish diplomat and novelist he was fond of quoting: "Politics is a noble adventure." Then he clapped his brother on the back and marched out the door. Bobby never saw him again.

AS A BOY GROWING up in the tiny East Texas farm town of Chandler, Ralph Yarborough liked to hunt. But when he went into the woods by himself, a fear would always creep over him. This is something just built into a youngster, he would remark years later. Stalking his prey under a dark canopy of trees, accompanied only by his hunting dogs, he would get the shivers sometimes until he finally reached the open light. The same feeling of dread came over Yarborough on the afternoon of November 22, as he rode through the shadowy canyon of downtown Dallas, two cars behind the president.

The senator was squeezed into the backseat of a convertible between the vice president and his wife, Lady Bird—a cozy proximity that pleased neither of the men, who were pitted bitterly against one another in the Texas Democratic Party feud. LBJ still resented Yarborough for breaking ranks with the Texas delegation at the 1960 Democratic convention and throwing his support to Kennedy instead of Johnson, the state's favorite son. And Yarborough felt, with considerable cause, that the conservative Johnson-Connally wing of the state's Democratic Party had been seeking to punish the renegade liberal ever since. When the president's plane landed at Love Field at 11:38 that morning, Kennedy—desperately trying to smooth over the dispute during his trip—had to order Yarborough to ride in Johnson's car. White House aide Larry O'Brien backed up the president's demand by shoving Yarborough into the vehicle at the airport and slamming the door behind him to ensure the bickering politicians presented a harmonious face to the Dallas crowds.

As the motorcade left Love Field, heading down Mockingbird Lane toward downtown, the senator, who could turn on the folksy charm when he needed to, quickly slipped into his proper role, shouting "Howdy thar!" to the spectators lining the streets, while Johnson sat sullenly beside him.

When the motorcade began gliding down Main Street, underneath the dark towers of corporate Dallas, Yarborough's mood began to change. The old boyhood fear came upon him. On the street, the crowd—which was now ten to twelve people deep—seemed exuberant, raucously cheering the president and first lady, who was making her first trip to Texas. But the senator did not like what he saw when his eyes scanned the office building windows. The people standing there—businessmen and their secretaries—stared with eerie silence at the passing spectacle. "They stood there rather stonily," Yarborough would recall. "They just stood there looking at the president. And they weren't saying anything . . . I'd look up there on the second, third floor, I'd see people through glass windows up there, standing back. . . . They'd be looking down at the president, it looked to me like, with positive hate. I saw them, and I grew apprehensive." Among the grim-faced office building spectators was ultra-right oil tycoon Hunt, who gazed down at the president from his seventh-floor perch in the Mercantile Building, flanked by two secretaries.

Yarborough was afraid that someone would throw a pot of flowers or something and hit the first lady. As the presidential cavalcade moved slowly down Main Street's sunless gulch, the senator strained to see the open light, as he had on his boyhood expeditions through the woods. If they could just get through the dark shadows of downtown, he felt they would be safe.

When the motorcade reached sun-spangled Dealey Plaza, Yarborough breathed a sigh of relief. It was like finally coming out into the open fields with his dogs when he was twelve. "I thought, 'I'm glad to see daylight. I'm glad we're through.' I felt safe the minute we got [there]. It's all over."

But as the column of cars turned left on Elm Street, heading for the expressway to the Dallas Trade Mart, a noise rang out that snapped Yarborough immediately back to his childhood terrors. This time he felt like the hunted, not the hunter. It was the unmistakable sound of a rifle shot, quickly followed by more shots. The day froze dead in its tracks. And then he caught a sharp whiff of gunpowder on the breathless air.

Hunted down, ambushed—these were the ways that passengers in the motorcade would describe their doomed feeling that day. They were trapped in a crossfire. And the prey, the president of the United States, was defenseless. For the rest of his life, Yarborough would wonder about the peculiar

stone-footed reaction of the Secret Service that day. "Here stood the Secret
Service men around that car in front of me like a bunch of dupes," he would
spit. "They didn't do anything. They stood and stared around." Everyone except agent Clint Hill. After he threw himself into the presidential limousine
as it suddenly began to accelerate from its near dead stop on Elm Street, Hill
beat his hand on the back of the car. Yarborough never forgot the awful sight.
"He had all kinds of anguish written on his face and despair and everything
else." Seeing that, "I knew they had either killed or seriously wounded the
president."

John F. Kennedy had been gunned down at high noon, in a Dallas plaza
named for the frontier-era father of Kennedy-hater Ted Dealey. JFK, the avid
reader of history, would have appreciated the ripe irony.

Americans would get some sense of the utter horror—the visceral obscenity—of Dealey Plaza, when a home movie of the assassination made by
a fifty-nine-year-old Dallas dress manufacturer named Abraham Zapruder
was finally excavated from the *Life* magazine vault where it had been kept
for years and widely exhibited. The infamous twenty-six-second film clip of
the president's final moments—culminating in the repulsive frame where a
searing bolt slams his head viciously backwards, tearing off a shard of his
skull in a spray of bloody mist—will forever punish the souls of those who
watch it. Zapruder himself paid a terrible price for being the nation's eyewitness. Amazingly, he kept steadily filming the horrible spectacle as it unfolded in graphic detail before his camera. Then he clambered down from
his vantage point—a concrete abutment on the grassy knoll overlooking the
crime scene—and stumbled back to his office in a daze, screaming, "They
killed him, they killed him, they killed him!" Afterwards, he sat at his desk
sobbing.

A terrible thought flashed across Zapruder's mind as he watched his president being executed before his eyes. "I just felt that somebody had ganged
up on him." His words—conjuring the image of the most powerful man in the
country bullied into bloody submission by anonymous assailants—are still
deeply troubling.

Zapruder, a Russian Jewish immigrant who came to America as a teenager, never recovered from the shock of what he intimately observed through
the lens of his Bell & Howell 8mm movie camera. For the rest of his life, he
suffered recurring nightmares. When he was called before the Warren Commission in July 1964, he broke down in tears as he relived the afternoon. At
the end of his testimony, he apologized abjectly for his outburst of emotion.
"I am ashamed of myself," he told the staff attorney taking his testimony. "I

didn't know I was going to break down, and for a man to—but it was a tragic thing, and when you started asking me that, and I saw the thing all over again, and it was an awful thing—I know very few people who had seen it like that—it was an awful thing and I loved the president. And to see that happen before my eyes—his head just opened up and shot down like a dog— it leaves a very, very deep sentimental impression with you. It's terrible."

Wesley Liebeler—the assistant counsel who was dispatched to belatedly and perfunctorily take Zapruder's eyewitness account—was not interested in hearing about his trauma. Nor was the attorney particularly interested in his observations that the shots "came from right behind me" on the grassy knoll—the spot where most eyewitnesses and police bystanders that afternoon immediately suspected the sniper's nest was located. The Warren Commission, which originally did not plan on interviewing Zapruder at all, treated him as an afterthought. But his 486-frame film would reveal more about the death of the president than the vast twenty-six-volume report delivered by the commission chairman, Chief Justice Earl Warren, to President Johnson on September 24, 1964. Zapruder's handheld horror movie would live on long after his death in 1970, a haunting testament to how President Kennedy was "ganged up on" in Dealey Plaza by more than one assailant—gunmen firing shots from the front as well as rear of the presidential limousine.

As dreadful as it was, the Zapruder film did not capture the full mayhem inside the presidential limousine during the explosion of violence in Dealey Plaza. But the wives of the two men shot that day—Jackie Kennedy and Nellie Connally—would insist on telling everything they witnessed. It was Jackie's wrenchingly matter-of-fact account, delivered to *Life* magazine correspondent Theodore White in an extraordinary interview at the family's Hyannis Port compound one week after Dallas, that most vividly conveyed the unfiltered horror of it all. This—along with the interview she gave William Manchester, the family's authorized chronicler of the assassination—would be the only times she ever publicly discussed November 22, 1963. Sitting on a sofa, dressed in black slacks and a beige pullover—her dark eyes "wider than pools"—she told her unspeakable story to White in a remarkably calm voice. The words poured out of her as if she were in a trance. "I realized that I was going to hear more than I wanted to," White later wrote—an odd comment for a journalist who had just scored the scoop of his career.

White's employer shared his tender sensibilities. Once again, *Life* would find it necessary to suppress a terrible document of Dealey Plaza, publishing a soothingly expurgated version of the interview in its December 6, 1963, issue. The brief article, "An Epilogue for President Kennedy," focused on JFK's love of the musical *Camelot*, helping turn his story into a gauzy Arthurian legend instead of the monstrous crime mystery it was. Missing was the eyewitness testimony of a woman still scorched by what she had endured just one week earlier. But over three decades later, following the death of Jacqueline Kennedy Onassis in 1994, the Kennedy Library finally released White's "Camelot documents," including his handwritten notes from the interview. Despite the passage of time, Jackie's account was still awful to read. And media coverage of the documents' release was still decorous, pulling a veil over the grisly details that Jackie could not forget.

The motorcade from the airport that afternoon put her in mind of the first couple's tumultuous procession through the streets of Mexico City the previous year, Jackie told White. It was "hot, wild" and the sun was blazing in her eyes. Jack had asked her not to wear her sunglasses for fear it would make the first lady look too much like an aloof movie queen to the people on the Dallas streets. She was happy to oblige him, knowing how important the Texas trip was to her husband's political fortunes. After suffering the death of their newborn son Patrick in August, the couple seemed closer than they had been in a long time. Jackie had grown weary of the political circus, but riding with her husband that day was an expression of her love. JFK, who took pleasure from the electric effect that his wife had on crowds, deeply appreciated her company on the trip. Even without their sunglasses, the couple emitted a starry glow as they waved to the boisterous crowds lining the streets. Sitting in the press bus several cars behind the Kennedys' limousine, Robert Donovan, the *Los Angeles Times* Washington bureau chief, mused that "if Hollywood had tried to cast a president and his wife, they could never have dreamed up John F. Kennedy and Jacqueline Kennedy. They were just two beautiful people that day, glamorous, and they had a screaming reception. There was never a point in the public life of the Kennedys, in a way, that was as high as that moment in Dallas."

Nellie Connally was relieved and elated by the cheering crowds. As their car turned slowly onto Elm Street, she shifted around in the jump seat where she was riding next to her husband, and beamed at Kennedy: "Mr. President, you certainly can't say that Dallas doesn't love you!" His eyes grew wide with excitement. Dallas had surprised him, thought Nellie. And then the plaza rang with the first gunshot.

The first bullet tore through Kennedy's throat, and his arms went up as if to block himself from further injury. His wife turned to him, and just as she did, another bullet shattered his head. The picture of her husband in his final moment of life seared itself into her memory. She remembered the strange elegance of his demeanor. "His last expression was so neat; he had his hand out, I could see a piece of his skull coming off; it was flesh-colored not white. He was holding out his hand—and I can see this perfectly clean piece detaching itself from his head; then he slumped in my lap."

Later in her interview with White, Jackie returned to the moment of her husband's death. It was an odd association to make, but something about his face brought back the alert play of his mind at press conferences. "You know when he was shot. He had such a wonderful expression on his face. You know that wonderful expression he had when they'd ask him a question about one of the ten million gadgets they'd have in a rocket? Just before he'd answer, he looked puzzled; and then he slumped forward."

Now the contents of her husband's precious brain were spilled all over the car. They splattered everyone riding in the limousine. To Nellie Connally it felt like she was being tattooed by "hot hail." Even the motorcycle cops riding uselessly behind the presidential vehicle were splashed with Kennedy's life matter.

The first lady tore the air with her frantic screams: "Jack, Jack!" And then: "They've killed my husband! I have his brains in my hand!"

Nellie Connally could offer no help. She was bent over her own husband, who was gushing blood through his shirt. By holding him tightly, Nellie Connally would save her husband's life, blocking the gaping hole in his chest. "My God, they are going to kill us all!" the governor blurted before sagging forward. The Connallys would forever insist—contrary to the Warren Report, which strained to limit the number of bullets fired that day to fit its lone gunman theory—that the bullet that ripped into the governor's back was not one of those that hit the president.

Suddenly the first lady, her pink suit drenched in her husband's gore, was clambering onto the trunk of the moving limousine. She needed to retrieve the missing fragment of her husband's skull. It was the only way that she could save him, that she could make him whole again. The sprinting Clint Hill pushed her back into the car, just as it suddenly sped off to Parkland Hospital. "We all lay down in the car and I kept saying, 'Jack, Jack, Jack' and someone was yelling, 'He's dead, he's dead,'" she told White. "All the ride to the hospital, I kept bending over him saying, 'Jack, Jack, can you hear me, I love you, Jack.' I kept holding the top of his head down trying to keep the . . ." She could not finish the sentence.

At the hospital, sitting in the terrible Lincoln—"long and black as a hearse," in Nellie's words—Jackie could not let go of her broken husband.

"The seat was full of blood and red roses," she recalled. Everywhere else during the trip, they had given her the yellow roses of Texas. But at Love Field, she had been presented a bouquet of red American Beauties. Secret Service men were suddenly swarming everywhere, screaming, "Mr. President!" They pleaded with Jackie to get out of the car. "These big Texas interns kept saying, 'Mrs. Kennedy, you come with us.' They wanted to take me away from him. Dave Powers came running to me; my legs, my hands were covered with his brains. When Dave saw this, he burst out weeping. From here down"—and here, she made a gesture indicating her husband's forehead—"his head was so beautiful. I'd tried to hold the top of his head down, maybe I could keep it in . . . I knew he was dead.

"They came trying to get me; they tried to grab me, but I said, 'I'm not leaving.' When they carried Jack in, Hill threw his coat over Jack's head [but] it wasn't repulsive to me for one moment—nothing was repulsive to me. And I was running behind this big intern, I was running behind with the coat covering it. I remember this narrow corridor. I said, 'I'm not going to leave him, I'm not going to leave him, I'm not going to leave him.'" She remembered the grueling back operation that had nearly killed him when they were newlyweds. She had promised him that she would not leave his side during the surgery, but they had taken him away and she had not seen him again for hours. "They're never going to keep me away from him again," she told herself at Parkland.

Dr. Malcolm Perry, the surgeon working on her dying husband, did not want her in the operating room, but she forced her way in. She told him, "It's my husband, his blood, his brains are all over me." There was nothing Perry and the other doctors could do to save her husband. A priest was summoned to deliver the final rites. "There was a sheet over Jack, his foot was sticking out of the sheet, whiter than the sheet. I took his foot and kissed it. Then I pulled back the sheet. His mouth was *so beautiful*, his eyes were open. They found his hand under the sheet, and I held his hand all the time the priest was saying extreme unction."

In the months following Dallas, the fallen president's deeply despondent widow sought counsel from a Jesuit priest named Richard McSorley. She was plagued by something from that day, she told McSorley. Her husband was already dying from the fatal second shot before she realized it. "If only I had a minute to say goodbye. It was so hard not to say goodbye, not to be able to say goodbye."

Later, in the hot confines of Air Force One, which Lyndon Johnson insisted stay on the Love Field tarmac until he was sworn in as the new president of the United States, everybody urged her to wipe her husband's dried blood off her face. A photographer was going to commemorate the historic ceremony and Johnson wanted Jackie by his side. She stared at herself in the mirror. "My whole face was splattered with blood and hair. I wiped it off with a Kleenex." But she immediately regretted it. "One second later I thought, why did I wash the blood off? I should have left it there, let them see what they've done." That's what she told Bobby when she saw him later. They should have seen her with her painted face and clotted hair when the famous photo was taken on Air Force One; her horrible visage would have condemned them for all time.

But, widowed at thirty-four, she already felt herself fading into history. White's notes are filled with the word. She repeated it often during the interview. "History," she said inexplicably at one point, as if describing herself, for that's what she was becoming. As Air Force One flew through the darkening sky to Washington, events were already sweeping past her. "I thought no one really wants me here."

For a brief, savage moment, Jacqueline Kennedy considered playing the role of a raging truth-teller from a Greek tragedy. This is how they killed the king! This is how they spilled his beautiful mind into my hands! But she would soon allow herself to be turned into "the Widder Kennedy," as she mocked her image—the stoic woman who taught a nation how to mourn.

IN THE CHAOTIC HOURS after Dealey Plaza, the world tilted off its axis. Global leaders wondered whether the assassination of the U.S. president meant the beginning of nuclear war. The newly inaugurated president was not certain if he could control the shock waves from Dallas. Like his predecessor, he did not feel in full command of the country's military machine. Would he be history's master, or its victim, wondered Lyndon Johnson as Air Force One carried him, along with Kennedy's remains and his shattered retinue, back to Washington?

Bill Moyers, Johnson's young protégé, had rushed to his side as soon as he heard about the assassination, chartering a private plane in Austin, where he had been overseeing the final leg of the Texas trip, and flying to Dallas before Air Force One took off. Johnson—surrounded by angry, distraught Kennedy loyalists—was relieved to see the fresh-scrubbed face of the former Baptist seminarian on board. The two Texans were closely connected by what Moyers called an almost-familial "umbilical cord." Johnson—who knew that the Kennedy circle liked the bright, young Texan, who was serving as Sargent Shriver's Peace Corps deputy at the time—needed him more than ever now. While Air Force One was still in the air, the new president re-cruited him to be his special assistant.

At one point during the flight, Moyers noticed his old mentor sitting by himself, gazing intently at the passing clouds outside his window. "What's on your mind, Mr. President?" asked Moyers. A grim-looking Johnson turned to him and said, "I wonder if the missiles are flying." Moyers was puzzled by the remark at the time. If the United States was launching a nuclear attack, certainly the new president would know it. But, in the frantic aftermath of Dallas, Johnson was clearly unsure who was running the country.

"The thought in Johnson's mind at this time could only be that there had been a coup, and that once the airplane took off from Love Field for Wash-ington, the country would spin into the hands of the button-pushers," ob-served James K. Galbraith, a political historian at the University of Texas's Lyndon B. Johnson School of Public Affairs, in a recent interview. Galbraith, the son of the late economist and Kennedy advisor John Kenneth Galbraith, added that "Johnson knew that this was the moment of maximum strategic advantage" for national security hard-liners who yearned for a final confron-tation with the country's enemies. For nearly three years, Kennedy and Mc-Namara had held off these rabid advocates of a final nuclear solution. But with JFK bluntly removed from the chain of command, there was no telling what they would now attempt.

These same fears were gripping the two foreign leaders most likely to be attacked by unhinged nuclear warriors in the United States. In Cuba, Fidel Castro was eating lunch with Jean Daniel, the French journalist who had brought peace feelers from President Kennedy, at the Cuban leader's Varadero Beach residence when he received the stunning report about Dallas. "This is bad news," a dazed Castro repeated three times after putting down the phone.

After their long and bitter jousting, Castro had begun to see Kennedy as an agent of change. "He still has the possibility of becoming, in the eyes of history, the greatest president of the United States, the leader who may at last understand that there can be coexistence between capitalists and social-ists, even in the Americas," Castro told Daniel during an all-night interview session on the eve of Dallas. "He would then be an even greater president than Lincoln. I know, for example, that for Khrushchev, Kennedy is a man you can talk with. I have gotten this impression from all my conversations with Khrushchev."

Then Castro broke into what his French visitor described as a "broad and boyish grin," pledging to help Kennedy in his reelection campaign: "If you see him again, you can tell him that I'm willing to declare Goldwater my friend if that will guarantee Kennedy's reelection!"

But on the afternoon of November 22, as Castro and Daniel huddled over a radio, listening to an NBC News broadcast from Miami, the Cuban leader's mood grew dark and foreboding. When Kennedy's death was confirmed, Castro stood up and said, "Everything is changed."

Then, as the radio played "The Star Spangled Banner," Castro, surrounded by a circle of worried aides, made an astute prediction: "You watch and see, I know them, they will try to put the blame on us for this thing." Later, as they rode in Castro's car, the radio reported that Lee Harvey Oswald, the accused assassin, was married to a Russian. "There! Didn't I tell you; it'll be my turn next," erupted the Cuban leader. Minutes later, it was. The American broadcaster reported that Oswald was a Castro admirer who belonged to the Fair Play for Cuba Committee. At first he tried to shrug it off, calling it an obvious "propaganda device. It's terrible. But you know, I'm sure this will all soon blow over. There are too many competing policies in the United States for any single one to be able to impose itself universally for very long."

But as the radio announcer ominously confirmed that Kennedy's assassin was a "pro-Castro Marxist" and the tone of the reports grew increasingly shrill and aggressive, Castro's equanimity began to fail him. He started grilling Daniel about what he knew of the new U.S. president. What were Johnson's relations with Kennedy? With Khrushchev? What was his position on the Bay of Pigs? And then, "finally and most important of all," Daniel recalled, Castro asked him: "What authority does he exercise over the CIA?" It was a question that Lyndon Johnson was asking himself at the very same time.

Meanwhile, in Moscow, the roly-poly leader who, clowning and growling, had at first tried to intimidate the young, untested American president—and then, after he had taken his measure of the man, settled into a mutually respectful quest with him for world peace—was utterly undone. Hearing the news from Dallas, Khrushchev broke down and sobbed in the Kremlin. He took the news as "a personal blow," said one aide. For several days, he was unable to perform his duties. Khrushchev was convinced that Kennedy was killed by militaristic forces in Washington bent on sabotaging the two leaders' efforts to reach détente. Would they now launch a nuclear strike on the Soviet Union? Would the Soviet leader be ousted by hard-line forces in his own government?

"Khrushchev needed Kennedy and thought Kennedy needed him," observed Khrushchev biographer William Taubman. Together, they were staking out a course that was steering the two countries away from nuclear brinksmanship to a new world harmony. Even administration tough guy Bobby Kennedy looked forward to a second summit meeting, where—unlike the abrasive posturing of Vienna—the two leaders could "calmly sit and talk everything over." Now Khrushchev's essential partner was gone.

At the White House reception for the foreign dignitaries who attended Kennedy's funeral, the guests were surprised to see the president's widow coming downstairs to greet them, despite everything she had been through. In the receiving line, the Russian representative—Khrushchev's old warhorse deputy, Anastas Mikoyan—approached Jackie, visibly trembling. She clasped both his hands in hers and in a voice filled with deep emotion, said, "Please tell Mr. Chairman President that I know he and my husband worked together for a peaceful world, and now he and you must carry on my husband's work." The old Bolshevik blinked and hid his face with both hands.

A week later, Jackie Kennedy followed up her remarks to Mikoyan by writing a letter directly to Khrushchev, to make sure he clearly understood her message. The day of the funeral had been so "horrible" for her, she explained in the letter, that she did not know how lucid she was in her brief conversation with his representative. She told Khrushchev how her late husband had regarded him as an integral force for peace. And then she made a revealing reference to the obstacles that Kennedy had faced in his search for détente—one that certainly would have resonated with the Russian leader, who confronted similar opposition at home. "The danger troubling my husband was that war could be started not so much by major figures as by minor ones," wrote Mrs. Kennedy. "Whereas major figures understand the need for self-control and restraint, minor ones are sometimes moved by fear and pride. If only in the future major figures could still force minor ones to sit down at the negotiating table before they begin to fight!"

Jackie's letter appeared to reinforce the confidential message that she and Bobby sent to the Soviet leadership that same week through their trusted friend Bill Walton: President Kennedy had been the victim of a conspiracy of small-minded men.

After Kennedy's death, Khrushchev's own days in office were numbered. In October 1964, less than a year after JFK's assassination, the Soviet leader was removed from power in a shake-up engineered by his more stolid, less imaginative rival, Leonid Brezhnev. Ironically, it was a bloodless coup.

Living out his final years in domestic exile, sequestered in a log cabin on the banks of the Istra River, Khrushchev pursued his own personal glasnost.

He bitterly complained about how the Brezhnev regime was reversing his reforms. Listening to the BBC and the Voice of America on an old Zenith short-wave radio given to him years before by an American businessman, he grew increasingly impatient with the heavy-handed propaganda of the Soviet media. "This is just garbage!" he fumed, flipping through *Pravda*. He read a samizdat copy of *Dr. Zhivago* and regretted that his government censors had banned it. "I should have read it myself," he said. He denounced the jailing of dissident Soviet writers and expressed disgust over the 1968 invasion of Czechoslovakia. "What kind of socialism is this? What kind of shit is it when you have to keep people in chains?"

Towards the end of his life, Khrushchev began work on his memoir. When the news reached Moscow, the Politburo demanded that he immediately stop and hand over what he had written to the Central Committee. He defiantly refused and after completing the manuscript, like a dissident writer, he had it smuggled out of the country and published in the West, where it became an instant bestseller. In the book, titled *Khrushchev Remembers*, the retired autocrat wistfully recalled his days with Kennedy, whom he praised as a "real statesman" despite his youth. If Kennedy had lived, he wrote, the two men could have brought peace to the world.

On September 11, 1971, less than a year after his memoir was published in the United States, Khrushchev died of a failed heart. The Central Committee decreed there would be no fanfare and no formal Red Square funeral. His wake was held in a drab red-brick building and he was quietly buried in the remote corner of a Moscow cemetery next to a sixteenth century nunnery. Only a small crowd of determined mourners was allowed through the lines of police, who photographed them as they entered the cemetery. It would take four years for his family to get permission to put a monument at the head of his grave.

IN THE WEEKS AFTER Dallas, as political leaders and intelligence services all over the world were struggling to make sense of the assassination, so was Robert Kennedy. But his was a deeply emotional, as well as political, struggle. As the days went by, his rush to uncover the mystery faltered. Overtaken by the enormity of his loss, his investigative zeal began to ebb away. His brother was the center of his orbit, and his sun had fallen from the sky. What difference would it make to solve Jack's murder, he would tell people—it wouldn't bring him back. But as Robert Kennedy slowly emerged from his tomb of mourning, his quest for justice was reborn as well.

Robert Kennedy wore the burden of that mission uneasily. At times he did not want to face the truth. He suspected that the conspiracy involved elements of his own government, and he realized that following its dark trail could tear apart the country. He also feared that the quest would highlight the brothers' own fatal errors—and reveal how his own passions had stirred up the furies that took Jack's life. And, finally, he knew that the search would put him in mortal danger. But, in the end, Kennedy could not help but pursue the truth.

6

THE AWFUL GRACE OF GOD

In moments of national crisis, the public's desire to huddle together and put its trust in the country's leadership can be frantically powerful. Such was the mood of the country in the days and weeks after Dallas. The government declared that the calamity that had befallen the nation was the work of one misfit, and that his shocking elimination two days later was the work of another distraught individual. The press rushed to endorse this conclusion. There was only one lingering mystery, the public was reassured—that of the human soul. Whatever prompted Lee Harvey Oswald to kill the president— a man whose civil rights record he was said to admire—was a secret that he took with him to the grave.

It takes a certain temperament to challenge a national consensus with the near compulsory power that the lone gunman theory had in the aftermath of John F. Kennedy's assassination. A pugnacious self-righteousness and a charmless egocentricity are certainly essential ingredients of this personality. And these happened to be defining characteristics of a thirty-six-year-old crusading New York attorney named Mark Lane. He would become the first American to throw himself in front of the freight car of official opinion, declaring that Oswald had been railroaded to infamy without an honest public hearing and that "the assassin of President Kennedy remains at large."

Less than a month after the assassination, in the December 19, 1963, issue of a left-wing national weekly paper called the *Guardian*, Lane published a ten-thousand-word broadside that punched disturbing holes in the official version of the crime. The attorney highlighted a list of inconvenient facts about the case, including several that would become the cornerstone of conspiracy research for decades to come. How could Oswald have been the lone gunman, firing from his perch in the Texas School Book Depository behind the president's car, when Parkland Hospital doctors declared that one of the bullets fired at Kennedy struck him in the throat? How could a gunman using a rudimentary, bolt-action rifle that he had purchased for $12.78 squeeze off three expertly aimed shots in less than six seconds—a feat that even the skilled marksman who headed the National Rifle Association was unable to match? Why would alleged left-winger Oswald kill a president who was intent on improving relations with the Soviet Union and Cuba—a man whom Fidel Castro believed could become "the greatest president of the United States"?

Despite the marginality of the *Guardian*—where Lane was forced to take his work after getting rejections from a wide range of U.S. publications, including *Life*, *Look*, the *Saturday Evening Post*, the *Nation*, and *Fact* ("the magazine of controversy")—his article created a sensation. When the issue promptly sold out on the newsstands, the *Guardian* printed thousands of extra copies of the article in pamphlet form. Blacked out by the American media, Lane found an eager audience in the European press. He also formed a Citizens Committee of Inquiry, which began interviewing Dealey Plaza witnesses, and he rented a New York theater, where each evening for many months he presented his case against the lone gunman theory.

On January 14, 1964, Oswald's mother, Marguerite, hired Lane to represent her son before the Warren Commission. Portrayed in the media as a figure of frazzled pathos, the plump, matronly Marguerite would insist in her testimony before the commission that her son was a U.S. "intelligence agent" and that he was "set up to take the blame" for the assassination. When Lane himself later went before the commission, he insisted the session be held in public—the only time the secretive panel did so—and the confrontation was heated. "We had very, very little trouble of any kind" during the hearings, Supreme Court Chief Justice Earl Warren—the panel's chairman—later recalled, "except from one fellow by the name of Mark Lane. And he was the only one that treated the commission with contempt."

Lane knew the Kennedy brothers slightly from the 1960 campaign, when he ran successfully at the bottom of the Democratic ticket for a New York assembly seat. The young attorney was part of a reform movement that was trying to wrest control of the city's Democratic Party from the corrupt Tammany Hall machine. When Bobby met with the group at the Kennedys' Car-lyle Hotel suite, he shocked the West Side liberals by bluntly telling them their righteous battle to clean up New York city politics was not as important as getting his brother elected president. "Once he's elected we don't give a damn if blood runs in the streets of New York," Bobby informed them. After-ward, the reformers clucked in outrage. But Lane did not share their indigna-tion. "Bobby might be lacking in tact, courtesy and manners," he felt. "His honesty was commendable, however."

Bobby did not return Lane's admiration. Despite his own hard-nosed reputation, Kennedy was often rubbed the wrong way by abrasive personali-ties. "He just didn't like him," recalled Kennedy aide Frank Mankiewicz. "I'm really sorry that Mark Lane jumped in [to the assassination inquiry] so quick. He gave the whole thing a kind of a queer, bizarre tone."

In January 1964, Bobby returned to what was now his forlorn post at the Justice Department. His law enforcement team was drifting without his en-ergetic direction. "We need you," Walter Sheridan had told him. "Yeah, I know," Bobby had replied, "but I don't have the heart for it right now." Later that month, his friends in the administration arranged for Kennedy to make an official visit to Indonesia, to take his mind off his loss. The trip briefly restored his sense of purpose. But Dallas was looming for him as soon as he returned. Among his first callers after arriving back in Washington was Mark Lane.

"I said, 'I'd like to see you,'" recalled Lane. "He said, 'All right. Lunch tomorrow?' I said, 'OK.' And then he said, 'But you're not going to talk about *that*, are you?'" Kennedy still could not bring himself to give the assassina-tion its name.

Lane's notoriety as an assassination researcher was already on the rise and he knew exactly what "that" meant. "Yes, that's what I want to talk to you about," Lane told Kennedy. And then the attorney made the mistake of play-ing a card that was far too explosive with Kennedy. He told Bobby, "You know, you have an obligation—" Before he could finish his sentence, Kennedy sharply cut him off. "Don't you tell me about my obligations to my family." The conversation skid to an abrupt conclusion. "If that's the only thing you want to talk about, Mark," said Kennedy, "then we're not going to meet." The two men never spoke again.

The chilly exchange between Kennedy and Lane set the stage for Bobby's awkward and volatile relationship with assassination watchdogs for years to come. Kennedy could not stop himself from avidly following their activities, and even sometimes personally engaging with them. But he was easily put off by their often tactless or eccentric personalities, and seemed relieved when this gave him an excuse to dismiss their investigative work, no matter how valid it might be. Their very existence shamed and disturbed him, because their inquiries were boldly public, while he felt forced to carry out his own search in dark privacy.

In the gray, lifeless winter months following the death of his brother, Bobby lacked the will to face what had happened in Dallas. His burst of investigative passion in November quickly drained out of him, replaced by a paralyzing sense of loss. Nevertheless, Kennedy's friends felt driven to keep bringing information about the assassination to his attention. In December, Arthur Schlesinger was impressed enough by a sober and meticulous dissection of the lone gunman theory that appeared in the *New Republic* two days after the publication of Lane's essay to send a copy to Bobby. Titled "Seeds of Doubt," the article—written by scholars Jack Minnis and Staughton Lynd—raised many of the same questions about the case as Lane did, but without his rhetorical flourishes. Concerned citizens also wrote Kennedy's office to express their fears of a conspiracy. "To paraphrase Shakespeare, there is something rotten in Dallas," University of Illinois psychology professor Charles E. Osgood, a former chairman of the American Psychological Association, declared in a letter to the attorney general.

In March, Kennedy was urged to contact two journalists whose work on the case was beginning to attract the same florid attention as Lane's— syndicated gossip columnist and game show celebrity Dorothy Kilgallen and a Paris-based American journalist named Thomas Buchanan. Writing in the French newsweekly *L'Express*, Buchanan had created a stir by charging that President Kennedy was the victim of a far-right plot. His *L'Express* articles would become the basis for the first JFK conspiracy book—*Who Killed Kennedy?*—which was released in May by a British publisher.

Buchanan's articles were part of a wave of European press coverage that tartly questioned the official version of Kennedy's demise. While the U.S. press accepted the soothing reassurances of Washington officials, European publications cried out that something dark and foul had occurred in Dallas. As Raymond Cartier wrote in *Paris-Match*, the *Life* magazine of France, "Europe, almost in totality, rejects" the official view of the crime. "Europeans are convinced the Dallas drama hides a mystery, which, if uncovered, would dishonor the United States and shake it to its foundations."

Buchanan alleged that Oswald was a low-level CIA agent who had been assisted by others in the crime. The petty crook who dispatched him, Jack Ruby, was a coconspirator known to Oswald. The motive for the assassination, according to Buchanan, was to disrupt the developing détente between Washington and Moscow, which threatened the weapons industries on which the plotters depended. "I believe [Kennedy] lived for something, and I think he died for something," Buchanan would conclude in his book. "Any man is measured by his enemies. The list of those who hated Kennedy the day he died does honor to him. It must never be forgotten that he went to Dallas to combat these men, to tell the people of that city, of the nation and the world beyond, that peace is not a sign of weakness."

Like Mark Lane, who was ridiculed in the U.S. media as paranoid (while his phones were being tapped and offices bugged by the FBI), Buchanan received rough treatment in his native country. *Washington Post* columnist Chalmers Roberts notified his readers that Buchanan had been fired in 1948 as a *Washington Star* reporter after confessing a brief membership in the Communist Party. (Blacklisted at home, Buchanan had been forced to go overseas to find employment.) "On the face of it, it is absurd to call Buchanan, an admitted former Communist now living in Paris, a 'rival' to the group of seven distinguished Americans headed by the Chief Justice of the United States," sniffed Roberts. But that is just the predicament that the Warren Commission found itself in, lamented the columnist, after Buchanan "sowed vast quantities of seeds of doubt about the assassination."

But Ben Bradlee, JFK's press pal who was destined to take over Roberts's newspaper the following year, had a higher estimation of Buchanan. On March 9, 1964, Bradlee phoned Bobby Kennedy at the Justice Department, getting his efficient secretary Angie Novello, who told him the attorney general was in New York for the day. Bradlee left a message for Kennedy, urging him to meet with Buchanan, who was visiting the United States at the time. Buchanan was "one of the most articulate writers on the assassination," according to the message Novello relayed to Kennedy, and "is most anxious to see you without going to the FBI." Novello asked Bradlee if Buchanan "had some information" for Kennedy "and Ben said he did, but he also wanted some information" from the attorney general.

Bobby apparently did not meet with Buchanan. Instead, he directed him to his brother Ted, who in turn steered him to Nick Katzenbach, the Justice Department official whom RFK had asked to serve as his liaison—or, more accurately, his screener—with the Warren Commission. Katzenbach dutifully met with Buchanan for an hour and then passed him on to a commission staff member, who took the journalist's material and dropped it deep in the panel's voluminous files.

The same day that Ben Bradlee was trying to set up a meeting between

RFK and Buchanan, Pierre Salinger was intervening with Kennedy on behalf of Dorothy Kilgallen. "[Salinger] says Kilgallen has been calling him for an appointment with you," read a phone message for Bobby, because "she has some information she wants to turn over to you."

There is no evidence that Kennedy and Kilgallen met to discuss Dallas. But the Hearst newspaper columnist—known to millions for her sensational scoops as well as her regular guest slot on the popular Sunday evening game show *What's My Line?*—was digging more and more into the assassination. Kilgallen would become a thorn in the side of the Warren Commission, running a leaked copy of Ruby's testimony—which exposed the hapless quality of the panel's interrogation, prompting an FBI investigation of the newspaperwoman—and later scoring her own jailhouse interview with Oswald's killer. She hooked up with Mark Lane, who began feeding the columnist provocative items from his investigation. When Lane referred to Kilgallen's coverage of the assassination in his lectures, audiences would snicker at the mention of the gossip queen's name. But he admired her courage—she was the only prominent journalist in the country willing to take on the case, declared Lane.

After her exclusive interview with Ruby, Kilgallen began telling friends that she was going to "break the real story" behind the Kennedy assassination, that she was going to have "the biggest scoop of the century." But she never revealed in her newspaper column what Ruby—the only key figure in the case who was in custody—had told her. Apparently she was holding on to the scoop for her forthcoming book—a collection of the crime stories she had covered, titled *Murder One*—to ensure that it would be a blockbuster. But the book was never published. On November 8, 1965, Kilgallen was found dead in her Upper East Side townhouse, a victim of what police said was an overdose of alcohol and Seconal. The draft of her Jack Ruby chapter, and her notes for it, were never found. The Kilgallen story would become one more mysterious footnote in the aftermath of Dallas. For some it represented the deeply sinister aspect of the case, and the lengths that the conspirators would go to cover up their crime. For others it was simply another tawdry aspect of the world of conspiracy enthusiasts, a gaudy carnival peopled by hard-drinking, pill-popping gossip peddlers like Kilgallen.

While Bobby avoided controversial sleuths like Lane, Buchanan, and Kilgallen in the months after the assassination, he did not reject their suspicions about the case. But he was determined to keep his own inquiries into Dallas private. He was seen taking long walks in a Washington park with Allen Dulles, the former CIA director who had returned from the exile imposed on him by President Kennedy to become the dominant force on the Warren Commission. But Bobby never revealed what the two men discussed during these lengthy conversations. CIA veteran Sam Halpern later told *Washington Post* reporters Walter Pincus and George Lardner that RFK also secretly recruited a mobster from upstate New York to dig into his brother's assassination. But the late Halpern was an unreliable source on the Kennedys, one of those CIA officials eager to portray the brothers in the most unflattering ways. And having Bobby, of all people, consort with mobsters would be a particularly lurid way of tarnishing his image.

Still, Kennedy was obviously in emotional extremis in these early months after Dallas, the kind of punishing state of mind where a man feels driven to take extraordinary steps. One day, Bobby went as far as to arrange a secret meeting with the man he considered Public Enemy Number One.

EARLY ONE MORNING IN March 1964, Secret Service Agent Mike Howard and his partner had a surprise encounter with Attorney General Robert Kennedy. Howard was one of the agents assigned to protect Jackie Kennedy in the months after Dallas. His eventful career had also included overseeing the Fort Worth leg of JFK's Texas trip and taking Marina Oswald and her children into protective custody for a week after the assassination at a Six Flags motel outside Dallas. Years later, Howard would guard former President Johnson when he retired to his Texas ranch. While on duty with the former first lady, the agent sometimes drew the midnight shift. Sitting outside her bedroom, he would hear Jackie's screaming nightmares.

One morning around seven, after another graveyard tour of duty—this time at Wexford, the weekend manor that Jackie had built in the Virginia horse country the last year of JFK's life—Howard and his partner were leaving when they came upon Bobby Kennedy in the kitchen, drinking a cup of coffee. "Will you fellows, ah, be going past Dulles?" Kennedy asked the Secret Service agents. When Howard told him they would, he asked if he could ride with them.

Howard wondered why the attorney general did not have FBI men to ferry him around. But he later learned that J. Edgar Hoover, who had once been eager to put FBI cars at Kennedy's service, had cut off all amenities for the attorney general after his brother's assassination. As Howard soon discovered, it was not just transportation Bobby needed that morning. It was the Secret Service men's intimidating presence.

Bobby asked the agents if they could stop at Dulles Airport on the way back to Washington, directing them to a remote spot on the tarmac where private planes landed. "I'll need you to drive me out onto the air field and I'd like you to stay with me," said Kennedy, and the two agents agreed. After the car was parked, Bobby got out and began walking toward a small plane that was sitting about fifty yards away, followed by Howard and his partner. About forty feet from the plane, Bobby turned to the agents and said, "Fellows, you wait right here." As Kennedy approached, a fireplug of a man got off the plane followed by two hulking sidekicks. The Secret Service agents instantly recognized him: Jimmy Hoffa. To the agents' amazement, Kennedy and Hoffa greeted each other and began conversing, as the attorney general showed a document to the Teamster leader, and Hoffa alternately nodded and shook his head. As the two men talked, Howard and his partner warily eyed Hoffa's bodyguards. "One was built like a Green Bay Packer," Howard recalled, "and the other wore dark shades and there wasn't any doubt about what he had under both armpits—he was loaded."

Howard and his partner could not believe what they were witnessing. "We weren't expecting something like this at all," he said. "This wasn't part of our routine duty. We weren't even supposed to be there!

"We could hear Bobby and Hoffa talking, but we couldn't hear what was being said. But the thing that was a concern to us was what was going to happen. Hoffa had made it clear, at one time, that he would kill this son of a bitch if he got the chance. All of a sudden, I wasn't sleepy anymore, I can guarantee you. We were wide awake, because we didn't know whether there'd be a shoot-out right there or not."

Later, as Kennedy and the Secret Service men drove back to Washington, there was no conversation in the car. "He didn't say a word about it—not a word," Howard recalled. And the Secret Service men were too professional to ask anything about the extraordinary meeting. "That was something you didn't do."

Why did Kennedy confer with his long-time nemesis that day? His Justice Department had finally won a conviction against the slippery Hoffa, on jury tampering charges in Nashville, and the following month it would put the Teamster boss on trial again, for defrauding the union's Central States Pension Fund of $20 million. This might have been the subject of the two men's conversation that morning on the landing field. But as investigative journalist Gus Russo has speculated, it might also have been Dallas. Perhaps Kennedy wanted "to look into Hoffa's eyes while asking him if he had anything to do with his brother's killing—as he had done with, among others, John McCone of the CIA."

It has long perplexed assassination researchers why Robert Kennedy did not put the formidable power of the Justice Department behind the probe of his brother's murder. If anybody had the means and motive to solve the crime, it was the attorney general of the United States. Kennedy's inertia is partly explained by the enervating gloom that settled over him in the months after Dallas. But another explanation is suggested by Howard's remarkable story. When Kennedy did marshal the energy to pursue leads on his brother's case, he could not rely on the government's investigative apparatus. Kennedy's official power began slipping away the minute his brother was killed. It was so weakened by March 1964 that he could not depend on the FBI to protect him during a nerve-twisting meeting with his top criminal target. There is something deeply poignant about the attorney general of the United States reduced to hanging around his sister-in-law's kitchen in hopes of borrowing her Secret Service protection.

Increasingly marginalized by Lyndon Johnson—a man he regarded as a usurper and who eyed him in return with burning suspicion—and the new president's malevolent courtier, Hoover, Kennedy was powerless to mount a full assassination investigation in 1964, even if he had possessed the will. It was the FBI chief who moved quickly to bring the investigation under his control, ignoring the attorney general in the process.

Hoover's contempt for Kennedy's authority became so blatant after Dallas that Ed Guthman, the tough newspaperman who was still serving as the attorney general's press secretary, stormily confronted Hoover deputy Cartha DeLoach over lunch in early March. Guthman was outraged at the way that Hoover and his coterie—before "the president's body was even cold"—had begun to snub the attorney general, communicating directly with the new occupant of the White House and feeding LBJ's rampant paranoia with tales of Bobby's disloyalty. "It pissed me off. I mean what the hell . . . to get fucked around like that by Hoover," Guthman later told me. "As soon as President Kennedy was killed, Bob Kennedy might just as well not have existed as far as he was concerned."

After an initial exchange of pleasantries that afternoon, the lunch meeting soon grew heated. Guthman was blunt in his assessment of the FBI director's behavior: it was "chickenshit" and "unmanly." The words surely inflamed the hypersensitive Hoover when "Deke" DeLoach dutifully reported back to his boss—a man of "monstrous ego," in the deputy's own words, who ruled the FBI like "the Great and Powerful Oz."

Hoover and his men were clearly moving "to consolidate [their] position with President Johnson," Guthman observed, "and went out of their way to really stick it in, and hard" against Kennedy. At a time when Bobby could barely function, lost in his fog of grief, Guthman found the FBI czar's behavior "cruel and unnecessary . . . we had no illusions about what had happened or what changes in power [had taken place]." But Hoover needed to keep reminding Kennedy of his fall, to punish the young man—once called the second most powerful person in Washington—for his short-lived dominion over him.

There was a time when Kennedy would have directly confronted Hoover himself. But in his final months at the Justice Department, sleeping and eating intermittently, he seemed to shrink even physically before the eyes of his friends and colleagues. Bobby took to wearing JFK's old clothes, but wrapping himself in the comforting leather skin of his older brother's bomber jacket, he seemed like a lost boy. "He looked to me like a man who is just in intense pain," said his friend John Seigenthaler, after visiting Washington to check in on Bobby. "He looked to me like a man hurt, I mean, you know, just physically hurt."

Bobby Kennedy once charged through Washington's bureaucratic fortresses like a blazing revolutionary, determined to inflame the government with a sense of Kennedy mission. The attorney general "was frequently an insurgent, and his country was the beneficiary of the insurgency," Edward R. Murrow would tell Bobby in a wistful thank-you note after receiving a pair of the cufflinks that were given to the core members of the Kennedy administration on Christmas 1963. But without his inspirational leadership, Kennedy's crusades at the Justice Department began to lose their fervor and some of his young prosecutors began to drift away.

When Bob Blakey—who had served on his organized crime task force and would one day play a key role in reopening his brother's case—dropped by Kennedy's office to say goodbye, he was stunned by the transformation his once-dynamic boss had undergone. "He seemed absolutely devastated. He used to have these piercing eyes—when he was looking at you, you knew it. The day I came into his office, he was idly playing with that big dog of his, Brumus. He looked at me with vacant eyes. Instead of his usual vigorous handshake, his hand felt like a piece of meat."

To friends like Seigenthaler, it seemed as if Kennedy's body-wracking grief after Dallas was intensified by something else, a haunting sense of remorse. It was as if he felt responsible in some way for his brother's murder. "That must have been part of his agony," Blakey observed. "This terrible sense—is there something I did, or failed to prevent, that backfired against the president?" He was supposed to be his brother's sleepless watchman, but he had failed him.

There was something else that undoubtedly weighed on Kennedy in those dark months, another reason he seemed immobilized, unable to confront the truth about his brother's assassination. It was first speculated about in a provocative monthly magazine called *The Minority of One* that was published by a brilliant, Polish-born survivor of Auschwitz named Menachem Arnoni.

The Minority of One, whose board of sponsors included Albert Schweitzer, Bertrand Russell, and Linus Pauling, lived up to its defiant motto: "the independent monthly for an American alternative dedicated to the eradication of all restrictions on thought." Its founder, known to his readers as M. S. Arnoni, ran his magazine with the fearless abandon of a man who had "lived a thousand lives, and . . . died a thousand deaths," as he declared in a 1965 speech on the Berkeley campus, where he addressed the audience in the striped uniform of a Nazi concentration camp inmate. With his tragic, European sense of the world, Arnoni inveighed against the dangers of militarism and the threat of a new and final world war, displaying a passion and intellectual acuity rarely evident in the American press. Long before Walter Cronkite signaled the mainstream media's disaffection with the war in Vietnam, *The Minority of One* was regularly denouncing it as a moral disaster. And while the rest of the press was rushing to close the case on the assassination of President Kennedy, Arnoni insisted on raising sharp and disturbing questions about the official version, publishing the work of pioneering dissidents on Dallas like Lane, Sylvia Meagher, and Vincent Salandria. The monthly's carefully documented dissections of the Warren Report and intriguing explorations into the identities of Oswald and Ruby would catch the attention of men in Bobby Kennedy's circle, who read and corresponded with the journal.

The most disquieting essay on the assassination ever published by Arnoni might have been one he wrote himself in the January 1964 issue. In the piece—which ran on the cover of the magazine under the title "Who Killed Whom and Why? Dark Thoughts About Dark Events"—Arnoni raised the chilling possibility that Kennedy's assassination was a regime change engineered at the top levels of government. Deep into his essay, Arnoni made another disturbing conjecture—one that might further explain Bobby's paralyzed condition after Dallas. "The possibility can by no means be dismissed that important men in Washington do know the identity of the conspirators, or at least some of them, and that these conspirators are so powerful that prudence dictates that they not be identified in public," Arnoni suggested. "Let us make the 'fantastic' assumption that President Lyndon Johnson and

Attorney General Robert F. Kennedy know or believe that the murder was planned by a group of high-ranking officers who would stop at nothing to end American-Soviet negotiations. However strong their desire to avenge John F. Kennedy, what course would be open to them? To move against such formidable conspirators might start a disastrous chain of events. It could lead to American troops shooting at other American troops. It could lead to a direct take-over by a military clique. To avert such catastrophes, it might well be considered prudent to pretend utter ignorance, in the hope that the conspirators might be removed from power discreetly, at a later date, one by one."

This seems a sharply intuitive reading of Robert Kennedy's mind at the time. As soon as RFK concluded his brother was the victim of a high-level plot—which he communicated to family members and even the Soviet government within days of the assassination—the very next thought that must have occurred to a passionate patriot like Bobby, someone who had dedicated his life to the service of his country, was surely enough to freeze his heart. *If I move against the conspirators at this point, with a slipping grasp on the machinery of government, it could spark an American inferno.* In fact, this is precisely what Kennedy later suggested to an old family friend. "If the American people knew the truth about Dallas," RFK told him, "there would be blood in the streets."

Once, Bobby had been renowned for his prosecutorial zeal. But now, emotionally and politically unable to bring his own brother's killers to justice, he seemed hollowed out, drifting listlessly through his days. In his deepening gloom, he sought counsel—not from a psychiatrist, but in the Irish way, from a priest. Worried about Jackie's state of mind, Kennedy had recruited his old friend, Father Richard McSorley, a liberal Jesuit theology teacher at Georgetown University, to talk with her, under the guise of giving her tennis lessons on the backyard court at Hickory Hill. Jackie confided in the priest that she was plagued by suicidal thoughts. Would she be punished in the afterlife if she committed this mortal sin, she asked McSorley? "Do you think God would separate me from my husband if I killed myself? It's so hard to bear. I feel as though I am going out of my mind at times. Wouldn't God understand that I just want to be with him?"

Bobby too tried to comfort his sister-in-law, but all he could offer her was stoic advice. "Sorrow is a form of self-pity," he told her. "We have to go on." He also chided his colleagues at the Justice Department about their downcast moods. "Robert Kennedy Defeats Despair," proclaimed the headline of a January 9, 1964, article in the *New York Times* by his friend Anthony

Lewis—as if by telling it to the press Bobby could make it true. But Father McSorley realized that it was not just Jackie who desperately needed help.

In a letter he wrote in early summer 1964, McSorley consoled Bobby for his irreplaceable loss: "Your grief goes as deep as your love. Because you were close to him, you received the impact of his rare personality more fully than others. Yours was the inspiration of constant, daily, personal contact." But he then encouraged Bobby to turn grief into action, by picking up his brother's fallen banner. "I look at you as [Jack's] twin spirit," wrote the priest. "No one is in a better position to lead those whose hearts have caught fire from his flame than you."

But it would take time before Kennedy was ready to resume his brother's mission. In the meantime, the man of action found solace in literature and philosophy. It was Jackie who helped guide him this time, giving him a copy of *The Greek Way*, the minor 1930 classic by retired headmistress Edith Hamilton that extolled the glory that was briefly Athens. Kennedy devoured the book during a trip he took with Jackie and a small group of family and friends to the island of Antigua in March 1964, retreating to his room in a borrowed seaside villa to read and heavily underline it. The tragedy of Athens—its 150-year reign as a cradle of democracy and art, before succumbing to the corruptions of empire—must have echoed his own gloomy thoughts about the perils of a life devoted to politics. And he took deeply to heart the ancient counsel of the great tragedians whom Hamilton celebrated, particularly Aeschylus—the poet who had once been a warrior, hero of Marathon, a man whose wisdom was born of life's cruel strife. Kennedy found particular comfort in these lines from the playwright; they would guide him through his bleakest days: "He who learns must suffer. And even in our sleep pain that cannot forget falls, drop by drop, upon the heart, and in our own despair, against our will, comes wisdom to us by the awful grace of God."

EARLY IN 1964, BOBBY arranged to meet in Miami one last time with Angelo Murgado and his compadres, Manuel Artime and Manuel Reboso. Kennedy was closing his Cuban accounts. The farewell meeting between Kennedy and his Cuban intelligence team was deeply painful, recalled Murgado. "We sat down with him, and man, it was highly emotional. Everybody was in tears. It took us about five minutes to regain control. You should have seen the guy, Jesus Christ! He had lost weight. He was in such pain. He had just come down to talk about what happened and to say goodbye. And that was the last time we ever spoke."

Murgado said he and his colleagues did not bring up the name of the man

whose spectral presence loomed over the meeting, Lee Harvey Oswald—
the man Kennedy had told them months earlier was safe to ignore, since
he seemed to be under the direction of the FBI. "Why the hell would you put
alcohol in the wound, you understand? He said goodbye and that was it."

Murgado and his pro-Kennedy allies in the exile community had been
stunned on November 22 when the man they had been tracking in New
Orleans was suddenly identified as the suspect in the assassination of the
president. "When that happened, we shit in our pants." Afterwards, he and
his fellow exiles anxiously huddled to try to make sense of the events in Dallas. They quickly came to the conclusion that the assassination was the work
of their employer, the CIA. "When the thing happens, we sit down and we
talk. We realized, 'My God, we've been used like toilet paper. Who the hell
is behind all this?' And we knew that the plot could come from only one
source—the CIA. The whole infrastructure, the logistics—it was the CIA.
We all believed the same thing. It was a highly sophisticated operation. Look,
they were so good at it that, even today, nobody knows exactly what happened. There's only one enterprise that can pull off shit like that. It was the
CIA, but not alone. It was the CIA plus something higher."

Murgado uses the term "invisible government" to describe the high-level
source of the plot. He believes these high officials eliminated Kennedy because he broke from their Cold War ranks: "JFK was another victim of the
Bay of Pigs . . . he was ahead of his time."

But Murgado won't speculate on the names of people who might have
been involved in the conspiracy, especially those of other Cuban exiles. "Anything you want to know about me, related to Bobby, I will tell you. The rest,
forget about it. Because that would create a lot of static. And remember, in
the Cuban environment, you don't create a lot of static."

In any case, said Murgado, it's too late—those who could shed light on
the plot are long gone. "Everybody is dead—or other guys have disappeared.
And I respect that. You fade away and I respect that. I ain't going to bring
nobody out of the shadows to come up with the truth." Murgado doubts that
the American people even want the truth. "You know that line from the
movie? It's the best line I've heard for this country: 'You don't want the truth,
you can't handle the truth.'"

In the months after Dallas, Robert Kennedy seemed eager to distance
himself from Cuba, the battleground that had once absorbed so much of his
aggressive energy. It was also the cauldron of intrigue that he associated with
his brother's murder. Reminiscing about the Kennedy administration over
dinner with Bill Moyers in spring 1968, soon before his own assassination, a

wistful Bobby remarked that he "wondered at times if we did not pay a very great price for being more energetic than wise about a lot of things, especially Cuba."

Immediately after JFK's assassination, the CIA and its Cuban assets began systematically promoting the idea that the Castro regime was behind the violent assault on the U.S. presidency. Robert Kennedy himself was one of the targets of this disinformation campaign. On November 27, 1963, someone identifying himself as Mario del Rosario Molina mailed a letter to Kennedy from Havana, informing him that a Castro agent in the United States named Pedro Charles had paid Oswald $7,000 to assassinate his brother. "Pedro Charles reached an understanding with Lee Harvey Oswald, an expert marksman, for the President to be killed and for an international scandal to be unleashed so that all the blame would fall on the racists and the extreme-rightists of the State of Texas," read the letter. The mysterious communication had all the markings of the CIA's anti-Castro propaganda campaign, and it failed to convince Bobby that the Cuban leader was behind his brother's murder.

More important, Lyndon Johnson also resisted the intense pressures building within the government, refusing to be stampeded into declaring war on Havana. LBJ moved swiftly to defuse the ticking Cuba bomb, suspending CIA-sponsored raids on the island in January and making it clear to Erneido Oliva there would be no U.S.-backed invasion led by the Bay of Pigs veterans. At Johnson's request, Bobby Kennedy accompanied Oliva to the White House the day LBJ delivered the bad news. The president wanted to make it clear there would be no more vague Kennedy promises of liberating Cuba. In a brusque, sixteen-minute meeting in the White House library, recalled Oliva, Johnson "flatly told me my program with the Cubans had to be terminated. Bobby didn't say anything. You know they didn't get along well. [Bobby] told me before that he had tried to persuade him . . . but he didn't try and persuade the president of the United States in front of me. He was only listening, his head bowed, pretty sad."

But the CIA would prove unresponsive to Johnson's leadership, just as it was under Kennedy, continuing to sponsor unauthorized raids and assassination attempts on Castro. In February, the agency was soon back to its old game, trying to manufacture excuses to invade the island. This time it was reviving a scheme from the final days of the Kennedy administration.

On November 19, three days before he was assassinated, President Kennedy was startled when Richard Helms opened a canvas air travel bag in the

Oval Office and pulled out a submachine gun. The weapon, Helms claimed, was part of a Cuban cache that had been found on a beach in Venezuela—dramatic proof of Castro's brazen effort to subvert his neighbors' governments. Helms's message was all too predictable: it was time to get tough on Castro. But Kennedy seemed more disturbed by the fact that the CIA official had been able to blithely slip an automatic gun into the Oval Office unmolested by his Secret Service centurions. "It gives me a feeling of confidence," he dryly told Helms.

After Kennedy's death, the CIA resumed flogging the Venezuela weapons caper in hopes of driving a wedge between Cuba and the Organization of American States and establishing a pretext for war. The agency was having a hard time making its case, even within its own bureaucracy, where one official later declared himself "not too impressed with the evidence," which struck him as suspiciously "manufactured."

On February 28, 1964, Des FitzGerald paid a visit to Bobby Kennedy's office to show him a copy of the "Spectrum Paper"—the latest CIA scenario for war on Castro—in hopes of enlisting his support. FitzGerald was under no obligation to seek Kennedy's approval that day, since the new president had removed Cuba from RFK's portfolio, but John McCone had suggested the visit, undoubtedly as a courtesy to the man who once spearheaded the government's crusade against Castro.

As the attorney general perused the Spectrum Paper that day, it soon became clear he no longer had the heart for anti-Castro intrigue. He surprised FitzGerald by asking him whether the CIA's Board of National Estimates "had ever directed its attention to the question of whether or not the United States could live with Castro." The answer was obviously no—and the agency was not about to change now. And LBJ—to the agency's delight—had made it clear he agreed with the agency, declining to pursue the backchannel peace negotiations initiated in JFK's final months.

But FitzGerald found Kennedy strangely persistent. "[Kennedy] wondered whether it might not be a good idea for such [a peace assessment] to be produced," FitzGerald later noted in his memo on the meeting. No, FitzGerald flatly told the attorney general, it was not a good idea to explore the peace option with Havana.

This post-Dallas picture of a wan and powerless Robert Kennedy is painful to behold. Here he is, facing a CIA official he once made tremble and all he can do is feebly suggest that the agency completely reverse its course on Cuba. FitzGerald and his colleagues back at Langley must have gloated at the fall of their rude overseer. The suspicions that Kennedy harbored about a CIA involvement in his brother's murder must have made meetings like this all the more excruciating for him.

Kennedy did not suspect FitzGerald in particular of participating in any plot. In fact, the CIA official apparently shared RFK's doubts about the lone gunman proposition. Watching TV with his wife on the morning of November 24 when Ruby suddenly burst in front of the cameras and shot down Oswald, FitzGerald began to cry. "Now we'll never know," he said. When FitzGerald dropped dead of a massive heart attack in July 1967 while playing tennis, Bobby Kennedy was among those who attended his funeral.

In the months after Dallas, Kennedy also seems to have maintained a civil relationship with CIA director John McCone, who often phoned Bobby at the Justice Department and invited him and Ethel to dine at his home. But this was not the case with other CIA officials.

Like McCone, Dick Helms—the real power at the agency—also strove to maintain close contact with Kennedy, offering to brief him on intelligence matters even though Johnson had ordered McCone to inform Bobby that he would no longer enjoy the same intelligence access in the new administration. On January 22, 1964, Helms wrote Kennedy a warm note, attaching a tribute to JFK that had been written by an editor of the *London Sunday Telegraph*. On March 4, 1964, Helms phoned Kennedy to congratulate him on the Hoffa conviction, making an appointment to see him the following week, without specifying the reason. The spymaster would call Kennedy's office to see him at least twice more before he stepped down as attorney general in August. It is unclear why Helms continued to pursue a relationship with the lame-duck attorney general; it was certainly not out of affection for him. Helms had feared and reviled Kennedy when he reigned over the agency.

For the wily Washington operator, it must have been a case of keeping an enemy close. Helms was not interested in befriending Kennedy or consoling him, said RFK aide John Nolan, who observed the CIA official continue to court Kennedy when he became a senator. "Dick Helms was not a warm and cuddly guy. He was a consummate bureaucrat, and in that sense a savvy operator in Washington power games. . . . Calling Bob Kennedy every morning . . . was his way of either currying or maintaining favor with Bob Kennedy."

Bobby clearly felt no warmth for Helms. The day after the assassination, the deputy CIA director handwrote a condolence letter to Kennedy on his home stationery. "There is nothing for me to say that has not been said better by many others," wrote Helms. "When you sent me to see the president Tuesday afternoon [to discuss the Cuban arms allegedly found in Venezuela], he never looked better, seemed more confident or appeared more in control of the crushing forces around him. Friday struck me personally. Mrs. Helms and I extend our deepest sympathy and heartfelt condolences to you and the family. We pray that you will continue to give us your leadership. Respectfully and sadly, Dick Helms." Helms's letter was smoothly crafted— down to his less-than-sincere "prayer" that Bobby remain the CIA's master. But it apparently left Kennedy unmoved. "Dear Dick," he perfunctorily replied two weeks later. "My thanks to you." Condolence letters from a range of other well-wishers—Kirk Douglas, Hugh Downs, even Soviet ambassador Dobrynin—elicited warmer responses from Kennedy.

As Hoover did with the FBI, Dick Helms—working with his old mentor Allen Dulles—made certain that the CIA was insulated from the Warren Commission's investigation. Dulles was the most diligent member of the commission. "I don't think Allen Dulles ever missed a meeting," Warren later recalled. Mark Lane would comment that the assassination panel should have been called "the Dulles Commission." The former CIA chief had lobbied hard to get appointed to the panel. He lost no time in establishing himself as its dominant player, expertly deflecting the investigation away from the spy agency and herding his fellow panelists toward the lone gunman conclusion. No one in the mainstream press commented on the striking irony of the man whose career had been terminated by President Kennedy leading the inquiry into his murder. After being forced into political exile by JFK in 1962, the embittered Dulles found it hard to adjust to life outside Washington's whirling power center. "He had a very difficult time to decompress," observed James Angleton, who made a point of visiting his old colleague two or three times a week at his house. His service on the commission brought Dulles back to life. Though no longer on the CIA payroll, he served as the agency's undercover man on the commission, leaking information to Angleton, with whom he continued to confer regularly.

Meanwhile, Helms moved swiftly to limit the CIA's own probe of the assassination, taking the case away from the bright, aggressive official to whom it was originally assigned—a well-respected forty-three-year-old covert operations veteran named John Whitten—and handing it to the spooky wizard Angleton. Helms removed Whitten from the investigation at a December 6, 1963, meeting after the conscientious agent complained that information about Oswald—on whom the CIA had maintained files for at least three years—and his Cuba-related activities was being withheld from him. With Whitten out of the picture, the CIA's probe of the Kennedy assassination soon became mired in Angleton's misty swamps, where he and his counterintelligence sorcerers strained mightily to draw a connection between Dallas and Moscow.

Angleton, whose counterintelligence unit was in charge of monitoring defectors to the Soviet Union like Oswald, drew gauzy theories about the ex-Marine's alleged KGB role. But Bobby Kennedy and his Justice Department team did not buy the spook's theories. "A stranger man I never met—he just gave me the creeps," said Nick Katzenbach, who talked to Angleton on several occasions. Angleton was known to loathe President Kennedy, whom he came to regard—in his alcohol-fueled paranoia—as an agent of the Soviet Union. If the Soviets had launched their doomsday missiles, he darkly muttered to reporters late in his career, the Kennedys "would have been safe in their luxury bunker, presumably watching World War III on television, [while] the rest of us would have burned in hell."

Years later, as newly appointed CIA director William Colby prepared to sack Angleton in a sweeping effort to purge the agency of its past sins, the fallen spymaster made a strange and airy remark apparently related to the Kennedy assassination. In December 1974, pursued by the dogged Seymour Hersh, who was then investigating the CIA's illegal domestic operations for the *New York Times*, Angleton suddenly blurted to the reporter, "A mansion has many rooms . . . I'm not privy to who struck John." What did the cryptic remark mean? "I would be absolutely misleading you if I thought I had any fucking idea," says Hersh today. "But my instinct about it is he was basically laying off [blame] on somebody else inside the CIA, and the whole purpose of the conversation was to convince me to go after somebody else and not him. And also that he was a completely crazy fucking old fart."

In May 1978, John Whitten again surfaced in relation to the Kennedy probe, appearing before the House Select Committee on Assassinations to discuss his aborted investigation. Testifying for seven hours in secret session, using his old CIA code name "John Scelso," the former agent—then living in Austria, where he had fled the intelligence world to sing with the Vienna Men's Choral Society—drew a disturbing picture of the machinations of his former bosses, Dick Helms and Jim Angleton. Helms hid the CIA's assassination plots against Castro from him, Whitten told the two committee investigators who were questioning him. If he had known about the plots, testified Whitten, he would have zeroed in on the CIA's Miami station and conducted a thorough investigation of its activities. He told the congressional investigators that he was stunned to learn that Helms had chosen Bill Harvey—a "ruthless guy who was, in my opinion, a very dangerous man"—to run the assassination operation against Castro. When Harvey brought mobster Johnny Rosselli into the fold, Whitten added, it reenforced the sinister character of the scheme. "The very thought of Helms entrusting Harvey to hire a criminal to have the capacity to kill somebody violates every operational precept, every bit of operational experience, every ethical consideration." Moreover, Whitten declared, it was a "morally highly reprehensible act" for Helms to withhold the Castro assassination plots from the Warren Commission. He had obviously done so "because he realized it would have cost him his job and precipitated a crisis for the agency."

Then Whitten was asked an even more explosive question: Could Harvey have been involved in the assassination of President Kennedy? His elliptical reply was worthy of a longtime spy. "He was too young to have assassinated McKinley and Lincoln," Whitten said.

Whitten also offered an unsettling view of Angleton. He regarded him as psychologically unsound, finding his "understanding of human nature . . . his evaluation of people, to be a very precarious thing." Then came another provocative question: Did Angleton have ties to organized crime? This time Whitten's answer was blunt: "Yes." Angleton had covered for his Mafia associates in federal investigations, added Whitten, and he had used them in Cuba operations.

If John Whitten and his thirty-agent team had been allowed to carry out the CIA's investigation of the Kennedy assassination, the Warren Commission would have found itself deeply enlightened by their work. But Richard Helms and James Angleton made sure that did not happen. "Whitten was a rare CIA hero in the Kennedy assassination story whose personal odyssey is a poignant but unsettling reminder that inquiries into national tragedy can be compromised early on," *Washington Post* reporter Jefferson Morley has observed. Without an investigative unit of its own, the Warren Commission was utterly dependent on the information provided by Hoover at the FBI and Helms and Angleton at the CIA. The commission boasted some of the most distinguished names in Washington—from Supreme Court Chief Justice Earl Warren on down—but its mission was compromised from the very start by its investigative weakness. The blue-ribbon panel would be the helpless pawn of two agencies that Robert Kennedy considered his mortal political enemies.

"NICK, WHAT DO I do?" wrote Bobby in his tight, tiny script on the letter he received from Earl Warren on June 12, 1964. There was a plaintive quality to Kennedy's question, which was directed to his deputy, Nicholas Katzenbach, the man he had asked to take over Warren Commission-related duties at the Justice Department. Kennedy was in a dilemma. He had so far avoided testifying before the Warren Commission, but now the chairman—a man he greatly respected—was writing to tell him that before the panel wrapped up its investigation, it needed to hear directly from the attorney general. "In view of the widely circulated allegations on this subject," Warren wrote, "the Commission would like to be informed in particular whether you have any information suggesting that the assassination of President Kennedy was caused by a domestic or foreign conspiracy. Needless to say, if you have any suggestions to make regarding the investigation of these allegations or any other phase of the Commission's work, we stand ready to act upon them."

Kennedy had made it clear to Katzenbach that he wanted nothing to do with the Warren Commission. "He said he didn't give a damn whether there was any investigation," the former Kennedy aide recalled. " 'What's the difference? My brother's dead.' That's what he would say to me." But as Katzenbach suspected, that was not the full story behind Bobby's refusal to cooperate with the commission.

Kennedy was not ready to publicly reveal everything he knew, and he certainly was not going to tell it to the Warren Commission—a panel that, despite its august composition, was under the control of his political enemies at the FBI and CIA. In true Kennedy fashion, he wanted to control any investigation of the crime—not only to ensure its authenticity, but to prevent any damage to his brother's legacy and his own political future. Bobby knew that if the Kennedy administration's secret war against Castro—a war that he was supposed to be overseeing—was revealed as the source of the plot against his brother, the family's image could be badly tarnished.

Like others close to Kennedy, Katzenbach sensed that he was plagued by feelings of guilt over Dallas. "My own feeling was that Bobby was worried that there might be some conspiracy and that it might be his fault," Katzenbach says today, sitting in the comfortably stuffed study of his stone house outside Princeton, New Jersey. "I think the idea that he could be responsible for his brother's death might be the most terrible idea imaginable. It might very well have been that he was worried that the investigation would somehow point back to him."

Kennedy's political enemies—including Lyndon Johnson—were quick to play on his sense of guilt when it suited their purposes. Within days of the assassination, LBJ—irritated with Kennedy for a series of real and imagined slights, including brushing past him to embrace Jackie when Air Force One returned to Washington—was making incendiary comments to former

JFK aides, knowing they would get back to Bobby, suggesting that the Kennedys themselves were responsible for the terrible fate that had befallen Jack. "I want to tell you why Kennedy died," Johnson told White House staffer Ralph Dungan. "Divine retribution . . . divine retribution. He murdered Diem and then he got it himself." The accusation was not true—JFK had dithered on the decision to back the coup in Saigon, and was appalled by its bloody outcome—but it was an expertly aimed dart at a man haunted by the notion that he and his brother had been "more energetic than wise on a lot of things."

Now Earl Warren was asking Bobby to resolve his inner turmoil about the assassination and tell everything he knew about Dallas. But he simply could not do it. Kennedy turned to Katzenbach to get him out of his predicament.

Conspiracy researchers would later blame the deputy attorney general for playing a key role in the government's cover-up of the assassination. "The public must be satisfied that Oswald was the assassin; that he did not have confederates who are still at large . . . [and] speculation about Oswald's motivation ought to be cut off," wrote Katzenbach in a post-assassination memo that would be widely quoted as evidence of his complicity in a cover-up. But Nick Katzenbach was a Kennedy loyalist—the man Bobby had called upon many times in the heat of battle, including the raging night at Ole Miss—and in the traumatic days after Dallas he was primarily responding to signals from his boss.

Katzenbach worked out a deal for Kennedy with Warren and the commission's chief counsel, Lee Rankin. In return for being excused from testifying before the commission, Bobby would be required to sign a letter written by Warren Commission attorney Howard Willens, which read, "I would like to state definitely that I know of no credible evidence to support the allegations that the assassination of President Kennedy was caused by a domestic or foreign conspiracy." After hesitating for several weeks, Kennedy finally signed the letter, though he knew it to be untrue, and had it delivered to Willens on August 4.

The pact Robert Kennedy made was a fateful one, for it would put his name on record as endorsing the Warren Report—a document that, as time passed, would be widely condemned as a monumental government fraud. For the rest of his life, Kennedy would be forced to publicly defend the official version of his brother's assassination—a predicament that filled him with increasing turmoil over the years, since he believed that its central conclusion about a lone assassin was false.

Kennedy made his first public statement about who was responsible for his brother's murder during a trip to Poland in late June 1964. Despite a cool reception from the Communist authorities, Bobby and Ethel were given a raucous greeting by the Polish people. In the town square of Cracow, the old university town, a youthful crowd thronged their car, pelting them with flowers and serenading them with "Sto Lat"—"May you live a hundred years!"—while the Kennedys responded with an improvised version of a favorite family song, "When Polish Eyes Are Smiling." The emotional Polish crowds—which unnerved government officials in Warsaw as well as in Washington—were the first sign of the Kennedy cult that was starting to sweep the world. The long-dispirited Bobby came alive in the crush of the crowds, climbing on top of the U.S. ambassador's car with Ethel and denting the rooftop (to the horror of the rigidly proper envoy), and clasping the beseeching hands that reached out to him.

Later, at a public forum in Cracow, a nervous twenty-five-year-old Polish student leader first put the question to Bobby. "We always greatly respected President Kennedy and we are very interested in your version of his death," said the young man. "We hope you will forgive us for asking such a direct question, but we really would like your view."

Kennedy seemed to take the question in stride, calling it "a proper question which deserves an answer." He told the audience that his brother's assassination was the work of a solitary "misfit" by the name of Oswald, who was motivated by a vague dissatisfaction "with our government and our way of life" rather than a specific ideology. "There is no question that he did it on his own and by himself. He was not a member of a right-wing organization. He was a confessed Communist, but even the Communists would not have anything to do with him. Ideology in my opinion did not motivate his act. It was the single act of an individual protesting against society."

Kennedy seemed to be signaling to the authorities back home that they had no cause for concern—he would stick closely to the government's line, an official story that was intended to put the public's fears to rest, rather than exhume the truth.

But three months later, on September 28, 1964, when Earl Warren presented his commission's voluminous report to President Johnson in the White House, Kennedy could not muster the same enthusiasm. Bobby, who was then campaigning for the Senate in New York, issued a brief statement on the Warren Report, repeating the comments he had made in Poland and declaring that he was "completely satisfied that the commission investigated every lead and examined every piece of evidence." But Kennedy felt obliged to add this caveat: "I have not read the report, nor do I intend to." This would become part of his obligatory response on the subject whenever he was asked about it, a kind of escape clause that might become important in the future when he would undertake his own inquiries.

The release of the Warren Report seemed to cast a pall over Kennedy. He canceled his scheduled campaign appearances in Manhattan that morning, overcome by what aides said were the "sorrowful memories" provoked by the report, and retreated behind closed doors with Jackie. In the afternoon, as he flew upstate to address rallies in Ithaca, he seemed "subdued," according to the *New York Times*, sitting by himself on the plane and staring out the window. Later, "he smiled wanly during his speeches, which lacked fire," reported the *Times*.

Kennedy was trapped in an impossible position. Privately, he contemptuously dismissed the Warren Report as nothing more than a public relations exercise designed to reassure the public. But unwilling at this point to publicly challenge it, he was stuck with supporting it. Perfunctorily giving the report his stamp of approval was his way of deflecting any further press inquiries about the assassination. *You know my position, let's move on.* In 1964, he was in no political—or emotional—condition to do anything more. "He always stood by the Warren Commission in public—he thought that was the right political thing to do," said RFK aide Frank Mankiewicz, who knew that Kennedy privately harbored very different views about Dallas. "He didn't want to talk about it. I think he was physically unable to talk about it."

The Warren Report won unanimous praise in the U.S. press, with the *New York Times* and *Washington Post* setting the euphoric tone of the coverage. Writing in the *Post*, Robert J. Donovan hailed it as a "masterpiece of its kind."

"For the stamp of honesty, authenticity and fact is on this report," effused the *Post* correspondent. "It surely will convince reasonable men beyond a reasonable doubt that Lee Harvey Oswald, a malcontent of questionable sanity, assassinated President John F. Kennedy while acting alone on his own impulses."

Both newspapers took pains to assure their readers, in a fusillade of articles, that the report once and for all "Knocks Props From Under All Plot Theories," as a *Post* headline definitively announced.

Press coverage of the Warren Report's release followed the line that, ironically, had been set months earlier by *New York Times* reporter Anthony Lewis, who was close to Bobby Kennedy. Lewis's promotion of the report—which began with a page-one story that ran on June 1, nearly four months before the report was released—reflected Kennedy's own public position on the commission's views. This was part of a pattern that started soon after Dallas and continues today, in which RFK friends—out of a sense of loyalty to the man they understandably deferred to on the assassination—stick closely to his public declarations about the crime. His mantra became their own: *Lone misfit, nothing will bring him back, it's morbid to dwell on the past.* The tragedy, of course, is that—unknown to most of these friends—Robert Kennedy actually believed something quite different. In truth, Kennedy was one of the first—and among the staunchest—believers in a conspiracy.

Unaware of this, Lewis took the lead in knocking down conspiracy theories, quoting anonymous Warren Commission staff members at length in his advance story on their investigation as they predicted that their final report would silence their critics once and for all. Lewis' story singled out Thomas Buchanan and Mark Lane, whom his commission sources seemed particularly eager to discredit. Their report would "completely explode" these men's theories, they told a sympathetic Lewis.

Over the years, Lewis would continue to disparage critics of the Warren Report, but he seemed to become less certain of his convictions. He later intimated to reporters for the *Village Voice* that his coverage of the Warren Commission was colored by his close ties to the Kennedy family—specifically Bobby Kennedy—making the subject "very painful to me personally. Over the years I felt I did not want to get involved as a counterexpert or expert. Maybe with all that has happened, Vietnam and Watergate, today's reporters would have come to it with more resistance."

In its eagerness to embrace the Warren Report, the press failed to discover that among the study's most prominent critics were some of its own authors, including Senators Richard Russell and John Cooper and banker-diplomat John McCloy, whose illustrious resume earned him the media moniker "chairman of the Eastern establishment." All three of these commission members privately expressed strong skepticism about the single bullet theory—the shaky proposition that JFK and Governor Connally were hit by the same "magic bullet," on which teetered the entire lone gunman belief system. But it was Russell in particular who would prove troublesome as the commission sought an elusive unanimity of opinion.

LBJ had strong-armed a reluctant Russell to serve on the Warren Commission, feeling that his old Senate mentor would bring prestige to the panel and trusting that he would be able to work smoothly with the CIA, since Russell was one of the senators responsible for overseeing the agency. "You're my man [on that commission] . . . period," Johnson declared, closing his sales job on the venerable senator from Georgia. But Russell would be troubled by his service on the commission for the rest of his life. He came to the Warren Commission believing that the burst of gunshots in Dealey Plaza resulted from a conspiracy, and he left with the same suspicion, despite the panel's reassuring conclusions.

As the commission drove toward its goal of a unanimous report, Russell held out. At an executive session on September 18, ten days before the final report was released, the senator forced the commission to include a disclaimer stating that the possibility Oswald had coconspirators "cannot be rejected categorically." Unknown to Russell, chief counsel Lee Rankin later had the disclaimer purged from the commission's records, to expunge all signs of discord on the panel. But the legislator steadfastly clung to his suspicions. In January 1970, suffering from the lung cancer that would kill him within a year, Russell gave a final interview to Atlanta-based Cox Television in which he aired his doubts about the Warren Report. He "never believed that Lee Harvey Oswald assassinated President Kennedy without at least some encouragement from others," Russell said. "And that's what a majority of the committee wanted to find. I think someone else worked with him on the planning."

PERHAPS THE MOST SURPRISING Warren Report skeptic was the man who cobbled together the commission and herded it toward its reassuring conclusion—none other than President Lyndon Johnson. Working closely with J. Edgar Hoover—with whom he had developed a pragmatic relationship over the years that served both men's interests—LBJ had moved aggressively to wrap up the case. "The thing I am most concerned about . . . is having something issued so that we can convince the public that Oswald is the real assassin," Hoover told Johnson in a phone conversation two days after the assassination, which echoed the new president's own sentiments.

But privately, Lyndon Johnson was haunted by Dallas. LBJ began anxiously conjecturing about a conspiracy immediately after the assassination, while still at Parkland Hospital, and he clung to his suspicions until he died. He shifted blame for the assassination over the years, sometimes focusing his suspicions on Cuba and sometimes on the CIA, depending on the person with whom he was airing his thoughts. There seemed to be a strategy behind his speculations.

Deke DeLoach, Hoover's liaison with the White House, dismissed the president's dark mutterings as simply his efforts to reassure himself that the Warren Report was correct. But Dick Helms, another audience for Johnson's suspicious ramblings, probably had a more accurate read of the president: he was on a fishing expedition and he wanted to see who bit. "I didn't know whether [Johnson's conspiracy talk] was just like the fly fisherman flick over the water to see if he has any takers, or whether he really believed it," remarked the spymaster. The relationship between these two consummate power players was fraught with hidden meaning. In 1966, Johnson would finally give Helms the top post at the CIA he had long coveted. But there seems to have been little trust between the two men. When Johnson asked Helms if the CIA ever plotted to kill foreign leaders, the CIA official flatly denied it to the president's face. There were certain matters that were above the president's pay grade, Helms believed.

Johnson's suspicions about JFK's demise always seemed mixed with fears for his own safety. At Parkland Hospital, he asked White House press aide Malcolm Kilduff to delay announcing Kennedy's death until he was safely back aboard Air Force One. "We don't know whether this is a worldwide conspiracy, whether they are after me as well as they were after President Kennedy," he told Kilduff. Later, on the presidential plane, Johnson's fears briefly blossomed into a full-blown panic attack. Searching for LBJ to get his approval to take off, Brigadier General Godfrey McHugh, Kennedy's Air Force aide, found him "hiding in the toilet . . . muttering, 'Conspiracy, conspiracy, they're after all of us!'"

After moving into the White House, Johnson again grew agitated when he saw the blood-red rug that Jackie had installed in the Oval Office before the Dallas trip. "It reminded him of the president being assassinated, and he put another rug in the Oval Office with the presidential seal on it," DeLoach recalled. Johnson did not trust the Secret Service with his life after Dallas and demanded that the FBI protect him even though it was not part of its job description. "Just honestly, Mike," LBJ told Senate Majority Leader Mike Mansfield in a September 1964 phone conversation recorded by the president's Oval Office taping system, "—and I wouldn't have this repeated to anybody—my judgment is that they're more likely to get me killed than they are to protect me."

DeLoach sympathized with Johnson's security concerns, but gently rejected his request. "He was not a coward," insisted the FBI official, although that's precisely what Bobby Kennedy believed about him, ever since he witnessed Johnson's shaky performance during the Cuban Missile Crisis. "The president was a very courageous man. He was a very strong man, but he wanted that added protection. . . . For example, he would call and ask me to put an FBI agent on Air Force One on almost any trip. A lot of times, he wanted me to go personally and I, frankly, couldn't turn loose of my responsibilities and handle such assignments and I diplomatically told him that."

From time to time, Johnson would unsettle DeLoach by bringing up Kennedy's violent end and speculating about "who may have caused it." The FBI man would rush to assure him that his fears of a conspiracy were groundless. "He indicated that, 'Could it have been the CIA?' And I said, 'No, sir.' And he didn't think so himself, he was just rambling in his conversation. 'Could it have been Castro? Could it have been the Soviet Union?' And I told him no, that the investigation had been very thorough, that the Warren Commission had confirmed the conclusions of the FBI, that there was no conspiracy involved and that Lee Harvey Oswald—and Oswald alone—did it."

But Hoover's man in the White House failed to put the president's mind at rest. After Johnson was driven from office in 1969, a nearly broken man, historians would conclude that he was a victim of the war in Vietnam. But as Max Holland, a scholar of LBJ's White House tapes, has observed, "The assassination weighed on him as heavily as did the war." Back home on his Texas ranch, smoking and drinking heavily again in defiance of his failing heart, Johnson continued to speculate about the dark trauma that had given him the terrible gift of the American presidency. In a 1969 interview with Walter Cronkite of CBS, he raised the possibility of an international conspiracy, but then quickly tried to shove the disturbing idea back in its bag, pressuring CBS to cut this exchange for reasons of "national security." Nonetheless, Johnson could not contain his disturbing thoughts.

One day, lounging in his swimming pool on the ranch, he brought up Dallas with his Secret Service guard Mike Howard, who he knew had some connection to the case.

"What do you think of this Oswald fellow?" Johnson asked Howard.

The Secret Service man dutifully gave the former president the official line: he was a "deranged young man who had delusions of grandeur."

"So you think he did it by himself?" asked LBJ.

"I sure do," said Howard.

Johnson squinted in the sun at the agent. "Uh huh." That was all he said.

Historians have cautioned that not much should be made of Lyndon Johnson's dark speculations about Dallas, since his mind was given to conspiratorial brooding. But he was not alone in Washington power circles in his suspicions. One of the most startling and little-known facts about this chapter in American history is how much of the political elite believed Kennedy was the victim of a conspiracy. While the country's ruling caste—from President Johnson on down—muttered among themselves about a conspiracy, these same leaders worked strenuously—with the media's collaboration—to calm the public's fears.

LBJ's suspicions about the Castro regime's involvement in Dallas were fed to him by the CIA's McCone and Helms. But it is uncertain whether he actually believed them. Abe Fortas—the trusted legal advisor Johnson asked to scrutinize the Warren Report and report back to him—was among those in the president's inner circle who poured cold water on the theory. The CIA and the U.S. ambassador to Mexico, Thomas Mann—a hard-line Cold Warrior who came from the CIA-connected United Fruit Company—began spinning LBJ on the false story that Oswald was a Castro agent immediately after the assassination. But Hoover, whom Johnson found a more trustworthy source of intelligence, informed the president that the photographic and audio evidence the CIA was using to prove Oswald had visited the Soviet and Cuban embassies in Mexico City appeared to be faked—a disturbing piece of information that both men certainly recognized pointed back at the CIA itself.

Johnson knew that he was being hustled into war with Cuba by forces within his own government. The Warren Commission would become his way of heading off this military showdown, which he realized could lead to nuclear war. Johnson famously overpowered Chief Justice Warren's resistance to chairing the assassination commission by painting a cataclysmic vision of the future if the hysteria about a "Red plot" was not put to rest—his picture of a scorched world with 40 million dead brought tears to the seventy-two-year-old jurist's eyes. But it was not simply another melodramatic Lyndon Johnson performance. The president believed these were the stakes.

"Once you hear the conversations that Johnson had with Warren and Russell, you recognize the commission was not set up to search for the truth about the assassination," remarks James Galbraith, political historian at the University of Texas's Lyndon B. Johnson School of Public Affairs. "Nonetheless, it had a very high purpose, which was to protect Johnson from the far right, from being stampeded into nuclear war. This is the haunting risk that keeps Johnson awake nights throughout his presidency."

Lyndon Johnson was too shrewd a master of Washington power not to sense the dark forces at work that had resulted in his occupancy of the White House. The shadow over his ascension to the exalted office would forever plague him. Robert Kennedy was not the only haunted figure in Washington after the assassination. "Johnson was weighed down by a lot of guilt feelings too," observed Katzenbach. To begin with, the despicable crime had occurred in his home state. "Of all the places in the world!" Katzenbach exclaimed. "Johnson knew that was the kind of thing that could start all sorts of rumors."

Robert Kennedy and Lyndon Johnson were legendary antagonists. They warily circled one other, brimming with wounded emotions and scalding resentment. But, ironically, they shared similar suspicions about the events in Dallas. The only way that the truth about the assassination could have been wrung out of the government is if these two formidable personalities had joined forces to demand it. But considering their poisoned chemistry, and their lifelong predilection for secrecy, this was asking the impossible.

Meanwhile, the Kennedy band of brothers, following Bobby's lead, also stayed largely silent about Dallas. They looked to RFK as the future king, convinced that his succession was inevitable. In the meantime, they waited. They were always waiting for Bobby.

BACKSTAGE AT THE CHANNEL 9 studio in Los Angeles, Arthur Schlesinger was having his makeup removed after being interviewed by local TV newsman Stan Bohrman for his afternoon talk show. Before he left the station, Schlesinger was asked by Bohrman if he would meet with a Los Angeles assassination researcher named Ray Marcus, who had brought some evidence to show him. It was 1967 and conspiracy theories about Dallas were now in full bloom. Schlesinger himself had long been a skeptic about the Warren Commission's lone gunman conclusion, and had even called for reopening the case. But he had stopped short of joining the conspiracy camp. Still, the Kennedy court historian agreed to meet Marcus, who was waiting to see him in an adjoining room.

Ray Marcus, who was forty at the time, was a respected figure among the first wave of Warren Report critics. He ran a small business, distributing "Keep Off the Grass" and other household signs to retail stores, but was able to leave it in the hands of a trustworthy partner, allowing him ample time to delve into the case. In a later generation, the dedicated citizens like Marcus who threw themselves into the deep arcana of the assassination would have been bloggers. Some were frenzied—even decidedly mad—in their devotion to the case; others, like Marcus, were solidly grounded. He had been pulled down "the rabbit hole," as some researchers called the labyrinth of their obsession, on the very first day. "I've always been a newshound and I was glued to the TV set on November 22," he recalled. "I knew that when they began saying Oswald had acted alone, they were either telling a lie or saying something that could not possibly have been proven by that time."

Working in the pre-Internet era, Marcus produced sober, well-documented monographs on the assassination, which he published and distributed himself. He also closely examined the photographic evidence from Dealey Plaza, cutting out frames from the Zapruder film that were published in Life magazine and the Warren Report and turning them into four-feet-long photo displays to graphically demonstrate how JFK must have been shot from more than one direction.

Like the other assassination critics, Marcus was tormented by the idea that the American people had been deceived by the government, the legal system, and the media. The Warren Report, he declared at the time, was "the most massively fraudulent document ever foisted on a free society." Marcus conceded that his photographic analysis might be "completely unscientific. But my answer to people saying, 'You're no expert' is 'Where are the experts?'"

Marcus thought it was important for President Kennedy's key courtiers to see his photographic evidence and he made a strong effort to contact them. When Bohrman, who knew of his work, offered to introduce him to Arthur Schlesinger, he jumped at the chance.

But when Schlesinger walked into the backstage room at Channel 9, he was not prepared for what he saw. After shaking the historian's hand, Marcus directed his attention to the photo display that he had set up on a table. Included in the blow-ups was notorious Frame 313, where President Kennedy's skull explodes in a halo of bloody mist. Schlesinger glanced at the photos and visibly paled. He turned immediately away. "I can't look and won't look," he said. There was no further conversation. Schlesinger left the studio and Marcus never saw him again.

"I can't look and won't look"—it was a perfect summation of the attitude toward the horror of Dallas that was widely held in the Kennedy circle. Many of the president's men were plagued by doubts about the Warren Report, but they could not muster the political and emotional fortitude to grapple with the case. Instead, they waited for Bobby. And while they waited, they mulled over the unspeakable crime quietly among themselves.

Courtney Evans, the FBI agent with the unenviable task of serving as RFK's and Hoover's go-between, recalled the intense discussions about Dallas among Kennedy's Justice Department brotherhood. Evans was inclined to believe Oswald had acted alone, but not everyone agreed. "I still think Oswald was the assassin, a man who had fallen under the influence of certain groups and ideas," Evans says today. "The old crowd at the Justice Department—Katzenbach, Ramsey Clark—we used to talk it over, the subject came up whenever we were together. There was ambivalence within the group about who was responsible for the assassination. But there just wasn't much factually to prove there was a conspiracy."

Why didn't RFK's elite Justice Department team—the young, hard-charging prosecutors, former investigative journalists, and loyal FBI men like Evans—use their formidable talents to solve the case? Evans said he was restrained by his boss. "Hoover kept me as far away as possible from the Warren Commission. He made sure I was kept busy with other tasks. Of course, he put nothing in writing—the subtle word was put out orally."

Evans was one of the few FBI men who had clearly shifted his loyalty to the Kennedys. "I felt the Kennedys were trying to do a wonderful service for the country," he said. "President Kennedy had a strong feeling that we should change the course of the country." But after Johnson took over, realizing he had no future at Hoover's FBI, Evans resigned from government service. "I was certainly disillusioned with Hoover and the bureau. He would have sent me to Anchorage. Obviously I was not going anywhere in the FBI. It's been published that Hoover knew JFK was going to replace him in his second term—maybe he was taking that out on me."

Oddly, despite the well-known strains between RFK and Hoover, the attorney general's team trusted the FBI to investigate the assassination. According to former organized crime prosecutor Ronald Goldfarb, not even the mob-connected Ruby seemed to ring alarm bells. "You have to go back to those times," he said. "It was a time we believed government, it was pre-Watergate and all that stuff." And, like everyone else in the Kennedy circle, Bobby's prosecutors were following his lead. "I remember people saying, 'Who's got a greater motive than Robert Kennedy to get his brother's murderer?'" recalled Goldfarb.

To his Justice Department team, it seemed that Bobby had delegated the assassination investigation to Herbert "Jack" Miller, the chief of the department's criminal division. But, Miller insists today, "Bob didn't ask us to—he knew damn well we would." Miller said that he and his staff investigated a possible Mafia connection to Dallas. "We ran all the traps we could and we found no evidence."

But some of Kennedy's prosecutors wondered why Miller was taking the lead on the investigation. He did not seem like the kind of bulldog Bobby would pick to go snuffling about the gutters—and suites—of America to find his brother's killers. A lifelong Republican, Miller had been plucked by Bobby from the plush world of Washington corporate law because his legal background included a skirmish with the Teamsters. After his stint at the

Justice Department, Miller would resume his lucrative law practice, representing such elite clients as Richard Nixon, for whom he won a presidential pardon.

"If Bobby was going to get the truth, I know who he would have chosen," said Goldfarb. "He would have chosen Walter Sheridan. Because he trusted him, he was tough, they knew each other for a long time."

What Goldfarb, and other Justice Department lawyers, did not know was that Kennedy had indeed tapped Sheridan—secretly—to dig into the crime. But the two close friends were biding their time, waiting until Kennedy had the political power to make their investigation official.

With Bobby keeping his suspicions about Dallas quiet, his circle of colleagues and friends were left to figure out their own views about the crime. James Symington, Kennedy's former administrative assistant, had gone to work in Abe Fortas's Washington law firm by the time of the assassination. Fortas, charged with reviewing the Warren Report by his longtime friend and client Lyndon Johnson, delegated the task to his young employee, dropping the massive tome on his desk with a thud. "I never talked to Bob about the assassination," Symington told me. "I was not in his inner circle. But I had to read the entire Warren Report before it was released, and it seemed to me like an effort by people who were very anxious to put the case to rest without looking into every nook and cranny. It was a long and windy thing and was concerned mostly with Oswald's background and showing that he acted alone. But I could never bring myself to think that—that he acted alone. Because of the way the bullets struck Kennedy and because Oswald's motivation was never clear to me. Why the hell would he do that? It was never made clear. And then there was the totally unbelievable situation of Jack Ruby walking up to him in the police station and killing him. As if to make sure he would never talk. There were just too many loose ends."

Nick Katzenbach is one of the Justice Department veterans who has consistently defended the Warren Report over the years. "I think the Warren Commission had the facts right," he told me recently. "I have absolutely no doubt." But even Katzenbach concedes the flaws in the official investigation. In his 1978 testimony before the House Select Committee on Assassinations, he was scathing in his description of how the CIA and FBI had manipulated the commission. "Cooperation?" he laughed bitterly at one point. "I don't think the term is applicable. It's unbelievable some of the stuff they concealed from the commission." Katzenbach was "astounded" by how Allen Dulles—who he said was "obviously the CIA's spy on the commission"—hid crucial information like the CIA-Mafia plots from the blue-ribbon panel. As for the FBI's role in the investigation, Katzenbach testified, "Hoover was impossible in those days. His real talent was running over people and covering up in the process." Today, Katzenbach even suggests that Oswald might have been backed by others. "I'm as certain as one can be there was no other gun shot," he told me, characterizing as "silliness" views to the contrary. "But it's not silliness to speculate that somebody was behind Oswald. . . . I'd almost bet on the [anti-Castro] Cubans. If I had the choice, if it had to be one of the three," he said, referring to the CIA, Mafia, and Cuban exiles, "I'd say the Cubans probably had the worst judgment."

Doubt and confusion about the assassination also reigned in Kennedy circles outside the Justice Department. In a newspaper interview, former White House press aide Malcolm Kilduff established his respectability by taking the obligatory swipe at conspiracy theories as "garbage," but then expressed profound skepticism about the Warren Report's magic bullet. Fred Dutton, JFK's Cabinet secretary and later RFK's behind-the-scenes campaign manager in his 1968 presidential race, told me shortly before his death in 2005 that he agreed with Bobby's characterization of the Warren Report as a PR job. Dutton was convinced "there was more to it than we've gotten, and yet I don't know what that is." According to their sons, Larry O'Brien—JFK's savvy congressional liaison—and Chicago Mayor Richard Daley—the Kennedys' key political ally—also both suspected a conspiracy. "I would have put my dad in the camp of someone pretty suspicious of the Warren version," Bill Daley says today.

But no former Kennedy administration official ever created a public furor over Dallas. It would become clear that if one wanted to remain a member in good standing in Washington political and social circles, it was wise not to say anything intemperate about the assassination. This expedient position was couched as doing what was right for the country, and helping it get on with its business. "I think he accepted the Warren Report, but did he believe it? That's another matter," said Carol Bundy, daughter of the late William Bundy, one of the cerebral, well-bred brotherly duo who served President Kennedy as foreign policy advisors. "I think he thought it was for the good of the country—this is what we put together and now we need to move forward. When I brought up the subject, he would say there's probably a lot of evidence we don't know about, but that doesn't necessarily mean there was a plot. The point was to stabilize the country after the assassination—let's get on with the ship of state."

Despite his emotional ties to the Kennedy family, Robert McNamara took the same practical attitude as fellow Establishment figures like Bundy.

Did the Warren Report get it right? "Well, you know, the answer is that I have made no effort to find out," McNamara informed me. "The answer is I do believe it's the most likely [explanation]. I just don't know." Then he laughed—a queer, uncomfortable laugh. So, in his mind, the case has been settled? "You know, it was a terrible loss. I think the world would be different today had not the two Kennedys been assassinated. But it's done, it's past. I can't do anything about it."

Arthur Schlesinger found his own sentiments on the subject harder to contain. Despite his avowal to Marcus that he would not look, he did look many times through the years. He would talk to Bobby about it; he would read the assassination books. In later years, he even gave a measured endorsement to one of the best such books, *Conspiracy* (later retitled *Not in Your Lifetime*), by investigative journalist Anthony Summers. But in public he would go no further than declaring himself "agnostic" on the question of whether Oswald acted alone. It was a position that even his own wife found inadequate. During a March 2001 conference in Havana to mark the fortieth anniversary of the Bay of Pigs, film producer and former John Kerry speechwriter Eric Hamburg found himself seated next to Schlesinger's wife, Alexandra. At one point, she surprised Hamburg by leaning over and asking to look at his copy of *ZR Rifle*, a JFK conspiracy book by Brazilian journalist Claudia Furiati that draws heavily on Cuban intelligence files. "I used to have a copy," she said, "but I've lost it. I'm sure this book is right. I'm absolutely convinced there was a conspiracy." Then Alexandra Schlesinger nodded towards her husband and whispered confidentially, "He's an agnostic, but I'm not."

But Schlesinger's wife made it clear that she had problems with one of Furiati's charges—her allegation, credited to the Cuban State Security Department, that Richard Helms was "the ultimate author" of the assassination plot. "I can't believe the part about Dick Helms," she told Hamburg. "He was a friend of ours. We played tennis with him."

The Kennedy circle's overlapping relationships with the Georgetown CIA set made it hard for many of them to make this unnerving leap, to conclude that JFK's assassination was—like the slaying of Julius Caesar—an inside job. Some of the Kennedy men, including Schlesinger, had known CIA officials like Helms since their days together in the OSS. Some drank martinis with them at Joe Alsop's salons. Or played tennis with them. Or lived next door to them.

Long-time Kennedy friend Marie Ridder—who party-hopped in Georgetown with a young Jack before his marriage ("I'm the only person I know,"

she quips today, "who went out with Jack and didn't get propositioned!")—
is among those who cannot bring themselves to suspect the CIA. A spunky
former Knight-Ridder newspaper reporter and widow of publisher Walter
Ridder, Marie Ridder now lives in active retirement in a sun-dappled clap-
board house on a rolling, green bluff overlooking the Potomac. She greeted
me one day in rumpled slacks and blouse, fresh from her garden, and over a
lunch of chilled sorrel soup and hamburgers on her backyard patio, reminisced about the Kennedys and her old Georgetown friends. "Jim Angleton
was, of course, kind of an evil genius," Ridder remarked at one point. "But I
don't think he'd be involved in killing his president. I really, truly don't. He
used to have the land over there," she said, pointing to the lushly landscaped
house next door. "He was a fabulous gardener. And a man who is a fabulous
gardener is not going to kill off a president, I'm sorry."

And Helms? "Helms was a very sweet, well-meaning man," said Ridder.
"He would not have been in a murder conspiracy," she added, overlooking his
confessed role in the plots against Castro.

With other Kennedy intimates, the very subject of the assassination is an
emotional minefield that must be gingerly navigated. Theodore Sorensen
quickly makes it known when the subject arises in conversation that it is still
too painful for him to contemplate, even at this late date. An interviewer
feels sadistic to press on. New Frontiersmen like Sorensen are in their autumn days now; they have lived long, eventful lives. But nothing filled them
with as much pulsing sense of purpose as their time with Jack and Bobby
Kennedy. Their eyes pool with tears as they relive those days, when they
were the young and the chosen and were changing the world, before something was cut from their hearts.

Like Schlesinger, Sorensen says that he is "agnostic" on the question of
Dallas. "I have never seen any hard evidence that contradicted the Warren
Commission conclusion that Oswald acted alone," he tells me, making it
clear that he would prefer to change the subject.

Sorensen seems weighted down with the melancholy burden of history.
He knows that John F. Kennedy lived for a purpose; he just can't bring himself to believe he died for one. "It's terribly painful. You see, there's emotion
on both sides internally. On the one hand, if I can know that my friend of
eleven years died as a martyr to a cause, that there was some reason, some
purpose why he was killed—and not just a totally senseless, lucky sharp-
shooter—then I think the whole world would feel better. That brave John F.
Kennedy, with all these courageous positions, went into Texas knowing that
it was hostile territory, and he ended up dead. But I just think that's a fanciful

theory as of now, and comforting as it may be, I'm not going to embrace it, because there's no evidence of it."

But Kenny O'Donnell—Kennedy's vigilant watchdog, the politically shrewd White House aide who wielded the most influence over the president—did see evidence of a conspiracy. He saw it with his own eyes in Dallas. And it would torment him the rest of his life. Among the Kennedy brotherhood, Kenny O'Donnell's story looms as the saddest of them all.

KENNY O'DONNELL AND HIS fellow Irish mafia warhorse Dave Powers were eyewitnesses to history on November 22, 1963. Riding immediately behind the president's limousine in the Secret Service backup car, the two men saw it all that day. Before the motorcade began, JFK—attentive as always to political details—had asked them to take seats in the follow-up car so they could closely observe the reactions to him and Jackie from the crowds. The two men could never forget what they saw that afternoon. As the shots rang out, Powers blurted, "Kenny, I think the president's been shot." O'Donnell quickly made a sign of the cross. As both men stared intently at the man they had loved and served ever since he was a scrawny young congressional candidate, a final shot "took the side of his head off," O'Donnell would later recall. "We saw pieces of bone and brain tissue and bits of his reddish hair flying through the air. The impact lifted him and shook him limply, as if he was a rag doll, and then he dropped out of our sight, sprawled across the back seat of the car. I said to Dave, 'He's dead.'"

O'Donnell and Powers, both World War II veterans, distinctly heard at least two shots come from the grassy knoll area in front of the motorcade. But when they later told this to the FBI, they were informed that they must be wrong. If they did not change their story, it was impressed on the men, it could be very damaging for the country. So O'Donnell altered his account to fit the official version, testifying before the Warren Commission that the shots had come "from the right rear"—the direction of the School Book Depository. Powers, however, could not be fully shaken from his story. Even though one of the Warren Commission employees who took his statement kept interrupting him, Powers insisted that he "had a fleeting impression that the noise appeared to come from the front" as well as from behind—which is probably why Powers was not invited to testify before the commission as the more amenable O'Donnell was.

Five years after the assassination, O'Donnell confessed to his friend, Boston congressman (and future Speaker of the House) Tip O'Neill, what he had dutifully hidden from the public—he heard two shots from behind the fence on the grassy knoll. O'Neill, who was dining with O'Donnell and a few other people at Jimmy's Harborside Restaurant in Boston, was stunned. "That's not what you told the Warren Commission," he said.

"You're right," replied O'Donnell. "I told the FBI what I had heard, but they said it couldn't have happened that way and that I must have been imagining things. So I testified the way they wanted me to. I just didn't want to stir up any more pain and trouble for the family."

"I can't believe that," said O'Neill. "I wouldn't have done that in a million years. I would have told the truth."

"Tip, you have to understand. The family—everybody wanted this thing behind them."

It's clear from O'Neill's account—and one given by Dave Powers, who suggested that Hoover himself pressured O'Donnell to change his account—that the FBI played a key role in this fateful distortion of the record. But it's equally obvious that O'Donnell was also responding to signals from the Kennedy family, and that could only mean his close friend Bobby, the man with whom his life and career had been completely intertwined ever since they were Harvard roommates. The intensely loyal O'Donnell, who was as close as a brother to Bobby, would never have changed his story without first checking with Kennedy. And Bobby had made it clear that he was not ready to publicly question the official story about the assassination.

Whatever his reasons for hiding the truth about Dallas, O'Donnell's decision weighed heavily on him. The Kennedys had been his life. Tough, taciturn, and utterly dedicated, he had put in slavish hours at the White House. But he laughed at the notion it was a sacrifice. "Tough job my ass. It was the best job I ever had," he would say. Now the man he had served was gone. He wished the bullets had hit him instead, he told his wife. And instead of helping bring the president's killers to justice, he was misleading the country. "The assassination was the end of his life," his son Kenny Jr. told me. "He never was the same again. None of the men around Kennedy were. But especially him."

O'Donnell confided what he really witnessed in Dealey Plaza to his son as well. "He said there was fire from two different directions," recalled the younger O'Donnell. And his father would bitterly complain about his experience with the Warren Commission to his son. "I'll tell you this right now," he told him, "they didn't want to know." O'Donnell called the inquiry "the most pointless investigation I've ever seen." Pulling out the records of his testimony to show Kenny Jr., he would point to a passage with disgust and say, "Look, this is ridiculous—they weren't even looking for an answer to this."

O'Donnell might also have been disgusted with his own performance before the commission.

In the months after Dallas, O'Donnell would devote himself to helping Jackie. The two had clung to each other like old soldiers ever since the assassination. As they flew back to Washington that day, both were stained with Jack's blood. Kenny and Bobby found solace by gathering friends at Jackie's Georgetown house and entertaining her with old stories about Jack.

But O'Donnell could not put Dallas behind him. What he and Dave Powers witnessed that day continued to work inside them. O'Donnell experienced wrenching bouts of nausea for six months after Dallas. Powers began suffering violent headaches. The pain was focused in the same part of his skull where he had seen the bullet blow off the top of his friend's head. He couldn't get the "sickening sound" out of his own head—like "a grapefruit splattering against the side of a wall."

O'Donnell began drinking heavily. When friends warned him to go easy on the stuff, the man nicknamed The Cobra would fix them with a cold glare and tell them, "Go to hell and mind your own business." But he listened when Jackie and Bobby sat him down and talked to him. "It worked," observed his daughter, Helen. "He seemed to step forward into human company again."

But Kenny O'Donnell never fully recovered. "He just lived the rest of his life with a heavy heart," said his son. He ran twice for the Democratic nomination for governor in Massachusetts, in 1966 and 1970; but his political talent was as a behind-the-scenes man, not as a campaigner, and he lost both times. Bobby's assassination was the final blow. Kenny Jr. was with his father the night he heard. His father had just spoken to RFK on the phone about the California primary results. "It's over," his father told him after hearing that history had repeated itself. "That's all he said," recalled Kenny Jr. "That was the absolute end."

When O'Donnell died in a Boston hospital in September 1977 at age fifty-three, his family requested that the cause of death be withheld, but the press reported he had succumbed to a liver ailment. There was no more Bobby to tell him to put down the bottle. His memorial service was held at St. Matthews Cathedral, where he had escorted Jack's casket fourteen years before, walking slowly up Connecticut Avenue from the White House. At the Irish wake held afterwards at the Mayflower Hotel, a Boston pol reminisced about his fallen friend. Without the Kennedys, he said, "O'Donnell was the music without the harp."

• • •

ONCE AGAIN, ED GUTHMAN was worrying about his friend Bob Kennedy's life. It was fall 1964. Kennedy's campaign for the Senate was under way and everywhere he went, the candidate spiked into deep wellsprings of emotion. The people strained against police lines, they lunged to touch him. Whites, blacks; the young and old; men, women. It was a longing that went beyond politics. Americans needed to feel that not all hope had died on November 22. Here he was in the flesh, a living reminder that the Kennedy dream was still alive. After the long months of mourning, when nothing seemed right anymore about the country, the very sight of Bobby set off explosions of ecstasy.

But Guthman knew that passions about Kennedy ran in opposite directions. As he marched along the New York campaign trail, less the happy warrior than an ashen penitent, Bobby also stirred darker thoughts. Guthman, who had left the Justice Department with Kennedy to work on the Senate campaign, heard about the constant stream of death threats. The FBI would call nearly every morning with another warning about their campaign destination that day. Were they all real? Was Hoover exaggerating the threats to disrupt the campaign or make his bureau seem more vigilant than it was in protecting his brother? Guthman took the threats seriously enough to talk to Jim King, the NYPD detective who was traveling with the campaign. But both men knew it was useless to say anything to Bobby; he would never let security precautions dictate his campaign style. The people needed to touch him; he needed to touch the people. It was the only thing that seemed to bring him alive.

On September 29, the campaign rolled through Rochester. It was the hometown of his incumbent Republican opponent, Kenneth Keating, but as usual, the Kennedy crowds were boisterous. Still, Guthman felt that dark undercurrent.

Earlier that day, a man with a rifle who had asked about Kennedy's motorcade route was arrested by the police. (They released him after he convinced them he was a deer hunter on his way home from a gun shop and was trying to avoid traffic.) But Kennedy did what he always did—he went into the poorest, most crime-ridden neighborhoods, including the ghetto that had been torn by rioting in July. He climbed onto car hoods to speak to the surging, grasping crowds—alone, with no guards. In Rochester, he reminded people what America should stand for.

It was the day after the Warren Report's release, but Bobby came out of the gloom that had descended over him when he was asked at a press conference to define his foreign policy differences with his opponent. Keating was a genial, white-maned, ruddy-faced uncle figure with a progressive record on civil rights. But he had played a provocative role during the Cuban Missile Crisis, using information leaked from the CIA to goad the Kennedys into a combative stance. Bobby told the press that day he stood for a strong military. But, he immediately added, America's military prowess must be coupled with "the inner strength and wisdom not to use that military strength precipitately or indiscriminately." He said that in the end communism would only be defeated "through progressive practical programs which wipe out the poverty, misery and discontent on which it thrives." He suggested that true national security would come from strongly supporting the United Nations—"mankind's noblest experiment"—and helping lift the world's two billion poor from their wretched fate. Finally, he declared, America would only command the world's respect if it practiced what it preached at home, upholding democratic principles and working towards racial equality.

"We cannot expect an African to believe we are on the side of equality and human dignity when his own ambassadors are not served in our restaurants. We cannot expect countries with far lower standards of living to respect our belief in human dignity if their aged are venerated and ours are neglected. We cannot expect nations to join us in combating poverty if in the midst of unprecedented wealth, six million families live in poverty."

Giving voice to these New Frontier ideals lifted Kennedy from his doldrums of the previous day, as if borne aloft by his brother's soaring rhetoric. But if Bobby was conjuring his brother's spirit, Guthman was concerned with keeping this living, breathing Kennedy safe from bodily harm. "I was with him that day in Rochester," he recalled, "and it appeared to me to be a kind of dangerous situation. So I went up to these news photographers who were covering the campaign and I asked them to gather around him, to give him some protection."

It's astonishing in today's political climate to consider a media pack agreeing to do this—to put themselves in the line of fire for a candidate. But that's precisely what the photographers did, said Guthman. "Look, a *lot* of people would have taken a bullet for Bob Kennedy any day of the year." Would Guthman have done so? "Absolutely, without hesitating."

Robert Kennedy's 1964 Senate campaign rolled forward on a wave of popular sentiment, a yearning that he realized had more to do with his brother than with him. After a hectic day of campaigning, Guthman rejoiced in the clamorous receptions that Kennedy had received. "I've never seen crowds like you're getting, they've got to be a good omen," he told Bobby.

But Kennedy looked at Guthman with a melancholy expression. "Don't you know?" he said. "They're for him—they're for him."

Kennedy's race for the Senate was the critical first step in his strategy to regain the White House, where, he had vowed, he would continue his brother's policies. But Bobby's heart was clearly not in the campaign. He had announced his Senate candidacy at the last moment, on August 25, after declaring he would not run just two months earlier. The decision came after an overwrought process, in which he first considered running for governor in Massachusetts (finally rejecting this option out of concern he would be stepping on brother Teddy's turf) and then allowed himself to be briefly pushed forward by supporters as Lyndon Johnson's vice presidential running mate. Both men knew it would be a disastrous match and LBJ summoned Kennedy to the White House on July 29 to make his decision official. The meeting was deeply awkward for both men. As Bobby later recounted to Kenny O'Donnell, Johnson told him that "he wanted a vice president who could help the country, help the party, and be of assistance to him . . . and he concluded by saying that person wasn't me." Kennedy, who knew that Johnson needed to establish an independent political base, took the decision in stride. "Aw, what the hell," he laughed, after telling his Justice Department colleagues what happened, "let's go form our own country." From then on, Bobby and his circle would be "the government in exile," as Ethel accurately jested.

Kennedy's outsider status would be driven home at the Democratic Party convention in late August. Bobby announced his Senate candidacy the day before the convention began in Atlantic City, but Johnson was so fearful that his rival would spark a delegate stampede for the vice presidential—or even presidential—nomination that he took the unprecedented step of ordering the FBI to keep Kennedy under surveillance. Cartha DeLoach and a thirty-man FBI team swept into Atlantic City to monitor every move of the attorney general of the United States—the man who was officially still their boss. The FBI spies, who flashed fake NBC News press passes and other bogus credentials, had special instructions to look for any contacts between Kennedy and Martin Luther King Jr.—a charismatic combination that could have swept the convention hall. Johnson's chief of staff, Marvin Watson, even instructed former JFK advance man Jerry Bruno to keep a close eye on Bobby. "We are not going to let Bobby and Jackie Kennedy steal this convention," Watson told him. Bruno, a Kennedy loyalist, was stunned by the order. He would stick with RFK at the convention, but as a friend not a spy.

Johnson did not have to worry. Bobby was in such fragile shape during the convention, where his brother's ghost hovered everywhere, that he could never have mounted a political rebellion. When he climbed onstage to introduce a film tribute to JFK—a speech that the nervous Johnson had rescheduled from the beginning of the convention to lessen its impact—Kennedy was greeted with a massive ovation. He stood on the podium, while it washed over him in unending waves, for twenty-two long minutes. "Mr. Chairman," he would begin as the applause finally began to wane. But then it would rise up again from some new corner of the cavernous hall. Wearing the same black suit and tie he had worn almost continuously since the assassination, he fought back tears as he looked over the cheering crowd. His eyes, red and glistening in the spotlights, were filled with the sorrow of the past nine months. Finally he began his speech. There was nothing political about it— he said nothing of the forces that had cut down his brother. But even his sentimental references to the fallen president would be interpreted by his enemies in the Johnson camp as political attacks. "When he shall die, / Take him and cut him out in little stars," said Bobby, quoting Shakespeare's *Romeo and Juliet*—an addition to the speech suggested by Jackie. "And he will make the face of heaven so fine / That all the world will be in love with night / And pay no worship to the garish sun." Supporters of the garish Texan were quick to take offense. Other observers interpreted the extended ovation for Kennedy as a slap at party bosses. But after he finished his speech, Bobby simply retreated to the fire escape outside the convention hall, where he sat sobbing for fifteen minutes.

He had been raised to believe that "Kennedys don't cry," passing this stoicism along to his own children. But he found it hard to live by on the Senate campaign trail, even in public. At Columbia University, a student confronted him with the dreaded question. Did he believe the Warren Report's conclusion about a lone gunman? For several minutes, Kennedy stood speechless, while the audience murmured nervously. Finally he responded irritably, "I've made my statement on that." But as he began to rehash what he had said months earlier in Poland, Kennedy's voice suddenly cracked. He dropped his head and tears began streaming down his face. The man whom colleagues found astonishingly honest could not bring himself to repeat what he did not believe.

With Kennedy unable to shake free of his grief, his desultory campaign was headed for defeat. Paul Corbin—the ruthless political operator whom some called "Bobby's dark side"—was the only one with the nerve to confront him. "Get out of your daze," he scolded his boss. "God damn, Bob, be yourself. Get hold of yourself. You're real. Your brother is dead."

"It was painful to watch him on the campaign trail—he was depressed and the crowds sensed it," recalled Justin Feldman, the reform Democrat who first approached Bobby to run for the New York Senate seat and later worked as his campaign coordinator. Feldman urged him to go on the attack against Keating, but Bobby did not have the stomach for it. "He told me, 'Well, he hasn't been that bad of a senator, has he? Everybody says I'm so ruthless.'"

Then, as Keating seemed coasting to victory, he made a "fatal mistake," said Feldman. "And it made Bobby finally come alive." At the end of September, trying to drive a wedge between Kennedy and the Jewish vote, Keating dredged up the old Nazi appeasement charges that had haunted the Kennedy family. He suggested that as attorney general, Kennedy had settled a World War II–era case in favor of a chemical company with Nazi ties in order to please his father. Bobby, the family protector, was outraged that Keating would use such a tactic. He had lost a brother and a brother-in-law to the war, he reminded voters. Left unsaid was that his family had just given another son to the country. "Bobby went nuts," said Feldman. "He no longer thought Keating was this benign force in politics. He denounced his charges as outrageous demagoguery. After that, Bobby became a campaigner."

In the end, Kennedy won by over 700,000 votes. But he needed the coattails of his brother's successor, who carried the state by two million more votes than Bobby won, to do it. Even in victory, Bobby seemed melancholy. Congratulated by his bodyguard Bill Barry during the raucous election night party, Bobby said, "If my brother was alive, I wouldn't be here. I'd rather have it that way." Later, sitting at the Johnson inauguration with his old friend Joe Tydings—who had also just been elected to the Senate from Maryland—Bobby grew teary watching the ceremony that should have ushered in his brother's final term. "We quietly cried together when LBJ was sworn in," said Tydings, "when, you know, President Kennedy should have been there."

UNLIKE HIS BROTHER TED, Robert Kennedy's interest was not engaged by the day-to-day business of the Senate. But he quickly seized it as a platform to highlight the national and international issues that he deemed most urgent. "He thought that the way the Senate ran was archaic," Pierre Salinger recalled. "He didn't see it as a real action place. And I think he was rather restless with the Senate. . . . I'd go up and sit in the Senate office for four or five hours at a time. And he would spend most of his time talking to people on problems which were not at all directly related to his Senate duties." Kennedy met with foreign dignitaries Salinger introduced to him such as French politicians Pierre Mendes-France and François Mitterand. And he would discuss the intractable problems of poverty with activists from Mississippi and the Indian reservations.

Quietly, Bobby also began to show renewed interest in his brother's assassination. On November 16, 1964, shortly after he won his Senate seat, RFK flew to Mexico City, where he spoke at the dedication ceremony for a workers' housing project named after President Kennedy. At a press conference, he was again asked about the Warren Report and he again endorsed it—but this time he added an intriguing qualifier, saying he believed in its veracity, "as far as the investigation went."

Though he attended a flurry of events during his two-day visit and dined with U.S. ambassador Fulton Freeman at the fashionable San Angel Inn, Kennedy made it clear to embassy officials that he also wanted private time while he was in Mexico. But the visiting U.S. senator could not escape official supervision. Newly released Mexican government documents show that RFK was put under surveillance by the *Dirección Federal de Seguridad*, Mexico's FBI—an agency with close ties to the CIA station in Mexico City. CIA station chief Winston Scott, who was kept informed of Bobby's comings and goings during his visit, learned that the senator was gathering information about Lee Harvey Oswald while he was there. Scott noted in a memo for agency files that playwright Elena Garro de Paz, wife of novelist Octavio Paz, was among those trying to pass information about Oswald to Kennedy during his stay.

Mexico City was one of the most intriguing chapters in Oswald's murky life before his collision with history in Dallas. The alleged lone assassin had traveled there in late September 1963, according to the CIA, to get a visa from the Cuban embassy. But, as Hoover had informed LBJ, the evidence suggesting Oswald was urgently trying to visit Cuba was apparently falsified by the CIA. Was Oswald the object of a U.S intelligence operation or a Cuban operation? The Warren Report had left pressing questions like this about Oswald's Mexico City trip unresolved. Bobby was interested in finding out more about Oswald's mysterious trip during his own visit.

In the months after his election, Kennedy also took time from his Senate duties to meet and correspond with assassination researchers. In August 1965, Ray Marcus mailed a packet of his Dealey Plaza photographic evidence to Kennedy. In his cover letter, Marcus apologized for sending the senator material that would certainly cause him "personal anguish," but said he felt an "overriding obligation" to bring this evidence of a conspiracy to

Kennedy's attention. To the researcher's surprise, Bobby responded in a letter dated September 16. "I just wanted you to know that your interest is appreciated," wrote Kennedy.

Bobby also agreed to meet in his Senate office with Penn Jones Jr., a
crusading Texas publisher who had turned his small-town newspaper, the
Midlothian Mirror, into a forum for assassination muckraking. Jones—a
short, feisty former boxing champ at the University of Texas and World War
II hero—realized there was something absurd about a cow-town newspaper
taking on the political crime of the century. But he didn't see the big media
guns taking on the job and he refused to sit idly by. He became convinced
that JFK's murder was a "coup d'état" involving the Joint Chiefs of Staff and
the CIA. Puzzled by Bobby's silence about Dallas, Jones decided to fly to
Washington to present his research to the senator and encourage him to
speak out about the case. Greeting the publisher in his office, Kennedy told
him, "Look, I'll listen to what you have to say. I won't necessarily agree or
disagree, but I'll listen." Afterwards, Bobby autographed Jones' copy of *Profiles in Courage*, next to the signature that JFK himself had scrawled in the
book during his Texas trip. RFK then asked his limousine driver to take Jones
to JFK's final resting place at Arlington, which the publisher wanted to visit
before returning home.

In his speech at the 1964 Democratic convention, RFK had urged the
delegates not to be swept away in the mists of the past, but to "look forward"
as President Kennedy did. Bobby once chided Jackie for immersing herself
in Kennedy Library work, telling her it was morbid to dwell on the past. But
Bobby too could not forget. "The senator is still haunted by memories," a
New York Times reporter observed in June 1965, describing one corner of his
Capitol Hill office as "a small shrine to President Kennedy—pictures, books,
the restored image of the fallen leader."

Everywhere he went, Bobby carried Jack's old overcoat. "He hardly ever
wore it, but he was always taking it with him," remembered his aide Ronnie
Eldridge. "He always forgot the damn overcoat, he'd carry it with him and
then leave it in different places. So we were always scurrying around, looking
for the overcoat."

Bobby's friend Marie Ridder speculates that his ongoing interest in the
assassination was part of his inability to let go of the past and accept his
brother's death. "I wonder how I can put this," she said. "My first husband
was killed in World War II, at the Battle of the Bulge. I went to Germany
right after the war and I used to look at all the soldiers there to see if by
chance Ben was there. I mean, I absolutely knew he wasn't. I knew that. I

had his clothes. But I emotionally couldn't let go. I think that's the nearest parallel [with Bobby's belief in a conspiracy]. . . . It's not rational, but I understand why he'd do it."

But the men in whom Kennedy confided his suspicions about Dallas did not regard them as irrational.

"WE KNOW THE CIA was involved, and the Mafia. We all know that." Dick Goodwin is speaking over the phone from his home in Concord. His voice is matter of fact. "But [exactly] how you link those to the assassination, I don't know." Goodwin has suspected there was a conspiracy behind the assassination of JFK for more than four decades now. But who precisely was involved and how the plot was carried out—these crucial questions remain a mystery to Goodwin. He never investigated the case himself. Like other members of the Kennedy inner circle, he was waiting for Bobby to do that. And he remains convinced to this day that Kennedy would have done that, if he had made it back to the White House. "Whatever way he went about it, he would have tried to find out if there was more there, once he had the power to actually get information. That was always my assumption."

Goodwin was one of the few people with whom Bobby discussed his suspicions about Dallas. It took someone Kennedy trusted—and someone with Goodwin's blustery personality—to force the conversation. It happened on the evening of July 25, 1966, at Kennedy's fourteenth-floor UN Plaza apartment overlooking the East River, where Goodwin had returned with him following dinner to spend the night. Bobby used his six-room suite in the luxurious glass tower, which was also home to Truman Capote and Johnny Carson, as his crash pad when he stayed in New York, and it had more the feel of a hotel than a home.

Goodwin was not one of the band of brothers whom Bobby had drafted into the Kennedy administration, and the two men were not particularly close during JFK's presidency. After Dallas, there was some strain between the men when Goodwin decided to accept LBJ's offer and stick with the new president as a speechwriter and civil rights advisor. Goodwin felt obliged to defend his decision in a letter to Bobby, arguing that by staying on, he would be able to help protect JFK's legacy. "I feel strongly that I am doing a service—small as it is—not only to the president and the country, but to your brother whom I idolized," he wrote. Goodwin was bemused by Bobby's grudging response: "I wish you wouldn't [take the job]. But I guess you have to. After all, if any one of us is in a position to keep him from blowing up Costa Rica, or something like that, then we ought to do it."

But as time went by, Goodwin developed warmer feelings for Bobby. Just before joining Johnson's White House staff, he attended a reception at the Venezuelan embassy where he watched Kennedy deliver a brief speech thanking the Venezuelan government for its contribution to the Kennedy Library. "It is curious—he doesn't have the intellectual depth of his brother," Goodwin later jotted down in his notes on the evening—a perspective he would later change. "But he has a feeling for the needs and mood of other people which few politicians possess. I am constantly wavering in my opinion of RFK. He is, after all, only where he is because of birth. He has a great tendency to divide the world between the good guys and the bad guys. On the other hand he has intuitive understanding of the complexities and subtleties of other people's motivations. His weakness is probably to act quickly, from emotion—to have too emotional a response to events, although when he has thought them out he is very good."

It was a description that in some ways matched Goodwin himself. And by July 1966, when the two men sat talking late into the night in Bobby's apartment, with the lights of the vast sprawl of the outer boroughs of New York twinkling in the distance, they were fast friends. Goodwin would later call it the closest personal relationship he ever made in politics—"indeed, a friendship as important to me as any I ever had."

The day before, Goodwin had rocked the capital by writing a laudatory review in the *Washington Post* of Edward Jay Epstein's systematic critique of the Warren Report, *Inquest*. Epstein's book was a landmark in the assassination case. Like other Warren Report critics, Epstein found the blue-ribbon study deeply flawed and unconvincing. But Epstein, who had written the book as his master's thesis for Cornell, took a dry, meticulous approach, seeking to avoid what he considered the pitfalls of other Warren Report commentary, which he characterized as either works of "blind faith" or conspiratorial "demonology." In his review, Goodwin wrote that Epstein presented his case "with a logic and a subdued tone which have already disturbed the convictions of many responsible men." The former Kennedy aide then dropped a bombshell. He called for an independent panel to review the Warren Report's work, and if it was found defective, he proposed a new inquiry into President Kennedy's murder. A startled *New York Times* observed that Goodwin was "the first member of the late president's inner circle to suggest publicly that an official re-examination be made of the Warren Report."

It was not the first time Goodwin had displayed an interest in the assassination. Earlier that year, in March, he had mailed Kennedy a request, asking if he might be able to help him get a copy of a thirty-three-page letter written by Jack Ruby that had been sold at a New York auction. "P.S.," he scribbled at the bottom of the letter, knowing Bobby's acute sensitivity on the subject. "Don't worry—I am not writing anything on this subject."

But the Epstein book did compel Goodwin to air his views. The evening after his review ran in the *Post*, Goodwin was eager to discuss his urgent misgivings about the government's investigation with Bobby. Over night-caps in Kennedy's living room, he launched into his analysis of the Epstein book. But, as usual, Bobby instantly withdrew into a self-protective silence, twirling the Scotch in his glass and staring down at the floor while Good-win spoke. Finally, he looked up and said, "I'm sorry, Dick, I just can't focus on it."

Goodwin was acutely aware of how painful the subject was for Bobby. Most of Kennedy's friends would stop as soon as they saw the anguished expression come over his face. But Goodwin decided to press on. "I think we should find our own investigator—someone with absolute loyalty and discretion."

Suddenly, Kennedy did focus. Goodwin was on the right track. It was precisely what he was contemplating. "You might try Carmine Bellino," Bobby said. "He's the best in the country."

It was a revealing suggestion. Like Walt Sheridan, Bellino was a key member of the elite investigative team that Kennedy had assembled during the Senate rackets probe and later kept on Hoffa's trail at the Justice Depart-ment. But these were Bobby's men, not Goodwin's. There was no way that Goodwin could initiate an investigation without Bobby's nod. Both men knew this. Goodwin understood that it was Kennedy's way of saying, *Let's drop the subject for now. You know who will carry out the investigation for me when the time comes. But for now we have to wait.* The conversation moved on to other topics—the Vietnam War, civil rights, the war on poverty and whether Americans were too selfish to enlist in it. (With the right leadership, Bobby thought they could be properly inspired.)

As the two men finally rose from their armchairs at 2:30 in the morning and made their way down the hallway to their bedrooms, Bobby suddenly paused. "About that other thing," he began, his eyes unable to meet Goodwin's. His friend knew immediately what he meant. "I never thought it was the Cubans. If anyone was involved it was organized crime. But there's nothing I can do about it. Not now."

In his memoir, Goodwin wrote that he and Kennedy never discussed the assassination again. But Adam Walinsky remembered other times that Goodwin would raise the subject when Bobby was present. Walinsky was a young Yale Law graduate who had briefly served in Kennedy's Justice Department before going to work in his Senate office as his legislative assistant. With his crusty demeanor, keen intelligence, and soft heart, Walinsky quickly endeared himself to the senator, who relied on his sharp young aide to keep him current on the most important new books, articles, and ideas. "I was his intellectual valet," said Walinsky, smiling, in a recent interview.

Walinsky shared Goodwin's skepticism about the Warren Report, whose ballistics theory he found "completely tortured and strange." But, following his boss's lead, he learned to keep his suspicions about Dallas to himself. Goodwin, on the other hand, "would talk openly about the assassination," said Walinsky, launching into an imitation of his distinctive mumbling growl. " 'It was the CIA, the Mafia . . .' The senator would be in the room or around. But he was always extremely guarded. One of the things you learned when you were around Kennedy, you learned what it was to be serious. Serious people, when faced with something like that—you don't speculate out loud about it. You might ask a question. That's all. It's a matter of mental discipline."

Until he could win the White House, Kennedy was convinced, there was nothing he could do to solve his brother's assassination. And even then, Bobby realized, his task would be daunting. "He had an acute understanding of how difficult that kind of investigation is, even if you had all the power of the presidency," Walinsky said. "If there is something there, you can't possibly find it out unless you're the president of the United States. And even then you may not, but that's the only chance."

And so Kennedy bided his time, waiting for his opportunity to return to power. But, in the meantime, events started to rush past him. By 1967, a decisive majority of Americans—60 percent—believed that President Kennedy's assassination was a conspiracy. Public opinion had shifted dramatically since the publication of the Warren Report, when only 31 percent of the country suspected a plot. This was largely the result of the tireless assassination critics, whose voluminous work Kennedy's staff struggled to stay up with. "We were drowning in it," Walinsky recalled. "You can't believe how much of that stuff there was. I had a big shelf with all that stuff. But we never discussed it. Never." Everyone in Kennedy's office knew the number one goal: to get him elected president. Until that was accomplished, nothing was possible.

Still, the pressures mounted on RFK to comment on the Warren Report.

A *London Observer* review of the Epstein book, reprinted August 13, 1966 in the *San Francisco Chronicle*, pointedly commented, "How long the dead president's political heir can manage to maintain even a non-committal attitude is perhaps the most intriguing question in American politics today."

Bobby was asking himself the same question. In October 1966, drinking into the wee hours with Arthur Schlesinger at P.J. Clarke's saloon, his favorite New York watering hole, RFK wondered "how long he could continue to avoid comment on the [Warren] Report," Schlesinger later noted. Bobby believed the report was "a poor job," the historian observed, but he was still "unwilling to criticize it and thereby reopen the whole tragic business."

Kennedy's silence on the issue was used by Warren Report defenders to fend off critics. Surely if the president's own brother—the top lawman in the country at the time—did nothing to pursue the case, there must be nothing there, they said. It must have been particularly galling for Bobby to hear this from one of President Johnson's advisors. John P. Roche, a Brandeis University professor on leave as LBJ's "intellectual in residence" at the White House, denounced conspiracy researchers as "marginal paranoids" in a widely publicized letter to the *London Times Literary Supplement*, arguing that RFK's support for the Warren Report was proof of its validity.

If he had known about it, Kennedy would have found even more grotesque a secret CIA document that recommended using his silence on the Warren Report to counter critics. The January 1967 memo—which was distributed to CIA media assets at the *New York Times*, CBS, NBC, ABC, and elsewhere—suggested ways of "countering and discrediting the claims of conspiracy theorists," whose growing impact on public opinion at home and abroad the agency found alarming. "Innuendo of such seriousness affects . . . the whole reputation of the American government," the memo grimly noted—including that of the CIA itself. "Conspiracy theorists have frequently thrown suspicion on our organization, for example by falsely alleging that Lee Harvey Oswald worked for us." The memo listed a number of arguments that could be used by CIA-friendly journalists to knock down the work of conspiracy authors. Among them: "Note that Robert Kennedy, attorney general at the time and John F. Kennedy's brother, would be the last man to overlook or conceal any conspiracy."

At least one of Bobby's friends in the press, CBS News producer Don Hewitt, found the nerve to confront him on the growing controversy over the assassination. Hewitt—who produced the legendary Kennedy-Nixon debates in 1960 and later created *60 Minutes*—was drinking iced tea with Kennedy one morning in the backyard of Hickory Hill when he decided "with more guts than brains to ask him the big one, the million dollar question—'Bobby, do you really believe Lee Harvey Oswald, all by himself, killed your brother?'

"He dismissed the question with almost studied indifference," Hewitt later recalled, giving the TV newsman his usual conversation-stopper. "What difference does it make? It won't bring him back."

But the savvy journalist knew when he was being handed a line. "I never believed that Bobby believed 'What difference does it make.' I've always believed that he knew something he didn't want to share with me or anyone else."

Hewitt himself came to suspect that JFK was the victim of a conspiracy—because of "things I've learned since," he told me recently. "Like Lee Harvey Oswald and Jack Ruby were not strangers. Ruby was a gangster of sorts who was asked by Oswald's uncle to take good care of his nephew. I've always believed that Ruby went to that police station on a mission to make sure that Oswald didn't talk. . . . So many things [about the case] just don't add up."

The broadcast news veteran speculates that "disgruntled CIA types" might have been behind the assassination. "I have heard from some of those White House plumber types that their real bitch with Jack Kennedy was denying air cover for their comrades at the Bay of Pigs, and maybe someone decided to get even for that. That's the best theory I can come up with." Unknown to Hewitt at the time, Bobby was thinking along similar lines.

Hewitt is certain that Kennedy would have gone after his brother's killers with a vengeance when the time was right. "Bobby was relentless in his pursuit of wrongdoing," he said. "When he said that to me about it not making a difference, I couldn't help thinking, Bobby, you're fucking lying to me."

In 1967, a gaudy Louisiana legal spectacle would make it harder than ever for Kennedy to keep his silence.

7

NEW ORLEANS

As New York's junior senator, Robert Kennedy continued to draw on the services of the Irish mafia loyalists who had long served him and his brother, like political aide Joe Dolan. But his Senate staff included some new faces as well—men who were neither Boston Irish nor Harvard intellectuals. One day, during a meeting in his Capitol Hill office, Kennedy gazed at the men around him. Frank Mankiewicz. Adam Walinsky. Peter Edelman. Jeff Greenfield. There was not a Catholic among them. "You realize, fellows, that I'm the only one here who is going to go to heaven," he dryly observed.

He inspired an intense devotion among his staff. He was tough, but had a wounded vulnerability; he was demanding, but returned their unstinting loyalty. He combined a shrewdness about American politics with a soaring view of the country's possibilities that his aides found utterly unique and intoxicating.

Mankiewicz—who had gone to work as Kennedy's press secretary at age forty-two, making him one of the older staff members—first fell under RFK's spell in 1965 during a State Department meeting where Bobby discussed his forthcoming trip to Latin America. Mankiewicz was head of the Peace Corps' Latin American division at the time. He had abandoned a promising career at a Hollywood law firm to join JFK's New Frontier. "My wife, Holly, and I decided that if I stayed with the firm, within ten years we'd have this terrific house and a lot of money, but nobody would care if we had lived or died, except perhaps our mothers," Mankiewicz later recalled.

After JFK's death, Mankiewicz stayed on with the new administration, but his heart was with the Kennedy cause. At the State Department meeting, RFK and President Johnson's Latin American team—headed by a prickly bureaucrat named Jack Vaughn—stared frostily at one another across the conference table. Bobby inquired what he should say when he got to Brazil and was asked about the brutal CIA-backed military coup that had recently overthrown the elected government there. The Brazil desk officer, consulting a piece of paper, responded, "You could say, 'While we regret that a great power has decided to temporarily suspend democratic liberties—'" Kennedy quickly cut off the bureaucratic cant. "I don't talk like that," he said firmly.

Mankiewicz, who had been pushed to the left by his Latin American experience, was impressed by Kennedy's refusal to mouth the administration line. At the Peace Corps, he had found that the young volunteers were always on the side of social change in the medieval societies in which they were assigned to work. "But whenever people in Latin America tried to emulate the American Revolution," Mankiewicz observed, "the U.S. government tried to emulate George III. It radicalized me." Now, sitting before him was a political leader who shared his views about the role the United States should play in poverty-stricken Third World countries. Shortly after the State Department meeting, Mankiewicz signed on with Kennedy as his press spokesman.

The balding, rumpled Mankiewicz had an unusual background for a Senate aide. He came from a legendary Hollywood family. His uncle, the writer-director Joseph Mankiewicz, won an Academy Award for *All About Eve* and produced other screen classics like *The Philadelphia Story* and *Woman of the Year*. His father, Herman, won an Academy Award for writing *Citizen Kane*. Herman Mankiewicz had come west to make his fortune after working as the drama editor for the *The New Yorker*. "Millions are to be grabbed out here and your only competition is idiots," he notified his friend and fellow journalist Ben Hecht in a telegram. "Don't let this get around." Notoriously boozy, and belligerent to his Hollywood paymasters, Mankiewicz sought refuge from the crass torments of the movie industry by recreating his old Algonquin Round Table in his Beverly Hills home. Luminaries like Scott and Zelda Fitzgerald, the Marx Brothers, Greta Garbo, James Thurber, and Orson Welles traipsed through young Frank's childhood.

"Nobody would give you an argument if you said my father was a self-destructive man," Mankiewicz would later remark. To ensure that the screenwriter completed the masterpiece that would make them both legends, *Citizen Kane* director Welles had his often thirsty co-creator locked away in a

cabin in the dreary desert town of Victorville. Nonetheless, the elder Mankiewicz instilled in his son the values that would draw him to Robert Kennedy.
"He was a gambler, and he probably was an alcoholic, but those are not sins,"
Frank recalled about his father. "He never stole from the poor, he never fired
anybody on Christmas. He was a good man. Most of all, he was funny and
furious. I thought he was a terrific father. He told me what things were important. I believed him. I still do."

With Kennedy, Mankiewicz could dream about all the ways the country
might change, and since Kennedy was widely assumed to be in line for the
throne, there was always the expectation it could all come true. "As a senator,
Bobby got a deeper and deeper sense that race and poverty were tearing
apart the country, how these problems could destroy us," Mankiewicz said
recently. He was sitting in his office on the sixth floor of the Watergate building, overlooking the Potomac. In his mid-eighties now, he wears hearing aids
in both ears; grayer and rounder, he huffs as he hefts his body around in his
swivel chair. But he still works every day as a Washington lobbyist, holding
the title of vice chairman at Hill & Knowlton, the public relations power-
house. It's the longest job he's ever held down, but he knows that when he
dies, the headlines will identify him as a "Kennedy aide" and that will be fine
with him. On the walls, next to posters of *Citizen Kane* and other movies
written by his father, are framed memorabilia of his years with Bobby, including a Camus quote that was a Kennedy favorite: "I should like to be able to
love my country and still love justice."

"Every once in a while, at the end of the day in the Senate, when Bobby
didn't have to rush off somewhere, we would drift into his office and sit and
talk," Mankiewicz continued. "He'd ask us, 'What's going on? Frank, what
are you reading? Adam, Peter, who's doing the best work on education these
days?' I remember when the race riots were raging in Newark and Detroit
and LBJ was calling for a day of mourning—as if that were going to do anything. And we asked him, 'If you were president, what would you do?'

"He thought about it and then he said, 'I'd call in the heads of the three
TV networks and I'd sit them down and tell them what a terrible problem
this was for the country and I would tell them that they should devote a
whole month of prime-time programming to what it was like to be black in
America, what it was like to live with two or three generations of poverty, to
have your brother be the first one to graduate from school and still not be
able to get a job, to wake up in the morning and see rats around your baby's
crib.' He said that you could show all that graphically on TV, and it might be
able to change things."

Though Mankiewicz had not been one of Kennedy's band of brothers at the Justice Department, he soon established himself as one of his trusted inner circle. The Californian was the type of man whom Bobby felt he could rely on, with the requisite combination of brains, guts, and heart. Despite his privileged background, Mankiewicz had served as an infantryman in Europe during World War II. "Very few people there were from Beverly Hills," he remarked. He later worked briefly as a journalist before studying law at Berkeley and becoming an entertainment industry lawyer. Kennedy trusted his press aide's shrewd instincts.

When the controversy around the Kennedy assassination reached a fever pitch in early 1967, as news broke that New Orleans District Attorney Jim Garrison was reopening the investigation, Mankiewicz was one of the select few to whom Bobby turned to help him get a better grasp of the case. One day, walking together through an airport, Kennedy and Mankiewicz were confronted with the suddenly omnipresent face of Jim Garrison—his wide-set eyes burning with a messianic intensity—on a newsstand's magazine racks. Bobby pointed at the magazine covers and asked his aide, "Does that guy have anything?"

"I'm not sure that *he* does, but there is something there," Mankiewicz replied. Kennedy's aide had never accepted the Warren Report. "I just didn't believe that a high-school dropout could've planned the whole thing."

"I want you to look into this, read everything you can," Kennedy instructed Mankiewicz, "so if it gets to a point where I can do something about this, you can tell me what I need to know."

Mankiewicz turned himself into "an assassination buff," he later recalled, poring over the piles of books and monographs on the subject and quizzing conspiracy researchers like Ray Marcus, who brought big blowups of his Dealey Plaza photos to Mankiewicz's Maryland home. "I came to the conclusion that there was some sort of conspiracy, probably involving the mob, anti-Castro Cuban exiles, and maybe rogue CIA agents," said Mankiewicz. "Every so often I would bring this up with Bobby. I told him who I thought was involved. But it was like he just couldn't focus on it. He'd get this look of pain, or more like numbness, on his face. It just tore him apart."

Mankiewicz's conclusions about the assassination mirrored those of Kennedy himself. Hearing them voiced by a trusted aide must have made them starkly real for Kennedy. And they must have, once again, filled him with an immobilizing sense of guilt, since the conspiracy described by his aide grew out of the very groups he was supposed to be controlling for his brother. The prospect of confronting this conspiracy, with its powerful government connections, was clearly still paralyzing for Kennedy.

In public, Kennedy continued to deflect questions about the assassination with an icy resolve. Joe McGinnis, a *Philadelphia Inquirer* columnist at the time, observed the senator during one such painfully awkward moment in December 1966. After a long day of visiting antipoverty centers, Kennedy was waiting on the platform at the North Philadelphia train station to ride back to New York. As usual, there were no bodyguards to fend off overly friendly or threatening intrusions. It was just Bobby, standing without a topcoat on the frigid platform, brushing back his shock of wind-swept hair. "He looked small and cold and, for just those few seconds, like a little boy who was lost," McGinnis observed. Suddenly, a radio reporter pushed his way through the small circle gathered around Bobby, and after exchanging some idle remarks with Kennedy, he inched his way toward the inevitable question. McGinnis knew what it was "and it made you want to leave because you knew what was going to happen would be awful."

Taking a deep breath, the radio reporter began, "Senator, with all the recent criticism of the Warren Commission . . ."

Kennedy immediately cut him off. "I don't discuss that." His voice, hard and sharp, would have silenced all but the most persistent journalists. As Kennedy batted away the question, the muscles in his clenched face visibly twitched. But, horribly for everyone witnessing the spectacle, the radio man pushed on. It was his job, and he was gutsy to do it.

"I know you haven't discussed it in the past, but our district attorney here, Arlen Specter—" The reporter got no further than invoking the name of the former Warren Commission attorney (and future senator from Pennsylvania) who helped concoct the magic bullet theory. Again, Kennedy cut off the reporter. "I said I don't discuss that. At all." And this time his voice was full of such barely suppressed rage that even the dogged reporter fell silent.

Everybody looked down at their shoes until the train "mercifully" came, recalled McGinnis. And then, as he stepped forward to board the train, Kennedy did something to pull the reporter out of the hole where he had banished him, "even though," observed McGinnis, "he must have wanted to put the radio man's head on the tracks and let the train run over his mouth." Kennedy stretched out his hand to the man, and looking him directly in the eyes, said, "Goodbye. Nice to have seen you."

To McGinnis, Kennedy's parting gesture "showed an awful lot of class."

But it was surely more than that. It was Kennedy's way of acknowledging that the reporter was not out of line. The press, and the public, had the right to know more about his brother's death. He simply could not help them yet.

AMONG THOSE ELECTRIFIED BY the Garrison investigation in New Orleans was a maverick man of letters named Chandler Brossard, a self-educated literateur and journalist who wrote hipster novels like *Who Walk in Darkness*, which was set in bohemian Greenwich Village, but paid the rent by working as an editor at magazines like *The New Yorker*, *Time*, and *Coronet*. In 1967, Brossard, who was working as a *Look* magazine senior editor at the time, convinced his boss—William Attwood, who had been hired as *Look*'s editor-in-chief the year before—to meet with Garrison in the magazine's New York office. Attwood, JFK's old prep school mate and secret liaison with Castro in the administration's final days, had begun to have his own suspicions about the events in Dallas by then. He agreed to meet with the New Orleans prosecutor and Brossard, and the three men's discussion of the case spilled into the evening, through dinner and drinks, not ending until one in the morning. After finally bidding goodnight to Garrison, Attwood was so fired up about the prosecutor's case for a conspiracy that he phoned Bobby Kennedy from the New York Press Club, where he had dined that night.

Like everyone else in the Kennedy circle, Bill Attwood was waiting for Bobby Kennedy to do something to finally solve his brother's murder. "Bill thought that Bobby was a real tough guy," recalled his widow, Simone. "One of the things he thought about the assassination was that, if anybody knew what was going on, Bobby did. That Bobby was very much on top of things and not about to just lie down and say, 'That's the way it is' and just accept the official story."

Attwood, a man whom Bobby respected for his diplomatic service during the Kennedy administration, urgently told the senator that Garrison was on to something. The editor intended to throw the weight of *Look*, a lively written picture magazine second only to *Life* in national influence at the time, behind Garrison's investigation. He strongly encouraged Kennedy to commit himself to reopening the case. In response, Bobby told Attwood that he agreed his brother had been the victim of a conspiracy. "But I can't do anything until we get control of the White House," Kennedy told him. Soon after hanging up the phone, Attwood suffered a major heart attack and was rushed in the early morning hours to St. Vincent's Hospital. It took him three months to recover enough to return to work. *Look* magazine never jumped on Jim Garrison's bandwagon.

"I can't do anything until we get control of the White House." It became Bobby's standard reply whenever those in his circle pushed him to take a stand on the assassination controversy. But as the Warren Report became increasingly besieged in 1966 and '67, it grew more and more difficult for Kennedy to hold to this position. Public opinion was racing ahead of his presidential timetable.

By this time, dissension over the Warren Report was even starting to embroil elite circles. In February 1966, an independent New York researcher named Charles E. Stanton took it upon himself to mail a rudimentary survey about the assassination to a sprawling spectrum of prominent personalities in the United States and abroad. The questionnaire—which asked whether or not respondents believed the Warren Report and whether or not they suspected that the government was suppressing evidence of a conspiracy—was accompanied by a heartfelt letter, appealing to the illustrious recipients' sense of history. One "Kennedy intimate" had chided Stanton, he confessed in his letter, criticizing his survey for being "in bad taste, if not actually morbid." But "would it not be provocative to read the reactions of Abraham Lincoln's contemporaries—Disraeli, Karl Marx, Mark Twain, Jules Verne, Garibaldi, Oscar Wilde—and what they thought of the disastrous assassination?" Stanton pleaded.

The researcher sent out more than three hundred questionnaires between February 1966 and January 1968, addressing them to a politically diverse group that spanned from Fidel Castro to Francisco Franco. Many— including U.S. media luminaries like Walter Cronkite and Eric Sevareid and political potentates like J. Edgar Hoover, Senators Barry Goldwater and William Fulbright, and lawyer Roy Cohn—predictably dodged Stanton's questions. But the responses Stanton did receive provide an illuminating snapshot of an elite class in turmoil over the Kennedy assassination. He never published the results of his work, but the handwritten scrawls of these famous Kennedy contemporaries—now stored at the Kennedy Library—are fascinating to read.

Among those who endorsed the government's version of the assassination were Pierre Salinger (who would change his mind later in life), journalists Harrison Salisbury and Stewart Alsop, movie mogul Dore Schary, poets Richard Wilbur and Carl Sandburg, historian James MacGregor Burns, politically divergent intellectuals William F. Buckley and Dwight Macdonald, and socialist leader Norman Thomas. The researcher also heard back from the two principal architects of Kennedy's Bay of Pigs disaster, former CIA officials Allen Dulles and Richard Bissell. Unsurprisingly, Dulles expressed

his unswerving confidence in the government investigation that he had assiduously guided to its foregone conclusion. But the assassination survey
clearly got under Bissell's skin and he could not stop himself from scrawling
in large, bold script in the "Comments" section: "Who cares? Let's get our
minds—if we have any—on something else."

Ironically, adding his Warren Report endorsement to those of the two
CIA men with whom he and his brother had bitterly clashed, was Senator
Robert F. Kennedy. "The Warren Report was prepared by highly competent
and respected people after intensive study, and there is every reason to have
confidence in their findings," read the reply on Kennedy's Senate stationery.
Adding to the irony, Bobby's response was penned for him by his aide Joe
Dolan, a man who harbored even more explosive suspicions about Dallas
than RFK.

The list of those who believed Kennedy was the victim of a plot was
equally impressive: poets Robert Graves, Allen Ginsberg, Thomas Merton,
and Kenneth Rexroth; novelists Katherine Anne Porter, Terry Southern, Ir-
ving Wallace, and Ray Bradbury; dramatist Paddy Chayevsky; sociologist
Andrew Hacker; journalist and Kennedy peace emissary Norman Cousins;
Norwegian seafaring adventurer Thor Heyerdahl of *Kon-Tiki* fame; British
scholars Arnold Toynbee, Bertrand Russell, and Hugh Trevor-Roper. Among
the more passionate hand-written comments came from Southern, whose
screenplay for *Dr. Strangelove* had been inspired by the doomsday militarists
with whom JFK had dueled. "The absurdity of the Warren Report is patent
and overwhelming," he angrily scrawled at the bottom of the survey. "One
has only to browse through any of the 26 volumes to know at once what a
complete farce, charade and incredible piece of bullshit it is. The impressive
thing about it is its insulting artlessness. It is as though they imagined that
not ONE SINGLE PERSON in America would take the trouble to look at the un-
abridged version."

With the country's political leadership and news media refusing to exhume the JFK case, it fell to a few intrepid celebrities to speak out about the
mystery that was haunting America. In June 1967, onstage at the now legendary Monterey Pop Festival, David Crosby of the Byrds stunned the audience, as well as his fellow band members, by making a shocking statement
about JFK's assassination: "President Kennedy wasn't killed by one man—he
was shot from several directions. The truth has been suppressed. You should
know that. This is your country."

Comedian Mort Sahl emerged as the most prominent critic of the Warren Report in the entertainment industry, putting his career on the line by

turning his popular nightclub act into a running critique of the official investigation and charging that JFK was the victim of a government plot. Kennedy was "the only president that ever went up against" the country's national security complex, Sahl told an alternative newspaper in March 1968. "And see what happened to him for his pains." Onstage, he would poke holes in the government's cover-up, reading in scathing tones from the twenty-six Warren Report volumes piled around him as props.

Sahl's once lucrative career began to suffer, with his income plummeting from $1 million a year to $13,000. "Working on the Kennedy assassination caused people to accuse me of not being funny or beloved anymore. In the eyes of show business, those are the greatest crimes of all," he said. Sahl had avoided the obscenity legal battles and drug woes that had brought down fellow comedian Lenny Bruce, who broke in with him in the early sixties in San Francisco nightclubs like the hungry i. But now his friends warned him that his "obsession" with the Kennedy case would be his own demise. He could not bring himself to stop.

Sahl had supplied JFK with gags during the 1960 campaign but had fallen out with the Kennedy camp after the election, when he switched back to his role as political satirist and began tweaking the new president. Old Joe Kennedy thought you were either with the family or against it. He didn't laugh when Sahl sent him a congratulatory telegram: "You haven't lost a son. You've gained a country." But Jack was different. He knew how to laugh at himself. Sahl admired his grace and humor. He thought his American University peace speech should be taught in schools. He thought his murder was "the foulest event of our lives." That sort of thing was not supposed to happen in America. And where were the watchdogs of the American press? He was revolted by the sentimentalization of Kennedy's death, the way that Walter Cronkite led the nation in an orgy of "communal crying." He took a savage view of the news media's supine acceptance of the Warren Report: "Hitler said that he always knew you could buy the press. What he didn't know was you could get them cheap." When Jim Garrison announced he was reopening the case, Sahl flew to New Orleans and volunteered to help him. Finally, someone was doing something to solve the crime of the century.

By late 1966, it was becoming impossible for the establishment media to stick with the official story. Shamed by the growing cultural ferment around the Kennedy assassination—and prodded by best-selling conspiracy books by authors like Mark Lane, Edward Jay Epstein, and Josiah Thompson, a Haverford College philosophy professor whose *Six Seconds in Dallas* presented a carefully constructed case for three assassins and at least four bullets in Dealey Plaza—the media began to finally take a skeptical attitude towards the Warren Report.

On November 25, 1966, *Life* magazine questioned, "Did Oswald Act Alone?" in a remarkable cover story that suggested he did not. The report was the work of a team that included Haverford's Professor Thompson. It marked a stunning shift for the Luce publication, which had played a key role in the crime's cover-up by buying the original Zapruder film and locking it away. This outrageous action—which was ordered by *Life*'s publisher, C. D. Jackson, who, like his boss Henry Luce, was a fervid anticommunist with strong ties to the CIA—allowed the magazine to repeatedly distort what the Zapruder film actually depicted, publishing frames and captions that misled the public into believing JFK was struck only by shots from the rear. But by late 1966, Jackson was dead and Luce near the end of his life, and the growing cracks in the Warren Report forced even *Life* to shift direction.

The next month, the *New York Times* quietly announced that it was forming a special task force to investigate the assassination. The team was headed by Harrison Salisbury, then the editor of the *Times*' op-ed page, who announced that his reporters would "go over all the areas of doubt and hope to eliminate them." Even the *Saturday Evening Post*—showcase of all-American, Norman Rockwell values—was moved to declare that there was "something rotten" about Dallas, running a major excerpt from Thompson's book on its cover with the blaring headline: "Three Assassins Killed Kennedy." An accompanying editorial declared, "We believe the Kennedy mystery has not been solved, that the case is not closed."

All these ripples of activity around the Kennedy assassination would be swallowed in 1967 by the tidal wave of Jim Garrison's investigation. It was a roaring media spectacle that swept everything before it. The probe dredged up a florid cast of characters—including CIA mercenaries, violent Cuban refugees, street hustlers, and of course Clay Shaw, the elegant gay business leader with murky intelligence affiliations who became the central focus of Garrison's case.

Robert Kennedy had been quietly waiting until he was able to win the White House—a race he was planning to make, at this point, in 1972 after Lyndon Johnson completed his second full term. Then RFK would enlist the powers of the federal government in his hunt for his brother's killers. But he had not counted on Jim Garrison. The prosecutor's raucous investigation would force Bobby out of the shell where he was biding his time, compelling him to try to make sense of the Garrison cavalcade—and to take steps to avoid being run over by it.

• • •

IT TOOK A MAN with the bravura of Jim Garrison to be the first law enforcement official in the country to reopen the Kennedy investigation. Known in New Orleans as "the Jolly Green Giant" for his oversized frame—six feet, seven inches and 240 pounds—and glad-handing personality, he cut a colorful swath in a showy town. As he began his legal career, Garrison brought with him an eccentric résumé, but it was not a liability in the Big Easy. His father was a shady character who had done time for larceny and selling illegal hootch to Indians. During World War II, Garrison served with distinction as a combat pilot in Europe. But when he was called back to active duty during the Korean War, he was beset with anxieties and was discharged for psychiatric reasons. He joined the FBI, but abruptly quit less than four months later. After being elected district attorney, Garrison made a name for himself by strapping on a pistol and leading well-publicized raids on the fleshpots of Bourbon Street. But he himself was a notorious ladies' man with a strong penchant for the pleasures that the French Quarter offered.

In March 1962, Garrison worked his Louisiana political connections to finagle an audience with the dazzling young president of the United States. Instead of taking his wife, Liz, with him to Washington, he brought his girlfriend of the moment, a flight attendant named Judy Chambers. The night before his meeting with JFK, the fun-loving district attorney and his mistress partied so exuberantly that he overslept his appointment at the White House. Garrison was able to pull himself together, however, for a Justice Department meeting with Bobby Kennedy at 1:30 that afternoon. If JFK discovered the reason that Garrison stood him up, he was likely amused. But Bobby, who never put pleasure before business, did not hide his irritation with Garrison. When the D.A. returned to New Orleans, a friend asked him how the trip went. "Well, I met Bobby," Garrison replied. He was then obliged to explain why he had missed his meeting with the president. But he was not the least contrite. "You can always meet a president," Garrison informed his friend. "But you can't always get a piece of ass like that!"

Garrison was "flamboyant," as he bragged to the press, but he was no buffoon. Like most Americans, he accepted the government's version of the assassination until one day in November 1966 when venerable Senator Russell Long from Louisiana, with whom he was sharing a flight to New York, made some disturbing remarks about the Warren Report. "Those fellows on the Warren Commission were dead wrong," Long, the Senate's majority whip, told Garrison. "There's no way in the world that one man could have shot up Jack Kennedy that way." Senator Long's comments launched Garrison on his mission to find the truth about what had happened to JFK in the streets of Dallas. "For me," he said, "that was the end of innocence."

After plowing through the voluminous Warren Report—a study, he became convinced, designed only to "tranquilize the American public"—and the work of the leading conspiracy researchers, Garrison came to the conclusion that Kennedy was the victim of a well-organized plot with roots in New Orleans, where Lee Harvey Oswald had spent the summer before the assassination. Despite its reputation for a tropical, easygoing tolerance, the city was a hotbed of anti-Kennedy extremism. JFK himself confided to Louisiana congressman Hale Boggs, while waiting out a rain delay in the dugout during an opening day baseball game in April 1962, that he dreaded a forthcoming trip to New Orleans because of the murderous passions against him there. "I'm not sure about going to New Orleans," the president told Boggs. "I've got reports that it's so tense down there that something could happen."

As Garrison began investigating Oswald's ties to local Kennedy haters, he zeroed in on the peculiar office building at 544 Camp Street where a former FBI agent and far-right zealot named Guy Banister and his eccentric associate David Ferrie oversaw a buzzing beehive of anti-Castro activity that included the young man later arrested for Kennedy's murder. The prosecutor came to the conclusion that Oswald was a pawn in a complex plot, framed as a Castro-loving Marxist to take the blame for the assassination. The real masterminds behind the conspiracy, he decided, could be found in the CIA and Pentagon. "President Kennedy was killed for one reason," Garrison began to tell the press. "Because he was working for reconciliation with the [Soviet Union] and Castro's Cuba. . . . President Kennedy died because he wanted peace."

The United States, Garrison concluded, had been taken over by the military-industrial complex that Eisenhower had warned about. "In a very real and terrifying sense, our government is the CIA and the Pentagon, with Congress reduced to a debating society," he declared in 1968. "I've learned enough about the machinations of the CIA in the past year to know that this is no longer the dreamworld America I once believed in. . . . I've always had a kind of knee-jerk trust in my government's basic integrity, whatever political blunders it may make. But I've come to realize that in Washington, deceiving and manipulating the public are viewed by some as the natural prerogatives of office. Huey Long once said, 'Fascism will come to America in the name of anti-fascism.' I'm afraid, based on my experience, that fascism will come to America in the name of national security."

Guy Banister had died of a heart attack in 1964, so David Ferrie became

Garrison's chief suspect. Ferrie was a pilot and soldier of fortune who had been fired by Eastern Airlines after he was arrested on sex charges involving adolescent boys. Ferrie had known Oswald since he was a teenage cadet in the Civil Air Patrol, where the older man was a trainer. Ferrie moved in a shadowy world of anticommunist adventurism, where intelligence types, gangsters, and Cuban exiles all intermingled. As Edward Jay Epstein mordantly observed, he "was bizarre even by the relaxed standards of the French Quarter." The victim of a disease that had robbed him of all his hair, Ferrie wore ill-fitting, homemade reddish wigs and dabbed on greasepaint to cover his missing eyebrows, giving his face the appearance of a "ghoulish Halloween mask," in Garrison's estimation. His filthy, ramshackle apartment was filled with cages of squealing white mice that Ferrie was using for cancer experiments—tests, he told some, to find ways of injecting Castro with the disease.

Garrison first brought Ferrie in for questioning a few days after the assassination, when he heard that he had made a mysterious trip to Texas on the day of the crime. He was on the verge of hauling Ferrie before a grand jury in February 1967 when word of Garrison's investigation leaked in the press, and Ferrie suddenly found himself in the eye of a media storm. Though Garrison's suspect was growing increasingly frantic in the public spotlight, the D.A. decided to hold off on bringing him in, apparently to sweat him a while longer. It was a fateful decision. Just as Garrison was telling his staff to "stay cool, hold our fire, and wait a little longer," he received a call that Ferrie had been found dead in his apartment. The coroner ruled that the forty-eight-year-old man had died of natural causes—Ferrie suffered from high blood pressure and some of his friends speculated that his fatal brain hemorrhage was brought on by the stress of Garrison's investigation. But Garrison always suspected it was a suicide or murder. Ferrie, he said, was a victim of forces much larger than himself, "swept up in the gales of history."

By now, the New Orleans D.A. was also swept up in a tempest, a political and media hurricane never seen before in his city. Hundreds of reporters and camera crews from all over the world were swarming his office. The White House, Justice Department, FBI, and CIA were intensely focused on his underfinanced investigation. With Ferrie's death, Garrison's key suspect was gone and he suddenly had a gaping hole in his case. But the prosecutor was riding a wild animal, and instead of getting off the snorting, steaming beast to which he was strapped, he held on and declared that he had a new suspect.

In March 1967, Garrison announced he was arresting a New Orleans civic leader named Clay Shaw for the murder of John F. Kennedy. The stunned city knew Shaw as the respected founder of the International Trade Mart. But to Garrison, he was a CIA-linked international businessmen and—like David Ferrie, a man familiar to Shaw through gay circles—he had served as one of Oswald's handlers in New Orleans. Shaw would not be brought to trial until January 1969. But in the intervening months, Garrison's investigation sucked virtually all JFK activity into its swirling vortex. Among the millions of Americans who were riveted by the case was Robert F. Kennedy.

ONE EVENING SOON AFTER David Ferrie's death, the phone rang at the home of Dr. Nicholas Chetta, the New Orleans coroner who had conducted the autopsy on the man who had been at the center of the Garrison whirlwind. The phone was answered by Chetta's teenage son, Nicky Jr., who by then was growing fed up with the incessant calls from the press that had been set off by Ferrie's sudden death. Garrison was not the only one who found the timing of his demise suspicious.

"Hello, this is Robert Kennedy," the caller said. "May I speak with Dr. Chetta?"

"Yeah, and I'm the Lone Ranger," replied the doctor's son, who was in no mood for prank calls, slamming down the phone.

Shortly after, the phone rang again. "This is Robert Kennedy and I insist on speaking with Dr. Chetta." This time the teenager surrendered the phone to his father, who held a hushed conversation with Kennedy for several minutes. The senator wanted to assure himself that Garrison's key suspect was not the victim of foul play.

As Garrison sparked fireworks, Bobby Kennedy began taking steps to determine the validity of his investigation. His direct call to Chetta notwithstanding, Kennedy relied on his usual method of using surrogates to look into the New Orleans probe. Among those he pumped for information was his old friend and former press spokesman, Ed Guthman. After leaving the Justice Department in August 1964, shortly before his boss, Guthman had returned to the newspaper business, as the national editor of the *Los Angeles Times*. Guthman insists today that Kennedy did not ask him to investigate Garrison. He says that he decided on his own to put five of his best reporters on the story. He even traveled to New Orleans himself to look into the case, taking Garrison and one of his investigators—a private eye named Louis Gurvich—to lunch. Despite Guthman's insistence today that his motivations were journalistic, the two men assumed that he was on a mission for Kennedy. "He probably was sizing up our intelligence quotient for Bobby," said Gurvich at the time. "Bobby's always been leery of the kooky [assassination] critics."

Guthman's team of reporters descended on New Orleans shortly after the news broke about Garrison's case in February 1967 and stayed with the story into the fall. They quickly developed a scornful attitude towards the prosecutor and his case, after interviewing sources like Jack Ruby's sister, whom they found in Southern California; Perry Russo—the handsome, twenty-five-year-old insurance trainee and self-described "sexual freak" who became Garrison's star witness after tying Ferrie, Oswald and Shaw together in the plot against JFK; and, most important, Gurvich's brother and investigative partner, William, who had become one of Garrison's most damaging critics after breaking with him on the case. Fed numerous tales of Garrison's eccentricities by William Gurvich, one *Times* reporter filed a memo with Guthman that seethed, "If it weren't so deadly serious because of the injury it is doing to innocent people, [the Garrison investigation] would be comic, a burlesque."

Guthman's reporters convinced him that Garrison was "a phony." Looking back on the case today, he says, "I sent some of our best people down there, mostly from our Washington bureau, great reporters like Jack Nelson. And I went down there myself. But all my guys concluded there was nothing to it. And they were damn good reporters."

Guthman later met with Kennedy in Washington and reported to him what the *Los Angeles Times* team had decided about Garrison. "I talked to Bob. He wanted to know what we had found out and I told him. So he accepted that. My feeling was that it was possible [there was a conspiracy], but with Garrison, the evidence wasn't there."

But the man who had the most impact on Kennedy's view of the New Orleans investigation was Walter Sheridan. The former chief of RFK's "Get Hoffa" squad at the Justice Department played a central, yet little-known, role in Kennedy's secret search for the truth about Dallas. There was no person in his inner circle on whom Bobby depended more to help him ferret out the full story of what happened to his brother. Sheridan's word on Garrison was bound to carry enormous weight with Kennedy. Bobby once confided to New York reporter Jack Newfield, who had drawn close to the senator while covering him, that he had "assigned different aspects of the assassination case to Goodwin, Mankiewicz, and Sheridan." But Newfield knew that the key player here was Walt Sheridan. He was the man whom Kennedy intimates assumed would one day lead the way in cracking the case.

Kennedy's deep trust and affection for Sheridan had been forged during the Senate rackets investigation and then reinforced during their long quest to put Jimmy Hoffa behind bars. He was slight and soft-spoken but—like Bobby—fierce and unrelenting when on the trail of corrupt figures like Hoffa, a man to whom they both applied the word "evil." Kennedy and Sheridan shared a black and white view of the world, rooted in their Catholic faith, when they joined forces in the 1950s. They were determined to cleanse government—which they believed, like the Church, was meant to uplift the needy and suffering—of the moral rot they feared had spread even to the loftiest echelons of Washington. "We must kindle an enthusiasm for the good and the right and the just," Sheridan told the Adoration Society, a Catholic group in his native Utica, New York, in 1960. "It is time to reaffirm the basic toughness and moral certitude that motivated our country to its position of greatness." Bobby's Justice Department crusade against organized crime would become Sheridan's vehicle for the nation's moral revival. The crusade would take both men into the darkest corners of American power, expose them and their families to frequent physical danger, and finally bond them like soldiers who had shared the same blood-soaked trench.

Sheridan was loved "as a brother and as a member of the family," recalled Teddy Kennedy. He and Bobby, who were born on the same day, celebrated their birthdays together. He and his family were frequent guests at Hickory Hill, where despite his unimposing build, Sheridan was an enthusiastic participant in the Kennedys' rough and lawless touch football games, once suffering a near concussion when he bashed heads with charging former All-American Byron "Whizzer" White. Sheridan's wife, Nancy, was equally fond of Bobby, who often invited the Sheridans' five children to parties in the Justice Department courtyard and spoke at their daughter's high school graduation.

And so it was the trusted Walt Sheridan to whom Kennedy immediately turned on November 22, 1963, dispatching him to Dallas to find out what he could. Even from the outset, neither man trusted the FBI to get to the bottom of the crime. At the beginning of his career, Sheridan had spent four years with the FBI, recruiting Communists as undercover agents. But he finally quit after getting fed up with Hoover's extremism. "I was a cut liberal, and the FBI is a right-wing organization," he later explained. He would denounce the FBI chief as "somewhat of a dictator and somewhat of a son of a bitch." After he quit, his fellow FBI agents were warned to have no contact with him. It must have galled Hoover when Sheridan's name began being floated in the press as a possible replacement for the aging "dictator" in a second Kennedy term. When Sheridan dug up evidence within forty-eight hours of JFK's assassination that Jack Ruby had received a "bundle of money" from a Hoffa associate, the FBI showed no interest in pursuing this tantalizing piece of evidence.

Sheridan and Bobby Kennedy quickly came to the same conclusion: JFK was the victim of a powerful conspiracy. But for the rest of his life, Sheridan was extremely cautious in his public remarks about the assassination. Another trait the Kennedys deeply valued in the investigator was his discretion. A submarine sailor during World War II, Sheridan knew how to "swim underwater," one Kennedy aide remarked. "Business or pleasure, secrets were safe with Walter," an appreciative Teddy Kennedy eulogized Sheridan at his 1995 funeral. "Whether working on an investigation or planning a surprise party, nothing ever leaked. On that point we all agreed—Walter Sheridan kept his mouth shut."

Nonetheless, Sheridan shared a crucial piece of information with his wife—he and Bobby were determined to crack the assassination of President Kennedy. When first contacted for this book, Nancy Sheridan was as reticent as her late husband to talk about the assassination. But gradually, during five separate interviews extending over a two-year period, she revealed more about the two men's collaboration on the case.

Sheridan's widow stated that Walt and Bobby pursued leads in the years after Dallas and planned to reopen the case if Kennedy succeeded in winning the presidency. "They continued working on the case even after Bob left the Justice Department. The two of them would sometimes go back to the Justice Department to look over evidence together," she said, sitting in her modest, one-story home in suburban Maryland. She spoke in a soft, halting voice, choosing her words carefully.

While Nancy Sheridan knew that her husband was working on the highly sensitive case with Kennedy, Walt never told her what they were finding. "He didn't tell me anything specific," she said. "That would have been a major obligation, a terrible burden on his family."

"You mean that he did not want to put his family at risk?" I asked.

"Yes."

In a later interview, she reiterated this point. "I've said to our children, 'Whatever Walt knew about what went on in Dallas, he took with him.' He would never put that responsibility on his family."

Again, seeking to be certain of what she was saying, I asked, "Because he didn't want to put the family in jeopardy?"

"Well," she replied, "it would be an awful responsibility for anybody, don't you think?"

Did Sheridan ever write down his thoughts about the case?

"No, he wouldn't have written that down."

In February 1965, Sheridan left Kennedy's staff to pursue a career as an investigative journalist, taking a job as a producer with NBC News. "I want to hit people between the eyes. I want to talk about things that have not yet been talked about," he announced. Before he started his new job, he made an agreement with Kennedy not to investigate Dallas for NBC. They would wait until they could reopen the case together. "When Walt was offered the job at NBC," Nancy recalled, "he went to Bob and said, 'This is what I'm going to do, what do you think about it?' And their decision was, the only thing Walt wouldn't do for NBC was to investigate the assassination. It was because they had something going together."

Two years later, the Garrison probe exploded in the press. Kennedy and Sheridan were both eager to find out what the D.A. had. Bobby told Arthur Schlesinger that he thought Garrison might be onto something. But Sheridan, who decided to go to New Orleans to check out the investigation, quickly came to a different conclusion, putting the Kennedy camp and the Garrison camp on a fateful collision course.

Like Guthman, Sheridan insisted he did not go to New Orleans on Kennedy's behalf. But soon after arriving there, he began feeding his former boss information about the investigation. Sheridan's scathing reports on Garrison would turn Kennedy against the prosecutor, and his scorching NBC special—"The JFK Conspiracy: The Case of Jim Garrison"—would turn the media tide sharply against the New Orleans lawman.

According to Nancy Sheridan, her husband decided that Jim Garrison was "a fraud—a dishonest man, morally and intellectually" within twenty-four hours of his arrival in New Orleans. "He talked to enough people to say this guy's crazy—and crooked," she recalled. As with Guthman's Los Angeles Times team, Garrison defector Bill Gurvich was a principal source for Sheridan as he reached his withering assessment of the prosecutor. After abandoning Garrison's camp, Gurvich would be described in the press as the D.A.'s chief investigator. But Garrison himself would dismiss Gurvich as merely a chauffeur and photographer, one of the many people who floated through his rambling, disorganized operation, which was soon peppered with colorful personalities from all over the country, including informants for the CIA and FBI.

Sheridan thought enough of the disgruntled Garrison employee to set up a meeting for him with Kennedy at Hickory Hill on June 8, 1967. Their ninety-minute conversation continued in a cab ride to the airport and ended as the two men sat on a luggage conveyor. Gurvich later explained that he had met with Kennedy because he worried that he would think "there actually was something in New Orleans and might be overly optimistic and hopeful" about solving his brother's murder. In their conversation, the investigator bluntly told Kennedy, "Senator, Mr. Garrison will never shed any light on your brother's death."

"Then why is he doing this?" Kennedy asked him.

"I don't know," Gurvich replied. "I wish I did."

Walt Sheridan had his own explanation for Garrison's media-circus investigation. He thought the D.A. was trying to deflect the spotlight from New Orleans godfather Carlos Marcello and his banker, Jimmy Hoffa—two men who were high on Sheridan's list of suspects in the assassination. Sheridan believed that Garrison was on Marcello's payroll. Why else didn't the prosecutor pursue the gangster, who had more obvious ties to David Ferrie than Clay Shaw did? At the time of the assassination, Ferrie and Banister were both working as investigators for Marcello in the deportation case brought against the Mafia lord by Bobby Kennedy's Justice Department. Ferrie was also reported to have flown Marcello back from Guatemala, after Kennedy's men grabbed him under dubious legal circumstances and hustled him out of the country in 1961. But curiously, Jim Garrison never bothered to investigate Marcello's connections to Dallas, a city that was under his criminal dominion and whose local Mafia underboss—Joseph Campisi—was the first person to visit Jack Ruby in jail. Since Ferrie and Banister also did work for the CIA, the agency that he believed had masterminded the plot, Garrison chose to focus only on this aspect of their employment record.

Throughout his years as district attorney, Garrison gave Carlos Marcello a pass, going so far as to insist that the mobster, who called himself a tomato salesman, was "a respectable businessman." In his 1988 memoir, Garrison wrote that he never came "upon evidence that [Marcello] was the Mafia kingpin the Justice Department says he is." He conceded that the Mafia sometimes acted as a shadowy partner of the CIA, but the only significant role he believed the mob played in Dallas was as a convenient scapegoat for the intelligence agency. Kennedy had a more astute understanding of the way power in America worked; he recognized that institutions like the CIA sometimes became so entwined with the criminal underworld, it was difficult to tell them apart at the operational level.

Sheridan felt his suspicions about Garrison were confirmed in late June

1967, when—locked in what was now a very public brawl with the NBC producer—the D.A. leaked word to the press that he was investigating Ed Partin for a possible connection to the Kennedy assassination. Partin, the renegade leader of the Teamsters' Baton Rouge local, had been the key witness in the Kennedy-Sheridan case against Jimmy Hoffa. After Hoffa was finally convicted and sent to jail in March 1967, the Teamsters and their organized crime allies began pulling every string they could to pressure Partin into switching sides and helping free Hoffa. Sheridan immediately concluded that Garrison's press leak about Partin was the latest move in this campaign on Hoffa's behalf. For Walt Sheridan and Bobby Kennedy—who had devoted much of their professional lives to hunting down Hoffa—there were few other affronts they would have taken more seriously than tampering with their hard-won conviction of the Teamster boss.

Only one other Garrison move would have agitated Sheridan and Kennedy more: steering his investigation into the dark waters of the anti-Castro plots that had been supervised by Bobby and inquiring how they might have backfired against JFK in Dallas. This is precisely what Garrison began doing, to what must have been Kennedy's horror. The prosecutor began stumbling around the Cuba minefield, looking into whether Oswald might have been part of a CIA plot to kill Castro and whether the operation was approved by Attorney General Kennedy. Even assuming that RFK did not approve the Castro assassination schemes, there was enough in the Cuba catacombs to have haunted Bobby ever since the shots rang out in Dealey Plaza. This angle of Garrison's investigation could only have intensified Kennedy's feelings of guilt and his fears that the New Orleans case was going to blow up in his face.

In May 1967, Sheridan—who had discovered Garrison's alarming line of inquiry—took the extraordinary step of approaching the CIA to see if the agency might be willing to cooperate with his NBC investigation of the D.A. On May 8, Richard H. Lansdale, a lawyer for the agency, disclosed in a memo that he had been approached by a Sheridan representative—Washington lawyer Herbert "Jack" Miller, the former criminal division chief in the Kennedy Justice Department. Miller told the CIA counsel that Sheridan had learned Garrison was trying to develop an explosive "thesis" about Oswald. The prosecutor was attempting to prove that the alleged assassin "was a CIA Agent, violently anti-Communist, recruited by the Agency for an operation approved by Robert Kennedy to kill Castro. When Oswald killed President Kennedy, the thesis is, it was necessary to show Oswald as a Communist in order to cover up the original plan." Three days later, Lansdale reported that

Miller had contacted him again on behalf of Sheridan, telling him that Sheridan "has indicated a willingness, if not a desire, to meet with CIA under any terms we propose. He would outline Garrison's schemes and intentions as he understands them and would receive from us anything, if any, we want to say. This could become part of the background in the forthcoming NBC show."

The fact that the Kennedy camp and the CIA—with their long, dark history of hostile relations—discussed the possibility of joining forces against Garrison shows how anxious they both were about the events in New Orleans. The agency took aggressive steps to infiltrate and disrupt Garrison's investigation. And during the trial of Clay Shaw—who Dick Helms later admitted was a CIA asset, providing information on overseas businessmen traveling behind the Iron Curtain—the CIA director repeatedly asked his top deputies whether "we are giving [the Shaw defense team] all the help they need?"

But Sheridan had a more demonstrably damaging impact on the Garrison investigation when NBC broadcast his hour-long news special on June 19, 1967. The program ripped into the D.A. for cobbling together a rickety case against Shaw by bribing, intimidating, and manipulating witnesses. The results of Garrison's prosecutorial mayhem, the show's host concluded, "have been to damage reputations, spread fear and suspicion, and, worst of all, to exploit the nation's sorrow and doubts about President Kennedy's death." The NBC show was a devastating blast, and it marked a turning point in Garrison's fortunes. After Sheridan's indictment, the D.A.'s public image began shifting from crusading to kooky.

The wounded Garrison demanded—and got—equal time from NBC to defend himself. But he also reinforced his image as an out-of-control backwater despot by turning the tables on Sheridan and arresting *him* for bribing witnesses. (The charges were later dropped.) The Sheridans feared that the D.A. was trying to throw Walt in jail so he could do him "some bodily harm," said Nancy. Kennedy rushed to Sheridan's defense, declaring that "his personal ties to President Kennedy, as well as his own integrity, ensure that he would want as much as, or more than any other man, to ascertain the truth about the events of November 1963."

By now, Kennedy himself was aroused to oppose Garrison. When he learned that Mort Sahl had landed an appearance for the D.A. on Johnny Carson's *Tonight Show*, Kennedy tried unsuccessfully to get Carson to withdraw the invitation. CNN political reporter Jeff Greenfield, who was a young Kennedy aide at the time, remembers walking into his Senate office and overhearing Bobby lobbying Carson on the phone. "He was telling Carson that Garrison was full of crap. Bobby was saying, 'Don't believe him. If I thought there was anything to this, I would have done something. Don't you think I would've pursued it vigorously?'" Carson went ahead with the interview, but his questions—which Sheridan helped supply him—were surprisingly hostile for the genial talk show host and prompted numerous viewer complaints. Nevertheless, Garrison performed like the smooth courtroom lawyer he was, expertly taking the interview out of Carson's hands and raising provocative questions of his own about the assassination. The TV host was so annoyed that he later took it out on Sahl, banning the comedian from his show.

For the rest of their lives, Garrison and Sheridan would regard each other with a poisonous contempt. Even today, among Garrison supporters, the name Walter Sheridan elicits a furious reaction. They accuse him of doing the CIA's bidding when he went to New Orleans. Those close to Sheridan, in turn, scorn the New Orleans D.A. as a corrupt demagogue. In reality, neither man is so easy to dismiss.

It is certain that Sheridan was acting on Robert Kennedy's behalf, not as an intelligence agent, when he went to New Orleans. His loyalty—from the time he went to work for Bobby Kennedy's rackets investigation in the late 1950s to the final chapter of his career in the 1980s, when he worked as a Senate investigator for Teddy Kennedy—was unquestionably to the Kennedy family. Walt Sheridan brought a religious devotion to the Kennedy cause, one that he could never have divided on behalf of another master. Jack Kennedy "asked the best of all of us and we all eagerly gave it," he once said, looking back on his service in JFK's administration. "Politics became a noble profession again, as it had been in Ancient Greece." He embraced this view of the Kennedy years throughout his life. In Sheridan's mind, Bobby only took the mission higher.

It is true that Sheridan had an intelligence background when he came to work for Bobby Kennedy. After quitting the FBI in 1954, he received a security clearance to join the CIA. He decided to work for the National Security Agency instead, but after only three years, he left that organization—a covert labyrinth dedicated to the cracking of foreign codes—because, he said, "I felt cut off from the world." There is no evidence that Sheridan continued to play an intelligence role in his career with the Kennedys. Nancy Sheridan said that her husband shared Bobby's suspicious view of the CIA. "They didn't trust it," she said simply.

It is easy to understand why the approach that Sheridan made to the agency in the midst of his Garrison research raises eyebrows among his critics. But the CIA, which ordered a background check on Sheridan after hearing from him, was clearly as leery of him as he was of the agency. Langley officials might have feared that Sheridan and Kennedy were not only investigating Garrison but were on a fishing expedition to find out what the agency knew about the assassination. In any case, the incident reveals more about the two parties' mutual distrust of Garrison than it does about their trust in one another. And there is no evidence Sheridan and agency officials did in fact end up joining forces against the D.A.

Walt Sheridan went to New Orleans for reasons that had nothing to do with U.S. intelligence. He went to size up the Garrison probe, and then—after quickly deciding it was a threat to Bobby Kennedy's political interests and his future chances of reopening the case—to sabotage it.

If Sheridan was no spook, Jim Garrison was not simply a pawn of organized crime. He had a troubling blind spot when it came to Carlos Marcello. And he certainly was not the shining knight portrayed by Kevin Costner in Oliver Stone's *JFK*. But Garrison was more heroic than Sheridan believed.

To Bobby's incorruptible crime-hunter, Garrison carried a repellent, swampy odor because of his willingness to overlook the criminal exploits of men like Marcello. But Sheridan was too quick to dismiss the entire Garrison enterprise because of this. The prosecutor was, after all, a creature of his environment, and this was hothouse New Orleans, where few public officials did not have to change shirts now and then to stay clean. Despite this, Garrison's outrage over the unsolved murder of the president was genuine. And it put to shame the many public officials in Washington who were in a much grander position to do something about the crime, yet chose to do nothing.

Garrison also might have erred badly by targeting Clay Shaw after the deaths of the two more central figures in his case, Guy Banister and David Ferrie. But, as the House Select Committee on Assassinations would confirm a decade later, the New Orleans prosecutor did succeed in shining a light on a crucial corner of the conspiracy—a world of zealous CIA plotters, Cuban expatriates, far-right militants, and mercenaries, where President Kennedy was considered a traitor.

There is a tragic sense to the blood feud that broke out between Jim Garrison and Walter Sheridan. These two men probably knew more than anyone else in the country, besides the conspirators themselves, about the plot that cut down JFK. But, like the competing heirs to the Kennedy legacy—RFK and LBJ—they were doomed to clash rather than cooperate. You could not find two more different men—one big, loud-mouthed, and brash; the other slight, tight-lipped, and circumspect. Garrison was a man of outsized appetites and ambitions; Sheridan was a devoted family man and squeaky-clean public servant who had submerged his own dreams in those of Robert Kennedy. But it was not their clashing personalities that ultimately drove them to opposing corners. It was Kennedy's need to control the search into his brother's killing. Even without his obvious flaws, Garrison would have been unacceptable to Bobby. When it came to solving the crime, RFK trusted only himself and a few men, like Sheridan, who served him.

ONE EVENING, WHILE HE was volunteering as Jim Garrison's media advisor, Mort Sahl was invited to a Washington dinner party by his friend, NBC News anchor David Brinkley. Sahl was seated next to Bob McNamara, while his wife, China, sat next to a nervous Bobby Kennedy. Everyone avoided The Topic hovering in the air. "The conversation was so innocuous that it had to be an effort," Sahl recalled. "Weather was a recurrent topic, and no one ever took a position on it." Ethel Kennedy finally broke the strained mood by getting drunk and dancing on the table. "Ethel, please, my career," cracked Bobby.

Finally, at eleven o'clock Sahl left to do his nightclub show, leaving his wife with the jittery Kennedy, who was ripping napkins into shreds and making paper pyramids. Only after Sahl had gone did Bobby work up the nerve to ask China, in roundabout fashion, about the controversial turn her husband's career had taken. Why was Mort fired from his popular talk show on a Los Angeles TV station? Kennedy asked her. But he already knew the answer—Sahl had been terminated for talking too much about his brother's assassination. Finally, after Bobby kept pumping her for information, the sharp-tongued China cut him off: "You had him next to you for two hours. Why didn't you ask him then?"

Sahl was exasperated by the reticence of Bobby Kennedy and his circle to publicly confront the subject for which he was sacrificing his career. On another occasion, while escorting the wife of NBC newsman John Chancellor, who was working that night, to a White House dinner, the comedian bumped into Ted Kennedy's wife, Joan. When he told her that Bobby had invited him to his Senate office the next day, she burbled, "Oh, so he's not angry at you anymore?"

"Angry about what?" Sahl erupted. "I'm destroying my career trying to find out who killed his brother!"

The next day, when the comedian visited him in his Capitol Hill office, Bobby once again assiduously avoided the topic. Kennedy wanted to know what the prevailing opinion of LBJ was on the college campuses where Sahl frequently performed. "They hate him," Sahl said.

"It's probably time for someone to make a move," Bobby obliquely commented.

Sahl cut to the chase. "You might just save the country."

It was the upcoming presidential race that preoccupied Kennedy. All his future plans depended on his occupancy of the White House.

According to Sahl and Mark Lane, who also moved to New Orleans to work on the case, the Kennedy and Garrison camps occasionally sent back-channel messages to each other despite the blazing feud between the D.A. and Sheridan. This was far from a formal arrangement, and indeed it seems to have consisted largely of gossip and bits of information passed back and forth by a colorful intermediary named Jones Harris. A New York man about town whose social circle overlapped with the Kennedys', Harris turned himself into a dogged assassination researcher after Dallas, traveling to Dealey Plaza and later New Orleans. The out-of-wedlock son of Broadway producer Jed Harris and actress Ruth Gordon, Harris had a waspish wit and a theatrical flair, showing up in Garrison's office in a straw hat that he rarely took off, even indoors. He had dated Jackie's White House appointment secretary (and JFK mistress) Pamela Turnure and partied with the Kennedy crowd in Newport when Jack was still alive—he once told Jackie that her glamorous husband should go into movies and let Peter Lawford run the country. Garrison found Harris intriguing and the New Yorker became one more member of the vivid cast of characters surrounding the prosecutor.

Shuttling between New York and New Orleans, Harris would pass along information about the Garrison investigation to Kennedy clan insiders like Steve Smith—the husband of Bobby's sister Jean and manager of the family's finances—whom he bumped into at Manhattan watering holes like P. J. Clarke's saloon. Harris would then relay messages from Bobby Kennedy's circle back to Garrison.

According to Sahl, the message from Bobby was always the same: I must wait until I reach the White House. Then I will "get the guys who killed Jack." Perhaps this was Kennedy's way of signaling to Garrison that it was time for him to step aside—he was going to take over the investigation. But Garrison told Sahl that Bobby would not live long enough to win the nomination. The prosecutor sent back word to Kennedy that his only chance was to speak out about the conspiracy that killed his brother, which might make his enemies think twice before moving against him. But the advice was not well received by Bobby's camp, according to Sahl. The message that came back through Harris was, "What are we going to do—listen to the people in Washington who have worked with the Kennedys forever, or to a nightclub comedian and a Southern cracker sheriff?"

Sahl shakes his head. "I don't think he'd be under that everlasting flame today if he'd listened to us."

Even at the height of his battle with Sheridan, Garrison never turned his fury against Bobby Kennedy. The only sharp public remark Garrison made about Bobby came after the D.A. ordered Sheridan's arrest, when Kennedy rushed to his friend's defense. Bobby didn't want the "real assassins" caught, Garrison acidly commented, because it "would interfere with his political career."

Privately, with his staff, a pained and confused Garrison would wonder out loud about the strange quiescence of the Kennedy brothers' circle. One day the prosecutor turned to Sahl, who was the only member of his team who had ever met the Kennedys, and in "utter frustration," asked him, "You knew them—what kind of friends did those guys have?"

"If they killed my brother," Garrison added, "I'd be in the alley waiting for them with a steak knife, not sitting at the Kennedy Center watching a ballet with them."

Sahl, too, was scathing in his assessment of the Camelot round table and their failure to pursue their leader's killers. The old Kennedy crowd was so worried they would stop being invited to parties if they stirred up trouble, sneered the comedian. "Even if the party had become one long funeral party."

Even the president's widow—at first so righteous in her fury against her husband's despicable killers—had gone mute. One day, while walking along Madison Avenue near Seventy-fourth, Sahl came upon Jackie, peering into the store windows and art galleries in the neighborhood. Their eyes met. She knew what Sahl had been doing for her fallen husband. "Hey," said Sahl. "I know, I know, I know," Jackie muttered, and then quickly walked on.

IN THE END, JIM Garrison's trial of Clay Shaw did exactly what Kennedy and Sheridan had feared it would. It contaminated the JFK assassination investigation for years to come.

After deliberating for less than an hour, the jury filed back into a New Orleans courtroom shortly after midnight on March 1, 1969, and declared that Shaw was an innocent man. While the jury members made it clear that they were not endorsing the Warren Report—graphic evidence like the Zapruder film, which Garrison repeatedly played in the courtroom, had made a strong impression on them—they explained that the D.A. had simply failed to present a strong enough case against Shaw. In the eyes of the media, however, the verdict was a resounding vindication for the government's lone gunman theory. For at least another decade, until Congress finally reopened the case, research into the killing of John F. Kennedy would carry the taint of cultism or lunacy because of Garrison's spectacular courtroom failure. Even some of the leading assassination critics who originally supported Garrison, like Harold Weisberg, turned bitterly against him in the end.

"Let justice be done though the heavens fall," Garrison had thundered. And the skies did indeed crash down on him after the collapse of his investigation. Though he beat back attempts to jail him for corruption and run him out of public office, Garrison never again rode the crest of history as he did during his two-year Kennedy investigation.

By the time of Garrison's downfall, Robert Kennedy was dead. And Walter Sheridan would never complete their mission of bringing JFK's killers to justice. As the years went by, Sheridan avoided talking about the assassination. "He was the keeper of confidences, the sphinx of secrets," remarked journalist Jack Newfield, who tried unsuccessfully to persuade Sheridan to appear in his 1992 *Frontline* documentary about Mafia involvement in the Kennedy assassination. In public, Sheridan claimed he believed the lone gunman theory, but he clearly did not want to linger on the subject. "If there was a conspiracy, I would have been the one to find it out," he told investigative reporter Dan Moldea, author of a book on Jimmy Hoffa. Off the record, however, he conceded that there might be something to Moldea's suspicions about the Teamster leader and Mafia bosses Marcello and Trafficante.

As they grew older, some of Sheridan's children found it harder to accept their father's terse endorsement of the Warren Report. Walt Jr., who remembers playing at Hickory Hill and Hyannis Port as a child, began to suspect there was more to the crime than Oswald and was keen to hear his father's views. "To me, it is the biggest deal politically that ever happened in my life, the biggest question that goes unanswered today," he said. "To me, it *is* the day the music died."

Every time Walt Jr. asked his father whether he believed the lone gunman theory, Sheridan insisted that he did. But shortly before his death, Sheridan finally told his son what he really believed. They were sitting in Sheridan's living room after dinner one evening, when Walt Jr. raised the old question once again.

"Isn't it realistic to think there was something else going on in Dallas besides Oswald?" he asked his father.

There was a pause, and then Sheridan simply said, "Yeah."

"To me, it was such a major victory after all those years to hear my father finally say that out loud. Because I always knew there was something there. And when he said it, I didn't even respond, I just sank back in my chair and said to myself, 'Thank God.'"

Walter Sheridan died of lung cancer in January 1995 at the age of sixty-nine. His obituaries cited his long, successful career as a crusading investigator for the American public, including his battles against Teamster corruption, abuses in the pharmaceutical industry, dangerous working conditions in the mines, and the exploitation of farm workers. His eulogies highlighted his family devotion and his strong convictions. "He had a heart as large as his ability, and his courage and dedication to justice and the public interest were unmatched by anyone," said Teddy Kennedy. "In a sense, Bobby lived on through Walter. In the nearly twenty years that he worked with me in the Senate, I never met with Walter or talked with Walter or laughed with Walter that I didn't think of Bobby."

Despite his many accomplishments, Sheridan became deeply despondent before his death over his failure to close the Kennedy case. Jack Newfield, who stayed in touch with Sheridan, used the word "suicidal" to describe his state of mind near the end of his life. When I asked Nancy Sheridan if it was true that Walt had become seriously depressed, I expected her, ever protective of her husband's memory, to deny it. But she said, "Yes, that's true. He was so close to Bob. He felt very strongly about him. And I believe that the two of them did crack the case. But Walt was never in a position to do anything about it after Bob died."

Why didn't Sheridan pursue the investigation after Bobby's death? "He did not have the mandate or power to do anything," said Nancy. "And he had promised Bob not to do anything without him. So he was honoring that agreement even after Bob was gone." Even in death, Kennedy was the man they followed.

At a Cabinet Room meeting in April 1961, one week before the Bay of Pigs invasion, the operation's CIA masterminds, Allen Dulles and Richard Bissell, were full of confidence. Sitting from left to right are Defense Secretary Robert McNamara, Joint Chiefs of Staff chairman Lyman Lemnitzer, Dulles and Bissell. Intelligence officials did not inform President Kennedy that, by the agency's own estimates, the invasion was doomed to fail unless the U.S. threw its military might against Castro's forces. "I've got to do something about those CIA bastards," JFK raged after the ensuing fiasco. *Courtesy Woodfin-Camp NYC, photo by Jacques Lowe*

The president and first lady welcome the recently freed leaders of the Bay of Pigs brigade at a December 1962 Orange Bowl ceremony in Miami. Though Kennedy had no intention of launching a U.S. invasion of Cuba, he raised the Cuban exiles' hopes during his speech by declaring that the rebel flag they had presented him "will be returned to this brigade in a free Havana." *Courtesy Getty*

Members of the Joint Chiefs of Staff gather in the White House for a meeting with President Kennedy. From left to right are Admiral Arleigh Burke; General Andy Goodpaster, a military aide to former President Eisenhower; Marine General David Shoup; Army General George Decker; and Joint Chiefs chairman Lemnitzer. Kennedy had a deeply strained relationship with his military commanders. He became so concerned with the mutinous atmosphere in some military quarters that he persuaded friends in Hollywood to alert the public by making a film version of *Seven Days in May*, the bestselling novel about an attempted coup in Washington.
Courtesy Woodfin-Camp NYC, photo by Jacques Lowe

Defense Secretary McNamara and General Maxwell Taylor, who took over from Lemnitzer as Joint Chiefs chairman, confer with JFK in the White House. Kennedy tried to impose control over the restive armed forces with the help of McNamara and Taylor, two men deeply distrusted by the military establishment. Kennedy saw McNamara as a key ally in his drive for a more peaceful and stable world. But after Kennedy was replaced by Lyndon Johnson, McNamara would earn a more bellicose place in history. *Courtesy JFK Library, © Robert L. Knudsen, White House*

Richard Helms, who maneuvered his way to the top of the CIA in the 1960s, kept the agency's secrets from presidents and congressional overseers. He approved the CIA's recruitment of Mafia assassins to kill Castro, without informing the Kennedys. And he later made sure that the Warren Commission remained ignorant of dark agency secrets like this. *Courtesy Getty*

The strange and spectral James Angleton also played a key role in misleading the Warren Commission and spreading disinformation about JFK's assassination. After his ouster from the CIA, grisly morgue photos of Robert Kennedy were found in his office vault. *Courtesy Corbis*

Cord Meyer and Mary Meyer, shown here after their 1945 marriage, shared a youthful vision for global peace after the slaughterhouse of World War II, which took the life of Cord's twin brother and left him partially blinded. But after he joined the CIA, where he fell under the spell of Angleton, Meyer grew increasingly gloomy in his world views. After Mary left him, to pursue the life of an early '60s bohemian, she became romantically involved with President Kennedy. CIA officials like Angleton, who kept a creepy watch over Mary, suspected that she was leading Kennedy down the path of peace, love, and drugs. *Courtesy Corbis*

David Atlee Phillips, the CIA's propaganda chief for the Bay of Pigs operation, was among those who were deeply embittered by President Kennedy's refusal to rescue the doomed invaders. Investigators for the House Select Committee on Assassinations later zeroed in on Phillips' possible ties to JFK's murder, but their inquiries were aborted. "I was one of the two case officers who handled Lee Harvey Oswald," Phillips wrote in a proposal for a strangely confessional novel before his death in 1988.

David Morales, the paramilitary chief for the CIA's JM/WAVE station in Miami, carried out a variety of dark assignments for the agency. Morales, who grew close to Mafia confederates like Johnny Rosselli, later told his lawyer he was in both Dallas and Los Angeles when John and Robert Kennedy were assassinated.

Mafia emissary Johnny Rosselli arrives on Capitol Hill in June 1975 to testify before the Church Committee about the CIA's pact with the mob. The following year, after Rosselli was called to testify further, his dismembered body was found stuffed in a rusting oil drum, floating in the waters off Miami. "Rosselli was killed every way you can be killed," said committee member Gary Hart. *Courtesy Corbis*

As the Kennedy family laid the fallen president to rest, Bobby and Jacqueline Kennedy's rage at the "they" who had killed JFK was replaced by a paralyzing sense of loss. To close friends, it seemed Bobby's crushing grief was compounded by a profound guilt, the feeling that he could have prevented his brother's murder if he had only been more vigilant. *Courtesy Woodfin-Camp NYC, photo by Jacques Lowe*

Bobby Kennedy could not bring himself to accept Lyndon Johnson, "the garish sun" who had replaced his brother as president. Ironically, the two bitter rivals shared a deep suspicion that JFK was the victim of a conspiracy. While Washington's political elite muttered darkly among themselves about the plot that had ended the Kennedy presidency, the media continued to reassure the public that the assassination was the work of a lone misfit. *Courtesy JFK Library, photo by Edward Ozern*

While inspecting the miserable conditions for farm workers in upstate New York, Senator Robert Kennedy speaks with the young son of a farm worker family who lived in the hulk of an abandoned car. Always attuned to the feelings of children, Kennedy developed a deep sense of empathy for America's afflicted after his brother's assassination, an empathy that reflected his own wounded condition. *Courtesy Adam Walinsky*

Bobby strides briskly outside the Capitol Building with his two young Senate aides, Peter Edelman (center) and Adam Walinsky. RFK's staffers pushed him toward his inevitable showdown with President Johnson over the Vietnam War. Who were we, Kennedy declared in a passionate Senate speech co-written by Walinsky, "to play the role of an avenging angel pouring death and destruction" from above on the people of Vietnam? *Courtesy Adam Walinsky, photo by George Tames: © New York Times Magazine/ Redux*

Bobby waves to ecstatic supporters during his tumultuous 1968 presidential race, surrounded by a tumbling Ethel and several of their children, as aide Fred Dutton (far right) walks alongside the campaign car and bodyguard Bill Barry keeps a protective hold on the candidate. Despite the physical dangers, Kennedy gave himself to the crowds, wading into the wounded heart of American democracy with heroic confidence. *Courtesy JFK Library*

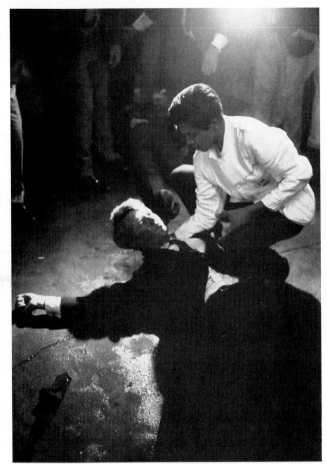

Seconds after being shot in the head, Kennedy lies in a pool of blood on the kitchen floor of the Ambassador Hotel, held by seventeen-year-old busboy Juan Romero. Bobby's face "had a kind of sweet acceptance to it," observed reporter Pete Hamill—he looked like a man who had been released. *Photograph by Bill Eppridge/LIFE/©Time Inc.*

Press secretary Frank Mankiewicz wipes away tears as he announces the death of Senator Robert F. Kennedy on June 6, 1968. Bobby had asked his trusted aide to help him find the truth about Dallas. Now their mission would never be completed. *Photo by Bill Eppridge*

8

THE PASSION OF ROBERT KENNEDY

O ne evening in late spring 1966, Kennedy aide John Nolan—who was in Johannesburg helping to organize the senator's forthcoming historic trip to South Africa—dropped by the home of South African tennis player Abe Siegel. While he was visiting Siegel, the Kennedy aide's car was broken into and a bag containing his passport stolen.

"This scared the bejesus out of Siegel and his wife," recalled Nolan. "They thought it was the South African secret police." Kennedy's trip, which was scheduled for June, was a source of growing tension within the apartheid regime, which feared the U.S. senator's arrival would set off a wave of unrest against its racist policies. But it was not only the South African government that was keeping a watchful eye on Kennedy's travel plans. His own government was also tracking him. Despite the regime's barbaric treatment of its nonwhite population, Pretoria was viewed as an important Cold War ally in Washington. Once again, Kennedy's political opponents thought his free-wheeling diplomacy was damaging United States' security interests.

Despite his host's anxieties, Nolan was not too unnerved by the theft of his belongings until he returned home to Washington. "I had a little trouble getting a new passport and so on, but we managed to do that and I flew back on schedule," Nolan said. When he reported back to Kennedy's office, the senator asked him about the car break-in, wondering if any sensitive notes on the trip also might have been stolen. Nolan, who had not told Kennedy about the burglary, was stunned.

"How did you know about that?" he asked him.

"Dick Helms called me," Kennedy replied. "He followed you day by day, every step of the way across South Africa."

To Nolan, Helms's close monitoring of his trip was another example of how the spymaster tried to ingratiate himself with Washington VIPs, by showing that he was always "on the ball." But Helms, who would soon be promoted to the top of the CIA by President Johnson, was also conveying another message to Kennedy: The agency is watching you.

In the last years of his life, Bobby Kennedy became increasingly estranged from Washington's political elite. His growing commitment to a new, multiracial America—which allied him with the crusade of Martin Luther King Jr.—was viewed with alarm by J. Edgar Hoover, who regarded both men as dangerous. And his critique of American foreign policy, which became more passionate as the war in Southeast Asia dragged on, drew the baleful eye of the White House and CIA, which began spying on Kennedy as if he were a hostile foreign agent.

When Kennedy and his small party—Ethel, Angie Novello, and Adam Walinsky—finally arrived in Johannesburg on June 4, 1966, the regime—which had held up the trip for five months—greeted him with frosty contempt, declaring it would not allow the senator's trip to be "transformed into a publicity stunt . . . as a buildup for a future presidential election." But as Kennedy disembarked from his plane just before midnight and exited the airport, he was welcomed by a boisterous crowd of young people, who screamed his name and tore his cufflinks from his sleeves.

During his South Africa odyssey, Kennedy directly challenged the moral basis of apartheid. Unintimidated by the coldly watchful regime, he denounced its brutal subjugation of its black citizens and urged his largely white university audiences to muster the courage to overthrow the cruel system of racial separation. In a soaringly inspirational speech at the University of Capetown on June 6—a speech Schlesinger called the greatest of Kennedy's life—the senator reminded his audience that history is moved forward by countless small acts of heroism. "Each time a man stands up for an ideal, or acts to improve the lot of others or strikes out against injustice, he sends forth a tiny ripple of hope, and crossing each other from a million different centers of energy and daring, those ripples build a current which can sweep down the mightiest walls of oppression and resistance." The speech, which was written for Kennedy by Walinsky and Goodwin, would later be chiseled on his Arlington resting place.

At a dinner party with a group of politicians, business leaders, and newspaper editors in Pretoria, Kennedy drew fire. How could he attack South Africa when it was such a loyal ally in the world struggle against communism? But fighting one form of tyranny doesn't excuse another, Kennedy responded. "What does it mean to be against communism if one's own system denies the value of the individual and gives all the power to the government—just as the Communists do?" The Cold War had long provided a cover for despotic U.S. allies to abuse their own populations. But Kennedy was declaring those days must end.

Everywhere the senator went, he challenged his white hosts to question their deepest assumptions. At the University of Natal in Durban, one audience member observed that the church to which most of the white population belonged taught that black inferiority is divinely ordained. "But suppose God is black," replied Kennedy. His remark was greeted by stunned silence. Afterward, returning to his hotel, Kennedy came upon a group of black South Africans and he joined them in singing the stirring U.S. civil rights hymn, "We Shall Overcome."

As the Kennedy cavalcade rolled across South Africa, he created his own, ever-expanding ripples of hope. At first, "his only crowds were the students," Walinksy observed. "But then somewhere as the thing started to get across . . . there were just thousands of ordinary citizens . . . pulling at him and tugging at him and cheering him and it was really fantastic." In Soweto, the sprawling black ghetto Kennedy called "a dreary concentration camp," he waded through cheering and chanting throngs, climbing up the steps of a church and onto the roof of a car to address them. He visited banned opposition leaders in their homes, including the aging Chief Albert Luthuli, for whom he played a recording of JFK's landmark 1963 civil rights address.

The Pretoria regime was greatly relieved when it finally came time for Kennedy to go. He too sensed the revolutionary fervor his trip had unleashed. As his plane lifted off the runway, Kennedy remarked with a wry smile, "If we stayed another two days, we could have taken over the country."

During his years in the Senate, Robert Kennedy undertook a remarkable mission—the forging of an independent foreign policy. He was intent on showing the world that there was another America—one aligned with his brother's ideals instead of the Johnson administration's policies. As the United States' image turned darker overseas, where the country was seen as increasingly militaristic and business-driven, Kennedy strived to make a separate peace with the world. Trying to avoid a traumatic rupture with Johnson, RFK was compelled to convey this message with diplomatic finesse. But his message to the world, particularly those countries where anti-

American sentiments were on the rise, was clear: Take heart. The United States once stood for negotiation, not war; social reform, not oppression. And it will once again. The message carried weight, since Kennedy was no ordinary senator. He was his martyred brother's heir; an aura of righteous ascension hung over him.

The first clear sign of Kennedy's diverging foreign policy came in April 1965 when Johnson responded to a leftist uprising in the Dominican Republic by storming the impoverished island with 22,000 Marines. LBJ's heavy-handed action had been prompted by the CIA, which relayed false and inflammatory messages about decapitations in the streets and other unverified reports of Communist mayhem. Kennedy thought the U.S. invasion was an "outrage," and he took to the Senate floor to denounce it. Johnson undoubtedly found Kennedy's impassioned protest bitterly ironic, coming as it did from the man who once led the covert war on Castro. But by then Kennedy had mellowed so far on Cuba that he was not even agitated by its ongoing efforts to arm other Latin revolutionaries. Cuban guns were no longer the problem in Kennedy's mind, said Walinsky—it was the medieval condition of Latin societies. "I mean, hell, anybody can get guns—the question is what people want to do with them. I think he felt that if people really want to overthrow the government, then they're going to do that whether they get guns or not."

Looking back today at Kennedy's political evolution, Walinsky insists that RFK's growing sympathy for Che Guevara and his revolutionary mission has been wildly exaggerated by left-leaning writers. "There has been all this romanticism—people treat him as if he were sort of Che without the beard. It's such utter drivel. I can't begin to express my horror at that kind of view." But Kennedy himself called Guevara "a revolutionary hero." And when, in October 1967, a sick and exhausted Che was tracked down and killed in the jungles of Bolivia by a CIA-led team of hunters, who sawed off his hands and buried him in an unmarked ditch so his grave could not become a shrine, Ethel was moved to mourn his passing at a Washington party.

As with Che and other icons of the sixties, a struggle has raged over the decades to define Robert Kennedy's political identity. Walinsky—who later in life became associated with conservative issues such as welfare reform and police training—is among those who have emphasized Kennedy's more traditional values, including his devotion to family, country, and religion. He points out that Kennedy too became increasingly critical of the welfare state, decrying how the bureaucratization of modern life robbed the individual and the family of their power. But, as Walinsky acknowledges, this is not just a conservative critique—it was a radical one, and it was also espoused by the 1960s New Left, which sought to empower communities, not the federal government. (Though some liberals squawked about it, even RFK's law and order fervor as a Senate investigator and attorney general had a progressive focus, targeting the corrupt politicians, union bosses, and gangsters who preyed on working Americans.) One thing is clear, looking back at Kennedy's storied political odyssey in the sixties. The message of self-determination and human dignity that he brought to his fellow citizens—as well as to those in the countries he visited—was undeniably radical. In the highly polarized atmosphere of the day, Kennedy had an electrifying—and dangerous—impact.

This was demonstrated during the tumultuous, three-week tour of South America that RFK made in November 1965. Kennedy said his trip to Peru, Brazil, Argentina, and Chile was motivated by his concern that the Alliance for Progress—which he saw as an important part of his brother's legacy—was being gutted by the new administration. Soon after JFK's assassination, Johnson promoted Thomas Mann—the hard-line ambassador to Mexico who had tried to connect Oswald to a Communist conspiracy—to the State Department post in charge of Latin American affairs. Mann quickly turned his attention to the Alliance, the centerpiece of Kennedy's Latin reform policy, and began turning it into a tool of American corporations. Tom Mann was the type of "colonialist" who believes that the "natives . . . need to be shown who is boss" and "who feels the principal job of the United States in Latin America is to make the world safe for W.R. Grace and Company," moaned Dick Goodwin when he heard about his appointment. Mann himself summed up his philosophy years later like this: "I never believed we should compete with the revolutionaries." But this is precisely what the Kennedys had in mind when they launched the Alliance. They would try to steal the Communists' thunder by offering the downtrodden of Latin America not only aid but the stirring vision of democracy.

The political passion displayed by Kennedy in South America—and later in South Africa—resonated around the world. These two memorable journeys would set the stage for Robert Kennedy's most heroic expedition of all, the 1968 presidential campaign.

Kennedy's party—including Ethel, Walinsky, Goodwin, and John Seigenthaler—began their Latin America trip by swooping into Lima on November 10, 1965. U.S. embassy officials immediately wanted to hustle the senator off to a white-tie reception for the King of Belgium. "Robert F. Kennedy doesn't even own a white tie," an aide informed the officials.

Instead Kennedy met with students at a local university, where he quickly struck the insurgent theme of his trip. "The responsibility of our time," he told them, "is nothing less than a revolution." This cataclysm, said Kennedy, would "be peaceful if we are wise enough; humane if we care enough; successful if we are fortunate enough. But a revolution will come whether we will it or not." Then, as if to underscore why this sweeping change was inevitable, Kennedy threw himself into Lima's deepest holes of misery, the teeming barriadas built on the city's red-clay hillsides, where he stepped over acrid streams of sewage to play with the listless, half-naked children who clustered outside their mud huts. He was appalled to find out that the slums had no running water because U.S. aid to Peru had been suspended after the Peruvian government got into a conflict with the local subsidiary of Standard Oil. "What has aid got to do with company profits!" Kennedy angrily demanded of a hapless embassy official. "You mean to say we can't get a water tank for these people because of an oil dispute?"

He followed this volatile pattern in each country he visited—delivering provocative speeches to campus audiences, touring the shanty towns and plantations where the continent's semifeudal conditions were on shocking display, and angrily confronting local patricians and U.S. officials at the lavish receptions in his honor. "Don't you know you're making way for your own destruction!" he snapped at a sugar cane company representative in Brazil after hearing about the cane cutters' slavelike working conditions.

The grotesque disparities in Latin societies began to wear on the nerves of Kennedy and his group. One evening—after coming down from the Andes, where the once-proud citadels of Inca civilization were now overrun with children whose bellies were swollen from hunger—the senator was invited by a friend of President Fernando Belaúnde Terry to his lavish estate. Belaúnde was known by Latin American standards as a Kennedy-style reformer. But his friend was one of the country's wealthiest landowners, and as Bobby's group entered the aristocrat's mansion, walking past machine gun-toting guards into the great hall, they were stunned by the baronial opulence on display. "It's a sight I'll never forget," Walinksy remembered. "The room was about a hundred feet long and about three stories high. It was their living room. And it had a fireplace that was big enough for eight men to stand in. . . . Above the fireplace was the head of an elephant, and on either side of the fireplace there were two rhinoceros heads and two hippopotamus heads. And then stretching all along the walls . . . were [more] animal heads. There were conservatively a thousand heads of animals. There was a great long table with maybe twenty-five chairs, and the chairs were all covered in zebra hide. The ash trays were made out of leopard claws. I mean there just wasn't anything in the room that wasn't a dead animal. And a case of maybe thirty or forty guns. And we were all, I mean we were all just struck dumb. And I almost went insane because literally every head up there in front of my eyes turned into the head of one of these Indians, because it was the same thing of course."

In the backyard was a vast, sunken private museum filled with the plundered treasures of Inca civilization, room after room with display cases of gold artifacts, breast plates, knives, shields. This is where the wealth of Peru's Indian population had disappeared—buried in the backyard of one obscenely fortunate man.

Kennedy's growing sense of outrage began to focus on the strutting Latin generals, with their rows of self-bestowed medals, who acted as the enforcers for these corrupt regimes. "He had a deep distrust and abhorrence of the military in general," observed Walinsky, "and of the kind of repressive military that you got in Latin America in particular." Kennedy found it intolerable to see the blank-staring soldiers with their ominously pointed machine guns everywhere on the streets. As the crowds surged around Kennedy, the soldiers were always roughly shoving people and beating them with their gun butts. Once, in exasperation, Ethel punched a policeman in the stomach outside a reception where people were being brutally handled.

Kennedy also turned his anger on the U.S. officials who served to prop up the exploitive system—a system from which American corporations reaped huge rewards. "I mean in Latin America what you were talking about basically was a kind of cabal between the Johnson State Department . . . and these companies to just basically rape the countries they were dealing with," said Walinsky, reflecting Kennedy's attitude.

The senator knew that he was being carefully monitored by his own government during his trip. At U.S. embassy meetings, he would delight in calling on the CIA agents in the room to identify themselves. Once, in Recife, Brazil, a man actually did raise his hand. "Absolute fool," spat Walinsky, who shared Kennedy's disgust with the agency's local representatives. Kennedy dismissed the CIA men they encountered on the trip as "just awful, just morons."

The CIA agent in Recife tried to scare Kennedy out of appearing at a local college, telling him the crowd would be "too dangerous, too left-wing." Police had just arrested three local students for plotting to throw acid in the U.S. senator's face—although the credibility of such official claims was always questionable under Brazil's new military dictatorship. Kennedy blew off the CIA man's warnings. The audience turned out to be "the mildest kind of students in the world, and 90 percent of them were girls," Walinsky recalled.

Kennedy was not greeted as a liberator everywhere in South America. In some places, the Kennedy name still meant the Bay of Pigs and the assassination attempts on Castro. "I'm tired of all these Latins attacking me for going after Castro," he griped to Goodwin. "The fact is that I'm the guy who saved his life." Kennedy was still in the dark about the CIA's ongoing efforts to kill the Cuban leader, which continued even then, long after he and his brother thought they had put a stop to the plots.

At Concepción University in Chile, a hundred Communist students in the audience heckled him, spit on his face, and threw eggs at him. They missed, splattering his aides instead. "If these kids are going to be young revolutionaries," he told Seigenthaler as they emerged from the barrage, "they're going to have to improve their aim."

But everywhere else he went, the crowds exulted over Kennedy. Later, in the streets of Concepción, the throng of people who pressed around him grew so frenzied that he clambered on top of a police car and sang "The Battle Hymn of the Republic" to calm them. They threw flower petals at him in Linares, Chile, and he was given a standing ovation by a hundred thousand people at a soccer game in Rio. It was not simply his reform brand of Catholicism that connected Kennedy to the South American crowds, said Walinksy—it was more his Irishness. It had to do, he said, with "that whole history of the Kennedys and the Fitzgeralds . . . with that whole thing about what it was to come to this country Irish and to struggle your way up in Boston." It was a heritage that had kept the younger Kennedys "from being a bunch of stiff rich prigs," said Walinsky. "Understanding, really in your gut, something of what it was to have been poor and to have struggled up."

As he did later in South Africa, Kennedy came to see that he could profoundly shake up the South American societies he visited. "He really did conceive of this as a kind of international politics in which he was trying to bring about changes in policy inside those countries," Walinsky said. "You may think that's a great act of hubris, but indeed he had the potential to do it and to some degree he probably did."

But Kennedy knew that his power came from his brother's legacy, and he could only complete JFK's mission by embroiling himself in the growing political maelstrom back home. His brother's ghost was everywhere he went in South America, from the moment he landed in Lima to the end of the trip. Walking off the plane with Bobby in Lima—to ecstatic shouts of "Viva

Kennedy!"—Dick Goodwin dropped his luggage, overcome with the melancholy echoes of the past, when he had heard the same chant for another visiting Kennedy. The cheer was appropriate this time, thought Goodwin; after all, Bobby had the same name. "Yet it was not because of him that they were shouting; but because he was the blood heir to someone admired almost to the point of reverence."

In Brazil, on November 22, as he commemorated the third anniversary of his brother's death, Bobby had a mournful day. Tears came to his eyes as he placed a wreath at a JFK bust in the small farming town of Natal, and he openly wept in Salvador when young women at a center for unwed mothers sang "God Bless America." He told a group of shoeless kids at a community center named for JFK that his brother was very fond of children and, in a soft voice, he asked them to do a favor for the late president. "Stay in school, study hard, study as long as you can, then work for your city and Brazil."

If Bobby was haunted by the past, he was equally haunted by the future. He knew what awaited him as he faced the political crucible back home. Sitting in an outdoor café in Rio two days after the horrible anniversary, Kennedy was jolted from his seat by the explosive crackle of a backfiring car. Realizing it wasn't gunfire, he settled back in his chair, but there was no relief in his face. "Sooner or later," he told his companion. "Sooner or later."

Bobby and his advisors wanted to wait until 1972 to launch his inevitable campaign for the presidency, after Lyndon Johnson had served his final term and the way to the White House was clear. But, again, history would not wait for Robert Kennedy.

AROUND 4:30 P.M. ON February 6, 1967, a bitterly cold winter afternoon in Washington, Bobby Kennedy arrived at the White House for a meeting on the Vietnam War with President Johnson. Returning to the White House always filled Kennedy with a disorienting sense of melancholy. But this occasion would leave him feeling more agitated than somber. Kennedy had just come back from a European tour, during which he had met with French president Charles de Gaulle, a strong critic of the war, and the French diplomat in charge of Asian affairs, who passed along a significant peace feeler from Hanoi to Kennedy. If the Johnson administration would extend the bombing halt it had recently declared, Kennedy was told, the North Vietnamese government would be willing to negotiate with the United States. Kennedy was eager to communicate this message directly to Johnson and he arranged for the White House meeting as soon as he arrived back in Washington.

But Johnson was in no mood to hear about peace talks—particularly from an emissary like Kennedy. His political rival's global wanderings in pursuit of a separate U.S. foreign policy were bad enough. But sticking his nose into the Vietnam War—which by then had become the central agony of Lyndon Johnson's life—was more than the president could bear. Once again, Kennedy seemed to be running his own presidency, treating Johnson as if he were simply a squatter in the White House. LBJ remained silent as Kennedy presented Hanoi's message and his own suggestions for how Johnson could finally bring the war to a conclusion. The senator argued for a permanent end to U.S. bombing and an internationally monitored cease-fire accompanied by negotiations. But as soon as Kennedy finished speaking, Johnson erupted. "Well, I want you to know that I'm not going to adopt any single one of those suggestions because we're going to win the war, and you doves will all be dead in six months." It was a sharp slap in the face. Kennedy knew LBJ meant politically dead. But he was infuriated by his insulting tirade. "I don't have to take that from you," Kennedy hissed, getting to his feet. Back in his office, he told his aides, "You know, what I have just been through is just unbelievable. . . . Do you know what that fellow said? That marvelous human being who is the president of the United States?" He later reported to Jack Newfield that Johnson had been "very abusive. . . . He was shouting and seemed very unstable."

The flooded dam of mutual resentment and hostility that Robert Kennedy and Lyndon Johnson had struggled for years to contain—for their own political reasons—was about to explode. Long engaged in covert political war, the two men were now on the brink of taking their brawl into the streets. Their epic battle was fueled by countless personal and political grievances. But at its heart was the ageless hatred of two contenders for the same throne. The wrong man was sitting there, in Bobby's eyes. It was that simple. It should be Jack. And if not his brother, then it should be him. No one else could carry on the Kennedy legacy. Least of all, the braying Texan who had taken up residence in the White House. "When this fellow looks at me," Johnson complained about Bobby to John Connally, "he looks at me like he's going to look a hole through me, like I'm a spy or something."

In Bobby's eyes, Johnson had taken the Kennedy dream of hope and freedom that had briefly made the United States a beacon around the world and dragged it through the mud of the Dominican Republic and Vietnam. And in Johnson's view, RFK was an arrogant princeling whose diplomatic dabblings were giving aid and comfort to the enemy.

LBJ passed word to the press that Kennedy was little more than a Communist dupe who had allowed himself to be used in Hanoi's "psychological warfare offensive." And a week after their White House meeting, Johnson let the world know what he thought of Kennedy's peace initiative by renewing the rain of bombs on North Vietnam. Kennedy told his aide Peter Edelman "that Lyndon Johnson was so insane that he would literally prolong the war simply because Bobby Kennedy was against it."

After the acrimonious White House meeting, Kennedy was unleashed. He no longer saw any reason to soften his criticism of Johnson's Vietnam policies. Bobby began reaching out to antiwar movement leaders like Tom Hayden and Staughton Lynd (the academic who had authored one of the earliest magazine critiques of the lone gunman theory). Kennedy—who had recently read the two men's book on their trip to Hanoi, *The Other Side*— asked Jack Newfield, who had been encouraging him to speak with Hayden, to set up the meeting. To avoid the inevitable uproar from his pro-war critics, Kennedy asked the two men to slip quietly into his New York apartment on the early evening of February 13. It was a largely uneventful summit. At one point, Bobby, noticing a thick bank of smog rolling up the East River, jumped up to call Con Edison to complain about the pollution from the utility company's Fourteenth Street power plant. The men's discussion of the war was interrupted again when Lynd's young son spilled some Coke on the carpet. "Don't worry about that," Bobby—as always, tuned in to kids' feelings— told the boy. "It makes the rug grow better." It was the deeper feeling of the conversation, more than anything that was said, that later stayed with the three men.

Here was the most celebrated member of the U.S. Senate, a man with enormous political expectations on his shoulders, and he was meeting with two activists who not only belonged to the radical wing of the antiwar movement but had traveled to the enemy's capital. It was the kind of political risk that no other American politician with an eye on the White House would have dared. But it showed how unmoored Robert Kennedy had become from the weight of political tradition. As the country fractured over both the war and racial conflict, and as the certainties in his own life fell away, Kennedy was a man in open, breathtaking flux.

On March 2, 1967, Kennedy delivered a watershed speech about Vietnam on the floor of the Senate. All Washington had been anticipating his gunshot across Johnson's bow. That morning—after Bobby stayed up until 3 a.m. polishing the speech with Goodwin, Walinsky, and Mankiewicz—Ethel greeted him in the kitchen at Hickory Hill: "Hail, Caesar." Kennedy had crossed his Rubicon. He was now on his way into the lion's den on Capitol

Hill. The speech, which called for a bombing halt and negotiated settlement of the war, was full of beautiful Goodwin-Walinsky language. Though the war was a distant cannon and did not directly affect most Americans, Kennedy called upon his fellow citizens to imagine the horrors that were being visited on Vietnam in their name. War, he said, was "the vacant moment of amazed fear as a mother and child watch death by fire fall from an improbable machine sent by a country they barely comprehend." Who was America to play God in this way? Who were we "to play the role of an avenging angel pouring death and destruction" from above?

Walinsky himself thought the speech did not go far enough, that it failed to question "the basic premises of the war, or the administration's rationale." Edelman, the other young dove in Kennedy's office, called it "mushy." Still, it was enough to inflame Washington hawks. Richard Nixon said Kennedy's speech would have "the effect of prolonging the war by encouraging the enemy." Barry Goldwater charged that Kennedy was out of control. "This is another case of getting his foot in his mouth. And if he doesn't stop, he's going to have an orthopedic mouth."

Johnson was enraged by Kennedy's high-profile attack on his management of the war, charging that Bobby was proposing a "dishonorable settlement." Many in the senator's camp thought LBJ took revenge by leaking an explosive story to syndicated columnist Jack Anderson, one aimed directly at Bobby's most sensitive spot. On March 3, a day after Kennedy's Vietnam speech, Anderson wrote, "President Johnson is sitting on a political H-bomb, an unconfirmed report that Senator Robert Kennedy may have approved an assassination plot [against Fidel Castro] which then possibly backfired against his late brother." The syndicated story had so little foundation that the *Washington Post* and *New York Post* spiked it. But LBJ tried to turn it into a federal case by urging Attorney General Ramsey Clark to pursue an investigation and Dick Helms to make a full CIA report on the charges.

No amateur when it came to playing Washington hardball, Kennedy immediately moved to shut down the story. He requested a copy of the FBI memo on the 1962 Justice Department meeting when he was first informed by the CIA about the Mafia plots, to prove his reaction had been withering. And then he phoned Helms to ask him to lunch. There is no record of what the two men discussed at this March 4 meeting. But it can be safely assumed that it was not simply a pleasant discussion of old times. The two men had a barely restrained loathing for one another, and a tense understanding of some sort was certainly hammered out. What is known is that on May 10, when Helms presented the CIA's internal report on the Castro murder plots to Johnson in the White House, it did not pin the blame on Robert Kennedy.

LBJ knew that Bobby Kennedy was a formidable political adversary. Over the years, Kennedy had amassed a vast amount of information about Johnson's corrupt dealings. RFK was no doubt prepared to use this poison arsenal should their political battle ever escalate. This is what made Robert Kennedy such a rare and potent force in American politics—he was a man who could call on the higher instincts of our nature and he also knew how to fight with his bare knuckles.

This time, Kennedy and Johnson fought each other to a standstill. Two weeks after the Anderson column ran, Bobby delivered a curiously effusive speech about LBJ at a Democratic Party fund-raiser in New York, calling him "an outstanding president." And Johnson never again used the Cuba bombshell against Kennedy.

But as the months went by, it became clear that Kennedy and Johnson were headed for a final political showdown. As Bobby edged closer to challenging Johnson for the presidency, he understood that he must be prepared for one of the most brutal campaigns in American history.

It was an excruciating decision. Most of the old guard from the Kennedy administration—including Sorensen, Schlesinger, and Dutton—warned him not to enter the 1968 campaign, fearing he would tear apart the Democratic Party and ruin his long-term chances for the White House. The Washington press corps was hostile, interpreting his growing opposition to the war as a personal vendetta against Johnson. By running, Kennedy would not only be breaking sharply from tradition by challenging a sitting president in his own political party. He would finally and irrevocably be turning his back on his brother's administration, since the key policymakers behind the war were holdovers from the Kennedy years—McNamara, Bundy, Rusk, Rostow. But entering the race was also the only way to redeem his brother's legacy, by showing the country—and the world—that Johnson's disastrous Cold War policies were a violation of his brother's ideals.

Bobby was trapped in the swirling political passions around the war, torn at from both sides. His young aides and antiwar leaders beseeched him to take on Johnson, telling him the fate of the nation was in his hands. But still he hesitated. He knew that if he ran, he risked everything.

Through all his agonizing over Johnson and the war, there was one high administration official to whom Kennedy remained close—Bob McNamara. It was a relationship that utterly baffled the young firebrands on his staff like Walinsky, who was filled with contempt for the leading intellectual architect of the war, a man the young Kennedy aide felt had sacrificed his conscience in the name of bureaucratic loyalty. As the war steadily escalated and Johnson kept promising there was a light at the end of the tunnel, McNamara grew quietly disenchanted. But he kept sending more troops and expanding the bombing campaign.

Even in McNamara's final hours in office—as LBJ prepared to shuffle the increasingly tormented defense chief out of the Pentagon to the World Bank—Kennedy held out the hope that he would reject Johnson's consolation prize and finally break with the president in public over the war. Kennedy knew it would make a major impact on the political establishment if Robert McNamara joined him in opposing the war. Kennedy met with McNamara after his departure from the administration was announced, and Edelman thought his boss even urged the once mighty defense czar to run with him on an antiwar presidential ticket.

But instead, McNamara—ever the company man—went along with what Johnson asked of him, exchanging one powerful Washington post for another. At his farewell press conference, choking back tears, he came to Johnson's defense. "Many in this room believe Lyndon Johnson is crude, mean, vindictive, scheming, untruthful. Perhaps at times he has shown each of these characteristics. But he is much, much more."

Walinksy was disgusted. "I mean, the country's falling apart over a war that he's pretty much started and has been running all this time—and then all of a sudden, he just walks away from it, without saying another word. Excuse me?" In response, Walinsky wrote a scathing analysis of the Johnson-McNamara relationship, which he suggested had perverse master-slave tones. Titled "Caesar's Meat," the essay was avidly circulated within the Kennedy circle, where Ethel was among those who praised its insights. McNamara had a choice, wrote Walinsky. "In a dozen ways, he could have preserved his dignity and his freedom; not just the freedom to speak out on the war, now or later, not just the freedom to join Robert Kennedy if that would be his choice: but his freedom as a man, freedom from manipulation, freedom from the domination of a meaner and pettier man. Instead he chose submission."

By crushing McNamara's spirit, Walinsky continued, LBJ was sending a message to Kennedy: "You think to challenge me. Then watch carefully what I am about to do. I will take this man—with all he means, all he is, all his power and ability and character—I will take this man and break him into nothing. I will reach in and tear out his spine, and he will say 'thank you, sir.'"

Kennedy himself would not hear any criticism of McNamara. When a young speechwriter named Phil Mandelkorn who had just joined the senator's staff dashed off a memo to Kennedy counseling him to distance himself from McNamara "because history was going to show he is to blame for killing an awful lot of people," he was promptly told that Kennedy and McNamara were friends and that the senator did not need his unsolicited advice. The staffer who conveyed this message to Mandelkorn—Walinsky—had certainly been told the same thing.

To Bobby, McNamara still carried the aura of those years with Jack. For him, the defense secretary would always be the imposing intellect who stood up to the generals, the man who took the Kennedy brothers' side during the Cuban Missile Crisis and helped keep a world that was spinning towards oblivion in the safe grasp of their humane logic. After Jack was gone, Bobby wrote McNamara a letter: "Dear Bob, I just want you to know that I don't want to be in Washington when you are no longer Secretary of Defense or something even higher than that. You are the one that makes the difference for all of us." Though he knew how poisoned the Johnson-Kennedy relationship was, McNamara continued to socialize with Bobby and his family and shared with him his growing doubts about Vietnam.

But now Bobby was on his own. The former defense chief would not risk his prestige by joining Kennedy's insurgent campaign. Nonetheless, McNamara would make a lesser gesture on Kennedy's behalf. Late in Bobby's campaign, shortly before it came to its violent end, McNamara agreed to appear in a TV endorsement for Kennedy. In the spot, the former defense secretary offered praise for RFK's cool-headed performance during the Cuban Missile Crisis. "I wasn't stupid," McNamara told me, recalling his decision to help Kennedy. "I knew that it would be taken as a political violation of my position at the World Bank. And in fact I later got all kinds of hell at the bank for doing it—there were calls for my resignation and so on. But I went ahead and did it. And thank God I did. It was filmed in early May 1968. And of course he was killed shortly after that. I would have felt awful if I hadn't done it."

HE STOOD IN THE ornate, chandeliered caucus room of the Old Senate Office Building on Saturday morning, March 16, 1968—the same room where his brother had announced his quest for the American presidency eight years before. "I do not lightly dismiss the dangers and difficulties of challenging an incumbent president," declared Robert Kennedy, flanked by the familiar faces of past campaigns. "But these are not ordinary times and this is not an ordinary election. At stake is not simply the leadership of our party and even our country. It is our right to moral leadership of this planet."

And so began one of the most terrible and most beautiful journeys in American political history—the passion of Robert Kennedy. He saw his race for the presidency in missionary terms; he thought America's salvation hung in the balance. But there was almost a weary resignation in his decision to finally join the epic battle.

It was the Tet offensive at the end of January 1968 and Senator Eugene McCarthy's near upset of President Johnson in the New Hampshire primary on March 12 that finally forced Kennedy into the race. The sweeping Viet Cong assault on American strongholds, timed for the country's lunar new year, dramatically exposed the Johnson administration's empty promises of imminent victory. And McCarthy's surprisingly strong showing in the first Democratic primary exposed the president's political weakness. With the Johnson White House unalterably wedded to its disastrous course in Vietnam, and another Democratic dissident threatening to steal his antiwar base, Kennedy could no longer sit on the sidelines.

There was no euphoria around RFK's announcement. He was entering the race late, and by the time he got in, McCarthy had already captured much of the rebellious energy in the party with his youth-driven "children's crusade" against Johnson. The McCarthy camp bitterly resented the sudden intrusion of their more glamorous rival. The pro-Johnson Democratic Party establishment was also unnerved and enraged by Kennedy's entry. And the political pundits were deeply skeptical of his motives. As he announced his daunting bid for the highest office, Robert Kennedy seemed more isolated than ever. Even some key Kennedy loyalists, like Dick Goodwin, were missing, after joining the McCarthy campaign in frustration while Bobby had dithered.

And then there was the awful air of danger that hung over his announcement. Kennedy's 1968 presidential bid was not only politically risky, it was physically perilous. Kennedy knew how many lethal enemies he had, he knew that the men who had plotted his brother's murder were still at large. He was surprised, after Dallas, by the fact they hadn't killed him instead of Jack. Since then, he had been the target of numerous death threats.

A few days after RFK's announcement, Jackie Kennedy took Arthur Schlesinger aside at a party in New York. "Do you know what I think will happen to Bobby? The same thing that happened to Jack." In fact, she pointed out, Bobby aroused more hatred among his enemies than Jack did. "I've told Bobby this," she said, but he had brushed aside her fears.

After watching Kennedy's announcement speech on a hotel room TV in Portland, Oregon, where he was campaigning for the Republican nomination, Richard Nixon turned off the set and then stared at the blank screen for a long time. Finally he spoke, shaking his head. "We've just seen some very terrible forces unleashed," Nixon told the four or five aides in the room. "Something bad is going to come of this." He gestured toward the screen. "God knows where this is going to lead."

At a meeting of FBI officials that was held as Kennedy's campaign got off the ground, Clyde Tolson—Hoover's longtime intimate and assistant— shocked the group by spitting out his hatred for Bobby. "I hope that someone shoots and kills the son of a bitch."

Kennedy sensed the danger, but he plunged forward with his campaign, unshielded from the crowds' manic energy and whatever else was coiled and ready to greet him. "Living every day is like Russian roulette," he told New-field. He had taken to heart an Emerson maxim, copying it down in his notebook and underlining it: "Do what you are afraid to do."

Though the political establishment was deeply wary of Kennedy, the crowds that poured into the streets and packed auditoriums to see him as he took his campaign through the Midwest, and out to the West Coast that spring, were frantic in their need to touch him. It was more like religious ecstasy than political celebration. They clawed at him, they tore at his hair and clothes, they even pulled his shoes from his feet. After years of death, of riots and war, they wanted to hope again.

JFK, with his body always tightened against pain, had flinched from the physical hurly burly of campaigning. He did not like to be grabbed and em-braced. But Bobby exulted in it. His pain was of a different sort. And it found release in the crush of the crowd. He wore the scratch marks, the split lips, the shredded shirtsleeves like a holy scourge. As he waded into the scream-ing, shoving melees that inevitably greeted him—into this wounded heart of American democracy—Kennedy sometimes had a stricken look on his face. But he never held himself back from the crowds. He knew that this torrent of popular energy swirling around him was the only force that could over-come the political machinery stacked against him.

His aides were sick with fear about the physical risks he was taking. One day in suburban Sacramento, Kennedy climbed on a ladder inside a shop-ping mall to address a sprawling, boisterous crowd. His speeches were never stemwinders in the old Boston fashion; they were more halting and reflec-tive. But he knew how to touch emotional chords with his audiences, and that day he touched the hearts of the rambunctious crowd by evoking the personal tragedies of the war. "Which of these brave young men dying in the rice paddies of Vietnam might have written a symphony," he said in a quiet voice. "Which of them might have written a beautiful poem or might have cured cancer? Which of them might have played in the World Series or given us the gift of laughter from a stage, or helped build a bridge or a university? Which of them might have taught a small child to read? It is our responsibility to let those men live."

The eloquent speech elicited a long, sustained wave of applause. But afterward, as Kennedy made his way toward the shopping mall exit, the crowd "suddenly became a live and dangerous thing," in the words of a reporter who was there. Navigating his way through the surging mass of people, Kennedy had to reach down to rescue children who had been toppled to the ground. When he finally made it back to his open convertible and climbed on the trunk, he was almost yanked off the car. Kennedy bodyguard Bill Barry, a former college football star and FBI agent, fell to his knees and locked his strong arms around Bobby's waist to keep him from being swallowed by the crowd.

Barry was the only protection Kennedy had that day, as he was during most of Bobby's tumultuous campaign. "I loved him intensely as a human being, and for his qualities," Barry later said. "I wanted him to be president of the United States for the sake of my children and generations to come. It was not just a professional job with me. It was something my life qualified me for. This would be my juggler's gift." The candidate had made it clear to his staff that there were to be no cordons of guards around him, no barriers between him and the crowds. Poor Barry was Kennedy's only full-time security person. It was a terrible responsibility to put on one man. And it would haunt Barry for the rest of his life.

Kennedy's closest political confidants told him that Bill Barry was not enough—he needed more protection. Ed Guthman, as usual, was one of them. Taking a break from the *Los Angeles Times*, he went out to Indiana to observe the primary campaign there for a couple of days. "I was amazed at what I saw, no security at all," Guthman told me. "I called Bob up and he said, 'Let's go for a walk.' Well, I knew what that meant. The next morning, we got up at 6 a.m. and went for a walk in some field behind the motel where they all were staying. And I told him, 'I was watching last night, Bob—you didn't have a lot of protection.' And he said, 'Aw, I don't want a lot of cops around.' I told him, 'Look, let's put aside the fact that you have a wife and ten kids, with an eleventh on the way—you're very important to this country.' But he wouldn't do anything."

In early April 1968, the Kennedy campaign headed for a series of major rallies in Indianapolis to build momentum for the important Indiana primary election. As a Kennedy advance man made preparations for Bobby's upcoming appearances in the city, federal documents later revealed, he was being spied on by the FBI. On April 3, the FBI official in charge of the local office noted ominously in a memo that "the Kennedy rallies scheduled for April 4 in Indianapolis might be subject to some violence simply to embarrass Senator Kennedy." The heavily blacked out document—which was obtained by scholar Joseph A. Palermo under the Freedom of Information Act—suggests that the Kennedy campaign was being targeted by the same well-documented FBI dirty tactics that were being used against Martin Luther King's organization and other activist groups.

But it was a far greater calamity that disrupted Kennedy's campaign plans in Indianapolis. As his plane landed in the city that evening, the candidate was informed that the Reverend King had died, after being shot through the jaw by a sniper while the civil rights leader was standing on a motel balcony in Memphis. King had gone to Memphis to lead a march of striking black garbage workers, part of his growing campaign to link the race problem with the issue of economic exploitation.

When Kennedy got the news, he was headed for one of the poorest black neighborhoods in Indianapolis, where he was to formally open the state's Kennedy for President headquarters at an outdoor rally. The chief of police warned him not to go into the ghetto. Fiery riots sparked by King's murder were already spreading across the country, including in the nation's capital, where flames lit up the sky just blocks from the Capitol building. But Kennedy insisted on going ahead with his appearance. When he arrived at his destination, it was dark and cold. He made his way through the crowd and climbed onto a flatbed truck illuminated by floodlights that cast a flickering, funereal glow in the blustery wind. It was Kennedy who brought the people the terrible news that night—the crowd expelled a loud moan as if punched in the gut. And it was he who consoled them. He was the only white leader in America they would have allowed to do it.

There was no speech making that night—when an aide rushed up to him beforehand with a sheet of talking points, Kennedy crumpled the notes and stuffed them in his pocket. He talked to them from his heart, softly and slowly, like he was comforting them in their living room after giving them news of a loved one's death. And they listened quietly in the evening gloom because, as he reminded them, he too had suffered the death of a loved one.

"For those of you who are black and tempted to be filled with hatred and distrust at the injustice of such an act, against all white people, I can only say that I feel in my own heart the same kind of feeling. I had a member of my family killed, but he was killed by a white man. But we have to make an effort to understand, to go beyond these rather difficult times." It was the first time Kennedy had ever invoked the death of his brother in a public speech in the United States. And then he shared with the crowd how he had learned to bear what was unbearable. Quoting the Aeschylus passage he knew by heart, he reminded them what they already knew, that only time would turn their misery into something higher: "In our sleep, pain which cannot forget falls drop by drop upon the heart until, in our own despair, against our will, comes wisdom through the awful grace of God." Finally, he urged them not to lash back in anger, but to honor King's message of peace. "What we need in the United States is not division; what we need in the United States is not hatred; what we need is not violence or lawlessness; but love and wisdom, and compassion toward one another, and a feeling of justice toward those who still suffer within our country, whether they be white or they be black."

Unlike many other U.S. cities, Indianapolis was not set on fire that night. The crowd listened to him because they knew it was not just more words, that Bobby would continue King's crusade.

But Kennedy himself knew how impossible his task was, how torn and bleeding the country was. One night after King's death, Bobby dropped by the Los Angeles home of Pierre Salinger, high atop Coldwater Canyon. At one point during the evening, Salinger's sixteen-year-old son Stephen found himself alone with Kennedy, and the teenager put one of his favorite songs on the living room stereo to play for Bobby. The song was Simon and Garfunkel's "7 O'Clock News/Silent Night," a bitter juxtaposition of jarring news headlines backed by the soothing strains of the Christmas carol. While a radio announcer briskly reports a grim barrage of news—Vietnam, civil rights battles, mass murders, celebrity drug overdoses—the duo sweetly sing that "all is calm, all is bright." As the song played in the Salinger living room, Kennedy stared silently out the picture window at the twinkling lights in the San Fernando Valley below. "After it was over, Bobby turned around," said the younger Salinger, recalling the moment many years later. "And his eyes were filled with tears. He didn't say anything."

"WE WANT TO KNOW who killed President Kennedy!" a young woman in the crowd screamed. Other students picked up her cry, yelling, "Open the archives!" Bobby tried to ignore them at first, but finally he relented. "Your manners overwhelm me," he quipped irritably. "Go ahead, ask your question."

It was March 25, 1968, a blazing hot afternoon on the campus of San Fernando Valley State College in Northridge, California. Kennedy had just delivered a campaign speech to a tumultuous crowd of twelve thousand people, who jammed the campus and stood on rooftops to hear him. But afterwards, during the question period, he was finally confronted with the tormenting query that he knew would inevitably arise after he got into the race. If elected president, would he reopen the investigation into his brother's murder?

For years he had routinely endorsed the Warren Report in public, while pursuing his own investigative path in private. But Kennedy hated the rampant lying in political life—seeing LBJ as one of the worst perpetrators—and the growing "credibility gap" between those in power and the public. By the 1968 race, he was clearly finding it more difficult to keep misleading the public about his true opinion of the Warren investigation. And yet he fully realized how explosive the reaction would be if the headlines suddenly blared, "Kennedy Rejects Warren Report." Not only would it turn the assassination into the leading campaign issue—instead of Vietnam or the country's growing social divisions—but it might put Kennedy in more danger on the campaign trail. The assassination question was a growing dilemma for Kennedy that promised to ensnarl his campaign more and more as the race progressed.

When he was suddenly confronted with this conundrum by the student hecklers on the San Fernando Valley State campus, Kennedy seemed ready for it, and his reply was subtly—and intriguingly—different from his standard response in the past. In effect, he split the difference, once again endorsing the Warren Report (although more haltingly this time), while at the same time leaving the door open for reopening the case. Rick Tuttle, a young campaign coordinator seated right behind the candidate that day, later recalled Kennedy's manner as he responded to the emotionally and politically charged question: "I remember there was a slight trembling of the hands, which happened every so often when Kennedy spoke, there was a slight tensing. But I also remember saying to myself, 'He was prepared for that question.' I remember he handled it well. Don't forget—at this point, we're past the mourning period and he is running for president and he had entered that world. He was prepared to handle it. It was not one of those times when he stammered badly or fell apart or got mournful."

This is precisely what Kennedy said that day, as recorded by a radio reporter for Los Angeles station KLAC: "You wanted to ask me something about the archives. I'm sure, as I've said before, the archives will be open."

The crowd responded to this by cheering and applauding. "Can I just say," continued Kennedy, "and I have answered this question before, but there is no one who would be more interested in all of these matters as to who was responsible for uh . . . the uh, uh, the death of President Kennedy than I would. I have seen all of the matters in the archives. If I became president of the United States, I would not, I would not, reopen the, uh, Warren Commission Report. I think I, uh, stand by the Warren Commission Report. I've seen everything in the archives, the archives will be available at the appropriate time." At this, the crowd again broke into loud cheers.

Kennedy's statement was a careful tightrope walk. So cagily constructed was his reply that some assassination researchers later concluded it was simply another example of Kennedy's perplexing refusal to push for a new investigation. But that's not how Kennedy's reply was heard that afternoon by the students. They were moved to cheer because Kennedy agreed that the government's assassination archives should be opened—and opening the archives meant reopening the investigation. When they heard Kennedy pledge that the government's investigative evidence "will be made available at the appropriate time," to them this clearly meant when Bobby became president.

The students who cheered Kennedy were not the only ones who interpreted his answer this way. So did his press secretary Frank Mankiewicz, a man who closely monitored everything the candidate said in public and who had been asked by Kennedy to accumulate assassination information for a future investigation. In short, Mankiewicz was the ideal person to accurately read the nuances in Kennedy's reply—and to realize the significance of what Kennedy was saying. There was no doubt in Mankiewicz's mind: Kennedy was calling for his brother's assassination to be reopened one day. "I remember that I was stunned by the answer," recalled Mankiewicz. "It was either like he was suddenly blurting out the truth, or it was a way to shut down any further questioning. You know, 'Yes, I will reopen the case. Now let's move on.'"

The following month, Kennedy again spoke revealingly about his future investigation plans, this time with a small group of campaign aides in his room at San Francisco's Fairmont Hotel. It was late in the evening on April 19, and Kennedy had just returned from a raucous appearance at the University of San Francisco, where a small group of antiwar radicals had charged at him, trying to hit him as he got out of his limousine. When he tried to deliver his speech, they shouted him down, screaming "Victory for the Viet Cong" and calling him a "fascist pig." Decompressing in his hotel room later,

Kennedy was in a particularly voluble mood, wanting to talk about the chaotic state of the nation and his plans to restore the country's sanity if he reached the White House. Emboldened by Kennedy's expansive mood, one of his aides mustered the courage to ask him about his brother's assassination. Richard Lubic, a campaign media consultant who was in the room, later made notes on what Kennedy replied: "Subject to me getting elected, I would like to reopen the Warren Commission."

BY THE TIME HIS campaign reached the pivotal California primary, Bobby Kennedy was beginning to wrestle with a variety of formidable problems that he knew would confront him as president. One of them was the CIA. What was he going to do with it, he wondered out loud one day on the campaign plane with Pete Hamill, one of the journalists who grew so close to Kennedy that he briefly wrote speeches for him. "I have to decide whether to eliminate the operations arm of the agency or what the hell to do with it," Kennedy told Hamill. "We can't have these cowboys wandering around and shooting people and doing all these unauthorized things."

Fred Dutton, the political veteran who served as Kennedy's informal campaign manager, later confirmed that the candidate was starting to confront the CIA problem. Kennedy thought the agency "was out of control," said Dutton. "The CIA would come up in discussions" during the race, said the Kennedy advisor—"just his disgruntlement over it." But the agency's abuses never became a campaign issue. "My reaction at the time was let's win the campaign and we'll worry about that problem later," Dutton said.

Kennedy's epic battle for the presidency was all coming down to California. He had won his first primary contests, in Indiana and Nebraska, but his campaign was far from the "well-oiled machine" that Richard Reeves had declared it in the *New York Times* magazine. It rumbled along with a rickety, improvised organizational structure and a spontaneous energy. There was no strong hand running it, as there was in JFK's 1960 race. "Bobby did not have a Bobby," said Edelman.

The campaign's weaknesses were glaringly exposed on May 28 when Kennedy lost the Oregon primary to McCarthy—the first electoral defeat ever suffered by a Kennedy. If he lost California the following week, Kennedy's campaign would likely be finished.

Kennedy was fighting a tough, two-front war, battling not just the rival peace candidate but the party establishment's choice, bland and genial Hubert Humphrey, whose front-runner status was ensured by the backroom process of selecting candidates that was still in operation in 1968. Humphrey, LBJ's vice president, had entered the race, in effect, as Johnson's pro-war surrogate. Johnson had stunned the nation on March 31 by announcing he would not run for the presidency. The wounded leader could not bring himself to risk defeat at the hands of his longtime enemy. But the Johnson-Kennedy rivalry continued as a shadow play with Humphrey's entry in the race. Though he had promised to stay neutral in the Democratic contest, LBJ worked closely with Humphrey behind the scenes to thwart Kennedy whenever he could. Loath to test his popular appeal against that of Kennedy by entering the primary races, Humphrey quietly used the party machinery to amass delegates while stand-ins took his place on the state ballots. (In California, the Humphrey place-holder was the state attorney general, Tom Lynch.)

Meanwhile, McCarthy fought bitterly on. Despite his victory in Oregon—where the white suburban population responded to the former professor's cerebral charm—even McCarthy, a quirky and diffident campaigner, knew his chances of winning the nomination were remote. Instead, he seemed increasingly intent on spoiling Kennedy's chances. McCarthy never let go of his resentment of Kennedy for entering the race, after he had taken the initial risk of challenging Johnson.

As the California campaign heated up, the Humphrey and McCarthy campaigns seemed to be collaborating to drive Kennedy out of the race. The ties between the two campaigns began to grow when a former CIA official named Thomas Finney, who was close to Humphrey, took over as McCarthy's new campaign manger in the final weeks of the Oregon campaign. Finney's sudden emergence as McCarthy's campaign boss—and reports that Humphrey partisans had funneled $50,000 to McCarthy—drove some of the peace candidate's staff to resign in protest. It is possible that the CIA and the Democratic Party establishment were working to split the peace vote to hand the nomination to Humphrey. But McCarthy himself was surprisingly popular in CIA circles, where Kennedy was reviled and there was growing disaffection with the war, which some intelligence officials believed was damaging the country's national security interests. Dick Helms—who advised President Johnson in a secret 1967 memo that the CIA believed he could withdraw from Vietnam without any permanent damage to the United States—was one of the McCarthy sympathizers in the agency's upper ranks. Over the years, Helms wrote in his memoir, he and the Minnesota senator "lunched occasionally and encountered one another at the usual Washington events, or as guests in owner Jack Kent Cooke's box at Redskin football games. McCarthy was always good company, intelligent and witty."

Reeling from his Oregon loss and ganged up on in California by his two Democratic rivals, Kennedy was facing political disaster. If his campaign crashed on the West Coast, not only would it be a personal humiliation for Bobby but the end of his national crusade to revive the Kennedy dream. But California was not Oregon. It was densely populated with the white blue-collar workers and the black and Hispanic voters who were his base. It was also a media-saturated state that thrilled to his starry aura. And in the weeks leading up to the June 4 California primary, Kennedy's supporters roared to life. As he trekked up and down the nation-sized state, putting in seventeen-hour days, Kennedy was swarmed by screaming mobs. In the overgrown Central Valley farm town of Fresno, the crowd toppled the barriers at the airport as he got off his plane and engulfed him. "I touched him. I touched him!" shrieked one girl. "I won't wash this hand for a week!"

His motorcades through the streets of California were pageants of ec-static democracy. By the time his campaign convertible had completed its slow, meandering journey through the shouting swarms, Kennedy's shirt would be hanging out and matted to his back with sweat, his forearms would be scratched and bleeding, and his cufflinks and PT-109 tie clip long gone. But the candidate's spirit would be rejuvenated.

In the black neighborhoods of South Central Los Angeles, teenagers ran alongside his car, lunging for his outstretched hands as Bill Barry crouched beside him, holding onto Bobby's slight frame with all his might. Women came running out of their homes and beauty parlors in curlers, men came running out of bars—they all wanted to see him, shout out to him, touch him. Reporters riding with the candidate stared with stunned disbelief at the explosive energy he unleashed. "These are my people," said Kennedy. It was the race of his life and Kennedy was pouring his very soul into it. And the people in the streets responded with a fervor that was like a wild hunger.

Kennedy was greeted with the same frenzied celebration in Latino neigh-borhoods, where crowds shouted, "Viva Bobby!" and mariachi bands sere-naded him with brassy versions of Woody Guthrie's populist anthem, "This Land is Your Land." The state's large Mexican-American vote was mobilized by the United Farm Workers union, whose charismatic leader, César Chávez, had been devoted to Kennedy ever since the senator took up the UFW cause. In 1966 Kennedy held hearings in California on behalf of the union, whose nonviolent Catholic leadership and bitter struggle with the state's agribusi-ness industry deeply appealed to the senator's sense of justice. The senator hauled union-busting local sheriffs before his panel—the kind of redneck lawmen who had been harassing California farm workers since the *The*

Grapes of Wrath era—and subjected them to the same grilling that gangsters once suffered at Kennedy's hands, acidly suggesting that they read the U.S. Constitution before they illegally arrested any more UFW members.

Most of the labor movement was under the control of pro-war union leaders who were solidly behind Humphrey. But UFW members fanned out all over the state to campaign for Bobby, including Chávez himself, who—still debilitated from a long hunger strike to protest farm workers' conditions—pushed himself so hard on Kennedy's behalf that he was bedridden for the following year. The union's all-out drive would prove critical for Kennedy. "It was," said Chávez, "a product of respect, admiration [and] love." Kennedy had come to the farm workers' aid when they needed it most—now they were doing the same for him.

By the final days of the campaign, Kennedy was so drained that he seemed to be sleepwalking through his events. On a plane ride to Los Angeles, the candidate grabbed Jack Newfield as he walked down the aisle with a Bloody Mary in his hand and steered him into the empty seat next to him. He wanted to talk about Bob Dylan, whose music Newfield had been urgently recommending to him. Kennedy had a hard time listening to Dylan's voice, which he found whining. But after hearing Bobby Darin, whose vocal style was more to this taste, sing "Blowin' in the Wind" at a campaign rally, he was suddenly intrigued by the songwriter. "Do you think you could introduce me to Dylan?" he asked Newfield. Talking with him up close on the plane, the reporter was taken aback by Kennedy's haggard appearance: "His face looked like an old man's; there were lines I had never noticed before. The eyes were puffy and red and pushed back into his sockets. His hands shook, as they often did when he was speaking in public."

June 3, the last day of the race, was the most punishing of all, a twelve-hour marathon that took Kennedy from Los Angeles to San Francisco to Long Beach, through Watts, then to San Diego for a late-night rally and finally back to Los Angeles. In San Francisco, he rode through Chinatown as always, in an open car so the people could see him. "He felt he had to ride in a convertible because his brother had been killed in a convertible," Newfield observed. When a string of Chinese firecrackers suddenly shattered the air, violent as gunfire, Ethel—pregnant with their final child—collapsed into a protective fetal crouch on the car seat, visibly trembling. "I was walking alongside the car," remembered John Seigenthaler, who had taken a leave from the *Nashville Tennessean* to help his old friend's campaign. "I saw the sheer terror in Ethel's eyes. It scared the hell out of me too." But Bobby kept standing and waving, refusing to show any fear.

By the time they reached Long Beach, Kennedy was groggy with fatigue, stumbling almost incoherently through his speech. When he got back to the car, Fred Dutton stated the obvious: "You had a little trouble with some words that time." Kennedy confessed that he did not feel well, something he would have normally hidden from his staff.

The final event of his long day's journey was a rally at the El Cortez Hotel in San Diego. The crowd was so massive that it had to be divided in half and Kennedy was forced to deliver two back-to-back speeches. After the first one, he walked offstage and collapsed into a chair, burying his face in his hands. Bill Barry and Rafer Johnson, the former Olympic athlete who had begun to help out as a volunteer bodyguard, eased the ailing Bobby to a men's room. He didn't vomit, he later insisted to Dutton, he was just dizzy for a few minutes. "I just ran out of gas," he said. But he gathered himself one more time to return to the stage and deliver his last speech of the campaign. And then it was over. Robert Kennedy's political fate was in the hands of the California people.

ON ELECTION DAY, KENNEDY recuperated at the Malibu beach house of John Frankenheimer with Ethel and six of their children. The director's Cold War movies, *The Manchurian Candidate* and *Seven Days in May*, had been embraced by JFK as warning messages against totalitarian impulses in Washington. And when Bobby jumped into the presidential race, Frankenheimer volunteered to direct his TV ads, trying to capture the electricity of the campaign by following the candidate around with his camera. The two men grew close on the campaign trail, and Frankenheimer even got Bobby to talk about his suspicions about Dallas. But when the director gingerly touched on one aspect of the case—Joe Kennedy's ties to organized crime and how the Mafia might have felt betrayed by the family—Bobby made it clear that area was off-limits. Frankenheimer was sensitive enough to drop the subject, and Kennedy felt sufficiently comfortable with the director to accept his invitation to use his beach house as a retreat from the campaign's tumult.

Nine days before Election Day, Kennedy had been relaxing on a Sunday afternoon at Frankenheimer's house with a group of his supporters from the entertainment world, including Warren Beatty, Shirley MacLaine, Burt Bacharach, Angie Dickinson, and actress Jean Seberg. While talking with Kennedy, Seberg's husband, French novelist Romain Gary, suddenly said out loud what everyone found too terrible to mention: "You know, don't you, that somebody's going to try to kill you?" The room fell deathly silent. But Kennedy, sitting cross-legged in his swim trunks on the floor, simply stared into a glass of orange juice that he was swirling in his hand and answered, "That's the chance I have to take."

Then, taking the same blunt Gallic approach, he challenged Gary: "Take De Gaulle. How many attempts on his life has he survived, exactly?"

Gary shrugged. "Six or seven, I think."

"I told you," said Bobby, with a soft chuckle, "you can't make it without that good old bitch, luck."

There was more drama at the Frankenheimer house on Election Day. As Kennedy and his kids romped in the surf, his twelve-year-old son David was suddenly caught in a strong undertow and Kennedy had to dive in to rescue him. The candidate came back to shore with a red bruise on his forehead that Frankenheimer covered with theatrical makeup, in preparation for the big evening that awaited him.

The rest of the day was less stressful, and the exhausted Bobby napped in the bright sun, stretched limply over two chairs by the pool. Coming upon his lifeless form, Dick Goodwin flinched, before realizing he was only sleeping. "God," thought Goodwin, who had returned to the Kennedy fold, "I suppose none of us will ever get over John Kennedy."

Later, Frankenheimer offered to drive Kennedy to his election night headquarters at the Ambassador, the grand old hotel in downtown Los Angeles, packing the candidate and Dutton into his Rolls-Royce and tearing off down the Pacific Coast Highway. The director had taken race car driving lessons from Carroll Shelby and was eager to show off his high-speed skills to the candidate. But Kennedy kept telling Frankenheimer to slow down, they would live longer.

As the polls closed at 8 p.m. and it began to become clear that the massive pro-Kennedy vote in Los Angeles would inevitably put RFK over the top, the uproar in the hotel's Embassy Ballroom—thronged by young men in Kennedy straw hats and young women in white blouses, blue skirts, and red Kennedy sashes—grew deafening. Upstairs in his suite, Kennedy finally started to relax, smiling and joking with his staff and taking congratulatory phone calls from friends and key Democratic figures around the country. The most important call came from Chicago mayor Dick Daley, the powerful kingmaker whom Kennedy had pronounced "the ball game" when he got into the race. Daley, who had long ties to the Kennedy family and had grown disenchanted with the war, favored Bobby from the start. But he needed to see Kennedy build popular momentum in the primaries before he was willing to throw his considerable clout behind him. Now Daley was calling to make it official. The man who would be running the Democratic convention in Chicago was on his side. Salinger was sitting next to Kennedy while he spoke with Daley. As the phone call ended, he remembered, "Bobby and I exchanged a look that we both knew meant only one thing—he had the nomination."

Salinger's euphoria was probably premature—there was a lot more campaigning and political maneuvering before Kennedy could finally claim the nomination. But with victory in California assured, Kennedy clearly had the look of a winner. He also looked, for the first time in his political life, like his own man. Kenny O'Donnell, who was planning to fly to California the next morning to join his old comrade's campaign, later said, "He had arrived. He had won the biggest state in the Union—not as Jack Kennedy's brother, not as Bobby Kennedy, but as Robert Kennedy." Observing the candidate in his increasingly boisterous hotel suite, Newfield jotted down the word "liberated" in his notebook. "That's how Kennedy seemed to be that last night."

Late in the evening, Kennedy began to let his imagination roam. He sat on the floor, smoking a thin cigar with Newfield, Hamill, and his friend, screenwriter Budd Schulberg, and began to dream out loud about the kinds of new programs he envisioned for the country. He asked Schulberg about the Watts Writers Workshop that he had started for promising young blacks. "He was saying, 'I'm going to replicate that all over the country, we'll make a federal writers workshop program,'" recalled Newfield.

And then it was time to go downstairs and declare victory. At quarter to midnight, he rode down the service elevator and walked through the kitchen, shaking hands with the workers. The ballroom was hot and blindingly bright as he entered, overheated by the TV lights and the densely packed bodies of his screaming supporters. On the platform, Kennedy kept his speech short and upbeat, knowing how sweltering the room was becoming. The film footage of his beaming face and loose, wisecracking demeanor is still too awful to bear for those who watched his victory speech that night and are forever tormented by what came next. "Mayor Yorty has just sent me a message that we've been here too long already." He smiled, tweaking the conservative Los Angeles mayor, whom he had turned into a running campaign gag. "So my thanks to all of you, and now it's on to Chicago and let's win there." Those were his parting words to his supporters. Then he flashed a V for victory sign—which in those days was also a peace sign—and brushed his forelock off his brow one more time, and he was gone.

The moments afterwards are a flash of searing images now iconic in American history. After conferring with Bill Barry, Dutton had decided that Kennedy should exit the back way, instead of wading into the ballroom crowd, which, he later said, was "rather unruly. Some people in the crowd had too much to drink." Stepping down from the stage, Kennedy made his way back toward the hotel kitchen, the quickest way to a press room where print reporters were waiting for the candidate. In the crush of people—who were loudly chanting, "We want Bobby! We want Bobby!"—Kennedy became separated from Barry and Dutton. As he headed toward the kitchen—led by the hotel's assistant maître d', Karl Uecker—the candidate was about to violate several fundamental security rules, a rueful Joe Dolan said years later, as if he still wanted to grab Kennedy by the shoulders and make him stop. "He wasn't with his security guy, Bill Barry. He was always supposed to stay right next to the guy who was carrying him. We used to say to each other, 'Who's got the package?'—meaning who was responsible for moving him around. But we lost him that night. Another rule was don't go through the kitchen. And the third was don't reach into the crowd."

Barry rushed to catch up with Kennedy—along with Rafer Johnson and former Los Angeles Rams star lineman Roosevelt Grier, who were also providing the candidate with muscular, but untrained, protection that night. But, slowed by the swarm of people, they had not reached him yet as Kennedy entered the kitchen pantry—a "long, grubby area," as Hamill later described it, that "was the sort of place where Puerto Ricans, blacks, and Mexican-Americans usually work to fill white stomachs." The service area was lit by the dull glow of fluorescent lights and there was a rusty ice machine on one wall and a steam table stacked with dirty plates and glasses along the other. A row of cooks and busboys in white uniforms lined each wall, eagerly waiting for the chance to shake Kennedy's hand as he made his way through the gauntlet.

One of them, a seventeen-year-old Mexican-American busboy named Juan Romero, had met Kennedy earlier, after the candidate's entourage checked into the hotel. Romero had offered to pay another kitchen worker if he let him take a room-service cart to Kennedy's room. The busboy was not politically involved, but he was intrigued by the famous politician. Romero had seen photos of the Kennedy brothers in people's homes back in Mexico and he knew that Bobby had rolled up his sleeves for California's farm workers. When he pushed the food cart into Kennedy's room that day, the candidate shook his hand "as hard as anyone had ever shaken it. I walked out of there twenty feet tall, thinking, 'I'm not just a busboy, I'm a human being.' He made me feel that way."

Now, as Kennedy edged his way through the pantry, Romero reached out to shake his hand once more, when suddenly he felt a flash of heat in his face

and heard a loud pop. The busboy saw Kennedy fall backwards. As the room
exploded in screams and whirling motion, he knelt down on the greasy pantry floor and cradled Bobby's head in his hand. He felt the warm blood ooze
through his fingers. Romero leaned down and asked him if he could stand
up. Kennedy was saying something in a faint voice and the busboy bent his
ear closer to hear him. "Is everybody OK?" whispered Bobby, the watchful
guardian to the end. Then Ethel and others were there, nudging Romero out
of the way. "Oh, my God," she sighed softly, kneeling next to her husband,
who seemed to turn towards her with recognition as she took his hand. She
crouched over him, in her orange and white party dress, whispering to him
and stroking his bare chest and brow. Romero asked her if he could give
Bobby his rosary beads, but she didn't answer so he slipped them into one of
the senator's strong hands, wrapping them around his thumb so they wouldn't
fall off.

Hamill had been a few paces ahead of Kennedy, walking backward and
taking notes, when he heard the small, sharp explosions—pap, pap, pap. He
saw the young, curly-haired man with the outstretched gun—his first impression was that he was Cuban—and he was one of the first people to slam
into the assailant. "Get the gun! Get the gun!" men were screaming. Hamill
quickly gave way to the bigger men who were wrestling for the revolver, including Barry, Johnson, Grier, and writer George Plimpton. Barry, who had
reached Kennedy just as the shots were fired, hit the gunman twice in the
face so hard that he thought he was going to kill him. To control his fists, he
threw his arms around him in a stranglehold. The big man who had wrapped
his arms protectively around Kennedy throughout the campaign had lost his
"package" for just a minute, and now he was locking his arms instead around
a man who had shot at Kennedy.

By the time Hamill could get a look at Kennedy, he knew his friend was
beyond help. His face "had a kind of sweet acceptance to it," thought Hamill—he looked like a man who had been released. "His eyes were glassed
over, but open. There was a sort of flicker on his face, an ironic smile as if he
had been expecting this all along." Bobby's last words before slipping into
unconsciousness, someone later told Goodwin, were, "Jack, Jack."

While Bobby lay bleeding on the scummy kitchen floor, a wrenching
moan—*not again, not again*—sped like electricity down the grimy corridor,
like the shock of recognition that passes down a line of cattle on the way to
the killing floor, and then it jolted the still crowded ballroom next door. As
the sense of what had happened filled the big, bright, chandeliered room, a
wave of revulsion—so powerful it was almost a physical thing—rolled through

the crowd. Rick Tuttle was standing near the TV camera platform at the back of the ballroom with another young campaign worker—the woman who would become his wife—when the wave hit. "There's a literary phrase—'the room heaved.' That's exactly what it did. Something made it heave and then it heaved again, like an undulating ripple. And, of course, it was the word from the pantry."

The howls from below began rising to the upstairs rooms. Goodwin, still in the Kennedy suite, ran to the TV in one of the bedrooms to see what had happened. There, sitting on the other bed, silently staring at the television's unwatchable images, was another Kennedy veteran, Ted Sorensen. "We just looked at each other and we both knew that he was dead," Goodwin remembered.

Outside the hotel, Frankenheimer and his wife, Evans, were waiting in their Rolls-Royce to drive Bobby and Ethel to the victory party, which was to be held at the Factory, the trendy new disco that Salinger co-owned with celebrities such as Peter Lawford, Sammy Davis Jr., and Paul Newman. A policeman suddenly banged on the Rolls and barked, "Get this car out of here." The director started to explain that they were waiting for Senator Kennedy, when he and his wife heard the screams: "Kennedy's been shot! Kennedy's been shot!" Forced by the cop out of the Ambassador driveway, the Frankenheimers drove through downtown L.A., which was desolate at night, frantically looking for a phone booth. The car radio said Kennedy had been taken to Good Samaritan Hospital, and after finally finding a gas station with a pay phone, the director managed to reach Goodwin in the hospital waiting room. Since all the Kennedys' clothes and belongings were back at the Malibu house, Goodwin advised them to go back there and help gather them.

Evans Frankenheimer later recounted the ghostly feeling of the house when they arrived. As soon as they got inside, they turned on the row of TVs that Frankenheimer had installed for the Kennedy team to watch the building excitement of Election Day. Instead, there were chilling scenes from the Ambassador and shots of the police cordon outside the Good Samaritan and of sobbing people standing vigil. The Frankenheimers walked into the bedroom where Bobby and Ethel had been staying. All their clothes were still there, including the gaudy pink and green Hawaiian swim trunks that Bobby had worn that afternoon. "Two campaign assistants later showed up to get Bobby's clothes, and one of them just started throwing them in a heap in the suitcase," Evans recalled. "John became absolutely apoplectic and said, 'Fold those! Fold those!' So they had to take them out again and John stood there helping them fold Bobby's clothes.

"In the heat of it all, they forgot the damn swim trunks. I found them later. There they were, still wet and blobbed up in the sink."

At the Good Samaritan, the dark vigil dragged on. A team of six surgeons labored over Kennedy for nearly four hours. But as time wore on, it became clear the vigil was a death watch. Kennedy had suffered three bullet wounds—one grazed his forehead, another lodged in his neck and the final, most serious, shot had struck him behind the right ear and penetrated his brain. As the doctors struggled against the inevitable, family and friends gathered in a hospital suite. When Kennedy was wheeled unconscious into the room after surgery, the doctors' mood was grim. They took aside Mankiewicz, who had been giving medical progress reports to the press, and told him the truth. "They told me they took some pieces of bullet out of his brain, but they couldn't get it all. They were as gloomy as doctors can be. It seemed to me this was the end."

Walking by the bathroom in the hospital room, Mankiewicz noticed Ted Kennedy standing there, bent over the sink and splashing water on his face. He started to say something to the remaining Kennedy brother, but then he saw his face. "I have never seen as agonized a look on anyone's face in my life," said Mankiewicz years later. "It just tore me up. I mean it wasn't like a mother whose son has died in combat or a father whose daughter has been kidnapped. It was something beyond that. I just thought, 'Oh, the hell with it. I'm not going to say anything.'"

It was Frank Mankiewicz who finally had the task of telling the world that he was dead. The press aide had been at Kennedy's side nearly every day for the past three years. And now he was walking into a press room for the final time to make an announcement about the senator. The statement came in the haunted early morning, nearly twenty-six hours after Kennedy was shot. "I have a short announcement to read which I will read at this time," said an exhausted Mankiewicz, in a voice he struggled to keep under control. "Senator Robert Francis Kennedy died at 1:44 a.m. today, June 6, 1968. With Senator Kennedy at the time of his death were his wife, Ethel; his sisters, Mrs. Stephen Smith and Patricia Lawford; brother-in-law Stephen Smith; and Mrs. John F. Kennedy. He was forty-two years old." He later added the name of his brother, Senator Edward Kennedy.

The country—staggered by Dallas, by Vietnam, by King's death, by the exploding cities, by the spiraling feeling of chaos and doom—was now forced to make sense of this latest calamity. This second assault on a dynastic family in which so many Americans had invested their hope. One would have to go back to ancient Rome to find a precedent in the stunning back-to-back assassinations of two brothers at the height of their political glory—all the way to the second century B.C., when Tiberius Gracchus and then his younger brother Gaius were viciously hacked to death after each was elected tribune of the people and antagonized the Roman aristocracy with their democratic reforms.

Even in death, Robert Kennedy remained an object of perverse fixation for J. Edgar Hoover. The first autopsy photos of Kennedy's remains were rushed to the FBI chief, who locked away the grisly trophies in his infamous "official and confidential" files—the only celebrity death pictures preserved like this by Hoover. The gruesome, color autopsy pictures also found their way into the safe of James Angleton—as his CIA successor was repulsed to discover years later when he cracked open the fired spook's secret vault.

BOBBY'S DEATH SHATTERED THE Kennedy dream forever. The men who had served the brothers were blown to their separate fates, to try to recover and to find their way down new paths. But none of them would ever reach the same political heights, the same pinnacle where it once seemed they could have changed the course of America.

Daniel Ellsberg, the young defense intellectual who had broken from the government to advise Kennedy on Vietnam, was in Chicago, attending a conference on the war, when a friend told him to turn on the TV set in his hotel room. "Bobby's been shot," she told him. He sat on his bed as he watched the horrible images from Los Angeles, his chest heaving uncontrollably. All his hopes had been on Bobby. "I was thinking: Maybe there's no way, no way to change this country."

Later, after flying back home to Los Angeles, Ellsberg took a long walk on the Malibu beach. Bobby's funeral train was moving slowly down the tracks from New York to Washington, past the same crowds—white and black, young and old—who had once swarmed his motorcades, but were now standing as somber sentinels to salute him one last time. The train was filled with Kennedy's comrades, but Ellsberg didn't want to be on it. He wanted to be as far away as he could. As he watched the waves roll onto the Malibu shore, he dropped some LSD that a neighbor had given him. "I wanted to be on the moon, I wanted to be away from everything."

Some of the Kennedy team would drift away altogether from liberal politics. "After Bobby was shot, the lights went out for me," said Fred Dutton, who had dedicated nearly eight years of his life to the Kennedy cause, but later became a Washington lobbyist. When Dutton died in June 2005, the *Los Angeles Times* would note in his obituary that his disillusionment with politics after the second Kennedy assassination "helped explain to many why the unabashedly liberal Mr. Dutton . . . later agreed to represent the conservative Saudi Arabian government."

Dick Goodwin stayed in politics for awhile, rejoining the McCarthy campaign, although he knew it had no hope, and drafting the doomed peace plank at the 1968 Democratic Convention—a gathering that, instead of uniting party warhorses like Mayor Daley and the antiwar movement as RFK's nomination would have ensured, pitted them violently and disastrously against each other. Afterward, Goodwin dropped out of the action. "Dick went kind of nuts after Bobby's murder," Newfield told me before his death. "He moved up to Maine and invited me up there to do rifle practice. He told me, 'They got my friends, but they're not going to get me.' He had a dark view of the whole thing." Today, Goodwin makes light of the rifle practice but confirms that he was in a bad way. "I had to get away. I was very disturbed by what happened."

For the Kennedy circle, once again, the world was off its axis, and this time the country seemed an even more strange and threatening place. On Bobby's funeral train, Jacqueline Kennedy—so stoic after Dallas—threw herself on his coffin, sobbing, "Oh, my God, oh, my God." It was McNamara who finally calmed her down, grabbing her and holding her in his arms. Later, her sorrow turned to bitterness. "If they're killing Kennedys, then my children are targets," she said. "I want to get out of this country." She would soon find a way, by marrying Greek shipping tycoon Aristotle Onassis.

John Frankenheimer too would flee the country, moving to Europe for five years, drinking heavily and largely ignoring his movie career. That night at the Ambassador sent him to a dark place, the director later recalled. "If you want to date a moment when things started to turn, it was after that night. I went through sheer hell. I went to Europe, and I just lost interest. I got burned out. I was really left very disillusioned and went through a period of deep depression. It took a long time to get it back."

Bobby Kennedy himself would have scorned this feeling of alienation, Adam Walinsky contends today—this growing dread that America was lost. "He would have had no tolerance or patience for such a sentiment. His reaction would have been, 'What do you mean we've lost America? It's a great country—are you telling me the whole heritage of Washington and Lincoln and everything that Americans and their ancestors have done is all going down the drain because I'm not around? What the fuck is the matter with you? Grow up, get to work, cut that out!' "

But Bobby was no longer there to rally his family and fellow warriors. The flag carrier they had always looked to had been carried from the field. JFK's death had been cataclysmic. But they still had Bobby. For years, after Dallas, he had been the one they looked to, the one who kept the mission alive. His disappearance left a final void.

There was also no Bobby to hunt relentlessly for the truth about what happened in those chaotic moments at the Ambassador Hotel. And so the men who had followed him grappled privately with their suspicions, and many never reached a satisfying conclusion about his death. Some thought Sirhan Bishara Sirhan—the luckless young Palestinian immigrant who was arrested and convicted of the murder—was the whole, pathetic story. Others thought the assassin, who seemed in a trance that night, was programmed— or that he was not the only shooter, perhaps even a decoy. Ironically, Sirhan had brushed by Frankenheimer during Kennedy's victory speech, as the di- rector stood watching Bobby on a TV monitor in the ballroom's archway. "It was *The Manchurian Candidate*," Frankenheimer later said. "I felt this shak- ing inside me."

As pandemonium swept through the pantry that night, Jesse Unruh, the powerful California politician and Kennedy supporter, had shouted, "We don't want another Oswald!"—urging the enraged crowd that swirled around Sirhan not to kill him. But for many people in the Kennedy circle, that's pre- cisely what that night at the Ambassador would become—another Dallas, with the same type of mysterious gunfire, murky characters, and shockingly inept investigation.

Mankiewicz and Hamill were among those who accepted the official ver- sion of Robert Kennedy's death—that Sirhan alone put an end to everything that night. While both men strongly suspected that JFK had been the victim of a conspiracy, they believed that Bobby simply had been dispatched by "a pimply messenger . . . from the secret filthy heart of America," in Hamill's disgusted words. This was the anguished, metaphorical way that the Ameri- can liberal media generally reacted to RFK's murder. As time went by, Hamill would see the convicted assassin in less symbolic terms. Sirhan was the kind of Palestinian extremist you would later find blowing up cafes in Israel, Ha- mill says today. "It just seemed weird at the time because we didn't know anything about Palestinians."

But others who were in the Ambassador pantry when the shots rang out were deeply disturbed by what they witnessed. They could never reconcile their observations with the official version of Kennedy's killing. Gunpowder burns found on Kennedy's right ear during the autopsy indicated the fatal shot was fired directly behind his head, from a distance of only three inches or less. But not one witness saw Sirhan shoot Kennedy in the back of his skull at point-blank range. According to witnesses, Sirhan attacked Kennedy from the front, and he was standing between three and six feet away from his victim.

Frank Burns, a lawyer and aide to Jesse Unruh, was standing at Kennedy's right shoulder when the gunfire erupted. He was among those who jumped on Sirhan, who held on to his gun like a man possessed while much bigger men wrestled to disarm him. "There is no question that Sirhan was trying to assassinate Kennedy," Burns told me. "But I don't believe that Sirhan's gun got within a couple of inches of Kennedy's head, as the powder burns showed. So I've never been able to reconcile that. And I was standing right there. Now Kennedy *could* have circled completely around into the muzzle of the gun while we were waltzing with Sirhan—but I didn't hear any other shots while we were wrestling with him.

"In the years since Bobby's assassination, every conspiracy researcher in the world has called me up, from Dan Rather on down. But what it all comes down to for me is that the official story is just not believable—nor are other explanations and theories for who could have killed him. It's still an unsolved mystery in my mind."

Dr. Thomas Noguchi, the Los Angeles coroner who conducted the autopsy on Robert Kennedy, came to the same unsettling conclusion—though it received surprisingly scant attention when he revealed this in his 1983 memoir. Disturbed by the gunpowder evidence, eyewitness testimony, and indications that twelve bullets were fired that night—more than Sirhan's eight-bullet revolver could hold—Noguchi wrote that it "all seemed to indicate there may have been a second gunman," speculating that Sirhan's role might have been to divert attention from Kennedy's principal assailant. The coroner acknowledged that "crowd psychology" during moments of mayhem like the night at the Ambassador often made eyewitness testimony unreliable. Nonetheless, Noguchi wrote, "Until more is positively known of what happened that night, the existence of a second gunman remains a possibility. Thus I have never said that Sirhan Sirhan killed Robert Kennedy."

Richard Lubic, the Kennedy media consultant, did see another drawn gun that night. He too was standing next to the senator as he was shot. As Lubic kneeled down to help the fallen Kennedy, he saw a security guard with a gun in his hand, pointed toward the floor. The guard, Thane Eugene Cesar, was standing behind Kennedy when he was shot. He later insisted he did not fire his gun that night, but police never tested it. And Cesar—who held strong anti-Kennedy, racist views, telling one interviewer that the Kennedys had "sold the country down the road . . . to the commies" and minorities— has long since figured in conspiracy theories about RFK's death.

After the assassination, Lubic was visited at his home by members of Special Unit Senator (SUS), the Los Angeles police task force set up to investigate the crime. To Lubic, the investigators from SUS, which had ties to U.S. intelligence, seemed like "government people." When he tried to tell them about Cesar—asking them, "Why would a security guard have his gun pointed toward the floor, instead of at Sirhan?"—they cut him off. "It's none of your business," the investigators told Lubic. "Don't bring this up, don't be talking about this." Later, at Sirhan's trial, Lubic was never questioned about the mysterious security guard.

Frank Burns discovered the same lack of curiosity when he was called to the witness stand. He was never asked about the position of Sirhan's gun. "Everybody was certain they had the right guy—Sirhan was convicted before the trial ever began," Burns said. "I had felt the same way until I began to see some of the evidence about the bullet holes and trajectories and so on."

Within weeks of RFK's death, questions began to emerge about the LAPD investigation, including charges of destroying evidence and intimidating witnesses. "Big Daddy" Jesse Unruh, California's most formidable Democrat, was disturbed by what he was hearing about the investigation, and he alerted the Kennedy family. But irreparably broken by the death of Bobby— who, even more than Jack, had been the heart of the family—the Kennedys were in no condition to focus on the mysteries of the case. According to Burns, "Unruh talked to Kenny O'Donnell and Steve Smith. He told them we had some questions about the investigation in L.A. And he wanted to know if they had any concerns and if they had anything they wanted us to pursue. If the family had been troubled by any concerns, Jess would have been willing to do whatever he could to look into them. After all, he had a lot of clout, he was the California Speaker. But the answer came back from the Kennedy camp: 'No, we don't want to pursue it.' The family's attitude was clearly, 'Thanks for your concerns, but please butt out.'"

Ted Kennedy was now the head of the family, but he lacked Bobby's burning sense of political mission—nor did he have his brother's investigative drive. Family members became consumed by their own private torments. No Kennedy would take up Bobby's secret quest to solve Jack's murder, and none would dedicate himself or herself to ensuring justice for Bobby.

Allard Lowenstein, the bespectacled whirling dervish of liberal activism, made the RFK assassination a cause until his own strange murder in 1980 by one of his former political protégés. And, over the years, various lawyers for Sirhan tried without success to reopen the case. But, overshadowed by the JFK mystery, Bobby's assassination received scant media scrutiny.

WITH JOHN KENNEDY'S DEATH had come the birth of Camelot—endless TV specials and magazine spreads on the dashing, storybook king and his tragic, inexplicable end. With Robert Kennedy's assassination, the Kennedy Curse was born—countless media ruminations on the once charmed family's dark fate. This gauzy coverage had the effect of making the double killing of the Kennedy brothers seem like something preordained, something the family had brought upon itself like characters in a Greek tragedy.

Ted Sorensen tried to counter the creation of the Kennedy Curse. At a memorial service held at his New York law firm the day after Bobby's death, he delivered an eloquent tribute to the fallen brothers. John and Robert Kennedy were killed not because they were cursed, Sorensen declared, but because they dared to change history. "There is no curse upon the Kennedys," Sorensen told his colleagues. "They have met their share of ill-fate because they had more than their share of the courage and the conviction required to dare and to try and to tempt fate. . . . They died heroic deaths because they lived heroic lives."

As time passed, it became clear that the curse was not on the Kennedy brothers. It was on America. Years would go by, and no new leader would appear to take the country to the same heights.

"We've been on an endless cycle of retreat ever since the Kennedys," Goodwin remarked. "A retreat not just from liberal ideals, but from that sense of excited involvement in the country. I was asked by a magazine once what I thought John Kennedy's greatest contribution was, and I said, 'He made us feel that we were better than we thought we were.' That was the big loss. There's so much a president can do to inspire a nation—it's hard to even remember that nowadays. I mean JFK just liberated an enormous energy in the country. And Bobby would have done even more, I think."

Once again, Walinsky intervenes to put the Kennedy memorializing in perspective. He refuses to indulge in the senseless "what if they had lived" ritual. "I was at one of those memorial events once," Walinsky recalled, "and Arthur [Schlesinger] got up and went into this long deal about if John Kennedy had lived, this would be different, that would be different, and this struck me wrong. So when it came my turn to talk, right after Arthur, I just put aside what I was planning to say and I said, 'Look, the entire time I worked for Robert Kennedy, I never heard him say, 'If only President Kennedy had lived, this would be different.' Because to him that would have been a statement of weakness. That would have been saying, 'My brother didn't succeed in doing it, therefore we can't.' The question to him was not 'what if?' It was 'what now?' He felt 'Here we are, we are responsible, it's up to us.' And there's a real logic in this. Because if you say, 'Too bad President Kennedy isn't still alive'—why stop there? What about Lincoln, Washington—isn't it a pity George Washington isn't still here with us! And how about Socrates, Moses? Jesus could walk among us again! The fact is, other people can't solve your problems for you—they can only give you an example of how to live, then it's up to you what to do about it."

With his gleaming shaved head, flashing eyes, and disputatious style—a cross between a courtroom lawyer and Talmudic scholar—Walinksy presents himself as the tough, unsentimental guardian of Robert Kennedy's legacy. As Bobby himself would insist after Jack's death, Walinsky doesn't want to be caught up in the misty past. But as he's talking, sitting in a sunny breakfast nook off the kitchen of his Scarsdale home, he's watched over by another saintly photo of Bobby. This one is a black-and-white picture of Kennedy with the small child of migrant farmworkers, crouching in the dirt next to the family's home, an abandoned, rust-eaten car. Walinsky is not so different from the other men who served John and Robert Kennedy. The Kennedy years remain their touchstone, their reminder of what is best in them. Like the others, Walinsky's eyes are sometimes stung with tears as a particular memory comes suddenly to mind. And like the others, his house is filled with Kennedy memorabilia. The mementos—framed photos, stirring quotations, political cartoons—cover the walls in these men's studies, living rooms, even breakfast nooks. These men's homes are shrines to that heroic past, when they all were young and the country was beginning anew. When Robert Kennedy called to them, telling them, "Come, my friends, it's not too late to seek a newer world." And they believed him.

9

TRUTH AND RECONCILIATION

> "Never let me hear that brave blood has been
> shed in vain; it sends an imperious challenge
> down through all the generations."
> —SIR WALTER SCOTT

After Robert Kennedy was killed in 1968, there was no major figure in Washington with the drive to solve the JFK assassination—or investigate the lingering questions around RFK's own death. But in the early 1970s, the Watergate scandal began to lift the cloak that hid some of the country's darkest secrets. "There is a crack in everything, that's how the light gets in," Leonard Cohen sings. And Watergate—along with years of senseless bloodletting in Vietnam—cracked the system enough to let the light seep in.

The closest the U.S. government came to solving the JFK mystery was in the post-Watergate period, as the Church Committee and then the House Select Committee on Assassinations reexamined the Warren Commission's conclusions. These congressional inquiries unearthed important new evidence of a conspiracy and raised troubling questions about the role of government agencies in the assassination cover-up, if not the crime itself. But, in the end, these probes were frustrated by political limits imposed from within and without. They underlined how doomed any investigative effort was bound to be that depended on the voluntary cooperation of agencies like the CIA and FBI—deeply secretive institutions that had already blatantly misled the Warren Commission and would prove equally obstructionist during the 1970s inquiries.

The Church Committee was convened in January 1975 under the leadership of Frank Church, the Democratic senator from Idaho, to investigate abuses of power in the CIA, FBI, and other intelligence agencies. The committee produced a string of revelations—from the CIA's illegal opening of American citizens' mail to the FBI's pathological obsession with Martin Luther King Jr. But its most explosive discovery was the CIA's secret efforts to assassinate hostile or simply inconvenient foreign leaders, including Castro, Patrice Lumumba of the Congo, Rafael Trujillo of the Dominican Republic, Ngo Dinh Diem of South Vietnam, and Chile's General Rene Schneider, who was seen as an obstacle to the overthrow of President Salvador Allende. It was news of the CIA's assassination program that made the deepest impact on the American press and public, leading to cries for more congressional oversight of the agency—which Senator Church famously castigated as a "rogue elephant."

Among those who were shaken by the CIA assassination disclosures was Senator Richard Schweiker of Pennsylvania, one of the more active members of the Church Committee. A moderate Republican who had been inspired by JFK's call for a new era of public service, Schweiker was stunned to learn how the CIA and FBI had withheld critical information from the Warren Commission, including the CIA-Mafia collaboration against Castro. And he began to wonder what more the Senate committee would learn if it turned its spotlight on Dallas. In late 1975, as the panel was winding down its investigation, Schweiker persuaded Church to let him set up a subcommittee—composed of himself and Gary Hart of Colorado, a young post-Watergate reformer recently elected to the Senate—to investigate an assassination closer to home, that of JFK.

The time was right for a reopening of the case. Watergate, and the earlier Church Committee revelations, had raised dark questions in the public's mind about its own government. The American people's confidence in the government was shaken further that year when television viewers watched the first national broadcast of the Zapruder film, after TV news showman Geraldo Rivera pushed ABC to air the horribly revealing footage on its late-night *Good Night America* show.

Schweiker, regarded as something of a Boy Scout by his Senate colleagues, was equally dazed by what he was discovering in the catacombs of his government as he sifted through piles of evidence and declassified documents in the National Archives related to JFK's assassination. After hearing of the CIA-Mafia plots against Castro, Schweiker initially suspected Kennedy was the victim of retaliation by the Cuban dictator. "But we never produced any evidence that Castro was involved," recalled Dave Marston, the senator's legislative counsel and his lead man on the subcommittee's investigation. Schweiker's suspicions then began to head in an even more explosive direction. "We don't know what happened, but we do know that Oswald had intelligence connections," Schweiker told the press. "Everywhere you look with him, there are the fingerprints of intelligence."

Marston, who later left Schweiker's office to become U.S. attorney in Philadelphia and is now in private practice, is still convinced of this. "Oswald could not have acted alone," he says today. "His global wanderings clearly point to something bigger going on. There were so many CIA people and other government agents scheming in Florida and New Orleans, doing the crazy things they do—it's inconceivable that they didn't know about Oswald."

Gary Hart was amazed to hear Schweiker voice his suspicions during meetings of the Church subcommittee. "Dick made a lot of statements inside the committee that were a lot more inflammatory than anything I ever said, in terms of his suspicions about who killed Kennedy," Hart said in an interview for this book. "He felt, this is outrageous, we've got to reopen this. He was a blowtorch."

But Hart's mind was also blown by what they were finding. As the Church subcommittee dug deeper into the swamps of anti-Castro intrigue that festered in Florida during the Kennedy years, Hart was stunned by the complexity of the anti-Kennedy ecosystem and by the intricate web that linked the CIA, Mafia, and Cuban exiles. "I think the whole atmosphere at the time was so yeasty," he said. "And I don't think that anybody had control of the thing. There were people plotting with people, the Mafia connections, the friendships between the Mafia and the CIA agents, and this crazy exile community. There were more and more layers, and it was honeycombed with bizarre people. I don't think that *anybody* knew everything that was going on. And I think the Kennedys were kind of racing to keep up with it all.

"If there was anybody who was on top of it, it was Dick Helms—the man who kept the secrets," Hart added. "He would have been closer to knowing what was going on than anybody else, but I don't think even he did. There was no mastermind there. There was too much going on, involving too many people. Too many rogue elephants all over the place. Too many ad hoc operations. It was just a nightmare. I think a big book could be written on Florida in the early sixties, just a huge book."

Hart makes clear that he doesn't believe the assassination of JFK was an official CIA operation—his suspicions focus more on the Mafia. But he doesn't rule out rogue agents who were working closely with the Mafia. And he believes the agency was involved in the cover-up. "If there was any lock-down, I'm sure Helms would have been part of it," Hart said.

In the course of the Church investigation, it became shockingly clear that the Senate panel was confronting ruthless forces. In June 1975, Chicago godfather Sam Giancana was shot to death in the basement of his home, one week before he was to testify in Washington. Soon after, Johnny Rosselli—the key liaison between the Mafia and CIA—was called before the committee on two occasions to answer questions about the Castro assassination plots. The following year, Schweiker subpoenaed Rosselli once more to answer questions about the Kennedy assassination in a tightly guarded session of his subcommittee. He was hoping to grill the gangster more, when—on July 28, 1976—Rosselli's dismembered body was found stuffed in a rusting oil drum, floating in the waters off Miami. It was obvious that Rosselli's former confederates would stop at nothing to prevent the Senate investigators from getting at the truth.

"Rosselli was killed every way you can be killed," Hart said. "He was garroted, his arms and legs were sawn off, he had a bullet hole in his head. I went down on behalf of the subcommittee, in secret, to meet with the Miami detectives and the Dade County sheriff's office. And they showed me pictures of when they pulled him out of the water—terrible, the worst things I'd ever seen in my life. They told me it was a Mafia hit. It wasn't amateur night." Church Committee staff investigators concluded that Rosselli's execution, as well as Giancana's, had been ordered by Florida godfather Santo Trafficante, another key suspect in the Kennedy conspiracy.

Stonewalled by CIA witnesses like Helms and violently deprived of key witnesses like Rosselli and Giancana, the Church probe finally ran out of time and political momentum. Frank Church went off to pursue the 1976 Democratic presidential nomination, which he lost to Jimmy Carter. And Richard Schweiker was lured away from his Kennedy probe by Ronald Reagan, who was hoping to soften his image in his ill-fated challenge of President Ford by adding the moderate Pennsylvanian to his ticket.

Looking back at his probe today, Schweiker is still perplexed by the lingering questions. The CIA's rank duplicity deeply bothers him. "My opinion of the CIA has greatly diminished through the years," he told me. Like Hart, he believes the agency engaged in a cover-up—and some of its rogue operatives might have been involved in the assassination itself. But the former senator has come to conclude that the JFK assassination was a Mafia plot. "I've gone through a lot of phases on this, but I now really think the assassination was basically a mob hit—it was the mob trying to get back at the Kennedys for cracking down on the Mafia." But when Oswald comes up, Schweiker seems less certain that the assassination was a mob operation. The accused assassin was the product of a fake defector program run by the CIA, Schweiker observed. "And then he went haywire." Schweiker is still clearly unsettled when he retraces Oswald's footsteps before Dallas. "I certainly don't believe the CIA gave us the whole story."

As for Hart, he too suffered disappointment in his later bid for presidential glory. He was knocked out of the 1988 Democratic nomination race when the press exposed his affair with model Donna Rice, after *Miami Herald* reporters hid in bushes outside his Washington home to catch him in the act. Hart tried to weather the political storm, arguing that a politician's private life should not be exposed to peeping-tom journalism. But it was 1987, and in these pre-Clinton years, the media's powers as morality enforcer were still largely unchallenged. Armed with a comical photo of the candidate cavorting with the blonde beauty on a luxury yacht appropriately named *Monkey Business*, the press soon pummeled Hart's political career into the dirt.

In later years, Hart salvaged his public reputation, serving with distinction as the co-chairman of a pre-9/11 commission that tried to warn the country of the dangers of terrorism and turning himself into a voice of reason against the Bush administration's overreliance on a military response to the Al Qaeda threat. He still takes pride in the Church Committee's efforts to subject the country's shadowy intelligence apparatus to democratic controls—a struggle that has assumed new significance today.

As he looked back at the Church Committee's limited probe of the Kennedy assassination, Hart—a tall, fit, ruddy-faced man with a penchant for cowboy boots—suddenly made a startling charge. Whenever he was asked by reporters about the Kennedy assassination during his 1984 and 1988 presidential runs, Hart said, "I would tell the press that, based on my Church Committee experience, I believe there are sufficient doubts to justify reopening the files of the CIA, particularly in relationship to the Mafia. And I think that I signed *my* death warrant when I did that. I didn't realize it at the time . . . but I think what happened to me in 1987 was a pure setup. I think what people discovered then was you can assassinate somebody without using a bullet."

Hart did not want to linger on this explosive assertion. He does not want to appear "wacky" or "obsessive"—labels, he pointed out, that are quickly applied to any politician who dares to call for reopening the JFK case. "You have to be very careful about falling into the conspiracy category," he observed. But when pushed, Hart said that he received tips after the scandal broke that suggested a possible Mafia involvement in the *Monkey Business* affair. A prominent investigative reporter told Hart that after he began calling for a new JFK probe, close associates of Florida godfather Santo Trafficante expressed their strong displeasure with the senator. "We don't think [Hart's] any better than the Kennedys," one of the mobsters told the reporter. But Hart chose not to pursue these leads. "I just didn't want to make it my life cause," he told me.

It is easy to understand why Hart did not want to make this claim—that he was the victim of character assassination because of his stand on the JFK case—too loudly. The press had already pilloried him back in 1987 when he tried to make reporters' window-peeping the issue, instead of his own sexual indiscretion. He was flayed for trying to dodge responsibility for the humiliating fiasco. Hart's assertion that his political downfall was related to the JFK conspiracy would certainly have driven the media into a new frenzy. Since Hart himself has declined to pursue the matter, it would be hard to prove that he really was set up during the 1988 campaign. But what's intriguing is that Hart believes it might be true. One of the few Washington officials to aggressively—if briefly—investigate the Kennedy assassination, Gary Hart came away from the experience with the belief that he was up against powerful forces that, years after JFK's murder, were still determined to keep the truth from being revealed.

SOON AFTER HE WAS hired as the deputy chief counsel of the House Select Committee on Assassinations in December 1976, Robert Tanenbaum came to see Richard Schweiker in his Senate office. The Assassinations Committee was picking up the investigation where Schweiker and Hart had left it, and Schweiker was going to hand over his JFK file to the recently formed panel. Tanenbaum was a thirty-three-year-old, streetwise product of legendary New York D.A. Frank Hogan's office, where he had won every one of his murder cases, rising to become deputy chief of the homicide bureau. When the young prosecutor was recruited by the chief counsel of the Assassinations Committee, Richard A. Sprague, he made clear that he would only take the job if he could treat the JFK investigation like one of his New York homicide cases—with no political compromises, no interference. Sprague, the former district attorney of Philadelphia, assured Tanenbaum that he had the same philosophy and the two men began assembling an aggressive team—including investigative reporter Gaeton Fonzi, an experienced holdover from the Schweiker subcommittee, and Cliff Fenton, a savvy, black homicide detective whom Tanenbaum brought with him from New York.

But as soon as Tanenbaum began talking with Schweiker that day, he realized he had been very naïve. There was no way that this case would follow the usual steps of a homicide investigation. "First of all," Schweiker told Tanenbaum, after asking all staff members to leave his office, "you should know that they're going to stonewall you." While the young prosecutor was trying to absorb this startling idea—that duly elected representatives of the American people should expect to be defied by forces more powerful than themselves—Schweiker told him something even more shattering. "In my judgment," the senator said, "the CIA was involved in the murder of the president."

Tanenbaum physically recoiled. "When I heard that, every capillary in my body went into electrified shock," he recalled. "This was a United States senator telling me this!"

That night, Tanenbaum took the Schweiker file home to the townhouse near American University he had rented after moving to Washington. He and Cliff Fenton pored over the stack of papers until three in the morning. When they finally finished, Fenton got to his feet and made his way to the door, with Tanenbaum following him outside. Standing on the brick sidewalk in the early morning chill, the homicide cop looked at his boss and said, "We are in way over our heads. And there's no Frank Hogan here to protect you." Tanenbaum knew he was right.

Nonetheless, the prosecutor plowed forward. He and Sprague began to subpoena CIA officials, bringing them before the House Committee to undergo aggressive questioning for the first time about the assassination of President John F. Kennedy. When Tanenbaum first joined the committee, he had no strong opinions about the case—for years, he had assumed the Warren Commission had got it right. But as he and his investigators dug deeper, he came to the same conclusions as those of a long line of Washington insiders, from Bobby Kennedy to Richard Schweiker. "The more we looked into it, the most productive area of investigation was clearly the CIA—namely, those operatives who had worked with the anti-Castro Cubans," Tanenbaum said in an interview.

One of the CIA veterans who aroused the congressional investigators' particular interest was David Atlee Phillips, the CIA disinformation specialist who had masterminded the propaganda campaigns for the Guatemala coup and the Bay of the Pigs invasion. Phillips was based in Mexico City when the CIA station there apparently falsified evidence to show that Oswald visited the Cuban and Soviet embassies just weeks before the assassination. Furthermore, Gaeton Fonzi came across explosive information that indicated Phillips had met with Oswald in Dallas in September 1963. But when the veteran spy appeared before an executive session of the Assassinations Committee, he put on an artful performance like the former actor he was, lying about his Mexico City role and his Oswald surveillance.

It was a dramatic confrontation. On one side of the table was Bob Tanenbaum, the blunt-spoken, Brooklyn-born prosecutor—a hulking man who had attended the University of California's Berkeley campus on a basketball scholarship. On the other was David Phillips, a tall, blond Texan with a long, deeply lined face who was nearly two decades Tanenbaum's senior—a smooth, chain-smoking man from a Fort Worth family of fallen fortune who had risen to become chief of the CIA's Western Hemisphere division. Phillips had recently stepped down after a quarter century in the spy business to become a CIA advocate as the head of the new Association of Retired Intelligence Officers.

Phillips had mastered the aloof, country-club attitude of the agency's WASP elite. Like his boss, Dick Helms, he acted as if he were doing committee members a favor by granting them his time. "They are very antiseptic people," Tanenbaum said of Phillips and the other CIA overlords with whom he clashed. "I don't know what world they're living in. But they're not in the world of ordinary America, of taking subways, hailing cabs, shopping at grocery stores."

Despite his other-worldly bearing, Phillips did not intimidate the Assassinations Committee deputy counsel. Tanenbaum had tangled with Mafia bosses, he had tried and convicted members of the Columbo crime family. He was not going to back away from the likes of David Phillips. "These guys act like they're totally above the law," Tanenbaum said. "But they were exactly the kind of guys I thought should be brought down, if in fact they were proven guilty."

As Tanenbaum was interrogating Phillips, the congressional investigator had in his possession an FBI memo that indicated Oswald had been impersonated by somebody else in Mexico City—a disturbing piece of evidence that suggested the accused assassin was the focus of a U.S. intelligence operation. CIA bugging equipment taped a man purporting to be Oswald phoning the Soviet and Cuban embassies. When Tanenbaum pushed Phillips to tell him where those audio tapes could be found, the former spy insisted they had been destroyed. But Tanenbaum knew he was lying. Since the FBI had listened to the CIA's "Oswald" tapes, they clearly had not been immediately "recycled" as Phillips claimed.

Under the counsel's relentless questioning, Phillips started getting entangled in his story's inconsistencies. It was a taste of what might have been, if key suspects in the JFK assassination had been thoroughly subjected to this type of skilled prosecutorial scrutiny.

"When he told us the tapes were gone," Tanenbaum recalled, "I told him, 'Well, the bottom line is there are three people in this room who know you just lied—Detective Fenton, me, and you.' And then I had Cliff hand him a copy of the FBI memo."

Tanenbaum was astonished by what Phillips did next. "He read the memo. And then he just folds it up and leaves the room." That is what David Phillips thought of Congress's right to oversee U.S. intelligence.

Tanenbaum wanted to drag the former CIA official back for another round of questioning. "Call him back," the deputy counsel told the Assassinations Committee. "He's in contempt, he committed perjury. Let him know it." But committee members were beginning to get cold feet about their staff's energetic methods. Tanenbaum wanted the spy agency to deliver unredacted documents to his office. But the committee wouldn't back him up. "They were pulling the rug out from under us."

The assassination investigation started coming under fire in the press. A New York Times article clawed through Sprague's past as a Philadelphia prosecutor, suggesting he was no stranger to controversy. An op-ed piece in the Times blasted the committee's "McCarthy-era" tactics. Congressional funding for the investigation began to run out and Sprague and his staff stopped getting paid.

Seeing the writing on the wall, Tanenbaum met with Sprague and convinced him that since they were not prepared to compromise their investigation, the only honorable course for them was to resign. "I didn't want to participate in an historical fraud," Tanenbaum later explained. "My daughter, when I was in Washington, was three years old . . . and I didn't want to look at her years later and put my rubber stamp on a report that I knew was a fraud because it looked good on my résumé."

Sprague resigned as the Assassinations Committee chief counsel in March 1977, returning to Philadelphia to practice law. Soon after, Tanenbaum followed him out the door, moving to California, where he branched out from law to serve as mayor of Beverly Hills and to pursue a successful new career as the writer of best-selling legal thrillers. Corruption of Blood, his 1996 novel, would tell the dark tale of what happened when Manhattan prosecutor Butch Karp went to Washington and tried to solve the Kennedy assassination.

Sprague was replaced as chief counsel by G. Robert Blakey, a Cornell law professor and organized crime expert who had written the Racketeer Influenced and Corrupt Organizations (RICO) Act, the 1970 law that would finally bring the powerful Mafia families to their knees. There was a poetic justice to Blakey's role in creating RICO—he was, in effect, finishing the crime-busting crusade he had begun under Bobby Kennedy as a young Justice Department lawyer. And, by taking on the Assassinations Committee job, he was continuing Bobby's mission to crack the murder of JFK. Blakey was a Kennedy loyalist and he was dedicated to getting to the bottom of the mystery that still haunted America. But, unlike Sprague and Tanenbaum, he was also experienced in the Byzantine ways of Washington bureaucracy and he was determined to save the besieged investigation by steering clear of explosive confrontations.

To do this, Blakey made a fateful decision—in effect, he accepted the investigative limits that his predecessors had stormily challenged, choosing to take the CIA's word that it was fully cooperating with his probe and handing over all relevant documents. After the Assassinations Committee released its final report in 1979, Blakey crowed that his strategy of voluntary cooperation had worked: "In point of fact, the committee ultimately obtained from the CIA every single document that it wanted. No limitations were put on it. We got deeper and wider in the agency files than any other congressional committee in the history of Congress—bar none."

But the young staff investigators who had been given the job of prying information out of the CIA knew differently. They had been stonewalled by the agency every step of the way. One of these investigators was Dan Hardway, a long-haired Cornell law student from West Virginia whom Blakey had brought with him to Washington. Hardway would roll into the CIA headquarters' parking lot every day in a chopped, circus-red VW dune buggy blasting Talking Heads out of oversized speakers, accompanied by his equally energized fellow investigator Eddie Lopez, a Puerto Rican New Yorker also from Cornell Law School.

"We were not popular in Langley," chuckled Hardway years later. The two youthful Blakey aides were investigating Oswald's links to the CIA and his murky visits to Mexico City. But as they tried to track down relevant documents in the agency's labyrinthine citadel, a veteran agent named George Joannides—the former Helms man who had been brought out of retirement to serve as the CIA's liaison with the Assassinations Committee—suddenly appeared to block them. "They brought him in to shut us down," says Hardway flatly today.

Hardway and Lopez complained to their law professor that Joannides was obstructing their investigation. But when Blakey took their grievances to the CIA, intelligence officials assured him that they were fully cooperating, telling him that his investigators were just hot-headed kids. Blakey chose to believe the agency.

Hardway felt that Joannides was hiding evidence of a conspiracy that involved CIA officers. Like Tanenbaum, he came to suspect David Phillips, who he believed had run the disinformation aspect of the assassination. Immediately after JFK was shot, Phillips's operation began to spread bogus stories linking Oswald to Castro—with a speed that made the propaganda campaign seem preplanned. When the retired spy was finally brought back before the committee, it was the law student—wearing a red cotton plaid shirt and faded jeans—who grilled Phillips this time. If Phillips thought the long-haired coal miner's son with the West Virginia twang could be easily brushed off, he soon found out he was wrong. As Hardway bore down on Phillips, the retired spook fidgeted and chain-smoked his way through the interrogation. At one point, Phillips had three or four cigarettes going at once. "The thing that got him so nervous was when I started mentioning all the anti-Castro Cubans who were in reports filed with the FBI for the Warren Commission and every one of them had a tie I could trace back to him. That's what got him very upset. He knew the whole thing could unravel."

But in the end, the House Select Committee on Assassinations chose not to pursue Phillips or other suspicious CIA figures and its final report let the agency off the hook. The study found that President Kennedy "was probably assassinated as a result of a conspiracy"—an historic break from the federal government's lone gunman dogma. And it pointed a finger at the Mafia and Cuban exiles, declaring that the conspiracy might have involved members of those groups. But the report cleared the intelligence agency, even though a number of the committee's own staff members—including Hardway and Fonzi—believed that some CIA officials were deeply implicated.

Though the committee's final report was circumspect about the principal source of the plot, Blakey himself pulled no punches. "I think the mob did it," he bluntly told the press. Over the years, Blakey would be sharply criticized by Fonzi and other assassination researchers for his single-minded focus on the Mafia. Some of them, including Hardway, argued that the Mafia vs. the CIA debate about the assassination was a false dichotomy. At the operational level, the two organizations had merged in shadowy enterprises like the Castro murder plots. And Hardway was convinced that rogue agents had joined with gangsters and anti-Castro militants to kill JFK.

Hardway—who through the years kept in touch with his old professor, for whom he still felt great respect and affection—would continue to thrash out this old debate with Blakey whenever they talked. "I don't know how many times since 1978 that Bob and I have had this conversation," said Hardway, who is now a small-town lawyer in North Carolina. "I will tell him, 'Bob, you're right—the mob was involved. But Bill Harvey, David Phillips, and some of the people from the CIA were also involved.' He'll say, 'No, they weren't, Dan.' I'll say, 'Yes, they were, Bob.' "

In April 2001, something happened that shook Bob Blakey's certainty. That month, the weekly *Miami New Times* published a story on George Joannides—the veteran CIA agent whom Hardway and Lopez had accused of blocking their investigation. The article revealed that Joannides, who was based in Miami in the early 1960s, was the agent in charge of DRE—the CIA-financed Cuban exile student group that had worked hard to implicate Oswald as a Castro stooge, before and after Dallas. In other words, Joannides had played an intriguing role in the Oswald mystery, but had chosen to keep this hidden from Blakey's committee. Meanwhile, the career spy—who died in 1990—had used his liaison position with the committee to deflect scrutiny from the CIA. The *New Times* article, which was written by *Washington Post* reporter Jefferson Morley, stunned and outraged Blakey. Over two decades earlier, he had praised the CIA for its cooperation with his investigation. Now the law professor realized his young investigators had been right about the CIA—he had been duped.

A furious Blakey told the press that if he had known who Joannides was, the agent would not have been his CIA liaison—he would have been sworn in as a witness and forced to testify: "Joannides's behavior was criminal. He obstructed our investigation." The CIA had manipulated the Warren Commission, Blakey fumed, and now he knew that it had also deceived the House Select Committee on Assassinations. "Many have told me that the culture of the agency is one of prevarication and dissimulation and that you cannot trust it or its people . . . I am now in that camp."

Blakey's credulity had allowed Joannides to stonewall the investigation and had helped suspicious CIA figures like David Phillips to slip away from the congressional spotlight. But late in his life, Phillips would become oddly confessional, providing a curious coda to the Assassinations Committee saga.

In a July 1986 conversation with a former committee investigator, Phillips remarked, "My private opinion is that JFK was done in by a conspiracy, likely including American intelligence officers."

The former spy—who, in retirement, tried his hand at a literary career—elaborated on this assassination scenario in notes for a novel that he planned to write, but apparently never completed. The novel—whose working title, *The AMLASH Legacy,* was inspired by the CIA code name for one of its assassination plots against Castro—portrayed the slaying of Kennedy as a hideous, unforeseen offshoot of the agency's Cuba scheme. In Phillips's scenario, it was the Soviets—working with a wealthy, CIA-hating American leftist—who subverted the anti-Castro operation, turning it into a JFK assassination plot that would destroy the CIA.

"I was one of the two case officers who handled Lee Harvey Oswald," Phillips has the CIA official based on himself declare in the book outline. "After working to establish his Marxist bona fides, we gave him the mission of killing Fidel Castro in Cuba. I helped him when he came to Mexico City to obtain a visa, and when he returned to Dallas to wait for it I saw him twice there. We rehearsed the plan many times: In Havana Oswald was to assassinate Castro with a sniper's rifle from the upper floor window of a building on the route where Castro often drove in an open jeep.

"Whether Oswald was a double-agent or a psycho I'm not sure, and I don't know why he killed Kennedy, but I do know he used precisely the plan we had devised against Castro. Thus the CIA did not anticipate the President's assassination but it was responsible for it. I share that guilt."

Whether this labyrinthine literary exercise was a partial confession—or one last attempt by the disinformation master to muddy the assassination waters—is not clear. While Phillips felt compelled to at least "share" the guilt for JFK's murder, he did so in a weirdly cloaked manner. And he still placed the primary blame on the CIA's old nemeses—Moscow and the American left.

Shortly before his death in 1988, however, Phillips revealed more. According to the CIA veteran's nephew, Shawn Phillips, the ailing spy confessed something to Shawn's father, James, that he could never bring himself to tell Congress. The two brothers had grown estranged after James began to suspect David was involved in the JFK assassination. Suffering from late-stage lung cancer, David phoned his brother to attempt a final reconciliation. "Were you in Dallas on that day?" James asked him. "Yes," David replied. James hung up the phone and never spoke to his brother again.

• • •

AFTER THE HOUSE SELECT Committee on Assassinations found evidence of a JFK conspiracy, the panel recommended that the Carter Justice Department pursue the numerous tantalizing leads that it had developed. But, predictably, there was no further government action, and as the Reagan administration took power in 1981, the reign of secrecy in Washington only hardened.

With the government incapable of investigating itself, it fell to the media to shine a light on the dark corners of the Kennedy assassination. There was overwhelming public support for such scrutiny, with polls over the years showing that anywhere from 50 to 85 percent of Americans believed the official version of the JFK assassination was a fraud. But instead of aggressively investigating the many lingering questions about Dallas, the mainstream media continued to discredit conspiracy theories, straining harder with each passing decade to prop up the increasingly moth-eaten Warren Report. The most prestigious news institutions—the ones with the power to unearth new information—put themselves instead at the government's service. The special reports on the assassination produced with numbing regularity by the *New York Times*, *Washington Post*, CBS, NBC, ABC, *Time*, and *Newsweek* inevitably rallied to the defense of the lone gunman theory—with editors, reporters, and producers taking their cues in many cases from Warren Commission members, CIA and FBI officials, and media executives close to these government agencies. On some occasions, journalists who were intelligence assets simply funneled the government's version of Dallas directly into the press. As Carl Bernstein reported in an explosive 1977 *Rolling Stone* article, the CIA alone had over four hundred American journalists secretly at its service. And declassified documents reveal that some of these journalists did the CIA's bidding as the agency worked to tilt press coverage of the JFK mystery.

The American media's coverage of the Kennedy assassination will certainly go down in history as one of its most shameful performances, along with its tragically supine acceptance of the government's fraudulent case for the wars in Vietnam and Iraq. Assassination critics have long railed at the media's obedient embrace of the Warren Report, a credulousness that grows more and more bizarre with the passage of time and accumulation of contrary evidence. But even more confounding is the failure of JFK's close friends in the press to investigate the monumental crime. Some of these Kennedy intimates occupied influential positions high on the media ladder.

Critics see their failure to look into JFK's murder as not only a dereliction of professional duty but a personal betrayal.

The legendary newspaperman Benjamin Bradlee—who reigned for years as the executive editor of the *Washington Post*, including during its Watergate-era investigative glory days—comes immediately to mind in this regard. As I researched this book, I began to wonder why the man who was JFK's closest friend in the Washington press corps—a man who had the power to help bring down the Nixon presidency—apparently did nothing to reveal the truth behind Kennedy's murder.

Bradlee's deep affection for JFK shines through his 1975 memoir, *Conversations with Kennedy*—a book, along with Red Fay's *The Pleasure of His Company*, that offers the most intimate view of JFK, and is, essentially, a love story. Bradlee and his second wife, Tony, Mary Meyer's sister, socialized regularly with the Kennedys at the White House, Camp David, Palm Beach, and Newport. Late at night, after one champagne-carbonated soiree, Jackie drew Bradlee aside to tearfully confide that "you two really are our best friends." Unashamed of his unique relationship with the president, the journalist later wrote that his friendship with JFK "dominated my life." Kennedy, he gushed, was "graceful, gay, funny, witty, teasing and teasable, forgiving, hungry, incapable of being corny, restless, interesting, interested, exuberant, blunt, profane, and loving. He was all of those . . . and more." And yet, under Bradlee, the *Washington Post* showed little curiosity about how his extraordinary friend had died.

The same year Bradlee published his Kennedy memoir, journalist Robert B. Kaiser—writing in *Rolling Stone*—explored the media's disturbing lack of interest in the JFK assassination. The *Washington Post's* failure to commit investigative resources to the case was "especially puzzling," Kaiser observed, because of the newspaper's "courageous handling of Watergate and the intimate friendship Bradlee had with President Kennedy." When the *Rolling Stone* journalist asked Bradlee to explain his lack of interest in the case, he snarled, "I've been up to my ass in lunatics"—a reply that revealed not only his contempt for conspiracy researchers but his oddly passive view that the *Post's* role was simply to sift through the "lunatics" instead of directing its own investigative firepower at the story. "Unless you can find someone who wants to devote his life to [the case], forget it," Bradlee added. This comment also struck me as strangely resigned, especially for the man who had famously declared that reporters should be willing to "give their left nut" for a great story.

There must be other reasons for Bradlee's inaction, I concluded, after reading the *Rolling Stone* article years later. So I decided to visit the man himself—the man whom I, like the rest of those inspired by Watergate to enter journalism, had long regarded as a craggy icon of Fourth Estate integrity. Bradlee was long retired as the *Post*'s executive editor when I spoke with him in 2004. But, at age eighty-three, he retained emeritus status at the paper—as well as a small, unassuming office, which is where he agreed to meet with me. Dressed informally in a buttoned sweater and slacks, the legendary editor still exuded the feisty energy that had driven him to the top of his profession.

We began by talking about Bradlee's memories of Bobby Kennedy, with whom he had a somewhat prickly relationship. "I think that he maybe resented my relationship with Jack," Bradlee said. I told him about my book, and how my research showed that, after the shots rang out in Dallas, Bobby immediately suspected the CIA and its henchmen in the Mafia and Cuban exile world. Bradlee did not seem surprised. "Jesus," he said, in his trademark growl, "if it were your brother . . . I mean if I were Bobby, I would certainly have taken a look at that possibility." Then Bradlee made a truncated, but revealing remark. "I've always wondered whether my reaction to all of that was not influenced by sort of a total distaste for the possibility that [Jack] had been assassinated by . . ." He did not finish the sentence, but the rest was clear: "by his own government."

I pursued this angle with Bradlee. He had been the brother-in-law of CIA golden boy Cord Meyer; he socialized, like other Cold War liberals in the Washington press, with the agency's top men at Georgetown salons. Did he ever make discreet inquiries in these CIA circles, I asked Bradlee, about what happened in Dallas?

"I'm sure I talked to Helms about it privately, but as usual he dusted me off," he answered.

"He was good at that, wasn't he?" I said.

"Oh, yeah, he'd ask you to have lunch with him and you'd think, 'Oh, God, we're going to get a real good juicy pearl'—and you got nothing."

Then I asked Bradlee the question that had been looming throughout the interview. Why didn't he do more as the editor of the *Post* to get at the truth? "It was the fall of '65 when I became managing editor here," he replied, "and I've got to tell you that . . . I was so busy with trying to, in the first place, trying to build a staff. . . . And so I spent an enormous amount of time trying to decide who to hire." It was a weak explanation, and we both knew it.

I pushed him again. "In retrospect," I asked, "do you think the *Post* should have taken a harder look at the assassination?" And then Bradlee, who surely finds it hard to bullshit other journalists, gave me a brutally honest reply. He didn't do more to investigate his friend's death, Bradlee told me, because he was concerned about his career. "I think I probably felt that since I had been a friend of Kennedy's that—you know, this is just [two] years later, and the first thing that he does is come over to the paper that he's hopefully going to run for a while—and he concentrates on *that*?" He was afraid, Bradlee continued, "that I would be discredited for taking the efforts [of the *Post* newsroom] down that path."

And then he added a wistful little kicker that was stunning in its understatement. If his newspaper *had* solved the monstrous crime, "it would have been fantastic."

Yes, I nodded. "It would have been an amazing story."

"Yeah, yeah," said Bradlee.

And that was it. No angst about the way he had put his ambition ahead of his loyalty to a friend, no moaning about what letting a crime of this magnitude go unsolved does to the soul of a nation. I knew Bradlee was old school—journalists don't blubber, and all that. You cut your losses and move on. But his attitude was still weirdly emotionless, even by his hard-bitten standards.

I later spoke with Don Hewitt, another prominent journalist who knew the Kennedys. As we have seen, the *60 Minutes* creator has long harbored suspicions about Dallas, wondering whether "disgruntled CIA types" were behind JFK's assassination. Like Ben Bradlee, Hewitt—as the long-reigning executive producer of the most successful and esteemed investigative news show in television history—was in a position to dig deeply into the case. And that's just what he did, Hewitt insists today.

I talked to Hewitt in 2005, the year after he stepped down as the *60 Minutes* mastermind. During his thirty-seven years at the helm of the CBS program, the show did not break one major investigative story on the assassination. But, Hewitt told me, it was not for lack of trying.

"We tried and tried and tried," Hewitt said. "We went to Dallas, had marksmen shoot bullets out the window [of the Texas School Book Depository], tried to figure the trajectory of where it would have come from . . . I sat in that window and looked out that window for an hour, trying to figure out—I just never believed [the official story] for one second. And it's the biggest mystery of my life, [why the real] story has never surfaced."

Hewitt talked more about the obvious falsity of the official version of Dallas and how major political figures of the sixties like Richard Nixon privately rejected it. A top Republican once told Hewitt he had asked Nixon what he knew about JFK's assassination. "You don't want to know," Nixon had replied. Even in retirement, Hewitt was clearly vexed by the dark crime.

Later, bidding me farewell, the broadcast news legend wished me luck in my attempt to shed more light on the case. "Well, go, man—because it's the mystery of my life," he repeated, adding that he was mystified why more journalists had not devoted their "all-consuming" energy to the story. "Go man," he said one last time. "Big story."

It did not sound like a brush-off. It sounded more like Hewitt was passing the baton than passing the buck.

I know the criticisms of *60 Minutes*-style investigative reporting—that Hewitt made a great show of dramatic confrontations, but lacked the guts to take on the most potent forces in American life. (Just ask ex-producer Lowell Bergman about the show's surrender to Big Tobacco and network politics.) But Hewitt's parting words sounded like they were from the heart. And I took them to heart. He had failed to crack the political crime of the twentieth century, but at least he had tried. So far, my generation of journalists has done no better.

FOR OVER A DECADE, the JFK case remained stuck where the House Select Committee on Assassinations had left it. Then Hollywood stepped in, as the dream factory sometimes does when the country is gripped by a nightmare and is unable to wake itself. In response to the long paralysis of the political and media establishments came the shock therapy of Oliver Stone's 1991 movie, *JFK*.

The film, a glorified account of Jim Garrison's bold carnival of criminal pursuit, burrowed deeply into America's most hidden fears, suggesting that Kennedy was killed by a national security cabal intent on driving the country to war. The political and media elites denounced the film, calling it "paranoid," "twisted history," a "big lie" of Hitlerian proportion, and wondering whatever possessed Warner Brothers to release it.

But one former Kennedy confidant risked his reputation to support Stone—Frank Mankiewicz. He shocked the Beltway crowd—including the Kennedy family—by going to work as the Washington publicist for *JFK*. "Every American owes [Oliver Stone] a debt of gratitude," Mankiewicz announced. "He kicked open a door that had been closed too long."

Mankiewicz took an aggressive media strategy, returning the pundits' fire with equal scorn. "The political writers, the Establishment writers, the editorialists, and the thumb suckers were almost unanimous in attacking *JFK*, because it challenged the work they had done in the 1960s—which was very little," he acidly remarked. Guided by an aggressive Mankiewicz media playbook, Stone sharply responded to the numerous attacks on him in the *New York Times* and *Washington Post*. "History may be too important to leave to newsmen," the director opined in a *New York Times* op-ed piece. In January 1992, Stone went before the National Press Club in Washington, armed with a two-fisted, Mankiewicz-written speech. How could plush-salaried press sages like Tom Wicker, Dan Rather, and Anthony Lewis pooh-pooh the idea of a conspiracy, he declared, when they had never roused themselves to investigate the dark possibility—and when they worked in a capital city replete with conspiracies, from Watergate to Iran-Contra to the 1980 Reagan campaign's "October Surprise"?

The Kennedy family passed word to Mankiewicz that they did not approve of his high-profile advocacy of *JFK*. They had decided years before to follow Bobby's public vow to focus on the future instead of the past, even though—as some family members certainly knew—RFK was privately following a very different path. Mankiewicz stopped receiving invitations to family events. But the former Kennedy aide was undeterred. What he was doing was in the spirit of his old boss, Bobby, who years earlier had given him the assignment of digging into the assassination.

"I worked on the film's behalf because I believed in it," he says today. "Oliver was the first serious player to tackle the subject. The *Washington Post* and the rest of the media could sort of piss on the people who came before him and insult them. But Oliver had two Academy Awards and he had a $40 million budget for *JFK*. He could take them on."

In the end, Oliver Stone did not prevail in the media arena, where he is still a figure of ridicule. But the director did succeed in the marketplace, where the public swarmed into movie theaters and made *JFK* a box office hit. The controversial movie also succeeded in shaking loose an avalanche of secret government documents about the assassination. Stone had been persuaded by researchers Kevin Walsh and James Lesar to add a crawl at the end of the film, stating that the files of the House Select Committee on Assassinations had been sealed until the year 2029. When Capitol Hill offices were promptly flooded by thousands of angry letters, a heroic Rep. Lee Hamilton of Indiana—later co-chair of the 9/11 Commission and the Iraq study panel—ushered the 1992 JFK Assassination Records Collection Act through Congress, which resulted in the declassification of thousands of revealing documents.

Stone had accomplished overnight what hard-working assassination critics—and a passive Washington press corps—could not in decades. There were no smoking gun memos in this paper flood—and it is wishful thinking to believe that if there ever was such clear documentation of a conspiracy buried somewhere in government files, it would not have been shredded years ago. Nonetheless, the documents released under the JFK Act helped researchers fill in a subterranean picture of the Kennedy administration, with its heated schisms and scheming over Cuba and other Cold War flashpoints. The records provide more context for why Bobby Kennedy, among others, immediately suspected his brother was the victim of "a large political conspiracy."

Like the congressional investigations of the 1970s, the Oliver Stone movie opened up a new spirit of inquiry in the nation, one that affected even presidential contender Bill Clinton. On the 1992 campaign trail, Clinton and his running mate, Al Gore, responded to questions about *JFK* by saying all relevant government documents should be released.

When Clinton moved into the Oval Office, one of his first directives to Webster Hubbell—the Arkansas golfing buddy he named associate attorney general—was to find out "who killed JFK." There was a touching innocence to the young president's query, a naïve optimism that presidents could easily get to the bottom of such a deep, dark hole—something that Lyndon Johnson and Richard Nixon could have set straight for him. Hubbell, who was later driven from office in scandal, looked into the Kennedy case but reported that he "wasn't satisfied with the answers I was getting."

The new wave of skepticism inspired by *JFK* proved to be short-lived. In 1993, a former lawyer named Gerald Posner published a new brief for the Warren Report, *Case Closed*. The media quickly rallied around the book, making it a best seller. The book—which concluded that "a sociopathic twenty-four-year-old loser in life, armed with a $12 rifle and consumed by his own warped motivation, ended Camelot"—not only had a reassuring simplicity, it let the press off the hook. The journalists who had taken the government's word about the assassination all along felt vindicated.

By 2003, Posner himself no longer seemed so certain that the case was closed. After learning of journalist Jefferson Morley's revelations about CIA agent George Joannides and the Assassinations Committee, Posner wrote an essay for *Newsweek* calling on the intelligence agency to come clean about Dallas. The CIA's deception of Congress "is not a performance that inspires public confidence," Posner wrote. "Needless conspiracy speculation is only fueled by the CIA's stonewalling. The American public has a right to know everything that its government knows about the president's murder and Lee Harvey Oswald."

But the media continued to insist that the case was closed. Nearly a half century after the assassination of JFK, the story seemed lost in a limbo, caught somewhere in the public consciousness between Stone and Posner. Then, in late 2006, a flurry of events began to shake up the long dormant case.

IN NOVEMBER 2006, THE BBC program *Newsnight* aired a provocative report by filmmaker Shane O'Sullivan alleging that three CIA operatives were caught on camera at the Ambassador Hotel on the night of Robert Kennedy's assassination and suggesting that they were involved in his killing. The BBC report identified the three men as veterans of the CIA's Miami-based anti-Castro operation: George Joannides, the senior officer who had misled investigators for the House Select Committee on Assassinations in 1978; David Morales, the head of the JM/WAVE station's paramilitary operation and, like Joannides, long suspected of ties to the JFK conspiracy; and a man whom filmmaker O'Sullivan identified as Gordon Campbell, deputy station chief of JM/WAVE. O'Sullivan presented conflicting testimony about the identities of the three men who were photographed and filmed that night. Some former associates said the men were indeed Joannides, Morales, and Campbell, while others disputed this. Despite the mixed evidence, O'Sullivan concluded, "My gut feeling is that these three senior CIA operatives were behind the assassination of Robert Kennedy." The CIA, he told the BBC audience, "owes the public an explanation before the truth behind the Robert Kennedy assassination is lost to history."

Shortly after the BBC report aired, I joined with the *Washington Post's* Jefferson Morley, an expert on Joannides and the CIA's anti-Castro war, to look into the charges about the spy agency and the Ambassador Hotel. Morley and I traveled widely, interviewing dozens of relatives, friends, and former colleagues of Morales, who died in 1978, and Joannides, who died in 1990. We found that the BBC report was seriously flawed. The real Gordon Campbell turned out to be an Army colonel attached to the JM/WAVE station, and he died in 1962, making it impossible for him to have been filmed in 1968 at the Ambassador Hotel. (When asked about this, O'Sullivan suggested that the man caught on camera might have taken the dead man's name as an alias, since taking false names was a common practice among CIA covert operatives.) In addition, Morley and I found photographic evidence that seemed to disprove that the tall, dark-skinned man filmed by TV news cameras at the Ambassador was Morales. The evidence we gathered on the alleged Joannides photograph was more intriguing, but in the end proved inconclusive. Some people who knew the CIA operative identified the erect, bespectacled man in the photo as Joannides, but other credible sources insisted it was not him.

While our investigation cast strong doubt on the BBC story, Morley and I unearthed new evidence that tied Morales and other JM/WAVE veterans to the assassination of President Kennedy, and possibly to the killing of Bobby Kennedy as well. In the course of our reporting, Morales—a key link between the CIA and the criminal underworld who died shortly before he was to be interviewed by the House Assassinations Committee—began to loom as a particularly interesting figure. As we talked with people who knew Morales, a picture emerged of the late covert officer as a violent and ruthless man, driven by a supercharged sense of patriotism and a poisonous hatred for anyone he considered a traitor, including the Kennedys.

Morales was raised in a Mexican-American family in Phoenix that was so poor, he and his brother had to share a pair of shoes, so each boy could only attend school on alternate days. After joining the Army at the end of World War II, Morales was recruited by the CIA while serving in post-war Germany, becoming an intensely loyal "Company" man. His impoverished background and dark Indian features contrasted sharply with the elite, Ivy League breeding of the agency's overseers. But Morales was willing to carry out whatever orders were given him by the organization that had rescued him from his hardscrabble youth and given him a glamorous, high-stakes life of international adventure.

Though he rose to a position of prominence in the CIA, Morales was the agency's "peon," said one family member, who asked to remain anonymous. "He did whatever he was told. They gave him a lifestyle that he would never have had under any circumstances . . . He did everything for the Company. His family wasn't his life—the Company was his life."

Wayne Smith, a twenty-five-year veteran of the foreign service who worked with Morales at the U.S. embassy in Havana before Castro took power, said, "Dave Morales did dirty work for the agency. If he were in the mob, he'd be called a hit man."

After running the CIA's anti-Castro paramilitary program in Miami— where he was closely associated with gangsters like Johnny Rosselli— Morales was stationed in Southeast Asia, where he took part in the agency's notorious Operation Phoenix program, targeting people suspected of Viet Cong ties for assassination. He has been connected to a bloody trail of CIA exploits, from the 1954 Guatemala coup, to the hunting and execution of

Che Guevara in 1967, to the violent overthrow of Chile's Salvador Allende in 1973. (Morales later stated that he was in the palace when Allende was killed.)

It's easy to believe that Morales would have participated in the JFK assassination, a relative told me—not on his own, that was not in his character, but if ordered to do so. "When they call him a 'rogue,' that's bullshit. He was extremely loyal [to the agency]. But I can see him being told to do something, and do it. With no questions asked." One of Morales's jobs was to consort with the criminal element on behalf of the agency, added the family member. Morales might have been ordered to recruit "those sleazy guys" and "get them to wherever they were supposed to go" for the Dallas operation.

According to his lawyer, Robert Walton, Morales revealed that he was involved in both Kennedy assassinations. Walton has told this to several researchers over the years, including former congressional investigator Gaeton Fonzi, who recounted the story in his 1993 book, *The Last Investigation*. Walton repeated the story on camera to Shane O'Sullivan for the BBC report. According to Walton, Morales told him "I was in Dallas when I, when we got that mother fucker, and I was in Los Angeles when we got the little bastard. What was said to me was that he was in some way implicated with the death of John Kennedy, and let's go one step further, and also with Bobby."

Ruben "Rocky" Carbajal—who was one of Morales's closest friends, from childhood until the day the CIA operative died—has told researchers a similar story, but does not directly implicate his old friend in the killings. I visited with Carbajal in Nogales, Arizona, the border town where he has retired, chatting with him for hours in the bar and dining room of his favorite hangout, the Americana Motor Hotel, and at his hillside home overlooking the parched, scrubby terrain of Mexico. Carbajal, who was celebrating his eightieth birthday with a group of his old compadres over beers and glasses of Scotch when I found him, is a blunt-spoken, profane man. Short and spry, with well-groomed white hair and mustache, he was dressed sharply—in tan leather jacket, beige velour pullover, tailored brown slacks, and two showy rings—and carried himself like a scrappy bantamweight despite his advanced years. He and Morales grew up together in the tough streets of Phoenix, fighting with "the Okies" and playing together on the Phoenix Union High School football team, where Carbajal was the quarterback and Morales was his wide end. The two boys were closer than they were to their own brothers; they went everywhere together, with the bigger Morales acting as his friend's bodyguard. Morales's father abandoned the family when he was only four, and the Carbajal family—which owned a popular Mexican restaurant named El Molino that was frequented by Barry Goldwater and other Arizona VIPs— embraced Morales as one of their own.

Nearly three decades after Morales's death, Carbajal is still intensely loyal to the memory of the man he calls "Didi." Carbajal regards his late friend's covert assignments for the CIA as courageous missions that bestowed on him heroic stature. "When some asshole needed to be killed, Didi was the man to do it," Carbajal told me, drinking Bud Lites and chain-smoking Marlboros in the Americana dining room. "You got that right. That was his job."

"He was very patriotic. He believed in his job to protect the United States and he was going to go after anyone who was against it," he added the next day, sitting on a leather couch in his home's fully stocked bar room whose walls were covered with Hollywood celebrity stills, cheesecake shots, and posters of Aztec warriors with swooning maidens. "He didn't give a damn. If his own brother would have talked against the United States, he would have blown his ass apart."

Was his friend involved in the Kennedy assassinations? Carbajal wouldn't answer directly, only saying that Morales was "maybe" in Dallas and Los Angeles on those days. There were "eight million people in Los Angeles . . . when Bobby Kennedy got hit, so there may not be any significance to that," he observed, adding that Morales might simply have been visiting family members there at the time. In any case, said Carbajal, neither he nor Morales mourned RFK's death. "We didn't give a shit. Good riddance. Whoever did it, I want to thank them —thank you very much."

Carbajal does know who killed JFK—it was the CIA, he said, without naming any individuals. Morales and his close CIA colleague Tony Sforza both told him the agency was behind the Dallas plot. The Kennedys got what was coming to them, Carbajal insisted. "[President] Kennedy screwed up, caused all those deaths at the Bay of Pigs, he pulls off the planes, the men get caught on the ground. You want me to respect a president like that? Or an asshole like his brother?" The Kennedys, he added, had also given "the damn nation to the blacks."

Didi and he both felt that JFK had violated their code, said Carbajal. "If the son of a bitch caused the deaths of all these people [at the Bay of Pigs], he deserved to die. You should never go around lying to your people. You go back on your word, you ain't no good. My dad taught me that. I don't give a shit who it is. If it was my own father and he lied to me, he deserves to die. 'Cause you're no good. I was brought up that way. And Didi was that way too, see?"

Despite all the dangerous dirty work that Morales performed for the CIA, in the end, Carbajal believes, the agency turned on his friend. He suspects that Morales's sudden illness and death in May 1978 at age fifty-two was induced by his intelligence associates, who feared that he would talk openly about JFK's murder to the House Select Committee on Assassinations, which was planning to question him. "I think that's why they knocked him off, 'cause they didn't want him to say nothing," Carbajal said. Was the agency right to fear Morales's honesty? "You're goddamn right," said Carbajal. "You ask him a question, like you ask me a question, and he got right to the point, boom, no horse-shitting around. . . . You want the truth, here it is."

The overweight Morales, who chain-smoked unfiltered Pall Malls and often finished off a bottle of Johnny Walker at night, began experiencing heart trouble after flying home to Arizona from Washington, where, he told Carbajal, he had been drinking Scotch with agency colleagues before boarding the plane. He died that weekend in a Tucson hospital. According to a family member, there was no mystery to his death. "He had a heart attack. At home. Maybe [the congressional investigation] was running through his mind and it stressed him out, but the heart attack was there, ready to happen." As soon as Morales died, his family was visited by CIA officials at their Willcox home in remote Apache country. "They were there making sure he was dead," said the relative, who was at the Morales home at the time. "Was he dead or was he not dead?"

Our reporting led Morley and me into the catacombs of the old CIA war on Cuba—the underworld that Robert Kennedy suspected had spawned his brother's assassination. We spoke with another ghost from those long-lost days, fabled anti-Castro militant Antonio Veciana, still vibrant at seventy-eight. Sitting in the backroom office of his boat supply store in Miami, Veciana—leader of Alpha 66, a CIA-sponsored exile group that launched terrorist attacks and raids on Cuba—told us point blank that he thought the CIA was involved in the assassination of President Kennedy, "but I don't know [exactly] who." He repeated what he told House Assassination Committee investigators three decades ago, saying he once saw his CIA handler—a man he knew as Maurice Bishop, but whom congressional investigators identified as David Phillips—talking with a man he would later recognize as Lee Harvey Oswald in the lobby of a Dallas building where Veciana had gone to meet the CIA officer. "Goddamn it, what a fucking mess I'm in!"

Veciana later exclaimed when he saw Oswald's photo in the press. He speculates that the agency wanted to pin JFK's assassination on Castro, as a pretext for invasion. But Veciana makes it clear that he never believed his hated
adversary was behind the Dallas plot.

The man who once swore a fight to the death with Castro seems to have
accommodated himself to history, predicting that as the Cuban leader finally
fades into the sunset, there will be a diplomatic reconciliation between
Washington and Havana. "I don't agree with it, but it's a reality," shrugged
the graying, bespectacled warrior, who still looks like the Havana banker
he was before he fled the revolution. Back in 1979, as he was leaving his
store one evening, Veciana was shot in the head by assassins, on orders, he
believes from Fidel. But that all happened so long ago, in another century.
It's hard to believe these days that so much blood and treachery flowed
around the island, enough passion, perhaps, to have claimed the life of a
president.

One of the more intriguing pieces of evidence we came across during our
reporting was an eleventh-hour confession by a legendary veteran of the war
on Castro. Ever since Kennedy assassination researchers began airing their
theories, they have been confronted with the skeptical response, "If there
was a conspiracy, someone would have talked." But the fact is, over the years,
a number of important figures—beginning with Lee Harvey Oswald himself,
and including several people long tied to Dallas, such as Johnny Rosselli,
David Phillips, and David Morales—did begin to talk before their deaths.
And in February 2007, Morley and I discovered the final testament of
E. Howard Hunt, another CIA veteran around whom JFK assassination rumors had long swirled.

Hunt's confessions began with *American Spy,* the memoir he completed
shortly before his death in January 2007. Like the aborted O. J. Simpson
confession, Hunt took an oddly speculative tack on the crime of the century,
writing that if the CIA *did* carry out the assassination of President Kennedy,
this is how it probably happened

Hunt suggested that several prominent CIA officials might have been
involved in the plot, including Cord Meyer—whom the book's original ghost
writer, Eric Hamburg, conjectured was a WASP-elite stand-in for Richard
Helms, the top agency man Hunt still could not bring himself to name.
(Helms "was very careful to keep his skirts clean—very, very careful," Hunt
intriguingly told Hamburg.) The other CIA suspects Hunt named in his book
were William Harvey and Morales, a "cold-blooded killer," Hunt observed,

who like his boss Harvey, was "possibly completely amoral." While vigorously proclaiming his own innocence, Hunt speculated that Harvey—"a strange character hiding a mass of hidden aggression"—might have played the lead role in organizing the assassination, hiring Mafia sharpshooters "to administer the magic bullet" in Dallas. Hunt even went so far as to raise the possibility that Harvey was acting on orders from Lyndon Johnson.

These speculations by Hunt—a colorful and controversial spy whose intelligence career ended after he was arrested for his role in the Watergate break-in—were, of course, just that—speculations. More significant was what Hunt left out of the book—an eye-opening account that was brought to our attention shortly after Hunt's death.

The aging spy had begun the confessional process in 2004, at the prodding of his oldest son, St. John, who felt that his father owed history—and his own family—the truth. St. John was a colorful character in his own right, who as a seventeen-year-old had helped his father destroy evidence as Watergate investigators bore down on Hunt—tossing the burglars' surveillance equipment into a Potomac canal late one night with his father. On another occasion, at his father's request, St. John got rid of a typewriter by throwing it into a neighbor's backyard pond; he later learned that his father had used the typewriter to forge cables showing that JFK had ordered Diem's assassination.

"I didn't resent him asking me to help him get out of trouble," St. John insisted. "I was glad to do it. I knew that I hadn't lived up to his dreams as a son. I was not a great student, I didn't go to Choate or Exeter. I wasn't the son that he had hoped for. So doing all these things for him gave me an emotional strength. My dad needed me."

In later years, St. John Hunt led the rambling life of a post-sixties rock musician, consuming and dealing more than his share of drugs, until after two felony convictions for peddling speed and finding himself and his children on the streets, he abruptly shifted gears, kicked drugs, and began living a law-abiding life in the appropriately named north coast town of Eureka, California. He recently earned a degree in hotel management from a local college, but keeps in practice as a guitarist, playing with a blues-rock band called Saints and Sinners on weekends.

"I convinced my dad to tell his story after writing him a letter, imploring him to tell the truth before it was too late. His health was starting to decline, he was suffering from cancer, recurring pneumonia, he had just had a leg amputated, just one thing after the other," St. John recalled, sitting in the dining room of the Red Lion Hotel in Eureka. A compact, handsome man in his early fifties, he was dressed in the style of a cool, aging musician—black suit and shirt—and sported a brief, trim goatee.

Urged on by his son, Hunt began to open up about his murky past, writing provocative notes on the JFK assassination, adding more in an audiotape he mailed to St. John, and finally sitting down to talk for an hour about Dallas on video camera, prodded by questions from St. John and Hamburg, who is well versed in Kennedy literature.

Hunt's last will and testament—for that is how it sounds, as the gray-bearded figure struggles to speak in the video and on the tape recorder, gasping for air between snatches of his story—is a remarkable American tale. "He felt that he had to come clean—not just for his conscience and history, but also to leave behind something for his family, in case the book made some money. He always deeply regretted that his family had been destroyed by Watergate." St. John said that his two sisters never forgave their father for his part in the scandal that tore apart their family and led to the death of his mother, Dorothy, in a mysterious 1972 plane crash.

St. John believes that his father was willing to open up to him, in particular, because of the risks his son had taken for him during Watergate. "We had a relationship built on trust, based on all of that . . . So years later, when I implored Papa to tell me everything he knew about JFK's killing, he was open to it."

But this confessional process was abruptly cut off when Hunt's second wife, Laura, and their two grown children intervened—worried about the possible fallout from his unexpurgated account. "Papa was under huge pressure from his second family," St. John said. "They were telling him, 'Howard, what are you doing—you're opening up all these doors from the past.' It became a huge family issue. I told them, 'This happened to *my* family, before *you*.' I felt very entitled to hear him tell that story—I resented his second family telling me what I could talk to my father about. But Papa was so torn. He was old and worn out by then. He told me, 'Saint, this is my family now. You are my family too. But these are the people I have to live with. I'm too old to be put in the middle of a war between my two families.'" Unwilling to accept family-imposed constraints on the project, St. John and Hamburg ended their involvement in it, and another ghostwriter was hired to finish Hunt's memoir.

Laura Hunt, an elementary schoolteacher in Miami, confirmed that she was opposed to reopening the Kennedy assassination in her husband's memoir. "Things were a little strained" within the family, she acknowledged. But she does not repudiate the book, and she emphasizes that Hunt, though ailing, was of sound mind when he was working on it. She also denies that Hunt's speculations about a CIA role in the JFK assassination were prompted by any bitter feelings he might have harbored about the agency for not coming to his aid during Watergate. "He never felt bitter with the agency," she said. He was not trying to "get some body back. Howard Hunt wasn't made that way."

Hunt's most explosive revelation about the CIA and the Kennedy assassination is not contained in his book. Before he stopped telling his oldest son about his buried past, however, the old spy unburdened himself of a stunning secret. And this revelation was not speculative, but an eyewitness account. In 1963, Hunt recalled, he was invited by Frank Sturgis—the mob-friendly anti-Castro operative who later joined Hunt's Watergate burglary team—to a clandestine meeting in a CIA safe house in Miami. At the meeting, a group of men—including David Morales—discussed what was referred to as "the big event," which, it soon became clear, was a plot to kill President Kennedy. After Morales left, Sturgis asked Hunt, "Are you with us?" Hunt said he was "incredulous."

"You guys have everything you need—why do you need me?" Hunt asked Sturgis.

"You could help with the cover-up," Sturgis suggested.

Hunt was no Kennedy lover. He once told St. John he wanted to have a bumpersticker made reading: "Let's finish the job—let's hit Ted." But Hunt insisted he did not join the plot, because he learned that Bill Harvey was involved, a man he regarded as "an alcoholic psycho."

After Kennedy was shot down in Dallas, Hunt recounted, he was "haunted" by the assassination "like the rest of the country." He felt "lucky" that he had not played "a direct role" in the conspiracy. But Hunt left his exact role in the plot hazy. In the audiotape he sent St. John in January 2004, he said, "I was a benchwarmer in [the plot]," adding cryptically, "I had a reputation for honesty and information was brought to me."

Sitting in the Red Lion as the winter sun sank into the Pacific and the shadows fell over the coastal redwoods, St. John Hunt tried to make sense of his father's truncated confession. Was his father a co-conspirator in the killing of President Kennedy? "At the end of the day, I just don't know. But I do know that he at least had foreknowledge of it. He certainly knew a lot more than he said about it. I was just starting to get a lot out of him when they shut him up."

Whatever Hunt did in his life, his son has found a way to forgive him. The eulogy that St. John delivered for his father at his funeral in Miami was an outpouring of love for the swashbuckling spy he called "the classic CIA man; an American James Bond." If he was guilty of base deeds, it was out of a misguided sense of mission. "My personal feeling," St. John told the assembled mourners, who included Hunt's fellow Watergate convict Bernard Barker and aging anti-Castro militants like Felix Rodriguez, "is that my father's deep sense of loyalty and patriotism for this was country was exploited by men of petty concerns and vastly inferior moral fiber."

He has no qualms about making public his father's JFK confession, St. John said later. Why? "Because it's the truth. And I don't see it as that terrible. Assassination is part of the American political culture. It was going on long before Kennedy and it will be going on long after us."

IN RECENT YEARS, THE Kennedy legacy has been clouded by a spate of books, documentaries, and articles that have attempted to demythologize Camelot by presenting JFK as a drug-addled, sex-deranged, mobbed-up risk taker. While Kennedy's private life would certainly not pass today's public scrutiny, this pathological interpretation misses the essential story of his presidency. There was a heroic grandeur to John F. Kennedy's administration that had nothing to do with the mists of Camelot. It was a presidency that clashed with its own times, and in the end found some measure of greatness. Coming to office at the height of the Cold War and held hostage by their party's powerful Southern racist wing, the Kennedy brothers steadily grew in vision and courage—prodded by the social movements of the sixties—until they were in such sharp conflict with the national security bureaucracy and Southern Democrats that they risked splitting their own administration and party. This is the fundamental historical truth about the presidency of John Fitzgerald Kennedy.

And yet, caught up in the fashionable anti-Kennedy backlash of the times, prominent journalists like Christopher Hitchens dismiss JFK as "a vulgar hoodlum." One result of this relentless Kennedy bashing has been to diminish the public outrage over JFK's unsolved murder. After all, if President Kennedy really was such a sleazy character, where is the tragedy in his violent demise?

It has also become fashionable in all the media babble about Dallas that fills the air each year around November 22 for commentators to opine that "we will probably never know the truth about John F. Kennedy's assassination"—a self-fulfilling prophecy that relieves them of any responsibility to search for the truth. Ironically, some of the more politically backward coun-

tries where Bobby Kennedy took his rapturous mission in the 1960s—
including South Africa, Argentina, and Chile—have made strenuous, if
painful, efforts to confront the deepest traumas of their past, including assassinations, kidnappings, and torture. In South Africa, this post-apartheid
process of political and moral self-examination became known as "truth and
reconciliation." But in the United States, the darkest political mysteries of
recent decades—including the assassination of President Kennedy—have
yet to be fully explored. From Dallas to Vietnam to Iraq, the truth has consistently been avoided, the perpetrators have never fully answered for their
actions. When the nation *has* mustered the courage to impanel commissions,
these investigations soon come up against locked doors that remain firmly
shut to this day. The stage for this reign of secrecy was set on November 22,
1963. The lesson of Dallas was clear. If a president can be shot down with
impunity at high noon in the sunny streets of an American city, then any kind
of deceit is possible.

Assassination researchers insist that it is not too late, even at this remote date, to revive the JFK investigation. Most people who could have
shed light on the crime are now dead, researchers acknowledge, but the
trail has not receded entirely into history's far horizons. Researchers list a
variety of actions that can still be taken. The government should be compelled to release the estimated 1,100 JFK files it is still withholding. The
CIA should also be required to disclose the phone and travel records of
agents suspected of involvement in the JFK—and RFK—assassinations,
such as David Morales. Washington should follow this by making a formal
request to the Cuban and Mexican governments to release all their secret
files on the case. The Justice Department should offer amnesty and waive
government secrecy pledges for all those who step forward with relevant
testimony. Lingering technical disputes about the events in Dealey Plaza—
such as the hotly debated "acoustic fingerprints" on the Dallas police motorcycle Dictabelt that apparently indicated that as many as five shots were
fired that day—should be resolved by utilizing the most sophisticated forensic resources, including those of the federal Lawrence Livermore Laboratory, which has oddly refused to take on the case. Finally, the Kennedy
family should be persuaded to completely open the papers under their
control—including those of John and Robert Kennedy and Jacqueline Kennedy Onassis—which are still subject to frustrating restrictions.

The assassination researchers are, of course, indefatigable by nature.
That's what has allowed them to carry on, through years of government ob-

struction, media ridicule, and the bewilderment of family and friends. But outside this shrinking community of hardy souls, a malaise hangs over the JFK crusade.

Some of those with a long history of involvement in the case are deeply pessimistic. When I visited Bob Blakey in November 2003, the week before the fortieth anniversary of the JFK assassination, he seemed resigned to the idea that the crime would never be solved. We spoke in his home near the University of Notre Dame campus, where he teaches law, sitting in over-stuffed chairs in his dimly lit study, where the flickering flames in the fire-place warded off the chill of an overcast afternoon. Near the end of the interview, Blakey told me that the Kennedys no longer seem important, at least not to those Americans who were born after JFK was shot. "The Kennedys are not part of this generation," he said. "I teach this generation. [The assassination] is not a big deal for them. They grew up in a different world."

So how will history resolve the Kennedy mystery? I asked him. "My guess is that the Warren Commission will carry the day," said the man whose con-gressional investigation offered the first—and last—official challenge to the Warren Report. The lone gunman theory has the virtue of simplicity, Blakey explained. It was a dreary place to circle back to, after forty long years of exploration.

A couple of years later, I found myself at the Museum of Television and Radio in Beverly Hills, sitting in a quiet cubicle and reeling through Bobby Kennedy's life in video. Maybe Blakey is right, and the Kennedy story is no longer relevant for many Americans. But the black and white footage flashing before me that day seemed to be loaded with painful meaning, even now.

The last reel I looked at was Bobby in 1968, and it included his appear-ance on a San Francisco public TV talk show called *Kaleidoscope* as he geared up for his final campaign. The interviewer asked pointed but polite ques-tions, in a public television kind of way. But Bobby seemed pained and the interview took on the strained intensity of a psychodrama. In close-ups, the camera captured his raw, weather-ravaged face and scabbed lips. The coun-try was angry and demoralized, the interviewer observed. He could also have pointed out that it was suffering a kind of moral rot and vacancy of the soul because of the ugly, no-exit war that had begun seeping into every corner of American life. In these brutal circumstances, why would he commit himself to the political arena? Kennedy was asked. Working for the public good was "no sacrifice," Bobby replied. "The most unhappy people in the world are those who are involved in just themselves."

But, even though he was on the eve of the political adventure of his life, Bobby did not seem happy. There was never a mask with Bobby. On camera that day, he was quiet, wistful, ironic. He was constitutionally incapable of the cheerful artifice and empty bravado that is required of American politicians. And yet, he really did believe in America—he simply refused to give in to what it was becoming.

After a long discussion of the country's woes, the interviewer asked Bobby, "But you are an optimist?" Kennedy nodded and smiled his weary-eyed smile. "Just because you can't live any other way, can you?" he replied. He was America's first and last existential leader.

We live in a dark age of clashing fundamentalisms. The country is ruled by an administration that has made a cult of secrecy and obedience. We are caught up in another endless war, this time on "terror"—or perhaps it's a struggle with fear itself. But in this bleakest of times, Bobby Kennedy's message seems more compelling than ever. *We can't go on, we must go on.* Do Americans still want the truth—starting with Dallas and going all the way to Guantánamo? Do they want to take back their country? I don't know for certain. But I have to be optimistic. Just because there really is no other way, is there?

NOTES

1: NOVEMBER 22, 1963

1   was eating lunch: William Manchester, *The Death of a President*, 146.

1   "I have news for you": Ibid., 195.

2   "told me with pleasure": Author interview with Nicholas Katzenbach.

2   "on the faculty of Howard University": Quoted in Anthony Summers, *The Secret Life of J. Edgar Hoover*, 364.

2   "amazing computer brain of his": Author interview with Jack Newfield.

3   "riding into an ambush": Quoted in Lamar Waldron, with Thom Hartmann, *Ultimate Sacrifice: John and Robert Kennedy, the Plan for a Coup in Cuba, and the Murder of JFK*, 15.

4   inscribed a picture, Edward Guthman, *We Band of Brothers*, 7.

4   "so much bitterness": Ibid., 244.

4   "He distinctly said 'they' ": Author interview with Guthman.

4   encircled Kennedy's estate: Ibid.

5   "built like a tank": Quoted in William Doyle, *An American Insurrection: James Meredith and the Battle of Oxford Mississippi, 1962*, 68.

6   Bobby was "president": Quoted in Waldron, 69.

6   a stunning outburst: Seymour Freidin and George Bailey, *The Experts*, 85. The authors did not cite a source for this revealing account. But co-author Freidin, the former foreign affairs editor of the *New York Herald Tribune*, was later revealed by columnist Jack Anderson as a paid informant for the CIA in the 1950s and '60s. (According to Anderson, Freidin also spied on the Humphrey and McGovern presidential campaigns for Richard Nixon). So presumably Freidin got his scoop about the Kennedy phone call directly from his CIA contacts.

6   "seized with the horror of it": William Manchester interview with John McCone, CIA-DCI file, declassified October 9, 1998.

6   "if they had killed my brother": Quoted in Arthur Schlesinger, *Robert Kennedy and His Times*, 616.

7   blessed by the pope: McCone letter to Robert Kennedy, Attorney General papers, December 20, 1962, JFK Library.

7   two shooters in Dallas: Schlesinger, 616.

8   "no such thing as organized crime": Author interview with Guthman

8   "open some doors": Quoted in Seymour Hersh, *The Dark Side of Camelot*, 450.

8   "numerous federal marshals": Author interview with Walter Sheridan, Jr.

9   "in any foxhole": Sen. Edward M. Kennedy's eulogy for Walter Sheridan, JFK Library.

9   "a news flash": Quoted in Walter Sheridan, *The Fall and Rise of Jimmy Hoffa*, 299.

9   "One of your guys did it": Quoted in *Washington Post*, April 17, 1981.

10   "passionate parish priest": Author interview with Haynes Johnson.

10   "it was a shocking thing": Ibid. This is the way Johnson originally reported the phone conversation in a April 17, 1981 article for the *Washington Post*. But in a November 20, 1983 story in the *Post*, Johnson implied that Kennedy told him, not Ruiz-Williams. The two different accounts have led to some confusion over the years. Today Johnson insists that the original version is accurate: Kennedy was talking to Ruiz-Williams when he said, "One of your guys did it."

10   shuttled in and out of Cuba: Gerald D. McKnight, *Breach of Trust: How the Warren Commission Failed the Nation and Why*, 10.

11   "they make me crazy": Quoted in Waldron, 139.

11   "expecting to see a very impressive guy": Quoted in Haynes Johnson, *The Bay of Pigs*, 290.

11   "an old-fashioned buccaneer type": Author interview with Johnson.

11   [RFK] sent Harry to Miami: Waldron, 131.

11   Miami had already been ruled out: *Newsweek*, May 13, 1963.

12   "keep a sharp look on our Cubans": Author interview with Angelo Murgado.

12   like a Welsh collie: *New York Times Magazine*, May 28, 1961.

13   "I don't have any recollection": Author interview with Robert McNamara.

13   "Let them see what they've done": Quoted in Manchester, 348.

13   "I want his friends to carry him down": Ibid, 386.

14   the hot, bright streets of Dallas: Ibid, 392.

14   "You do that": Ibid., 391.

14   "accepted that there was a conspiracy: Vincent Palamara, *Survivor's Guilt: The Secret Service and the Failure to Protect the President* (self-published manuscript).

15   an organized plot more powerful than the presidency: James Hepburn, *Farewell America: The Plot to Kill JFK*, 10.

15   "looking burned alive": Quoted in Manchester, 406.

15   "three-ring circus": Quoted in McKnight, 154.

16   "you just follow orders": Quoted in Jim Garrison, *On the Trail of the Assassins*, 248.

16   he also discussed taking possession of JFK's death limousine: Attorney General Robert F. Kennedy phone logs, February 24, 1964, JFK Library.

17   JFK was the target of a conspiracy: Henry Hurt, *Reasonable Doubt: An Investigation into the Assassination of John F. Kennedy*, 49. Burkley had avoided the subject years earlier when an oral historian from the John F. Kennedy Presidential Library asked him about the autopsy evidence used by the Warren Report. "I would not care to be quoted on that," Burkley, who died in 1991, told the library interviewer—a cryptic remark that was nonetheless revealing.

17   "the greatest treasure in my life": Quoted in Manchester, 428.

17   "I just heard him sobbing": Charles Spalding oral history, JFK Library.

18   "in the White House with the president of the United States": Research associate
      Karen Croft interview with Milt Ebbins.

18   [Kennedy said] they were facing a formidable enemy: The source for this story is a
      Los Angeles man named Andy Harland, a movie props supplier who became friends
      with Lawford later in his life. Since Lawford became a notorious alcoholic and
      drug addict in the years after the assassination, this account must be regarded with
      a certain amount of suspicion. But in an interview for this book, Harland insisted
      that Lawford was sober when he related this story. And the statements attributed
      to Bobby correspond with the views he was expressing that week. According to
      Harland, Bobby told Lawford that the plot against JFK had grown out of a secret
      anti-Castro operation codenamed "Project Freedom."

19   blatant show of disrespect for McNamara: Manchester, 494.

19   "he could stay up there forever": quoted on Arlington National Cemetery Web site,
      www.arlingtoncemetery.org/visitor_information/JFK.html.

19   an old Edward G. Robinson gangster movie: Manchester, 526.

19   "some kind of goddam banana republic": Author interview with Matthew Walton.

19   Eisenhower was put in the same bitter frame of mind: Manchester, 260.

20   "was killed to keep him from talking": Quoted in McKnight, 22.

20   "Bobby . . . turned it off": Croft interview with Ebbins.

21   "Jack Ruby was visiting Syndicate members": Confidential communication to U.S.
      Attorney General Robert Kennedy and CIA Director Allen Dulles, December 1,
      1963, declassified on August 12, 1993, National Archives and Research Adminis-
      tration (NARA) document number 1993.08.12.17:17:16:960005.

21   Sheridan reported . . . that Ruby "had picked up a bundle of money": FBI memo,
      November 24, 1963, declassified October 26, 1992, record number 124-10072-
      10228. Kennedy assassination researchers Lamar Waldron and Thom Hartmann
      supplied further evidence about Hoffa's payoff to Ruby in their 2005 book, *Ulti-
      mate Sacrifice*. The researchers interviewed a friend of Pierre Salinger, a business-
      man named Jim Allison, who reported that he had witnessed the payoff at the
      coffee shop of a Chicago hotel on the weekend of October 27, 1963. According to
      Allison, the payoff was made by a bagman with ties to Hoffa and the Mafia with
      whom he was dining. The bagman handed Ruby a business envelope with a stack
      of $100 bills which the authors estimated to total $7,000.

      Herbert "Jack" Miller, chief of the Justice Department's criminal division, also
      checked out the story on a trip to Dallas to pursue assassination leads. According
      to a November 25 FBI memo, Miller determined that two newspapermen—John
      Mashek of the *Dallas Morning News* and Tony Weitzel of the *Chicago Daily News*—
      were the sources for the story. Miller called off Justice Department attorney Pelo-
      quin and terminated the investigation into the payoff after he determined the story
      "was based on speculation of reporters only," according to the memo. But Waldron
      and Hartmann suggested that a more compelling reason the Justice Department
      aborted the Ruby probe was to avoid compromising its ongoing case against Hoffa.
      As the FBI memo stated, "Miller expressed concern to Peloquin that there would
      be publicity regarding the Weitzel story which would give Hoffa and the Teamsters
      an opportunity to criticize the Department by alleging that Department was trying
      to tie Hoffa in with President's murder."

      It is unclear whether Bobby approved ending the Ruby payoff probe or whether

Miller made this decision on his own. Miller, one of the few Republican holdovers in Kennedy's top ranks at the Justice Department, would surface again in the assassination saga, during Jim Garrison's investigation in New Orleans. More on Miller can be found in Chapter Seven.

21   "I do wish Department would mind its own business": FBI memo from chief of Chicago office to FBI director, November 25, 1963, NARA record number 124-10077-10016, NARA.

21   Draznin . . . provided further evidence about Ruby's [mob] background: National Labor Relations Board memo, November 27, 1963, NARA record number 179-40005-10028, declassified October 22, 1993. The report Draznin prepared on the mobbed-up Ruby, with his "wide syndicate contacts," seems to blatantly contradict what he later told journalist Seymour Hersh. "I picked up nothing at all tying [the assassination] to Chicago mob men," Draznin told Hersh for his 1994 book, *The Dark Side of Camelot*, adding, "Ruby thought [killing Oswald] was a patriotic act. I believe it to this day."

21   [Bobby] quietly asked Daniel Moynihan to explore . . . whether the Secret Service had been bought off": William Turner, *Rearview Mirror: Looking Back at the FBI, the CIA and Other Tails*, 123.

22   Rowley . . . was adamantly opposed to the bill: Warren Commission hearings, Vol. V, 473.

22   "Clint Hill, he loved us": from unpublished notes of Theodore H. White interview with Jacqueline Kennedy for *Life* magazine, released May 26, 1995, JFK Library.

22   all of whom said the order came from Secret Service officials: Palamara, 8.

23   "never interviewed a more tormented man": Mike Wallace, *Between You and Me: A Memoir*, 15.

23   But he waved them off: Manchester, 70.

23   "He was never afraid": Author interview with Guthman.

24   the two knelt and prayed: Evan Thomas, *Robert Kennedy: His Life*, 282.

24   "It was a bleak day": *New York Times*, November 29, 1963.

24   Bobby and Ethel "were putting up their usual good fronts": Walter Sheridan oral history, JFK Library.

24   "I remember telling him what Hoffa had said": Ibid.

25   "he was the most shattered man I had ever seen": Pierre Salinger oral history, JFK Library.

25   "The key name was Marina Oswald": Author interview with Richard Goodwin.

25   "Bob . . . was going to deal with truth": Author interview with Guthman.

25   "I was even in his bedroom in the White House": Clay Blair Jr. interview with William Walton, Blair papers, American Heritage Center, University of Wyoming.

26   "just a wonderful-looking, kooky, young" photographer: Ibid.

26   "can't resist those Marlboro men!": Walton papers, JFK Library.

27   "she caught us on his bedroom floor": Walton oral history, JFK Library, courtesy of Matthew Walton.

27   "the only civilizing influence": Author interview with Gore Vidal.

27   "Jackie flung herself on the bed—free!": Vidal, *Palimpsest: A Memoir*, 374.

28   "Jackie . . . dared not look in": Ibid., 375.

28   "gay as a goose": Quoted in Sally Bedell Smith, *Grace and Power: The Private World of the Kennedy White House*, 136.

28   "There are certain visceral dislikes": Author interview with Vidal.

28   "The two people Bobby most hated": Vidal, 350.

28   "They completely trusted him": Author interview with Justin Feldman.

28   "My father was a believer": Author interview with Matthew Walton.

29   "He was not out to get glory for himself": Vidal, 360.

29   Walton visibly sagged: Manchester, 252.

29   "He was exactly the person": Author interview with Vidal.

30   "Poets in Moscow have fans": Notes on Moscow trip, Walton papers, JFK Library.

30   invited to take tea with Mrs. Khrushchev: Ibid.

30   "He was a man of peace": Ibid.

30   Walton "detested" the new president: Aleksandr Fursenko and Timothy Naftali, *One Hell of a Gamble: The Secret History of the Cuban Missile Crisis*, 402.

31   "One time Bob wanted to invite Georgi to a party": Author interview with James Symington.

31   "He gave me the creeps": Robert Kennedy, *In His Own Words*, 338.

31   "You son of a bitch": Quoted in Michael R. Beschloss, *The Crisis Years: Kennedy and Khrushchev 1960–1963*, 578.

32   Bobby heatedly confronted his Russian friend: Pierre Salinger, *P.S.: A Memoir*, 254.

32   He said that Bobby and Jackie believed that the president had been killed by a large political conspiracy: Fursenko and Naftali, 345. Fursenko and Naftali based their account of the Walton-Bolshakov meeting on a memo that Bolshakov prepared for the GRU. Fursenko also interviewed Bolshakov in January 1989 before he died. In an interview for this book, Naftali observed, "It's possible that Bolshakov exaggerated what Walton said to him to remind his superiors how close he was to the Kennedys. Bolshakov clearly liked the fact that he had become a player, and it's possible he exaggerated a bit to get back into the inner circle. But I'd be surprised if he invented it out of whole cloth." The authors note in their book that "the GRU material on Bolshakov has been corroborated in other cases and some of the details in this document have been corroborated."

33   "irresponsible . . . act of backdoor diplomacy": Thomas, 289.

33   "He just wandered around his office": Quoted in Salinger, *With Kennedy*, 363.

2: 1961

35   "All war is stupid": Quoted in Thurston Clarke, *Ask Not: The Inauguration of John F. Kennedy and the Speech that Changed America*, 109.

35   "the principal reason Kennedy ran for the presidency": Author interview with Theodore Sorensen.

37   "I had no choice": Richard Nixon, *RN: The Memoirs of Richard Nixon*, 221.

37   "one foot in the Cold War": Harris Wofford, *Of Kennedys and Kings: Making Sense of the Sixties*, 68.

38   "the Goths have left the White House": Quoted in Clarke, 208.

38   "I have never heard a better speech": Admiral Arleigh Burke oral history, JFK Library.

38   "through a membrane in time": Clarke, 200.

38   "The line in the inaugural address that is the most important": Author interview with Sorensen.

39   "the only human being who mattered to me": Quoted in Beschloss, 126.

39   a "puppet who echoed his speechmaker": Quoted in *New York Times*, June 19, 1962.

39   "a little boy in so many ways": Quoted in Clarke, 66.

39   Nixon himself was more generous: *New York Times*, June 19, 1962.

40   "I was against killing": Author interview with Sorensen.

40   Sorensen was raised to view war with a deeply skeptical eye: Victor Lasky, *JFK: The Man and the Myth*, 164.

40   Ted would meet his first wife: Author interview with Sorensen.

41   "I'm sure that would have provoked them further": Ibid.

41   Barry Goldwater promptly turned the *Tribune* article into a political issue: *Newsweek*, October 9, 1961.

41   "It didn't bother him at all": Author interview with Sorensen.

42   "He's all hopped up!": Quoted in Beschloss, 187.

43   Bissell wrote a friend: Richard Bissell Jr., *Reflections of a Cold Warrior*, 159.

43   Bill Walton was stunned to hear Dulles: Walton oral history, JFK Library.

44   "I'm not going to be able to change Allen": Quoted in Peter Grose, *Gentleman Spy: The Life of Allen Dulles*, 408.

44   "gentlemen" . . . were not bound by the same moral code: Ibid, 484.

45   "We've got to persuade the president!": Quoted in Peter Wyden, *Bay of Pigs: The Untold Story*, 270.

45   "It was inconceivable to them": Walt Rostow, *The Diffusion of Power*.

46   The invasion was "on the brink of failure": Bissell, 189.

46   the brigade leaders were to mutiny: Johnson, 75.

46   Burke . . . had also flirted with insubordination: Mario Lazo, *Dagger in the Heart! American Policy Failures in Cuba*, 294.

47   "but we *are* involved!": Quoted in Wyden, 270.

47   "they had me figured all wrong": Quoted in Kenneth P. O'Donnell and David F. Powers, *Johnny, We Hardly Knew Ye: Memories of John Fitzgerald Kennedy*, 274.

47   "our concept . . . is now seen to be unachievable": Quoted in *Miami Herald*, August 11, 2005.

47   "The CIA knew that it couldn't accomplish this": Ibid.

48   "There was some indication that the Soviets": Quoted in *Washington Post*, April 29, 2000.

48   "So I took the information to Allen Dulles": Author interview with Charles Bartlett.

49   "at the decisive moment of the Bay of Pigs operation": Quoted in Bissell, 191.

49   Kennedy was "surrounded by doubting Thomases": Quoted in Beschloss, 134.

49   "I was probably taken in by Kennedy's charisma": Quoted in Gus Russo, *Live By the Sword: The Secret War Against Castro and the Death of JFK*, 61.

49   "criminal negligence": Quoted in Don Bohning, *The Castro Obsession: U.S. Covert Operations Against Cuba, 1959–1965*, 48.

49   "the boys killed during the botched Bay of Pigs operation": Robert Maheu, *Next to Hughes*, 156.

50   "The [Bay of Pigs] failure was Kennedy's fault": Quoted in Russo, 20.

50   "absolutely reprehensible": Quoted in Wofford, 350.

50   the worst American defeat "since the war of 1812": Quoted in Beschloss, 129.

50   "Mr. Kennedy . . . was a very bad president": Burke oral history, U.S. Naval Institute. By August 1961, Burke would be eased out as Navy chief, the first of several Joint Chiefs and high-ranking officers whom Kennedy would force into retirement as he struggled to exert his authority as commander-in-chief. After retiring from the Navy, Burke became chairman of the new Center for Strategic Studies at Georgetown University. Out of uniform, Burke lobbied against Kennedy's policies and

continued to fume about the "amateurs" in the White House who were imperiling the nation. He made dark comments about the administration's dictatorial tendencies, denouncing its drive to muzzle dissent within the government. He charged that his offices at Georgetown University had been broken into, suggesting the Kennedy administration was behind it.

51   "Those sons-of-bitches . . . just sat there nodding": Quoted in Richard Reeves, *President Kennedy: Profile of Power*, 103.

51   Never again . . . would he be "overawed by professional military advice": Quoted in Arthur Schlesinger Jr., *A Thousand Days: John F. Kennedy in the White House*, 290.

51   "Nobody is going to force me": Quoted in Paul B. Fay Jr., *The Pleasure of His Company*, 161.

51   "Kennedy had contempt for the Joint Chiefs": Author interview with Schlesinger.

52   "The episode seared him": Quoted in L. Fletcher Prouty, *JFK: The CIA, Vietnam and the Plot to Assassinate John F. Kennedy*, 155.

52   Bradlee had urged him to replace [Dulles]: Benjamin C. Bradlee, *Conversations with Kennedy*, 33.

52   JFK "came into government the successor to President Eisenhower": Robert Kennedy, 246.

52   He asked Sorensen to start advising him on foreign affairs: Beschloss, 146.

53   where the Kennedy administration began becoming "a family affair": Author interview with Peter Dale Scott.

53   "The two brothers often held these sessions": Author interview with Fred Dutton.

53   There could be "no long-term living with Castro": Quoted in Beschloss, 375.

53   "I am almost a 'peace-at-any-price' president": Quoted in Schlesinger, *Robert Kennedy and His Times*, 430.

54   JFK "brought . . . the knowledge of history": Quoted in "Recollecting JFK with Theodore Sorensen and Robert McNamara," JFK Library forum, October 22, 2003.

54   "This nation is without leadership": Quoted in Reeves, 196.

54   Because we live in a free society: Quoted in A. M. Sperber, *Murrow: His Life and Times*, 628.

56   "I had no doubt he had come to talk to me": Richard N. Goodwin, *Remembering America: A Voice from the Sixties*, 197.

56   "My experience in government": Quoted in *New York Times*, June 29, 1961.

57   "Since I have no greeting card": Quoted in Goodwin, 195.

57   "when the people of Cuba once more have regained their freedom": Quoted in *New York Times*, August 17, 1961.

58   "We are the revolutionary generation": Goodwin papers, JFK Library.

59   "You should have smoked the first one": Quoted in Goodwin, 202.

59   His enthusiasm for Guevara's peace feeler: Goodwin papers, JFK Library.

60   Don't make Cuba a geopolitical obsession: Goodwin, 203.

60   "kid playing with fire": Quoted in Goodwin, 205.

60   Goodwin's appearance quickly turned into a "pleasant session": *New York Times*, September 1, 1961.

60   calling on President Kennedy to get rid of the men who had been "wrong from start to finish": Quoted in *New York Times*, November 13, 1962.

61   "I felt put down": Laura Knebel oral history, JFK Library. Knebel later reported Kennedy's provocative comments back to Guevara himself. "I'm going to tell you something funny that President Kennedy said after my last visit here, when he asked me about you," the journalist confided to Che—an intimate gesture which

does indeed seem on the flirtatious side. But Guevara did not want to play along. "He was a dedicated revolutionary not given to personal chitchat," Knebel later recounted, seeming a tad disappointed. "He had a wife to whom he was devoted, and such frivolities as Kennedy's remark, I think, were beyond him." In truth, the womanizing Che's devotion to his wife was a flexible proposition.

61   "They had never met but were fascinated by each other": Tad Szulc, *Fidel: A Critical Portrait*, 532.

62   democracy had an "unparalleled power": Quoted in *New York Times*, December 18, 1961.

62   "the most significant turn in U.S. hemispheric foreign policy.": *New York Times*, July 22, 1962.

63   "Latins were astonished that this young Yankee": Quoted in Goodwin, 194.

63   "There's even one from that bastard Somoza": Ibid, 146.

64   "then I got it from these old-line CIA guys": Author interview with Goodwin.

64   "our public posture toward Cuba should be as quiet as possible": Goodwin memo, U.S. State Department, *Foreign Relations of the United States, Vol. X, Cuba: 1961– 1962*, 646.

64   "we did not control the Joint Chiefs of Staff": Author interview with Schlesinger.

65   "something would go wrong in a *Dr. Strangelove* kind of way": Quoted in *Boston Globe*, July 28, 1994.

66   "like the cockroaches they were": Gen. Curtis LeMay oral history, Lyndon Baines Johnson Library.

66   The Air Force chief stunned the capital: *Washington Post*, July 19, 1961.

67   "LeMay's view was very simple": Author interview with Robert McNamara.

67   "I went out to SAC for a meeting with Tom Power": Author interview with Carl Kaysen.

68   "A prick like LeMay": Author interview with Charles Daly.

69   presented the doomsday plan "as though it were for a kindergarten class": Schlesinger, 483.

69   "The Kennedys used intimidation": Hanson Baldwin oral history, U.S. Naval Institute.

69   "Nuclear conflict was very much in the air": James K. Galbraith, *American Prospect*, September 21, 1994.

70   the "little brother" whom Clay said he could "not abide": Quoted in Beschloss, 333.

71   "tasks many officers pursued with gusto": Joseph A. Califano, Jr. *Inside: A Public and Private Life*, 95.

71   "General Walker . . . thought Harvard was the bad place": *Newsweek*, December 4, 1961.

72   "I feel the general is being crucified": Quoted in the *New York Times*, September 21, 1961.

72   Walker's indoctrination program had been endorsed by . . . General Lemnitzer: Richard Dudman, *Men of the Far Right*, 59.

72   they wondered if there was the . . . possibility of such a coup: Ibid, 36.

73   "a serious blow to the security of the United States": Quoted in Fred J. Cook, *The Warfare State*, 266.

73   "If the military is infected with the virus of right-wing radicalism": Ibid, 270.

74   "the intervention of the military in politics has had disastrous consequences": *Washington Post*, September 13, 1961.

74   "certain Pentagon brass hats": *Washington Post*, September 18, 1961.

74   "trapped McNamara": *Newsweek*, September 18, 1961.

75   the Fourth U.S. Army sponsored a two-day propaganda show: *Washington Post*, September 28, 1961.

75   the Armed Services Committee announced it would subject the McNamara crackdown: *New York Times*, October 6, 1961.

75   suggested a coup was in order: Cook, 265.

75   "you are riding Caroline's tricycle": Ibid, 29. When an account of this hostile exchange was later leaked to Kennedy friend Charlie Bartlett, who promptly reported it in the *Chattanooga Times*, Dealey denied that JFK made the icy response. "Bartlett's quotations are unfamiliar to me," said Dealey. "I think the whole story was cooked up by the administration."

76   The president took the "frenzy of the far right a lot less seriously than I": Vidal, 361.

76   He dispatched Bobby to meet with the Reuther brothers: Rick Perlstein: *Before the Storm: Barry Goldwater and the Unmaking of the American Consensus*, 149.

77   "a scornful 21-gun presidential blast": *Los Angeles Times*, November 19, 1961.

78   [JFK] would be forced to confront their passions in a surprising place: *Los Angeles Times*, November 20, 1961.

78   praising Welch as a "dedicated anticommunist": Dudman, 77

79   "riding on the left wheel all the time": Quoted in *New York Times*, November 19, 1961.

80   "You must read the University of Washington speech": Author interview with Sorensen.

80   "General Eisenhower listened intently": *New York Times*, November 19, 1961.

80   "I don't think the United States needs super-patriots": Quoted in *New York Times*, November 24, 1961.

81   when he "saw a band of black baboons": Quoted in Wofford, 371.

81   "The tone of [the] meeting was deeply disturbing": U.S. State Department, *Foreign Relations, 1961–1963, Vol. XII, American Republics*, documents 300–326. Bowles also wrote in his memo that White House aide Dick Goodwin, who attended the meeting, "vigorously supported" Bobby's rash approach on the Dominican Republic. But in a recent interview, Goodwin denied Bowles' account: "I never heard anybody saying we were going to burn down the consulate or do things like that." Goodwin suggested that Bowles's report on the meeting might have been colored by his bitter relationship with Bobby. "There was already an open feud between the two, which Bowles was destined to lose of course."

82   "The McCarthy years had pounded into [the Kennedy crowd's] heads a sense of inferiority": Bowles oral history, JFK Library.

82   "Kennedy's inability to . . . draw on the wisdom of Bowles": Wofford, 381.

82   Kennedy bowed to the political pressure: Goodwin, 213.

82   "Fucked again": Quoted in Beschloss, 296.

83   The president was in a reflective mood: Fay, 221.

84   "I asked him how he was feeling": Quoted in Amanda Smith, *Hostage to Fortune: The Letters of Joseph P. Kennedy*, 697.

84   The stress on the father must have been terrible: Thomas, 165.

84   "Typical Mafia killing": Author interview with Vidal.

3: 1962

85 "When he lost his temper": Author interview with Fred Dutton.

86 "a definite impression of [his] unhappiness": Lawrence Houston, Church Committee testimony, June 2, 1975.

86 "I trust that if you ever do business with organized crime again": Thomas, 171.

86 They would say that Kennedy was simply scolding the CIA: In 1975, Richard Bissell—the CIA official who initiated the Mafia plots in August 1960, in the final months of the Eisenhower administration—was quizzed about the dark pact by the Church Committee. Bissell testified that he had briefed Bobby about the CIA-Mafia partnership in spring 1961 during the Bay of Pigs postmortem review overseen by RFK and General Maxwell Taylor. But Taylor told the Senate panel that Bissell never mentioned an assassination effort against Castro. Considering Bissell's record of shading and concealing the truth with the Kennedys, it seems likely he kept them in the dark about the murder plots.

86 Kennedy "was disgusted that he had been placed in that position": Houston, Church Committee testimony.

86 "Bob . . . was absolutely furious": Author interview with John Seigenthaler.

87 "McCone was out of the loop": Ibid.

88 "Helms said all these stories are just the tip of the iceberg": Quoted in Newsweek, October 12, 1998.

88 "We were caught in the reality of the Cold War": Author interview with Seigenthaler.

89 "Are you Southerners always late?": Quoted in Helen O'Donnell, A Common Good: The Friendship of Robert F. Kennedy and Kenneth P. O'Donnell, 134.

90 "He was completely candid with me": Schlesinger, 190.

90 Seigenthaler decided [to do] "everything in my power": John Seigenthaler oral history, JFK Library.

90 "It's terrible. There's not a cop in sight": Quoted in Wofford, 154.

90 "Never run for governor of Alabama": Quoted in Schlesinger, 297.

91 "I need you in this government": Ibid., 229.

91 "You won't have any trouble finding my enemies": Quoted in Life, January 26, 1962.

91 "It showed either . . . guts or no sense at all": Quoted in Schlesinger, 23.

92 Bartlett did not see Jack's subtlety of mind in Bobby: Charles Bartlett oral history, JFK Library.

92 He struck Sorensen as "militant": Quoted in Thomas Maier, The Kennedys: America's Emerald Kings, 282.

92 "I have a pretty good character": Quoted in Smith, 306.

92 "everything was black and white for Bobby": Salinger oral history, JFK Library.

92 "there was less hidden business with Jack": Author interview with Benjamin Bradlee.

93 a beast of "passable intelligence": Look, May 21, 1963.

93 Guthman realized . . . he was the oldest person in the room: Guthman, 94.

93 Bobby's mandate was clear . . . "to murder Fidel Castro": Hersh, 268.

93 "What would you think if I ordered Castro to be assassinated?": Quoted in Szulc, 558.

94 "I don't think someone as media-savvy as Kennedy": Author interview with Goodwin.

94 "we would all be targets": Quoted in Szulc, 558.

94 "Jack and Bobby had nothing to do with the plots": Author interview with Robert Kennedy Jr.

94 "You could never be sure with the CIA": Author interview with Goodwin.

94 "Tell them no more weapons": Goodwin, 210.

95 "My idea is to stir things up on the island": Handwritten notes, November 7, 1961, Attorney General Robert F. Kennedy papers, JFK Library.

97 suggesting they go around . . . "the CIA palace guard": Lansdale memo, November 24, 1961, Attorney General Robert F. Kennedy papers, JFK Library.

97 Lansdale complained that the CIA's "smash and grab" raids: Lansdale memo, December 7, 1961, in U.S. State Department, *Foreign Relations of the United States, Cuba 1961–1962, Vol. X*, 692.

97 "Americans once ran a successful revolution": memo, February 20, 1962, ibid., 746.

97 "When the Huks came": Quoted in Jonathan Nashel, *Edward Lansdale's Cold War*, 40.

98 the tale "makes Filipinos vomit": Ibid., 42.

98 Goldwater was denouncing the administration's "do-nothing policy": Quoted in *New York Times*, April 19, 1962.

99 "He asked me if I thought we would have to go into Cuba": Burke memo, July 26, 1961, *Foreign Relations of the United States, Vol. X*, 635.

99 "something must be done about Cuba": Quoted in *New York Times*, September 5, 1962.

100 "Cuba was the key to all of Latin America": McCone memo, August 21, 1962, *Foreign Relations of the United States, Vol. X*, 955.

100 Bobby acknowledged that the Mongoose effort was "disappointing": Ibid, 850.

100 the CIA man realized he didn't have one of the "customary" autographed pictures of JFK: Richard Helms, *A Look over My Shoulder: A Life in the Central Intelligence Agency*, 227.

101 "There were many divorces": Author interview with Cynthia Helms.

101 what she called his "Oriental look—totally inscrutable": *New York Times Magazine*, April 18, 1971.

101 "He just had a martini on Friday nights": Author interview with Cynthia Helms.

101 "My husband was not particularly an admirer of Robert Kennedy's": Ibid.

102 [a] CEO type who "stepped straight from central casting": Quoted in Helms, 195.

102 "A former foreign correspondent, he observes much": *New York Times Magazine*, April 18, 1971.

102 "there seemed to be more than a whiff of disciplinary flavor": Helms, 207.

102 no "more than pinpricks" against Castro: Ibid, 202.

102 "getting my ass beaten": Quoted in Evan Thomas, *The Very Best Men: Four Who Dared—The Early Years of the CIA*, 300.

103 "I didn't trust Helms": Author interview with Seigenthaler.

103 When the James Bond-bedazzled JFK: Joseph J. Trento, *The Secret History of the CIA*, 207.

103 Harvey called the Kennedy brothers "fags": Ibid., 212.

104 "Bill gets chewed out by Bobby Kennedy": Quoted in Bohning, 110.

104 "What will you teach them . . . Babysitting?": Quoted in David Corn, *Blond Ghost: Ted Shackley and the CIA's Crusades*, 82.

105 the CIA . . . "relegated Cubans to the status of tools": CIA memo, July 5, 1962, NARA record number 104-10171-10378.

105 Ford reported to his CIA superiors that one of the ELC men . . . was tied to a suspected Castro spy: CIA memo, September 28, 1962, NARA record number 104-10171-10355.

105 "Substantial numbers of Castro's forces would survive": Kent memo, *Foreign Relations of the United States, Vol. X,* 783.

107 "We could foster attempts on lives of Cuban refugees in America": Pentagon memo, March 13, 1962.

107 "I sure as hell would have rejected it": Author interview with McNamara.

107 "McNamara's arrogance was astonishing": Quoted in James Bamford, *Body of Secrets: Anatomy of the Ultra-Secret National Security Agency,* 82.

107 "until he made the mistake of coming into the White House . . . in a sport jacket": Quoted in Beschloss, 474.

107 He thought their administration "was crippled . . . by inexperience": Quoted in Bamford, 82.

107 Lemnitzer was summoned by President Kennedy . . . for a discussion of Cuba strategy: Lansdale memo, March 16, 1962, NARA, released under JFK Act, March 28, 2005.

108 "The Joint Chiefs of Staff recommend . . . military intervention in Cuba": Pentagon memo quoted in Bamford, 82.

109 He gave Rosselli the false cover of an Army colonel: Charles Rappleye and Ed Becker, *All American Mafioso: The Johnny Rosselli Story,* 223.

110 "I was not dealing with the Mafia as such": Harvey testimony, Church Committee, June 25, 1975.

110 "He became best friends with Rosselli": Author interview with Gary Hart.

110 "I told Bill Harvey . . . to close it down": Helms, 202.

110 "I don't want anybody on this committee to think I'm being slippery": Helms testimony, Church Committee, July 17, 1975.

111 The CIA death plots against Castro preceded the Kennedy administration: Contrary to some accounts, the Kennedy brothers' Operation Mongoose was not an assassination program but a subversion operation aimed at inciting an internal Cuban uprising. Defense Secretary McNamara did float the idea of "liquidating" Castro at a Mongoose meeting on August 10, 1962. But in an interview with the author, he dismissed this as "idle chatter," insisting that he never seriously "proposed or would have supported assassination." When Lansdale recorded the off-hand remark in his memorandum of the meeting, McCone strongly objected, saying the U.S. government should "not consider such actions on moral or ethical grounds." When he phoned McNamara to emphasize this, McCone later recalled, the defense secretary "agreed with me wholeheartedly and the words were eliminated from the memorandum." Lansdale later told the Rockefeller Commission that the Mongoose group raised the assassination idea only as a "possibility," but quickly rejected it. He testified that the reaction against it was "quite sharp by members of the group, including the attorney general, McCone, and McGeorge Bundy, among others."

112 "[Helms] was very clear that this was something that had been canceled": McCone testimony, Church Committee, October 9, 1975.

112 "The fact that this happened is very disturbing to me": McCone testimony, Rockefeller Commission, May 5, 1975.

113 Assassination . . . "was totally foreign to [JFK's] character": Sorensen testimony, Church Committee, July 21, 1975.

114 "It would have made whoever ate the sugar feel very lousy": Author interview with Carl Kaysen.

114 the United States simply arranged for a sugar firm to buy the cargo: William Sturbitts deposition, Rockefeller Commission, April 16, 1975.

115 "I'm going to come back here and run against you": James Donovan speech to Inland Daily Press Association, published as "Cuban Negotiator's Own Story," April 18, 1963, Attorney General Robert F. Kennedy Papers, JFK Library.

116 "Viva Donovan!": Bohning, 168.

116 "Bob wanted me to deal with Donovan": Author interview with John Nolan.

116 "Castro was never irrational": Nolan oral history, JFK Library.

117 "we should start thinking along more flexible lines": Quoted in Bohning, 168.

117 "Before falling asleep at night": Author interview with Nolan.

118 CIA spokesman Sam Halpern claimed it was not: Bohning, 182.

118 the former Kennedy aide . . . confront[ed] a CIA official: Author interview with Nolan.

118 Shackley . . . wrote a memo to his CIA boss: CIA memo, March 19, 1964, NARA record number 104-10072-10289. Burt, who was one of several Miami journalists given the CIA cryptonynm "AM/CARBON" (the "AM" denoted a Cuba connection and "CARBON" referred to print journalists), later denied that he knowingly served the agency as a media asset. "Calling me a propaganda outlet was bureaucratic boasting on his part," Burt said of Shackley, in an interview for David Corn's 1994 biography of the CIA official.

119 "She was fiercely independent": Author interview with Nolan.

120 "do something about that son of a bitch Bobby Kennedy": Quoted in Sheridan, 216.

121 "We know where your kids go to school": Quoted in Warren Rogers, *When I Think of Bobby: A Personal Memoir of the Kennedy Years*, 53.

122 "If you want to kill a dog": Quoted in John H. Davis *Mafia Kingfish: Carlos Marcello and the Assassination of John F. Kennedy*, 34. Years later, while serving prison time, Marcello launched into another of his many anti-Kennedy tirades, telling an FBI informant on December 15, 1985, "Yeah, I had that son of a bitch killed. I'm glad I did it. I'm sorry I couldn't have done it myself."

122 "He is going to be hit": Ibid., 37. Like Marcello, Trafficante also confessed a role in the JFK assassination late in his life. Shortly before his death on March 17, 1987, the ailing Florida crime lord told his lawyer that he and Marcello had "fucked up in getting rid of [JFK]—maybe it should have been Bobby."

122 Kennedy's "soft" policies toward the Castro regime: Frank Ragano, *Mob Lawyer*, 358.

122 "I don't know how Bobby Kennedy squared that": Quoted in Hersh, 287.

123 "I'm not working with guys outside the system": Quoted in *New York* magazine, April 18, 2005.

123 "whether I was directed to sally forth and initiate contact with . . . the underworld": Charles Ford memo for the record, September 19, 1975, NARA record number 104-10303-10001.

124 Bobby Kennedy "has so many enemies": Quoted in Davis, 19.

124 "You can't touch me. I've got immunity." Quoted in Waldron, 357.

125 Bobby found himself . . . digging in an Illinois farm field: Robert F. Kennedy, *The Enemy Within*, 184.

127 "They have the smooth faces and cruel eyes of gangsters": Ibid, 88.

127 "So you're Joey Gallo": Quoted in *Life*, January 26, 1962.

128 the two men clashed with a kind of fury she had never seen: Schlesinger, 142.

128 "The old man saw this as dangerous": Quoted in Russo, *The Outfit:The Role of Chicago's Underworld in the Shaping of Modern America*, 313.

128 "I definitely know you have the goods": Smith, 147.

128 "I wouldn't be too discouraged": Ibid., 549.

129 "Yes, he was amoral": Blair interview with Arthur Krock, Blair papers, American Heritage Center, University of Wyoming.

130 "Bob was a little keyed up": Ruth Watt oral history, JFK Library.

130 Bobby was "the least like his father": Schlesinger, 97.

130 still calling Bobby her "own little pet": Smith, 535.

130 "The scariest one" was Vito Genovese: Watt oral history, JFK Library.

131 "Two tousle-haired brothers from Boston": *U.S. News & World Report*, April 12, 1957.

131 "They feel they're above the law," Kennedy told Paar's audience: Hoffa later filed a $2 million libel suit against Kennedy and *The Tonight Show* host. Kennedy laughed off Hoffa's showboating tactic, but he couldn't help needling Paar, who took the lawsuit seriously. "What are we going to do? We are in trouble," a nervous Paar phoned Bobby. "We certainly are in trouble," Kennedy told him, "if you don't have your half."

132 "We're exempting everyone but hoodlums": Newsreel footage featured in the 1992 PBS *Frontline* documentary, "JFK, Hoffa and the Mob."

132 "We were like flint and steel": Quoted in G. Robert Blakey and Richard N. Billings, *Fatal Hour: The Assassination of President Kennedy by Organized Crime*, 220.

133 "he directed the same shriveling look at my brother": Kennedy, *The Enemy Within*, 74.

133 "All this hocus-pocus . . . is a smoke screen:" Quoted in Ronald Goldfarb, *Perfect Villains, Imperfect Heroes: Robert F. Kennedy's War Against Organized Crime*, 188.

134 "A Saturday night ice cream": Ragano, 181.

134 "for real debauchery he turns to chocolate ice cream": *Life*, January 26, 1962.

134 "I'm no damn angel": Quoted in Richard D. Mahoney, *Sons & Brothers: The Days of Jack and Bobby Kennedy*, 38.

134 "It just killed him": Ibid., xv.

135 "Henry the Fourth. That's my father": Ibid., 376.

135 the FBI was "the greatest organization in the Government": Smith, 680.

135 "every gangster chief in the United States was there": Quoted in Anthony Summers, *The Secret Life of J. Edgar Hoover*, 310.

136 Kennedy [met] with Chicago godfather Sam Giancana: Hersh, 135.

136 "The Republicans stole as many votes": Salinger oral history, JFK Library.

137 "He challenged them": Author interview with William Daley.

137 "Jack's hair would have turned white": Quoted in Russo, *The Outfit*, 366.

137 "the old man is hurting you": Ibid.

138 he "was in the soup worse than ever": Quoted in Dan E. Moldea, *The Hoffa Wars: Teamsters, Rebels, Politicians and the Mob*, 109.

138 "My boss, Jack Miller, called me in one day": Author interview with Goldfarb.

139 "He was burning the candle at both ends": Ibid.

140 "They treat him like a whore": Quoted in Rappleye, 235.

140 "Why, oh why, did Joe get that fucking stroke?" Quoted in Summers, *Sinatra: The Life*, 287.

141 "Christ, how can I silence that voice?" Quoted in Russo, 243.

141 "that little son of a bitch is breaking my balls": Quoted in Rappleye, 231.

141 "we felt that we could not look to the FBI": Author interview with John Cassidy.

141 "we formed our own intelligence unit": Author interview with Guthman.

142 "it is such nonsense to . . . waste time prosecuting the Communist Party": Quoted in Summers, *J. Edgar Hoover*, 327.

142 "My father would send us kids into Hoover's office": Author interview with Joseph Kennedy II.

142 "And having Brumus": Author interview with Kathleen Kennedy Townsend.

142 "he was saving everything he had on Kennedy": William Sullivan, *The Bureau: My Thirty Years in Hoover's FBI*, 50.

142 Bobby said that . . . [Hoover] was . . . a "menace to democracy": Quoted in Jack Newfield, *Somebody's Gotta Tell It, A Journalist's Life on the Lines*, 162.

143 "He's rather a psycho": Quoted in Summers, *J. Edgar Hoover*, 323.

143 we "thought we could control him": Edwin O. Guthman and Jeffrey Shulman, editors, *Robert Kennedy In His Own Words*, 134.

143 the Kennedy brothers knew Hoover "wore funny clothes": Author interview with Kenny O'Donnell Jr.

143 "I think you should know that [the Kennedys] are fags": Quoted in Salinger oral history, JFK Library.

144 "something at the core of our society was beginning to rot": Quoted in Sheridan, xxxi.

144 some studios were under the direct control of the Mafia: Ibid, xv.

144 One star . . . told the screenwriter he was afraid: Ibid.

145 He confronted the military man with . . . evidence of his treason: Fletcher Knebel and Charles W. Bailey II, *Seven Days in May*, 313.

146 Knebel . . . got the idea . . . after interviewing . . . LeMay: *New York Times*, February 28, 1993.

147 "Stock, do you think I'll be assassinated?": Blair interview with Grant Stockdale's widow, Blair papers, American Heritage Center, University of Wyoming. Stockdale himself met a tragic end ten days after Kennedy's assassination when he fell to his death from his thirteenth floor Miami office. He did not leave a suicide note but his friend, Senator George Smathers, said he was deeply depressed by JFK's death. Some assassination researchers, however, have suggested that he was pushed out his office window because he knew too much about his friend's murder. Before his death, Stockdale was caught up in a scandal with Washington lobbyist Bobby Baker, with whom he was partners in a vending machine company that had government contracts. The company was also tied to mobsters, including Sam Giancana. The day before he died, an anxious Stockdale spoke with his attorney, William Frates. "It didn't make much sense. He said something about 'those guys' trying to get him. Then about the assassination."

147 Knebel was sharply challenged by [Kennedy] on the facts: Knebel oral history, JFK Library.

148 "Kennedy wanted *Seven Days in May* to be made as a warning": Author interview with Schlesinger.

148 "The Pentagon didn't want it done": Quoted in Schlesinger, 450.

149 JFK "was really interested in the facts of the project": Sinatra interview, 1988 video release of *Manchurian Candidate*.

149 "The Secret Service was alarmed": *Look*, November 19, 1963.

149 The studio yanked the ad: *Variety*, December 4, 1963.

150 "The world is on too short a fuse": Quoted in *Los Angeles Herald-Examiner*, March 5, 1964.

150 Quoting . . . Arleigh Burke to support his case: *Los Angeles Times*, February 6, 1964.

150 Melvin Laird . . . called for the movie to be clearly labeled fiction: *Variety*, May 13, 1964.

150 American democracy "as an excitingly perilous arena": *New York Times*, September 14, 2003.

150 "Paranoia only exists if the circumstances are totally untrue": HBO Web site interview with John Frankenheimer, http://www.hbo.com/films/pathtowar/artist_inter views.shtml.

151 Could a military coup really happen here?: Fay, 162.

151 "I haven't had such an interesting time since the Bay of Pigs": White House recording quoted in Jonathan Rosenberg and Zachary Karabell, editors, *Kennedy, Johnson and the Quest for Justice: The Civil Rights Tapes*, 66.

152 "Stay right by Meredith": Ibid., 78.

153 "Guthman's so scared": Ibid., 71.

153 "Well, you know what happened to those guys": Quoted in Guthman, 204.

154 "we could have a hell of a battle": Rosenberg, 65.

154 "Damn army!": Ibid., 73.

155 "we . . . didn't have the foggiest idea where the town of Oxford was": Unpublished Henry Gallagher memoir, courtesy of Gallagher.

155 "I would think they'd be on that fucking plane in about five minutes": Rosenberg, 74.

155 "People are dying in Oxford!": Quoted in Doyle, 233.

156 "We are very panicked by all this right now": O'Donnell oral history, courtesy of Helen O'Donnell.

157 "I could not believe I was on the campus": Quoted in Doyle, 237.

158 "There was no discussion of Walker's rights": Califano, 105.

158 "The president, angry and distraught, goes home": O'Donnell oral history.

159 "The problem with you people": Quoted in Rosenberg, 31.

159 "I'm afraid that the moral passion is missing": Quoted in Wofford, 129.

159 "If Khrushchev was running against Kennedy": Quoted in *New York Times*, August 4, 1963.

159 white Southerners would embrace "another Civil War": Quoted in *New York Times*, October 7, 1962. Faulkner himself embodied the South's deep psychological and moral divisions over race. He knew that the region's racial apartheid was a stain that had to be removed, but he appealed for more time. "Let us sweat in our own fears for a little while," he wrote in 1956. If he were forced to take a stand at that moment, declared Faulkner, he would "fight for Mississippi against the United States even if it meant going out into the streets and shooting Negroes." But it is unlikely he would ever have taken up arms for the South's dying order. A year later, following the federally enforced integration of schools in Little Rock, Arkansas, Faulkner observed in a letter to the *New York Times* that "white people and Negroes do not like and trust each other and perhaps never can." But, he added, "what is important and necessary and urgent . . . is that we federate together, show a common unified front, not for dull peace and amity, but for survival as a people and a nation."

160 "Later I told the troop of my call": Quoted in Doyle, 312.

160 primitively racist artifacts: Oxford leaflets and pamphlets, Attorney General Robert F. Kennedy files, JFK Library.

161 "One preacher let me into his church": Author interview with Symington.

162 "I was there as a soldier": Quoted in Doyle, 295.

162 "I just hope the song could be heard": Quoted in Perlstein, 169.

163 "I thought it was rather ridiculous": General David Shoup oral history, JFK Library.

163 LeMay . . . had been advocating a preemptive nuclear strike on Russia: Thomas M. Coffey, *Iron Eagle: The Turbulent Life of General Curtis LeMay*, 331.

163 LeMay . . . recommended that the U.S. "fry it": Dino A. Brugioni, *Eyeball to Eyeball: The Inside Story of the Cuban Missile Crisis*, 265.

164 "Can you imagine LeMay saying a thing like that?": Quoted in O'Donnell and Powers, 318.

164 LeMay bluntly declared that "we don't have any choice except direct military action": White House recording, quoted in Ernest R. May and Philip D. Zelikow, editors, *The Kennedy Tapes: Inside the White House During the Cuban Missile Crisis*, 113.

166 "what LeMay said is almost out of *Seven Days in May*: Author interview with Sorensen.

166 "you're screwed": May, 122.

166 pouring out in a torrent of "insubordination": Author interview with Sorensen.

167 "I was sitting next to Bob McNamara in Havana": Author interview with Schlesinger.

167 The Joint Chiefs . . . "were certain that no nuclear warheads were in Cuba": Quoted in "On the Brink: The Cuban Missile Crisis," JFK Library panel, October 20, 2002.

167 "There isn't any learning period with nuclear weapons": Quoted in *New York Times*, October 14, 2002.

168 "I don't give a damn what John Paul Jones would have done": Quoted in Max Frankel, *High Noon in the Cold War: Kennedy, Khrushchev and the Cuban Missile Crisis*, 127.

168 "Mr. Secretary, you go back to your office": Admiral George Anderson oral history, Naval Institute.

169 the agency began leaking information about the missiles to friendly reporters like Hal Hendrix: Corn, 114.

169 "Of course, I was furious": *Robert F. Kennedy In His Own Words*, 378.

169 "Harvey has destroyed himself today": Quoted in Thomas, *The Very Best Men*, 291.

169 "McCone felt it would be appropriate to move Harvey": FBI memo, October 30, 1962, NARA record number 124-90092-10010.

170 "Who was Brutus?": Quoted in Trento, 253.

170 Harvey continued to stay in touch with his old Mafia comrade:Rappleye, 225.

170 Johnny Rosselli was a man of "integrity as far as I was concerned": Harvey testimony, Church Committee, June 25, 1975.

170 "Thank God for Bobby": Quoted in Dave Powers oral history, JFK Library.

170 "What . . . gives . . . any government the moral right": Quoted in Schlesinger, 529.

171 Bobby Kennedy "was almost crying": Nikita S. Khrushchev, *Khrushchev Remembers*, 551.

171   "JFK had a great capacity to resist pressures from the military": Author interview with Schlesinger.
171   "we had felt there was a danger that the president would lose control of his military": Khrushchev, 552.
172   "It's the greatest defeat in our history!": Quoted in Beschloss, 544.
172   "We had a chance to throw the Communists out": Quoted in Coffey, 391.
172   "There was virtually a coup atmosphere": Author interview with Daniel Ellsberg.
173   "Operation Mongoose died": CIA memo, November 5, 1962, NARA record number 1781-0004-10128.
173   "Talk about the word treason at the Bay of Pigs": Quoted in Bohning, 125.
173   "People no longer thought that world war": National Security Archives interview with Sorensen, http://www.gwu.edu/~nsarchiv/
173   it was up to Kennedy and him to stop tugging on the "knot of war": Khrushchev, 555.
174   his military advisors had "looked at me as though I was out of my mind": Beschloss, 523.

4: 1963

175   "Don't go there": O'Donnell and Powers, 277.
176   JFK went "off script": Author interview with Goodwin.
176   "it was the worst possible gesture": O'Donnell and Powers, 277.
176   During JFK's Orange Bowl appearance, an assassin lurked: Mahoney, 220.
178   A secret Defense Department background sheet on [Artime]: U.S. Army memo, undated, NARA record number 198-1004-10060.
178   [Murgado] and Artime first met with Bobby at the Kennedys' [Palm Beach mansion]: Author interview with Angelo Murgado.
179   where he came across a curious gringo named Lee Harvey Oswald: Murgado claims that he crossed paths on one other occasion with Oswald, when he and fellow Brigade veteran Bernardo De Torres spotted him while paying a visit to the Dallas apartment of Silvia Odio, a Cuban exile tied to JURE, a left-wing anti-Castro group. "She was a heck of a nice piece of ass, that's all," Murgado says bluntly, by way of explaining his visit.
      This encounter is laden with significance, and controversy, in JFK assassination research circles. Some claim that De Torres was the infamous "Leopoldo" and Murgado the "Angel" who showed up on Odio's doorstep on September 25, 1963. Odio told government investigators that the two exiles were accompanied by a man whom she later identified as Oswald. Shortly after the visit, according to Odio, Leopoldo phoned her and made some chilling remarks. He told her that Oswald was an ex-Marine marksman who thought JFK should have been shot after the Bay of Pigs. "He says we should do something like that," Leopoldo told her. Some researchers believe the Odio encounter was an attempt to frame Oswald and implicate the left wing of the anti-Castro crusade in the JFK assassination.
      Did Murgado and De Torres show up on Odio's doorstep with Oswald in tow—or was he already sitting in her apartment when the two men arrived? It is easy to understand why neither Murgado nor Odio want to be associated with the man whose name would go down in infamy. But even if Murgado is shading the Odio story for obvious self-serving reasons, there is no indication he is doing the same with his Bobby Kennedy account.

181 The Kennedys had sold out the liberation movement: *Newsweek*, April 29, 1963.

182 "there is not going to be any invasion": Quoted in CIA memo, April 7, 1963, NARA record number 104-10233-10029.

182 Miró proudly retorted "that he could never be a traitor": CIA telegram, April 9-10, 1963, Attorney General Robert F. Kennedy confidential file, JFK Library.

182 "a formal request for the return of the Brigade flag": CIA memo, April 11, 1963, NARA record number104-10306-10015.

182 Nixon chided the White House for its flip-flopping Cuba policy: *Newsweek*, April 29, 1963.

182 He worked feverishly to make sure that Brigade veterans . . . were taken care of: RFK memo to Army Secretary Cyrus R. Vance May 8, 1963, Attorney General Robert F. Kennedy papers, JFK Library; also State Department memo, June 17, 1963, RFK confidential file, JFK Library; also RFK memo to Goodwin, March 25, 1963, JFK Library.

183 "I do think he felt a sense of guilt or obligation to them": Author interview with Nolan.

183 The two men were attempting to "organize an exile raid": State Department memo, July 19, 1963, RFK confidential file, JFK Library.

185 "the Russians would be immediately invited to Goldwater's ranch": Nathaniel Weyl, *Encounters with Communism*, 143.

186 "There are no rules in such a game": Quoted in Max Holland, "A Luce Connection: Senator Keating, William Pawley and the Cuban Missile Crisis," *Journal of Cold War Studies*, 1.3, 1999.

186 he blamed the disaster on President Kennedy's "betrayal": Thomas G. Paterson, *Contesting Castro: The United States and the Triumph of the Cuban Revolution*, 211.

186 "I think we have to drop ten thousand Marines in the environs of Havana": Quoted in Holland.

187 Clare Booth Luce referred to the three-man crew . . . as "my young Cubans": Quoted in Warren Hinckle and William Turner, *Deadly Secrets: The CIA-Mafia War Against Castro and the Assassination of JFK*, 148.

187 "The information they came out with was remarkably accurate": Quoted in Holland.

187 he had tried to talk his old friend Fulgencio Batista into leaving: Hinckle and Turner, 192.

188 "The Russians would be photographed on board": Weyl, 143.

188 [the friendship] was undisturbed even when Kennedy slept with Clare: Clarke, 97.

188 "It was a memorable moment in my life": Henry Luce oral history, JFK Library.

189 "The Kennedy clan is fun to watch": Quoted in Holland.

189 Clare lectured him that Cuba was an issue . . . "of American survival": Hinckle and Turner, 186.

189 If his son ever "shows any signs of weakness": Luce oral history, JFK Library.

190 "The pain is more than I can bear": Quoted in *New York Times*, January 8, 1977.

191 its claim that Kennedy was backing a coup/invasion plan . . . was unconvincing: The book's other major conclusion was even less persuasive. Waldron and Hartmann asserted that the Mafia masterminded the assassination of JFK, after infiltrating the Cuba plot, knowing that the government could not prosecute the mob for fear of exposing its top-secret coup/invasion plan. This thesis failed the basic credibility test in numerous ways. One of its biggest puzzles was why the Mafia would

choose to knock off Kennedy just as he was preparing to knock off Castro, paving the way for the mob to regain its fabulously lucrative sin franchise in Havana.

191   arousing so much anticipation in his Cuban friend that he began naming Cabinet ministers: Waldron, 145.

191   he asked them to lay off "because of the increasing frequency of rumors": CIA memo, July 17, 1963, NARA record number 104-10240-10326.

191   was scheduled to meet with them again on November 21 or 22: Army memo, December 11, 1963, NARA record number 198-10004-10011.

191   That is why he continued to believe in the Kennedys: Erneido Oliva, "Why Did the Assault Brigade 2506 Give Its Flag to President Kennedy for Safekeeping?" published on Cuban-American Military Council Web site.

192   He was "also afraid of the dentist": Quoted in Johnson, 186.

192   RFK "could not admit to them": Califano, 119.

192   There will be a point when "the national interests of the United States": William Turner interview with Harry Ruiz Williams, courtesy of Turner.

193   "No, absolutely not": Author interview with McNamara. The idea that Kennedy would have kept secret from McNamara an imminent invasion of Cuba—which was suggested by Waldron and Hartmann in their book—is exceedingly far-fetched. McNamara was not only the top civilian chief of the country's military forces, he was the Cabinet member most respected by the president and his brother.

193   "Why would we have done it?": Author interview with Goodwin.

193   "The phone would ring and it would be Robert Kennedy": Croft interview with Barbara Lawrence.

194   "tying a rock to a wire": Quoted in Fursenko and Naftali, 329.

194   [Artime's] exotic girlfriend aroused agency suspicions: Corn, 98.

195   "My bust is bigger than yours": Quoted in Bradlee, 147.

195   "So there I was, the 'beard' for Mary Meyer": Quoted in Ralph G. Martin, A Hero for Our Time: An Intimate Story of the Kennedy Years, 398.

196   "I don't care how many girls" Jack has slept with: Quoted in Bedell Smith, 352.

196   circumstances . . . forced him to learn how "to destroy": Cord Meyer, Facing Reality: From World Federalism to the CIA, 8.

198   "he became more Catholic than the Pope": Thomas Powers, The Man Who Kept the Secrets: Richard Helms and the CIA, 63.

198   "Cord entered the agency as a fresh idealist": Quoted in Frances Stonor Saunders, The Cultural Cold War: The CIA and the World of Arts and Letters, 342.

198   Joe Alsop found him repellent: Washington Post, February 7, 1978.

198   "Such a thing can either make or break a marriage": Quoted in New York Times Magazine, January 7, 1973.

198   Cord "acted like a 17th century cuckold": Quoted in Nina Burleigh, A Very Private Woman: The Life and Unsolved Murder of Presidential Mistress Mary Meyer, 151.

199   "When he was with her, the rest of the world could go to hell": Herbert Parmet, JFK: The Presidency of John F. Kennedy, 305.

199   They "were in love": Quoted in Trento, 280.

199   "I think [Angleton] was perhaps even in love with Mary": Author interview with Bradlee.

199   Meyer and Kennedy took one low dose of the hallucinogen: Burleigh, 212.

200   "Dr. Leary, I've got to talk to you": Timothy Leary, Flashbacks: An Autobiography, 128.

201 "Mary was so much more outgoing [than Cord]": Leo Damore interview with Timothy Leary, courtesy of Peter Janney.

201 "You have to live with sorrow": Quoted in *Washington Post*, February 7, 1978.

203 "None of us has any idea what Angleton did with the diary": Bradlee, *A Good Life: Newspapering and Other Adventures*, 271. In a letter sent to newspapers that carried reviews of Bradlee's memoir, Anne Truitt and Angleton's widow, Cicely, disputed his version of the diary caper. The two women claimed that Mary Meyer had asked that Angleton "take this diary into his safekeeping" in the event of anything happening to her. The CIA official had undertaken his search for the diary with Tony Bradlee's consent, the women insisted. When Tony Bradlee found the diary and several papers bundled together in her sister's studio, she handed them over to Angleton, requesting that he burn the documents. The spy followed Tony Bradlee's instructions by burning the loose papers, and complied with her dead sister's request by storing away the diary. When Tony Bradlee later asked for the diary, Angleton gave it to her, after which she burned it in Anne Truitt's presence. The letter only added to the confusion around the incident.

203 "I thought Jim was just like a lot of men": Author interview with Bradlee.

203 Helms could not recall just what it was about Mary's passing: Burleigh, 17.

204 "What *are* they looking for in my house?": Ibid., 226.

204 "The same sons of bitches that killed John F. Kennedy": Quoted in Heymann, *The Georgetown Ladies' Social Club*, 168.

204 "Mary Meyer became a female type": Burleigh, 227.

204 "Suppose the Russians did something now": Ibid., 212.

206 it elicited only 896 letters from the public: Beschloss, 601.

206 Khrushchev used it to win points with his Central Committee: *New York Times*, June 29, 1963.

206 "the world would have been different": Author interview with McNamara.

208 "You want me to accept President Kennedy's good faith?": Quoted in Norman Cousins, *The Improbable Triumvirate*, 99.

209 "The language in the speech is Unitarian language": Author interview with Sorensen.

210 "in that terrible era known as the nuclear age": "What Would JFK Do?" forum, April 21, 2002, JFK Library.

210 Khrushchev's eyes filled with tears: Reeves, 549.

211 "They literally hid him!": Author interview with Kaysen.

211 The attorney general worried that . . . McCone . . . might be disloyal: Beschloss, 632.

211 "I speak to you tonight in the spirit of hope": Quoted in Reeves, 549.

212 asking him to help activate "a whirlwind campaign": Cousins, 127.

213 "Mr. President, you're a hell of a horse trader": Quoted in Beschloss, 635.

213 "The whole bosom of God's earth": Quoted in Reeves, 594.

214 "This one is mine": Quoted in O'Donnell and Powers, 381.

215 "I think the issue of how JFK would have acted differently than LBJ [in Vietnam]": Quoted in *Boston Globe*, June 6, 2005.

215 JFK told O'Donnell that . . . the United States must withdraw: O'Donnell and Powers, 16.

216 but he never put it in writing: Author interview with Ellsberg.

217 "He never made a decision": Author interview with Sorensen.

218 "This is disorderly government": *New York Times*, October 3, 1963.

218   brought cries for Congress to "turn a permanent floodlight on the [CIA]": *New York Times Magazine*, October 26, 1963.

218   "He literally blanched": Robert McNamara, *In Retrospect: The Tragedy and Lessons of Vietnam*, 84.

219   JFK called Mary Meyer: Bedell Smith, 422.

219   "we must have a means of disengaging from this area": McNamara, 79.

219   "I don't want to talk about that": Author interview with McNamara.

220   "Kennedy would have had a hell of a problem": Ibid.

221   "He kept the peace": O'Donnell and Powers, 343.

222   "So, yes, that's how McNamara lives with himself": Author interview with Ellsberg.

222   "it would not have bothered me": Quoted in *New York Times*, February 6, 2004.

224   "Castro hadn't taken his boots off": Quoted in Summers, *Not in Your Lifetime*, 304.

224   Castro "made love to me efficiently": Author interview with Fritzi Lareau.

224   McCone sternly advised that the "Lisa Howard report be handled in the most limited and sensitive manner": Quoted in Peter Kornbluh, "JFK & Castro: The Secret Quest for Accommodation," *Cigar Aficionado* magazine, September-October 1999.

225   "She liked powerful men": Author interview with Lareau.

225   He looked with dismay on "the creeping police state" mentality: William Attwood, *The Twilight Struggle: Tales of the Cold War*, 142.

226   "the word 'America' made Che think of a huge hand pressing down on his head": Ibid, 251.

226   "we have something to gain": State Department memo, September 18, 1963, NARA record number 176-10010-10052.

227   he felt the peace dialogue was "worth pursuing": Quoted in Kornbluh.

227   JFK was even more enthusiastic: Ibid.

227   "if we recognize Cuba, they'll buy our refrigerators": Croft interview with Ebbins.

227   "he didn't think there was any reason [to confront] Cuba": Author interview with Paul "Red" Fay.

227   Schlesinger . . . later told Attwood that it was meant to help his diplomatic effort: Attwood, 262.

228   JFK's speech "may have been meant for potential dissident elements": Quoted in Waldron, 134.

228   "Mother was very naïve": Author interview with Lareau.

228   Helms urged that the administration slow down the Attwood initiative: Bohning, 172.

229   "and to hell with the president it was pledged to serve": Attwood, 263.

229   "It wasn't that I was being smart or tricky": Helms testimony, Church Committee, June 13, 1975.

230   "Bobby wouldn't have backed away [from the Cubela meeting]: Thomas, 300.

230   Oswald "has been heralded as a pro-Castro type": White House memo, November 25, 1963, NARA record number 178-10003-10066.

230   "a good opportunity to punish Bobby": Author interview with Vidal.

231   "She's being canned": Quoted in *New York Times*, November 19, 1964.

231   "Lisa Howard Pleads to Be Visible Again": *New York Times*, December 23, 1964.

231   "He is too inefficient to be ruthless": RFK letter, June 1, 1965, Senator Robert F. Kennedy papers, JFK Library.

231 "Mother was . . . having a mental breakdown": Author interview with Lareau.

232 "She was determined to die": Ibid.

232 Attwood told Schweiker . . . he had some suspicions: Attwood letter, October 16, 1975, William Attwood papers, State Historical Society of Wisconsin.

232 "This is why Kennedy was killed," Castro told him: Attwood memo on Cuba trip for Secretary of State Cyrus Vance, February 28, 1977, ibid.

233 Arthur Schlesinger concurred with Attwood's assessment: Summers, 307.

233 "We thought there was more to Dallas": Author interview with Simone Attwood.

233 "the secret negotiations with Cuba were the last straw": Tomlinson notes on Attwood conversation, January 29, 1986, courtesy of Anthony Summers.

234 "These were fairly nutty people": Quoted in *New Canaan Advocate*, June 12, 1980.

5: DALLAS

236 he mused that he found the job "rewarding": televised JFK press conference, October 31, 1963, Museum of Television and Radio, Beverly Hills.

237 "Scramble is putting it mildly": Author interview with Sorensen.

238 "the American people are going to save this country next year": Quoted in *Dallas Morning News*, November 19, 1963.

238 "Barry Goldwater could give Kennedy a breathlessly close race": Quoted in Perlstein, 234.

239 "a juicy steak for Connally, a sandwich for me": Jerry Bruno and Jeff Greenfield, *The Advance Man*, 88.

239 "Yarborough . . . felt the trip was too heavy on visits with fat cats": Ben Barnes, *Barn Burning, Barn Building: Tales of Political Life from LBJ to George W. Bush and Beyond*, 65.

239 "The president is not coming down to be hidden under a bushel basket": Quoted in *Washington Post*, November 20, 1988.

239 "I told the driver to step on it": Stanley Marcus oral history, Sixth Floor Museum, Dallas.

240 the American eagle [was turning] into a "dead duck": "Walker Speaks Unmuzzled" pamphlet, General Edwin Walker collection, Sixth Floor Museum.

240 calling Dallas "a very dangerous place": Quoted in Mahoney, 283.

240 "the president would have thought I had gone out of my mind": O'Donnell and Powers, 18.

240 "It turned my father and brothers and sisters and I upside down": Quoted in Edward J. Renehan, Jr., *The Kennedys at War: 1937–1945*, 2.

241 "I felt a surge of the intellectual power": Robert MacNeil, *The Right Place at the Right Time*, 200.

242 "We're heading into nut country today": Quoted in O'Donnell and Powers, 11.

242 Vallee . . . claimed that he was framed by someone with special knowledge of his . . . "CIA assignment": Quoted in Waldron, 630.

242 "The Tampa attempt . . . had even more parallels to Dallas": Ibid., 653.

243 a suspicious group of exiles moved into the house next door: Ibid., 683.

244 "Politics is a noble adventure": Quoted in Kerry McCarthy speech, JFK Lancer conference, November 22, 1997.

245 "They stood there rather stonily": Ralph Yarborough oral history, JFK Library.

247 "his head just opened up and shot down like a dog": Abraham Zapruder testimony, Warren Commission.

248   Hollywood "could never have dreamed up John F. Kennedy and Jacqueline Kennedy": Quoted in Cathy Trost and Susan Bennett, editors, *Kennedy Has Been Shot: The Inside Story of the Murder of a President*, 16.

248   "you certainly can't say that Dallas doesn't love you!": Nellie Connally, *From Love Field: Our Final Hours with President John F. Kennedy*, 7.

249   "His last expression was so neat": Theodore White's unpublished notes on his interview with Jacqueline Kennedy, November 29, 1963, JFK Library.

249   Connally would save her husband's life: Connally, 43.

250   "If only I had a minute to say goodbye": Quoted in Maier, 477.

251   "My whole face was splattered with blood and hair": White interview with Jacqueline Kennedy.

252   "I wonder if the missiles are flying": Author interview with James Galbraith.

252   "This is bad news": Quoted in *New Republic*, December 7, 1963.

253   Khrushchev took the news as "a personal blow": Quoted in William Taubman, *Khrushchev: The Man and His Era*, 604.

254   "I know he and my husband worked together for a peaceful world": Quoted in Manchester, 610.

254   "The danger troubling my husband was that war could be started": CNN.com report, "Letters reveal Soviet-U.S. dance following JFK assassination," August 5, 1999.

254   It was a bloodless coup: According to former KGB chief Vladimir Semichastny, Brezhnev did in fact seriously consider killing Khrushchev, asking the intelligence czar whether his rival could be poisoned or his plane sabotaged. But Semichastny claimed that he refused to carry out the assassination plot, insisting that he was "not a murderer."

255   "What kind of socialism is this?" Quoted in Taubman, 626.

255   If Kennedy had lived, the two men could have brought peace: Khrushchev, 557.

6: THE AWFUL GRACE OF GOD

258   a ten-thousand-word broadside that punched disturbing holes in the official version: the *National Guardian*, December 19, 1963.

258   Marguerite would insist . . . that her son was a U.S. "intelligence agent": *New York Times*, February 13, 1964.

258   "he was the only one who treated the commission with contempt": Earl Warren oral history, LBJ Library.

259   "we don't give a damn if blood runs in the streets of New York": Quoted in Mark Lane, *Plausible Denial: Was the CIA Involved in the Assassination of JFK?* 11.

259   "He just didn't like him": Author interview with Mankiewicz.

259   "but I don't have the heart for it right now": Sheridan oral history, JFK Library.

259   "But you're not going to talk about *that*, are you?": Author interview with Lane.

260   "there is something rotten in Dallas": Letter to RFK, November 28, 1963, Justice Department file, NARA record number 186-10003-10051.

260   "Europeans are convinced the Dallas drama hides a mystery": Quoted in Thomas G. Buchanan, *Who Killed Kennedy?* 150.

261   "I think he died for something": Ibid, 206.

261   Buchanan "sowed vast quantities of seeds of doubt about the assassination": *Washington Post*, May 2, 1964.

261   Buchanan "is most anxious to see you without going to the FBI": Attorney General Robert F. Kennedy phone logs, March 9, 1964, JFK Library.

261 a commission staff member . . . took the journalist's material and dropped it deep in the files: Buchanan would find a more curious reception for his conspiracy theories with a long-time adversary of Bobby Kennedy's—Ernesto "Che" Guevara. Today, decades after Che was hunted down by CIA-led trackers in the jungles of Bolivia, visitors to his home in Cuba can still see the books he was reading before he left on his fateful mission. There in his cramped upstairs office—in an alcove underneath his desk, next to several books on Bolivia, Africa, and the Algerian revolution—sits a French edition of Buchanan's book.

262 Kilgallen "has some information she wants to turn over to you": Attorney General Robert F. Kennedy phone logs, March 9, 1964, JFK Library.

262 she was going to have "the biggest scoop of the century": Quoted in Lee Israel, *Kilgallen: An Intimate Biography of Dorothy Kilgallen*, 382.

262 He was seen taking long walks . . . with Allen Dulles: Author interview with G. Robert Blakey.

263 that RFK also secretly recruited a mobster from upstate New York: Author interview with George Lardner Jr.

263 Mike Howard . . . had a surprise encounter with Attorney General Robert Kennedy: Author interview with Howard.

264 Perhaps Kennedy wanted "to look into Hoffa's eyes": Russo, *Live By the Sword*, 574.

265 "to get fucked around like that by Hoover": Author interview with Guthman.

265 who ruled the FBI like "the Great and Powerful Oz": Cartha D. "Deke" DeLoach, *Hoover's FBI: The Inside Story by Hoover's Trusted Lieutenant*, 13.

265 Guthman found the FBI czar's behavior "cruel and unnecessary": Guthman oral history, JFK Library.

266 "He looked to me like a man who is just in intense pain": Seigenthaler oral history, JFK Library.

266 The attorney general "was frequently an insurgent": Letter to RFK, January 11, 1964, Attorney General papers, JFK Library.

266 "He seemed absolutely devastated": Author interview with Blakey.

268 "Do you think God would separate me from my husband": Quoted in Maier, 472.

268 "Sorrow is a form of self-pity": Ibid., 470.

268 "Your grief goes as deep as your love": Ibid., 479.

269 "Everybody was in tears": Author interview with Murgado.

271 a wistful Bobby . . . "wondered at times if we did not pay a very great price for being more energetic than wise": Quoted in Wofford, 426.

271 a Castro agent in the United States . . . had paid Oswald $7,000: Letter to RFK, November 27, 1963, NARA record number 157-10002-10120.

271 Johnson "flatly told me my program with the Cubans had to be terminated: Quoted in Bohning, 244.

272 "It gives me a feeling of confidence": Quoted in Helms, 227.

272 one official later declared himself "not too impressed with the evidence": Joseph B. Smith, *Portrait of a Cold Warrior: Second Thoughts of a Top CIA Agent,* 383.

272 he no longer had the heart for anti-Castro intrigue: CIA memo, February 28, 1964.

273 "Now we'll never know": Quoted in Thomas, 308.

273 Helms phoned Kennedy to congratulate him on the Hoffa conviction: Attorney General Robert F. Kennedy phone logs, March 4, 1964, JFK Library.

273 "Dick Helms was not a warm and cuddly guy": Author interview with Nolan.

274 "Friday struck me personally": Attorney General Robert F. Kennedy correspondence file, JFK Library.

274 "I don't think Allen Dulles ever missed a meeting": Warren oral history, LBJ Library.

274 The former CIA chief had lobbied hard to get appointed: Trento, 269. Max Holland, a controversial figure in assassination research circles, has written that Robert Kennedy recommended Dulles's appointment to the Warren Commission. But considering the strains between Dulles and the Kennedy brothers—and Bobby's efforts to distance himself from the commission—this is unlikely. Dulles biographer Peter Grose concluded that there is "no evidence that the younger Kennedy played any role in the composition of the commission." As Warren Report chronicler Gerald McKnight has observed, none of the commission members was tied to the Kennedy wing of the Democratic Party.

274 "He had a very difficult time to decompress": Angleton testimony, Church Committee, February 6, 1976.

275 "A stranger man I never met": Author interview with Katzenbach.

275 the Kennedys "would have been safe in their luxury bunkers": Quoted in Heymann, *RFK*, 537.

275 "I'm not privy to who struck John": Quoted in *New York Times*, December 26, 1974.

275 "I would be absolutely misleading you if I thought I had any fucking idea": Croft interview with Hersh.

275 he was stunned to learn that Helms had chosen Bill Harvey: John Whitten testimony, House Select Committee on Assassinations (HSCA), executive session, May 16, 1978.

276 "Whitten was a rare CIA hero": *Washington Monthly*, December 2003.

276 "Nick, what do I do?": RFK's handwritten note on Warren letter, June 12, 1964, Attorney General papers, JFK Library.

277 "he didn't give a damn whether there was any investigation": Author interview with Katzenbach.

278 "I want to tell you why Kennedy died": Quoted in Max Holland, *The Kennedy Assassination Tapes: The White House Conversations Regarding the Assassination, the Warren Commission, and the Aftermath*. 236.

278 "The public must be satisfied that Oswald was the assassin": Quoted in Schlesinger, 615.

278 "I know of no credible evidence": RFK letter, August 4, 1964, Attorney General papers, JFK Library.

279 his brother's assassination was the work of a solitary "misfit": *Washington Post*, June 29, 1964.

280 "I have not read the report": *New York Times*, September 28, 1964.

280 he seemed "subdued": *New York Times*, September 29, 1964.

280 nothing more than a public relations exercise: Thomas, *Robert Kennedy*, 284.

280 "He always stood by the Warren Commission in public": Author interview with Mankiewicz.

281 Their report would "completely explode" these men's theories: Quoted in *New York Times*, June 1, 1964.

281 the subject [was] "very painful to me personally": Quoted in *Village Voice*, March 12, 1992.

281 "You're my man . . . period": Quoted in Holland, 151.

282   "I think someone else worked with him on the planning": Quoted in McKnight, 297.

282   which echoed the new president's own sentiments: Ibid, 19.

283   "just like the fly fisherman flick over the water": Quoted in Rhodri Jeffreys-Jones, *The CIA and American Democracy*, 140.

283   the CIA official flatly denied it to the president's face: Katzenbach testimony, HSCA, September 21, 1978.

283   "We don't know whether this is a worldwide conspiracy": Quoted in Holland, 14.

283   "hiding in the toilet . . . muttering 'Conspiracy' ": HSCA interview with Godfrey McHugh, May 11, 1978.

283   grew agitated when he saw the bloodred rug: DeLoach oral history, LBJ Library.

283   "they're more likely to get me killed": Quoted in Holland, 261.

284   "Could it have been the CIA?": DeLoach oral history.

284   "The assassination weighed on him as heavily as did the war": Holland, xxi.

284   "What do you think of this Oswald fellow?": Author interview with Howard.

285   Abe Fortas . . . poured cold water on the theory: Holland, 408.

285   "it had a very high purpose": Author interview with James Galbraith.

285   "Johnson was weighed down by a lot of guilt feelings": Author interview with Katzenbach.

286   "they were either telling a lie": Author interview with Ray Marcus.

287   "Where are the experts?": Quoted in the *New Yorker*, June 10, 1967.

287   "I can't look and won't look": Author interview with Marcus; also "Truth vs. Political Truth," self-published monograph by Marcus, August 2001.

288   "the Kennedys were trying to do a wonderful service": Author interview with Courtney Evans.

288   "It was a time we believed government": Author interview with Goldfarb.

288   "he knew damn well we would": Author interview with Herbert Miller.

289   "He would have chosen Walter Sheridan": Author interview with Goldfarb.

289   "I had to read the entire Warren Report": Author interview with Symington.

289   "It's unbelievable some of the stuff they concealed from the commission": Katzenbach testimony, HSCA.

290   "I'd say the Cubans probably had the worst judgment": Author interview with Katzenbach.

290   "there was more to it than we've gotten": Author interview with Fred Dutton.

290   "I would have put my dad in the [conspiracy] camp": Author interview with Daley.

290   "he thought it was for the good of the country": Author interview with Carol Bundy.

291   "I have made no effort to find out": Author interview with McNamara. McNamara's reluctance to focus his considerable intellectual energies on the assassination was made clear in an earlier interview, with JFK researcher Noel Twyman. But the former defense secretary, who agreed to talk with Twyman at his Georgetown house in October 1994 after meeting him on a hiking trek in the high Sierras, did grapple with the idea of a Dallas conspiracy in the course of their long dinner conversation. While McNamara insisted that it was impossible for top CIA officials like Allen Dulles and Richard Helms to have been involved in the assassination, he conceded that rogue agents might have played a role. "I absolutely don't think the CIA assassinated Kennedy, although I don't rule out some renegades," he told Twyman.

291   "He's an agnostic, but I'm not": Quoted in Eric Hamburg, *JFK, Nixon, Oliver Stone & Me: An Idealist's Journey from Capitol Hill to Hollywood Hell*, 272.

291 "We played tennis with him": Author interview with Hamburg.

292 "a man who is a fabulous gardener is not going to kill off a president": Author interview with Marie Ridder.

292 "It's terribly painful": Author interview with Sorensen.

293 "We saw pieces of bone and brain tissue": O'Donnell and Powers, 27.

294 "That's not what you told the Warren Commission": Tip O'Neill, *Man of the House: The Life and Political Memoirs of Speaker Tip O'Neill*, 178.

294 Hoover himself pressured O'Donnell: Waldron, 902.

294 "they didn't want to know": Author interview with Kenny O'Donnell Jr.

295 He couldn't get the "sickening sound" out of his head: Quoted in Melanson, 76.

295 "He seemed to step forward into human company": Helen O'Donnell, 339.

295 "the music without the harp": Quoted in *Washington Post*, September 30, 1977.

297 America's military prowess must be coupled with "the inner strength and wisdom": Quoted in *New York Times*, September 30, 1964.

297 "a *lot* of people would have taken a bullet for Bob Kennedy": Author interview with Guthman.

298 "They're for him": Quoted in Guthman, 294.

298 "he wanted a vice president who could help the country": Quoted in Helen O'Donnell, 346.

298 "let's go form our own country": Quoted in Schlesinger, 661.

298 "We are not going to let Bobby and Jackie Kennedy steal this": Quoted in Helen O'Donnell, 349.

299 Kennedy's voice suddenly cracked: Thomas, *Robert Kennedy*, 298.

299 "God damn, Bob, be yourself": Ibid., 299.

300 "Everybody says I'm so ruthless": Author interview with Justin Feldman.

300 "We quietly cried together": Joe Tydings oral history, JFK Library.

300 "He didn't see it as a real action place": Salinger oral history, JFK Library.

301 the visiting U.S senator could not escape official supervision: *Direccion Federal de Seguridad* memos, November 16 and 17, 1964, courtesy of Jefferson Morley.

301 Scott noted . . . that playwright Elena Garro de Paz: John Newman, *Oswald and the CIA*, 382.

302 Bobby also agreed to meet . . . with Penn Jones Jr.: Author interviews with Penn Jones III, Gary Shaw and David Wrone; also *Dallas Morning News*, November 22, 1992.

302 "a small shrine to President Kennedy": *New York Times Magazine*, June 20, 1965.

302 "He always forgot the damn overcoat": Author interview with Ronnie Eldridge.

302 "My first husband was killed in World War II": Author interview with Ridder.

303 "We know the CIA was involved, and the Mafia": Author interview with Goodwin.

303 "I feel strongly that I am doing a service": Goodwin letter, undated, Attorney General Robert F. Kennedy papers, JFK Library.

303 "I wish you wouldn't": Quoted in Goodwin, 254.

304 "he doesn't have the intellectual depth of his brother": Ibid., 299.

304 the closest personal relationship: Ibid., 433.

304 Goodwin was "the first member of the late president's inner circle": *New York Times*, July 24, 1966.

304 help get him a copy of a thirty-three-page letter written by Jack Ruby: Goodwin letter, March 2, 1966, Senator Robert F. Kennedy papers, JFK Library.

305 Over nightcaps in Kennedy's living room: Goodwin, 463.

306 Walinsky [found] the Warren Report . . . "completely tortured and strange": Author interview with Adam Walinsky.

306   And so Kennedy bided his time: According to Walinsky, Kennedy knew how to be patient. Once Walinsky relayed some disturbing information to RFK that he had learned about high-ranking CIA officials. The Kennedy aide had been informed by a close friend—a psychiatrist at the National Institutes of Mental Health who treated "the top CIA wives"—that the upper ranks of the intelligence agency were filled with sexually deviant personalities. "[My friend] came to me," Walinksy recalled in an oral history for the JFK Library, "and he said, 'Listen, I want you to know that the people who are running the CIA are really very, very, very sick and disturbed individuals. I mean, like they're the kind of people who make their wives tie them up to the bed and beat them with whips at night . . . I mean, you know, real fetishes and crazy sado-masochistic behavior. . . . He was talking about the *very* top level people." When Walinksy reported this to Kennedy, the senator made it clear to him that it was "just something you've got to tuck away and wait . . . until you get the levers of power."

307   RFK wondered "how long he could continue to avoid comment": Schlesinger, 616.

307   John P. Roche . . . denounced conspiracy researchers as "marginal paranoids": Quoted in *New York Times*, January 3, 1968.

307   "Note that Robert Kennedy . . . would be the last man": CIA memo, document number 1035-960, January 4, 1967, reprinted on JFK Lancer Web site, http://www.jfklancer.com/CIA.html.

308   "Bobby, do you really believe": Don Hewitt, *Tell Me a Story: Fifty Years and 60 Minutes in Television*.

308   Lee Harvey Oswald and Jack Ruby were not strangers: Author interview with Hewitt.

7: NEW ORLEANS

309   "but nobody would care if we had lived or died": Quoted in *People*, May 24, 1982.

310   "I don't talk like that": Mankiewicz speech, Robert F. Kennedy memorial, November 16, 2005, U.S. Capitol building.

310   "the U.S. government tried to emulate George III": *People*, ibid.

310   "Nobody would give you an argument": Quoted in "The Battle Over *Citizen Kane*," PBS series, *American Experience*.

311   "He was a gambler": *People*, ibid.

311   "I'd call in the heads of the three TV networks": Author interview with Mankiewicz.

312   "Very few people were from Beverly Hills": *People*, ibid.

312   "I'm not sure that *he* does": Author interview with Mankiewicz.

313   "He looked small and cold": *Philadelphia Inquirer*, December 7, 1966.

314   "Bill thought that Bobby was a real tough guy": Author interview with Simone Attwood.

314   [Attwood] strongly encouraged Kennedy to commit himself to reopening the case: Author interview with William Pepper.

316   Joe Dolan, a man who harbored even more explosive suspicions about Dallas than RFK: "I think [Lyndon] Johnson was part of the plot to kill the president," Dolan told me in a 2005 interview. Dolan could not provide any evidence to support his assertion. And there is nothing to indicate that Robert Kennedy shared his suspicion.

316   "The truth has been suppressed": David Crosby biography, A&E Biography Channel.

317 "see what happened to him for his pains": Quoted in Santa Barbara *Argo*, April 1–15, 1968.

317 "caused people to accuse me of not being funny": *PR Newswire*, January 6, 1992.

317 an orgy of "communal crying": Mort Sahl on *Fresh Air*, NPR, December 23, 2003.

317 "Hitler said that he always knew you could buy the press": Quoted in *Newsweek*, August 9, 1976.

318 his reporters "would go over all the areas of doubt": Quoted in *Newsweek*, December 12, 1966.

319 "You can always meet a president": Quoted in Joan Mellen, *A Farewell to Justice: Jim Garrison, JFK's Assassination and the Case that Should Have Changed History*, 23.

319 "Those fellows on the Warren Commission were dead wrong": Quoted in Jim Garrison, 13.

320 "For me . . . that was the end of innocence": *Playboy* interview, October 1967.

320 "I'm not sure about going to New Orleans": Hale Boggs oral history, LBJ Library.

320 "President Kennedy was killed for one reason": *Playboy*, ibid.

320 "our government is the CIA and the Pentagon": Ibid.

321 Ferrie was . . . "swept up in the gales of history": Ibid.

322 "Yeah, and I'm the Lone Ranger": Quoted in Russo, *Live by the Sword*, 403.

323 "if it weren't so deadly serious": Jerry Cohen memo to Guthman, August 18, 1967, Edwin Guthman papers, JFK Library.

323 "I sent some of our best people down there": Author interview with Guthman.

323 [Kennedy] had "assigned different aspects of the . . . case": Author interview with Newfield.

325 When Sheridan dug up evidence . . . that Jack Ruby had received a "bundle of money": FBI memo, November 24, 1963, NARA record number 124-10072-10228.

325 Sheridan knew how to "swim underwater": Author interview with John Cassidy.

325 "secrets were safe with Walter": Senator Edward M. Kennedy eulogy, January 17, 1995, Sheridan papers, JFK Library.

325 "They continued working on the case": Author interview with Nancy Sheridan.

326 "I want to hit people between the eyes": Quoted in *Newsweek*, October 23, 1967.

327 Gurvich . . . worried that [Kennedy] would think "there actually was something in New Orleans": Quoted in Patricia Lambert, *False Witness: The Real Story of Jim Garrison's Investigation and Oliver Stone's Film JFK*, 117.

327 Campisi . . . was the first person to visit Jack Ruby in jail: Blakey and Billings, 360.

327 Garrison gave Carlos Marcello a pass: Ibid., xxxi. According to Zachary Sklar, co-writer of *JFK*, Oliver Stone's glorification of Jim Garrison, even Stone was initially suspicious of Garrison's benign view of Marcello. "Before he made the final decision to make the movie," Sklar informed me in a March 2005 e-mail, "[Stone] had a researcher compile every nasty story about Marcello she could find, and Oliver threw every allegation at Jim. At the end, he said to Oliver: 'Are you finished?' Oliver said yes. Jim said, 'Then I suggest you take your cameras up the river about ten miles where Carlos Marcello is in jail, and you go make a movie about Carlos Marcello.' Oliver was astonished. 'Are you serious?' 'Dead serious,' said Jim. Oliver left, and called back the next day: 'You mean you'd give up a movie about yourself?' 'Well, you seem more interested in Carlos Marcello than me, so just go make a movie about him. That's fine.' Oliver never asked another question about Carlos Marcello."

328   Sheridan . . . took the extraordinary step of approaching the CIA: CIA security file on Walter Sheridan, NARA record number 104-10305-10003.

329   [Helms] repeatedly asked his top deputies whether "we are giving [the Shaw defense team] all the help they need: Quoted in Garrison, 234.

329   "his personal ties to President Kennedy, as well as his own integrity": Statement of Senator Robert F. Kennedy, Sheridan papers, JFK Library.

329   "He was telling Carson that Garrison was full of crap": Author interview with Jeff Greenfield.

330   "Politics became a noble profession again": Sheridan dedication speech, John F. Kennedy Junior High School, December 1, 1965, Sheridan papers, JFK Library.

330   "I felt cut off from the world": Quoted in *Newsweek*, October 23, 1967.

330   "They didn't trust it": Author interview with Nancy Sheridan.

332   "The conversation was so innocuous": Sahl, *Heartland*, 148.

333   the message from Bobby was always the same: Ibid, 149.

334   "What are we going to do—listen to . . . a nightclub comedian": Author interview with Sahl.

334   Bobby didn't want the "real assassins" caught: Quoted in Lambert, 124.

334   "what kind of friends did those guys have?": Author interview with Sahl.

335   "He was the keeper of confidences": Newfield, *Somebody's Gotta Tell It*, 161.

335   he conceded there might be something to Moldea's suspicions: Author interview with Dan Moldea.

335   "there was something else going on in Dallas": Author interview with Walter Sheridan Jr.

336   Newfield . . . used the word "suicidal": Author interview with Newfield.

336   "He did not have the mandate": Author interview with Nancy Sheridan

8: THE PASSION OF ROBERT KENNEDY

337   "This scared the bejesus out of Siegel and his wife": Author interview with Nolan.

338   would not allow the senator's trip to be "transformed into a publicity stunt": Quoted in Schlesinger, 744.

339   "What does it mean to be against communism": *Look*, August 23, 1966.

339   "suppose God is black": Ibid.

339   he joined them in singing . . . "We Shall Overcome": Schlesinger, 746.

339   Kennedy called "a dreary concentration camp": Ibid.

339   "If we stayed another two days": Ibid., 748.

340   Kennedy thought the U.S. invasion was an "outrage": Ibid, 691.

340   "anybody can get guns": Walinsky oral history, JFK Library.

340   "There has been all this romanticism": Author interview with Walinsky.

340   Kennedy . . . called Guevara "a revolutionary hero": Schlesinger, 801.

341   Tom Mann was the type of "colonialist": Goodwin, 245.

341   "I never believed we should compete with the revolutionaries": Mann oral history, JFK Library.

342   "The responsibility of our time is nothing less than a revolution": Quoted in *New York Times*, November 13, 1965.

342   "we can't get a water tank for these people because of an oil dispute?": *New York Times*, November 27, 1965.

342   "you're making way for your own destruction": Ibid.

342   "It's a sight I'll never forget": Walinsky oral history, JFK Library.

344 "I'm the guy who saved his life": Quoted in Goodwin, 189.

344 "they're going to have to improve their aim": Quoted in Schlesinger, 696.

344 he clambered on top of a police car and sang: *New York Times*, November 17, 1965.

344 he was given a standing ovation: *New York Times*, November 21, 1965.

344 It had to do . . . with "that whole history of the Kennedys": Walinsky oral history, JFK Library.

345 "Yet it was not because of him that they were shouting": Goodwin, 435.

345 "Stay in school": Quoted in *New York Times*, November 22, 1965.

345 "Sooner or later": Quoted in Schlesinger, 698.

346 "you doves will all be dead in six months": Quoted in Joseph A. Palermo, *In His Own Right: The Political Odyssey of Senator Robert F. Kennedy*, 42.

346 "That marvelous human being who is president of the United States": Quoted in Thomas, *Robert Kennedy*, 333.

346 "he looks at me like he's going to look a hole through me": Ibid, 295.

346 Kennedy was little more than a Communist dupe: Palermo, 44.

347 "Lyndon Johnson was so insane": Ibid., 46.

347 "It makes the rug grow better": Quoted in Newfield, *RFK: A Memoir*, 135.

348 Edelman . . . called it "mushy": Quoted in Palermo, 45.

348 Nixon said Kennedy's speech: Schlesinger, 774.

348 Goldwater charged that Kennedy was out of control: *New York Times*, March 3, 1967.

348 Bobby was proposing a "dishonorable settlement": Quoted in Schlesinger, 774.

350 Edelman thought his boss even urged the once mighty defense czar: Peter Edelman oral history, JFK Library.

350 "Many in this room believe Lyndon Johnson is crude": McNamara, 317.

350 "You think to challenge me": "Caesar's Meat," Walinsky papers, JFK Library.

351 "history was going to show he is to blame": Mandelkorn letter, *The Hook* (Charlottesville, VA), April 8, 2004.

351 "You are the one that makes the difference for all of us": RFK letter, March 13, 1964, Attorney General Robert F. Kennedy papers, JFK Library.

351 "I wasn't stupid": Author interview with McNamara.

352 "Do you know what I think will happen to Bobby?": Quoted in Schlesinger, 857.

353 "Something bad is going to come of this": Quoted in John Ehrlichman, *Witness to Power: The Nixon Years*, 24.

353 "I hope that someone shoots and kills the son of a bitch": Quoted in Sullivan, 56.

353 "Which of these brave young men dying in the rice paddies": Quoted in Jules Witcover, *85 Days: The Last Campaign of Robert F. Kennedy*, 112.

354 the crowd "suddenly became a live and dangerous thing": Ibid, 113.

354 "I loved him intensely as a human being": Ibid, 114.

354 "I was amazed at what I saw, no security at all": Author interview with Guthman.

355 the Kennedy campaign was being targeted by the same . . . FBI dirty tactics: Palermo, 179.

356 the teenager put one of his favorite songs on the living room stereo: Author interview with Stephen Salinger.

357 "He was prepared to handle it": Croft interview with Rick Tuttle.

358 "I remember that I was stunned by the answer": Author interview with Mankiewicz.

359 Richard Lubic . . . later made notes: Robbyn Swan interview with Lubic, courtesy of Swan and Anthony Summers.

359   "We can't have these cowboys wandering around": Author interview with Pete Hamill.

359   Kennedy thought the agency "was out of control": Author interview with Dutton.

360   [Helms and McCarthy] "lunched occasionally": Helms, 247.

361   "I touched him!": Quoted in Hamill, *Irrational Ravings*, 264.

362   Kennedy had come to the farm workers' aid: Quoted in Palermo, 226.

362   "His face looked like an old man's": Newfield, *RFK*, 283.

362   "He felt he had to ride in a convertible": Ibid., 286.

363   "You had a little trouble with some words that time": Ibid., 287.

363   Frankenheimer even got Bobby to talk about his suspicions: Author interview with Evans Frankenheimer.

364   "you can't make it without that good old bitch, luck": Quoted in Salinger, *P.S.*, 186.

364   "I suppose none of us will ever get over John Kennedy": Goodwin, 535.

365   "Bobby and I exchanged a look": Salinger, 196.

365   "He had arrived": Quoted in Witcover, 257.

365   Newfield jotted down the word "liberated": Newfield, *Somebody's Gotta Tell It*, 205.

365   He asked Schulberg about the Watts Writers Workshop: Author interview with Newfield.

365   Dutton had decided that Kennedy should exit the back way: Author interview with Dutton.

366   "But we lost him that night": Author interview with Joe Dolan.

366   a "long grubby area": Hamill, 284.

366   "I'm not just a busboy": Quoted in *Los Angeles Times*, June 1, 2003.

367   His face "had a kind of sweet acceptance to it": Hamill, 285.

367   "an ironic smile as if he had been expecting this": Author interview with Hamill.

367   Bobby's last words . . . were "Jack, Jack": Goodwin, 538.

368   "There's a literary phrase—'the room heaved' ": Croft interview with Tuttle.

368   "we both knew that he was dead": Author interview with Goodwin.

368   Frankenheimer and his wife, Evans, were waiting in their Rolls-Royce: Author interview with Evans Frankenheimer.

369   "I have never seen as agonized a look": Author interview with Mankiewicz.

370   The first autopsy photos . . . were rushed to the FBI chief: Summers, *Official and Confidential*, 424.

370   The gruesome, color autopsy pictures also found their way into the safe of James Angleton: CIA document, "Extracts from CIA History," NARA record number 104-10301-10011.

370   "Maybe there's no way, no way, to change this country": Ellsberg, *Secrets: A Memoir of Vietnam and the Pentagon Papers*, 220.

370   "After Bobby was shot, the lights went out for me": Author interview with Dutton.

371   "why the unabashedly liberal Mr. Dutton . . . later agreed to represent the conservative Saudi Arabian government": *Los Angeles Times*, June 28, 2005.

371   "Dick went kind of nuts": Author interview with Newfield.

371   "I had to get away": Author interview with Goodwin.

371   Jacqueline Kennedy . . . threw herself on his coffin: Author interview with Bill Rosendahl.

371   "I went through sheer hell": Quoted in *New York Times*, July 7, 2002.

371   "He would have had no tolerance": Author interview with Walinsky.

372   "It was *The Manchurian Candidate*": Quoted in *People*, May 16, 1988.

372 "because we didn't know anything about Palestinians": Author interview with Hamill.

373 the autopsy indicated that the fatal shot was fired directly behind his head: Dr. Thomas T. Noguchi, *Coroner*, 103.

373 "I don't believe that Sirhan's gun got within a couple of inches of Kennedy's head": Author interview with Frank Burns.

373 it "all seemed to indicate there may have been a second gunman": Noguchi, 108.

374 the Kennedys had "sold the country down the road": Quoted in Melanson, 120.

374 "It's none of your business": Author interview with Lubic.

374 "Unruh talked to Kenny O'Donnell": Author interview with Burns.

375 "There is no curse upon the Kennedys": Tribute to Senator Robert F. Kennedy, June 7, 1968, RFK papers, JFK Library.

375 "We've been on an endless cycle of retreat": Author interview with Goodwin.

376 "I was at one of those memorial events once": Author interview with Walinksy.

9: TRUTH AND RECONCILIATION

379 "we never produced any evidence that Castro was involved: Author interview with Dave Marston.

379 "we do know that Oswald had intelligence connections": Quoted in Fonzi, 31.

379 "He was a blowtorch": Author interview with Gary Hart.

380 "My opinion of the CIA has greatly diminished through the years": Author interview with Richard Schweiker.

381 "I think what happened to me in 1987 was a pure setup": Author interview with Hart.

383 "every capillary in my body went into electrified shock": Author interview with Robert Tanenbaum.

385 A *New York Times* article clawed through Sprague's past: *New York Times*, January 2, 1977.

385 "My daughter, when I was in Washington, was three years old": Tanenbaum testimony, Assassination Archives Review Board, September 17, 1996.

386 "the committee ultimately obtained from the CIA every single document": Quoted in Fonzi, 303.

386 "We were not popular in Langley": Author interview with Dan Hardway.

388 "I think the mob did it": Quoted in *New York Times*, June 3, 1979.

388 "I don't know how many times since 1978 that Bob and I have had this conversation": Blakey seems willing to concede that someone "low-level" in the CIA like William Harvey might have been involved, or at least been aware, of the JFK plot. But, in his mind, this still does not implicate the agency itself. "If Harvey is involved in the conspiracy, you can't really attribute that to the agency itself—it's a rogue agent," he told me. But, if by "rogue agent," Blakey means someone in the lower rungs of the CIA who was operating on his own, this point is debatable. Bill Harvey was a CIA legend who had been entrusted with two of the agency's most sensitive operations—the Berlin station, at the front lines of the Cold War, and Task Force W, the heavily funded anti-Castro project. Harvey reported directly to Helms and could count on his bureaucratic protection. In his testimony before the Church Committee, Harvey insisted—and there is reason to believe him—that he never did anything that was "unauthorized, freewheeling or in any way outside the

[agency] framework." It is more likely that Harvey was a convenient agency fall guy than an out-of-control agent. The "rogue agent" scenario where that assassination researchers like Blakey—who recoil at the idea that the plot came from within the government itself, but nonetheless must contend with compelling evidence it did—often find a safe refuge.

388 The *New Times* article, which was written by *Washington Post* reporter Jefferson Morley: Morley had originally pitched the story to his editors at the *Post*, but true to form, the newspaper turned it down. "They all agreed it was an interesting story—there was no lack of intellectual curiosity in it," Morley wryly recalled. "There was just a lack of publishing interest."

388 "Joannides's behavior was criminal": Quoted in *Salon*, December 17, 2003.

388 "Many have told me that the culture of the agency is one of prevarication": Quoted on "Who Was Lee Harvey Oswald?" PBS *Frontline* Web site.

389 "My private opinion is that JFK was done in by a conspiracy": Quoted in Larry Hancock, *Someone Would Have Talked*, 126.

389 "I was one of the two case officers who handled Lee Harvey Oswald": David Atlee Phillips' novel outline for *The AMLASH Legacy*, courtesy James Lesar.

389 "Were you in Dallas on that day?": E-mail from Shawn Phillips, reprinted at http://www.jfkmurdersolved.com/phillips.htm.

390 the CIA alone had over four hundred American journalists secretly at its service: *Rolling Stone*, October 20, 1977.

390 some of these journalists did the CIA's bidding: see, for instance, a January 25, 1968 CIA memo on Hugh Aynesworth, who covered the JFK assassination, first for the *Dallas Morning News* and then *Newsweek*. Aynesworth—who at one time, according to the memo, "expressed some interest . . . in possible employment with the Agency"—was considered by the CIA to be a solid "Warren Commission man on the assassination." NARA record number 104-10170-10230.

391 [Bradlee's] friendship with JFK "dominated my life": Bradlee, *Conversations with Kennedy*, 9.

391 The *Washington Post's* failure . . . was "especially puzzling": *Rolling Stone*, April 24, 1975.

391 "someone who wants to devote his life to [the case]": The only *Washington Post* reporter who stuck doggedly with the assassination story over the years was George Lardner Jr.—among whose distinctions was apparently being the last person to speak with David Ferrie on the night of his death. Lardner is a controversial figure in assassination research circles for his image as conspiracy skeptic. He was the first reporter to target Oliver Stone, using a purloined copy of the controversial *JFK* script to attack the director—whom he accused of "assassinat[ing] the truth"—before the movie was even released. Despite his reputation, Lardner—now retired—told me that he came to believe in a JFK conspiracy after examining evidence unearthed by the House Select Committee on Assassinations. "I think the evidence indicates there was Mafia involvement in the killing," he said. But the *Post* never followed up on Lardner's suspicions by investigating a possible organized crime involvement.

392 "Jesus . . . if I were Bobby, I would certainly have taken a look at that": Author interview with Bradlee.

393 "We tried and tried and tried": Author interview with Hewitt.

394 "You don't want to know," Nixon had replied: According to H.R. Haldeman, Nixon's

White House chief of staff, Nixon apparently connected the Kennedy assassination to the CIA's Cuba plots. In his 1978 memoir, *The Ends of Power*, Haldeman told an eye-opening story about the time Nixon ordered him to pressure CIA chief Dick Helms into helping the president head off the looming Watergate scandal. Following Nixon's mysterious instructions, Haldeman sat down Helms in his office and warned him that Watergate "may be connected to the Bay of Pigs and if it opens up, the Bay of Pigs may be blown." To Haldeman's surprise, the normally self-contained Helms exploded at this, shouting, "The Bay of Pigs had nothing to do with this. I have no concern about the Bay of Pigs." Nixon's top aide later concluded that "Bay of Pigs" was Nixon's code for the Kennedy assassination.

394 "Every American owes [Oliver Stone] a debt of gratitude": Quoted in Associated Press syndicated article, October 21, 1992.

395 "because it challenged the work they had done in the 1960s": Quoted in *Regardie's* August 1992.

395 "History may be too important to leave to newsmen": *New York Times*, December 20, 1991.

395 How could plush-salaried press sages . . . pooh-pooh the idea of a conspiracy: Stone speech to National Press Club, reprinted in *JFK: The Book of the Film*, 407.

395 They had decided years before to follow Bobby's public vow to focus on the future: "For me to now get interested in [assassination research] would be going against a habit of forty years," Kathleen Kennedy Townsend, the daughter of Robert Kennedy and former lieutenant governor of Maryland, explained to me. The lesson that was drummed into her generation of Kennedys, she said, was "there is nothing you can do to bring somebody back. So the issue is what you can do with your life to go forward, to promote their ideals. And we were taught that's a better way to live life. That was the message, and it was very strong."

395 "I worked on the film's behalf because I believed in it": Author interview with Mankiewicz.

396 On the 1992 campaign trail. Clinton and . . . Gore [called for] relevant government documents [to be] released: Author interview with Palamara.

396 Clinton [asked] Webster Hubbell . . . to find out "who killed JFK": Hubbell, *Friends in High Places: Our Journey from Little Rock to Washington, D.C.*

396 The CIA's deception of Congress "is not a performance that inspires public confidence": *Newsweek*, November 24, 2003.

397 "My gut feeling": BBC *Newsnight* transcript, November 20, 2006.

397 O'Sullivan suggested that the man caught on camera: Author interview with Shane O'Sullivan.

398 Morales was the agency's "peon": Author interview with Morales family member.

398 "Dave Morales did dirty work": Author interview with Wayne Smith.

398 Morales..."was in the palace when Allende was killed": Summers, *The Arrogance of Power: The Secret World of Richard Nixon*, 336.

399 "I was in Dallas when...we got that mother fucker": *Newsnight* transcript.

400 "When some asshole needed to be killed": Author interview with Ruben Carbajal.

401 . . . the CIA was involved in the assassination . . . "but I don't know exactly who": Author interview with Antonio Veciana.

402 Hunt suggested that several prominent CIA officials might have been involved: E. Howard Hunt, *American Spy*, 134.

403 "I didn't resent him": Author interview with St. John Hunt.

405 he was invited by Frank Sturgis...to a clandestine meeting: Handwritten E. Howard Hunt notes, courtesy of St. John Hunt.

406 dismiss JFK as "a vulgar hoodlum": *Atlantic*, September 2006.

408 "My guess is that the Warren Commission will carry the day": Author interview with Blakey.

BIBLIOGRAPHY

Attwood, William. *The Twilight Struggle: Tales of the Cold War*. New York: Harper & Row, 1987.

Ayers, Bradley E. *The Zenith Secret*. Brooklyn, N.Y.: Vox Pop. 2006.

Bamford, James. *Body of Secrets: Anatomy of the Ultra-Secret National Security Agency*. New York: Anchor Books, 2002.

Barnes, Ben and Dickey, Lisa. *Barn Burning, Barn Building: Tales of Political Life from LBJ to George W. Bush and Beyond*. Albany, TX: Bright Sky Press, 2006.

Beschloss, Michael R. *The Crisis Years: Kennedy and Khrushchev 1960–1963*. New York: Edward Burlingame Books, 1991.

Bissell, Richard M. *Reflections of a Cold Warrior*. New Haven: Yale University Press, 1996.

Blakey, G. Robert and Billings, Richard. *Fatal Hour: The Assassination of President Kennedy by Organized Crime*. New York: Berkley Books, 1992.

Bohning, Don. *The Castro Obsession: U.S. Covert Operations Against Cuba, 1959–1965*. Washington, D.C.: Potomac Books, Inc., 2005.

Bradlee, Ben. *A Good Life: Newspapering and Other Adventures*. New York: Simon & Schuster, 1995.

Bradlee, Benjamin C. *Conversations with Kennedy*. New York: W. W. Norton & Company, 1975.

Brugioni, Dino A. *Eyeball to Eyeball: The Inside Story of the Cuban Missile Crisis*. New York: Random House, 1991.

Bruno, Jerry and Greenfield, Jeff. *The Advance Man*. New York: William Morrow, 1971.

Buchanan, Thomas G. *Who Killed Kennedy?* New York: G. P. Putnam's Sons, 1964.

Burleigh, Nina. *A Very Private Woman: The Life and Unsolved Murder of Presidential Mistress Mary Meyer*. New York: Bantam Books, 1999.

Califano, Joseph A. *Inside: A Public and Private Life*. New York: Public Affairs, 2004.

Clarke, Thurston. *Ask Not*. New York: Henry Holt and Company, 2004.

Coffey, Thomas M. *Iron Eagle: The Turbulent Life of General Curtis LeMay*. New York: Crown Publishers, 1986.

Connally, Nellie. *From Love Field: Our Final Hours with President John F. Kennedy*. New York: Ruggedland, 2003.

Cook, Fred J. *The Warfare State*. New York: The Macmillan Company, 1962.

Corn, David. *Blond Ghost: Ted Shackley and the CIA's Crusades*. New York: Simon & Schuster, 1994.

Cousins, Norman. *The Improbable Triumvirate: John F. Kennedy, Pope John, Nikita Khrushchev*. New York: W. W. Norton & Company, 1972.

Davis, John H. *Mafia Kingfish: Carlos Marcello and the Assassination of John F. Kennedy*. New York: New American Library, 1989.

DeLoach, Cartha D. "Deke." *Hoover's FBI: The Inside Story by Hoover's Trusted Lieutenant*. Washington, D.C.: Regnery Publishing, Inc., 1995.

Di Eugenio, James and Pease, Lisa. *The Assassinations*. Los Angeles: Feral House, 2003.

Doyle, William. *An American Insurrection: James Meredith and the Battle of Oxford, Mississippi, 1962*. New York: Anchor Books, 2001.

Dudman, Richard. *Men of the Far Right*. New York: Pyramid Books, 1962.

Ehrlichman, John. *Witness to Power: The Nixon Years*. New York: Pocket Books, 1982.

Ellsberg, Daniel. *Secrets: A Memoir of Vietnam and the Pentagon Papers*. New York: Penguin Books, 2002.

Fay, Paul B. *The Pleasure of His Company*. New York: Popular Library, 1966.

Fonzi, Gaeton. *The Last Investigation*. New York: Thunder's Mouth Press, 1993.

Frankel, Max. *High Noon in the Cold War: Kennedy, Khrushchev, and the Cuban Missile Crisis*. New York: Ballantine Books, 2004.

Freidin, Seymour and Bailey, George. *The Experts*. New York: The Macmillan Company, 1968.

Fursenko, Aleksandr and Naftali, Timothy. *"One Hell of a Gamble": The Secret History of the Cuban Missile Crisis*. New York: W. W. Norton & Company, 1997.

Garrison, Jim. *On the Trail of the Assassins: My Investigation and Prosecution of the Murder of President Kennedy*. New York: Sheridan Square Press, 1988.

Goldfarb, Ronald. *Perfect Villains, Imperfect Heroes: Robert F. Kennedy's War Against Organized Crime*. Sterling, VA: Capital Books, 2002.

Goodwin, Richard N. *Remembering America: A Voice From the Sixties*. Boston: Little, Brown and Company, 1988.

Grose, Peter. *Gentleman Spy: The Life of Allen Dulles*. Boston: Houghton Mifflin Company, 1994.

Guthman, Edwin. *We Band of Brothers: A Memoir of Robert F. Kennedy*. New York: Harper & Row, 1964.

Haldeman, H. R. *The Ends of Power*, New York: New York Times Books, 1978.

Hamburg, Eric. *JFK, Nixon, Oliver Stone & Me: An Idealist's Journey from Capitol Hill to Hollywood Hell*. New York: Public Affairs, 2002.

Hamill, Pete. *Irrational Ravings*. New York: Putnam, 1971.

Hancock, Larry. *Someone Would Have Talked*. Southlake, Texas: JFK Lancer Productions & Publications, Inc., 2003.

Helms, Richard. *A Look Over My Shoulder: A Life in the Central Intelligence Agency*. New York: Ballantine Books, 2003.

Hepburn, James. *Farewell America: The Plot to Kill JFK*. Roseville, CA: Penmarin Books, 2002.

Hersh, Seymour M. *The Dark Side of Camelot*. Boston: Back Bay Books, 1998.

Hewitt, Don. *Tell Me a Story: Fifty Years and 60 Minutes in Television*. New York: Public Affairs, 2002.

Heymann, C. David. *The Georgetown Ladies' Social Club: Power, Passion, and Politics in the Nation's Capital*. New York: Atria Books, 2003.

Hinckle, Warren and Turner, William. *Deadly Secrets: The CIA-Mafia War Against Castro and the Assassination of JFK*. New York: Thunder's Mouth Press, 1992.

Holland, Max. *The Kennedy Assassination Tapes*. New York: Alfred A. Knopf, 2004.

Hubbell, Webster. *Friends in High Places: Our Journey from Little Rock to Washington, D.C.* New York: William Morrow, 1997.

Hunt, E. Howard. *American Spy: My Secret History in the CIA, Watergate & Beyond*. Hoboken, N.J.: John Wiley & Sons, Inc., 2007.

Hunt, E. Howard. *Give Us This Day: The Inside Story of the CIA and the Bay of Pigs Invasion*. New Rochelle NY: Arlington House, 1973.

Hurt, Henry. *Reasonable Doubt: An Investigation into the Assassination of John F. Kennedy*. New York: Owl Books, 1985.

Israel, Lee. *Kilgallen*. New York: Dell, 1979.

Jeffreys-Jones, Rhodri. *Cloak and Dollar: A History of American Secret Intelligence*. New Haven: Yale University Press, 2002.

Johnson, Haynes. *The Bay of Pigs: The Leaders' Story of Brigade 2506*. New York: W. W. Norton & Company, Inc., 1964.

Kennedy, Robert F. *The Enemy Within: The McClellan Committee's Crusade Against Jimmy Hoffa and Corrupt Labor Unions*. New York: Da Capo Press, 1994.

Kennedy, Robert. *In His Own Words: The Unpublished Recollections of the Kennedy Years*. New York: Bantam Books, 1988.

Khrushchev, Nikita. *Khrushchev Remembers*. New York: Bantam Books, 1971.

Knebel, Fletcher and Bailey, Charles W. *Seven Days in May*. New York: Bantam, 1962.

Lambert, Patricia. *False Witness*. New York: M. Evans and Company, Inc., 1998.

Lane, Mark. *Plausible Denial: Was the CIA Involved in the Assassination of JFK?* New York: Thunder's Mouth Press, 1991.

Lasky, Victor. *J.F.K.: The Man and the Myth*. New York: Macmillan, 1963.

Lazo, Mario. *Dagger in the Heart: American Policy Failures in Cuba*. New York: Twin Circle, 1968.

Leary, Timothy. *Flashbacks: An Autobiography*. Boston: Houghton Mifflin Company, 1983.

MacNeil, Robert. *The Right Place at the Right Time*. Boston: Little, Brown and Company, 1982.

Maheu, Robert. *Next to Hughes*. New York: HarperPaperbacks, 1992.

Mahoney, Richard D. *Sons & Brothers: The Days of Jack and Bobby Kennedy*. New York: Arcade, 1999.

Maier, Thomas. *The Kennedys: America's Emerald Kings*. New York: Basic Books, 2003.

Manchester, William. *The Death of a President*. New York: Harper & Row, 1967.

Martin, Ralph G. *A Hero for Our Time: An Intimate Story of the Kennedy Years*. New York: Macmillan Publishing Company, 1983.

May, Ernest R. and Zelikow, Philip D. (Editors). *The Kennedy Tapes: Inside the White House During the Cuban Missile Crisis*. New York: W. W. Norton & Company, 2002.

McKnight, Gerald D. *Breach of Trust: How the Warren Commission Failed the Nation and Why*. Lawrence, Kansas: University Press of Kansas, 2005.

McNamara, Robert S. *In Retrospect: The Tragedy and Lessons of Vietnam*. New York: Vintage Books, 1996.

Melanson, Phillip and Klaber, William. *Shadow Play*. New York: St. Martin's Press, 1997.

Mellen, Joan. *A Farewell to Justice*. Washington, D.C.: Potomac Books, 2005.

Meyer, Cord. *Facing Reality: From World Federalism to the CIA*. Lanham, MD: University Press of America, 1980.

Moldea, Dan E. *The Hoffa Wars: Teamsters, Rebels, Politicians and the Mob*. New York; Charter, 1978.

Moldea, Dan. *The Killing of Robert Kennedy: An Investigation of Motive, Means, and Opportunity*. New York: W.W. Norton & Co., 1997.

Nashel, Jonathan. *Edward Lansdale's Cold War*. Amherst and Boston: University of Massachusetts Press, 2005.

Newfield, Jack. *RFK: A Memoir*. New York: Thunder's Mouth Press, 2003.

Newfield, Jack. *Somebody's Gotta Tell It: The Upbeat Memoir of a Working-Class Journalist*. New York: St. Martin's Press, 2002.

Newman, John. *Oswald and the CIA*. New York: Carroll & Graf Publishers, Inc., 1995.

Nixon, Richard. *RN: The Memoirs of Richard Nixon*. New York: Touchstone, 1978.

Noguchi, Thomas T., M.D. *Coroner*. New York: Simon and Schuster, 1983,

O'Donnell, Helen. *A Common Good: The Friendship of Robert F. Kennedy and Kenneth P. O'Donnell*. New York: William Morrow and Company, 1998.

O'Donnell, Kenneth P., and Powers, David F. *"Johnny, We Hardly Knew Ye"*: *Memories of John Fitzgerald Kennedy*. Boston: Little, Brown and Company, 1970.

O'Neill, Speaker Tip. *Man of the House*. New York: Random House, 1987.

Palamara, Vincent. *Survivor's Guilt: The Secret Service and the Failure to Protect the President*. © 2005 Vincent Michael Palamara (self-published manuscript).

Palermo, Joseph A. *In His Own Right: The Political Odyssey of Senator Robert F. Kennedy*. New York: Columbia University Press, 2001.

Parmet, Herbert S. *JFK: The Presidency of JFK*. Connecticut: Easton Press, 1986.

Paterson, Thomas G. *Contesting Castro: The United States and the Triumph of the Cuban Revolution*. New York: Oxford University Press, 1994.

Perlstein, Rick. *Before the Storm*. New York: Hill and Wang, 2001.

Powers, Thomas. *The Man Who Kept the Secrets: Richard Helms and the CIA*. New York: Alfred A. Knopf, 1979.

Prouty, Fletcher L. *JFK: The CIA, Vietnam and the Plot to Assassinate John F. Kennedy*. New York: Citadel Press, 1996

Ragano, Frank, and Raab, Selwyn. *Mob Lawyer: Including the Inside Account of Who Killed Jimmy Hoffa and JFK*. New York: Charles Scribner's Sons, 1994.

Rappleye, Charles, and Becker, Ed. *All American Mafioso: The Johnny Rosselli Story*. New York: Doubleday, 1991.

Reeves, Richard. *President Kennedy: Profile of Power*. New York: Touchstone, 1993.

Renehan, Edward J. *The Kennedys at War: 1937–1945*. New York: Doubleday, 2002.

Rogers, Warren. *When I Think of Bobby: A Personal Memoir of the Kennedy Years*. New York: Harper Perennial, 1994.

Rosenberg, Jonathan and Karabell, Zachary. *Kennedy, Johnson, and the Quest for Justice: The Civil Rights Tapes*. New York: W. W. Norton, 2003.

Russo, Gus. *Live by the Sword*. Baltimore: Bancroft Press, 1998.

Russo, Gus. *The Outfit: The Role of Chicago's Underworld in the Shaping of Modern America*. New York: Bloomsbury, 2001.

Sahl, Mort. *Heartland*. New York: Harcourt Brace Jovanovich, 1976.

Salinger, Pierre. *P.S., A Memoir*. New York: St. Martin's Press, 1995.

Salinger, Pierre. *With Kennedy*. New York: Doubleday & Company, 1966.

Saunders, Frances Stonor *The Cultural Cold War: The CIA and the World of Arts and Letters*. New York: The New Press, 2001.

Schlesinger, Arthur M., Jr. *A Thousand Days: John F. Kennedy in the White House*. Boston: Mariner, 2002.

Schlesinger, Arthur M., Jr. *Robert Kennedy and His Times*. Boston: First Mariner Books, 2002.

Scott, Peter Dale. *Deep Politics and the Death of JFK*. Berkeley: University of California Press, 1996.

Sheridan, Walter. *The Fall and Rise of Jimmy Hoffa*. New York: Saturday Review Press, 1972.

Smith, Amanda (Editor). *Hostage to Fortune: the Letters of Joseph P. Kennedy*. New York: Penguin Books, 2001.

Smith, Joseph B. *Portrait of a Cold Warrior*. New York: G. P. Putnam's Sons, 1976.

Smith, Louis J. (Editor). *Foreign Relations of the United States, 1961–1963: Cuba 1961–1962*. Washington: United States Government Printing Office, 1997.

Smith, Sally Bedell. *Grace and Power: The Private World of the Kennedy White House*. New York: Random House, 2004.

Sperber, A. M. *Murrow: His Life and Times*. New York: Freundlich Books, 1986.

Stockton, Bayard. *Flawed Patriot: The Rise and Fall of CIA Legend Bill Harvey*. Washington, D.C.: Potomac Books, 2006.

Stone, Oliver and Sklar, Zachary. *JFK, the Book of the Film*. New York: Applause Books, 1992.

Sullivan, William. *The Bureau: My Thirty Years in Hoover's FBI*. New York: Pinnacle Books, 1979.

Summers, Anthony and Swan, Robbyn. *Sinatra: The Life*. New York: Alfred A. Knopf, 2005.

Summers, Anthony. *Not in Your Lifetime*. New York: Marlowe & Company, 1998.

Summers, Anthony. *The Secret Life of J. Edgar Hoover*. New York: Pocket Books, 1993.

Szulc, Tad. *Fidel: A Critical Portrait*. New York: Perennial, 1986.

Taubman, William. *Khrushchev: The Man and His Era*. New York: W. W. Norton & Company, 2003.

Thomas, Evan. *Robert Kennedy: His Life*. New York: Simon & Schuster, 2000.

Thomas, Evan. *The Very Best Men; Four Who Dared: The Early Years of the CIA*. New York: Touchstone, 1995.

Trento, Joseph J. *The Secret History of the CIA*. Roseville, CA: Forum, 2001.

Trost, Cathy and Bennett, Susan. *President Kennedy Has Been Shot*. Naperville, IL: Sourcebooks, 2003.

Turner, William. *Rearview Mirror: Looking Back at the FBI, the CIA and Other Tails*. Granite Bay, CA: Penmarin Books, 2001.

Twyman, Noel. *Bloody Treason: The Assassination of John F. Kennedy*. Rancho Santa Fe, CA: Laurel Publishing, 1997.

Vidal, Gore. *Palimpsest: A Memoir*. New York: Penguin Books, 1995.

Waldron, Lamar with Hartmann, Thom. *Ultimate Sacrifice: John and Robert Kennedy, the Plan for a Coup in Cuba, and the Murder of JFK*. New York: Carroll & Graf, 2005.

Wallace, Mike. *Between You and Me: A Memoir*. New York: Hyperion, 2005.

Weyl, Nathaniel. *Encounters with Communism*. USA: Xlibris Corporation, 2003.

Witcover, Jules. *85 Days: The Last Campaign of Robert F. Kennedy*. New York: Ace, 1969.

Wofford, Harris. *Of Kennedys and Kings*. University of Pittsburgh Press, 1980.

Wyden, Peter. *Bay of Pigs: The Untold Story*. New York: Simon & Schuster, 1979.

INDEX

ABOUT THE AUTHOR

David Talbot founded and was long-time editor-in-chief of Salon.com, the award-winning website for news and commentary. Before founding Salon in 1995, he was the editor of the *San Francisco Chronicle and Examiner's* Sunday magazine and senior editor of *Mother Jones*. He has written for many national publications, including *The New Yorker, Time,* and *Rolling Stone*. He lives in San Francisco with his family.